Also

Twenty-Twenty

Ellis Sharp

Zoilus Press

A Zoilus Press paperback
First published in Great Britain by Zoilus Press in 2021

© Ellis Sharp 2021

A CIP catalogue record for this book is available from the British Library.

ISBN   9781999735982

Jacket photographs by the Mr Triangle Agency

Cover design by The Ever Shifting Subject

Typeset by Electrograd

ZOILUS PRESS
York, England

In memory of Frank Key

Of course when there is nothing to do there is always the wall to run your finger over. But the prisoner touches the wall of his cell only to remind himself of what keeps him shut in. Or perhaps he is driven by the faint hope that his fingers may tell him what his eyes cannot, that a crack has appeared in the wall, or that the crack which was already there has grown so large that he may just be able to squeeze through it to freedom.

Gabriel Josipovici

Returning home at twenty past midnight on the first day of that year Ellis opened the book he had been saving for 2020. Or rather he opened the first of two large-format paperback volumes of the novel, which was entitled *Anniversaries*. Long waves beat diagonally, he read, and continued reading as far as the sentence beginning The next morning, the earliest coast train to New York. That last sentence he read to the end and then put out the light and in time fell asleep. Next morning it was a grey, quiet day. Outside, the local streets seemed empty and there was almost no motor traffic. In the afternoon Ellis put sacks of rubbish in the wheelie bin, prior to its scheduled collection the next day. He moved the bin into the front garden. In the street a youth on a bicycle pedalled slowly past, in the company of another youth who was propelling himself backwards in a lightweight wheelchair. The wheelchair was of the type seen in hospitals, used to transport patients between wards. The youth in the wheelchair appeared to be fooling around. Later, a neighbour walked slowly by and Ellis said: Happy New Year! The neighbour returned the greeting, adding that it looked as if it was going to be a dry day. Ellis agreed that it did. Later, Ellis went online. He learned that Pope Francis had apologised for slapping a woman's hand during a visit to the Vatican's nativity scene the previous night. In Australia since Christmas Day nine people were confirmed dead in bushfires, with four missing. At Malua Bay 1,000 people spent the night on the beach to escape the flames. There was a strange calmness, one witness said. People were as close to the water's edge as they could get. They were literally just lying on the beach trying to keep out of the smoke and ash. Roaming further online Ellis came across a link to Arundhati Roy's article *India: Intimations of an Ending*, which he read, before moving to an armchair and reading more of *Anniversaries* Volume One. By 17.37 he had reached page 16. In the kitchen that night, preparing a meal of sliced ham, poached eggs and pan fried sugar snaps, Ellis listened to Van Morrison's *Three Chords and the Truth*. That evening he watched on DVD *Three Billboards Outside Ebbing, Missouri*, which he had not seen before. He liked the film very much. In bed he read two more pages of *Anniversaries*.

Thursday 2nd January 2020

Indonesia floods leave 17 dead and thousands homeless, Ellis read, one of the headlines on the website of Sky News. 'Do not be here' warning as New South Wales declares wildfire emergency. Ellis drank a cup of tea and ate a bowl of cereal. He shaved and dressed. Ellis washed the scarlet tablecloth with the Christmas design and placed it over the horse in the kitchen to dry. He read half a page of *Anniversaries* and then filled the washing-machine with towels and a plastic bulb half-filled with liquid detergent. He switched the washing-machine on. Next he brought the emptied wheelie bin in. In *Anniversaries* he reached August 28, 1967. By twelve minutes after noon he had reached September 2. Now the weekenders have left silence in their wake, he read. Ellis drank his third cappuccino of the day. Labour leadership: Sir Keir Starmer takes lead in race to replace Corbyn - poll. Later on Ellis listened three more times to *Three Chords and the Truth*.

Friday 3rd January 2020

Ellis woke and switched on the radio on his bedside table. He'd just missed the headlines but he suddenly became aware that the US had assassinated someone in the Middle East. It soon turned out that it was Iranian military commander Qassem Suleimani and Iraqi commander Abu Mahdi al-Muhandis. Ellis wondered if others had died in the explosion. A driver? Bodyguards? An interview with an Iranian Professor of Middle Eastern Studies followed. The professor said it was the equivalent of the Iranians killing a British general. Later two American presidential advisers said how gratified they were by the killing of Suleimani. Ellis went on Twitter to see what David Wearing had to say but evidently Wearing was still taking his Christmas break. Later Ellis read another page of *Anniversaries*. In the meantime, he read, of the seven hundred faces she has seen this morning, almost all have been forgotten. Now the smiling starts. At 6pm, while preparing an evening meal, Ellis listened to BBC Radio 4 News. Lyse Doucet, OBE, the BBC's chief international correspondent, said of Qassem Suleimani that 'he smirked at his enemies'. At 19.31 Ellis read that 10 people had died in the US terror attack. Ellis knew that the western media would never give their names. Victims of imperialist terror whose skins are brown are of no interest to award-winning news reporters.

Saturday 4th January 2020

The meandering main street reminded her of Gneez, Ellis read, as did the buildings that each had a separate façade, the small shops, the often overcrowded sidewalks. The translation was not into English but American. Gotten, not got. Ellis went out to buy a loaf of bread, a newspaper, a pack of 16 paracetamol and a carton of milk. Next he deposited bottles and jars in a bottle bank. The bottle bank was almost full, he noticed. Instead of dropping in the green bottles he had to hurl them to the back of the container. Late afternoon he read his emails, replying to one of them immediately.

Sunday 5th January 2020

The radio news reported that President Trump had announced that if Iran retaliated for the assassination of Qassem Suleimani then 52 sites in Iran would be attacked, including unspecified cultural ones. As he drank his morning cup of tea Ellis went online. On Twitter Colin Kahl, a former Obama administration official, said that targeting cultural sites is a war crime. Research by Oxfam showed that the average British person would emit more carbon dioxide in the first two weeks of 2020 than a citizen of seven African nations would do in the entire year. 19.23 GMT: Iran has announced that it will no longer abide by any of the limits imposed by the unravelling 2015 nuclear deal, and Iraq's parliament urged its leaders to expel troops from the US-led coalition, as the aftershocks of the assassination of Iranian general Qassem Suleimani reverberated through the Middle East, Ellis read online. Turning away, he winks at Mrs Cresspahl, Ellis read in *Anniversaries*. Tomorrow it will be September 22, 1967.

Monday 6th January 2020

Donald Trump has defended his threat to target Iranian cultural sites, Ellis read online, after listening to a fawning interview with an American imperialist by Justin Webb, BBC Radio 4's corporate pimp. BBC News, true to form, continued to use the sanitising phrase 'targeted killing', avoiding wherever possible the words 'assassination' or 'unlawful'. On bellicose form, the US president lashed out at Iraq, following its Parliament's demand for American troops to be expelled from that country. Trump vowed to respond with crippling sanctions. As Ellis read he drank his tea, a blend of Assam loose tea and Earl Grey loose tea. Ellis deplored teabags. Sites important to Iranian culture, Donald Trump threatened on Twitter, WILL BE HIT VERY FAST AND VERY HARD. Targeting cultural sites is prohibited by international conventions, signed in Geneva and at the Hague. In 2017 the United Nations Security Council passed unanimously a resolution condemning the destruction of heritage sites. The action previewed by Trump would almost certainly involve the deaths of civilians, Ellis read. He finished his tea. On Twitter he read Richard Seymour@leninology, who wrote of Rebecca Long-Bailey that 'I'd like her to win' and 'Politically she's solid'.

Tuesday 7th January 2020

Black night at 5.30am, still black night at 6.35am, gone seven the sky lightens, by 7.30am it's daylight but the drivers still keep their headlights on. On Twitter, Ellis read that Raytheon built the Multi-Spectral Targeting System for the MQ-9

Reaper drone that killed Qassem Suleimani. The names of eight of the victims of the assassination were never reported in the Western media. *Collateral damage.* Soon all TV journalists were using the phrase 'taken out' to describe the assassination. In July, 72 per cent of the American public were still in favour of continuing the war in Vietnam, Ellis read in the first book of *Anniversaries*. That morning Ellis rocked the pram and sang *Go to sleep my little one, Go to sleep, my little one,Go to sleep, Go to sleep,Go to sleep in the morning.*The child slept. Later she woke. Later she played with Baby Daddy, the largest of her soft toys. She hugged Daddy Baby and held an ointment pot to the doll's lips, mimicking feeding it. That evening Ellis drove to the local fish and chip shop. He ordered scampi and medium chips and a cod special. Like a dentistry or a surgery the fish and chip shop provided reading material for its clients. While he waited for his order Ellis sat on a stool and read the Christmas issue of *OK!* He learned about the royal family's Christmas dining arrangements and gazed at photographs of the interior of a famous television presenter's mansion. On its sound system the fish and chip shop was playing 'San Francisco' by Scott McKenzie. Later Ellis drove to the station to meet the London train scheduled to arrive at 8.30pm. At that time of night there was ample parking. In bed he read a description of a journey taken by Gesine and Marie. They travel through an area of low houses built far apart, past Emily Dickinson's birthplace, then up above the Connecticut River, the wide water they repeatedly glimpse drowsing between the tall firs of the riverbanks.

Wednesday 8th January 2020

The headline news this morning is that overnight Iran launched 17 missiles at the American Al-Asad airbase and 5 missiles at the American Erbil airbase in Iraq. No casualties are reported. The Iranian foreign minister Javad Zarif described this as 'proportionate measures in self-defence'. On Twitter Ellis watched a video posted by B'Tselem: *Footage from the olive harvest in Burin: settlers attack Palestinian harvesters and make off with stolen olives while soldiers remove the owners.* In *Anniversaries* Ellis read: True, our Upper West Side of Manhattan is only an imagined homeland. The novel is translated by Damion Searls, who the frontispiece explains grew up on Riverside Drive in New York City, three blocks away from Gesine Cresspahl's apartment. Ellis puts the book down. Soon he is singing.
Miss Polly had a dolly who was sick, sick, sick,
So she called for the doctor to come quick, quick, quick,
The doctor came with his coat and hat
And he knocked at the door with a rat-a-tat-tat.
He looked at the dolly and he shook his head
And he said 'Miss Molly, put her straight to bed'.

He wrote on a paper for a pill, pill, pill,
'I'll be back in the morning, yes I will, will, will.'

That night Ellis watched *White House Farm* on ITV at 9pm. It was the first episode of a six-part drama documentary about the massacre of Nevill and June Bamber, their adoptive daughter, Sheila Caffell, and Sheila's two children, Daniel and Nicholas, at White House Farm near Tolleshunt D'Arcy in Essex on the night of 6-7 August 1985. The Bambers' adoptive son Jeremy Bamber, 24, who lived nearby, told police that Nevill had telephoned him to report that Sheila had gone berserk with a gun. The police initially believed his story but later arrested him. He was subsequently convicted of five counts of murder. At 10pm Ellis started watching Sky News but stopped when he discovered that the lead story was about Prince Harry and his wife. Later he went to bed and read three more pages of *Anniversaries*.

Thursday 9th January 2020

A bright sunny day. Ellis went shopping. He bought two lightbulbs, six eggs, two packets of leeks. He returned two books to the library. He chatted to the librarian and then to a woman who came in who was a member of a book group that Ellis occasionally attended. Back home Ellis listened to Van Morrison singing 'Here Comes The Night' from the live double album *'...It's Too Late To Stop Now...'* Sorting through an old box of books and folders he came across *The Great Operas of Mozart*, published by The Norton Library (1964). It included an Introduction, Cast of Characters, Plot and Libretto to each of five operas. Ellis saw that he had ticked the three that he had seen: *The Marriage of Figaro*, *Don Giovanni* and *The Magic Flute*. But that was many years ago. The book contained two cuttings of a performance of *Don Giovanni* by the English National Opera at the Coliseum in London, which Ellis had attended. The first reviewer, Nicholas Kenyon, had not liked the production, remarking that 'the music - and the characterisations - are pretty thin'. The second reviewer, Peter Heyworth, was in raptures. One could spend a long time in the great opera houses of the world without encountering a Mozart performance as dramatically alert and musically stylish as this, he wrote. At 17.27 it began raining very heavily, just as Ellis had finished peeling six potatoes. He was drinking a bottle of Liberty Ale from San Francisco, a Christmas gift. That night Sky News reported Canadian leader Justin Trudeau's claim that the Ukrainian passenger aircraft which crashed shortly after take-off from Tehran airport killing 176 people had been shot down by Iran. Ellis was surprised to see that Trudeau had grown a short beard. In *Anniversaries* it is now October 22, 1967, a Sunday. Yesterday, Ellis read, Mrs. Ernest Hemingway complained to *The Times* of London about their publishing letters her deceased husband wrote between 1950 and 1956 to one Adriana Ivancich, a young woman who says she was the basis for the character of Renata in Hemingway's novel *Across the River and into the Trees*.

Friday 10th January 2020

A warm, sunny morning. Ellis drank a cappuccino and ate a buttered crumpet. Online he read that 'intelligence sources' had confirmed to the *Guardian* newspaper that two Iranian anti-aircraft missiles had brought down the Ukrainian airliner. Overnight airstrikes by unidentified planes in the Syrian province of Deir Ezzor killed at least eight members of an Iranian-backed militia. The attack was most likely carried out by Israel, Iraqi officials said. Israel regularly carries out airstrikes inside Syria, he read. Ellis finished his crumpet. The melting of Himalayan glaciers has doubled since the turn of the century, with more than a quarter of all ice lost over the last four decades. 10.38am: Ellis watched his neighbour J walk past, abruptly stop, then walk back to her house, evidently having forgotten something. He did not see her return, his attention having switched to *Anniversaries*. Later he returned another book to the local public library and bought some green beans and a pack of Lemsip. Here was where Crespall wanted to register the birth of his child, Ellis read.

Saturday 11th January 2020

Ellis went online and read that the inaugural Hay Festival Abu Dhabi had published its programme for next month. It included Booker-winner Bernardine Evaristo and Baillie Gifford Prize-winner Hallie Rubenhold as well as historian William Dalrymple, and Nigerian Nobel Prize-winner Wole Soyinka. Ellis learned that it would take place from 25th to 28th February at the cultural centre and theatre Manarat Al Saadiyat alongside other venues across the capital, supported by the UAE's 'Ministry of Tolerance'. In other literary news Ellis read that the novelist Rose Tremain, who was made a Dame in the New Year's Honours list, said the honour felt like 'a gleam of light' after suffering from cancer. In the afternoon, in the street, Ellis saw a tall, slim black man of about thirty approaching him. The man was wearing only a dressing-gown and blue socks. Ellis avoided eye contact as the man walked past. The Queen had convened a meeting of senior royals on Monday to discuss Megxit, the tabloids reported. And the leader of the Revolutionary Guard had apologised for shooting down the Ukrainian airliner, having mistaken it for an incoming US aircraft. Johnson sat slumped behind the green table, Ellis read, firmly covering his manuscript with his two hands, his bald head reflecting the spotlights, his eyes scanning the room from between his brows and the rims of his glasses.

Sunday 12th January 2020

Upon arriving home that morning Ellis saw movement in the window of the house next door. The neighbour came out with some news. C had died. Yesterday. She lived alone. Apparently she'd been diagnosed with cancer but had refused all treatment and had chosen to tell no one of her condition. It's a shock to everyone who knew her. On the news it was reported that within hours of the Board of Deputies of British Jews requiring contenders for the Labour leadership to abide by ten pledges including adherence to the International Holocaust Remembrance Alliance's woolly and rambling definition of anti-Semitism along with all its Zionist-inflected examples. The majority of hopefuls had capitulated to this impudent demand: Rebecca Long-Bailey, Emily Thornberry, Keir Starmer, Angela Rayner, Lisa Nandy, Jess Phillips, Rosena Allin-Khan and Ian Murray. Ellis was unsurprised to find the pseudo-Left candidate Long-Bailey among this collection of lickspittle careerists and reactionaries. We walked down Broadway from our house to Seventy-Ninth Street and back up via Riverside Park, Ellis read that evening.

Monday 13th January 2020

PRINCE HARRY TO ATTEND CRISIS TALKS WITH QUEEN AND SENIOR ROYALS TODAY was the headline everywhere on the corporate media. FIVE MAKE IT THROUGH TO NEXT ROUND OF LABOUR LEADERSHIP CONTEST was the headline on the *Guardian* website, reporting that Keir Starmer, Rebecca Long-Bailey, Lisa Nandy, Jess Phillips and Emily Thornberry were the candidates who had obtained enough support from members of the Parliamentary Labour Party and the European Parliament, having gained at least 22 nominations. What a pitiful assemblage of mediocrities, thought Ellis. On Twitter, Ellis read Mark Curtis @markcurtis30: *According to "Prince" William, Oman's sultan was "unwavering in his commitment to improve the lives of his people". Not only is this statement hideous and false, it's yet another political intervention by a "royal" family propping up Gulf repression.*

Tuesday 14th January 2020

Light at 7.20am, winter fading. On the radio it was reported that owing to financial difficulties the Flybe airline was seeking the abolition of Airline Passenger Duty. After half an hour Ellis switched off the radio and began listening to Rod Stewart's album *Blood Red Roses*. That morning he walked in the park. The child soon fell asleep in her pram and remained unconscious for one hour and twenty minutes. As she slept Ellis went on the internet. He scanned the various Twitter sites that he read usually on a daily basis. Later Ellis learned that strong winds this afternoon had brought a large tree crashing down across one of the major routes out of the city, blocking it for several hours. Mr. Josiah Thompson didn't believe the official report about the death of President Kennedy either, Ellis read.

Wednesday 15th January 2020

Now the clock in the Commerce Department in Washington, which records a new citizen of the United States of America every 14.5 seconds, advances a step. Now it's up to two hundred million, Ellis read. All morning it rained. Marmalade, he wrote on a shopping list. Stiff bristle brush. Carpet cleaner. Later he learned how to play Twinkle, Twinkle, Little Star on the xylophone. Red X 2. Dark green X 2. Blue X 2. Dark green X 1. Lime X 1. Yellow X 2. Orange X 2. Red X 1. Green X 2. Lime X 2. Yellow X 2. Orange X 2. Green X 2. Lime X 2. Yellow X 2. Orange X 1. At 9pm Ellis watched the second episode of *White House Farm*. It ended with Jeremy Bamber having the cute dog put down by a vet with a hypodermic needle. From a distance his girlfriend Julie Mugford watched. Bamber's guilt as a serial killer was underlined by the representation of his attitude to the cute dog, Ellis felt.

Thursday 16th January 2020

A bright clear day. Ellis surveyed the storm damage. A wooden panel had flown over railings and smashed against a parked BMW with a German number plate, denting and scratching the passenger door. Was this what insurers called an Act of God? Ellis wondered. Later it clouded over. Ellis went out to push a cheque through a letterbox, renewing his subscription to the local history society. Soon after his return it began raining. Indoors that afternoon it was dark. He switched the reading lamp on. Someday, Ellis read, she promised herself she would travel every subway line - all 238 miles, all 482 stations, day and night - with the single token coin you need for admission into the system. *Anniversaries* is a novel which records geographical locations in some detail - New York especially but also Richmond in London. In the kitchen Ellis listened to some tracks of *Bridges to Babylon* while making a cappuccino. Amanda is sure that she once ended up with some sperm on the lap of her overcoat in the pushing and shoving, he read. On the internet Ellis learned about comments which Rebecca Long-Bailey had made to Salford Catholics during the last month's election. She had said she did not agree with allowing abortion on the grounds of disability after 24 weeks. In those dark times, when I wonder if I am making the right decisions, my faith is often the only thing that keeps me going, she said.

Friday 17th January 2020

The cost of policing the UN climate conference in Glasgow this November could exceed £200m, according to Scotland's chief constable, Ellis read online. During the 12 days from 9 November, an estimated 90,000 visitors including about 200 world leaders will attend the UN's 26th conference of the parties, known as COP26, at the Scottish Event Campus (SEC) on the River Clyde in the centre of Glasgow. Elsewhere Ellis read that a counter-terrorism police document distributed to teachers and medical staff as part of anti-extremism briefings included Greenpeace, neo-Nazis, the ocean pollution campaign Sea Shepherd, the Palestinian Solidarity Campaign and campaigners against airport expansion, among other groups and organisations. The guide, produced by Counter-Terrorism policing, is used across England as part of training for Prevent, the anti-radicalisation scheme designed to catch those at risk of committing terrorist violence. Cresspahl had a hard time putting down roots in Jerichow, Ellis read. Then it was Christmas.

Saturday 18th January 2020

A bright sunny day, clear blue sky, where Ellis lived. Ellis, who was often slow to catch up with his newspaper reading, began reading a week-old gushing two-page profile of Samantha Power in *The Times*, 11 January 2020. She went viral, Ellis read, with an impassioned speech at the UN accusing Russia, Iran and the Syrian regime of having no shame. So, Ellis thought. Power - apt name - is just another pimp of US imperialism. As he read on he thought: why does this crap purport to be journalism? The author of this sycophantic profile was one Damian Whitworth. Ellis had never heard of Damian Whitworth. Damian Whitworth wrote that President Obama liked Power because she told him straight truths with Irish passion. The profile was a plug for Samantha Power's latest book, titled *The Education of an Idealist*. Idealist? thought Ellis scornfully, as he read on. At a UN Security Council session in 2016, he read, she confronted the Assad regime, Russia and Iran over the deaths of civilians, including children, in attacks on Aleppo. "Are you truly incapable of shame?" she asked. Reading this Ellis realised he loathed Samantha Power with an acute and visceral intensity. She was a classic blood-drenched Liberal imperialist of the type which Noam Chomsky had spent his entire career identifying and analysing. But even Damian Whitworth, to his credit, raised the issue of the Barack Obama's use of drones to murder hundreds of swarthy foreigners in their own countries. Samantha Power said that President Obama had a lot of discomfort with it. It was a system that was vulnerable to abuse and excess of mistakes. She, Samantha Power, had herself felt discomfort. But she was basically okay regarding the repeated assassination of swarthy foreigners because it was all in a good cause. She was privy to the threat streams and the intelligence. *An idealist?* Samantha Power was a type who infested the Western corporate media. Samantha Power was guaranteed respect in the pages of *The Times* or *The Guardian* or across the BBC. On the front page of today's *Times* there was a photograph of Lee Child, in Shakespearean-statue-thoughtful-pose. Lee Child has revealed that at 65 he is retiring from writing his Reacher novels. Why do you say England's not part of Europe? Ellis read later, in *Anniversaries*.

Sunday 19th January 2020

Ellis felt unwell and this morning he went back to bed and stayed there until mid-day. Heavens to Betsy, it is a car with a cooling unit too! he read. Further down the page: De Rosny's house is a stone's throw from the Long Island Sound in a parklike neighbourhood where even the streets are private property.

Monday 20th January 2020

Ellis read that Lord Hall of Birkenhead was standing down as the director general of the BBC. In an era of fake news we remain the gold standard of impartiality and truth, Lord Hall said. The arrogance and impudence of this grotesque corporation and its reactionary and poisonous management is stupefying, Ellis thought. In *Anniversaries* he read: And at least on the eleventh floor of the bank they couldn't get over the fact that it was thirteen degrees (55°) on a 19th of December. Apparently that hadn't happened in decades. Ellis reached the end of the first book in the sequence. He felt a little disappointed that in this translated edition the quartet had been split into two volumes, not four.

Tuesday 21st January 2020

I am not allowed back, Ellis read. It's a long way from here, more than 4,500 miles, and even after an eight-hour flight you have to travel on until dark, and you still won't be there. On the next page he read: She lives around here, on the corner of Riverside Drive and Ninety-Sixth Street. Thirty-four years old. Further down the page he read: December 21, 1967. In the Senate Foreign Relations Committee, some members are sceptical about whether the administration and Joints Chiefs of Staff told the truth in 1964, when they claimed that the destroyers *Maddox* and *Turner Joy* were attacked by North Vietnamese ships on August 4 of said year.

You saw yet again that grown-ups are strange, and still you couldn't let go of my hand in a place where the language, the colors of the cars, and the height of the buildings were strange, to say nothing of your mother, Ellis read. In Marks and Spencer he bought two shirts. The child gazed up at him from the pram, absorbing the wonder of the world, occasionally grinning. On the internet Ellis later watched a clip of an interview with Lisa Nandy conducted by Andrew Neil. Nandy, it was obvious from her banal responses was, where foreign policy was concerned, a typical Labour MP, vigorously committed to repression, injustice and Zionism.

Thursday 23rd January 2020

In Germany he'd had to add something, Ellis read. An admission that some of the money saved up in England would go every month for a boy that Mrs. Elizabeth Trowbridge had brought into the world without his knowledge. On the website of *The New York Times* Ellis read that world leaders had converged in Jerusalem to mark the 75th anniversary of the liberation of Auschwitz. What an obscene farce, Ellis thought, that this anniversary should be memorialised at a site remote from where it occurred, in the Middle East not Europe, in a viciously sectarian racist state dedicated to the expulsion of the original inhabitants. Worse, the chosen site was drenched in other bitter historical ironies of the sort enlarged upon in Max Blumenthal's *Goliath* - the sort no BBC news journalist would ever cite. Among the world leaders paying pious tribute were the murderous thug Vladimir Putin, the blood-spattered Christian fundamentalist Mike Pence and that fatuous and pompous sponger and ignoramus, the Prince of Wales. The fawning and uncritical *New York Times* reported on the 'proud if slightly bellicose address' of the Israeli leader Benjamin Netanyahu who used this supposedly solemn occasion to squeal about 'The tyrants of Tehran' who 'threaten the peace and security of the entire world'. The fawning and uncritical *New York Times* reported it as 'the biggest political gathering in Israel's history'. The fawning and uncritical *New York Times* reported on a speech by Rabbi Israel Meir Lau, described as 'the chief rabbi of Israel and a towering moral voice of his generation'. The fawning and uncritical *New York Times* reported on a speech by President Frank-Walter Steinmeir of Germany, who spoke of how hatred is spreading, citing as an example 'when crude anti-Semitism is cloaked in supposed criticism of Israeli policy'. This reactionary poltroon, who would no doubt have thrived under Hitler, squeaked 'We stand with Israel'. Later Ellis looked up Rabbi Israel Meir Lau and discovered that he was a characteristic Zionist bigot who, typically of Israel, was originally a European, and who had spent most of his life as a member of the master religion in a stolen land. Rabbi Israel Meir Lau described criticism of Israel as 'irrational'. In searching for material on Rabbi Israel Meir Lau Ellis was unable to find any reference to the Palestinians. Ellis learned that the rabbi had arrived in Palestine at the age of eight carrying a rifle given to him by an American soldier, who'd asked him what he wanted to do with his life and who answered 'I want to take revenge'. And this blood-spattered sanctimonious holy man has been ideologically sponsoring the murderous repression of the Palestinians for most of his adult life. The sectarian American Zionist *Jewish Times* describes how the future chief rabbi 'first set foot on the holy soil of the land of Israel' in 1945, not mentioning that Israel did not yet exist, and that this land was Palestine. When the Judge said, 'You are sick and require medical attention,' Jones replied: 'Not as sick as you are.' Ellis put out the light and went to sleep.

Friday 24th January 2020

A dark drizzly morning. The death toll from the coronavirus has risen to 26 in China, with 830 infected. Ellis looked up Leroi Jones, who had long outlived the author of *Anniversaries* and who had died at the age of 79 on 9 January 2014. He read that Jones had been arrested for alleged weapons possession and resisting arrest during the 1967 Newark riots. His poem 'Black People' was read out in court by the judge. It included the lines quoted by Uwe Johnson: All the stores will open if / you will say the magic words. / The magic words are: Up / against the wall motherfucker / this is a stickup! But in the Johnson version, which relied on the *New York Times*, the word motherfucker was changed to mother blank. That same pusillanimous spirit still existed in 2020, Ellis realised, as he mistakenly wrote mother fuckwr and Spell-check offered him five possible corrections, none of which was the most fucking obvious one. Tucker, sucker, pucker, ducker, bucker. Elsewhere on the internet Ellis came across a column by Hagai El-Ad, executive director of B'Tselem. It was headlined *Netanyahu Exploits the Holocaust to Brutalize the Palestinians*. Netanyahu didn't invent the idea of leveraging the Holocaust for political gain, Ellis read. Yet he is taking even that low to new depths, stripping Palestinians of basic human rights in the name of the survivors of the Holocaust. The Palestinians who live under Israel's occupation are a people bereft of rights. They cannot vote for the government that controls every aspect of their lives. They have no army to defend themselves. They do not control the borders of their own territory, or their ability to travel abroad, or even how long it will take them to get to the nearest Palestinian town - if they are allowed to do so. They also have no recourse to justice through Israel's legal mechanisms. Israel's prosecutors and judges process Palestinians in the occupied territories through a 'justice system' that delivers an almost 100 percent conviction rate. At the same time, this system works to ensure impunity for Israeli security forces who kill, abuse or torture them, Ellis read. Later that day Ellis read on the *Guardian* website that BBC journalist Orla Guerin had upset some prominent British Jews with her Holocaust Memorial Day report, which ended with young soldiers from the repressive so-called Israeli Defence Force visiting Vad Vashem. 'Young soldiers troop in to share the binding tragedy of the Jewish people', said Guerin (not mentioning that this is a regular rite of passage to psych up these prospective murderers before they go off to repress and brutalise the population of Gaza and the occupied West Bank). 'The state of Israel is now a regional power. For decades it has occupied Palestinian territories but some here will always see their nation through the prism of persecution and survival.' The former BBC Chairman Michael Grade and Danny Cohen, its former director of television, have criticised Guerin for her 'unjustifiably offensive' News at Ten report, Ellis read. Jewish leaders and the former BBC executives have criticised the report as anti-Semitic. Cohen said her report 'should be widely condemned. The attempt to link the horrors of the Holocaust to the Israeli-Palestinian conflict is deeply offensive and upsetting'. Ellis laughed hollowly at these remarks, or would have done had he been a character in genre fiction. Holocaust Memorial Day was established by that blood-spattered fanatic Tony Blair, at the behest of Zionists. It has nothing at all to do with learning any lessons from history and everything to do with promoting the violent sectarian Zionist state. The Campaign Against Antisemitism has made a formal complaint to the BBC, reported the *Guardian*, not mentioning that this so-called campaign consists of two individuals, both bellicose supporters of Israel. The CAA said the report broke the international definition of anti-Semitism, which has been adopted by the British government, which includes 'drawing comparisons between Israeli policy and the Nazis'. Another hollow laugh required here. Amanda Bowman, the vice-president of the Board of Deputies of British Jews, said the report was 'crass and offensive'. In 2004, the Israeli government accused Guerin of anti-Semitism and 'total identification with the goals and methods of the Palestinian terror groups'. A rancid publication called *The Algemeiner* carried a report by Benjamin Kerstein which spoke of 'outrage' which 'erupted' after Guerin had used the Holocaust commemoration 'to slam the Jewish state'. Benjamin Kerstein wrote that Orla Guerin 'has long been accused of bias against Israel'. He cited the reactionary and pompous Zionist historian Simon Sebag Montefiore, who frothed that Guerin's report was 'truly foul' and 'shamefully amoral + historically inaccurate'. Benjamin Kerstein quoted Gerald Steinberg, 'head of the monitoring group NGO Watch'. Ellis had never heard of this individual or organisation but guessed it was another aggressive Zionist outfit. Steinberg frothed that Guerin had 'a long history of #antiSemitism and Israel derangement going back at least 20 years'. Benjamin Kerstein quoted another Zionist outfit of which Ellis had never heard, Students Supporting Israel (SSI). American, perhaps. Ellis couldn't be bothered to check it out. The internet was overrun with sock puppet 'organisations' which consisted of one or two individuals. 'This @BBCNews report exposes the inherent problem and hate towards Jews & Israel in the British #Media,' frothed the SSI. A cruel smile flickered on Ellis's face as he suddenly realised that the acronym included the letters 'SS'. How apt! SSIsrael... The impartial and objective journalist Benjamin Kerstein reported that 'Guerin's distaste for Israel and biased reporting have been a focus of concern and derision for decades'. Blah, blah, blah. But nowhere did Ellis read of what had happened to Guerin. Back at the start of the century she had reported both on the deaths of Israeli Jews killed by Palestinian suicide bombers and on the deaths and suffering of Palestinians murdered by Jews. The Zionist community was outraged that any attention be given to Palestinians, let alone that 'the conflict' be contextualised. Only Jews are permitted to be victims. Ellis remembered well what had happened. That blood-soaked Jew Ariel Sharon, who never served a day in jail for his well-documented crimes against humanity, complained to the BBC. Its Director, an unprincipled careerist named Mark Thomas, promptly scuttled off to Israel to receive his orders. Upon his return Orla Guerin was relocated to Siberia (or was it Africa?) and replaced by BBC journalists who could be relied upon never to mention Palestinian suffering again. In bed that night Ellis read: The playground by Pier 52, bounded by Hudson, Gansevoort, West Fourth, and Horatio Streets, is now, since yesterday, named after John A. Seravalli.

Saturday 25th January 2020

'Come and say it to me outside the ground, you fucking four-eyed cunt,' the 2019 BBC Sports Personality of the Year was recorded as saying on the first day of the fourth Test against South Africa, Ellis read on the Sky News website, although two of those words on the screen, needless to say, largely consisted of asterisks. Media reports suggested a spectator had likened the cricketer to the singer Ed Sheeran, adverting in an uncomplimentary manner to ginger hair. It was another grey but mild day. On the internet Ellis looked up the playground mentioned by Uwe Johnson. On mommynearest.com he read THINGS TO KNOW ABOUT CORPORAL JOHN A. SERAVALLI PLAYGROUND. There was only thing to know. *This is a notoriously anti-dog playground and cops are not shy about giving tickets out to those who abuse the rule. Be careful, play nice and all will be good.* In the kitchen, making coffee, Ellis listening to the track 'Always Returning' on Brian Eno's album *Apollo*. After drinking his coffee, Ellis returned to the kitchen and listened to 'An Ending (Ascent)'. Later he looked at a tweet by Jonny Geller, literary agent and chairman of Curtis Brown, who frothed that Orla Guerin's Yad Vashem commentary was 'dishonest, damaging and obscene'. Ellis watched Mick Jagger sing 'Memory Motel' from the *Bridges to Bremen* tour. Back then Keith Richards seemed more wrinkled than Jagger, he thought. Ellis read that Rebecca Long-Bailey, supposedly the Corbyn candidate, had refused to support Salma Yaqoob, the Labour candidate for West Midlands Mayor. This was another symptom of Long-Bailey's slippery politics, Ellis thought. The settlement of his inheritance had been enough for his Lisbeth to set up a respectable apartment in Güstrow, not far from the new housing for the Reich Farm Bureau, Ellis read later, having settled down in a comfortable armchair with the first volume of *Anniversaries*. He was almost at page 500 and had read far more of the book than he'd anticipated this grey January. Now Griem is head sergeant or whatever with the Reich Labor Service, Ellis read on the next page. Ellis was reminded of a point someone had made years ago. He had forgotten who this person was but it was someone on the Left who was making a point about how language is used to sanitise or deflect the truth. For example, the German word 'reich' translates as 'empire'. But this accurate translation is far too close to the bone for the Western bourgeoisie, for it reminds everyone that imperialism is not simply a phenomenon of Germany in the period 1933-1945. Hitler's Third Empire is uncomfortably close, as language, to the British Empire. Therefore at some point - when and by whom? - the name of the Hitler government was blandly changed in translation from the Third Empire to the Third Reich. That evening Ellis watched *Once Upon a Time in Hollywood*. He found it disappointing. It did not live up to all the hype. It was competent but not exciting. The irony and humour was heavy-handed. *Maps to the Stars* was a far, far better modern movie about Hollywood. The commission finds that the communications industry is giving Americans a false image of the society in which they live, Ellis read in bed. But not *The New York Times*, right? A question posed by Uwe Johnson perhaps more than by his character Gesine Cresspahl.

Sunday 26th January 2020

Another grey day. Ellis pulled up some weeds. While at the front of the house he chatted to a neighbour about her abscess. He chatted to another neighbour about William Gladstone. He chatted to a third neighbour about pork pies. He applied wood stain to the exterior of his bike shed. It was a busy morning. Later, indoors, Ellis read on Tony Greenstein's blog a blistering critique of the Palestine Solidarity Campaign. According to Greenstein the organisation's Annual Report lacked any reference to 'Zionism' or 'Zionist' other than in resolutions from members. Greenstein wrote that this refusal to mention the word 'Zionism' was fundamental to the political cowardice and timidity of the organisation's leadership. It is pro-Palestinian without being anti-Zionist, Greenstein observed. It's like being a vegan whilst going hunting animals, he waspishly commented. Ellis liked Greenstein's blog and was a regular reader. Greenstein was both informative and politically shrewd. In bed that night Ellis read: The oration started well, with the occasion of farewell, but quickly veered off into the woods, never to return. He read: Twenty-one South Vietnamese wood-cutters were killed in an attack by American artillery and tactical aircraft in Tayninh Province, because they were working in a zone where anyone is regarded as a fair target. He read: She limped without the slightest impatience; she was not even four years old and she buckled a little as skilfully as an old woman. How many paperback novels in the current list of top ten bestsellers use a semi-colon? Ellis wondered.

Monday 27th January 2020

An American basketball player whom Ellis had never heard of (and whom he strongly suspected most British people had never heard of either) had died in a helicopter crash. The BBC 'Today' programme on Radio 4 gravely treated this as a major story. Barack Obama had issued a tribute. And Michelle Obama had won a prize at the Grammys. And the UK's Chief Rabbi, Ephraim Mirvis, was given yet another slot on the programme, on its infamously syrupy and platitudinous 'Thought for the Day'. For today was Britain's Holocaust Memorial Day, a concoction, along with Armed Forces Day, of that famous humanitarian, Anthony Charles Lynton Blair. Apparently the purpose of this pious 'day' was 'To stand together against all forms of prejudice, discrimination and hatred'. And for BBC Radio 4's 'Today' programme who better than Ephraim Mirvis to emit the standard platitudes about tolerance? Mirvis, a man who had participated in the 2017 Jerusalem Day 'March of Flags', described by Bradley Burston in *Haaretz* as 'an annual, gender-segregated extreme-right, pro-occupation religious carnival of hatred, marking the anniversary of Israel's capture of Jerusalem by humiliating the city's Palestinian Muslims. Marchers vandalized shops in Jerusalem's Muslim Quarter, chanted "Death to Arabs" and "The (Jewish) Temple Will Be Built, the (Al Aqsa) Mosque will be burned down," shattered windows and door locks, and poured glue into the locks of shops forced to close for fear of further damage'. Googling the Chief Rabbi, Ellis came across a December 2019 news item by Rosa Doherty about the proposed National Holocaust Memorial and Learning Centre to be established in Victoria Tower Gardens, London. The location has been criticised, he read, by those who have argued that it will ruin the park and result in the deaths of hundreds of ancient plane trees. 'Chief Rabbi Ephraim Mirvis was among those to support the £100 million project, which has almost doubled in cost this year.' Ellis read with a hollow, reverberating laugh that Lord Pickles was overseeing the scheme. This grotesque 'Memorial' would be the perfect symbol of Zionism, involving as it did the seizure of green and fertile public space and replacing it by what in every sense would be the concrete expression of the power, influence and blood-drenched smugness of the racist 'Jewish community'. No one was more morally blank than the Holocaust-memorial-mongers. On the *Guardian* website, Ellis came across a pious editorial, which once again underlined how Holocaust Memorial Day was an occasion for Zionist propaganda. Having described anti-Semitism on continental Europe the newspaper continued, 'in the UK, the Labour party's failure to effectively combat the use of antisemitic tropes by some members led to a breakdown in relations with the Jewish community'. Or to put it another way, the racist and sectarian 'Jewish community' lied, lied and lied again about supposed anti-Semitism, when all along it was objecting to criticism of the violent, cruel sectarian Jewish state. Ellis went to the Twitter account of Ben White @benabyad where he read, on Holocaust Memorial Day, the statement of the Israeli 'defence' minister: 'In no case, under no condition, will we allow for the establishment of a Palestinian state or recognition of such a state and we will not relinquish a single centimetre of the land of Israel to Arabs'. Scrolling down Ben White's Twitter page, Ellis came across a link to the website of the Prisoner Support and Human Rights Association and its report 'The Systematic Use of Torture and Ill-Treatment at Israeli Interrogation Centers. Cases of torture committed at the al-Mascobiyya Interrogation Center.' It reported that since 1967 a total of 73 Palestinian detainees had died during torture while being interrogated. 'The crime of torture is systematic and widely-spread with the complicity of the Israeli judicial system.' The report went on to examine the torture of prisoners who were subjected to severe physical and psychological torture and/or ill-treatment at the al-Mascobiyya Interrogation Center. It described how the torture methods used resulted in visible marks and bruises. Several prisoners were afterwards unable to walk or even move due to the beatings and stress positions they were subjected to. Israeli doctors were complicit in the torture. According to Israeli military law, a detainee can be held and interrogated for a total period of 75 days without being charged. A detainee is not permitted to see a lawyer for a period of 60 days. A detainee may appear in court without legal counsel. The role played by the interrogators, the doctors, and the judges at both courts are complementary. A court in Jerusalem banned the Prisoner Support and Human Rights Association from publishing any details of the torture inflicted on Palestinian prisoners. 'Despite the absolute and non-derogable prohibition against torture , enshrined under article (2) of the International Convention against Torture and ratified by Israel on 3 October 1991, torture against Palestinian detainees is systematic and widespread in Israeli occupation prisons and interrogation centers'. The Report described in detail the torture inflicted on Sameer Arbeed, 45 years old, Jamil Der'awi, 40 years old, Walid Hanatsheh, 51 years old, Abed al-Raziq Farraj, 57 years old, I'teraf al-Rimawi, 44 years old, Qassam Bargouthi, 26 years old, Yazan Mugamis, 26 years old, Mais Abu Gush, 23 years old, Rebhi Karajeh, 24 years old, Aysar Ma'rouf, 29 years old, Israr Ma'rouf, 21 years old, Ameer Hazboun, 22 years old, Tariq Matar, 31 years old,

Kan'an Kan'an, 33 years old. Later that day Ellis drove westward. He discussed with his passenger a variety of topics, including Christine Keeler. On the return journey she mentioned Burns Night and vegan haggis. Later, on the *Guardian* website, Ellis read a column by Rosena Allin-Khan, headed 'As Labour's deputy leader, I would rebuild trust with the nation'. Ellis was not remotely surprised to see that this slippery careerist was tub-thumping her credentials as a prole ('Growing up poor and cold while my single mum worked three jobs to support me and my brother') and as a perverter of history ('proud of the internationalist views of the Labour party' - the party which in government was complicit in the deaths of one million Biafrans, gave nuclear weapons technology to the sectarian and belligerent Jewish state, deported the entire population of Diego Garcia, and was instrumental in the deaths of over one million Iraqis) while simultaneously underlining her credentials as a sycophant to the vocal and bullying Zionist lobby. 'As deputy leader, my first major meeting would be with the Jewish Labour Movement - they are our official Jewish affiliate; we must listen. I want JLM to be at the forefront of this fight against antisemitism, especially when it comes to education at the grassroots level.' Plus many other cliché-strewn drivelling platitudes. Later still Ellis came across 'How I would take personal responsibility for tackling antisemitism', an article by Sir Keir Starmer published in the Zionist *Jewish News*. It was another platitudinous apologia to Zionists using Holocaust Memorial Day as a bouncy inflatable base. 'I share the anger, frustration and pain of many in the Jewish community over how anti-Semitism has been handled by the Labour Party in recent years,' blathered the knight of the realm. The clichés were piled upon clichés as this genuflecting reactionary promised 'to leave no stone unturned'. But beneath the marshmallow language there was also a threat. He would work 'to take hate off the internet'. Oh really? Ellis laughed hollowly again, his face twisted by a cruel smile, as he foresaw where *that* censorship would lead and who and which topics would be its real targets. In bed that night Ellis reached page 553 of the first volume of the New York Review Books edition of *Anniversaries*. The section beginning January 25, 1968, seemed to Ellis a very good example of Uwe Johnson's use of collage as his basic narrative method. It begins with what appears to be a news item, presumably drawn from *The New York Times*, followed by a second paragraph beginning 'The apartment is empty'. It describes the departure of some house guests, the Fleury family. The paragraph ends: 'What happened, Marie?' Is this Marie Cresspahl interrogating herself or Uwe Johnson playing a game with his character? Or is it, perhaps, some third party who seeks answers? The third paragraph is a news item about a young soldier who has been court-martialed for refusing to wear his uniform. The fourth paragraph puts forward Marie's explanation for the departure of Annie Fleury and her children. The fifth paragraph, a news story, is about an encounter between the wife of President Johnson and protesters. 'Try again,

Marie. That doesn't make sense.' Whose voice is behind the command at the start of paragraph six? Marie's? Or Uwe Johnson's? Or is it, perhaps, that of Gesine Cresspahl, her mother? Paragraph seven: another brief news story. 'No. Can you try one more time, Marie?' Paragraph eight: another explanation. Paragraph nine: a news story about a violent mugging on Seventy-Fifth St. Paragraph ten: the dialogue between Marie and this other voice continues, on the same subject. The eleventh paragraph, the final one for this day: a conundrum about morality addressed to *The New York Times*. It's a rhetorical question.

Tuesday 28th January 2020

A cold morning. In another victory for the corrosive spread of Zionism in British society the *Jewish Chronicle* reports that 639 MPs have now signed up to the verbose, muddled and Zionist-inflected IHRA definition of anti-Semitism. All SNP, SDLP and Green Party MPs have signed. Shame on spineless Caroline Lucas! Ellis thought: *whatever happened to this woman?* Those who have not signed are the seven Sinn Fein MPs who abstain from taking their seats and Labour MPs Graham Stringer, Tahir Ali, Andy McDonald and Grahame Morris. You can be sure the usual howling mob will be after them, screeching and frothing. The government's Communities Secretary Robert Jenrick has said that universities and councils that refuse to adopt the spurious IHRA definition are to be listed and could have their funding cut. He said that only 136 of the 343 councils in England had agreed to accept the IHRA definition when dealing with allegations of anti-Semitism. Meanwhile today's *Guardian* website carries yet another piece about 'Labour's anti-Semitism crisis'. Then came Sunday with its morning haze and fog, Ellis read. Talk returned again and again to the mysterious dead woman retrieved from Preetzer Lake. Cresspahl walked down Town Street carrying a wreath. Little Gesine walked at his side, a subdued child in wooden clogs.

Wednesday 29th January 2020

A day of bright sunshine. After the child had eaten breakfast and played for a while, Ellis rocked the pram and sang: *Go to sleep, my little one, Go to sleep, my little one, Go to sleep, Go to sleep, Go to sleep in the morning.* The child slept. Ellis read a few more pages of *Anniversaries*. Cresspahl believed a war was coming. His wife Lisbeth found it hard to foresee a time when the town of Jerichow and her own household would lack for shoes or clothes or even kitchen knives. She saw no shortages, no signs of impending war. Business seemed to be thriving. The local paper was filled with advertisements for Mercedes Typewriters, cigarettes with genuine Turkish tobacco, gas stoves… Later the child woke. She flinched and turned away when the bright sunlight fell upon her face. In the garden of the mock-Tudor house the three white geese screeched furiously, as if on Twitter. In the park the child beamed as Ellis pushed the swing. She was less enthusiastic about the rope swing shaped like a bowl, constructed to resemble a giant spider's web. Later that day Ellis read a critique by Hugh Lovatt of Donald Trump's new 'peace plan' for occupied Palestine. Lovatt was described as 'a policy fellow at the European Council on Foreign Relations'. Ellis had never heard of this Council. The Trump proposal, Lovatt said, 'would cement a one-state reality of open-ended occupation and unequal rights for Palestinians. The plan leaves Palestinians with an atrophied entity made up of disconnected Bantusans in the West Bank and Gaza devoid of meaningful sovereignty, lacking any control over its borders, airspace, territorial waters, and the bulk of its natural resources - and with no capital in East Jerusalem. Essentially, the deal represents a worsening of the current situation, with a US presidential seal of approval.' When she returns home from work Gesine finds her daughter with some pictures cut out from *The New York Times*. One shows the Chinese quarter in Saigon. Bombs, fires and fighting have reduced it to rubble. It resembles a dump, with fire and thick smoke rising upward. Her daughter tells Gesine that this couldn't happen in New York.

Thursday 30th January 2020

It is announced that Sarah Sands, the infamous editor of Radio 4's poisonous morning show 'Today', will be leaving in September, 'I am so proud of what we have achieved,' she said. 'We played a not inconsiderable role in representing Jeremy Corbyn and his supporters as deranged left-wing fanatics. Who can forget our pioneering news story describing how Corbyn supporters had marched on Saint Stella Creasy's house and assembled outside in a blatant attempt to intimidate her regarding her brave support for bombing Syria. The fact that this fake news story, which originated in a hoax Facebook account, was treated with great deference and made a top news story by BBC News, could scarcely be a better illustration of the organisation's unstinting hostility to anything remotely tinged with socialism. Not one of the 8,000 employees of BBC News made any effort to check out that utterly bogus story, such was the BBC's hatred of Corbyn and everything he stood for. And when, months later, BBC News acknowledged that the story was a complete fabrication, the organisation made sure that its grudging apology for communicating fake news was tucked away on a website where it would be seen by almost no one. The 'Today' programme itself never mentioned this belated correction, but then why should it? When we can persuade someone as inept and feeble as John McDonnell to apologise for the non-existent bullying of Stella Creasy, and who could then be relied upon to return to 'Today' and never mention this, why the fuck should we? So piss off, Corbyn, I did my little bit to ensure you would never win an election, and my efforts on behalf of Britain's blood-spattered and corrupt status quo will not go unrewarded.' Or so Ellis *felt* she should have said. What Sarah Sands *actually* said was: 'I am so proud of what we have achieved - blah blah - the Today programme is a beacon of news journalism.' No it isn't. Year after year its rabid obsession with non-existent anti-Semitism was on a par with that of Jonathan Freedland's rancid *Guardian*. A daily diet of manufactured outrage. In bed that night Ellis read: 'It was Gesine who heard the phone ring the next morning.' An ending long hinted at had finally happened. Jarringly, the bleak basic minimal fact led on to information about the average woman industrial worker in Czechoslovakia.

Friday 31st January 2020

Today is the day that the United Kingdom (irony) leaves the European Union (sardonic laugh), at 11pm GMT. At Garboldisham that afternoon there were a few drops of rain. You have the flu and a fever, Mrs. Cresspahl, Ellis read later that day. It's practically an epidemic. And eleven pages later: Now everyone ran at once from where they'd been standing off to the side and gathered around the open hole. It made Ellis think of the time he'd stood by Uwe Johnson's grave. A bleak cold day in a month he could no longer remember. By 10pm Ellis had reached page 684 of *Anniversaries*. By 11pm that night Ellis was fast asleep in his narrow single bed. *Fast Asleep* he thought. A good title for an unwritten Ellis Sharp novel.

Saturday 1st February 2020

A sunny morning. On the *Guardian* website Ellis read a lengthy complaint about Brexit by the writer Ian McEwan. McEwan argued that the Referendum result had been advisory, not binding. He spoke darkly of 'Russian involvement'. He blamed Jeremy Corbyn who, he asserted, had held open the door out of Europe for Boris Johnson to walk through. Later he denounced 'Corbyn and his grim lieutenants'. He praised the 'honesty' of Theresa May. As Ellis was reading the article on the *Guardian* website an advert flashed up offering advice on how to invest £1 million in a pension fund. Ellis finished the feature. It struck him as an admirable representation of the unbearable smugness of a certain sort of privileged Remainiac. There was the slippery attitude to democracy - the argument that only 37% of the electorate had voted for Brexit. This was a statistic which dishonestly marshalled those who hadn't bothered to vote on to the side of Remain. There was the reference to populism depending on governments who locate the source of grievance in some hostile outside element. In one sense this was a banal truism but McEwan's choice of examples was instructive: Stalin, Iran, Recep Tayyip Erdoğan. Not Trump, Netanyahu or

Narendra Modi. Besides, the leaders of Iran had every reason to be fearful of a hostile outside element, namely the US of A, which was seeking to overthrow it. The history of Western violence against Iran and the assaults on its democracy by Britain and the USA were erased from the consciousness of bourgeois liberals and all the others who were wholly silent about US and British imperialism, like McEwan. McEwan's feature oozed with the complacency of the globetrotting liberal intellectual. 'Take a long walk in the American Midwest,' invited our famous author. 'Take a round trip from Greece to Sweden, from Portugal to Hungary'. Ah, yes, *Hungary*… Number one in McEwan's list of these nation's cultural wonders was, needless to say, *food*. Jetting around the world, eating at the most marvellous restaurants - what joy indeed it is to be one of the moneyed cosmopolitan intelligentsia. And the EU itself - a stupendous political achievement, according to McEwan. Now, thought Ellis, while it might make sense economically, *capitalistically*, in a world of capitalist gangsters, to be a member of a gang, there was nothing intrinsically humane, liberal or democratic about the EU. McEwan's adulation of the EU stirred a memory of something Ellis had once read on Ali Abunimah's Twitter account. The spokesman for an EU campaign in Israel was someone who had once tweeted: *Fuck it. Wipe out Gaza.* (https://electronicintifada.net/content/fuck-it-wipe-out-gaza-says-spokesman-new-eu-campaign/21296) This did not quite gel with McEwan's starry-eyed adulation of the EU. Ali Abunimah had also written about an EU ambassador in Tel Aviv who had made no secret of his extreme pro-Israel views, namely one Lars Faaborg-Andersen. During his time as ambassador, Ali Abunimah wrote, Faaborg-Andersen and his EU colleagues have done all they can to advance Israel's war against the Palestinian struggle for survival and freedom, including funding Israel's arms industry and torturers, participating in Israel's attacks on the nonviolent boycott, divestment and sanctions movement and remaining fully complicit in Israel's brutal siege of Gaza. The EU embassy in Tel Aviv has also served as a training ground for members of the Israel lobby in Brussels. Surely, wrote Ali Abunimah, Faaborg-Andersen's most infamous personal achievement will be employing an open advocate of genocidal violence as the face of the European Union and its much trumpeted "values". Social media can be a powerful tool to shine light on wrongdoing by governments, wrote Ali Abunimah. In recent years, I have used Twitter to draw attention to the complicity of the European Union and its member states in Israel's brutal regime of occupation, apartheid and settler-colonialism. On Twitter, I was blocked by Hélène Le Gal when she was the French ambassador in Tel Aviv. I am blocked by Jon Hanssen-Bauer, the Norwegian ambassador to Israel. Last year, I was also blocked by the EU embassy in Tel Aviv. Mild words of protest, wrote Ali Abunimah, have no impact on a rogue regime like Israel's, especially when Belgium and other EU states continue to reward Israeli leaders for their crimes with closer cooperation and trade, including with Israel's war industry. In 2017, for example, Belgium transferred target-tracking technology and other weapons systems to Israel worth about $2 million. This included "computers used in bombing, guns and gun control systems for weapons". It is no wonder, wrote Ali Abunimah, that Belgian officials don't like anyone challenging their self-delusion that they are champions of human rights and supporters of peace for Palestinians. Ellis thought of *Heart of Darkness* and of the Belgian genocide of the Congolese and of how the EU HQ in Brussels is located at a site dedicated to the memory of the blood-soaked genocidal criminal King Leopold. Boris Johnson's cabinet, continued McEwan, project a special kind of smirk, 'perfected back in the days of the old Soviet Union'. Ah, Russia again, thought Ellis, growing weary of McEwan's sycophantic denunciation of official enemies. How bitterly and burningly ironic, thought Ellis, his pulse speeding up, that the author of *Saturday* should praise the Remainers for holding out for 'a kinder sort of world' with 'enormous and good-natured marches'. McEwan frothed with indignation at 'the bullying mob outside the Rees-Mogg home' - an episode which did not live up to McEwan's billing, involving a notorious attention-seeker and crypto-revolutionary named Ian Bone, who had once - irony - earned himself praise from one of the *Guardian*'s own drippy women columnists, Suzanne Moore. But one could understand that in McEwan's shoes any multi-millionaire might feel uneasy about someone turning up at their front door to protest about said multi-millionaire's politics. One wants some tranquillity in one's secluded mews home, does one not? And no mention from McEwan of the bullying-Corbynista-mob-outside-Stella-Creasy's-home story which had flooded the corporate media and which was entirely fabricated, with not an ounce of truth in it. But mention of another fake news story. 'The antisemitic emails from within the Labour Party were a disgrace,' thundered McEwan. Eh? What anti-Semitic emails? As usual with this spurious story there was no detail. No names, no dates, no citation. It did not escape Ellis's attention that McEwan favoured the Zionist spelling of anti-Semitism, which eliminated the hyphen. McEwan's mountain of indignation grew and grew. Most of 'the arts' were against Brexit! How Ellis laughed hollowly at this line of argument. How Ellis despised the craven British intelligentsia, who were almost to a man and woman silent about the daily repression of the Palestinians. What a collection of shallow narcissists, always willing to genuflect to royalty and the establishment and collect an Honour, like, say, Ian McEwan, Commander of the Most Excellent Order of the British Empire. *The British Empire*. That blood-soaked monstrosity. Not to mention FRSA and FRSL... Elsewhere on the internet Ellis learned that McEwan ranked 19th in the *Daily Telegraph's* list of the 100 most important people in British culture. Later Ellis read Richard Wilbur's 'Advice to a Prophet', which contains the lines 'we know to our cost / How the dreamt cloud crumbles, the vines are blackened by frost, / How the view alters.' Afterwards

29

Ellis watched a few scenes from an episode of *Katie Morag*. Later he learned that the motto of the town of Sunderland is *Nil desperandum*: never despair. Later he learned that for speech-making David Cameron had been paid £1.6 million since resigning as Prime Minister. Theresa May has been paid £400,000 in 5 months for ditto. Tony Blair is said to have amassed a fortune of £60 million from sources including property and consultancy fees since stepping down as Prime Minister. He has also claimed £1 million in public funds since leaving office in 2007. He has received £1,077,888 to cover the cost of public engagements. Later that day the *Guardian* website reproduces John le Carré's speech accepting the Olof Palme prize. Another smug, narcissistic writer, Ellis thought, reading the speech. 'Palme loved being the irritant. Relished it. Relished being the outsider voice,' le Carré remarked, adding 'And now and then, I have to say, it does the same for me.' David Cornwell an outsider? St Andrew's Preparatory School, Sherborne School and Lincoln College, Oxford. And what could be more banal and conformist than Cornwell's politics? Dutiful mention of North Korea, ISIS, Iran, Russia, China and talk of nuclear threats but complete silence about Israel's armoury, Egypt, Saudi Arabia, events in Yemen. A dutiful assault on 'Jeremy Corbyn's Labour Party' which, had it been elected, would have meant David Cornwell paying a great deal more in tax. The usual generalised reference to Labour anti-Semitism without a shred of evidence. Agreeable reflections about his privileged life as a globe-trotter. No mention of carbon footprints or climate catastrophe. A fabulously wealthy old man and potboiler king wallowing in self-satisfaction. No wonder that the right-wing Israel-loving literary agent Jonny Geller took to Twitter to hail it as 'a beautiful speech'. Ellis reaches February 28, 1968. The West German president is said to have signed construction plans for a concentration camp in 1944 but is uncertain if he did or not. Mrs. Ferwalter lost part of her life in the Germans' concentration camps. And on the next page: She has no tolerance for Negroes and believes in all seriousness that God made them to live in squalor, poverty, and sin.

Sunday 2nd February 2020

That evening, in the restaurant, unexpectedly, just inside the door, on the wall to the right as Ellis entered, there was a framed photograph of Samuel Beckett. And above the urinals: a photograph of Serge Gainsbourg leaning towards a woman whose face was largely obscured by her hair but who Ellis thought might be Catherine Deneuve. It was next to a photograph of a man skiing down the Champs-Élysées, towed by a motorcyclist. The cars in the photograph were very old ones. This was the first place with framed photographs above the urinals that Ellis had encountered since visiting Coxwold. They were everywhere, Ellis read later, in the spines of books, in seat cushions, in lamp sockets - each with five eyes, six legs, two highly sensitive antennae. And so she learned, Ellis read, that it's always the Year of the Roach in New York.

Monday 3rd February 2020

What he'd thought in the night was rain was no more than the wind pushing through the tall pines, creating a sound which resembled falling rain. Later, in the dark, at 7am, Ellis did not see the branch which lay across the pathway. Part of it wrapped itself around the rear wheel and the bicycle came to a halt. The chain had come off. Ellis wrenched away the twisted foliage and reattached the chain. In Garboldisham that morning it was dry. He looked old, shorter than they remembered, emaciated, Ellis read, later that day. Without warning there he was on Border Road, and Gesine knew he'd come to fetch her. On the next page there was information dumping. The history of brownstones - four-storey New York properties named for their original facades of reddish-brown sandstone. *The Affair* begins with the Solloway family leaving their brownstone home to go on holiday in Montauk. On the next page Ellis read that the Irish were the most powerful political group in the neighbourhood 'before the Jews arrived from Harlem, unable to cope with the growing proximity of the Negro'. On the next page Uwe Johnson - for let us not pretend that the narrator at this point is some 'character' whose thoughts are somehow distinctly separate from that bald man at his typewriter - remarks that although white American racism directed against black people 'may be incomprehensible' the prejudice nevertheless serves tangible economic self-interest in the spheres of education and income. In bed that night Ellis read *Anniversaries* until 22.45pm, then put out the light and fell into a deep sleep.

Tuesday 4th February 2020

On the radio the man who ran Heathrow Airport was smoothly explaining that a projected 70 per cent rise in airline passengers was entirely compatible with a zero emissions target for the year 2050. Later Ellis went into a local bakery and bought two croissants. Then he went to the supermarket and bought six bananas, a plastic-wrapped head of broccoli, a red pepper imported from Spain, a pack of Italian tomatoes, a tin of peach slices, a pack of desiccated coconut and two cartons of skimmed milk. It was a bright sunny morning but very cold. Ellis read: How do you pronounce that name: Crisspaw? And seven pages later: When German troops occupied Prague in March 1939, there were snowflakes floating in the air. The paper quality of this book was admirable, Ellis reflected. Smooth and agreeable to touch. He liked the font, too. Later, on Twitter, Ellis read: Five minutes ago @EUinIsrael was claiming Israeli annexation would not go "unchallenged." But it's actually business as usual as EU strengthens, rewards,

aids and abets the criminal regime. EU are bare-faced liars.
(https://twitter.com/AliAbunimah/status/1224657595866238977)

Wednesday 5th February 2020

It was a bright cold day. Ellis went up and down, up and down, on the swing in
the park. The photographs he took this morning featured long slender shadows
cast by the winter sun. Once again the child looked apprehensive when he
lowered her on to the spider's web rope swing. He quickly lifted her off. In
Anniversaries the collage technique includes the juxtaposition of scraps of
conversation. What we did to the Indians is basically what the Germans did to
the Jews, Ellis read. I'm still on Zurich time. Another good title for a novel, he
thought: *Zurich Time*. You must be exhausted, Mr. Kristlein. President Donald
Trump is acquitted in his Senate trial on both of the articles of impeachment.

Thursday 6th February 2020

The Scottish finance secretary has resigned over messages to boy, 16, was the
headline this morning. Ellis had never heard of this politician. Deaths from the
coronavirus outbreak have reached 563. *Emergency law aims to stop next terror
release.* The film star Kirk Douglas has died, aged 103. Ellis remembered him
best for *The Vikings* and the scene in which Douglas ran up a raised drawbridge
using axe handles. BBC Radio News solemnly announces that several Israelis
have been injured after a car was driven at them in Jerusalem. This is described
as a terrorist attack even though the victims were twelve Israeli soldiers. Eleven
of the twelve were lightly injured. The soldiers were from the Golani Brigade
and were on their way to the Western Wall in the Old City. Also Wednesday
overnight, *Haaretz* reports (but BBC News does not report) a 19-year-old
Palestinian was killed by live Israeli fire during an Israel Defense Forces
operation in the West Bank city of Jenin. 'Clashes had apparently erupted
between Israeli security forces and Palestinians who were in the area.' Ah yes,
thought Ellis. People in their own neighbourhood are described as being 'in the
area' as if they were intruders, while the armed Zionist intruders are described as
supplying 'security'. How corrupt is the language of this style of colonial
journalism, Ellis thought. During *the altercations* seven Palestinians were
wounded, among them a Palestinian Authority policeman, the *Haaretz* report
ended. Ah yes, thought Ellis. He remembered that the BBC also likes to use the
word 'clashes' to describe the murder of Palestinian civilians by armed Zionist
soldiers. Elsewhere the Zionist agenda of BBC News was in full flow. The
number of anti-Semitic hate incidents recorded in the UK has reached a record
high, Jewish charity the Community Security Trust says, BBC News reports, not
mentioning that the CST is a bellicose Zionist outfit and that its statistics have

long been regarded with justified scepticism. Zionist propaganda by the CST is all about propagating the idea that Jews face an existential threat to their existence, whereas in truth it is the Palestinians who face this threat daily at the hands of sociopathic Jews. But no corporate media institution in Britain will ever acknowledge this, nor that Britain is one of the safest places in the world for Jews, who experience no discrimination whatever, at any level. The news story on the BBC News website is illustrated by an old photograph of British Zionists holding up posters, two of which attack the Labour Party. The Zionist Home Secretary Priti Patel is reported as saying that the figures were 'appalling'. Further down the page is another photograph of a man holding a large Israeli flag and a poster reading ZERO TOLERANCE FOR ANTISEMITISM. Meanwhile on social media, where the truth is far more likely to be found than from BBC News, *The Palestinian Red Crescent is reporting 79 injuries in Bethlehem [4 ppl hit by rubber bullets, one of them shot in the head], during continuing incursion by Israeli forces seeking car that hit IDF soldiers near Mt Zion last night.* At 10.50am Ellis read on the Media Lens Twitter account a reTweet of Ben White's Tweet earlier today: *Killed by Israeli occupation forces since yesterday: Mohammad Suleiman Al-Haddad, 16 (Hebron) Yazan Munther Abu Tabikh, 19 (Jenin) and a number of others wounded.* Media Lens commented: *If they were Israeli teenagers, it would be headline news. But they're 'unpeople'. Our media are so institutionally racist they don't even perceive a problem.* Later Ellis read on Ben White's Twitter account: *Update. Third Palestinian killed by Israeli occupation forces since yesterday. Tareq Badwan has died of his injuries, after being shot by Israeli soldiers during the demolition raid in Jenin overnight.* It is reported that the literary archive of the dead novelist Andrea Levy has been acquired by the British Library. British Library curator Zoë Wilcox said it was an incredibly rich and important archive which illuminated the creative practices of 'an extraordinary writer whose literary significance will be celebrated for years to come'. It joins other modern literary archives at the Library, including those of Hanif Kureishi, Margaret Forster, Will Self and Ruth Prawer Jhabvala. How many more times will I be carried through the tunnels dug into the stone beneath the city of New York for its subways and arrive between the forest of pitprops at the station and intersection of Ninety-Sixth Street and Broadway? Ellis read. Today the child walked for the first time, tottering a few unsteady steps before collapsing on to her kneeling mother's lap.

Friday 7th February 2020

A bright crisp sunny morning. **Extinction Rebellion.** *Police Scotland sent out guide listing activists alongside neo-Nazis.* **Antarctica.** *Hottest temperature on record with a reading of 18.3C.* In the high street an accordionist is playing

33

'Wooden Heart'. A blind woman goes past with her dog. She carries a yellow
sign: PLEASE DO NOT CONTACT ME. In the café the painter shows Ellis her
latest painting. An abstract, with layers of blue at the base and layers of red in
the upper half. It might have been a seascape. The slanting sun is so bright that
Ellis changes seats, so that he is facing the painter rather than beside her at one
corner. The painter is sitting on the same chair that the actress Lily James once
sat on. Memory of that summer preserves the turnstile, the vacation, Ellis read.
It wasn't like that.

Saturday 8th February 2020

Grey, spitting with rain. It was reported that the Special Immigration Appeals
Commission tribunal consisting of Mrs. Justice Elisabeth Laing, Mr. Doron
Ze'ev Blum, and Mr. Roger Golland had upheld Sajid David's decision to strip
Shamima Begum of her UK citizenship, on the grounds that she had
Bangladeshi citizenship through her parents, even though Bangladeshi
government officials had previously said she was not eligible for citizenship
there. In *The Times* Anthony Loyd described how he had visited the al-Hawl
camp in 2019 and first encountered Shamima Begum, who was then 19 and nine
months pregnant. The veiled young woman had said to him: 'I'm a Bethnal
Green girl.' Her circumstances, wrote Anthony Loyd, 'suggested to me that Ms
Begum was worth of a second chance. She was a legal minor (15) when she left
the UK… As I wrote the story I presumed that it would ultimately lead to her
retrieval and rehabilitation' and that the UK would bring her home. 'How wrong
I was,' wrote Anthony Loyd. On the internet Ellis read about the suspension by
the Labour Party of Wirral councillor Jo Bird and Mohammed Azam, both
leading candidates for seats on the National Executive Committee. Ms Bird had
already won the endorsement of 45 constituency parties and was supported by
the Labour Left Alliance, the Labour Representation Committee and Jewish
Voice for Labour. Mr Azam, who in the past has served on the NEC and as a
councillor in Oldham, had won the endorsement of 26 constituency parties and
the support of the Campaign for Labour Party Democracy and the Labour
Campaign for Nuclear Disarmament. It was another transparent stitch-up by the
Blairite and Zionist wing of the party, underlining yet again the weakness and
pusillanimity of the so-called Left. On Twitter the campaigning journalist Asa
Winstanley (35K followers) wrote: Good morning! I have quit Labour. In a
longer piece he wrote: I did so to protest the party's illegal mishandling of my
private data, and because it is using its complaints system to conduct a political
purge of members who support Palestinian rights. Antarctica had hit its highest
temperature on record with a reading of 18.3C at Esperanza research station,
Ellis read. The increasing loss of ice from the continent affects all of us, Ellis
read, not just a few penguins. Colonies of bees flew in the sun, Ellis read. The

tree behind Cressphal's house was black with starlings. That evening Ellis watched *Rocket Man*. In bed he read a few more pages. The man had a forty-five minute walk to the sea, after his long trip, and Cresspahl sent him off alone.

Sunday 9th February 2020

Ellis woke at 4am and listened to the wind as it rushed past the house. Storm Ciara had arrived. Later, after breakfast, he came across a Tweet by the slippery careerist Owen Jones. Glad Asa Winstanley - who repeatedly suggested I was being used by the "Israel lobby" - has left Labour after being suspended, Jones wrote. Joey Calzone tweeted a retort: There is an Israel lobby, no need for inverted commas. Louis Allday tweeted: Reminder that Owen Jones opposes BDS on the completely spurious grounds it could target "random Jewish people". He uses the vague & meaningless phrase "Palestinian justice" - he is not committed to the Liberation of Palestine. Someone else tweeted a photograph of a smiling Owen Jones with his arm around the shoulder of the Zionist propagandist Alan Johnson of BICOM. Someone linked to a tweet by Matt Kennard, which displayed a photograph of a smiling Jones cosying up to prominent Zionist propagandists at a meeting of the rabidly pro-Israel Jewish Labour Movement, including Ella Rose. Matt Kennard commented: Owen Jones spoke at a JLM event even after it was revealed that its director, Ella Rose, had gone direct from working for the virulently racist far-right Netanyahu administration to the JLM. For many on the left, Palestininians are still Unpeople. Asa Winstanley is a noble exception. Rip Torn tweeted to Owen Jones: Your silence on the witch-hunt and smearing of pro-Palestinian campaigners is deafening. Ali Abunimah tweeted: BDS opponent @OwenJones84 once again proves what an unprincipled and willing tool he is of the Israel lobby. Ali Abunimah tweeted: @OwenJones84 claims to "champion Palestinian justice". Really? It's bad enough that he opposes BDS. But at every turn he has cheered the Israel's lobby's campaign of smears and lies aimed at @JeremyCorbyn and anyone on the left who genuinely works for Palestinian rights. Max Heder tweeted: Some day Lord Jones will have a nice ring to it. Ellis was reminded of the story he had written long ago, 'The Bloating of Nellcock', which forecast that the then supposed fiery left-winger Neil Kinnock - in reality just another slippery and wholly unprincipled careerist - would end up in the House of Lords. The wind continued to rush past. According to the weather forecast the wind speed at 10am was 67mph, rising to 72mph at noon. The time was 09:59. The wind continued all day. Ellis listened to 'When the Stars Fall from the Sky', a Stiff Little Fingers song. In the evening he watched the new Agatha Christie drama on BBC1. He suspected the second wife would turn out to be a killer. He would find out in a week's time. He also suspected that the characters whose hair was coming out had been poisoned, perhaps with arsenic. Nine more hours, Ellis read. One more day in front of the humming, hacking typewriter. He came to the last sentence on page 875. He read the first two pages of the Appendix to Part Two and then put out the light and quickly fell asleep.

Monday 10th February 2020

Ellis read a link supplied by the Twitter account of The Angry Arab, about the Israeli state's use of torture. A Palestinian prisoner was hospitalized with kidney failure and eleven broken ribs, he read. Another was nearly unrecognizable to his wife when he was wheeled into a courtroom. A third required stitches after being savaged by a security dog. Then the three Palestinians were returned to their Israeli interrogators. They had been swept up in a sprawling manhunt launched after a roadside bomb killed a 17-year-old Israeli girl and wounded her father and brother as they hiked down to a spring last August in the occupied West Bank. The Public Committee Against Torture in Israel says more than 1,200 complaints against the Shin Bet have been filed since 2001, without a single case going to trial. Only one criminal investigation has been launched, over a 2017 case involving alleged rape, and it is still open. Rachel Stroumsa, the executive director of the Public Committee Against Torture in Israel, said the allegations are "very credible" and line up with the testimony her group has gathered from other detainees over the years. "Somebody who is in good health is arrested and ends up two days later in hospital, incubated, on dialysis, with broken ribs," she said. "It's extraordinarily difficult for me to see how you could give it any other explanation than a severe suspicion of torture." Later, after a bowl of stewed apple and yogurt, Ellis read Owen Jones's latest Twitter attack on Asa Winstanley. Jamie Kennedy replied: You are a fraud, Owen. You have never meaningfully challenged Zionism. You have neither endorsed BDS, nor called out Israel as an ethno-nationalist, Jewish supremacist state, built upon the ethnic cleansing of Palestine. Neither of which are anti-Semitic. Someone else responded to Jones's tweet: This is obtuse as hell. What Asa is clearly referring to is Momentum's acquiescence in the McCarthyite witch hunt, which by definition inflates the size of the problem & targets innocent people, not Momentum's opposition to the pathetic 0.08% of Labour members who actually are AS. In reply to Owen Jones, Asa Winstanley retweeted his Tweet of 22 Aug 2019: 1) I have never called Momentum as a whole "Momentum Friends of Israel." I suggested the @PeoplesMomentum *Twitter account* may as well rename itself that because of the way it has pushed the bogus Labour antisemitism "crisis" smear campaign. Owen Jones did not reply. He replied to none of his critics. He replied to just one individual, 'Natty Bennett', who had 4 followers and whose tweet did not address the point in question. Ellis reflected that once again it illustrated what a slippery, untrustworthy character Owen

Jones was. He read a new Tweet by AliAbunimah: @OwenJones84's disgusting, unprincipled support for the smearing of @AsaWinstanley as an anti-Semite was overwhelmingly rejected by followers, so now Owen is doubling down on the smears and whining that he's the victim of a "pile on." So pathetic. Ellis stopped reading Twitter and returned to *Anniversaries*. The American translation sometimes grated. Obligated instead of obliged. And what on earth was 'the British Defense Department, Air Force Division'? From the context it appeared that Johnson was referring to an intelligence unit operated by the RAF. Had there been such a unit during the 1930s? Ellis didn't know. The Appendix reiterated elements of the foregoing narrative and supplied information about many of the characters directly associated with Gesine's father. Under LESLIE DANZMANN Ellis read: Such English matters have to be dealt with at length in fictional form first, in films or so-called popular nonfiction books, to make them more bearable for the public. Ellis read on. He reached page XX. He had finished reading Volume One.

Tuesday 11th February 2020

A cold, blowy day. Blue sky. On the first page of the second volume of *Anniversaries* the word 'empire' was once again left in the original German. Mecklenburg, formerly a province of the German Reich, Ellis read. In 1957, for twenty-four-year-old Gesine Cresspahl, baby Marie had been part of her, Ellis read. In Brooklyn they shot and killed Charlie LoCicero, a Mafia elder, in his corner luncheonette as he sipped a strawberry malted. She was no one, Ellis read. A field of memory in which strange grasses grew.

Wednesday 12th February 2020

Yesterday, in the middle of Times square, New York observed the anniversary of the Warsaw Ghetto uprising twenty-five years ago, and we missed it, Ellis read. Another bright sunny day. Ellis drank coffee and ate a hot cross bun in a room with four others. There was discussion of the events leading up to a recent arrest. A friend loaned Ellis a book by an author he had never heard of, on a subject which interested him. The book began in New York and contained embedded photographs. For lunch that day Ellis ate a slice of quiche, some tomatoes and a packet of salt and vinegar crisps. It did not become dark until 5.30pm. Pontiy came by to see Cresspahl but Ellis was tired. He put out the light and was soon asleep.

Ellis woke to another spurious anti-Semitism story conveyed by BBC news radio and the *Guardian*. The four candidates for leader of the Labour Party had appeared on BBC Newsnight, in debate. Ellis wondered why they had bothered to involve themselves with a reactionary programme like Newsnight, which had in the recent past doctored an image of Jeremy Corbyn to make his hat appear Russian and then pasted his image on to a background of the Kremlin. The sub-text could hardly have been clearer. Ellis regarded all four candidates for Labour leader as poltroons and reactionaries. None of them were prepared to stand up to the corporate media. On the contrary, they kneeled before it. If any of them ever achieved power they would each one be instrumental in promoting climate catastrophe and western imperialism. Their stunted politics and feebleness were exposed by their craven acceptance of the Zionist campaign to smear the Labour Party as seething with Jew-haters. Not one of them had the guts to stand up to right-wing bodies like the so-called Jewish Leadership Council and the Board of Deputies of British Jews and tell them they would not be bullied by apologists for Israel and its innumerable atrocities. Ellis reserved his strongest contempt for Rebecca Long-Bailey, supposedly the candidate of the Left. She was alleged to be the inheritor of Corbynism and did indeed seem to resemble him in his obtuse reluctance to challenge Zionist propaganda. On Newsnight, BBC radio news informed him, Emily Thornberry had criticised Rebecca Long-Bailey for not doing enough to combat anti-Semitism in the Labour Party. She denied this. 'We can never stop apologising for not attacking this issue as robustly in the way that we should have done,' simpered pitiful Rebecca Long-Bailey, adding 'we have not tackled this issue adequately'. Later Ellis went to a general store to buy eggs,a loaf of brown bread and a packet of frozen peas. From there he went to the bank. Afterwards he went to the post office, to collect a book which the postman had been unable to squeeze through the letterbox when he was out. From there he went to the library to collect two books which he had reserved. From there he went to the supermarket to buy onions, sweet potatoes, carrots, milk, honey, ground almond, desiccated coconut, Lurpak and a bottle of white wine. From there he went to the bottle bank. Later he read about Mayor John Vliet Lindsay. Marie didn't want to accept that the mayor might appear in front of both the enemies and the supporters of the foreign war, equally a friend to both, wanting all their votes equally for the period after December 31 of next year. She said something as she tore pages out of her scrapbook, but it won't get written down here, Comrade Writer. Three pages later Ellis put out the light and went to sleep.

Ellis woke to yet another spurious anti-Semitism story manufactured by BBC news. *Labour leadership: Candidates apologise over anti-Semitism.* The four candidates had abjectly turned up to hustings at a synagogue in north London prepared by Paole Zion, the Labour Party's affiliated Zionist organisation. It was chaired by the journalist Robert Peston. None of the candidates, least of all the feeble 'Left' candidate Rebecca Long-Bailey, was prepared to ask why the Labour Party still had an organisation affiliated to apartheid Israel. All candidates committed to implementing the recommendations of an ongoing inquiry into this non-existent issue by the risible Equality and Human Rights Commission, a reactionary establishment 'watchdog' which now had Zionists in leading positions. A BBC hack named Helen Catt supplied 'Analysis' on the BBC News website, which once again underlined how BBC News was a leading purveyor of Zionist propaganda. 'It was clear from the start of this hustings that the Jewish community would be looking for real answers on anti-Semitism,' wrote Helen Catt, concealing from the BBC's audience that, farcically, to be a member of the Jewish Labour Movement you do not have to be either Jewish or a member of the Labour Party - merely fully committed to Israel. The odious Dame Margaret Hodge was present in her new role as JLM leader. 'It is clear,' wrote Helen Catt, 'that the new leader will need to do much more than say sorry to repair Labour's relations with the Jewish community.' Yes, indeedy. Complete and total support for Zionism, sectarianism and atrocity and a total absence of support for the Palestinians is the bare minimum required. Ellis turned to Twitter to read what people were saying. *All these craven poodles willingly allow themselves to be "grilled" by an unelected anti-socialist group*, matched Ellis's own thoughts about this event. Antony Lerman wrote: *The existence of the Jewish Labour Movement as an affiliated society in the Labour Party is an anachronism. An affiliate promoting discriminatory ethno-nationalism should have no place in a progressive party.* True, thought Ellis. But is it not also delusional to regard the Labour Party as 'progressive'? Ellis found illuminating a report by Sienna Rodgers, who had been present. Asked about the IHRA definition of anti-Semitism, Long-Bailey squirmed and evaded answering. Asked about the *Panorama* hatchet-job Long-Bailey genuflected before her hosts. Unbelievably, Long-Bailey said she would welcome Luciana Berger and Louise Ellman back into the party. 'I agree with Israel's right to exist and right to self determine', the cretinous Long-Bailey gushed. (This is the individual who Richard Seymour backed - exposing the shrivelling of his former radical politics.) As for Keir Starmer… He summed up the rancid and reactionary condition of the Labour Party when he said: 'I understand, sympathise with, and support Zionism'. An extraordinary statement of the kind which passed without comment nowadays. As for Lisa Nandy… She was every bit as bad as the others. So too Emily Thornberry, of course, but she was an irrelevance, having the least support of any of this gang of four. She would plainly not be the next Labour leader. Later in the day, at the Lowry Centre in Salford, Rebecca Long-Bailey set out a four-point plan to rebuild the Labour Party. 'We are the party of aspiration and bettering peoples lives,' she gushed. She said she was ready to take up the mantle of socialist leadership, which produced another cruel, mocking smile on Ellis's face. From this news item Ellis turned to the Twitter account of Asa Winstanley, where he read: The Jewish Labour Movement/Labour Friends of Israel endorsement goes to Lisa Nandy - who claimed last night that it is "anti-Semitic" to describe the 1948 Nakba as racist. Vile statement. In his next tweet, Winstanley added: Supposed "leftist" Rebecca Long-Bailey also agreed with this disgusting anti-Palestinian racism, claiming it was racist for Palestinians to describe their own expulsion as racist. She didn't grovel hard enough though! Got only 1.4%. She deserves their contempt to be fair. Adverting to the various statements made at this hustings, Samir Eskanda tweeted: It's cool how none of the Labour leadership candidates knows what Zionism is but all claim to support it. The Cheshire Cat's grin followed me into my last dream, Ellis read. Minutes later the sun vanished behind a thick bluish curtain, the same way the Cheshire Cat's grin did before I woke up.

Saturday 15th February 2020

Ellis woke to BBC radio news describing the prevalence of anti-Semitism. A Jewish author was being interviewed. He said his next book would be on this subject. Later, there was an interview with a retired general about 'defence spending' (the BBC's term for Britain's armed commitment in support of a variety of dictatorships, absolute monarchies and torture states across the Middle East). The fawning interviewer asked the retired general about the terrible toll on civilians in Idlib, in Syria. The fawning interviewer was concerned about civilian suffering. The fawning interviewer's rhetoric reminded Ellis that this compassion was never available for Palestinian civilians. The craven BBC had described the massacre of over sixty unarmed protesters as an event in which protesters had died 'in clashes'. The BBC never contextualised these recurring atrocities. There would never be any mention of previous atrocities in Gaza, in which Jews had deliberately murdered civilians. Khan Unis, November 3 1956: 275 males shot. Rafah refugee camp, November 12 1956: 111 males shot. In other parts of Gaza in November 1956: 66 males shot. Saturday 15th February 2020: other news. Emily Thornberry is out. She failed to make it on to the final members' ballot after failing to get the required backing of at least 33 Labour Party constituencies. A cold, grey blustery morning. Storm Dennis was forecast to arrive later in the day, bringing winds of 60mph. By 1pm the weather was unchanged - cold, dry, blustery, but nothing out of the ordinary. As he ate a slice of bread and butter, some slices of cheese and a bowl of sweet potato soup, Ellis read a reTweet of a tweet by Mark Curtis, dated December 12 2019. Curtis wrote that a study had showed that in the 45 days since the general election was called there had been 1,247 articles on Jeremy Corbyn and anti-Semitism, of which most had appeared in *The Guardian*, which featured 164 articles, an average of 3.6 a day. The wind roared in the trees as Ellis walked down the dark road. The noise was as loud as machinery and at one point he turned, to check that some large object was not bearing down upon him. The hall was lit and filled with people. Ellis asked the woman beside him at the table if she was watching *The Pale Horse*. She was not. She did not like Agatha Christie. The wind roared all night. The chicken had escaped from the Kommandatura, Ellis read later, in bed. It had found some grain beside the trouser pockets of the corpses. In its confusion it was pecking at human flesh as well.

Sunday 16th February 2020

The noise of the wind roaring through the loft of the house woke Ellis at a little before 4am. Forty-five minutes elapsed before he slid back into sleep. In the morning the top story was about the suicide of a television presenter, a blonde woman. Ellis knew little about the show she had presented, never having watched it. He regarded the fact that this human story was the top news item, treated with enormous importance, with many tributes and opinions reported, as symptomatic of the decadence and narcissism of BBC News and those who managed it and presented it. Not that BBC News was particularly different to other corporate news media in this regard. But the BBC was forever insisting, with all the shrill, screeching repetition of the proverbial bird in a gilded cage, that it was simply the best and most impartial news service in the world, the world, the world, the best, the best, the best. But this news story blanked out a thousand more important events in British society and around the world. Later Ellis went out shopping. He purchased carrots, a red pepper, a head of broccoli, some large onions. He first checked that the red pepper did not come from Israel (it didn't, it came from Spain). Afterwards he had his hair cut and discussed police racism with his hairdresser. The hairdresser said her black boyfriend was regularly stopped and searched by the police. It was harassment. Later Ellis encountered a cat named Frank. On Ben White's Twitter account he read: Yesterday, Israeli forces in occupied East Jerusalem shot 9-year-old Malek Issa in the face with a sponge-tipped bullet, as he walked home from school. Malek suffered a fractured skull & is reportedly likely to lose one eye. In *Anniversaries* Ellis reached May 8 1968. Senator Robert F. Kennedy has won the Indiana primary. A young man stands outside the Cresspahls' doorway. He is wearing highly polished shoes. Ellis puts the book down and prepares for sleep. Outside, the wind roars.

Monday 17th February 2020

A bright sunny morning. The high winds are over. The news is all about
flooding in Wales and further commentary about the suicide of the television
presenter. Ellis went shopping and bought a piece of cod. He was startled to be
charged over £16 for it. Next he purchased two kitchen rolls which were on
special offer. After that he went to Tesco to buy two packets of hot cross buns.
In the street he talked to a neighbour about a tall tree which might well cause
substantial damage to property if it blew over in a storm. It was unclear whether
the tall tree was on land which belonged to the local highways authority or the
owner of the adjacent house. Thursday is the day that Gesine Cresspahl takes
Czech lessons. Why does she wish to acquire this language? At this stage in the
narrative it is uncertain. There's a Czech film showing with English subtitles.
Gesine has been studying the language for six months. She wishes to test her
grasp of it.

Tuesday 18th February 2020

Another bright sunny morning. On the morning radio news a Russian woman
who had been under house arrest described her situation as a dissident under
Putin. For Ellis this was yet another reminder of the numerous ways in which
BBC News blanked out Palestinian resistance to the ferocious and ever-
expanding Jewish settler state. No Palestinian political prisoner would ever get
on BBC radio news and be permitted to describe their treatment to a sympathetic
interviewer. Ellis simply couldn't remember the last time he had heard any
Palestinian speaking about anything on BBC radio news or seen a Palestinian
being interviewed on TV. Not in years and years and years. Later, on the station
platform, it was bitterly cold. It was the half-term holiday and there were
children on the platform with parents, evidently being taken on an adventure.
Ellis listened to Florence Welch's fourth studio album. He ate a packet of Kettle
lightly salted crisps. By 15.37 the day had changed. The sky was cloudy. Later it
rained. Ellis watched *Us*. A metaphor, he deduced. But for what? A form of self-
destruction. Firearms? Extreme wealth juxtaposed with extreme deprivation?
The narcissism and complacency of the black bourgeoisie? It was an interesting
movie, even though it seemed to unravel somewhat at the end. There was an
echo of *The Matrix*. The twist was neat. It reminded Ellis of *Use of Weapons*.
The evening television news was dominated by stories of flooded towns in
Wales. The jury was out in the Harvey Weinstein trial. *The Fifth Horseman is
Fear*, the Czech film showing with English subtitles, can be seen at the Baronet
on Fifty-Ninth Street. Gesine doesn't always understand what is being said. But
when she reads the English subtitles she is distracted by the difference between
the original and the translation. Ellis looked the movie up on Amazon. It had

once been available as an American DVD but now not even a second-hand copy was on sale. And now in Jerichow an open coffin is driven down Town Street. It contains the body of a young man who has died on the Rammin estate. Circumstances unknown. Ellis put out the light and was soon asleep.

Wednesday 19th February 2020

Another bright sunny morning. The River Severn was reported to be in danger of breaching flood barriers. The dead television celebrity's family had released an unpublished instagram post she wrote days before she died. On the blog of John Hilley, Ellis read a critique of the programme which had made the dead woman a television 'celebrity'. The idealised TV place was certainly no Love Island, wrote John Hilley. It's the latest variant of a deeply-exploitative fantasy-as-reality genre. This actual country, the place where so much discussion of this story is being conducted, is no island of love either. It's also a place of peddled illusions and false hopes. It is built on a system that stands for the antithesis of compassion, empathy or love, wrote John Hilley. It is a system predicated on competition, acquisition, consumer status, greed, vanity, envy, low esteem and the actual promotion of *unhappiness*. A system that relentlessly pushes market ideals of enterprise, fame and material success as capitalistic versions of - never-to-be-realised - fulfilment, harmony and contentment. Gray light in the park as if winter was on its way, employee Cresspahl is wearing a funereal dress. Employee Cresspahl retreats into a telephone booth. She dials the numbers that spell NERVOUS on the dial.

Thursday 20th February 2020

Cold, grey, rain on its way. Nine people are reported shot dead in two bars in Germany. The episode is as yet unexplained. Not on the radio or TV news: Israeli Prime Minister Benjamin Netanyahu announced plans today to build thousands of new homes for Jewish settlers in annexed east Jerusalem. We're adding another 2,200 units to Har Homa, Netanyahu said in a video message posted by his office. The contentious Har Homa community was first built in 1997, during a previous Netanyahu government. Netanyahu also announced approval to build a new settlement with several thousand homes in Givat Hamatos, next to the mainly Palestinian east Jerusalem neighbourhood of Beit Safafa. Watchdog Peace Now called the Givat Hamatos project 'a severe blow to the two state solution', as it would interrupt 'territorial continuity' between Bethlehem and east Jerusalem. The website of the *Jewish Chronicle* carried the following item. Audrey White: An apology. In February and March 2019, we published articles which made allegations about Mrs Audrey White, some of which were untrue. We have already published the IPSO adjudication in relation to these articles and have agreed to pay a sum in damages to Mrs White and her legal costs. We apologise for the distress caused. On Twitter Ellis read that John McDonnell MP had visited Julian Assange in Belmarsh Prison. A *Guardian* journalist named Ben Quinn tweeted 'Assange extradition hearing is "the Dreyfuss case of our age," says John McDonnell after meeting inside Belmarsh prison'. It did not surprise Ellis that a *Guardian* journalist was unable correctly to spell the surname of Alfred Dreyfus. Karen Pollock, Chief Executive of the Holocaust Educational Trust, sputtered that the analogy was 'so deeply offensive'. But then Zionists were perpetually quivering with indignation about innumerable matters, except for the behaviour of the Jewish state, which they only ever sought to excuse, never to condemn. Quinn's tweet included a photograph of McDonnell, standing alongside an unidentified male who Ellis instantly recognised as the author of *The Leveller Revolution*, a book which lay at his bedside but which he had yet to read. His current priority was Uwe Johnson's magnum opus. Cresspahl was stuck with the problems he had with his police force, Ellis read. Like the cuckoo's stuck with his song, in italics.

Friday 21st February 2020

Cloudy but dry, a little warmer than yesterday. Ellis noticed that Richard Seymour had an article on the *Guardian* website about the dead television celebrity and social media. He did not bother to read it. On Twitter he learned that Graham Durham, a candidate for the Labour Party's National Executive Committee, had been suspended for describing the Chief Rabbi as a Tory. Graham Durham tweeted: 'Really they don't want a socialist anti-racist in the ballot for the NEC.' Near Augustwalde she found herself on the autobahn to Berlin and under fire from Soviet strafers, Ellis read.

Saturday 22nd February 2020

Cloudy bright. Thirty-two British and European evacuees from the *Diamond Princess* are flying back from Tokyo to Boscombe Down Ministry of Defence base, after spending two weeks isolated on the Coronavirus-stricken cruise ship, it is reported. The Britons will then be taken to Arrowe Park Hospital on the Wirral for two weeks of quarantine. Prince Harry and Meghan will no longer use 'Sussex Royal' on their branding after April, it is reported. This will require modifications to the couple's website and Instagram account. Filming of *The Batman* is under way in Glasgow. Leading man Robert Pattinson was not present. His double was seen wiping the rain away from his goggles, with filming taking place amid a yellow weather warning as the country continues to suffer from the aftermath of last weekend's Storm Dennis. Ellis watched *Emma*, the version with Kate Beckinsale, Mark Strong and Samantha Morton. It was only when the credits rolled that he realised the actress playing the role of Jane Fairfax, who he'd believed to be Greta Scacchi, was actually Olivia Williams. Afterwards he went to bed. Cresspahl trusted this man Pontiy one too many times, Ellis read.

Sunday 23rd February 2020

Pouring with rain, cold and grey. Ellis wakes and listens to the 7am radio news. An area of Italy is being cordoned off by police to prevent the spread of the Coronavirus. Tyson Fury has defeated Deontay Wilder to become the WBC world heavyweight champion. Bernie Sanders has declared victory in the Nevada caucuses. Sir Keir Starmer has warned the Labour Party that it would experience its longest period out of power since the Second World War if it continued to focus on internal disagreements rather than confronting the Prime Minister. We can blame each other and argue, the knight of the realm said, or pull together and win. A boat race metaphor, Ellis noticed. A sport of the ruling class. Rowing was an important activity at many private schools. Some even owned their own river. Ellis remembered a scene from a book about wild swimming in which the swimmer had been threatened and shouted at from the grounds of a private school while daring to swim along a river in Winchester. Presumably private rivers were partly funded out of the tax breaks private schools were granted as charitable bodies. On Twitter Sir Keir Starmer was denounced as a hypocrite. He had been part of the attempted coup by Labour MPs to unseat Corbyn after his election. Nicola James tweeted: Aside from the cost to democracy and socialist policies within the Labour Party if poster boy Keir Starmer becomes leader, many are rightly asking WHO FUNDED the post sent out to 580,000 Labour members today? Postage costs alone = £353,800! Nicola James reproduced a doctored image of the poster, which read *Keir Starmer for leader: No integrity, authority or unity*. Ryan Tipton tweeted: Don't vote for someone that supports Trident. Ryan Tipton accompanied the tweet with film of the poster being inserted into a shredder. Cultural Groucho Marxist tweeted: In 5 years of the "cult of Corbyn", not once did I get sent a poster of Corbyn's face. So why am I getting sent one of Keir? Daniel Griggs retweeted an earlier tweet of his which reproduced Sir Keir Starmer's June 27 2016 letter of resignation as shadow Home Office minister and asked: Why did Keir Starmer write this 4 days after the Brexit referendum and 11 days after the murder of Jo Cox, in June 2016, as part of a 172-MP coup against Jeremy Corbyn at the exact moment Labour needed to hammer in the response to press lies about Brexit? Daniel Griggs commented: Let's just say, Keir Starmer's capable of being a two-faced back-stabbing lawyer at the drop of a hat. Ben@BenJolly9 commented: Keir Starmer should have called for unity in 2016. He chose to join the chicken coup instead which cost us the election in 2017.

Later Ellis ate his lunch at his desk, before his computer. He drank a glass of water and ate an avocado with some mashed potato and mayonaise. He read an article by Jonathan Cook on the Middle East Eye website entitled *Labour's next leader has already betrayed the left*. A politics of cynicism – dressed only loosely in progressive garb - has returned to replace Corbyn's popular democratic socialism, Cook wrote. Leadership candidates are once again carefully cultivating their image and opinions – along with their hairstyles, clothes and accents – to satisfy the orthodoxies they fear will be rigidly enforced by a billionaire-owned media and party bureaucrats. Whoever takes over the party reins, the most likely outcome will be a revival of deep disillusionment with British politics on the left, Cook wrote. The low-point of the candidates' campaigning, and their betrayal of the movement that propelled Corbyn onto the national stage, came last week at a "hustings" jointly organised by the Jewish Labour Movement and Labour Friends of Israel. These two party organisations are cheerleaders for Israel, even as it prepares to annex much of the West Bank, supported by the Trump administration, in an attempt to crush any hope of a Palestinian state ever being established. Later in the article Jonathan Cook wrote: At another hustings, this time staged by the BBC, all three candidates said their top priority, were they to become party leader, would be to tackle Labour's supposed "antisemitism crisis". That's right – the top priority. Not changing the public discourse on austerity, or exposing the Tory government's incompetence and its catastrophic version of a hard Brexit, or raising consciousness about an impending climate catastrophe. Jonathan Cook's brilliant article, which offered the kind of penetrating analysis you would never encounter in rags like the *Guardian* or the *Times*, concluded: The next leader of the Labour Party is already a prisoner to the "institutional antisemitism" narrative. That means their hands are chained not only to support for Israel, but to the reactionary politics in which Israel as a Jewish state makes sense – a worldview that embraces its style of ethnic, chauvinist, militaristic, segregationist politics. On the website of the *Jewish Chronicle* Ellis read that Tracey Emin, Grayson Perry, Yinka Shonebare, designer Thomas Heatherwick and Tate director Maria Balshaw were among prominent art and design world figures among more than 500 guests at a West End dinner and gala auction in support of the British Friends of the Art Museums of Israel (Bfami). Installation artist and filmmaker Isaac Julien was guest of honour. He recalled that the Israel Museum in Jerusalem was the first to acquire one of his works. The dinner, auction and associated events — including a party for Young Friends of the Art Museums of Israel — raised in the region of £750,000 for educational projects. Ellis was not surprised to see that talentless and narcissistic Emin was among the list of conscience-free celebrities but he was disgusted to see Grayson Perry's name listed. *23/02/2020: The Legal Centre for Arab Minority Rights in Israel sent a letter today, 23 February 2020, to Israeli Chief Military Advocate*

46

General Sharon Afek, demanding he immediately open a criminal investigation into an incident that occurred this morning near Khan Yunis in the Gaza Strip in which an Israeli armoured bulldozer was filmed dragging a human body along the ground and repeatedly lifting it up in the air and dropping it down in the mud. A video of the incident was shared on Twitter by the Shehab news agency. In the letter, Adalah Attorney Sawsan Zaher detailed a series of international laws - including the Rome Statute, the UN Convention Against Torture and Other Cruel, Inhuman or Degrading Treatment, and the Hague Regulations - which classify the Israeli military actions depicted in the video as war crimes and blatant violations of international criminal law, and international human rights and humanitarian law. And now the latest news from the British corporate media, which repeatedly omits to report Israeli atrocities. The family of Harry Dunn has urged the government to refuse the extradition of Julian Assange until the United States returns Anne Sacoolas, the American woman charged with causing the teenager's death by dangerous driving. Dunn family spokesman Radd Seiger accused the US of "hypocrisy" in seeking Assange's extradition, while refusing to extradite Sacoolas. The 19-year-old's parents have called on the British government to refuse any further extradition requests by the United States. This comes after the Foeign Office said it had no plans to launch a public inquiry into the teenager's death and the handling of the case. 18.37. Ellis sipped a glass of Tesco Finest Picpoul de Pinet. At £6.50 (special offer) it seemed remarkably good value. It tasted superior to the other, more expensive brand of Picpoul de Pinet which he occasionally drank. Meanwhile the child's ability to walk had improved considerably in the past 48 hours. The child walked from the conservatory past the kitchen and into the living room, clutching in one hand a plastic stalk with windmills attached to the end. The plastic windmills were brightly coloured. Close to the television, which was switched off, the child sank to her knees. For his evening meal Ellis ate nutmeat with mushroom sauce and salad, followed by cherry pie and ice-cream. He read how carriages from not long after the First World War stopped every mile at narrow, barely roofed platforms. Names flashed by - the Verrazano Bridge, Oude Dorp, Arrohar, Arthur Kill, Tottenville, Raritan Bay. Ellis read how Jakob still had a credit of grain from his wages, how he'd drily swallow a smile, how he went to Gneez and came back with a coffin. Ellis read how Gesine and Marie were on their way to Grand Central Station when the remains of the parade swung onto Ninety-Fifth Street.

Monday 24th February 2020

The alarm went off at 7am. A grey, miserable morning, rain beating down on the windows. The Austrian government is considering closing the country's border with Italy, to prevent the spread of the Coronavirus. The world is on the brink of the outbreak being declared a pandemic. Julian Assange is appearing in court to face extradition proceedings. Ellis could hear a builder's drill. It sounded much like a dentist's drill. He felt uncomfortable hearing the drill piercing the brickwork, as if the machine were digging into his own flesh. Later he went to the bakery, the bank, the bookshop, the supermarket and what in *Anniversaries* would have been called a liquor store. On this rainswept morning he purchased a variety of goods, including two chocolate croissants, two bottles of wine, a pack of tomatoes, a bag of baking potatoes. On his trip out Ellis chatted to three people he knew. With the first person he discussed Amsterdam and American books, with the second a games mistress at a local school, and with the third, swimming. It began to rain heavily. The sidewalks were full of puddles. Later, on the *Guardian* website, Ellis read a review of the new Hilary Mantel novel. He learned that the book was of epic proportions, thrilling, propulsive, darkly comic, stupendously intelligent, startlingly fresh in every moment, with a narrative voice which rides at times like a spirit or angel on thermals of vitality, a masterpiece. Not his kind of book, then, Ellis decided. He had completed one Hilary Mantel novel, which a friend had urged him to read, and he had not found it enjoyable or interesting. As for *Wolf Hall…* He had soon given up on that prose brick. Another outdoor conversation took place with the person who Ellis had earlier discussed swimming with. This new conversation turned to the topic of rheumatism. Swimming, he was told by the sufferer, was good for rheumatism. It continued to rain. Later, Ellis held a conversation with a fourth person. They discussed Florida, *Key Largo*, the Hemingway house and museum at 907 Whitehead Street. 5pm, the radio news. Film producer Harvey Weinstein has been found guilty of two counts in his sexual assault trial. He faces up to 25 years in prison, Ellis was informed. Vacation in the country, he read. Country rain.

Tuesday 25th February 2020

A grey, cold day. In the pedestrianised city centre, as so often in British pedestrianised city centres, there was a display of gleaming motor vehicles. One vehicle, Ellis noticed, was named a Raptor. A symbol of aggression and speed. But then Britain was a car-centric nation, in thrall to metal dinosaurs. Later, on Twitter, Ellis watched a clip of a bearded, elderly man at a meeting held by Rebecca Long-Bailey. 'The people who prevented Jeremy Corbyn from becoming leader most are people like Margaret Hodge, John Mann, Tom Watson, and they are all members of the Israeli lobby. Why on earth did you declare yourself to be a Zionist?' Long-Bailey's reply demonstrated how shallow and self-serving she was. She blathered about 'the right of Jewish people to self-determine', ignoring the fact that Jews are not a people - q.v. Shlomo Sand, *The Invention of the Jewish People* (2008) - and blandly passing over the reality that this fictitious 'right' was obtained in the most bloody, violent and sectarian of ways at the expense of a genuine people, the Palestinians. Long-Bailey said: 'I believe in a secure, viable Israel against - alongside - a viable Palestinian state.' The Freudian slip was interesting, Ellis thought, because, of course, it was and is the essence of Zionism to deny Palestinian self-determination, and the only real 'Palestinian state' was that which existed before Jews arrived to erase Palestine from the map. Long-Bailey was a fraud and a liar in pretending that a Palestinian state could somehow exist alongside the Zionist entity. It had always been the deliberate policy of the Zionists to fragment the Palestinian people and obstruct any return to national status. Long-Bailey exhibited a stupefying ignorance about Palestine and the idea that she was somehow the 'Left' candidate was astonishing. The Labour Party was now more reactionary than it had been in the apartheid era, when no one suggested a black South African state alongside the apartheid state was the solution to the whiter racist state. And Israel was in so many ways so much worse than apartheid South Africa. Long-Bailey was a mistress of empty platitudes, blathering about calling for 'a peaceful resolution to occur as quickly as possible'. The feebleness of the Labour left was underlined by a tweet from Dr Philip Burton-Cartledge, a prolific tweeter and blogger and Course Director, Law and Social Sciences and Lecturer in Sociology at the University of Derby. The questioner at the Long-Bailey meeting was defamed by Dr Burton-Cartledge, who called it 'a question framed in anti-semitic terms'. Someone on Twitter responded to Dr Burton-Cartledge, denying that the question was in any way anti-semitic and asking Dr Burton-Cartledge to explain in what way it was. But Dr Burton-Cartledge did not reply to that very reasonable question. Ellis remembered that Dr Burton-Cartledge used to illustrate his blog with a photograph of himself with Tony Benn. But when Jeremy Corbyn had first stood for Labour leader, and to everyone's surprise had won by a commanding majority, Dr Burton-Cartledge had revealed that the candidate he had voted for was Yvette Cooper. Another defamatory tweet came from Matt Zarb-Cousin, who tweeted: 'To be clear, the guy who asked this question was a racist crank.' And who was Matt Xarb-Cousin? The name was vaguely familiar to Ellis. He looked him up and discovered that Zarb-Cousin worked in 'public relations' and 'public consulting'. Zarb-Cousin had started his career as a researcher in the office of Andy Slaughter MP. He was subsequently the founder and director of an agency specialising in 'digital comms, crisis management and public relations'. A smoothie, then, Ellis thought. Zarb-Cousin was the media spokesman for Jeremy Corbyn (2016-2017), appointed at the age of 26. On the Politics Home website Ellis read an article by Kevin Schofield dated 21 September 2017, which stated that Zarb-Cousin was exploring the possibility of becoming a Labour candidate, his first choice Rochford and Southend East, his second choice Thurrock. An ambitious smoothie, then, Ellis thought. A bit of a

Stella Creasy type. But Zarb-Cousin was not an MP. He was currently Director of Communications of 'Rebecca Long-Bailey for Leader'. So in abusing the questioner, who presumably believed passionately in justice for the Palestinians, Zarb-Cousin was speaking in an official capacity on behalf of Rebecca Long-Bailey, the supposed 'Left' candidate. Later, on the *Guardian* website, Ellis read more banal platitudes by Long-Bailey. 'Labour can win in 2024 with my plan to tackle the climate emergency,' blabbered Long-Bailey, adverting to 'a 2030 decarbonisation target', 'ensuring our firefighters are properly funded, equipped and resourced', 'a Climate Justice Fund' and 'working with trade unions, community groups and the climate movement'. Ellis laughed hollowly. Trade unions were among the most reactionary forces in the land when it came to climate catastrophe. Airports and new runways meant jobs! The RMT union was an aggressive defender of the rights of black cab drivers to clog up London with their noxious presence, and to oppose cycling infrastructure. It was typical of Long-Bailey's slippery opportunism that she was silent about Heathrow's proposed third runway, which had the backing of Len McCluskey and the Unite union. On its website the Unite union welcomed the new runway 'as an important step on the road to securing much needed airport capacity and tens of thousands of new jobs for generations to come.' Later, on Craig Murray's website, Ellis read an account of the first day of the extradition proceedings against Julian Assange. That evening in the fish and chip shop, waiting for his order of scampi and chips (twice) and a large cod and chips, Ellis read two stories in the *Daily Mail*. One was about a woman who had been murdered and who was a neighbour of Stanley Johnson, the Prime Minister's father. The other was about Harvey Weinstein. The *Daily Mail* reproduced photographs of him with a variety of actresses, including Julia Roberts, Catherine Zeta-Jones, Gwyneth Paltrow and Keira Knightley. That night, in bed, Ellis read: Cresspahl's daughter reigned behind a threshing machine. And two pages later: The thick panes rattled under the blows of a normal New York rainstorm.

Wednesday 26th February 2020

A bitterly cold morning. On the *Press Gazette* website Ellis read a story headlined: *UK national newspaper sales slump by two-thirds in 20 years amid digital disruption.* For example, the *Guardian*. In January 2000 it was selling 401,560 copies a day. Ten years later sales were down to 302,285. And last month the *Guardian* sold only 132,341 copies a day. But it seemed to Ellis that although the internet undoubtedly was responsible for this general slump in newspaper sales, in the case of the *Guardian* there was an extra, unacknowledged dimension. This was quite simply that no socialist would want to buy this newspaper any more. Once upon a time Ellis had bought the *Guardian* and the *Independent* every day, and the *Sunday Times* and *Observer*

50

every Sunday. He had grown sick of the *Observer* first, with its interminable articles by the likes of Shirley Williams (who was evidently still alive). He had given up the *Independent* next, unable to stomach the cretinous outpourings of John Rentoul and the weekly Zionist diatribes by the vile Howard Jacobson. The *Guardian* he had finally given up on when it sacked Nicholas Lezard and transformed itself into a Corbyn-hating rag crammed with fake news about anti-Semitism gripping the Labour Party. Jonathan Freedland was simply the worst of a hideous crew. The *Sunday Times* was a reactionary rag but its culture section was far better than the *Guardian*'s. But in the end the *Sunday Times* induced too much nausea (although occasionally Ellis still bought it, respecting its occasional forays into genuine investigative journalism). The *Times* he still bought on Saturdays, mainly for the TV guide. On the Politics Home website Ellis read a news item by Matt Honeycome-Foster. Ellis's cruel, cynical smile deepened. Rebecca-Long Bailey's campaign to become Labour leader has been boosted by more than £200,000 of donations from Unite, new figures show. Hailstones crashed down at 4.30pm. The grassy slopes briefly turned white, resembling snow. But by the time of the 5pm radio news the downpour was over. The clouds rolled back and the sun shone. That night, in bed, Ellis returned to Cresspahl's imprisonment in East Germany. He had lain too long in his own filth, unconscious or asleep or whatever it was, he read.

Thursday 27th February 2020

Raining. Very cold. At 8.20am it began snowing, but not for long. On Twitter one Steve Clarke tweeted: 'Fact - on the BBC news site there is not a single mention of the most important extradition hearing ever in this country. Not one. You'll struggle to find a mention on other UK news sites - in fact the *Guardian* is more interested in the Weinstein fallout. What a bunch.' Later this morning the court of appeal ruled that plans for a third runway at Heathrow airport were illegal because ministers did not adequately take into account the government's climate change commitments. The £14bn runway would bring 700 more planes per day and a big rise in carbon emissions. Later Ellis went to a local library and borrowed *Don McCullin*, published in 2019 by Tate Publishing. Photograph 108 showed a puddled rough street with smoke drifting from a terrace of houses. At the centre of the image were six young men, one playing a mandolin. In the foreground was a corpse, its arms spread wide, almost like a crucified Christ. The features were indistinguishable. The photograph was captioned *Young Christian Youth Celebrating the Death of a Young Palestinian Girl*, Beirut (1976). That night, on the 10pm Sky TV news, there was a brief clip of the three Labour leadership candidates at a televised hustings recorded in front of a small audience in Dewsbury. It was a classic corporate media event, slick, glossy, devoid of passion or dissent. Whatever happened to heckling? Ellis wondered.

Incredibly, the three candidates were still apologising for the non-existent anti-Semitism 'crisis' in the party. Lisa Nandy was anxious to 'earn the trust of the Jewish community' (i.e. the racist Zionist community). Sir Keir Starmer said he lobbied the Shadow Cabinet successfully in favour of adopting 'the international definition of antisemitism' (which is a verbose and incoherent definition, established by Zionists to delegitimise any criticism). Rebecca Long-Bailey whimpered that Jewish voters 'were frightened of the Labour party, and we have to accept that has happened and we have got to rebuild that trust' - ignoring the fact that the overwhelming majority of British Jews had long voted Conservative. Flight, revolt, liberation - he was no longer suspectible to these things, Ellis read. Cresspahl the father was deteriorating as a prisoner of a Stalinist state. In Times Square people craned their necks, reading the line of news running around the building. Robert Kennedy had been shot. Robert Francis Kennedy: 1948. B.A. from Harvard. 'Correspondent for *The Boston Post* in the Arab-Jewish war'. A curious way of defining the ethnic cleansing of Palestine, Ellis thought. Few Arabs outside Palestine had ever been involved, contrary to Zionist mythology. Sirhan Bishara Sirhan, the assassin. Born March 19 1944 in Jerusalem, his father of the Greek Orthodox faith. 1948, Sirhan Bishara Sirhan witnesses Jews murdering relatives and friends. His family are displaced to East Jerusalem. Education: Lutheran Evangelical school. A Palestinian Christian. Regarded as the brightest of the five Sirhan boys. 1957, the family moves to the USA under a refugee-admission program. 1967: 'Loses his homeland' (writes Uwe Johnson's character, although it would be more accurate to say that that homeland was lost in 1948, when the Jews seized it by force). 'Gives tirades about the Israelis who have everything but still use violence to take Jordanian land'. An accurate diagnosis, but then Zionism is predicated on the expulsion of *all* the Palestinians from their country. June 4 1968, Sirhan Bishara Sirhan enters the Ambassador Hotel in Los Angeles. 12:17am, empties the magazine of his gun at Kennedy and his associates.

Friday 28th February 2020

Bitterly cold but not sub-zero. There was no frost on the tiles and no ice on the parked cars. From an upstairs window Ellis watched as a jackdaw pecked at the guttering of a house and extracted something, which it then swallowed. Ellis had never been particularly interested in Robert Kennedy and his knowledge of the assassination was minimal. He knew that the killer was a Palestinian but was vaguely somehow under the impression that the assassin had mental health issues. From Wikipedia Ellis learned that in 1989 Sirhan Bishara Sirhan said, 'My only connection with Robert Kennedy was his sole support of Israel and his deliberate attempt to send those 50 bombers to Israel to obviously do harm to the Palestinians.' The Wikipedia entry on this day asserted: 'Some scholars believe that the assassination was the first major incident of political violence in the United States stemming from the Arab-Israeli conflict in the Middle East.' The usual stale formulation. The conflict was between bellicose Jews and Palestinians, not 'Arabs'. Israeli Jews enjoyed substantial support from global Jewry, especially middle class Jews in Britain, the United States and continental Europe. Motive. From Wikipedia Ellis learned that Sirhan Bishara Sirhan was upset by Robert Kennedy's support for Israel in the June 1967 war. Kennedy had promised to send Israel 50 fighter jets if elected president. M. T. Mehdi believed that Sirhan had acted in justifiable self-defence, stating: 'Sirhan was defending himself against those 50 Phantom jets Kennedy was sending to Israel.' A year before the assassination Sirhan Bishara Sirhan had joined the Rosicrucians. Later that day Ellis read a feature about the drawings of a young artist who stayed at the Spread Eagle hotel in Epsom in June 1986. Ellis remembered his only visit to Epsom, long ago, to see a film which was showing nowhere else in the Greater London area. He had wanted his companion to see it. Her stubborness persists for a while yet, he read. The course of events has become predictable. Ellis felt exhausted. It was 10.38pm. He put out the light and was quickly asleep.

Saturday 29th February 2020

Cold, grey, wet. The rain grew in strength. The 7am BBC radio news. A man in Surrey is reported to have contracted the Coronavirus. Another Atlantic storm system, storm Jorge, is predicted to bring high winds and rain to Britain over this weekend. The USA and the Taliban are to sign a peace deal. Several actresses walked out of the César awards ceremony in Paris after Roman Polanski, who fled the US after his 1977 rape conviction, won best director. Ellis went out and bought a *Times*, two almond croissants, some Cox's apples. The rain kept falling. Rain, rain, rain. That evening Ellis watched *Official Secrets*. He liked it. It was a reminder of how little political cinema there really was in the world of mainstream corporate entertainment. It was a reminder that Tony Blair had never spent a single night in a prison cell for his many crimes against humanity. It was a reminder that the BBC and the *Guardian* still regarded Blair's vacuous and reactionary speeches as events of enormous significance, well worth solemnly presenting to society. It was a reminder that the English judiciary were corrupt, reactionary, vindictive and wholly politicised. Rain, rain, rain. Such an important character, Ellis read. Then she disappeared. She was gone from my life.

Sunday 1st March 2020

Bright, crisp, cold, sunny. A blue, cloudless sky. Sunlight slanting down upon the pale wall of a nearby house. In the event of a pandemic, retired NHS staff will be invited to return to work to assist with the Coronavirus. The Home Secretary, Priti Patel, is coming under pressure to respond to bullying allegations made by Sir Philip Rutnam, who has resigned as the top civil servant in her department. It was a windy day. A speck of grit blew into Ellis's eye, causing him discomfort. He was momentarily reminded of *Brief Encounter*. He remained in discomfort until he arrived back home. There, he filled an egg cup with water and held it against the affected eye. He kept his eye closed until the egg cup was pressed against his eyelid, then opened the eye. After several attempts the speck of grit seemed to go and his eye felt better again. Later Ellis went to see *1917*. He found it to be a strangely empty film. It began well enough but later became preposterous. After a while he wondered if the drama was supposed to be the dream of a dying soldier. Evidently not. The mood music he felt was against the grain of the historical experience which the film purported to represent. Also, it didn't rain once. As for that waterfall... The title seemed an odd one, irrelevant to the subject matter. Besides, that year was remembered first and foremost for the Bolshevik Revolution. Ellis yawned. He felt tired. Wild swans, he read. Wild swans. Wild swans. Northward. Northward. Northward!

Monday 2nd March 2020

Grey, cloudy, mild. Coronavirus: more than 3,000 people have now died from the virus. Ellis read a review on the *Guardian* website of a newly published novel by James Scudamore. The suspense builds in the beautifully paced closing section, he read. Next, on the same website, he read a review of the new Hilary Mantel novel, *The Mirror and the Light*. This is where Mantel's supreme artistry is most evident, he read. She creates suspense and apprehension where none should exist. The plot is shaped as meticulously as any thriller. The technical skill is breathtaking. The book is shot through with wry comedy. There is a glorious scene. It is a masterpiece. Her Cromwell novels are the greatest English novels of this century. And yet, thought Ellis, from the extracts quoted this is a quintessentially inauthentic text, bogus in its modernised 'Tudor' dialogue - truly mock-Tudor! - and preposterous in its representation of Thomas Cromwell's inner life. A banal middlebrow slab of escapism for readers who would flinch at a text which denied them the comforts of rounded character, plot, suspense. A jigsaw-puzzle trilogy. The child has been unwell over the weekend but today she shows signs of improvement, although her nose is still a little runny. It was interesting, thought Ellis, that the BBC and the *Guardian* were among the leading proponents of swooning admiration for Mantel's trilogy. Two mornings running Ellis had heard on the morning radio news a trailer for an interview with Mantel by corporate news pimp Andrew Marr. Mantel had said when people asked her about contemporary events she disclaimed all knowledge, saying 'I've been away'. She meant immersed in research into sixteenth-century history. Ellis knew that a shallow toady like Andrew Marr would never interrogate her about the blatant contradiction in that squeaky assertion. Mantel had spent the past seven or eight years composing her novel. Yet in October 2015 Hilary Mantel had joined J. K. Rowling and Simon Schama in opposing the cultural boycott of Israel, via a newly-minted Zionist propaganda outfit called *Culture for Coexistence*. Hilary Mantel had signed its letter endorsing a two-state solution and calling for 'open dialogue' and other flabby, wishy-washy evasions designed to perpetuate the continuing violent dispossession of the Palestinian people. Not a single Palestinian had signed this letter. Still, it was useful to have a list of the British intelligentsia with a colonialist mentality. It included Melvyn Bragg, leading BBC Zionist Danny Cohen, Wendy Cope, the writer Amanda Foreman, top literary agent Jonny Geller, the reactionary historian Tom Holland, the novelist Charlotte Mendelson, the publisher Gail Rebuck (Baroness Rebuck, DBE), the art historian Sir Charles Robert Saumarez Smith CBE, the biographer Sir Anthony Seldon FRSA, FRHist FKC (at first Ellis misread this last acronym as KFC), Clive Sinclair, Chloe Smith MP, the poet George Szirtes, the actress Zoë Wanamaker, Fay Weldon and the cyclophobe Robert Winston (Baron Winston). These apologists for the Zionist torture state were criticised by supporters of the cultural boycott. Miriam Margoyles said: 'It is Israeli policies towards Palestinians which are divisive and discriminatory. Artists used the tactic of boycott against apartheid in South Africa and we are doing it again in support of Palestine - because no one else is holding Israel to account.' Brian Eno said: 'What kind of dialogue is realistically possible between a largely unarmed and imprisoned people whose land is disappearing before its eyes, and the heavily weaponised state that's in the process of taking it?' Ahdaf Soueif said: 'Today there's no question: an artist or intellectual who collaborates with activities funded or approved by the Israeli state is complicit in Israel's ethnic cleansing of the Palestinians.' Leon Rosselson said of those who had signed the letter that he was 'shocked by their political illiteracy and their arrogance'. Sarah Irving wrote that the letter ignored how many Palestinian artists are barred from any kind of cultural engagement by Israeli military closures, illegal walls and checkpoints, and travel restrictions. What the letter doesn't make clear, Sarah Irving wrote, is that one of the driving forces behind 'Culture for Coexistence' is Neil Blair, J. K. Rowling's literary agent. Blair is also on the board of the UK branch of the Abraham Fund, sponsored by Hapoalim, an Israeli bank that finances the construction of Jewish-only settlements in the occupied West Bank. Another committee member of

'Culture for Coexistence' is Loraine da Costa, who is on the board of 'One Family', a group which calls itself 'the leading support organisation that deals with victims of terror in Israel'. Patrons of that organisation include notorious Israel apologist Alan Dershowitz. *Artists for Palestine UK* released a statement which said that the letter would have been more credible if the signatories had some record of engagement and empathy with the experience of Palestinians over the past half century and more. 'Instead, we find the list thickly populated with the names of those who have consistently devoted their time and energy to protecting Israel from criticism and accountability.' That grotesque, bloated figure Eric Pickles MP, for instance. Pickles was behind the April 2015 suppression of an academic conference, *International Law and the State of Israel: Legitimacy, Responsibility and Exceptionalism*, involving 52 speakers from 11 countries, at the University of Southampton. The acid of Zionism has eaten deep into British culture, Ellis thought. It corrupts and devours everything it touches. And what was going on in occupied Palestine while Hilary Mantel was engaged in promoting her new book? On 26 February 2020 an Israeli military court sentenced Palestinian artist Hafez Omar to 13 months in prison. An event unreported by the corporate media, and which troubles the conscience of no one on that 'peace, love and dialogue' list, least of all Hilary Mantel. And who is Hafez Omar? He is an artist and human rights defender, whose award-winning artwork has been widely used on posters and campaigns defending the rights of Palestinian prisoners and for the Boycott, Divestment and Sanctions movement. He had been working in his graphic studio on 13 March 2019 when he was arrested. He was not told why or what charges he faced. He was handcuffed and blindfolded. He was taken to the Israeli Military Interrogation Centre in Ashkelon. He was refused access to a lawyer. The following day Ofer Military Court ordered that he be detained for 12 days. There was no charge and no access to a lawyer. The detention of Hafez Omar was repeatedly extended. On 8 January 2020 he was accused of 'incitement', 'joining the youth movement' and 'helping a wanted person'. On 26 February 2020, the Ofer Military Court sentenced Hafez Omar to 13 months' imprisonment and a fine of 2000 NIS (approximately 520 Euros) for 'illegal assembly' and 'stone-throwing'. This is the kind of persecution which Hilary Mantel sanitises by signing up to fraudulent 'dialogue'. But there was one name on that list which was ambiguous. Was it Clive Sinclair the inventor and businessman or Clive Sinclair the novelist? After some internet research Ellis decided it must surely be the latter Clive Sinclair. This Clive Sinclair was Jewish. He had won the Somerset Maugham Award and had been on the 1983 Granta 'Best Young British Novelists' list. His writing had been published in *Encounter*, *New Review*, *London Magazine*, *Transatlantic Review*, *The Guardian* and *The Times Literary Supplement*. In 1988 he was the British Council's Guest Writer in Residence at the University of Uppsala. He was the British Library's Penguin Writing Fellow. He was a visiting lecturer at the University of East Anglia and the University of California, Santa Cruz. He was a Fellow of the Royal Society of Literature. He was a winner of the Macmillan Silver Pen Award and the *Jewish Quarterly's* Wingate Prize. And he was dead. Almost exactly two years ago, on March 5th 2018, aged 70. On Amazon there were just two titles by Sinclair in print, neither of them the titles for which he had won prizes. Ellis read some obituaries. He learned that Sinclair had been a friend of the Israeli novelist Aharon Appelfeld and had written an obituary of him. Ellis would have liked to read it but this did not seem to be available online. Elsewhere, Ellis came across a wide-ranging interview with Sinclair conducted by Matthew Asprey in early 2011 and one year later edited, restructured and revised by both interviewer and interviewee. A polished, considered text, then. One of the topics covered was Clive Sinclair's Jewish identity. He revealed that he had little direct experience of anti-Jewish prejudice: 'If you ask me, anti-Semitism in England is very overrated.' But then we come on to the question of Israel. 'There was the Six-Day War, which turned me into a Zionist overnight,' Sinclair confided. He was asked about his 1987 book *Diaspora Blues: A View of Israel* and how he would update it. 'In a reissued *Diaspora Blues* I would express more anger at the enemies of peace, not only at Hamas, Hezbollah, and Iran, but also at the baleful Israeli government, and the fascistic settlers who provide its backbone,' Clive Sinclair said. 'I am still sufficiently enamored by the creation and making of Israel to see its unmaking as anything other than a tragedy.' He added: 'I would append these thoughts to *Diaspora Blues Redux* in an appendix, set not in the disputed territories, but in the diaspora itself - in London's revived Globe Theatre. In many ways [this] theatre serves as a metaphor for Israel. For a start it was the brain child of another Jewish obsessive - Sam Wanamaker - who, like Herzl, did not live to see his dream become reality. And, just like Israel, it was born of a text - the First Folio.' Leaving aside these preposterous Shakespearean analogies, Ellis thought, Israel was born of two texts, not one. The first was Herzl's repellent tract *The Jewish State* (which bore some striking similarities to *Mein Kampf*) and the second and more important one was the Balfour Declaration. 'But I would write about only one of the dramas it contains: *The Merchant of Venice*. I would describe what happened on a summer night in 2012 when the Habima Theatre of Jerusalem brought their production to the Globe Theatre.' It displayed Clive Sinclair's utter lack of understanding of the Palestinian experience that this privileged middle-class Jew should be discommoded by 'a security check, manned by policemen'. Bag searches, sniffer dogs, full-body scans! Clive Sinclair mocked 'stern-looking citizens bunched under Palestinian flags. At their head was some Marianne who tunelessly sang songs of freedom.' Needless to say, Clive Sinclair played the standard Zionist card, insisting that 'anti-Semites (along others) tried to get [the performance] banned'. Ah yes, the usual all-embracing racist smear, devoid, naturally, of specific reference. A protester interrupted the performance, shouting 'Palestinians are human beings too!' - or as Clive Sinclair puts it, with a disdainful curl of the lip, 'Or something like that.' Another protester shouted 'Shame on you Habima!' and another 'Freedom for Palestine'. With another languid, disdainful curl of the lip Clive Sinclair confides: 'As a matter of fact, I probably sympathized with many of their views. After all, anti-Semites aren't a priori wrong on everything.' To which one can add: the Palestinians don't need the sympathy of a Jew who does nothing whatever to oppose their repression. And, note, too, that basic rhetorical sleight of hand of a racist sectarian Jew like Sinclair by which even to shout 'Freedom for Palestine' is an inherently anti-Semitic act. Yet Sinclair knew nothing about the identity or motivation of these individual protesters. He was a slanderer. But then he was a Zionist. And on and on this fatuous 'liberal' Zionist goes, bringing out the usual chestnuts. Sinclair found it 'worrisome' that Israel should be 'subject to a unique cultural excommunication'. He added, 'Look to your own histories before criticizing mine.' Another fatuous and banal observation, since the history of Israel is not directly Sinclair's history, who was not born in the Middle East and had no connections with Palestine until he chose to exercise his racist and sectarian privileges as a Jew. And since Israel was created out of the Balfour declaration and since its very existence was predicated on British imperial policy, where better to protest against the cultural ambassadors of Zionism than London? Sinclair grumbled that as he left the theatre he found himself being filmed 'by a fierce-looking mullah' (racial stereotyping, anyone?). 'One look at the mullah was enough to show me that his mind was beyond my reach.' (Martin Amis emitted something rather similar, once, Ellis remembered.) As Ellis continued reading the interview he found it more and more illuminating. Sinclair felt it was 'a threatening act' to be photographed by a protester, indicating yet again his utter lack of awareness of how the Zionist state maintains a massive database of its colonial victims, who are filmed, photographed and subject now, in Gaza especially, to the perpetual whine of surveillance drones. No surprise to discover that Sinclair was a fan of 'Rabin's policies'. No surprise to learn that Sinclair said he tried to visit Israel once a year, enjoying all the privileges extended to an English Jew but which are denied to Palestinians. 17.22, the sun still just above the horizon, a blue sky seamed with multi-coloured clouds. Pink and fluffy, elongated and greyish-blue. Streaky and empurpled, like the clouds in a painting by Edward Lear which Ellis recalled seeing years earlier. Ellis suddenly remembered to look up starfish. He learned that starfish are marine invertebrates which typically have a central disc and five arms. Starfish date back 450 million years. 17.29. The sun has vanished. The ragged edge of the cloud lying closest to the western horizon is lined with orange-gold light. The sort of consciously 'poetic' sentence you'd get in the genre of 'literary fiction'. But *Twenty-Twenty* is not a genre novel. It is at best (at worst) autofiction. Ellis returned to the writing of Uwe Johnson. Mrs

Cresspahl is traveling with her daughter through the towns and forests north of New York, he read.

Tuesday 3rd March 2020

7.11am. A bright clear blue sky. It is expected that the Coronavirus will sweep Britain. The government is making emergency plans. An investigation has been established into the behaviour of the Home Secretary, who enjoys the total support of the Prime Minister and the government benches. Comparing her to Margaret Thatcher, Julian Lewis MP called Priti Patel the iron lady of the Home Office. Cheers from the government benches. Ellis read Craig Murray's latest account of the Julian Assange extradition hearing. He went out and bought three packets of ground coffee, a jar of instant coffee, a cabbage, a bunch of bananas, two almond croissants. In the afternoon it clouded over. The upper edges of the buildings shimmered, he read. After ten blocks, Lexington Avenue itself was blurry.

Wednesday 4th March 2020

Birdsong some time after 5am. It was light by 6.30am. Ellis swerved round the floodwater which covered half the road. But round the bend there was more water, covering the whole of the road. Some thirty to forty metres of flooded road. Later, Ellis read Asa Winstanley's new article for the online *Middle East Monitor* website about the imprisoned Palestinian artist Hafez Omar. Hafez Omar is not a criminal, wrote Winstanley. He is not a "terrorist" and nor is he an "extremist". He is not even a resistance fighter. The only "crime" that he has committed is to stand up for the rights of his people, the people of Palestine. Israeli army thugs first kidnapped Omar in March last year, wrote Winstanley. During the interrogation process, the Israelis demanded to know about "his artworks and publications on social media, especially those in support of the rights of Palestinian prisoners." He was not accused of any wrongdoing, except the "crime" of inspiring his people to resist the Israeli occupation. My point, wrote Asa Winstanley, is that Hafez Omar is guilty of no crime. He has been jailed for almost a year by the Israeli dictatorship very simply because the occupation state considers the very existence of the indigenous Palestinian people to be a crime against their racist settler-colonial project fuelled by that pernicious ideology Zionism. Later, Ellis read an article on *The Canary* website. It was written by Graham Durham and titled: 'I was a candidate for Labour's NEC. Here's why I was suspended just days before ballots went out.' The article was highly revealing. It showed how Labour was enfeebled by the leadership of dismal, supine Jeremy Corbyn and his spineless acolyte, General Secretary Jennie Formby. The party was terrified of upsetting Zionists. Graham Durham's suspension was leaked to *Labour List* before he himself had been informed. 'There is an assumption that any criticism of the Board of Deputies of British Jews is, by definition, antisemitic,' Graham Durham wrote, 'and that the Chief Rabbi, who has frequently adopted political positions hostile to progressive politics and the Labour Party in particular, is beyond criticism.' Bright sun but a cold day. In the park Ellis wore a warm coat, a hat, gloves and a scarf. Charming four-story brownstones on numbered streets, Uwe Johnson had written. What could be their fate if not a return to being luxury houses for one family each? It made Ellis think of the Solloway family home in *The Affair*. I gave you a year, Ellis read. That was our agreement. Describe the year.

Thursday 5th March 2020

The airline Flybe has gone into administration. The number of people in the UK contracting the Coronavirus has jumped to 87. Scientists say that the recent winter in Europe was the hottest on record. Judges at the international criminal court have authorised an investigation into alleged war crimes and crimes against humanity in Afghanistan. At Waterstones Piccadilly hundreds of fans queued in the rain last night to be the first to obtain copies of *The Mirror & the Light* at midnight and to meet Hilary Mantel. I want to go back to the sixteenth century, said one fan. Waterstones is expecting *The Mirror & the Light* to be its biggest book of the year. *The Mirror & the Light* was shortlisted for the Women's prize even before it was published. It is widely predicted to win this year's Booker Prize. He was able to console himself for his ample corporeality with languid, brown-eyed glances, Ellis read. He wore something resembling a frock coat. But Gesine Cresspahl's past life is never quite as interesting as her present one, Ellis thought. She is high in the East Tower. An empty, dirty sky is behind her. The tops of skyscrapers reaching up into it. Airplanes there would be less unexpected. Future history is present, although the author, long dead, cannot know it. Gesine can sense de Rosny's gaze passing over her out of the corner of her eye.

Friday 6th March 2020

Bright and sunny. Blue sky. Cold. The number of people in the UK contracting the Coronavirus has jumped to 116. The first death in the UK has occurred. As of today the global death toll is 3,404 and more than 100,000 people have been infected in more than 80 countries. Ellis followed a link on Ben White's Twitter page and read an article published yesterday on the *Haaretz* website. The headline: **'42 Knees in One Day': Israeli Snipers Open Up About Shooting Gaza Protesters**. *Over 200 Palestinians were killed and nearly 8,000 were injured during almost two years of weekly protests at the Israel-Gaza border.*

Israeli army snipers tell their stories. By Hilo Glazer. I know exactly how many knees I've hit, says 'Eden', who completed his service in the Israel Defense Forces as a sniper in its Golani infantry brigade six months ago. For much of the time, he was stationed along the border with the Gaza Strip. His assignment: to repulse Palestinian demonstrators who approached the fence. I kept the casing of every round I fired, he says. I have them in my room. So I don't have to make an estimate – I know: 52 definite hits. The mass demonstrations on Israel's border with the Strip border began on Land Day, in March 2018, and continued on a weekly basis until this past January. These ongoing confrontations, in protest at Israel's siege of Gaza, exacted the lives of 215 demonstrators, while 7,996 were wounded by live ammunition, according to the UN Office for the Coordination of Humanitarian Affairs. I believe I was on the right side and that I did the right thing, said the Jew. He was happy to shoot unarmed demonstrators who were, in his words, inciters. Protesters with their backs to him, with megaphones. The fact that he 'also' killed a protester 'by mistake' doesn't rattle him. They are all terrorists, the Palestinian protesters. 'Eden' says he broke the 'knee record' in the demonstration that took place on the day the new US Embassy in Jerusalem was inaugurated, on May 14, 2018. He did it jointly: Snipers usually work in pairs. My locator wasn't supposed to shoot but I gave him a break, 'Eden' said, because we were getting close to the end of our stint, and he didn't have knees. In the end you want to leave with the feeling that you did something, that you weren't a sniper during exercises only. So, after I had a few hits, I suggested to him that we switch. He got around 28 knees there, I'd say. And so it went on, depravity after depravity. In the USA, meanwhile, the UK Chief Rabbi, Ephraim Mirvis, spoke to AIPAC, celebrating the defeat of the Labour Party under Jeremy Corbyn. Does Mrs Cresspahl own a house on Long Island? No. Her devoted attention is turned to Kennicott II and nothing seems to matter more to her than how it was on the Montauk line with eighteen out of twenty-four trains from Babylon not in service. Bettina had had her fine pale hair cut fashionably short and tousled. This fashion came from a movie based on a Hemingway novel.

Saturday 7th March 2020

Bright, sunny, cold. Frost whitening the roof tiles, ice across the windscreens of parked cars. The sign on the chemist's glass door read: SORRY NO HAND SANITIZER GELS OR FACE MASKS THANKYOU. Later Ellis held a conversation with an electrician about the installation of a new television aerial point. Fischland is the most beautiful place in the world, Ellis read. I say this as someone who grew up on a northern coast on the Baltic, somewhere else. In 1947, during the summer, I was in Fischland. Never again.

Northern Italy has been sealed off to contain the spread of Coronavirus. Milan and Venice are both affected. Across Italy all schools, museums, nightclubs and other venues will close until 3 April. Cloudy bright, with light showers. At this time on a Sunday morning the bookshop was closed. Ellis stared at the bookshop window, which had a promotional display of *The Mirror & the Light*, featuring an enormous leather-bound Bible and two large silver keys. The Bible, he suspected, was bogus, no more than a prop. He was pleased to be able to resolve the enigma of the ampersand, which had not appeared in last week's *Guardian* review. That the *Guardian* could not even get the title of Mantel's book right did not surprise Ellis. He drank a cappuccino and ate a buttered hot cross bun from Tesco. Later, he rested a plank on a wooden block and smashed it into pieces with a sledgehammer. He repeated this procedure with a dozen or so more planks. The pieces he placed in a plastic dustbin. Cresspahl asked what the date was. Because there'd been such a rush about getting the papers the previous morning in the Schwerin prison, plus he couldn't read the small print too well yet.

Monday 9th March 2020

A little before 6am a woman on the radio was talking about the green woodpecker. It was traditionally known as the rain bird. The green woodpecker spends much of its time on the ground, hunting for food. It has a retractable tongue, used for probing ants' nests. Its mating ritual involves a game of hide and seek around a tree. The prime minister is to hold an emergency Coronavirus meeting. Trevor Phillips, ex-chairman of the Equality and Human Rights Commission, has been suspended from the Labour Party over allegations of Islamophobia. Mr Phillips said Labour was in danger of collapsing into a brutish, authoritarian cult. He was among 24 public figures who wrote to the *Guardian* last year declaring their refusal to vote Labour because of its association with anti-Semitism. It was no surprise to Ellis that Phillips immediately appeared on the Today programme to be given the opportunity to slag off the Labour Party. It also transpired that Phillips had written an article attacking Labour in today's *Times*. BBC News described the wording of Phillips's suspension letter as 'menacing' even though it was the standard suspension letter. A rubber loop is coiled high around her chest, Ellis read. She has a metal plate affixed to each wrist.

Tuesday 10th March 2020

The number of confirmed Coronavirus cases in the UK has reached 373. A sixth person has died. The first trolley in the supermarket was broken. The supermarket was crowded. Ellis bought some canned tuna, tomato puree and toilet rolls. In one of the aisles a customer was having a coughing fit. Later, Ellis washed his hands for the required 20 seconds. Now it's happening, he read. We're on our way to Prague. Ellis went to bed early, at 9.45pm, exhausted.

Wednesday 11th March 2020

My poor baby, Ellis heard her cry. A frantic, anxious time. Later, things settled down and grew calmer. On the radio it was announced that Nadine Dorries, the Minister for Health and Social Care, had contracted the Covid-19 virus. Anton Lesser would be reading *The Mirror & the Light* aloud all next week on Radio 4. Not on the BBC, not on the corporate media: Israeli forces shot dead a 15-year-old Palestinian this morning in Beita, a village near the occupied West Bank city of Nablus. Mohammad Abed Al-Rahim Hamayel, 15, was struck in the head with live ammunition fired by Israeli forces during the early morning hours. He was transferred by ambulance to Rafidia hospital in Nablus where he was taken to the operating room and later pronounced dead. Israeli forces, including around 40 military vehicles and two bulldozers, deployed near the Jabal al-Arma area east of Beita around 5am, clashing with villagers for around two hours. Israeli soldiers fired live ammunition and rubber-coated metal bullets at demonstrators from less than 130 feet (40 metres) away. 'Israeli forces increasingly resort to the use of excessive force, recklessly firing live ammunition and rubber-coated metal bullets at civilians, including children,' said Ayed Abu Eqtaish, Accountability Program director at Defense for Children International - Palestine. 'Excessive force and misuse of crowd-control weapons have once again proved to be the norm for Israeli forces when attempting to quash protests.' This occurred as Israeli forces accompanied a group of Israeli settlers to Jabal al-Arma. At least seventeen Palestinians were wounded, mainly from rubber-coated metal bullets, though one person was reportedly injured in the leg with live ammunition. Mohammad Abed Al-Rahim Hamayel is the second Palestinian child shot dead by Israeli forces since the start of 2020. Previously, Israeli forces shot dead 16-year-old Mohammad Suleiman-Al-Haddad with live ammunition on February 5 in the occupied West Bank city of Hebron. In 2019, DCIP verified the deaths of 28 Palestinian children at the hands of Israeli forces or settlers across the occupied West Bank, including East Jerusalem, and the Gaza Strip. Children in the Gaza Strip accounted for 23 of these fatalities. *Since 2000, Israeli forces or settlers have killed at least 2,115 Palestinian children in the occupied West Bank, including*

East Jerusalem, and the Gaza Strip. A seagull sawing into the wind, Ellis read. Her shoulders were hunched as though she had a lot of fear left over from the twelve swastika years. A good phrase, Ellis thought: swastika years. What would one choose for Palestinian suffering at the hands of violent racist Jews? Blue star years, perhaps.

Thursday 12th March 2020

A bright cold morning. President Trump has announced a 30-days travel ban from all EU countries to the USA, excluding the UK. Panic- buying has begun. Ellis discovered that Tesco had sold out of paracetamol. He bought a packet of Norwegian salmon and a loaf of bread. An American soldier, another American and a British soldier were killed yesterday after a rocket attack on the Taji military base north of Baghdad. At least twelve people were injured. Eighteen small rockets struck the base at 19.35 local time (16.35 GMT). UK Defence Secretary Ben Wallace called the attack a 'cowardly and retrograde act'. He added: 'We shall not forget their sacrifice and will ensure those who committed these acts face justice.' Boris Johnson said the attack was 'deplorable' and 'abhorrent'. Ellis talked to a neighbour's dog-sitter. She said: I have something you might like. She went into the neighbour's house and came out with *The Daily Telegraph.* The neighbours subscribed to the newspaper but the dog-sitter had no interest in reading it as she preferred her own newspaper, the *Daily Mail.* Thank you, Ellis said. He always found reading *The Daily Telegraph* an illuminating experience when a copy came his way. On the front page there was a large photograph of a woman wearing a face mask looking down at her mobile phone. She was standing in front of a billboard bearing the words NO TIME TO DIE and an image of Daniel Craig as James Bond. Further down the page Ellis read that the gormless, grinning Duke of Cambridge had suggested the coronavirus crisis was being 'a little hyped up by the media' when he talked to a paramedic during a tour of Ireland, Scientists accused the Government of creating a massive breach of trust after officials said they would no longer publish daily updates on the geographical location of new cases. Dr Bharat Pankhania, a senior clinical lecturer at the University of Exeter Medical School, said: 'I disagree profoundly with this approach. Before I decide to take a journey, I want to know if the place I am going to is a hotspot for Coronavirus or not.' Professor Jonathan Ball, a molecular virologist at the University of Nottingham, said he was surprised by the change of approach. He said: 'It's very difficult for people to understand the local risk if they don't know where those infections are occurring. Germany, which has 262 cases, publishes regional breakdowns on a daily basis, as does Italy, which now has more than 3,000 cases and 107 deaths.' It's Marie's eleventh birthday. Gesine is going to marry Erichson in the fall, after the trip to Prague. Jakob had gone to St. Peter's for Easter 1949, for the sermon on the resurrection, Ellis read. It was twenty to midnight. He put out the light.

Friday 13th March 2020

A bright cold morning. Blue sky, no cloud. Ex-health secretary Jeremy Hunt says it is 'concerning' that the government has decided not to cancel public events over the Coronavirus outbreak. Ten people have now died of the virus in the UK. There have been 596 confirmed cases but the actual number of people infected could be between 5,000 and 10,000. Chelsea Manning has been freed from prison after a judge ruled that it was no longer necessary for her to testify in an inquiry into Wikileaks. The US has bombed five sites in Iraq in revenge for the rocket attack on the Camp Taji military base on Wednesday. Dry pasta had sold out in the supermarket, Ellis discovered, along with paracetamol and toilet roll. The aisles seemed busier than usual. Schoolgirl Cresspahl was eager to learn how you made charcoal for flatirons, Ellis read. Less than three hundred pages to go, now.

Saturday 14th March 2020

At 5am, on the World Service, there was actually a mention of the devastating consequences if Covid-19 reached the Gaza Strip, which had intensive care facilities for at most between 50 and at most 100 patients. Naturally the BBC could not bring itself to acknowledge the reason for this lamentable state of affairs. By 7am this fleeting news item had vanished. Several European states have closed their borders. New Zealand requires all new arrivals to undergo a quarantine period of fourteen days. President Trump may include the UK in his travel ban. A grey, mild day. Ellis went out and bought a *Times*, two almond croissants and four quiches. Later he watched *North by Northwest*. 229 scientists from UK universities have signed an open letter asserting that the British government's approach to tackling the Covid-19 virus will risk many more lives than necessary. Willem van Schaik, Professor of Microbiology and Infection at the University of Birmingham, said the UK is the only country in Europe that is following what he described as its 'laissez-faire attitude to the virus'. The claws of the Picasso dove of peace painted behind him seemed to have him by the neck, Ellis read, shortly before he put out the light.

Sunday 15th March 2020

Grey and mild. At 6.45am a man walked past with a sandy-coloured labrador. President Trump has tested negative for the virus. American Airlines is to suspend almost all of its long-haul international flights. The total of deaths from the virus in the UK has risen from 11 to 21. Ellis went out and bought a *Sunday Times*. He noticed that the shop shelves had been emptied of meat pies, pizza, mince and steak. But there was plenty of bacon. Later, drinking cappuccino, Ellis read Camilla Long's review of the week's television. Of *Return to Wolf Hall,* a documentary about Hilary Mantel on BBC2, she wrote: We followed her extraordinary form as it drifted across the Derbyshire landscape like a big chiffon-wreathed space hopper. Camilla Long observed how Hilary Mantel lisped in her strange chicken's whisper. Camilla Long surmised that Mantel had only agreed to appear in the film on the understanding that large chunks of her books would be read out by Ben Miles, like the time Adele granted an audience to Graham Norton. On the TV news that night there was a photograph of someone who had died of the Covid-19 virus. He was 59, a retired policeman. Volunteers were shown pushing leaflets through letterboxes, asking elderly residents if they needed someone to do their shopping. The government hinted that anyone over 70 might soon be required to stay indoors, possibly for four months. Schoolgirl Cresspahl rose, leaving Pius with all his thwarted manhood behind, and walked up to Bettina Selbich, perfectly calm, without any permission to do so, Ellis read.

Monday 16th March 2020

At 5am the BBC World News was all about the spread of the Coronavirus. A mild, cloudy day. A secret Public Health England briefing for senior NHS officials, leaked to the *Guardian*, says that Covid-19 is likely to circulate for another 12 months and could lead to 7.9 million people being hospitalised. Ellis went to the bottle bank. Later he bought a piece of cod. The fishmonger told him that at the weekend he had sold out of fish. But there was no shortage and he was resupplied each morning. Ellis told the fishmonger that there were still no supplies of toilet roll in local shops. The fishmonger replied that no one in possession of a newspaper need worry about that. Later that day Ellis watched Boris Johnson's address to the nation. The 10pm Sky News bulletin showed deserted streets in York and theatre-goers being turned away in the West End. It is suggested that a quarter of a million people in Britain may die of the virus. Ellis returned to the final volume of *Anniversaries*. You did the right thing, ma'am! Calling us right away, that takes care of it, he read.

Tuesday 17th March 2020

A little before 6am Ellis listened to the tale of Albert the black-browed albatross. It is estimated that between 35,000 and 50,000 people in the UK are now infected with Covid-19. The new Chancellor Rishi Sunak is expected to promise financial help for the airline industry, among other measures to mitigate the economic impact of the virus. Tucked away on the BBC News website, near the foot of the column, was an item by Roger Harrabin, BBC environment analyst. *Climate change: The rich are to blame, international study finds.* A study by the University of Leeds of 86 countries claims that the wealthiest tenth of people consume about 20 times more energy overall than the bottom tenth, wherever they live. The gulf is greatest in transport, where the top tenth gobble 187 times more fuel than the poorest tenth, the research says. That's because people on the lowest incomes can rarely afford to drive. Previous research has shown that 15% of UK travellers take 70% of all flights. 57% of the UK population does not fly abroad at all. The authors say governments could reduce transport demand through better public transport, higher taxes on bigger vehicles and frequent flyer levies for people who take most holidays. Professor Kevin Anderson from the Tyndall Centre in Manchester, who was not involved in the study, said that the climate issue was framed by high emitters - politicians, business people, journalists and academics. When they say there's no appetite for higher taxes on flying, they mean THEY don't want to fly less. The same is true about cars and the size of some homes. High emitters have convinced themselves that their lives are normal, yet the numbers tell a very different story. Transport energy could increase 31% by 2050. If transport continues to rely on fossil fuels this increase could be disastrous for the climate, the report says. Flying and driving large cars should face higher taxes. The report's authors note that the recent Budget declined to increase fuel duty and promised 4,000 miles of new roads. It did not mention home insulation. The Treasury was contacted by the BBC to discuss the taxation issues raised in the research, but declined to comment. On the television news that night there was footage of the curfew in France, with deserted streets and police patrols. An Italian doctor wearing a face mask spoke from a tent. Behind him patients lay prone in beds, immobile. Incidentally, Ellis read, we already know everything, FDJ Comrade Cresspahl, all we need is confirmation from you.

Wednesday 18th March 2020

Cloudy and mild. Ellis read an online article by Richard Horton, editor of *The Lancet*: 'Scientists have been sounding the alarm on coronaviurus for months. Why did Britain fail to act?' *The Lancet*, Richard Horton wrote, had published an article on the virus on 24 January. At that time 800 cases of the disease had been confirmed and more than half of sufferers had difficulties in breathing. A third of these patients had such a severe illness that they had to be admitted to an intensive care unit. Most developed a critical complication of their viral pneumonia - acute respiratory distress syndrome. Half died. The Chinese scientists recommended as a matter of urgency the provision of personal protective equipment for health workers. Testing for the virus should be done immediately a diagnosis was suspected. The scientists concluded that the mortality rate was high. They urged careful surveillance of this new virus in view of its pandemic potential. That was in January, wrote Richard Horton. Why did it take the UK government eight weeks to recognise the seriousness of what we now call Covid-19? Chinese scientists had learned the lessons of the 2003 SARS outbreak. Under immense pressure, as the epidemic exploded around them, they took time to write up their findings in a foreign language and seek publication in a medical journal thousands of miles away, wrote Richard Horton. Their rapid and rigorous work was an urgent warning to the world. But medical and scientific advisers to the UK government ignored their warnings. For unknown reasons they waited. And watched. Graham Medley, one of the government's expert scientific advisers, suggested that 'ideally' we might need 'a nice big epidemic' among the less vulnerable to acquire 'herd immunity'. Sir Patrick Vallance, the government's chief scientific adviser, intimated that the target was to infect 60% of the UK population. After weeks of inaction, wrote Richard Horton, the government announced a sudden U-turn on Monday, after new modelling by scientists at Imperial College indicated that several hundred thousand Britons might die. Many journalists, led by the BBC, reported that 'the science had changed' and so the government had responded accordingly. But this interpretation of events is wrong, wrote Richard Horton. The science has been the same since January. What changed, wrote Richard Horton, is that government advisers at last understood what had really taken place in China. In due time, Richard Horton wrote, there must be a reckoning for this failure of government policy. We have lost valuable time. There will be deaths that were preventable, wrote Richard Horton. It was, of course, Ellis reflected, that fawning Tory pimp Laura Kuenssberg, who asserted that 'The science has changed'. There was nothing Kuenssberg wouldn't do to promote the interests of Boris Johnson. Whereas if Corbyn had become Prime Minister, Kuenssberg would no doubt be quoting anonymous sources worried that Corbyn's complacency and inaction had condemned thousands of people to death. That was how BBC News worked these days. And had always worked. Today it is announced that all state schools will be closed after Friday. Eton, of course, had shut its doors some time ago. The welfare of the rich is always more important than the welfare of the poor. A photo that looks like propaganda; no news value whatsoever, Ellis read. Ah, yes!: she croaked in a bouncy voice: Ah to be sixty again! Ellis looked again to check that there was really a colon after that first exclamation mark. There was. *A handwritten autobiographical statement*, Ellis read. *(fourth draft)*

Thursday 19th March 2020

Cloudy and mild. Chinese media report that there have been no new domestic cases of the Coronavirus. In Wuhan people are being allowed out briefly after a six-week lockdown. Ellis looked out of the kitchen window. A robin pecking at some seed on the bird table was joined by a sparrow. The robin immediately launched a ferocious assault on the sparrow, driving it away. Ellis had always felt well disposed towards robins. But now he felt that this one, which had been loitering in the garden for several days, was somehow the quintessence of the Thatcher-Blair years which had shaped where England was today. On Twitter Ellis read a tweet by Jalal@JalalAK-jojo: The reality in Palestine does not change with COVID 19. Israel continues to dehumanize us, raid our homes, arrest, shoot, and kill us. The one constant that does not change, no matter what the general circumstance is. The tweet was accompanied by photographs of Israeli troops wearing face masks and protective gear. Ellis stayed in for the second day running. On the news that night the Prime Minister, Boris Johson, said: I think, looking at it all, that we can turn the tide within the next 12 weeks and I'm absolutely confident that we can send Coronavirus packing in this country. But pubs, bars and restaurants could remain open and there were no plans to limit freedom of movement. Ellis examined the Year Planner at the front of his 2020 diary. In 12 weeks it would be June 11. Later Ellis underlined in pencil the words *from personal experience, at least since September 11*. Class II-A-11 needed almost three weeks for the first six pages of the novella, Ellis read on the next page. How the time is running away from us! he'd cry, and this was late October, and we were on chapter two, Ellis read further down the page. It was not yet 11pm but he felt exhausted. He had put a navy blue blanket over the bed to keep him warm on this night of solitude. Ellis put out the light and fell asleep almost once.

Friday 20th March 2020

Shortly before 6am Ellis learned from the radio about the courtship rituals and plumage of the male ruff. Today there are 244,523 confirmed cases of Covid-19 infection worldwide, with 10,031 deaths. Gavin Newsom, the Governor of California, has ordered everyone in the state to stay indoors. The Olympic flame has arrived in Japan. China has reported no new locally transmitted cases for the second day running. In the USA there are 14,500 confirmed cases of Coronavirus with 205 deaths. A grey, cold day. Ellis listened to The Libertines singing *Music When the Lights Go Out* on his phone. You never run across an Ingeborg Bachmann, he read. Later, eating pan-fried salmon, mashed potato and salad, he listened to a few tracks of *Bridge Over Troubled Water*. He drank a glass of water, having decided to avoid alcohol for a while. Alcohol weakened the immune system, he'd read. After the salmon he ate a bowl of stewed apple with blueberries and yogurt. He read a profile of Sir Keir Starmer in the *Sunday Times Magazine*. His good looks are an obvious asset, the *Sunday Times Magazine* informed Ellis. One of the most important things for a post-Brexit UK is to reassert values of peace, of justice, reconciliation and compliance with international law, said the knight of the realm, who elsewhere had said: I sympathize with and I support Zionism. Sir Keir Starmer - just another smooth and pitiless Labour careerist; a craven conformist devoid of critical intelligence or morality, thought Ellis. On Twitter, Ellis read a tweet by Ben White@benabyad: Over two weeks (3-16 March), Israeli occupation forces: killed one Palestinian (16-year-old child), injured 199 Palestinians, demolished/seized 16 homes & other structures, while Israeli settlers: injured three Palestinians, vandalised 385 trees & 15 vehicles. That evening Ellis learned that the Prime Minister had changed his mind about eating and drinking out. Today would be the last day that cafes, pubs, bars, clubs and restaurants could stay open. After tonight they must remain closed for the foreseeable future. Cinemas, theatres, leisure centres and gyms must also close. The ban is advisory. If it is flouted further action will be taken next week by changing licensing conditions. The death toll from the virus has risen to 177, from 144 on Thursday, with almost 4,000 people testing positive. The Chancellor, Rishi Sunak, said funds would be made available to employers to pay 80% of workers' wages up to a value of £2,500 a month, to deter mass redundancies. That evening Ellis watched *Le Temps Du Loup*. Topical, but a little tedious, he felt. When I finished reading it, Ellis read, a look hung in the air between us of the kind you experience maybe three times in your life, at most, if you're lucky.

Saturday 21st March 2020

Supermarkets are hiring more staff to cope with the surge in demand. Sir Philip Green's Arcadia group is closing all its stores: Topshop, Topman, Dorothy Perkins and Miss Selfridge. Kenny Rogers has died. He had once been a member of First Edition, which had a hit with *Just Dropped In (To See What Condition My Condition Was In)* and later with *Ruby, Don't Take Your Love To Town*. After the group broke up in 1974, Rogers started his solo career as a singer of country ballads and had a hit in 1977 with *Lucille*. Ellis knew only those first two songs. He could hear them playing in his head. He had never heard of Rogers' other hits. Ellis went to the pharmacy to collect a prescription. The pharmacy was empty. He enquired if they still had any thermometers. No. He bought a bottle of cod liver oil, collected the prescription, and departed. Next he went and bought a *Times*, a loaf of bread and a cauliflower. That night he watched a *Downton Abbey* DVD. The family went to to Scotland, where Phoebe from *Brideshead Revisited* had turned into a monster and a control freak. Ellis went to bed. He was stubborn, Ellis read. Introverted.

Sunday 22nd March 2020

A blue bright sky, the sun casting long shadows. Not on BBC News: The first two cases of Covid-19 have been reported in Gaza, raising fears about how the besieged territory's overstretched health system will cope if the virus spreads through its population of 2 million. It could spread rapidly given the concentration of people in overcrowded cities and refugee camps. The territory has just 62 ventilators and is chronically short of drugs and equipment. The Israeli blockade has limited the importation of medicines and other essential items. Ellis went out to buy a *Sunday Times* and some hot cross buns. He obtained the paper but the store shelves had been stripped bare of all bakery products. He did not get his hot cross buns. Cheese and meat had gone. Even dishwasher tablets. Ellis walked past shuttered pubs. He took some photographs of shopkeepers' signs. WE ARE ALL IN THIS TOGETHER (handwritten). DON'T PANIC (done in coloured ink). Waterstones was still open. A sign on the door asked customers to respect social distancing. Ellis had no intention of entering a bookshop until the crisis was over. He had plenty of books to read. He had enough to keep him going for years, if necessary. The child sang recognisable versions of *Twinkle Twinkle Little Star* and *Heads, Shoulders, Knees and Toes*. She smiled and burbled and played with her toys, not knowing of the collapsing world around her. On television that night there was film of people filling London parks and at holiday resorts. There were complaints that people in campervans were fleeing to the Scottish Highlands and Snowdonia to self-isolate. Second-home owners had moved from London to the coastal resorts of Suffolk, Norfolk, Cornwall and Devon. The government asked people not to do this. More banal advice from a lacklustre right-wing libertarian government, thought Ellis. This strand of Conservativism had always insisted on individual freedom without responsibility - or to put it another way, freedom without consideration of the ways in which it might impinge on other kinds of freedom. The British had long been permitted to wink at laws and regulations. 'Road safety' had always been a farce. Speeding and driving while using a mobile phone had long been treated as trivial offences which merited neither serious enforcement nor punishment. Killer motorists regularly breezed out of court with a small fine. The right to drive was a right fiercely promoted by the entire culture represented by Boris Johson, no matter how reckless or blood-spattered an individual's driving record might be. But in his daily news briefing Johnson hinted that he might be forced to bring in more rigorous measures because of the extent of the flouting of social distancing. That evening James Daunt, owner of Waterstones, succumbed to hostile publicity about the poor treatment of his bookshop staff, who were given neither hand sanitizer nor facemasks.

Waterstones' staff said they were actively discouraged from wearing facemasks. They had bitterly protested on social media about the risk to their health posed by customers crowding into the stores, some coughing, handling books, browsing, licking their hands as they turned pages, coming very close. Waterstones shops would be closed as from tomorrow. On the last page of *Anniversaries*, which he read that night, Ellis came upon a shocking plot development. He died in a plane crash near Helsinki-Vantass Airport, Finland, Ellis read. On Saturday. At eight a.m.

Monday 23rd March 2020

Another bright sunny day without a cloud in the sky. But there was a chill wind, nevertheless. Pressure grows on Japan to cancel the 2020 Olympics in June. McDonald's is closing all its restaurants. New Zealand is to impose a four-week lockdown. Harvey Weinstein has tested positive for Coronavirus. New jury trials are halted over Coronavirus fears. 11.21 GMT: Confirmed UK cases - 5,683; UK deaths - 281. Ellis decided to stay in. On Steve Mitchelmore's twitter page Ellis came across a link to a letter from Dr Tali Marian Chilson resigning from the Labour Party after 11 years of active membership. She had been accused of anti-Semitism (Notice of Investigation Ref: L0119535 Case No: CN-3). The link - https://www.jewishvoiceforlabour.org.uk/article/labours-urgent-need-for-justice-and-due-process/- gave her reply to The Governance and Legal Unit of the Labour Party. It supplied another reason why no socialist would ever wish to be a member of a Party as reactionary as Labour. It underlined the uselessness of Jeremy Corbyn, who had been a catastrophe for the Left by his sheer feebleness and lack of fighting spirit. Corbyn had all the edge of a drugged dormouse. Ellis went on to look at Mitchelmore's other recent tweets. He smiled at the ones which featured Hilary Mantel. Ellis was surprised that Mitchelmore seemed to have watched the recent BBC TV documentary promoting Mantel's new book. The enthusiasm of the BBC and the *Guardian* for a middlebrow writer like Mantel expressed the cultural poverty of those outlets of the illiberal liberal bourgeoisie. Elsewhere, on Ben White's Twitter page, Ellis read extracts from a report by B'Tselem: Israeli-made nightmare scenario: COVID-19 in Gaza. Ellis followed the link. The spread of COVID-19 in the Gaza Strip will be a massive disaster, resulting entirely from the unique conditions created by more than a decade of Israeli failure: a failing healthcare system, extreme poverty, dependence on humanitarian aid, dysfunctional infrastructure and harsh living conditions that compromise public health - even before exposure to the new virus - combine with overcrowding to form a nightmare scenario, Ellis read. The healthcare system in the Gaza strip was already on the brink of collapse, even before receiving its first COVID-19 patient. Already it cannot meet the population's needs due to an acute shortage of medicine, equipment, doctors and professional training, Ellis read. The infrastructure has collapsed: almost all pumped water in the Gaza Strip is undrinkable and electricity is provided for only a few hours a day, preventing the water and sewage systems from functioning properly. At 8.30pm Ellis watched the Zionist Boris Johnson's address to the nation. It seemed to amount to: when you all start dying it will be YOUR fault for going for a walk outdoors. Meetings of groups of more than two would not be permitted. No more protests about anything, then, thought Ellis (even socially responsible protests with two metre social distancing). The speech was lamentably vague in detail. Would Homebase remain open? Would W. H. Smith? On Twitter people were having fun running recent clips of Boris Johson asserting that the best scientific evidence showed that there was no benefit in stopping public gatherings. Football matches and the Cheltenham races had gone ahead... Go ahead and ask, Ellis read, on p. 1536. I'm just slow.

Tuesday24th March 2020

Another bright sunny morning. Sports Direct have said that as the government wishes people to look after their physical and mental wellbeing they plan to keep their stores open. All employees were sent an email stating: Sports Direct and Evans Cycles stores will remain open where possible to allow us to do this (in accordance with the Government's current social distancing guidance). There is no one else that has the range of product and range of stores to make this reasonably accessible for the whole population. The first Twitter page that Ellis consulted on this day was Ben White's. The first tweet after the pinned tweet was posted 15 hours ago. It read: Last night, Israeli occupation forces killed Sufyan Nawwak-al-Khawaja in the West Bank village of Nilin. Soldiers shot him in the head, & took his body. *Army: forces opened fire on suspected stone-throwers. The family: Sufyan was out buying supplies.* On social media people continued to tweet photos of crowded tube trains. Global figures for coronavirus at 12.48 UTC: 392,331 confirmed cases, 17,155 deaths, 102,972 recovered. On the *Guardian* website Ellis read an article about Libya by Tarek Megerisi. Libya is not the Middle East's forgotten war, it is the ignored war, he read. Having burned for almost five years now, the country has almost entirely collapsed. A humanitarian disaster looms as more than two million people remain in Tripoli, suffering daily shelling, failing electricity thanks to an oil blockade, and threats to cut off its water supply. Libya has become the world's main theatre of drone combat, with the UAE and Egypt introducing Chinese-made drones to the field of Middle Eastern warfare. Sports Direct has now agreed to close its stores. Ellis did not go out. The sun continued to shine. A blackbird pecked in the grass. On the television news that night the mayor of New York begged the Federal Government to send ventilators. He said the coronavirus was cutting through New York like a bullet train. But President Trump said that in a couple of weeks the USA would have come through it. By Easter he hoped the country could get back to work. We begin to see the light at the end of the tunnel, the President said. The bus comes out of the tunnel south of Hoboken, Ellis read. And on the next page: a scabby landscape piled high with never-decomposing garbage at the edge of a putrescent river.

Wednesday 25th March 2020

Light already at 5.15am. A hot sunny day. India has gone into a three-week lockdown. In Britain, some prisoners could be released to stop the spread of the coronavirus in prisons. Doctors and nurses are threatening to quit because of widespread shortages of personal protective equipment, especially face masks and visors. There are now more than 52,000 confirmed cases of coronavirus in the USA and a death toll of 677. Ellis went on the Johns Hopkins University website. Its Coronavirus Resource Center reported a total of 438,749 infections from 172 countries/regions, with 19,675 total deaths. Ellis remained indoors. Roaming the internet he discovered that the daily circulation figure for the *Guardian* in February 2020 was 126,879. Shouts and the noise of machinery nearby indicated that the rubbish collectors had arrived. Ellis went to collect his emptied wheelie bin. Breaking news: Prince Charles has been infected with the virus, suffered only mild symptoms, and is now well. His wife, the Duchess of somewhere, has been tested and does not have it. BBC News seemed curiously evasive about giving a daily total of infections and deaths in the UK. Jeremy Corbyn made his final appearance as Leader of the Opposition at Prime Minister's question time. Ellis felt another pang of disappointment at how after all those years as a radical dissenter Corbyn had exposed his inner self - a toothless Parliamentarian. And now Parliament is taking an early break. And now *Anniversaries* moves to its end. In 1953 Gesine moves to West Germany. Her daughter is born in July 1957. Pius is briefly married to Masha. Pius dies. Annie returns to her husband. Anita returns to Jerichow on a visit. Perhaps D. E. is not dead after all. Each day a telegram arrives from Helsinki. Uwe Johnson introduces into the text a reference to Hitler's *Sippenhaft*. Not a word Ellis has encountered before. It means punishing an entire family for the transgressions of a single member. Ellis instantly thought that perhaps the only country in the world where this lives on as state policy is Israel. If a Palestinian kills an Israeli Jew then the state bulldozes the family home. This barbarism attracts not a whisper of comment from any government or prominent politician, and still less from that entity known to the British media and the present fawning candidates for leadership of the Labour Party as 'the Jewish community'. Gantlik, Dühr and Gesine Cresspahl are arrested. Gesine is interrogated by the Stasi for ten days. Lockenvitz's trial. Sentenced to fifteen years. We looked for the hotel where we stayed in 1962, like a princess and infanta; torn down, Ellis read.

Another bright day of sunshine and a blue sky. Anniversaries... Today was the seventh anniversary, Ellis reflected. In normal circumstances there would have been a celebration. A good meal, bubbly, friends round perhaps. Not this year. The government has ordered 10,000 ventilators from Dyson, the vacuum cleaner manufacturers. The man who attacked mosques in Christchurch, New Zealand, has pleaded guilty to 51 charges of murder. The *Daily Star* (of all papers!) asks why Prince Charles was given a test despite displaying mild symptoms and there being a reported shortage of testing for frontline NHS staff. It was noted that at the time the government was urging people not to flee to the coast or remote areas, the Prince and his consort had fled to Scotland to their isolated mansion. A home which was not very large, royal arselicker and sycophant-in-chief the BBC's 'royal correspondent' Nicholas Witchell assured viewers. But Sky News showed the house which was, in fact, very large indeed, and staffed by servants. One doctor reported to the British Medical Association that she was forced to use a pair of safety goggles from her nine-year-old daughter's science party bag. Midwives report having to make do with goggles from a DIY store. The child wore her new yellow boots and tottered around in them. She waved her dolly. She chuckled, oblivious to the big world and all its problems. As children always are. The US has charged the Venezuelan president Nicolas Maduro and 14 others with drug trafficking, 'narco-terrorism', corruption and money laundering, and offered a $15m reward for Maduro's capture. An extraordinary act of impudence by the terrorist US state at a time of global pandemic. Ellis received an email telling him that M------ had died that morning. He was shocked and surprised by the news, which was wholly unexpected. On Ben White's Twitter account Ellis read: In the middle of the #COVID-19 crisis, Israeli authorities today sent soldiers to a Palestinian village to confiscate tents used for a field clinic and emergency housing. I would write "unbelievable", but...that's apartheid for you. Ellis followed the link to the B'tselem website, which began: This morning, Thursday 26 March 2020, at around 7:30am, officials from Israel's Civil Administration in the West Bank arrived with a military jeep escort, a bulldozer and two flatbed trucks with cranes at the Palestinian community of Khirbet Izbiq in the northern Jordan valley. They confiscated poles and sheeting that were meant to form eight tents, two for a field clinic, and four for emergency housing for residents evacuated from their homes, and two as makeshift mosques. Later in the B'tselem report Ellis read: As the whole world battles an unprecedented and paralyzing healthcare crisis, Israel's military is devoting time and resources to harassing the most vulnerable Palestinian communities in the West Bank, that Israel has attempted to drive out of the area for decades. This is an especially cruel example of the regular abuse inflicted on these comunities, and it goes against basic human and humanitarian prtinciples during an emergency. Today, the Civil Administration also demolished three seasonal homes of farmers who are residents of Jerusalem, in the village of Ein ad-Duyuk at-Tahta, west of Jericho. Ellis knew that these events would never be reported by BBC news. And Jericho! Just one consonant away from Uwe Johnson's Jerichow. It was with a set of reproductions of the "Frieze of the Listeners" that Gesine Cresspahl moved to Hesse, Ellis read, to the Rhineland, to Berlin, and to Riverside Drive in New York City.

Friday 27th March 2020

Another day of dazzling sunshine. The USA now has more cases of Coronavirus than any other country. President Donald Trump predicted that the country would get back to work 'pretty quickly'. He has set Easter Sunday, 12 April, as the date the USA can reopen. Outside the store a dozen people were standing at two- metre intervals. Ellis went into the bank, which contained only one other customer. A strange individual, wearing a winter overcoat, a woolly hat and a scarf. The counter clerk wore blue gloves and rubbed the machine with antiseptic gel before asking Ellis to insert his pin number. Next he went to the supermarket. He stared in and was surprised to see it was empty. He went in and bought a cabbage, a bag of potatoes, a pack of mushrooms, two packs of blueberries, five bananas, a pot of Greek-style yogurt, and two cartons of skimmed milk. The blinds were down in M------'s house. On the way back Ellis observed a police car cruise by. Home, he ate a slice of buttered toast smeared with marmalade, with a cappuccino. Boris Johnson has tested positive for Coronavirus. So has Matt Hancock. A news item says that the 21-year-old woman who died did not die of Covid-19, as previously reported, but of a heart attack. Later Ellis listened for the first time to the newly released Bob Dylan song, *Murder Most Foul*. As he was listening his phone rang. A poet of his aquaintance, asking how he was. During their conversation Ellis suddenly heard a barking dog. He knew that the poet did not own a dog. She explained she was out for a walk. That evening Ellis learned that the death toll in the UK had risen by 181 to 759, and that the rate of infection was doubling every three to four days. Ellis watched episode three of *The Men's Room*. Harriet Walter lay naked upon Bill Nighy and simulated orgasm. On the ten o'clock Sky News there was a report of a hospital in New York being overwhelmed by sick patients with the virus. But no footage from inside. The weather forecast for tomorrow was: cooler, windy, dry. Ellis went to bed. The awareness of being implicated. The dirty Algerian War of the French, 1954 to 1962, Ellis read. He was near the end, now. 1962: Professor Doctor Erichson proposes marriage after he'd gotten to know Marie. A sentence which resonates since Nabokov. Perhaps Uwe Johnson was oblivious. 1965: the USAF starts to use napalm in Vietnam. Francine may have died; she is lost. By 1968 Gesine and Marie have been living in New York for eight years. Is D. E. dead? Johnson creates an ambiguity about the matter. But is seems he is. An airplane has carried him off, to his death. 1,652 pages. January 29, 1968 - April 17, 1983. New York to Sheerness. The End. Two blank pages and then the Translator's Acknowledgements. Finished. Over. Ellis put out the light.

Saturday 28th March 2020

A thin haze of cloud across the blue sky. Exactly fourteen identical birds perched on the TV aerial Ellis can see from his study window. Starlings? He saw a murmuration last Sunday. A sudden sweep, like a gigantic wing unfolding in the air. Then gone, as if momentarily hallucinated. Virus testing is to be rolled out for frontline NHS staff. Trump signs into law the largest bailout in US history. A robin swooped down and perched on a branch as Ellis crossed the unkempt grass. It was a bitterly cold morning. Catching up on old newspapers Ellis read the *Sunday Times* travel section, March 8. There were two letters gushing about the delights of holidaying in Israel. Amanda Kenton, London, wrote 'We visit several times a year, and we've seen an exponential rise in quality hotels and restaurants - particularly vegan options in Tel Aviv.' Patti Anderson, Wolverhampton, said that Jerusalem was the highlight of her visit. It had a 'vibrant atmosphere'. She was 'keen to return'. Were these real people? Ellis wondered. There was an Amanda Kenton who was involved with something called The Abrahamic Reunion England. Or was she Amanda Kenton of Soothing Spaces, feng shui consultant, who for a fee of between £150 and £600 will advise on furniture arrangement and 'beneficial directions'? Or was she neither of these Amanda Kentons? Was Patti Anderson of Wolverhampton Maureen Patricia Anderson of Wolverhampton, WV9? Or was she not? Whoever these individuals were - assuming they were real and not fake identities fabricated by a Hasbara operative, either freelance or an employee of the Israeli state - both were evidently, at best, ignorant and complacent, and at worst devoid of conscience. Of these two spectres, Amanda Kenton was the worse - a woman plainly indifferent to her carbon footprint, as well as a contributor to the economy of a blood-spattered sectarian terror state. Having finished *Anniversaries* it was time for Ellis to begin a new book. *Diaspora Blues* had once belonged to a synagogue. The imprint of a stamp lingered inside the book cover: the fragment of an indecipherable capital letter, then a W, then a space, then SYNAGOG. Then part of a capital letter which was plainly a U. Then a space with a tiny scrap of lettering, which was plainly all that was left of an E. The subtitle was *A View of Israel* and the author - remember him? - was Clive Sinclair. Ellis had two personal reasons for being interested especially in the late Clive Sinclair. An acknowledgments section listed various publications in which extracts of the book had originally appeared 'somewhat differently'.

Encounter, Index on Censorship, the *Observer*, the *Sunday Times*, the *Times Literary Supplement*, the *Guardian*, the *Jewish Chronicle*. And others. Sinclair had enjoyed a prominent cultural access as a Jewish intellectual. *Diaspora Blues* begins with a map - a very odd map, which shows a dotted line linking St Albans and Tel Aviv. The author's journey, Ellis assumed. Already a burglar alarm had started to scream - a piercing, unending sound. Sinclair, an English Jew, was making a journey forbidden to hundreds of thousands of Palestinian refugees, who were permanently locked out of their homeland. Would Sinclair acknowledge his sectarian privileges? Would he show the slighest awareness of why Israel was a pariah state? Ellis strongly suspected he would not. But he was prepared to read Sinclair's book and discover his book-length engagement with Israel. It begins as CS - he will be called CS from now on - rereads notes he took on a trip to the Jerusalem Book Fair in May 1985. Paragraph two begins: Monday, Jerusalem. Too vague. *Which* Monday? There are times and places where dates are of central importance. Paris, 17 October 1961, for example. My friends have rented the back half of an Arab house on Rehov Harakevet, CS writes; the front is a synagogue. Questions, anyone? History, anyone? That piercing, unending sound, again. Unheard by affluent cultured Jews having a most agreeable vacation. A somewhat dated vacation, now, with mention of a 'portable Sony telephone'. CS is visited by his friend Josanne, who has come from Herzlia Pituach. An affluent and agreeable neighbourhood of Tel Aviv; another site with a muffled history. Josanna and CS take a pleasant trip to Ein Kerem. Another name that passes by without notice in the merry tinkle of agreeable tourism. The poor things - horror! - lose their car keys. But then they find them again. A drama which CS finds worthy of record. Ein Karem (let's spell it the Palestinian way) was known as the most beautiful of all the Jerusalem villages. Its 3,000 villagers were forced out by Jewish terrorists in 1948 and the entire village was repopulated by Moroccan Jews. Today, Ein Karem is home to wealthy Israeli professionals enjoying a relaxing life in a beautiful village. Wednesday. CS has luncheon with a couple of friends in Kiryat Hayovel. A neighbourhood on Mount Herzl (a mountain named after the visionary racist fanatic, Theodore Herzl). Its name translates as Jubilee Town, commemorating the fiftieth anniversary of the racist and sectarian Jewish National Fund. Throughout its history this poisonous organisation has 'redeemed' land from Palestinians, for the exclusive use of Jews. At 8pm CS is driven to the Khan Theatre (history?). It is 1985 and Milan Kundera is to receive the Jerusalem Prize. Officially, this prize is given to the writer who, in the opinion of the Jewish judges, best expresses 'the freedom of the individual in society'. A sick joke, from an institution mired in sectarianism. In reality, an attempt to sanitise the violence and sectarianism of the Israeli state by enlisting chic writers to give it cultural credit. And it works, of course. Never underestimate the narcissism and greed of popular writers. Shame on you all, especially, in the recent period, J. M. Coetzee of apartheid South Africa, Don DeLillo of New York, Susan Sontag (ditto), Arthur Miller, Haruki Murakami, Joyce Carol Oates, and that posturing, text-bloating mirror-starer, Karl Ove Knausgaard. And, of course, wheedling Ian McEwan, who claimed he went 'to engage Israelis, not isolate them'. How thrilled Zionists are to reel in the famous and the fashionable! How pleasant to see how the intelligentsia are so susceptible to bribery! CS reports that the salutation in 1985 was from Père Marcel Dubois, a Christian Zionist, with agreeable employment at the Hebrew University. He claimed that in Czechoslovakia after the Soviet invasion of 1968 a banner was seen which read: PRAGUE, BIAFRA, ISRAEL. If true - and no one lies quite as compulsively, repeatedly and comprehensively as a Zionist (except Donald Trump, obvs) - it was an utterly fatuous banner, created by an obtuse poltroon. Biafra was about secession, tribalism and civil war. Prague was about the Stalinist suppression of an independent state. Israel was never anything other than a violent racist colonial settler state which serviced imperialism. Milan Kundera exposed himself as similarly obtuse in his gushing acceptance of his sack of shining shekels. Here, at the rotting heart of the chauvinist settler state, Kundera saluted the 'great cosmopolitan Jewish spirit' (evidently unaware of its shrivelled and acidic condition in, of all places, Jerusalem). He emits some astonishingly banal and acutely evasive platitudes about 'this city with its dramatic and cruel destiny'. Dead language. Cheap journalism. Kundera continued. He blathered about the most precious aspect of European culture: its respect for the individual, 'for his original thought and for his inviolable private life'. Kundera's masculine language was of its time. To talk of those things in that city at that time displayed the usual optics of a narcissistic culture's agent. When this drivel was over no doubt the applause was thunderous. CS's own palms no doubt collided vigorously. CS wants to know if Kundera still believes that Israel is 'the true heart of Europe'. In a way, yes - its heart of darkness, propped up by the EU as well as by the US and the UK. But it appears CS couldn't get close enough to Kundera to ask his question. The famous novelist was surrounded by groupies. CS cites Wallace Stevens's Thirteen Ways of Looking at a Blackbird'. Israel, asserts CS, presents just as many possibilities. It is a modern state, asserts CS. Yes, but only in terms of its infrastructure. In its sectarianism it is unique in the world. No other state defines citizenship by religion rather than place of birth. Secondly, CS calls Israel 'a biblical anachronism', which perhaps is a fuzzy way of conceding that no other state denies admission to people born within its borders while permitting a 'right of return' to foreigners with no connection whatever to its land. CS, wallowing in his privileges as a member of the master religion, seems curiously reluctant to recognise or concede or state in clear language this fundamental point. Israel is, asserts CS, 'a socialist experiment' - to which one can only echo Tony Soprano: You're shitting me. It is, CS whispers, a colonial outpost. Well, yes, but it could have been put more sharply. Racist sectarian colonial settler state is rather more accurate. CS asserts Israel is 'a democracy'. No, it isn't. It's a democracy for its chauvinist Jewish population. The population of Gaza and the West Bank are denied any say in those who control every aspect of their lives. Israel is, whispers CS, an occupying power. But this, too, is fuzzy. Israel is not like Czechoslovakia under Soviet rule. Israel is the state of pitiless and prejudiced Jews, who violently wiped Palestine off the map, ethnically cleansed the land, and have behaved like barbarians both before and ever since that happened. A settler state is different to a land under occupation. CS turns all geographical. Israel is a small country with a narrow coastal strip. A definition devoid of political substance. Israel is the centre of the world. Eh? Jerusalem once was, in Christian iconography of the Middle Ages. It is a characteristic Zionist sleight of hand to push the word Israel backwards in time, so that Palestine is obliterated in consciousness long before it was erased by bullets, bulldozers and blood. Israel is an orange, CS asserts. Here CS reveals his complacency, his ignorance, his chauvinism. Because at the end of the nineteenth century the Palestinian farmers of Jaffa produced oranges, lemons, pomegranates, watermelons and grapes, as well as other crops such as vegetables, cotton and mulberries which were used for growing silk worms. Jaffa's most famous export was the Jaffa orange. In 1879 some 5,000 people were employed in the harvesting and packaging of Jaffa oranges. By 1912, 5,189 acres were orange orchards. The vast majority were owned by Palestinians. Others, owned by Jews, depended on Palestinian labour. In 1939 two million boxes of Jaffa oranges were shipped to England. In 1947, the British government bought the entire citrus harvest of 12 million crates. And then came 1948, and the Jews poured across the land with their guns and explosives and their terrorism. The Palestinians were expelled from Jaffa and the villages of the region. 37,000 acres of citrus plantations were left to rot. The Jews had no use for them, because cultivation depended on Arab labour. Kibbutz and moshavim preferred field crops to oranges, which required intensive irrigation and substantial labour. Most of the orchards were cut down and built over. This was deliberate. The destruction of agricultural infrastructure meant the refugees could never return to their old homes and employment. The Jaffa orange is indeed the perfect symbol of Israel - but not in the way CS complacently believed. Meanwhile in 2020 an acclaimed paperback novel was to be found in the pre-virus bookshops. Éric Vuillard's *The Order of the Day* (translated from the French by Mark Polizzotti) seeks to educate a European and American readership about German companies implicated in the Holocaust - brand names which still exist today. BMW, Daimler, Siemens, ThyssenKrupp. The novel ends with Jews from Brooklyn demanding restitution. A slick, clever, very readable novel. But Éric Vuillard could have written a similar novel, set in the same era, about the Jaffa orange. But Jews behaving as barbarians is a taboo topic, is it not? Jaffa the novel would win no prizes, or be acclaimed as important, deeply disturbing, brilliant, astonishing, shocking. On the contrary. No agent would touch it, no corporate publisher would publish it. If such a novel appeared it would be shunned, marginalised, defamed by that bullying raucous entity known as 'the Jewish community'. A machine gun, writes CS. No doubt thinking of the Uzi, designed by Uziel Gal. It fired 9mm ammunition at a rate of 600 rounds a minute. Uziel Gal was born in Weimar in 1923. When the Nazis came to power he moved to Britain. In 1936 he went to Palestine, to join his father. He joined the Haganah paramilitary group, where he maintained weapons. During the ethic cleansing of 1948 he participated in several battles in northern Palestine - details non-existent. He served in the terrorist IDF until 1975. A website entirely lacking in irony solemnly states that Gal will be remembered for his distinguished service and contribution to Israeli national pride, for his extraordinary creativity, and for his humanistic approach to life. A gathering ground for migrating birds, writes CS, spraying the page with ornithology. Feathers flutter and songbirds chirrup. A homeland, writes CS, exhibiting in two words an absence of irony combined with the standard absence of moral awareness of a Zionist. An oppressor, tosses in CS, to bolster his threadbare liberal credentials. A holiday destination. The last resort (whatever that is supposed to mean). Above all - CS thumps the table - a nation that believes in the power of the word. And what word is that, one wonders? Theft? Supremacism? Terror? Vegetarian risotto for supper. Rice, cauliflower, carrots, peppers (Ellis had checked the label to make sure they were not from Israel; they were not, they were from Spain), courgette, mushrooms. In the bath the child grinned and played with a small green plastic boat, a sponge shark, and a bright red dinosaur. That night Ellis watched *The Graduate*, a movie he never tired of watching. In bed, he returned to the book. CS because it reminds Ellis of the gas. And gas has resonance, does it not? Gas is used to exterminate. But gas is also used to disperse protesters. CS gas is a control agent. It causes a burning irritation in your nose, mouth and throat. CS attempts to incapacitate the subject. It makes the subject weep. It may cause vomiting. And gas is also used by a dentist to render a patient unconscious. You slip away from the pain and the intrusion of metal and the squeal of the drill and the young woman with her squawking plastic suction tube. And it is what Jumping Jack Flash is. And where CS is concerned two of these are intertwined. You can always count on an apologist for Israel to play the Holocaust card, even though the Zionist greed for Palestine long pre-dated young Adolf. And having crashed down that card, eyes swollen with indignation, mouth stretched and lubricated, ready to propel those ballistic missile words 'anti-Semite!', and when the hot air and thin steam has cleared, you are left with the sickly almost overpowering aroma of apologetics. Ellis remembered that the clocks went forward one hour at 1am. He moved the hands of his bedside clock, so that when he put the light out it showed 12.20.

Sunday 29th March 2020

Another cold morning. It had rained in the night. A largely cloudy sky with patches of blue. Every household in Britain is to receive a letter from the Prime Minister. It will say that things will get worse before they get better. The Duke and Duchess of Cambridge have given their support to a campaign to protect people's mental health during the Cortonavirus outbreak (a solemn report from the BBC's royal arselicker-in-chief, Nicholas Witchell). President Trump has changed his mind about putting New York into quarantine. Alex Salmond's accusers say they are devastated by the not guilty verdict. The UK death toll has increased by 260, to 1,019. On the *Guardian* website Ellis read a news item about Ernest Hemingway's fury at a letter dated November 3 1932 received from Jonathan Cape. Cape had taken it upon themselves to censor *Death in the Afternoon*. Cape had changed Go fuck yourselves to Go hang yourselves. Elsewhere in the text fuck had been replaced with blast. Bugger was changed to hang. You are not my vicar, Hemingway told Jonathan Cape. Don't you understand that if any excisions or changes have to be made it is I who will make them? I will make my own bloody decisions as to what I write and what I do not write. I will be damned if I have any vicar pruning my books to please the circulating libraries. Elsewhere on the website one of the *Guardian's* resident band of harpies was, characteristically, screeching about Jeremy Corbyn. Barbara Ellen's contribution to fake news was to claim that Corbyn 'presided over a culture of (cough) "alleged" antisemitism now under investigation by the Equality and Human Rights Commission, and facilitated Brexit'. Yes, even Brexit was apparently all Corbyn's fault. No surprise to see the *Guardian* flogging the dead horse of the Labour Party and anti-Semitism all over again. How the Blair-worshipping *Guardian* had loathed Corbyn! The *Guardian* and the BBC had been at the forefront of trying to destroy him. But the truth was that they would not have succeeded if Corbyn himself had not spinelessly capitulated to his enemies, instead of coming out fighting. Ellis was surprised to see hailstones fall from the sky. They danced down the tiles and bounced around on the ground. The child squatted, as if in a yoga position. The meal that evening was roast chicken, with parsnip, roast potato, broccoli, a jug of gravy. Well done, cook! The Deputy Chief Medical Officer, a rather lacklustre woman named Jenny Harries, says it could be six months before life in the UK returns to normal. The number of dead from the virus in Britain has reached 1,228. The numbers would get worse over the next week, possibly two, and then we are looking to see whether we have managed to push that curve down and we start to see a decline, said the Deputy Chief Medical Officer. The *Sunday Times* has obtained footage of Gordon Jackson QC discussing the case against his client Alex Salmond on a train during the first week of the trial. Jackson names two of the women who accused Salmond. He says he plans to 'put a smell' on one of

Salmond's accusers, to discredit her evidence. Jackson says he himself believes that Salmond is 'a sex pest', 'nasty' and an 'objectionable bully'. The matter will be investigated by the Scottish Legal Complaints Commission. And now CS is reminiscing. In 1973 CS enjoys 'a short stay in Israel'. Five words which sum up the banal complacency of an English Jew enjoying his privileges as a member of the master religion. In 1978 he jets back there to visit a painter named Yosl. The painter lives 'in a narrow lane with low, homely buildings on either side, shaded in season by broad-leafed trees.' Questions, anyone? How lightly, how unironically, that word *homely* trips off CS's tongue. We learn that 'Yosl himself was born in Vienna'. He moved to Israel in 1950. A year when tens of thousands of Palestinians, denied re-entry to their homeland, rotted in tents, scattered across the Middle East. Such trifles do not perturb the conscience of an Austrian/Australian Jewish painter or a Jewish novelist from England. Like good Germans, they simply cannot smell smoke drifting in the air or unpleasant odours of any kind. Yosl's father, Melech Ravitch, was a poet and a friend of Isaac Bashevis Singer. His papers are held by the Hebrew University. CS visits the archive there. Ah, yes, the Hebrew University. A place of learning built on 825 acres of stolen Palestinian land. There was once a Palestinian village here named Sheik al-Badr. On January 14, 1948, armed Jews forced the villagers from their homes. Once the village was empty more Jews turned up. They looted and vandalised the homes, then set fire to the houses. Twenty years later land which belonged to this long-vanished village was handed over to the Hebrew University. Every institution in Israel is built on rotten foundations. But this is not the sort of history that CS acknowledges. The smoke from those burning houses still lingers in the air. The villagers are gone, nameless, to die elsewhere. They were not poets or novelists. They are dust. And now CS moves on to tell his readers about Yosl's uncle Monyeh, who shot himself. Then a stroll through Tel Aviv. And a few thoughts from the author. Israel was founded to redress an injustice, asserts CS. Well, yes and no. Zionism was always a reactionary response to anti-Semitism - to run away rather than to stand and fight. It also begged the question of where a state exclusively for Jews might be founded. Where on the planet is there an empty space? Antarctica? Zionism was also grounded in nineteenth century blood and soil nationalism. The parallels with Nazism are, well, ironic. Theodore Herzl was Hitler's twin. His *lebensraum* was predicated on expulsion. Zionism was always a sly, poisonous politics which actively colluded with anti-Semites. They wanted rid of the dirty Jews, and the Zionists were happy to oblige. Give us a land and we will rid you of our noxious presence! And the land was there, apart from its dirty natives, Arabs, the *untermenschen*. Zionism colluded with imperialism, which was happy to create a colonial settler state. A little Jewish Ulster, indeed... CS uses the term 'self-haters', apparently without irony. A category of Jew. CS adverts to Kafka's story 'Jackals and Arabs'. He interprets this story as Kafka satirising 'Western

Jewry'. The Acknowledgements to the book include that obscure publication *Lillit*, which is now identified as a defunct Israeli magazine. CS reveals he wrote for it after visiting Masada for the first time in 1970. So that makes three trips to Israel so far: 1970, 1973, 1978. CS confides that he protested against the Viet Nam War (which those pesky Vietnamese insist on calling The American War). He protested, he says, in London and San Francisco. But, he further confides, he was 'vexed by the fashion to equate the Viet Cong with the Palestinians and both with the Red Indians'. If any such connections were made they were surely at the extreme margins of protest, not at the centre. Hardly 'the fashion'. But let's leave that aspect to the historians of protest. If anyone at the time did make those connections they were surely right to do so. Not only right to do so, but possessed of an advanced political consciousness. The Viet Cong did have something in common with the *Fedayeen*. They were guerrillas fighting for an independent homeland. And the Palestinians, like native Americans, resisted a violent, genocidal occupying settler state, determined to dispossess them of their land and freedom. And the US of A was involved in all three conflicts. So, yes, there does seem to be a connection there, even though it makes CS quiver with indignation. In fact CS seems, in his rush to share his indignation with a Zionist readership, to be an absolute poltroon. 'Let the existence of Israel be a symbol of hope for the Red Indians.' What *in hell* is this idiot CS on about? He sidesteps from his argument to give us the thoughts of Jesaja Weiberg, first director of Beth Hatefutsoth, the Museum of the Diaspora. The only way of Jewish survival, asserts Jesaja Weiberg, is Israel. 'Herzl thought that we'll continue here European culture,' he explains. 'You know, he was very enlightened.' *Orientalism* - a concept alien to supposed Jewish intellectual Clive Sinclair (as is colonialism, as is the racist settler state). Part Two of this revealing book begins with autobiography. CS explains that his parents were named Smolinsky. His father changed it to Sinclair in 1939. CS might have been born Joshua Smolinsky but instead he became Clive John Sinclair. The year was 1948. I was born at a time when English history had run its course, he remarks - another bizarre and fatuous formulation. 'My writing is a search for a place in which I may feel at home,' explains a man who thinks he understands Kafka. Pages of autobiography, dull, unengaging. I became a regular at Wingate Football Club, our autobiographer informs his reader. *Wingate*. Let's leave the vibrations of that name until tomorrow. Ellis puts his reading glasses away. He turns out the light. He sleeps.

Monday 30th March 2020

Bright and sunny; warmer than yesterday. But more rain in the night, the ground wet. Death is a reliable outcome, remarks Neil Ferguson, professor of mathematical biology, on the BBC's Today programme, during a discussion of statistics and the virus. It is reported that President Trump has said that virus guidelines will be extended to 30 April. The highest point of the death rate is likely to hit in two weeks, he said. By June, said the President, the US 'will be well on our way to recovery'. Also: 'They must pay!' he has tweeted, regarding security for Prince Harry and Meghan, who are believed to have left Canada for California. On the internet Ellis caught up with an article by Ali Abunimah, entitled: Johns Hopkins COVID-19 map faulted for erasing Palestinians. The constantly updated world map and dashboard published by Johns Hopkins University's Center for Systems Science and Engineering has become a vital resource for everyone to track the COVID-19 pandemic. On 11 March the website merged figures from Gaza and the West Bank with the entry for Israel, erasing the previous designation of 'Palestine' and then 'oPt' (occupied Palestinian territories). As a result Palestinians were unable to use the dashboard to track the spread of COVID-19 in those areas. Johns Hopkins is home to the Caroline Donovan Professorship in English Literature. She was the wife of Joseph Donovan, a leading slave trader. The University is built on land stolen from the Piscataway tribe. In response to protests the website has now silently reverted to supplying an entry for: 'West Bank and Gaza'. It shows 91 confirmed cases. But this designation is inconsistent with international law since it follows the US State Department's imperial designations. As of last Friday, nine cases of infection were confirmed in Gaza.Ellis went on Ben White's Twitter account. Six hours ago Ben White tweeted: Israeli rights activists are urging authorities to stop the demolition of Palestinian homes and structures in the occupied West Bank. These demolitions - part of a deliberately discriminatory planning process - have continued during the #COVID19 outbreak. Ellis returns to CS's book. He was not seriously expecting the Wingate team to be named after *that* Wingate. After all, the *Jewish Quarterly*'s Wingate Prize isn't. But it turns out that this Jewish football team is, after all, astonishingly, named in honour of Orde Wingate, psychopath, religious maniac, murderer, war criminal, and dear friend of Zionism. It is here that CS reveals himself for what he is: a complacent apologist for violent Jewish sectarianism. CS describes fondly a club reunion held in 1986 at the Empire Rooms on Tottenham Court Road. This is an apt place for it to meet, but CS is immune to irony. CS reveals that the year before BBC2 had shown a feature about CS's novel *Blood Libels*, which, he states, has a lot about Wingate football club in it. The BBC had tracked down footage of the club playing in the 1950s. Ellis had not read the novel, nor had he seen the feature. But it did not surprise him in the slightest that the BBC should have given a lavish promotional plug to a novel now long out of print (except in Kindle) and largely forgotten, which, apparently, treated Orde Wingate and the team that bore his name in a whimsical yet respectful manner. But there was nothing remotely amusing about Orde Wingate. He was a terrorist in the most literal meaning of that word and a war criminal, who massacred civilians with impunity. That this depraved individual was regarded as a hero by many British Jews showed just how morally blank they were. And CS himself is a perfect examplar of the moral depravity and complacency of the Jewish intellectual. 'I am, literally, an alienated Israeli,' he writes. No, he isn't. He wasn't born in Israel and he had no connections whatever with it, until he chose to exercise his privileges as a Jew and become a Zionist. It becomes clear that CS is that most greasy and slippery form of Jewish racist, the liberal Zionist - charming, civilised, highly educated, and drowning everything in perfume. And out they tumble - all the clichés of the Zionist. The expressed end of the Palestinians, he writes, is to drive the Jews into the sea. But the only people ever driven into the sea were Palestinians, in 1948. But of course CS is not interested in factual history, only the sentimental myths of Zionism. CS is ignorant of the history of Haifa and Jaffa. And what a dismal, anti-climactic tale this pitiful English bourgeois CS has to tell. His father, he tells us, in his youth had gone down to the docks to take a boat for Spain to fight for the Republic. Adding: though he had, in the end, stopped short of going. And CS himself is keen to make himself of service to Israel at the time of the 1967 war. But he arrived too late. On 17 August 1967. So that's four visits our sectarian Jew has made in the course of this book. Four visits denied to a Palestinian whose land has been stolen, whose house has been seized without compensation, and who rots in a refugee camp, while our English novelist enjoys his Jewish privileges as a member of the master religion. Our brave little writer crosses into the West Bank but soon retreats, as he charmingly puts it, 'back into civilisation'. But we must not be permitted to forget the anguish of a Jewish supremacist. It is 'upsetting' to see film of Israeli soldiers beating Palestinian children, although he cannot resist adding 'whatever the provocation'. Yes, these children are asking for it, are they not? And CS would like us to know his distaste for 'the secretary-general of the Board of Deputies of British Jews' - he is not named - who defends 'the morally indefensible'. And yet 33 years later this rancid organisation thrives and today even the Labour Party is terrified of upsetting bigots and fanatics who happen to be Jewish. And now CS plays the card beloved of the liberal Zionist. The original Israel was fine, only after 1967 and the occupation of Gaza and the West Bank did paradise become tainted. And as usual the thieves and murderers present themselves as the victims: 'Something tragic is happening to the Israeli people - they are becoming brutalised because they have to protect themselves,' sobs the Board's June Jacobs. A lie. The Israeli state was made with bombs, bullets and ethnic cleansing on a spectacular scale. Israel is saturated in the blood of those, including Jews, who were murdered by Zionist thugs. But CS conjures all that away. He nowhere recognises or acknowledges the Nakba. He speaks of Palestinians but never goes to talk to them. With the languid melancholy of the smug, self-satisfied colonist, CS remarks: 'I regret, no one has come up with an antibiotic that will palliate Arab anti-Zionism.' A revealing formulation. Like all Zionists he prefers to use that all-encompassing word 'Arab' to the more geographically appropriate 'Palestinian'. And anti-Zionism, notice, is *a sickness*. The sun continues to shine. Ellis drinks another cappuccino. The hours pass. And then death comes. The child is oblivious, cannot help but be. In her blue woolly hat. Exploring familiar rooms. Opening cupboard doors and lifting out their contents to lay them on the floor, chuckling. Ellis fries some cod. That evening the final episode of *The Men's Room* appears on the screen. Then the 10 o'clock news, just the first few minutes. Then bed. The present, despised Jewish state affords a rehabilitatory glimpse of what those who speak of a democratic Palestine must have in mind, asserts CS, who more and more comes to seem a liberal fool, a silky apologist for terror, a man plunged so deep into his sectarian privileges that he cannot distinguish his elbow from a smaller, tauter, less bony part of his body. That sentence has not aged well. For what other solution can there be but a single state which gives equal rights to all? Ellis puts out the light.

Tuesday 31st March 2020

Bright and sunny again. Ellis makes his first trip to a shop in a week. He is surprised to discover that the shelves are even barer today than last time. Last week there was coffee, tea, breakfast cereal. Now all have gone. No toilet rolls, or kitchen rolls, or tissues, either. News stories about shelves returning to normal are not true for this part of England. And there is no restriction on people entering the store, which is busy. Social distancing is not working. It's a farce and a shambles. Ellis hurries on to another store. It's the same there. No limits on people entering. Busy. People too close to each other. The bakery section depleted, apart from sliced bread and croissants. Ellis buys the last jar of honey. No paracetamol. No toilet rolls, tissues or kitchen roll. No cereal. He goes on to W. H. Smith. Closed indefinitely. At home the answering machine is pinging. A friend, asking how things are. Ellis drinks a cappuccino and eats a supermarket croissant, with apricot jam. He reads his latest emails. He returns to CS's book. In May 1971 CS is back in the Jewish supremacist state, helping to produce the fifth issue of *Lillit*. What a pleasant time CS is having with Pamela and Jonathan. CS goes to the theatre. He sits under a palm tree in the lemon-scented atrium of a delightful hotel. CS takes photographs of Ronald Segal, editor of Penguin Books's Africa Library. What the hell is an anti-apartheid activist doing in apartheid Israel? wonders Ellis. He looks him up on Wikipedia and learns that Segal was born into a rich Jewish family. Ellis remembers now. In *Unbelievable Things* he made a passing satirical reference to Segal's book on Trotsky. He now discovers that Segal has written a book about Israel. Another apologia? Ellis is not at all sure he can be bothered to find out. Segal, like CS, has slipped away into obscurity. Few now will ever read any of his books. What interests Ellis more is that in looking up Segal he came across a reference to the Sharpeville massacre, 21 March 1960. This was that event in which the South African police opened fire on a crowd of protesters, killing 69 and injuring 180. Many were shot in the back, causing some to be paralysed. UNESCO commemorates the date of the massacre as International Day for the Elimination of Racial Discrimination. It is interesting to compare this to 14 May 2018, when Israeli soldiers massacred 60 Palestinians peacefully protesting in Gaza about the dispossession of their land. BBC News, dishonest and pro-Israel as always, said the dead had died 'in clashes'. And two days later Rabbi Hazzan Jeffrey Myers, of the Tree of Life Synagogue in Pittsburgh, displaying the characteristic moral blankness of the representatives of modern Judaism, rushed to exonerate the murderous psychopaths of the so-called Israeli Defence Force. It was all the victims' fault. Yet again Israel shoulders the blame, wrote Rabbi Hazzan Jeffrey Myers, for protecting its citizens as its enemies try to break through its borders. This moronic American Jew plainly did not comprehend that Gaza remains part of the Palestine that violent racist Jews have stolen. With more victim-blaming Rabbi Hazzan Jeffrey Myers wrote: 'Gazans are victims once again, which was the cynical goal of Hamas all along, as they have been sidelined due to other pressing world matters. They have achieved their goal.' Utterly disgusting. No one sought to claim that the victims of the Sharpeville massacre were attention-seeking. But then - irony of ironies - five months later Rabbi Hazzan Jeffrey Myers and his congegation are attacked by a lone neo-Nazi gunman, who kills eleven and wounds six. The deadliest attack on Jews in the USA in history. A statistic which underlines just how safe the USA has been for Jews, historically. And afterwards that slippery Zionist Michael Segalov rushed out an article in - natch - the *Guardian*, which peddled the questionable anti-Semitism statistics of the Community Service Trust and, thumping his fist down on the table, asserted: 'It means not turning moments like this into debates about Palestine.' Oh really? Why not? American Jews, by and large, have long been sponsors of the dispossession and violent repression of the Palestinian people by Jews. Why should anyone be bullied into silence by the likes of Michael Segalov? The connection is there for those who bother to look. After the massacre Ellis scrutinised the Tree of Life Synagogue's website. *A Special Blessing - Israel at 70!* gushed Karen Morris, TLC Principal, in a piece published on 3 May 2018. Exercising her sectarian privileges as a Jew, Karen Morris had returned from a delightful trip to the violent racist Zionist state. We attended the dedication of a new archaeological garden used for education, she wrote, with a complete absence of irony or understanding of the many ways in which Zionist archaeology is used to create myths, suppress historical realities and conceal the crimes of ethnic cleansing. We met young Russian olim (new immigrants) at the Karmiel absorption center, wrote Karen Morris, who plainly had not the slightest concern for Palestinians denied re-entry to their homeland, who rot in refugees camps, while Jews thrive on stolen land, in stolen property. Karen Morris reported back, without irony, on how Israelis felt about the 70th anniversary of their ethnic cleansing of the Palestinians: 'We are a young country, we have accomplished so much in a short amount of time, yet, we aren't perfect, we have our challenges and there is work to do.' Banal platitudes from a society which is one of the most chauvinist in the world, and which is propped up by American dollars and weaponry. Don't mention the Palestinians, demands Michael Segalov. But the Tree of Life Synagogue was - is -mired in Zionism and Jewish supremacism. Karen Morris, TLC Principal, wrote: 'Before I left for Israel, we did a fun activity about the Israeli National Anthem - Hatikvah, and its meaning. We teach Hebrew to our students, learn about Israel, Israeli culture and life. Our students learn Hebrew songs, Israeli dances, and have an opportunity to eat Israeli food. Our Jewish community, supported by Partnership 2gether brings Israelis from Karmiel/Misgav to Pittsburgh and we go to Israel to be part of their community. Our connections and community are strong.' Returning to CS's book Ellis reads how the editorial office of *Lillit* is on the campus of the Hebrew University. Another instance of literature resting on rotten foundations. But CS cannot smell smoke. Its pungent odour is extinguished by the lingering aroma of a lemon-scented atrium. CS pops along - how easy travel is for a pop-popping Jew, how difficult for a Palestinian - to visit Lionel Davidson in Herzliya. Herzliya is named after the racist Jew, Theodor Herzl, patron saint of blood-and-soil fascist Judaism. Cities, towns, squares, parks, streets - Israel is overloaded with the pious remembrance of racists, psychopaths, torturers, murderers and war criminals. It was from a covert landing strip in Herzliya that the Zionists were assisted in their ethnic cleansing project by the Czechoslovak state, which in defiance of an arms embargo sold 23 fighter aircraft to the Jews. The Avia S-199 was built from leftover Luftwaffe components and was popularly known as the Messerschmitt. And so leftover Nazi materiel was used to create the sectarian Jewish state - another reminder of those parallels between Israel and Hitler's Germany. Hitler-Herzl, visionaries, each man wanted to expel the *untermenschen*. Nazi-Zionist - each throbs with aggression and violence. Look: $^{na}Z^i$ and Z^{ionist}. Let us remember what Roland Barthes said. Z is the letter of mutilation. Z is like a blade. It cuts and slashes. And this is what the $Z^{ionists}$ have done. They have slashed Palestine to pieces. And even today, Tuesday 31st March 2020, they go on slashing. The Twitter page of Ali Abunimah, some footage shot through a window on a mobile phone: Enemy occupier thugs confiscate food parcels intended to be distributed to Palestinian families in the village of Sur Baher. The depravity of the Israeli state is boundless. Lionel Davidson. Ellis had heard of him but had never read any of his books. A thriller writer. Lionel Davidson, a Jew, had decided to relocate from England to Israel. How easy it is for a Jew to do that - and how impossible for a Palestinian refugee. In turning into an Israeli have you ceased to feel British? CS asks. 'No,' replies Lionel Davidson. 'It's an odd position, really, as an English writer coming to live in Israel, because, in a sense, you're an emigrant, and always will be.' True. But it seems he did not stay. By 1987 Lionel Davidson has returned to England, to live in Hampstead. Ellis looks him up on Wikipedia and discovers that Lionel Davidson died in 2009. There seem to be no books about him and no biography. In July 1973 CS pops off to Israel for a month. He interviews Yehuda Amichai. And then a rambling chapter about Shulamit Lapid, Josepf Chaim Brenner, Kafka, Shlonsky… On 20 December 1978 CS walks down David Street. Let's return to this later. Then a chapter on Shulamit Aloni, a chapter on Amos Kenan. All this agonising by liberals about Israeli identity. Things have changed, for the worse, it is claimed. CS wants to know when this happened. 'Was it the catastrophe in the Lebanon?' he asks. How lightly, how unself-consciously, that word *catastrophe* is used by our sensitive English Zionist intellectual. CS, unsurprisingly, is invited to a reception at Claridge's for Shimon Peres. 23 January 1986. CS gets to shake him by the hand. Shimon Peres, who Noam Chomsky once described as 'one of the great terrorist commanders' - a blood-spattered war criminal who (Chomsky again) directed the murderous IDF Iron Fist operations in occupied southern Lebanon in 1985. (Yes, the blood is still fresh on the palms of Peres as he gives CS's hand a friendly squeeze.) Shimon Peres, our genial Jew, who delightfully summed up the aspirations of Zionism, with a chuckle and a wink: "maximum territory and minimum Arabs". In the next chapter CS is back in Israel, having an agreeable conversation at The Writers' House in Tel Aviv. And in the next chapter - why, it's the wizard himself! Somehow it comes as no surprise to learn that CS is also best buddies with Amos Oz. Ellis had written about this slippery, bogus 'peacenik' before, in his short essays 'Pure Wizardry', 'The Amos Oz Hard Disk', 'Yet More Wizardy of Oz' and 'Even More Amazing Wizardry of Oz' (in *Sharply Critical* [2017], pp. 150-163). It would be tiresome to repeat those dissections of Oz's fraudulent humanitarian credentials, which the BBC and the *Guardian* - natch - had been so enthusiastic about promoting. No surprise to discover from *Diaspora Blues* that Oz was trading in racist stereotypes. The founders of modern Israel, Oz confides, secretly wanted to be like 'the Arabs'. In short: 'unintellectual, uncomplicated, simple, tough'. A bit like children, then… The usual colonialist claptrap. Patronising garbage. Oz clears his throat and, dewy-eyed, makes an anguished appeal for an end to conflict: 'We call on you, the Palestinians, to turn now to the path of peace, of compromise. Answer our uncreasing plea with your own - let us have peace now.' It is July 1985 when our shiny wizard utters this mendacious drivel. It gets worse. The ideologist of a violent settler state piously adds: 'Never shall we let ourselves answer hatred - no matter from whence it come - with hatred.' Which is chutzpah on a scale so colossal it makes Everest look like a molehill. And on the next page we learn that CS goes on to review the wizard's latest book for the

Sunday Times. What a cosy world of connections! And then CS treats us to a sugary anecdote about a little girl, four years old, who, after meeting this loveable and engaging wizard, 'ever after, will love Israelis'. Violins play, doves coo, the focus is soft. CS supplies a stage for the wizard to make a sly, meretricious assault on his old adversary, Edward Said. And there is room for one final disposition of poison coated in saccharine. 'We have made the Palestinians part of the Jewish family.' Oz is the kind of man who could make Auschwitz sound like Disneyland. 'Go to Ashdod,' pleads the wizard. 'It's a nice, pleasant, humane city.' Ah, yes. *Isdud*. In 1922 its population consisted of 2,555 Muslims and eleven Christians. By 1931 it had 3,238 Muslims and two Christians. In 1945 the town had a population of 4,620 Arabs and 290 Jews. And then between May 29 1948 and June 3 1948 the Jews came and bombed the town. And then the Jews came with 4.2 inch mortars and machine guns. They returned in October to bomb the town. Those Palestinians who had not already fled - some 300 civilians - were driven out by armed Jews. Isdud was seized by the Jews, who changed its name to Ashdod. By November the town had been comprehensively purged of its Palestinian population, who were forced away, to the Gaza Strip. CS has nothing to say about such matters. Ashdod is twinned with Wuhan, China. I was in Israel next in June 1984, writes our Jewish tourist. But Ellis has had quite enough of CS and his colonialist apologia for one day. He puts out the light and is soon asleep.

Wednesday 1st April 2020

A grey, cold, dull day. It is reported that nightingales have evolved smaller wingspans as a result of rising temperatures. This may hamper their ability to migrate. Outside, a tiny blue tit lands on the photinia. It pecks at the branches. Eating insects, perhaps? The kettle boils. Banks have been asked to suspend dividend payments and bonuses. A million smaller businesses nationwide may go bust in the next four weeks, unable to get the cash they need. Loss of smell and taste may be a symptom of COVID-19 infection. Hospitals should use spare laboratory space to test NHS staff, the Health Secretary Matt Hancock has said. Not on BBC News: NHS doctors are being gagged from speaking out about widespread shortages of personal protective equipment. A dossier of evidence collated by the Doctors' Association UK (DAUK) shows that tactics used by NHS management include threatening emails, threats of disciplinary action, and two cases where staff were sent home from work. There are no April Fool stories in the papers today, it seems. Perhaps having Boris Johnson as the British Prime Minister and Donald Trump as the US President at a time like this is sufficient as preposterously unbelievable tales go. Darkly comic, as a reviewer of a standard forgettable work of literary conformity might say in the pages of the *Times* or *Guardian*. On the Twitter page of the editor of *The Lancet*, Richard

Horton, Ellis read: The handling of the COVID-19 crisis in the UK is the most serious science policy failure in a generation. Last week, the Deputy CMO said, "there comes a point in a pandemic where that [testing] is not an appropriate intervention". Now a priority. Public message: utter confusion. Ellis glanced at the *Guardian* website. Global figures: 861,305 confirmed cases, 42,364 deaths. As of 09.25 UTC. A bitterly cold morning. Ellis talked to a neighbour. Indoors, the child played happily with her new pushchair, rolling it to and fro across the room. She put on one of her mother's slippers. She opened a cupboard and took out a packet. She banged her xylophone. On Ben White's twitter page there is a link to a new report by B'tselem, dated 29 March 2020 and headlined 'A "car-ramming" attack that never was: soldiers shoot and beat Palestinian teens after car crash'. It's a detailed account of an incident on Thursday evening, 20 February 2020, around 8.30pm, when four fifteen-year-old boys were forced off the road by an oncoming Irsaeli military jeep driving in the wrong lane against the traffic. Having caused the car to crash the Israeli soldiers opened fire, hitting one of the boys. All were dragged from the car and beaten. They were then taken away to be interrogated by civilian interrogators. Just another passing moment in the history of Israel. A robin landed close to where Ellis had been digging with his silver trowel. It quickly found two worms in the freshly unearthed soil and began to slice and devour them. On social media there is film of a London underground train pulling ito a platform. A dense crowd pours from the carriages, assembles on an adjacent platform, and then enters another tube train. Social distancing is non-existent. Ellis recalls yesterday or the day before hearing that bland nonentity Sadiq Khan, London's Blairite mayor, on the radio, evading the issue. It was Khan's decision to cut the tube train service which resulted in workers having to squash together into trains on the now much-reduced service. Sadiq Khan is enabling infection. No surprise, really. Khan is New Labour to his bones. A smooth, silky careerist. June 1984. CS pops to Israel and meets Dov Yermiya, described as 'an old soldier, who had fought with Wingate in Palestine'. Now this sounds interesting! But if CS asks any questions about those days he does not mention them, or supply his readers with the answers. Instead we hear how Dov Yermiya has turned into a liberal, a Zionist who has a dream 'of peaceful co-existence'. But that is a contradiction. Zionism is predicated on the expulsion of the Palestinians from their homeland. And the Jewish democratic state is itself a tautology because no genuine democracy can guarantee the supremacy of any religious or ethnic group. Israel is a gerrymandered democracy for Jews, not a democracy for all its people. But it seems that by Israeli standards Dov Yermiya is one of the good guys. During his military service he wrote a diary about what he'd witnessed in the Israeli invasion of Lebanon. The shelling, the killing and the destruction which was sheer brutality, sheer vandalism. I saw many dreadful things. I saw the torture of prisoners. And every night I wrote a new page. But when Dov Yermiya tried to find a publisher for his memoir no Israeli publisher would touch it. So it was self-published. After that he was kicked out of the army. It was published in Britain as *My War Diary*. Has CS read it? Not clear. CS interviews Joshua Sobol, who mentions an article by Martin Buber in November 1939, a year after *Kristallnacht*. Buber wrote that some Zionists said that Nazi ideology in itself was not bad, that it was the most effective ideology for a nation in a state of crisis. Buber wrote that if a day comes when the Jews adopt Hitler's god in Palestine and only change its name into a Hebrew one then 'we are lost'. Buber believed in a bi-national state. And now CS pops off to see - Ellis's pulse starts to race, seeing this name - Aharon Appelfeld. *Aharon Appelfeld*. Ellis has deconstructed at some length Appelfeld's tendentious memoir, *The Story of a Life* (see 'The Blindness of Aharon Appelfeld' in *Sharply Critical*, pp. 129-146). Ellis learns that Appelfeld lives at Mevasseret Zion. No surprise to learn that Appelfeld lives on ethnically cleansed land. But that is not the sort of history that Appelfeld is interested in. Appelfeld took me through his back garden, where he picked me a peach from his own tree, and pointed across the valley to the next hill, CS writes. The cairn of stones on top of the promontory is really the ruins of a fort, explained Appelfeld, hence its name, Castel. Appelfeld outlines its recent, heroic history: how, in 1948, it commanded the road to Jerusalem, how, with many losses, the Israelis took it from the Arabs. And now let us see what a Jew with a conscience has to say about the history of the Israeli novelist's pleasant neighbourhood. *Heroic?* There were a large number of defenceless Palestinian villages in proximity to the Jaffa-Jerusalem road, writes Ilan Pappe in *The Ethnic Cleansing of Palestine*. Within a few days most of them would be expelled forever from the homes and fields where they and their ancestors had lived and worked for centuries. As for that 'cairn of stones on top of the promontory': let Pappe explain. The memorial to the Haganah that Israel has sited on the Qastal fails to mention that at this very spot there was once a Palestinian village. All over Israel many new settlements and national parks have become part of the country's collective memory without any reference to the Palestinian villages that once stood there, even where there are vestiges, such as an isolated house or a mosque, which visibly attest to the fact that people used to live there as recently as 1948. Aharon Appelfeld speaks to his English guest about 'the antisemitic press in Britain'. He means the corporate media like the *Guardian* and *Times*, exposing his deep intolerance of even the mildest criticism of Israel. Whereas Dov Yermiya developed a conscience and was troubled by the barbarism of the Israeli army, Aharon Appelfeld excuses it. Lebanon, he coolly informs CS, was 'an international terrorist nation in the making'. At the end of the interview Appelfeld's eldest son Meir arrives, on leave from the Israeli army. CS swoons with admiration. Meir is carrying an Uzi sub-machine gun over one shoulder, and a violin over the other. 'You represent the best hope of our nation' CS thinks (even though his nation is England, not Israel). And CS, who is not shy about name-dropping, tells Philip Roth about this wondrous sight. That's too good to be true, chuckles Roth. You wouldn't dare to use it in a novel. But why not? There were members of the SS who were, it seems, exquisite musicians. Why not the IDF? When did playing a musical instrument somehow absolve you of crimes against humanity? Mention of Roth is itself ironic. It seems plain that CS basically wanted to be England's answer to Philip Roth. Explorations of Jewishness, with lashings (so to speak) of sex. But CS's career fizzled out, unlike Roth's. Roth ended up acclaimed as the greatest living American novelist, whereas CS, after those early successes and prizes and the BBC documentary, slowly faded away. Presumably he lacked a readership. Readers who had read a CS book were in no hurry to repeat the experience. CS never vanished completely, of course. But he drifted away to the sidelines and stayed there, becoming obscure, his books falling out of print. For his evening meal this day Ellis ate pasta with vegetables and salad. That evening, after a long day devoted to *Twenty-Twenty*, Ellis watched the first episode of Peter Kosminski's drama *The Promise*. It was promising… Afterwards Ellis watched the first five minutes of the 10pm Sky news. Oddly, for the first thirty seconds nothing was shown but a black screen. The presenter did not apologise for the glitch. Best to pretend it never happened, perhaps. The same testing centre for NHS staff was shown as had been shown for several nights running, although strangely the footage showed the site - unidentified but perhaps in London - deserted, apart from figures standing around in high viz jackets and some signs: STAY IN YOUR CAR. KEEP WINDOWS CLOSED. PRE-BOOKED APPOINTMENTS ONLY. HAVE YOUR NHS ID READY. Ellis quickly lost interest. The so-called news was really only good for anecdotes about victims. For the second night running the child of an NHS consultant who had died of the virus as a consequence of having no protective equipment spoke to the camera. Ellis took his reading glasses, his phone and CS's book upstairs. He brushed his teeth. He reached CS's chapter bearing the title: *David Grossman*. Tomorrow…

Thursday 2nd April 2020

The sun is shining but it feels cold. But now it is 7.40am and the sun has gone in. The sky is the colour of a bruised face. A pretty metaphor, *nicht wahr*? Almost one million people have applied for universal credit benefits in the past fortnight. It is revealed that only 2,000 out of half a million frontline NHS workers in England have been tested for COVID-19. British Airways are grounding most of their jets and laying off their staff. Russia has sent medical equipment to the US. The robin is back. It perches on the bird table. Ellis finds a bakery which is open. He buys two almond croissants and two packets of hot cross buns. In the greengrocers he buys some apples and a packet of Grape Nuts. In Tesco he buys a carton of ice-cream. The one item that is still unavailable is toilet roll. Later, he finds that the pharmacy is closed. Lunch: soup, bread, cheese. Spain death toll passes 10,000 with record single-day rise of 950. Confirmed UK cases: 29,474; UK deaths 2,352, as of 12.24 BST today. The robin is back. A cold wind continues to blow. Matt Hancock gives the daily virus briefing. He looks well after his infection. Ellis receives a text message, recommending *Atomic Blonde,* the movie. On Film 4, tonight at 9pm. But when he switches on at that time to watch it the TV screen reads: NO SIGNAL. So instead Ellis went back to reading *Diaspora Blues.* David Grossman. Another slippery liberal Zionist. Ellis had deconstructed Grossman's acrobatics back in his days as a blogger. Now here he is again. Grossman speaks of the *very heavy burden* of myths which Israelis are obliged to carry *since the day we were born and even before.* Even before? Is even spermatozoa weighed down by the burden of myth? *We have to relate to some ideal or some myth that we have to equal ourselves to, and we always lose because we cannot behave like mythological creatures.* He speaks of the war on Lebanon. *I spent thirty-five days there and it was very difficult.* He mentions the 1973 war, *which was quite a trauma for us in Israel. I was a soldier then, very young.* David Grossman says: *You cannot imagine how awful it was, it aroused all the memories - memories that I have never experienced myself, memories from other days, from the Holocaust - because we really felt that our existence was in danger.* David Grossman says: *It's very difficult being a writer in Israel.* The language of victimhood. *It's very difficult being a writer in Israel* - but not as difficult as being a Palestinian writer. Ghassan Kanafani, for example. Assassinated by Israel on 8 July 1972. One of the great cultural crimes of the twentieth century, and Ellis was still searching for any kind of cultural commentary on this atrocity. The fact that Kanafani had a child with him when the Jews blew up up his car with a bomb did not trouble them. Child murder is all in a day's work for Israel and has been since 1948. And since we are on the topic of children, Ellis reflected, let's note something David Grossman said to CS on 11 June 1986 at the Institute of Jewish Affairs, London. *There are people that really think we have only two choices: either we will conquer or we will be conquered. They cannot accept the possibility of having another choice, another alternative. There are people who are so afraid of this other alternative they prefer war to compromise. I really cannot understand it. They are exactly the people who would commit suicide in the case of Masada, yes? I will not do it. I will not kill my children and commit suicide.* Fast forward to 2006. Who is an enthusiastic supporter of Israel's war on Lebanon in July 2006? Yup, peacenik David Grossman. And on August 12 of that year Grossman's 20-year-old son Uri, of the 401st Armoured Brigade, died in southern Lebanon when his tank was hit by an anti-tank missile. A change of tune to those violins that played so softly and gently for CS. *There were people who stereotyped me, who considered me this naïve leftist who would never send his own children into the army. I think those people were forced to realise that you can be very critical of Israel and yet still be an integral part of it. I speak as a reservist in the Israeli army itself.* That's right, the blood-drenched, atrocity-mired IDF. Let's move on quickly to the next chapter. Steven Zipperstein? He sounds like a Philip Roth character. Plus a mysterious un-named Jew who was forced to resign as editor of *Jewish Quarterly*, for publishing 'renegade articles' in another, unidentified magazine. This sounds interesting - is this mysterious individual by any chance Antony Lerman? But CS can be studiously vague when it suits him. This is a self-congratulatory chapter. CS regards himself as a feisty rebel against Jewish orthodoxy. He stands alongside another of this brave band: a prominent female liberal rabbi. Step forward Rabbi Julia Neuberger. In 2019 Neuberger publishes a book entitled *Antisemitism*, which exposes her as a fairly standard-issue foam-flecked Zionist. In this shoddy, dishonest book Neuberger squeaks that calling Israel an apartheid state born out of ethnic cleansing is very upsetting for Jews. Hers is is not a book about anti-Semitism. It's an apologia for a state with which Neuberger has intimate connections. Rabbi Julia Neuberger is about as morally blank as they come. In the next chapter CS reveals a nastier side to his character. It's a sustained attack on Edward Said. Said has suffered a death threat from the Jewish Defense League. CS sniggers and chortles that this 'is a bit like saying he gets hot salt beef on rye from Blooms'. This entire chapter consists of a dwarf sneering at a giant. *Jews have spiritual as well as political rights in the Levant*, squawks CS, who has no connections whatever with that region and no innate property rights at all. Like any apologist for atrocity, CS is keen to blame the victims. He confides that his mates 'would embrace the Palestinians, given half a chance'. But those pesky natives don't want a hug, the ungrateful brutes. CS airily confides that if it was in his power he would 'give the Palestinians a state on the West Bank'. How generous of him! A true gentleman, CS, just like Mark Sykes and François Georges-Picot. Another chapter. CS is shocked that in an essay entitled 'Kitsch 22' Anton Shammas criticises Milan Kundera ('of all people' gasps CS) for toadying to his Zionist hosts at the Jerusalem Book Fair. But Shammas was right. Kundera did not distinguish himself by pimping for a repressive settler state. He has all the appearance of an unprincipled opportunist, which made the 2008 scandal of his possible role as a police informer - an episode still fiercely debated and unresolved - all the more interesting. Shammas does not want a Palestinian state. He wants 'the dejudification of Israel'. Exactly. That's what democracy and equal rights require. Next chapter. CS informs us that the Law of Return is 'racist legislation, in his opinion'. Don't you just love those three last words of qualification? And so it goes on. Israel, CS insists, is 'a refuge to Jews who are persecuted and who want to come to join the nation'. But Jews from Brooklyn are not persecuted, neither are Jews from Essex or Surrey. And neither is CS, who confides that he has been making enjoyable trips to Israel 'on a more or less annual basis' since 1967. A fascinating revelation. *Diaspora Blues*, published in 1987, is the record of twenty years in the life of a self-regarding British Jewish intellectual - a writer who confides that 'Israel is an immensely attractive place to stay awhile'. Twenty years of repression, atrocities and dispossession, which CS delicately averts his eyes from. CS never hears the cries which come from the cells where Palestinian children are tortured. CS, purveyor of kitsch, who hears an early morning bird, *whose voice runs over the landscape like honey on toast, illuminating Jerusalem with a golden light.* Like a good German, CS sees and hears and smells nothing but that which is sweet and soporific. Let us leave CS, as he strolls with David Grossman up to the kibbutz at Ramat Rachel, where they sit on the grass and admire the view and hold a delightful conversation about Bruno Schulz and Kafka and Anton Shammas and how proud Israelis are to have won the Eurovision Song Contest. As for those troublesome Palestinians, the matter 'solved it must be. And soon.' How ironic that the First Intifada erupted exactly six months after *Diaspora Blues* was published on 8 June 1987. It was put down with all the ferocious violence which has come to characterise the Jewish settler state. As for Ramat Rachel, in 2008 the Zionist state decided to steal more Palestinian land by building 4,690 housing units and a commercial centre, together with hotels, offices, parks and roads. This development scheme supplied the missing link which connected the belt of Jews-only settlements along the southern side of occupied East Jerusalem: Har Homa, Gilo, Giv'at Hamatos and East Talpiot. The expansion of Kibbutz Ramat Rachel, illegal under international law, resulted in the separation and isolation of the Palestinian communities of Sur-Baher and Um-Tuba. A physical barrier was thus created between the southern West Bank and East Jerusalem - an integral part of the overall Israeli plan to isolate Jerusalem from the West Bank and to break the physical contiguity of the West Bank. This sectarian Jews-only development scheme forms part of the Zionist state's demographic war against the Palestinians of Jerusalem, aiming to maintain a Jewish majority, particularly in occupied East Jerusalem. The overall goal of the Israeli municipality is to drain Jerusalem of its Palestinian population, or at least maintain their existence at a marginal level, Ellis read on the website of poica.org. The expansion of Kibbutz Ramat Rachel is consistent with the procedures used by successive Israeli governments to hinder Palestinian neighbourhoods' urban development: 1. Land confiscation 2. Restrictions on land use such as building codes and regulations 3. Constructing Jews-only settlements and Jews-only by-pass roads 4. Segregating Jerusalem from the rest of the occupied Palestinian territory 5. Imposing selective zoning classifications on Palestinian land. The expansion of Kibbutz Ramat Rachel is in defiance of United Nations resolutions 242, 298, and 465. These facts prepared by the Applied Research Institute, Jerusalem, Ellis read. Ellis was relieved to be finished with *Diaspora Blues* (although he knew he would return to it later in this year, 2020). As an antidote to its folksy, twinkly-eyed Zionist writer anecdotes he began reading *The Myths of Liberal Zionism* by Yitzhak Laor.

Friday 3rd April 2020

Another bright sunny morning. Staring out of the kitchen window Ellis sees what at first seems like a strange black mound in the garden. Further scrutiny reveals it's one of the neighbourthood cats: the sly, fat one. He opens the back door and steps outside, clapping his hands. The cat streaks across the garden and scrambles up the fence, vanishing behind a garden shed. Ellis returns to the kitchen and scatters some Kellogg Organic Wholegrain Wheat and Raisin into a bowl. Next he lays some stewed apple over the cereal. Next he coats this mixture with three desert spoons of Greek-style yogurt. Next he dips another desert spoon into a jar of liquid honey and lets it drip over the contents of the bowl. The news. There are now more than one million confirmed cases of COVID-19 infection worldwide. The USA has recorded the world's highest daily toll with 1,169 deaths. Ellis spent the morning downloading hostile reviews and reactions to *The Promise*. He would read them after he'd watched the series. Onion soup for lunch, with bread and cheese. Then sliced apple with yogurt. The child, more confident on her feet than a couple of weeks ago, walked to the glass door that led out to the garden. Then she returned and found her soft toy dog. She began singing the song that introduced the TV series Waffle the Wonder Dog. Ben White's twitter page leads Ellis to a news report in Haaretz: **As Coronavirus Spreads in West Bank, Palestinians Also Face Greater Settler Violence.** *A worrying rise in violence might correlate with Israel closing down educational institutions - and if there are no legal consequences, observers fear it will only get worse.* By Hagar Shezaf, 03.04.2020. Arua Nasan, of the village of Al-Mo'eir north of Ramallah, was on his way with his cousin to pick akub (dwarf chicory), a wild plant popular in Palestinian dishes at the Ein Samia spring. They met three teenage settlers who told them they were not allowed to visit the spring. One of the youths phoned someone and within minutes two cars showed up from the direction of the settlement of Kochav Hashahar. A group of settlers then proceeded to attack Arua. One Jew threw a hammer at him, hitting him the face. The others beat him with metal rods. At this point a military vehicle drew up and one carload of settlers fled. Arua was taken to hospital with injuries to the jaw and shoulder. No action has yet been taken against the attackers. Information gathered by the Yesh Din human rights NGO shows that 91 percent of the cases opened by Israeli Police in the West Bank following complaints of settlers' crimes are closed without charge. "The quantity and severity of the violent cases we've handled in recent weeks is mind boggling," says Yesh Din Director Lior Amihai. This online story was accompanied by security camera footage of a mob of Jews vandalising Palestinian vehicles. Just another day of sectarian violence in the land where CS had so many very pleasant holidays. Gaza, Ellis learned, has 65 ventilators for a population of 2 million people. Confirmed cases globally: 1,066,706. Deaths: 56,766. As of 19.25 UTC. UK infections: 38,168. Deaths 3,605. For supper: cheese soufflé with mashed potato, cabbage and roasted beetroot. Ellis watched the second episode of Peter Kosminski's *The Promise*. Ellis read José Saramago's Foreword to *The Myths of Liberal Zionism*. José Saramago wrote that the great majority of the Israeli population seemed to support its government's treatment of the Palestinians. This is treatment characterized, as we all know, by a contempt and an intolerance which, on a practical level, have led to the extreme of denying any degree of humanity to the Palestinian people, at times even denying their basic right to existence, José Saramago wrote. But this Foreword, written in 2009, displayed naivety on the part of the Portuguese novelist. He was excited that President George H. W. Bush was demanding the withdrawal of the settlements. But of course the President was merely engaging in rhetoric. He had no intention of making Israel cease its seizure of Palestinian land. Next Ellis read Yitzhak Laor's Preface. Yitzhak Laor noted that Israel resists a constitution that would guarantee equality before the law to all its citizens. Sectarian discrimination is even embedded in the Jewish language itself. The Hebrew word for nation - *umma* - refers exclusively to Jews. Violence and racism are embedded in the books which Israeli children read. Whereas British children had the adventures of The Famous Five and The Secret Seven, the children of Israeli Jews had Hasamba, tales of a group of Tel Aviv children who formed a secret military unit which fought the British, the Arabs and criminals. Their commander was Yaron Zehavi - courageous, sensitive and blond. A role model for Jewish fascism. Ehud Barak described Israel as a villa in the jungle - reiterating the racist tropes of Herzl. And while morally blank Jews like CS enjoyed their vacations in the villa, in the jungle life was rather different. A Palestinian boy born in Tul Karm not only has never seen the Mediterranean which is just a few miles away, but has never visited his grandmother, who lives, say, in Ramallah. Yitzhak Laor quotes a new report: the infant mortality rate among Arab citizens inside Israel is twice that of Jews. 8 per 1,000 live births, against 4 per 1,000 live births. In the occupied territories it is 25.3 per 1,000 live births. The Jewish state which supplied CS with a lifetime of enjoyable holidays and lots of agreeable literary chit-chat was a state which killed children, both with bullets and by denying them medical care. Ellis moved on to Yitzhak Laor's Introduction. Political Zionism took over and nationalised the Jewish religion, he wrote. Zionism went to the heart of the colonial hinterland of Europe, the East, not to become part of that East but in order to become representatives of the West "over there". Sky News at 10... But Coronavirus fatigue - or at any rate fatigue with its mediation by the corporate media - sends Ellis to bed.

Another bright sunny morning. In the USA there are now 245,573 confirmed infections, twice the number in Italy. More than 6,000 have died and the curve is rising exponentially. Hospitals in New York, New Orleans and Detroit are overwhelmed. This will be regarded as the worst public health disaster in America in a century, said Eric Topol, professor of molecular medicine at Scripps Research in San Diego. The root cause of the disaster was the lack of readiness to understand where, how and when the disease was spreading. Trump was not just killing Americans, of course. He was also killing Iranians and Venezualans and Iraqis and Palestinians. The Trump administration intensified economic sanctions earlier this week on Iran and Venezuala. And a consignment of face masks, coronavirus test kits and ventilators to Cuba was blocked because of US sanctions. Ellis went shopping. He bought an avocado, a pot of apricot jam, a pot of chutney, a chicken, a pack of six eggs and a *Times*. Keir Starmer has been elected leader of the Labour Party, with Angela Rayner as his deputy. How stunted and reactionary are the political sensibilities of the members of this party, Ellis thought. A spokesperson for the new leader said: This afternoon Keir Starmer spoke with the Prime Minister about the current national emergency. Keir offered to work constructively with the Government on how best to respond to the coronavirus outbreak, accepted the Prime Minister's offer to meet next week and agreed arrangements for Privy Council briefings and discussions. Richard Seymour tweeted: Rule of thumb over the next five years: whatever the most moronic, inept, short-sighted, self-defeating option is, the Labour leader will take it. The *Times of Israel* quoted Keir Starmer, who told *Jewish News*: I do support Zionism. I absolutely support the right of Israel to exist as a homeland... I said it loud and clear - and meant it - that I support Zionism without qualification. Those last five words should not be forgotten, Ellis felt. Elsewhere on twitter Ellis learned that Starmer had been elected on a 62.6% turnout. So, 37.4% of Labour Party members couldn't even be bothered to vote for their new leader! The child ran across the lawn to hug the white sheet dangling from the washing umbrella. Ellis ate the avocado he had bought. One end was soft, the other hard and stringy. After chipping away with a teaspoon and eating some of it, he threw it away. Yitzhak Laor's first chapter is about the use and misuse of the Holocaust. Auschwitz is everywhere, Yitzhak Laor wrote. Holocaust Remembrance Day has been constructed. But there is no international day to mark the extermination of Native Americans or the slave trade. The question of how the Allied powers and especially the USA treated Jewish refugees before, during and immediately after the Second World War is conveniently overlooked. Today the Holocaust has become the symbol of the war in its entirety - in the cinema, on television, in political clichés, school syllabuses and state commemorations. Reading this chapter Ellis was astonished to learn that in Berlin there are streets named after Yitzhak Rabin and Ben Gurion. First the Germans persecuted the Jews, then they persecuted the Palestinians, Ellis thought. Despite all the pious commemorations of the Holocaust the German nation has learned nothing at all from its history. Yitzhak Laor went on to criticise the reactionary French philosopher Alain Finkielkraut, apologist for the Zionist state. Finkielkraut was scandalised that anyone might think the Israeli Separation Wall was racist. 'For Finkielkraut,' wrote Yitzhak Laor, 'The Holocaust alone can provide the definition of evil.' Ellis thought the name of the Frenchman was familiar. He remembered now that there had been a story - where else? - in the *Guardian* about the Frenchman and the gilet jaune protests. Upon sighting him in the street, it was reported, a gilet jaune protester had shouted that Finkielkraut was a 'dirty Zionist shit' who should 'go back to Tel Aviv'. In reporting this episode (24 February 2019), the *Guardian* was naturally keen to provide a platform to attack Jeremy Corbyn. 'Finkielkraut says he is particularly concerned about Britain's Labour leader Jeremy Corbyn,' the gutter *Guardian* reported. 'Jeremy Corbyn is at the doors of power. If he gets into 10 Downing Street it will be the first time in post-Hitler Europe that a great nation would be led by a leader who quite clearly has antisemitic tendencies,' Finkielkraut said. 'And that for me is a very great worry.' As usual, the standard Zionist sleight-of-hand is performed, whereby the racist sectarian Jew converts the anti-racist into a person of prejudice. The story mentions the French politician Simone Veil - another example of a Holocaust survivor with a moral blind spot. 'She believes that the threat to Jews [in France] comes not from the far right but from the extreme left and supporters of the Palestinians. "I am very nervous and worried about this," she said, adding that she is also concerned about the pro-Palestinian stance of French Jewish intellectuals.' Ellis found this on Sheldon Kirshner's blog for the *Times of Israel*. Ellis noted that the *Guardian* was even using the fashionable Zionist spelling of 'anti-Semitic', which removed the hyphen. Ellis was a great believer in hyphens. Nothing annoyed him quite so much as people who referenced *Moby-Dick* and got the title wrong.

Sunday 5th April 2020

Another bright sunny morning. The Queen will urge self-discipline and resolve in her speech to the nation today, reports the fawning BBC. A woman who has gone out of her way to signal her absolute support for her repellent son, Prince Andrew. Ellis would not be watching her emit her platitudes. President Trump has said the USA is in for a tough week. Sir Keir Starmer appeared on the Andrew Marr Show. He sniped at Jeremy Corbyn, accusing him of 'crowing' over the Coronavirus pandemic and the government. "Would you support the government in closing down unnecessary workplaces?" asked Andrew Marr. "We'll follow what the government say" replied the inept knight. He blathered about anti-Semitism and bullying in the Labour Party and said he wanted to see people like Louise Ellman back in the party. Aaron Bastani of the Owen Jones Institute for Opportunism tweeted (@AaronBastani): *Impressive from @Keir_Starmer on #marr. It's day 2 & challenges ahead, but I saw something for first time in a while: A Labour politician from centre left not giving formulaic answers or cowed by interviewer. Sticking to line of 'mistake' of austerity after 2010. Excellent.* Corrie Drew commented (@CorrieDrew): *Aaron, after his response to the question of how the government are doing on Coronavirus, I'm startled you could describe him as impressive. He actually defended them!* Clancy Moped commented (@CreldBrumple replying to @AaronBastani and @Keir_Starmer) *austerity wasn't a mistake, it was a deliberate choice of policy to hurt the poorest in society.* 'hugo' wrote (@hdmarks replying to @AaronBastani and @Keir_Starmer): *That's the difference between him and Corbyn. He paints austerity as an honest 'mistake', Corbyn called it out plainly as a political choice. That's a huge gulf.* Gloria's Tweets commented (@glorias_tweets replying to @AaronBastani and @Keir_Starmer): *Doesn't seem to be a set of coat tails that you wouldn't be willing to ride on, Aaron. I wonder why no one takes you seriously?* Sir Keir Starmer had also written about his vision as new Labour leader in the *Sunday Times*. Closet Politics commented on the same Bastani thread (@closetpolitics replying to @AaronBastani and @Keir_Starmer): *writing for the times is a weird move. It's like his first move is to write an article that none of the people who voted for him can read.* Starmer was also criticised for blatantly misrepresenting the reality of what happened to Louise Ellman. A lengthy article on the Jewish Voice for Labour website deconstructed the fictions of the Zionist lobby inside Labour: https://www.jewishvoiceforlabour.org.uk/article/louise-ellman-and-the-war-on-riverside-labour-party-jvl-exclusive/ Ellis downloaded it to read later. He also came across a blog post by the Zionist Ruth Smeeth, who was instrumental in having the black activist Marc Wadsworth expelled from the Labour Party. Although Wadsworth was a long-term ally of Corbyn the then Labour leader exposed yet again the rubber condition of his spinal column by his failure to stand by his old comrade. Ruth Smeeth quoted yesterday's assertion by Sir Keir Starmer: *Antisemitism has been a stain on our party. I've seen the grief that it's brought to so many Jewish communities. On behalf of the Labour Party I am sorry. I'll tear out this poison by its roots and judge success by the return of Jewish members and those who felt they could no longer support us.* Sir Keir Starmer, Ruth Smeeth wrote: '56 words. That was all it has taken to reassure British Jews across the country that, finally, the Leader of the Labour Party was going to act against the evil of anti-Jewish hate inside our ranks. The new Leader of the Labour Party set the right tone within minutes of his election. Keir is someone who I call a friend and consider an ally. The pain we felt from the hatred directed at us compounded by friends of the former Leader and fringe groups with their #JC4PM badge label us as liars, that our grievances were just smears and that those who were brave enough to come forward were merely political opponents. Within hours of the result, Keir Starmer called me to discuss anti-Jewish hate in the Labour Party. He wrote to the Board of Deputies to both apologise and to set the wheels in motion for moving forward. He has asked the Board, the JLC, CST and JLM to 'virtually' meet with him next week to start the long process of rebuilding trust.' In short, reflected Ellis, the Labour Party had lost a leader who was not a racist but who was slandered as one and replaced him with a leader who is a Zionist and who is fully committed to racism when it is carried out by Jews. Ellis went out and bought the *Sunday Times* and a pot of beetroot chutney. It was a very hot day. The streets were deserted as people observed the lockdown. There were a few cyclists, a fair few pedestrians, and only one or two motor vehicles driving past. In her bath that night the child placed a green plastic toy on her head. Ellis put a green sponge on top of his head and the child laughed and began to clap her hands. They played this game for two or three minutes, with the toy and the sponge falling off their heads and being put back. Ellis watched the third episode of Peter Kosminski's *The Promise*, followed by the Sky ten o'clock news. Boris Johnson has been taken to hospital after ten days of displaying Coronavirus symptoms. Scotland's Chief Medical Officer has been forced to resign after twice visiting her holiday home on the coast of Fife, in defiance of her own advice to the public to stay at home and only go out for essential trips such as shopping or exercise. The Queen -

Monday 6th April 2020

A blue tit pecked at the pink fat stick in the wire bird feeder. Cloudy and warm. There was an enormous queue outside the post office. A police car rolled by. Rain was in the air. Ellis drank three cappuccinos. The child chuckled. Ellis put on a white beret and the child ran off to put on her own blue woolly hat. The child beat the floor with a stick and sang what might have been, in a distorted form, the first two lines of 'Twinkle Twinkle Little Star'. On the internet Ellis came across a new tweet by George Galloway, who wrote @georgegalloway): *Looking at social media today on #Richard Burgon I am reminded of a truth I have refrained from expressing explicitly, no doubt for psychological reasons. Some of the most vile individuals I have ever encountered in Britain are to be found in the ranks of the Labour Party.* Ellis found himself in agreement with this point of view. Galloway was reacting to responses to the sacking of Richard Burgon from the Shadow Cabinet, including that of Kevin Schofield, editor of *Politics Home*, who tweeted: *Labour MP: "I just feel sorry for the village that's getting its idiot back."* Burgon had a northern accent and was on the Left of the party. It was widely believed on social media that, if Schofield's quotation was

103

true and not a malicious fabrication, its source was probably Wes Streeting, a particularly fervent supporter of Israel. Ellis spent the rest of the day reading *The Myths of Liberal Zionism*. That evening he watched the final episode of *The Promise*. On the news it was reported that Boris Johnson was now in intensive care in St Thomas's Hospital. In bed Ellis began reading the Introduction to *Palestine in Israeli School Books: Ideology and Propaganda in Education* by Nurit Peled-Elhanan.

Tuesday 7th April 2020

Another hot sunny morning. The Prime Minister is not on a ventilator, says Michael Gove. To Ellis's dismay his toaster appeared to have stopped working. He unplugged it and shook out the crumbs. But still his toaster did not work. He put it on the kitchen table to look at later. Ellis did not leave the house today. On the Twitter account of Alex Nunns he read that there was an 'Excellent overview' of the rise and fall of Corbynism on the Verso Books website. Ellis clicked on the link and read the article. It confirmed his doubts about the perspicacity of Alex Nunns. The article was by one James Schneider and titled: 'Bridging the Gap: Corbynism after Corbyn'. Ellis thought its analysis contained significant absences and was at times simply wrong. For example, Schneider claimed that ' a socialist majority had taken the National Executive Committee and appointed a socialist, Jennie Formby, to head up the party bureaucracy'. Oh really? Socialists ought to have no difficulty in seeing off the bellicose Zionist lobby. Instead these supposed socialists capitulated. The NEC signed up to the incoherent redefinition of anti-Semitism promoted by the Zionist so-called 'International Holocaust Memorial Alliance', along with the examples, some of which were explicitly designed to disable and defame pro-Palestinian activism. Revealingly, Scheider made no mention of Corbyn and his advisers' abject and strategically catastrophic capitulation to the fraudulent anti-Semitism campaign promoted by an unholy combination of the Zionist lobby, reactionary Jews, right-wing Anglicans including that banal Old Etonian reactionary the Archbishop of Canterbury, innumerable Blairites, *Guardian* journalists and that ruling-class echo chamber known as the BBC. Corbyn's inept reaction to ferocious media hostility was matched by some of his closest associates, such as hopeless wibbly-wobbly John McDonnell. Schneider, laughably, speaks of a 'turbocharged...Corbynite intellectual space'. By this he means that lamentable crew of fairweather lefties at Novara, whose primary ambition appeared to be obtaining a column at the *Guardian* and appearing on corporate TV. The notion that Labour under Corbyn 'took an impressive leadership role' on the environment was, well, bizarre and devoid of substance. Schneider fails to mention perhaps the biggest problem of all: Jeremy Corbyn's leadership deficiencies. Corbyn was not a fighter and he was disloyal to his supporters, while repeatedly accommodating his enemies. Margaret Hodge should have been expelled from the party. Instead Chris Williamson was. As a commander Corbyn was paralysed. He had the strategic intelligence of a goldfish. He failed to rally his troops or to press home an advantage when it came his way. His defence of Tom Watson was pitiful to behold. His opposition to open selection sealed the fate of his supporters and the Left in general within the party. He failed to take on the dead weight of a party bureaucracy which tried to subvert him at every turn. As Tony Greenstein wrote on his blog: *Corbyn was theoretically lazy... Corbyn was never the brightest of MPs or even intellectually curious. He held positions without ever working them out.* Perhaps most astonishingly of all, a man who had long campaigned for the Palestinians ended up accusing a Carlos Latuff cartoon of anti-Semitism. As Greenstein wrote: *Corbyn's inability to understand what lay behind the false anti-Semitism campaign has been his single biggest error of judgement. It has sapped his strength and drained his leadership of direction and purpose. Corbyn comprehensively lost control of the narrative.* In the end, thought Ellis, Corbyn was a colourless mediocrity who had all the pace of an arthritic tortoise. There were even dark moments when Ellis wondered if Corbyn had not in some way reached an accommodation with the secret state. But Schneider himself seemed to be part of the problem. As Greenstein wrote: *Uncritical support was worse than the hostility of his enemies because it allowed Corbyn's mistakes to go unchallenged.* Schneider ends his piece on a note of optimism, gushing that 'socialist leadership has provided a project for power for progressive forces to work towards'. Revealingly, Schneider finds Sir Keir Starmer 'Hard to place' with probably 'progressive' tendencies. Oh really? A man who says 'I support Zionism without qualification' is unequivocally an anti-Palestinian racist and a reactionary. Ellis looked up James Schneider on Wikipedia, and was amused to find him categorised (self-categorised?) as a 'Political leader'. Born in 1987 to Jewish parents Schneider was educated at the ruling-class Dragon School, the ruling-class Winchester College and the ruling-class St Paul's School. He then went on to Trinity College, Oxford. While at Oxford he was president of the Oxford University Liberal Democrats. He joined the Labour Party in 2015, became a co-founder of Momentum with the Jewish pro-Israel multi-millionaire property developer Jon Lansman, and Adam Klug and Emma Rees. In 2016 Schneider was appointed as Director of Strategic Communications for the Leader of the Opposition, Jeremy Corbyn. Schneider is the son of the chief executive of a property company and a property consulant. He describes himself as 'culturally Jewish' (whatever that means). By 20.04 Ellis had still not looked at the toaster. He had spent part of this warm sunny day reading the hostile reactions of the Zionist lobby to *The Promise*. The devious Zionist historian David Cesarini - Ellis possessed a copy of his biography of Adolf Eichman and was struck by how Cesarini evaded the little matter of Eichman's trip to

Mandate Palestine to visit Zionists - was granted a column in (where else!) the *Guardian* to froth and rage about 'massive historical distortion'. Cesarini sputtered with indignation that the hero, a sergeant in the 6th Airborne Division, says that the British army has 'been here for 30 years keeping them [the Jews and the Palestinians] apart'. As an explanation for the British military presence in Palestine this is, of course, grossly inadequate. Cesarini is scandalised that no one mentions the Balfour Declaration. But then no one mentions the British army's four-year war of terror on the Palestinians which started in 1936. Cesarini doesn't grasp that in a drama a character may say what they *believe* to be true, not what actually *is* true. A sergeant in the 6th Airborne Division is unlikely to have possessed knowledge of the history of either Palestine or Zionism. And in citing the Balfour Declaration - 'His Majesty's government view with favour the establishment in Palestine of a national home for the Jewish people, and will use their best endeavours to facilitate the achievement of this object' - Cesarini displays the standard slipperiness of the Zionist intellectual. In the Declaration there is no full stop after that last word 'object' but rather a comma and the words 'it being understood that nothing shall be done which may prejudice the civil and religious rights of the existing non-Jewish communities in Palestine, or the rights and political status enjoyed by Jews in any other country'. Of course Cesarini's objection to *The Promise* has really nothing at all to do with its historical inaccuracy but rather its visceral accuracy in depicting Jews as terrorists and Palestinian civilians as victims. Rather weirdly Cesarini perceives 'the British' as being depicted as 'the prime victims' in this drama, which displays a curious blindness to the representation of the Palestinian family befriended by the sergeant. But then Cesarini is a careless viewer. He writes: 'In one scene [Kosminski] shows three off-duty tommies bleeding to death after an ambush, while Jews in surrounding cafes callously sip tea and eat cream cakes'. In fact only one of the soldiers dies. And the scene is interesting in two ways, as an authentic representation of the cold hostility of Zionist Jews to the British presence (and, arguably, the fear of non-Zionist Jews to assist the occupier - written out of history and memory is the ferocious violence of Zionism against non-Zionist Palestinian Jews). But secondly it works as a metaphor for the indifference of post-Holocaust Jews to suffering and violence perpetuated by Jews in the cause of Zionism. The Jews sipping their tea and ignoring the bleeding soldiers in this scene are an apt metaphor for modern Jews such as those of the Board of Deputies of British Jews and those vast swathes of middle-class American and British Jewry for whom no atrocity by the Israeli state cannot be excused, sanitised, denied outright, or written off as the fault of the victims. Likewise the scene in which the Palestinian child is shot dead by a Jew is the perfect symbol of the IDF and its history. On the Twitter page of Anthony Costello ('Ex-Director, WHO') Ellis read the prediction of the Institute for Health Metrics and Evaluation in the

University of Washington, advisers to the World Health Organisation, which predicted 66,314 deaths in the UK by August 4th 2020. That evening Ellis read a news item on the Guardian website: *Jewish leaders praise Keir Starmer for pledges on Labour antisemitism*. It revealed that Keir Starmer's top priority as leader was ensuring the Party's commitment to the violent dispossession of the Palestinian people. Meanwhile the UK recorded its highest daily number of recorded coronavirus deaths, at 854. So did New York - up from 4,758 to 5,489. Toothless Beth Rigby of Sky News, dressed as usual like a vampire, stood by the statue of Winston Churchill in Parliament Square. This corporate pimp was keen to press home a supposed resemblance between Churchill and Boris Johnson, still in intensive care in St Thomas's Hospital. In bed Ellis read more of the Introduction to *Palestine in Israeli School Books: Ideology and Propaganda in Education* by Nurit Peled-Elhanan.

Wednesday 8th April 2020

Another very hot sunny day. Ellis talked to a neighbour, who told him of a supermarket which yesterday had toilet rolls on its shelves. Ellis watered some plants in pots. Ben White tweeted (@benabyad): *Another attack by Israeli forces on Palestinians in the occupied and blockaded Gaza Strip - this morning, a fisherman was shot and wounded in the hand and leg with rubber-coated metal bullets, while working off Gaza coast*. The streets seemed busier than before, with many pedestrians and more motor vehicles. The government has announced that 938 people died of Covid-19 yesterday, bringing the total UK dead to 7,097. At 17.46. Ellis read a tweet by the slithery Owen Jones: *This, at the start of Passover, is unbelievably grim. Thoughts with the journalists at this horrible time*. There was a link to a news item on the *Guardian* website: **Jewish Chronicle and Jewish News to close and staff laid off**. Ellis chuckled with delight. These poisonous and reactionary publications in the UK were in trouble. It was plain, reading the uniformly hostile responses to Owen Jones's preposterous and illuminating tweet that Ellis was not alone in his reaction. The twitterati were also chuckling and cheering. Except for the usual right-wing toadies. Sadiq Khan sobbed: *This is very worrying news. The Jewish Chronicle and Jewish News are home to some outstanding journalists and are the true voices of the Jewish community in London and all over the country. I hope very much that they are able to secure their future*. Elsewhere, slithery pseudo-leftist Aaron Bastani tweeted: *Best wishes and solidarity to all those whose jobs are on the line - and I hope a buyer is found*. Michael Marshall tweeted in response to Bastani: *Here you go. This is how it's done, you hopeless sap*. Michael Marshall then retweeted Matt Kennard, who wrote: *The Jewish Chronicle is a vile publication that specialises in smearing left-wing Jewish people and Palestine activists. Let's replace it with someone like Arbeter Fraynd* ("Worker's Friend")

- the anarchist Yiddish weekly edited by Rudolf Rocker in London in early 20th century. On this day Saudi Arabia carried out the 800th execution since 2015, in the reign of King Salman bin Abdulaziz. That evening, after watching *Atomic Blonde*, Ellis read to the end of the Introduction to *Palestine in Israeli School Books: Ideology and Propaganda in Education* by Nurit Peled-Elhanan.

Thursday 9th April 2020

The wooden knight. Chess. *Wooden knight.* Sir Keir Starmer. These scraps floated around in Ellis's mind as he thrashed around in bed, sleepless, at 5.30am. That is what people should call Starmer, Ellis thought. The wooden knight. Because of his stiff manner, the dullness of his words, all the polished banalities. A charisma-void. A politics devoid of principle or passion. The leader-shell. Ellis slipped back into sleep. Cloudy and cool at 6.30am but by 8am the sun had started to emerge through the fast-melting cirrus. **'We won't get a refund on our £17,000 chalet'** was one of the top stories on the BBC News website. It told of the anguish of an IT consultant and his family who had booked a skiing holiday in France this month and now could not fly there and who had been refused a refund and advised to claim on their holiday insurance. Covid-19 global statistics as of 07.25 UTC today: 1,484,811 confirmed cases and 88,537 deaths. At 8.37am Ellis read Ben White's latest tweet, posted eleven minutes earlier. It summarised a new B'Tselem report on the violent terrorising of Palestinian civilians by the Israeli Police. Ellis clicked on the link and arrived at a report titled **Sponge round shooting in al-'Esawiyah: Three minors injured. Israeli Police "operation" continues**. The report began: *For about a year, the Israel Police has been conducting a harassment operation in the East Jerusalem neighborhood of al-'Esawiyah. As part of this campaign, many Border Police and Special Patrol Unit officers enter the neighborhood daily, for no apparent reason. Their very presence creates friction with the residents, including arguments and filming of police operations, and in some cases throwing of stones and shooting of fireworks at police officers. The police use these actions as justification for a violent response, which includes throwing stun grenades, firing sponge rounds, and physical assaults on residents...since April 2019 100 neighborhood residents have been injured by sponge rounds. Firing of sponge rounds in the midle of a residential neighborhood can lead to grave and even fatal consequences... in recent years, hundreds of Palestinians in East Jerusalem have been injured by sponge rounds... In three cases documented by B'Tselem in February and March 2020, three minors - 8, 9, and 16 - were injured by sponge rounds. One lost his eye as a result.* This was the barbarism which the Mayor of London, Sadiq Khan, and the new leader of the Labour Party, Sir Keir Starmer, were fully committed to perpetuating, thought Ellis. He returned to the material which he had downloaded regarding the reaction to *The*

Promise by Zionists. On the website *UK Media Watch* (dedicated to sniffing out the slightest sign of pro-Palestinian sympathies) he read an anonymous review produced by an outfit calling itself the British-Israel Group (BIG). *The Promise*, complained BIG, was 'built on a major historical falsehood'. Echoing Cesarini, the objection is to the explanation offered by the British commander to his troops: "You must understand, the Jews see it as their holy land. But the Arabs, who have been here for over a thousand years, see them as stealing their land. Our job is to keep the two sides apart." A perfectly plausible speech for an English officer to have made to his men in this place at that time. The indignant Zios then go off at a tangent: 'Ever since World War Two, the Arabs have seen the Jewish national enterprise as the consequence of Nazism. Without indigenous roots. And without historical legitimacy.' And who better than a Zio to mediate what 'the Arabs' are thinking? And how delightful that velvet phrase 'the Jewish national enterprise' sounds! So much sweeter than 'the seizure of Palestine and the expulsion of the natives'. The Palestinians know perfectly well that the seizure of their land was primarily accomplished in the years 1936-1939, when the might of the British Empire set out to smash them by force, to create a pro-British Jewish settler state on the Ulster model. That is not in the programme either. Later, on Twitter, Ellis came across Jonathan Freedland and Hadley Freeman blubbering about the demise of *The Jewish Chronicle*. Freedland asserted that it was the beating heart of the Jewish community, but someone responded by asking why, if this was true, there were, in 2018, only 17,000 copies sold each week (bearing in mind that there are estimated to be 240,000 Jews in Britain). Later, Ellis saw that the *Guardian* website was running yet another bogus article about the Labour Party and anti-Semitism. This was by David Feldman, who seemed to have his own cottage industry in his role as Director of something called The Pears Institute for the study of Antisemitism at Birkbeck College, University of London, where he was also a Professor of History. That Feldman was another propagandist was quickly revealed by an internet search which threw up (apt verb!) a piece in *Haaretz* on 27 November 2019 in which he cited Chief Rabbi Ephraim Mirvis, whose 'excoriating article' in the *Times*, designed to smear the Labour Party just before the general election, Feldman regarded as expressing the 'anxiety' of British Jews. Of course if it was true that Mirvis did speak for a significant constituency all it indicated was that that constituency was a Zionist one, determined to protect Jewish privilege and Jewish theft in Israel. As for the claim that 'Many members of the Jewish community can hardly believe this is the same party that they called their political home for more than a century' - that rather evaded the sociological reality that Jews had long since gravitated from the Left to the Right for reasons of class and affluence. The overwhelming majority of British Jews had long since ceased voting Labour. Indeed, even Ed Miliband, a Jew, was reported as having lost a chunk of his Jewish support because of his tepid liberal views on Palestine. Later that day the fact that Sir Keir Starmer was dragging the Labour Party to the extreme right was signalled by his appointment of Wes Streeting and shallow, gobby narcissist Jess Phillips to his shadow cabinet. Ellis pan-fried some cod and ate it with chips, tomatoes and peas. It was a warm night and he opened the bedroom window. He began reading the first chapter of *Palestine in Israeli School Books: Ideology and Propaganda in Education* by Nurit Peled-Elhanan.

Friday 10th April 2020

A bright and sunny Good Friday. The child pushed her toy pushchair. Later she put a woolly hat on and chuckled when Ellis did the same. Ellis removed it and balanced a tupperware box on his head. The child imitated him. Later the child sang the theme song of 'Waffle The Wonder Dog'. A police car cruised the streets. The UK has recorded its worst daily fatality rate yet with a record 980 people dying in hospital in the preceding 24 hours, bringing the total to 8,958. This figure excludes deaths outside hospitals, for example in care homes. Ellis watched mobile-phone footage of a blonde policewoman in Yorkshire harassing a working-class man by telling him he was not permitted to be in his front garden and should go indoors. In the background his children could be heard shouting. Elsewhere on the internet Ellis read that park closures in cities hit BAME and poor Londoners the most. People in deprived areas have less access to gardens and other green spaces, analysis showed. A third of all land in the wealthiest 10 per cent of London wards is taken up by private gardens. Meanwhile Robert Jenrick MP, who owns three houses - two £2 million properties in London and a £1.1 million manor house in Hertfordshire as well as very occasionally using a £2,000 a month rented property in his Newark constituency, billed to the taxpayer - left London on March 29 to drive the 150 miles to his holiday home in Herefordshire. He then drove 40 miles to travel to his parents' home on April 4 or 5, claiming to be bringing food and medication, even though neighbours said they were already delivering essentials. Jenrick claims his country mansion is his family home but his own website says the opposite. It states that he and his family 'live in Southwell near Newark, and in London'. His wife works as a partner in a major US law firm in the City. The thoroughly useless new Shadow Home Secretary, Nick Thomas-Symonds, said that if Jenrick had delivered medicine to his parents that clearly adhered to the guidelines. It was once again a warm night and Ellis opened the bedroom window. He continued reading the first chapter of *Palestine in Israeli School Books: Ideology and Propaganda in Education* by Nurit Peled-Elhanan. He had always noticed that apologists for the Israeli terror state usually preferred to use the all-encompassing word 'Arab' to the noun 'Palestinian' and he was interested to read Peled-Elhanan's analysis of the language of Israeli text books and the way in which the word 'Arab' was used for sectarian propaganda purposes to deny Palestinians a national identity.

Saturday 11th April 2020

Another very hot day. Blue sky and sunshine. The voice of David Miliband dripped from the radio. This sweating toad with a strange wispy moustache had suddenly become more prominent in the media since the Labour Party had been reclaimed for neo-liberal economics, nuclear holocaust and Zionist terror. Ellis left the bedroom and went to drink his mug of tea at the computer. He wrote: Ellis left the bedroom and went to drink his mug of tea at the computer. Ellis could hear birds singing but he could not see them. He wondered if the toad had fled downtown New York, like the rest of the rich whites. Holed-up in the Hamptons? Mewed-up in Montauk? The government, Ellis read, has declined to say how many healthcare staff in Britain have died after contracting Covid-19. Ian Sinclair tweeted: *Shockingly, BBC Radio 4's 08:00 news bulletin this morning did not mention the record 980 deaths yesterday in UK from Coronavirus (it did find space to mention that Paul McCartney's handwritten lyrics for Hey Jude were being auctioned though).* Later, the child held out two plastic toys, one orange, one green. Ellis found an old pack of blank CDs, still unopened, in an orange-coloured plastic wrapper. He placed it on his head and the child laughed and put the orange-coloured toy on her head. Ellis found a packet of green tea to put on his head. But by now the child had lost interest in the game. On Twitter, Ellis read Jonathan Cook's analysis of the front pages of today's British national newspapers: *Quite astounding. The entire corporate media 'spectrum' scrubs from their front pages the fact that the UK has just hit the highest daily death toll from Covid-19 in Europe. Instead it's all diversionary 'spirit of the Blitz' stories.* The child ran around on the lawn, in the sun. That evening Ellis watched *Basic Instinct*, for the first time in many years. The movie had worn well, he thought. In bed he read more of 'The Representation of Palestinians in Israeli School Books'. It unfolded the variety of ways in which Israeli Jews were educated to view Palestinians as terrorists, refugees or primitive farmers.

Sunday 12th April 2020

Easter Sunday. This was the day the USA would be back in business, the lockdown would be over, and the churches would be packed with worshippers. asserted President Donald Trump on 27 March. *Associated Press: The U.S. death toll from the coronavirus eclipsed Italy's for the highest in the world Saturday, surpassing 20,000, as Chicago and other cities across the Midwest braced for a potential surge in victims. With the New York area still deep in crisis, fear mounted over the spread of the scourge into the nation's heartland. Chicago's Cook County has set up a temporary morgue that can take more than 2,000 bodies.* A bright sunny morning, but cooler. Thunderstorms are forecast for this afternoon. A new opinion poll by Opinion Research recorded the Westminster Voting Intention as: CON: 55%, LAB: 29%. Poll taken on 7-9 April. The Conservative Party had continued to increase in popularity and the Government Approval Rating was 61% - an increase of 9% since the previous poll on 1-3 April. A report by Tom Rayner, political corespondent, had been posted on the Sky News website at 00.13, UK. It was headed Exclusive: **Labour antisemitism investigation will not be sent to equality commission**. Even Sky News had now decided to delete the hyphen in the word 'anti-Semitism', Ellis noticed. The sub-heading ran: *A report found factional hostility towards Jeremy Corbyn amongst former senior officials contributed to "a litanty of mistakes".* It began: An extensive internal investigation into the way Labour handled antisemitism complaints will not be submitted to the Equality and Human Rights Commission after an intervention by party lawyers. The 860-page report, seen by Sky News, concluded factional hostility towards Jeremy Corbyn among former senior officials contributed to "a litany of mistakes" that hindered the effective handling of the issue. The investigation, which was completed in the last month of Jeremy Corbyn's leadership, claims to have found "no evidence" of antisemitism complaints being treated differently to other forms of complaint, or of current or former staff being "motivated by antisemitic intent". Tom Rayner reported that the investigation had uncovered thousands of private WhatsApp communications between former seior party officals and singles out for criticism some who gave whistleblower evidence to last year's highly-critical BBC Panorama ~~hatchet job on Corbyn~~ investigation on antisemitism within Labour. These include the former General Secretary Lord McNicol and the former acting head of the governance and legal unit, Sam Matthews. The report directly addresses the EHRC on several occasions, including urging the watchdog to "question the validity of the personal testimonies" of former members of staff. However, Tom Rayner wrote, Sky News understands party lawyers have told the ~~useless and feeble~~ General Secretary Jennie Formby the report entitled: "The work of the Labour Party's Governance and Legal Unit in relation to antisemitism, 2014-2019", should not be submitted to the Commission, due to fears it could damage the party's wider case. But that decision, Tom Rayner wrote, has prompted widespread concern amongst those who worked in the most senior positions in the leadership office of Jeremy Corbyn, with one telling Sky News: "This report completely blows open everything that went on. We were being sabotaged and set up left right and centre by McNicol's team and we didn't even know. It's important that the truth comes out. [Iain McNicol was the Labour Party General Secretary from 2011 to 2018.] Tom Rayner added: The report claims private communications show senior former staff "openly worked against the aims and objectives of the leadership of the Party, and in the 2017 general election some key staff even appeared to work against the Party's core objective of winning elections". The examples from chat archives published in the document include: conversations which it is claimed show senior staff hid information from the leader's office about digital spending and contact details for MPs and candidates during the election; conversations on election night in which the members of the group talk about the need to hide their disappointment that Mr Corbyn had done better than expected and would be unlikely to resign; conversations in which the same group refers to Mr Corbyn's former chief of staff Karie Murphy as "medusa", a "crazy woman" and a "bitch face cow" that would "make a good dartboard". The investigation also accuses the former General Secretary Lord McNicol, and other senior figures of providing "false and misleading information" to Jeremy Corbyn's office. Asked to comment Lord McNicol said: "This is a petty attempt to divert attention away from the real issue". The report also claims Sam Matthews, who served first as Head of Disputes and then as acting Head of the Governance and Legal Unit, "rarely replied or took any action". The predicted afternoon thunderstorm did not occur. The child waved her plastic spoon. Ellis took two plastic spoons from a drawer in the kitchen and waved them back. The child chuckled. Ellis received 18 texts from the same person over a course of three hours. For supper he dined on fried sausages, mash and boiled cabbage. Afterwards he ate a small bowl of dates. There were noises which might have been aircraft but which he later decided were faraway thunder. The number of people with Coronavirus who have died in UK hospitals has topped 10,000. The total number of hospital deaths stood at 10,612 on Sunday, up by 737 from 9,875 the day before. There was, Nurit Peled-Elhanan wrote, a connection between the school books which Israeli Jewish children read, and the belief of adult Jewish Israelis that their Palestinian neighbours should be eliminated or, at best, excluded, marginalized, segregated and controlled.

Monday 13th April 2020

Ellis heard rain beating down in the night. In the morning it was cold and grey and a strong wind blew through the neighbourhood. BBC News this morning (brought to you on behalf of the Conservative Party) was focused on 200 soldiers who had been retrained to assist ambulance crews. And the price of oil had increased by 5 per cent a barrel after a deal had been struck between major oil producers. Two Italians had fallen in love from their balconies. Not on the BBC News was the remarkable revelation that only 1.4 per cent of businesses seeking a government loan designed to support small and medium-sized businesses had been successful in obtaining one. 4,200 out of 300,000. Not on the BBC News was the revelation of an astonishing leaked dossier indicating that senior Labour Party staff had actively sabotaged Corbyn, the 2017 election, and posted abusive and insulting comments about other members of staff. After a short search on Twitter, Ellis located a site which offered the opportunity to download the entire document. Ellis duly did so, onto his mobile phone. The document, he discovered, was entitled: **The work of the Labour Party's Governance and Legal Unit in relation to antisemitism, 2014 - 2019. The Labour Party, March 2020.** It was 851 pages in length. He spent much of this day skipping through extracts. It revealed that those working against Corbyn were: Emilie Oldknow (Executive Director for Governance, Membership & Party Services - now Assistant General Secretary of Unison and married to Jon Ashworth MP, Keir Starmer's Shadow Health Secretary), Iain McNicol (General Secretary), Tracy Allen (married to Phil Woolas), Nicola Murphy (married to Chris Leslie), John Stolliday, Sarah Mulholland, Patrick Heneghan, Greg Cook, Simon Jackson, Jo Green, Ali Moussavi, Sarah Brown, Sam Matthews, Mike Creighton, Julie Lawrence, Simon Mills, Patrick Heneghan. Emilie Oldknow was awarded an OBE for Political Service in the New Year's Honours list in 2019. Emilie Oldknow boasted that Tom Watson was working to embarrass Jeremy Corbyn by delaying a decision on Ken Livingstone. The report stated that half of all anti-Semitism complaints in 2019 were made by a single individual, Euan Philipps, of so-called Labour Against Anti-Semitism. Of the BBC's top one hundred news reporters not a single one of them tweeted once about this explosive report, one of the most extraordinary documents to be leaked in modern British political history. BBC News mirrored the Labour Party. Both institutions were rotten to the core, thought Ellis. He reached for the yellow tube and began to blow bubbles. The child grinned and grinned. Ellis ate an omelette. Later he read more of Nurit Peled-Elhanan's book.

Tuesday 14th April 2020

Cold. Grey. Cloudy. At 8.30am the landline started ringing. Ellis stayed in all day. It emerged that Sir Keir Starmer had been in possession of the leaked report for a week and had taken no action, indicating his desire to cover-up its damning contents. On Twitter Ellis read Darius363: *No suspensions. No resignations. Just imagine for a second if this leak had revealed abuse, racism, bullyng & corruption by people associated with Corbyn. Imagine if Jewish MPs had been abused instead of Diane Abbot and Dawn Butler.* Starmer had announced an investigation which seemed to be as much about finding out who was responsible for the report and who leaked it as about addressing its contents. In the afternoon Ellis went to bed to rest. Later he had a bath. He dressed and went downstairs. The child removed a sock and held it up. Ellis removed a sock and waved it. The child grinned. Later Ellis pan-fried some salmon and ate it with mashed potato and peas. He spent the evening reading. In bed he read that four generations of Jewish children in Israel had been educated using racist and sectarian textbooks. The Zionist hypotext, wrote Nurit Peled-Elhanan, is unaltered and is still compatible with the Israeli socio-political discourse that has prevailed since 1948.

Wednesday 15th April 2020

Once again it was a bright and sunny morning. The explosive Labour Party leak had already been marginalized to the point of invisibility, except on social media. This morning's BBC poison was squirted in the direction of China. Echoing Donald Trump, BBC News pointed the finger of blame. The unusual transparency of the Chinese state in communicating the dangers of the virus was nowhere acknowledged. Instead BBC News offered xenophobia. It was easy enough to see the agenda here. It was a crude attempt to divert attention from the incompetence of the British government, and the Conservative Party's long hostility to the NHS and its years of under-resourcing that institution. You would never learn from BBC News about the dummy-run for a pandemic which had been held in the recent past, the recommendations of which were coolly ignored by the Conservative Government. 'Blame China' followed on from the spurious 'panic buying' story and the moral panic about people sitting on park benches. Later Ellis discovered that toilet rolls had returned to the shelves. But there was no cooking oil at all and canned fish had almost sold out. He saw a police car enter an almost empty car park and cruise towards a red car parked at the far end. Ellis went to the bottle bank. Later he rang the hospital. Later the child picked up a circular blue biscuit tin. Ellis picked up a different circular blue biscuit tin. He banged it and the child grinned and banged her tin. It was a warm sunny afternoon but a cooler evening. Ellis watched the first two minutes of the Sky 10pm news, then switched the television off and went to bed. He felt exhausted. He read a few pages of Nurit Peled-Elhanan's book and learned more about the misrepresentations of Palestinian history in Jewish school text books. The massacre of the villagers of Dier Yassin (which included rape and the burning alive of a teenager) is justified on the grounds that it was 'a base for aggressive attacks on Jerusalem'. Which is a lie.

Thursday 16th April 2020

Another bright warm sunny day. Ellis felt tired and stressed. Texts, phone calls… The child held out a red plastic toy. Ellis took hold of a red stapler and balanced it on his head. The child chortled and attempted to balance her plastic toy on her head. The child produced Green Rabbit, followed by Miss Polly. The child ran out into the sunshine. Ellis watched the daily government virus briefing. Those journalists who did ask searching questions received by way of reply clouds of verbiage and perfumed promises of future action. Ellis sawed off two buddleia branches. He prepared pan-fried cod with mashed potato and peas. That evening, to take his mind off various matters, he watched *The French Lieutenant's Woman*. It was one of a small number of movies he never tired of watching. Afterwards he looked up the cast, to see what had happened to them since. Most were still working in movies, television or theatre. Penelope Wilton (Sonia) had become famous as Isobel Crawley in *Downton Abbey*. Jeremy Irons was still a star. Ellis had last seen him in *High-Rise*. Ditto Meryl Streep. Ellis had last seen her in (oh dear) *Mamma Mia! Here We Go Again*. John Barrett (the dairyman) had died on 22 May 1983. Patience Collier (Mrs Poulteney) had died on 13 July 1987. Leo McKern (Dr Grogan) had died on 23 July 2002. Charlotte Mitchell (Mrs Tranter) had died on 2 May 2012. Peter Vaughan (Mr Freeman) had died on 6 December 2016. Liz Smith (Mrs Fairley) had died on 24 December 2016. The ideological basis of geography teaching in Israel, Ellis read, consists of the Zionist message regarding the redemption and resettlement of the Homeland by the Children of Israel who, possessing exclusive historical rights to the Land, have returned home after 2000 years of exile. Geography books offer very little information about the region or about Arab-Palestinian life, be it agriculture, social settings, rural or urban changes, during the 2000-year Jewish 'absence', Ellis read.

Friday 17th April 2020

Cool and cloudy. The burial of the explosive leaked Labour report was now complete by the corporate media. The Today programme, which had obsessively promoted the fraudulent anti-Semitism story day after day for over two years, was maintaining its absolute silence. Few people in Britain today would ever have heard of Emilie Oldknow, whose name by now should have been infamous and a household word. Instead, true to form, the Today programme this morning fawned over Prince William and his wife. The brown-nosing of Nick Robinson, oozing good humour, had surely earned him a future knighthood. Once again Ellis felt tired and stressed. Texts, phone calls… Later, on social media, he came across a tweet by John McDonnell MP, tweeted on April 15th. It read: *The best piece I have read so far on the Labour Party report.* There was a link to an article by Andrew Fisher, posted on the inew.co.uk website, titled 'I experienced the hostility documented in the leaked Labour report - it has to be a turning point'. Ellis read it and thought how impoverished John McDonnell's politics must be to like such a reactionary article. Andrew Fisher wrote that the Labour Party was 'wrong not to have immediately adopted the International Holocaust Remembrance Alliance (IHRA) definition' of anti-Semitism. Oh really? Fisher displayed a naïve faith in Keir Starmer, whose actions showed conclusively that he was not seriously perturbed by the Report's contents. No action had yet been taken against a single one of the figures revealed in the report to be racist, sexist and wholly subversive of the party which employed them. What is this crap? Ellis thought, as he read Andrew Fisher's lapdog conclusion: 'A more united and effective party is possible, but we all need to play our part.' This crap was worthy of the Liberal Democrats, Ellis felt. At the foot of the article it was revealed that Andrew Fisher was Executive Director of Policy at the Labour Party from 2016 to 2019. Later Ellis spoke to friends on a laptop - six people who could each see each other. Four held up their drinks - cheers. There was discussion of a seventh friend, who had cancer. That evening Ellis caught up with an old, unread copy of *The Sunday Times*, dated 5 April. He read about the impact the pandemic was having on *Sunday Times* readers. I miss not being able to go to New York and Paris on a whim or visit friends in Spain, wrote Alison Donnell, Ayrshire. Later, after seeing the newspaper front pages for Saturday, Ellis went to bed. He had no wish to stay up watching the analysis of Toby Young and some hack from the *Mirror*. In bed he felt too exhausted to read even a page of a book. He put out the light and quickly fell into a deep sleep.

Saturday 18th April 2020

A grey, cloudy morning. Ellis switched on the radio and listened to the end of Farming Today. He dressed and went out to post a card in a nearby postbox. He had just posted the card when suddenly torrential rain began to fall. Ellis ran home, arriving back half-soaked. Later there was a small queue outside the store. It continued to rain on and off all day. Ellis glanced at *The Times*. He would read most of it another day. On social media he learned that Sir Keir Starmer's leadership campaign had been partly financed by a prominent wealthy lobbyist for Israel. Starmer was still refusing to provide information about his financial supporters. On social media there was criticism of Starmer's failure to suspend a single individual regarding the leaked report. John McDonnell was still huffing and puffing. McDonnell's grovelling towards the Equalities and Human Rights Commission (EHRC) exposed yet again the sheer feebleness of a man who simply didn't seem to understand that this laughable Blairite quango was highly politicized. The notion that the EHRC was some kind of neutral and objective arbiter of what constituted racism was absurd. But then McDonnell's inadequacies had been indicated in 2019 when he had denounced as 'anti-Semitic' the witty ISRAEL IS A RACIST ENDEAVOUR posters appearing at London bus stops (which had rightly mocked the Labour Party's craven acceptance of the Zionist redefinition of anti-Semitism to incorporate criticism of Israel). When the parliamentary so-called 'Left' consisted of individuals like John McDonnell and Rebecca Long-Bailey (and, yes, even Richard Burgon, whose backtracking over his 'Zionism is the enemy of peace' remark was lamentable to behold) it was surely time to terminate once and for all any illusions that Labour would ever become a socialist party, and that socialists who gave it their support were simply perpetuating the crisis of critical absence. That night Ellis watched *The Sense of an Ending*. He remembered reading the novel and not finding it at all engaging. He could no longer remember a single thing about it. As the movie ran on he still remembered nothing at all of the book. The cinematography was exquisite, the settings elegant, the acting of a high order. And there was Lady Mary from *Downton Abbey*! She had a cushion pushed under her jumper. And Lady Mary's husband was in it too, the one who died in a car crash. He was in flashbacks, as a class teacher in a private school. Allso Jim Broadbent, who in this movie, Ellis felt, was rather creepy. The McGuffin was a diary, though how it had come into the possession of the woman who had recently died, and why she had decided to leave it in her will to Jim Broadbent, were glaring plot holes the script never tried to patch. It amounted to the usual glittering vacuity, in the same category as *On Chesil Beach* and *The Bookshop*. In bed Ellis read *Palestine in Israeli School Books* and learned that Palestinians are rarely visualized at all and when they are it is never as modern, productive human beings but as stereotypes constituting 'problems' and 'threats' to Israeli Jews. All school geography books use racist images to depict Palestinian citizens of Israel as primitive and backward, an assemblage of thieves, parasites and social outlaws who constitute the enemy within.

Sunday 19th April 2020

Bright and sunny. As he ate his morning bowl of cereal Ellis read an article on the Guardian website by Toby Helm, Emma Graham-Harrison and Robin McKie, titled: **How did Britain get its response to coronavirus so wrong?** Now, 11 weeks on from the first cases being confirmed in the UK on 31 January - a period during which more than 14,000 people (and probably several thousands more once care home fatalities are counted) in the UK have died from Covid-19 - and with the country in lockdown, the economy facing prolonged recession as a result, schools closed, and no sign of an end in sight - hard questions have to be asked, Ellis read. The article noted that the World Health Organisation had issued an alert on 30 January that Covid-19 represented a 'public health emergency of international concern' - the highest-level alert the WHO can issue. On 11 March the WHO declared a global pandemic. On 14 March, Spain went into lockdown, with France doing the same on 17 March. In the UK there was government reluctance to ban mass gatherings and close pubs and restaurants. This did not happen until 20 March. Testing and contact tracing was at the heart of the approach advocated by the WHO, whereas the UK's chief scientific adviser preferred 'herd immunity', which allowed the majority of the population to contract the virus and develop antibodies. On social media Ellis read of a report in today's *Sunday Times*, which described a catalogue of failure. It was revealed that 190,000 people flew into the UK from Wuhan and other high-risk Chinese cities between January and March 2020. Up to 1,900 of these passengers probably had the virus. The last rehearsal for a pandemic was in 2016, codename Cygnus. It predicted a lack of PPE and ventilators. Its lengthy list of recommendations was never implemented. Elsewhere on social media Ellis read a description by Matt Kennard of some curious connections in Sir Keir Starmer's past: https://twitter.com/DCKennard/status/125034431577212 416. The list, drawn from official sources, included the record of a meal with the head of MI5 after Starmer, in his role as Director of the Crown Prosecution Service, had decided not to prosecute the service in a case involving rendition and torture. Ellis telephoned the hospital and spoke to a nurse named Laura. Later he received a lengthy call which afterwards made him consider an event supposed to have happened on 19 January 1990. The child held up a spoon. Ellis went to get his two plastic kitchen spoons: the yellow one and the purple and grey one. They played with their spoons. The child grinned. Later, at bathtime, the child waved her red plastic dinosaur. Ellis watched *The Terminator*, which he had seen many times before. In bed Ellis read about cartohypnosis, a concept he had not encountered before.

Monday 20th April 2020

Another blue sky and sunshine day. The Today programme, characteristically, had Tony Blair on, explaining at length what needed to be done to combat the coronavirus. No one adored this blood-soaked criminal more than BBC News and the *Guardian*. Later, on Twitter, Ellis smiled as he read the comment: *I suppose if there's anyone who qualifies as an expert on hundreds of thousands of avoidable deaths, it's Tony Blair.* In the bakery Ellis bought two almond croissants and a pack of four hot cross buns. He telephoned the hospital and spoke to Laura again. He wrote emails. The child smiled as Ellis placed a cloth doll on his head and promptly imitated him. Later he pan-fried some cod and ate it with mashed potatoes and peas, followed by stewed apple and icecream. In 1994, A. K. Henrikson had written, Ellis learned, that every map is is a device for getting you to look at the world according to the map-maker's perspective. *They do it by conveying they have no such interest. They are convincing because the interests they serve are masked.* Ellis put out the light.

Tuesday 21st April 2020

Ellis slept, until a movement in the night sent the bedside glass of water crashing to the floor, soaking the carpet. He slept once more, then woke some time after four, when he went to the bathroom to urinate. Back in bed again he slept until a sharp unidentifiable noise woke him around seven. The bedroom was full of light. Ellis wondered if the noise had been a bird. Pigeons and crows sometimes pecked at the moss-filled guttering. It was another day of sunshine with a cloudless blue sky. A cold wind blew. Outside, there seemed to be more people and motor traffic than yesterday. Ellis telephoned the hospital. He was told he would be phoned back. He was not. He rang again later. Later he read a recent post by Craig Murray about the leaked Labour Party report which had exposed the racism, sexism and obstructiveness of certain members of the Governance and Legal Unit. Corbyn's office showed an alarming willingness to throw good people under the bus on very flimsy allegations of anti-Semitism, wrote Murray. The report shows a serious inability to to distinguish between real, nasty anti-Semitism and opposition to the policies of Israel. Furthermore, continued Murray, this is the attitude of the authors of the report themselves. Later in his piece Craig Murray wrote: I have always found the discourse around the Nazi/Zionist links disturbing and anti-Semitic in motivation. Of course there may have been some contact at some early stage between Nazis who wished to eradicate Jews from Europe and Zionists who wished Jews to move to Israel. But what purpose is there in pointing that out? asked Craig Muray. Any misguided Zionist who tried to deal with the Nazis was not therefore a Nazi supporter, wrote Craig Murray. It is a pointless discussion with highly unpleasant undertones, he asserted. Murray, Ellis felt, did not really understand Zionism, which is a nineteenth-century blood and soil ideology with much in common with Nazism. But this was a topic to return to on another day. Murray did not help his argument by then proceeding to the case of Gilad Atzmon and defending him. The child placed a blue cup on her head and grinned as Ellis balanced a blue spectacles case on his own head. Later he ate asparagus in hollandaise sauce and a lamb steak and watched *Terminator: Dark Fate*. It was a great disappointment. Apart from its ability to generate a second, skeletal self the terminator was no different to the one in *Terminator 2: Judgement Day*. The plot was stale and the action sequences lazy and conventional. The car chase. The fight. The chopper. The fight on a plane which is on fire and falling from the sky. The sequence in a vehicle underwater. The final denouement in a large industrial building. Ellis was bored and disappointed. He had hoped the return of Linda Hamilton signified a return to the power of the first two films in the series. It didn't. The franchise had become flaccid and complacent. This in itself was not a new phenomenon. *The Matrix* had been dazzling in its originality but the sequels were banal and pointless. Like *Jaws*. Only the *Alien* quadrology had bucked the trend. Outside, the night was cool and the sky glittered with stars.

Yet another blue-sky sunshine day. The asparagus had produced the usual pungent aroma. The roads seemed busy again today. The pandemic sweeping the world has infected more than 2.5 million people and killed nearly 180,000. Ellis went to the postbox with a card. Two people waited outside the adjacent shop. A man ran down the centre of the road. Ellis telephoned the hospital. He was told that their patient believed the hospital wristband was a tracking device. Cognitive functioning was 'very poor'. The sun continued to shine, reminding Ellis of the first sentence of a work of fiction by Beckett. The child put a blue sun hat on her head. Ellis placed a hat on his head. The child grinned. Later, Ellis finished watching *Harry Potter and the Order of the Phoenix*. The title was something of a McGuffin, he felt. He threw the DVD in the bin, knowing he would never wish to watch this film again. But it had passed the time and kept his mind off the stress he felt. That evening he ate vegetarian risotto. He finished reading Nurit Peled-Elhanan's chapter on Israeli Jewish school geography text books. The unequivocal conclusion, based on numerous examples, was that these Jewish students are taught to see themselves as masters of the Land of Israel/Palestine, to control its landscape and its space as well as the Palestinians. They are educated to do whatever is necessary to increase Jewish domination and its "development", which means its expansion.

Thursday 23rd April 2020

Yet another blue sky sunshine day. Ellis spoke to Narissa. The child ate fruit at lunchtime. She held up a banana and Ellis waved a banana. The child grinned. Accessing the world wide web Ellis was delighted to see that Tony Greenstein had finally posted his analysis of the leaked Labour Party report. Ellis knew that this would be the shrewdest and most comprehensive analysis of any. Ellis discovered that Greenstien had so much to say that he had broken down his analysis into two parts, and this was only the first part. Ellis cut and pasted Part One to a file to read at leisure. It said a great deal about the parlous state of the Left in Britain today that Greenstein was something of a marginalized renegade. Greenstein's analysis was the high point of Ellis's day. The low point was the discovery that the *Jewish Chronicle* had been saved. It was plain that money had been forthcoming for the explicit purpose of maintaining this rag as the bellicose mouthpiece of British Zionism. The consortium behind the purchase is fronted by Sir Robert Gibb (the BBC's former head of political programming), William Shawcross (former Chairman of the Charity Commission), former Labour MP John Woodcock, BBC Panorama hatchet man John Ware, broadcaster Jonathan Sacerdoti, Rabbi Jonathan Hughes of Radlett United Synagogue, Tom Boltman (Kovrr), Mark Joseph (EMK Capital), Robert Swerling (Investec) and Jonathan

Kandel (Kirkland and Ellis). That foul individual Stephen Pollard was being retained as editor. David Wolfson QC, Chair of the *Jewish Chronicle* Trust, wrote on the *Jewish Chronicle* website: *The Trust's sole aim has been to see the Jewish Chronicle survive and flourish in good hands. As Jonathan Freedland wrote in last week's issue, it is the "beating heart" of Anglo-Jewry.* Which, if true, would indicate that the heart of Anglo-Jewry is a cold, dark chamber smeared with Palestinian blood and echoing to the muffled sound of weeping and screaming from those bereaved or tortured by fascistic Jews. Ellis watched *Layer Cake.* In bed he continued reading Nurit Peled-Elhanan's book. The author analysed a section of the text book *Modern Times Part II: The History of the People of Israel for Grades 10-12.* Nurit Peled-Elhanan noted the subtle bias of the photographs, in which Jews looked straight at the camera, whereas Palestinians are pictured at a distance. Nurit Peled-Elhanan detected a racist tone in the caption used, which identified a 'Palestinian problem' which 'ripened' like a malignant growth or a plague. A human catastrophe morphed into an ecological disaster which lacked specificity or agency.

Friday 24th April 2020

Bright and sunny at 6am but by nine it had clouded over and become cool and misty. Later the sun returned. There seemed to be even more motor vehicles being driven on the streets today, and more people out and about. On the news it was reported that President Trump had suggested that an injection of disinfectant might cure anyone infected by Covid-19. The child played in the garden with her new sand and water table. It currently lacked play sand, which was at present unavailable for purchase. The sand section was filled with brightly coloured plastic balls. Indoors, she played with a potato. Ellis held up a potato and waved it. The child grinned. Ellis finished reading Part One of Tony Greenstein's lengthy analysis of the leaked Labour Party report. As Greenstein had rightly concluded, even now John McDonnell didn't seem to grasp that the great hunt for anti-Semites had absolutely nothing at all to do with a genuine concern for racism but was simply used as a device to destroy the equally obtuse leader of the Party, J. Corbyn, who had colluded from the start with his biggest enemies while showing utter disregard for some of his oldest comrades. The name Marc Wadsworth came to mind. Later in the day it was reported that Public Health England had appointed right-wing Islamophobic establishment toady Trevor Phillips to investigate why so many BAME workers were dying in the NHS. It was as if every public institution in England was rotten, Ellis thought. The landline telephone rang and he held an hour-long conversation. Twenty minutes later it rang again and he held another lengthy conversation with the same person. On Twitter footage circulated of thuggish Israeli troops blindfolding a Palestinian child and parading him down a street while the Jews tossed explosive grenades at houses. The depravity of the Jewish state was boundless and unending. That evening Ellis pan-fried some salmon, eaten with mashed potatoes, peas and flowering broccoli. He passed the evening reading recent copies of *The Times*, including the final pre-lockdown restaurant review, which involved the reviewer - a brittle 'comic' Zionist - swigging a bottle of wine costing £120 at a restaurant which charged £13 for each langoustine put on the plate. It was an inventory of expensive excess, for which the term 'restaurant porn' was entirely accurate. It was food for the super-rich and high-earning professionals with lavish expense accounts. Readers were invited to share vicariously the consumption of shining, spectacular adjectives. In bed Ellis read Nurit Pelel-Elhanan's analysis of a photograph in *Modern Times Part II: The History of the People of Israel for Grades 10-12*. Included in the subject topic *The Palestinians: from refugees to a nation* is a section titled *The Palestinians wage a terrorist war against Israel*. It is juxtaposed with a photograph of an Israeli soldier carrying a wounded crying girl. The caption reads: *Galil Maimon rescuing his wounded sister*. For Israeli Jews this is an iconic image. Part of its power, Nurit Pelel-Elhanan suggests, is that it is a classic universal; image of rescue: a soldier rescuing an injured young girl. The soldier runs from an invisible danger. The fact that no Palestinians are shown in this chapter that is supposed to relate their history, writes Nurit Pelel-Elhanan, only the consequences of their criminal actions, already colours their route "from refugees to a nation" with the blood of innocent children. It is the only photograph in all the textbooks that shows blood. Jewish-Israeli children are indoctrinated with this horrific image just prior to their conscription into the Israeli army.

Saturday 25th April 2020

Grey and cold. But later hot and warm. A magpie seized some bread Ellis had put out for the birds. He had never seen a magpie in the garden before. He went out and bought a *Times*. The child ran around the house and the garden, happy. She brushed her hair. Ellis went to get his own hair brush and copied the child, who grinned. Next the child experimented with putting both her feet inside a shoe belonging to an adult. Ellis waited all day for the telephone to ring but it did not ring. That evening he ate gnocchi with mushrooms and spinach, followed by apple crumble and ice-cream. The film tonight was *Knives Out*. A slick, entertaining reworking of an ancient formula. As for Daniel Craig's Deep South accent... Ellis went to bed. In her fourth chapter Nurit Pelel-Elhanan analysed the ways in which even when the Israeli state educational system acknowledged the mass murder of Palestinian civilians by Israeli soldiers these crimes were legitimated with reference to security or by supplying only a less than comprehensive account of these atrocities and asserting fictitious connections between the victims and terrorism. She cited a book titled *Ethnocracy* by O. Yiftachel, which it seemed argued that apartheid Israel depended upon two key elements in perpetuating the chauvinism of its Jews: segregation and an ideology of justification. Among the components of Jewish identity was a fundamentalist belief in Jewish supremacism as the only acceptable form of citizenship, a complacent acceptance of the privileges which the state confers on Jews and denies to non-Jews, and a racist contempt for the Other which enthusiastically accepts the need for collective punishment and assassination. Israel is a militarised society whose population of Jews remains overwhelmingly supportive of war crimes, which is in part the consequence of an educational system which celebrates barbarism. Jewish teenagers are taught that the soldiers of Unit 101 who committed the Qibya massacre "excelled in their audacity" and were "superb warriors". And that bloated, blood-spattered monster Ariel Sharon is a hero of the Jewish nation. Which says everything.

Sunday 26th April 2020

The phone rang at 5.35am. Ellis listened to the message. He made a telephone call and talked to two people. Then he went back to bed, but could not sleep. It was another bright sunny morning. He drank a mug of tea, then ate a bowl of cereal. Later he made another telephone call. He then went off to write an email. While he was writing the email the telephone rang. Ellis was given some startling information. Afterwards he finished writing his email and sent it. Later, on Twitter, he read a tweet by Dr Matt Prescott: *Allegra STRATTON (former TIMES, INDEPENDENT, NEW STATESMAN, BBC, GUARDIAN, Robert PESTON), ITV NEWS EDITOR > Rishi SUNAK / TREASURY.* Allegra Stratton, Ellis learned, was married to James Forsyth, political editor of *The Spectator*. She was a vicious right-winger, infamous for one notorious television episode. On 23 May 2012 the BBC Newsnight programme broadcast a report which falsely portrayed a working single mother as an unemployed scrounger living off benefits as a lifestyle choice, using an interview by Political Editor Allegra Stratton with single mother Shanene Thorpe. Despite blatant misrepresentation Newsnight did not broadcast an on-air apology until more than three months later. Those centrally involved in this fake news production were programme editor Peter Rippon, BBC2 controller Janice Hadlow, BBC News executives Helen Boaden and Peter Horrocks, Newsnight presenters Jeremy Paxman, Kirsty Wark, Gavin Essler and Emily Maitlis, and then director general, Mark Thompson. A clip of her propaganda work for Newsnight was tweeted, and Ellis watched it. It was from 2015. Allegra Stratton reported that early signs that Jeremy Corbyn might win the election for new Labour leader was "scary for the Labour Party" and that when party activists contemplated the possibility that he might actually win they would no longer lend him their support. To discuss the horrifying possibility of a Corbyn victory who better for Stratton to choose for comment than John McTernan, a former adviser to Tony Blair, who attacked "moronic MPs" who had agreed to nominate him. Allegra Stratton and Kirsty Wark chuckled their implicit agreement. The reason why Corbyn might be experiencing a surge in support was off-limits. It was probably quite literally inconceivable to these three individuals sealed in their little bubble of power, privilege and wealth. Next Ellis looked up McTernan. He was a professional apparatchik, having served Blair and various other New Labour figures. He was Chief of Staff to the leader of the Scottish Labour Party, Jim Murphy, who managed to lose Labour every seat in Scotland but one. The swing to the SNP from Labour in Scotland under Murphy and his brilliant Chief of Staff was over 30%. Ellis learned from Wikipedia that *During the 2006-07 police investigation into the Cash for Honours political scandal surrounding the Labour Party, McTernan was twice questioned, under caution, by the Metropolitan Police. No criminal charges were ever brought against McTernan or anybody else.* John McTernan was paid to write a column in the *Daily Telegraph*. Following the 2016 revelations about David Cameron's earlier offshore earnings, and Corbyn's call for an investigation, McTernan argued in his newspaper column that tax avoidance is an expression of basic British freedoms. Wheels within wheels, Ellis thought. Returning to Allegra Stratton, Ellis read Mark Curtis's tweet: *UK elite society is a big revolving door, between media & govt, military & corporations, corporations & state. UK functions more as a private club than a country. It's an oligarchy. With democratic elements but which are largely a facade.* Every day Ellis learned far more from Twitter than he ever learned from the British press or broadcast media. Among today's nuggets was that Dominic Cummings is married to Mary Wakefield, commissioning editor of *The Spectator*. Wheels within wheels... Later, on the radio news, Ellis heard Mark Mardell gushing with excitement at the return of Boris Johnson tomorrow after his convalescence at Chequers. He is raring to go, said Mardell, using a phrase which had curiously been used by the gutter press and the rest of the corporate media that day, just as a few days earlier the adjective 'forensic' had been attached by innumerable corporate news pimps to the performance of the wooden, florid Sir Keir Starmer. Ellis remembered that this was the same Mark Mardell who had remarked on 'The World This Weekend' on 21 May 2017: 'One cynic told me expectations are so low, if Corbyn turns up and doesn't soil himself, it's a success.' A remark for which Mardell should have been fired but after which nothing at all happened, this incident only serving as yet another reminder of what a vile, degenerate institution BBC News was. The telephone rang and Ellis answered it. Later, the child sang her own version of 'Twinkle Twinkle Little Star' and waved her doll. Then it was time for tea. Fish fingers! At 7.22pm the sun was still shining. The latest Covid 19 statistics: 152,840 confirmed UK cases, with 20,732 deaths. On the 10pm Sky News the chief political correspondent Beth Rigby reported Boris Johnson's return to Downing Street. 'He really is raring to go,' she said. In bed Ellis read Nurit Peled-Elhanan's analysis of how an Israeli school text supplied a distorted, misleading and fundamentally dishonest account of the Kaffer Kassem (Kafr Qasim) massacre of October 29, 1956. Between 5pm and 6.30pm, in nine separate shootings, a platoon led by Lt. Gabriel Dahan killed a total of nineteen men, six women, ten boys (aged 14-17), six younger boys (aged 8-13) and six girls (aged 12-15). Many others were injured and left to bleed for 24 hours, unattended. The text conceals important facts, explained Nurit Peled-Elhanan, such as prime minister David Ben-Gurion's order to deny that any massacre had occurred, a lie which he maintained for six weeks, aided by a total ban on newspaper reportage of the massacre. A military cordon around the village prevented journalists from entering it to talk to residents. Blame was attached to the border guards, not to the army or the commanders. The border guards' brigade commander Colonel Yissachar Shadmi's derisory token fine of one Israeli cent is not mentioned by the text book, nor is the overwhelming support he received during his trial from senior army officers. Not mentioned is that all the killers were pardoned and released within months. Not mentioned is that all the killers regained their positions with the explicit help of Prime Minister David Ben-Gurion. In a further indication of the depravity and racism of the Jewish state the city of Ramla (occupied by Jews after the city's Arab majority population was driven out in 1948) put Lt. Gabriel Dahan in charge of 'Arab Affairs.'

Monday 27th April 2020

Sunny at first, then cloudy. A wren skipped about the garden. The child played with her shoes and a plastic spoon. More than 3 million people around the world are now confirmed to have been infected with Covid-19, with over 200,000 deaths. Ellis spent the afternoon and early evening waiting for a phone call which never came. He grated some cheese and scattered it over some warmed-up gnocchi. He read through days-old copies of *The Times*. There was a report in Saturday's issue about a libel case brought by Rachel Riley against Laura Murray. High Court Judge Matthew James Nicklin ruled that Murray's tweet calling Riley 'dangerous and stupid' was defamatory under common law. This was the same judge who had ruled that when the 'The Campaign against Anti-Semitism' described the Jewish anti-Zionist blogger Tony Greenstein as a 'notorious antisemite' on five occasions this was merely a matter of opinion, not fact, and therefore not defamatory. This was the same judge who had ruled in favour of Anna Turley MP, member of the Zionist JLM and Labour Friends of Israel, when she sued the trade union Unite and Stephen Walker, publisher and editor of *The Swawkbox*, for libel. One of the witnesses for Turley was Ruth Smeeth MP. In short, High Court Judge Matthew James Nicklin had form. There was a photograph of Nicklin on the internet which showed him posing in front of a bookcase lined with books the colour of dried blood. Law books, no doubt, representing the mummified relics of the English judicial tradition in all its violence, prejudice and aggressive determination to maintain the interests of the propertied, the powerful and the wealthy. High Court Judge Matthew James Nicklin: a smug-looking fat white man with a pudgy well-fed face, in a scarlet robe, with a silly wig. A hanging judge. In bed Ellis read some more pages by Nurit Peled-Elhanan. She described censorship by the Israeli ministry of education, which moved swiftly against a text book deemed guilty of 'criticism against the state'. Including an account of the 1948 Nakba and what it meant to Palestinians was intolerable: 'presenting Arab propaganda as equal in value to the Israeli version is like presenting the Nazi version as equal to that of the Jews regarding the Holocaust'. The book was removed and changes were required by the state before it could once again be set before Israeli teenagers. The legitimation of massacres in the school books studied here is mostly based on effect and utility, wrote Nurit Peled-Elhanan.

Tuesday 28th April 2020

A dull wet morning. Ellis made a 9am telephone call. The child balanced a yellow bucket on her head. Ellis emptied the wickerwork litter bin and placed it upside down on his head. New Covid-19 cases in the UK: 4,310. Data from Public Health England at 13:52 BST 28 April 2020. Ellis made a 10am telephone call. Ellis made a 12 noon telephone call. Ellis made a 12.40pm telephone call. In the afternoon he received a telephone call from a doctor. In her bedtime bath the child waved her blue shark. On the Sky 10pm news footage was shown of three UFOs filmed by American pilots. They were indistinguishable shapes at unknown locations with no estimates of size or distance supplied. In bed that night Ellis finished reading *Palestine in Israeli School Books*.

Wednesday 29th April 2020

A day of cloud and drizzle. The death was reported of the actress Jill Gascoine. A blackbird pecked in the gutter, extracting moss for a nest. The child put on her boots and yellow raincoat. She stared through the glass door at the lawn. She wanted to go out there, in the soft light rain. The corporate media swooned at the birth of the Prime Minister's child. Robert Peston was especially sycophantic. On somebody's tweet Ellis watched a clip of Piers Morgan trashing Home Office Minister Victoria Atkins, who had never heard of Exercise Cygnus. Later, glancing out of the window, Ellis saw that scraps of moss and dried compacted earth were scattered across the flagstones. Perhaps birds had been hunting for worms or insects there, as well as seeking nesting materials. Either way this was useful in helping to clear the clogged gutter. Ellis telephoned the hospital twice. He replied to texts and emails. In the evening he rang Kevin and held a short conversation. Later, Francis replied to his email. Ellis began to read a classic novel he had never read before. The road was now a black tunnel floored with the impalpable defunctive glare of the sand, he read. *Defunctive: adj. Having ceased to exist or live.* In bed Ellis reached page thirty.The blow fetched him completely to, Ellis read, and he opened the door and half fell to the ground and dragged himself up and turned towards the station at a stumbling run.

Thursday 30th April 2020

Awake in the night, Ellis heard torrential rain beating down outside. But when he woke in the morning the sky was blue and the sun was shining, though the ground was wet. He remembered that today is the day that Health Secretary Matt Hancock and government spokespersons have repeatedly insisted will be the day that 100,000 tests for Covid-19 will be carried out on NHS staff and family members and others qualifying for the test. Ellis also remembered that, having postponed reopening America at Easter as President Trump initially suggested on 27 March, today is the day that on 20 March the president said that strict social distancing measures could end and the US economy could reopen. Covid-19 cases in USA today: 1,078,476; deaths, 62,535, as of 18.38 GMT. Governor Gavin Newsom of California has shut down the beaches of Orange County. But Alabama moved to reopen its beaches, and Texas will do the same in parts of the state on Friday, even as health experts warn that doing so could produce a surge in new virus cases. In Maine and Tennessee stay-at-home orders will also expire, allowing restaurants and stores to reopen. Iowa, North Dakota and Wyoming are also planning to ease their rules. Retail stores, restaurants and malls will be permitted to reopen if they operate at 25% capacity. New Jersey reported 460 new virus-related deaths today, more than any other state in the USA. In the park the sun shone. The child walked through the puddle in her yellow boots. The water in the puddle was clear rainwater. The child stamped in the water and stared at the splash. She repeated this several times, taking in this new experience. Then she grinned and ran off. Later, the child waved her spoon and put a plastic bucket on her head. Ellis ate pasta with baked vegetables and a cheese sauce. He continued reading the classic novel. It was atmospheric, lush with adjectives, the language at times contorted. There was a mood of impending catastrophe. Everything seemed slightly blurred, the characters opaque. An event would occur - or would it? The pages nudged the reader towards the potential event in slow motion. By Chapter 15 the pivotal moment had occurred. She had never been given to talking, Ellis read, living a life of serene vegetation like perpetual corn or wheat in a sheltered garden instead of a field. He continued reading to the next page, then put out the light.

Friday 1st May 2020

Ellis woke in the night, hearing again torrential rain beating down. In the
morning there were puddles in the street. A weak sun glimmered through a sky
puffy with pale grey clouds. Ellis made 19 telephone calls before he was finally
able to speak to Beth. A day of sunshine and showers. He went on with the
classic novel. It lay in a sort of drugged immobility, like the children which
beggars on Paris streets carry, Ellis read. A bird crashed against the window.
Out back the robin skipped across the grass. The child went and lay on her back
on her nappy-changing mat. She took hold of the box of antiseptic wipes and
dragged it closer. Then, rolling off the mat, she walked to the corner of the room,
where the sack of disposable nappies stood. She dragged it back across the room
to where her mat was. Then she lay down again. Her mother laughed and
changed the old nappy for a new one. But it wasn't a game: the nappy she had
on was sodden. Matt Hancock said that in the 24 hours up to 9am today there
were 122,347 tests for Covid-19 infection in the UK, a big rise on Thursday's
figure of 81,611. But the Health Service Journal reported that the government
was fiddling the figures by including home-testing kits sent out by post, which
had yet to be returned with a sample, as well as kits ordered via the
government's online portal. This inflates the statistic by some 50,000. The
DHSC's permanent secretary, Chris Wormald (apt name!), had quietly signed
off this major unpublicised change to the way the headline daily number is
calculated. Ellis downloaded and read Tony Greenstein's authoritative and
penetrating analysis *Pt: 2 Labour's Leaked Report - the Sad, Sorry Story of how
Corbyn's Office Urged the Compliance Unit to Increase the Rate of Expulsions.*
That evening Ellis watched the first episode of the first series of *Better Call Saul,*
which he had never seen before. In bed he read the words: A car started beneath
the window with a grind of gears; again the faint bell rang, shrill and prolonged.
He was half way through the novel, now.

Saturday 2nd May 2020

A bright sunny morning, with a cloudless blue sky. The Food and Drug
Administration in the USA has authorised the use of the Ebola drug remdesivir
to treat people who are hospitalised with severe Covid-19. Kim Jong-un has
appeared in public for the first time in 20 days, North Korean state media says,
reports UK state media, the BBC. Ellis drank a mug of tea. He shaved and
dressed. I like that shirt, she said. But it's a devil to iron. Ellis made some
telephone calls. He read an article by Daniel Finn. The postman delivered a
package. Ellis put on a pair of gloves, opened it and let the paperback inside

drop to the floor. The packaging he quarantined beside the recycling bin. Later it was reported that 14,695 people were currently in hospital with Covid-19 in the UK. Once again the child went and lay on her changing mat, indicating a desire for a nappy change. Later, in the kitchen, Ellis listened to several tracks on *For Better, or Worse*. Johnny phoned and he and Ellis talked for fifteen minutes. The evening meal was lamb steak with mashed potato and cabbage, followed by stewed apple and ice-cream. The child grinned in her foamy bath. She played with her orange dinosaur and her blue shark. At 8.30pm, on BBC2, *The Guernsey Literary and Potato Peel Pie Society* was broadcast. It was not a film which, having watched it, Ellis had any desire to see again. He was in bed, Ellis read, in bed. He had been lying in the dark for about an hour, when the door of the room opened, felt rather than seen or heard. It was his sister.

Sunday 3rd May 2020

Overcast, with a bright saucer of light where the sun was shining beyond the cloud layer. The state radio reported that the Prime Minister needed litres and litres of oxygen in hospital. Shots have been exchanged across the Demilitarised Zone which divides Korea. Ellis looked up the filming locations of *The Guernsey Literary and Potato Peel Pie Society* and discovered that none had been on Guernsey. He read an article on the *Guardian* website by Rachel Clarke: 'NHS doctor: Forget medals and flypasts - what we want is proper pay and PPE'. The more I hear Conservative MPs applaud and fawn over NHS staff, the more I think back to the footage from 2017 of those same MPs in the Commons cheering as they voted down a proper pay rise for nurses, wrote Rachel Clarke. Tobias Ellwood was among them, alongside Rishi Sunak, Dominic Raab, Matt Hancock and Boris Johnson. Rachel Clarke wrote: Most iniquitous of all, of course, is the government's willingness to laud us as heroes even while watching us die without proper personal protective equipment. Rachel Clarke wrote: The dehumanising narrative of healthcare as heroism benefits political leaders by deflecting attention from their dismal failure to keep staff from avoidable harm. Elsewhere on this website Ellis encountered an enthusiastic review of a new book by Philippe Sands, described as a professor at UCL and renowned international barrister, as well as John le Carré's neighbour. Ellis distrusted Philippe Sands. He was supposed to be a smart guy, yet he had lent his name to a shoddy, meretricious Zionist apologia by Julia Neuberger. 'Passionate, principled and necessary' was the praise attached by Philippe Sands to Neuberger's rancid assault on Palestinian activism in her crappy little book *Antisemitism* (which was yet another attempt to redefine anti-Zionism as inherently anti-Semitic). Neuberger was a morally blank reactionary and a fervent apologist for the Jewish supremacist state. Ellis looked up Philippe Sands and discovered he appeared at events alongside the smug Zionist Adam

Wagner. Searching further Ellis discovered that Philippe Sands had joined in the Zionist smear campaign against the Labour Party. Philippe Sands had told the *Jewish Chronicle* that Jew-hate within the Labour Party "is plainly an issue". No, it isn't, thought Ellis. The great human rights lawyer Philippe Sands appeared to be struck dumb where Israeli atrocities and crimes against Palestinians were concerned. He had literally nothing to say. Or rather, when he did it was to deploy a bucket of cold water. At a conference organised by 'Independent Jewish Voices' and 'The Bruno Kriesky Forum', on the subject 'Equal Rights for All: A New Path for Israel-Palestine', held at Birkbeck College 14-16 March 2015, a critical online report by Blake Alcott ('Fifty Shades of Soft Zionism') acidly noted that *Philippe Sands for some reason found it necessary to tell us that while Return and compensation are non-abrogable rights, actually negotiations (should they come to pass) would involve only their partial and imperfect application. An audience member said that might be so, but that now is surely not the time to start compromising and fashioning collective deals. I agree.* Elsewhere on the internet Ellis found an old interview with Philippe Sands on the Mother Jones website. He spoke of President George W. Bush as having damaged 'America's commitment to the international rule of law'. What commitment? thought Ellis. The notion that Bush was somehow qualitatively worse than his predecessors struck Ellis as bizarre. 'I have great hopes for Senator Obama and his team. His foreign policy advisers, like Samantha Powers, recognize America's special role and responsibility.' And so on. Sands seemed to be a complete ignoramus when it came to the history of US foreign policy. And in 2016 it was reported that the Palestine Solidarity Campaign had objected to the appointment of Daniel Bethlehem QC, a legal adviser to the Israeli state, to lead the Foreign Office's legal team. In 2002 Daniel Bethlehem had advised Ariel Sharon to oppose a UN inquiry into Israeli atrocities carried out at the Jenin refugee camp. Two years later Daniel Bethlehem also represented the Israeli government at the International Court of Justice in The Hague to defend the separation wall being built across the West Bank. The question mark over Daniel Bethlehem's role in blocking any investigation into Israeli atrocities at Jenin was raised with the *Guardian* newspaper by a British lawyer, who requested anonymity. *Another lawyer, Philippe Sands QC, who knows Mr Bethlehem well, said: "He is a first-class international lawyer and an individual of impecable integrity."* But also willing to service the morally indefensible. Nuff said. The child once more went and lay on her changing mat, requesting a nappy change. Ellis read a week-old copy of *The Times*. In bed he continued with the clasic novel. The last sentence he read before putting out the light: The house was dark, still, as though it were marooned in space by the ebb of all time.

Monday 4th May 2020

A bright grey day. The sun lay behind a thin screen of cloud, a perfect white coin which even as Ellis watched grew brighter and brighter until he had to avert his eyes. Half an hour later the cloud had gone and the sun was shining. The robin was back, skipping around the garden. A man walked down the road with a dog on a long lead. Ellis made a telephone call but when he got through all he heard was a recorded voice. He terminated the call and went to make himself a cappuccino. As he drank it he read more of the novel. Later in the morning the telephone rang and Ellis held a long conversation with the woman who had called him. Later it was reported that Jennie Formby had resigned as Labour Party general secretary. Tony Greenstein in his recent analysis of the leaked report had exposed how politically shallow Formby had been in office, having eagerly embraced the cause of expelling Left activists to placate the bellicose Israel lobby. That afternoon the telephone rang. Ellis listened as the speaker explained about Stansted Airport and Air Force One. Afterwards he did some painting. That evening he read some more of the classic novel. In bed that night Ellis came to the last page. Rich and resonant the brasses crashed and died in the thick, green twilight, rolling over them in rich, sad waves.

Faulkner – Sanctuary

Tuesday 5th May 2020

The blue sky was a slender serpentine layer framed by clouds of an uneven colour. Yellowish and pale, greyish and empurpled. A pretty observation, quite possibly influenced by the novelist Ellis had been reading. The two TV aerials opposite lacked the usual perching birds. Wandering the internet Ellis learned that in a 2015 poll organised by the state broadcaster *The Waves* was voted the 16th greatest British novel ever written. Ellis drank a cappuccino. The Office for National Statistics states that the total number of deaths with Covid-19 mentioned on the death certificates was 32,313 by 2 May, making it the highest recorded Coronavirus death toll in Europe. At 13:43 Ellis went on the Media Lens twitter page, which commented one hour earlier: *Media around the world are headlining the big news that the UK now has the highest European death toll, 32,000. But not the BBC website.* Ellis switched to BBC News to check, and it was true. No headline about it at all. It wasn't even clear if BBC News was reporting this sensational new statistic at all, anywhere. The telephone rang. Ellis spent a long time in conversation with the woman at the other end of the line. The child sat in her high chair and ate a bagel with peas, followed by a bowl of yogurt. Ellis went on the internet. Until today Ellis had never heard of Paul Bogdanor. He read a feature on the *Rolling Stone* magazine website about Michael Moore's new documentary attacking Green energy activism. He read a review of two new books, one an anthology of Edward Said's writings, the other a collection of critical essays about his work. That evening Ellis read the Introduction to Ron Rosenbaum's *Explaining Hitler: The Search for the Origins of his Evil*. He finished this Introduction in bed. For a brief moment, Ellis read on its last page, a part of me felt a frisson of what I knew was false hope.

Wednesday 6th May 2020

The headline news was that Professor Neil Ferguson had resigned from SAGE (Scientific Advisory Group for Emergencies) after being exposed as someone who had not conformed to his own advice about the need for social distancing. The *Daily Telegraph* had somehow discovered that he had received visits at home from his lover Antonia Staats, 38, who lived in South London with her husband and children. On Twitter people were making jokes about stats and modelling. Outside the sun was shining and the blue sky was cloudless. Ellis joined the socially distanced queue outside the supermarket. Once inside he purchased the last pot of tartare sauce, the last packet of white rolls, the penultimate quiche. There was no desiccated coconut or tinned mackerel in tomato sauce. That morning he encountered a strange object on the ground which consisted of an elongated oval rubber object covered in small spikes, a yellow colour, attached loosely by rope to rubber balls at each end. They also were covered in small spikes. They greatly resembled the Coronavirus models which were shown on television. Ellis deduced this was a toy for a dog to chew on. Later, unexpectedly, he saw a heron which fluttered down and stood rigidly beside a distant ditch. He continued reading the Hitler book. It was racy and journalistic but seemed authoritative in its presentation of the facts and historical knowledge. The author mentioned Isaiah Berlin's 'borderland theory of charismatic political genius'. Hitler and Theodor Herzl were in the list. The 'peculiar psychology of many of the most charismatic, fanatic, possessed nationalist political leaders' could be traced back to their origins outside or on the margins of their societies. They had 'overwrought sensibilities' and a disposition to 'a neurotic distortion of the facts'. Rosenbaum visited the fragmentary remnants of Döllersheim, in search of Hitler's family background. The identity of the man who fathered Hitler's father remains ambiguous, and perhaps unknown. Was it, as one argument runs, a nineteen-year-old Jew, the son of wealthy parents, who impregnated a forty-two-year old unmarried serving woman named Maria Schicklgruber in 1836? Ellis read about Franz Jetzinger's pioneering 1956 book *Hitler's Youth*, based on exhaustive archival research. He came to Rosenbaum's analysis of the recollections of Hitler's associate, Hans Frank. Were they rooted in fact or were they a fabrication? Ellis went to sleep.

Thursday 7th May 2020

Lockdown restrictions will shortly be lifted. 400,000 protective gowns flown from Turkey by the RAF last month, amid much publicity, are currently stored in a warehouse, having failed to meet the required safety standards. Nine people have died and hundreds have been injured after a gas leak in the city of Visakhapatnam in India. The leak has been traced to the LOG Polymers plant. Ellis at once thought of the Bhopal disaster of 1984. On that occasion the factory had been owned by the American Union Carbide Corporation. But civic and criminal cases against the corporation and its chief executive Warren Anderson were routinely blocked by US courts, which claimed that the factory was independent of its owners. Outside, the sun was shining and the sky was blue. Ellis drank a mug of cappuccino. The telephone rang. It was a call from Sweden. Later he went to a pillar box to post two envelopes. He had just posted them when two people he knew turned the corner. They engaged in a five-minute conversation. Then Ellis saw a woman approaching with a letter and the meeting broke up. The child seemed unusually animated today. She wore a new dress with elephants along the base. The sun continued to shine. In the late afternoon Ellis read more of Rosenbaum's book, which he found compelling and persuasive. He was interested to learn that prior to taking power Hitler often successfully sued journalists for defamation, knowing that the right-wing judiciary would take his side, even though the stories which had been published were true. Rosenbaum believed that much more could be learned about Hitler's personality and character by studying the Munich years, rather than the Berlin ones. That night in bed Ellis finished chapter four.

Friday 8th May 2020

A very warm sunlit morning, the sky once again a sheet of bright blue, almost painful to look at. Confirmed UK cases of Covid-19 infection: 206,715. New cases: 5,614. Deaths: 30,615. Data from Public Health England at 09:50 BST. The telephone rang, twice. Ellis read more of the Rosenbaum book. The child found her shoes and socks. She wanted to go outside. In the distance an ice-cream van played 'Greensleeves'. Ellis glanced at the printed report of a conversation held years ago between Salman Rushdie and Edward Said. That night in bed he read more of the Rosenbaum book.

Saturday 9th May 2020

Hot and sunny. Just one phone call on the landline. Ellis did not go outside, apart from to spray a plant coated in blackfly with pesticide. He watched a scrap of film shot on a mobile phone which showed two cops confronting a black man at a garage in Manchester, while a child screamed Daddy! Daddy! One of the cops fired his taser gun at point blank range. The black man dropped to the ground, while the child continued to shout. By the time Ellis watched it the footage had been viewed more than 4 million times. Ellis looked Rosenbaum up on Wikipedia, which supplied a link to an article Ron Rosenbaum had written five years ago. Ellis was disappointed to discover that Rosenbaum was an ardent, even hysterical supporter of Israel, who cast the Palestinians as consumed by a desire for genocide. The standard victim-blaming by yet another obtuse Jewish intellectual. Rosenbaum seemed to have no understanding whatever of the twentieth century history of Palestine or the enormity of what Jews had done to that land, let alone the racism and barbarism which underlay the Zionist colonial project. A shame, as Rosenbaum's Hitler book was engaging, humane and at times drily ironic. It was a very warm day. The child tottered around in shorts and socks. She was fond of her red hat, which she wore repeatedly. That evening Ellis ate cold chicken, mashed potato and salad. He watched *High Fidelity* and then went to bed.

Sunday 10th May 2020

Ellis listened to the 6am news. He was informed that the government's new message would replace STAY HOME with STAY ALERT. Fuzzy rhetoric would replace the previous slogans. A representative of the Police Federation said that the police were losing the battle against people having picnics in parks in East London. It was a warm morning but the sky was a sheet of cloud. Ellis sat at his computer, wearing his striped dressing gown. He drank a mug of tea. Later the wind increased in speed and began to shake the trees. The child clapped her two red shoes together and grinned. There was a power cut. After some twenty minutes Ellis began boiling water in a pan to make coffee when the power was restored. He returned to his computer when the screen cut out. There had been a second power cut. Later, after power had once again been restored, Ellis pan-fried two fillets of salmon and boiled some new potatoes. In bed that night he began reading the sequel to the novel he had finished reading on Monday 4 May.

Monday 11th May 2020

Ellis woke at 6am and made himself a mug of tea. It was a wild, blustery morning, with brief interludes of sunlight breaking through scudding clouds. There was widespread criticism of the government's new slogan STAY ALERT, CONTROL THE VIRUS, SAVE LIVES, which replaced STAY AT HOME, PROTECT THE NHS, SAVE LIVES. Muddled and confusing and vague, said many. The leaders of Scotland, Wales and Northern Ireland refused to replace

135

the old slogan with the new one. Later that morning the landline telephone rang. Ellis talked to the mental health nurse. Outside, two heavily tattooed men walked past carrying large cardboard boxes and various items of furniture to a lorry. They were emptying a house. In the garden a blackbird pecked at a large fallen leaf, watched by a plump attentive pigeon. Ellis discovered that the members of the panel investigating the leaked Labour report had been named. The leader would be barrister Martin Forde QC, supported by three Labour peers who would decide the scope of the enquiry: right-winger Baroness Debbie Wilcox of Newport, Larry Whitty and Ruth Lister. A single thin almost unheard voice crying thinly out of the roar of a mob, Ellis read in bed that night : 'Wait, look here, listen ---- '

Tuesday 12th May 2020

A bright sunny morning, but cool. A cloudless blue sky. Steam rose from the boiler ventilation shafts at the sides of houses, a spectacle made more acute by low slanting beams of the early morning sun. On the Novara Media website Ellis read a critique by Nick Fitzpatrick of the projected investigation into the leaked Labour report. Fitzpatrick, described as a senior lawyer with significant experience of working on inquiries, criticised the appointment of Martin Forde QC to lead the inquiry. Forde's practice, he observed, was largely devoted to defending clients in matters of medical law. Moreover because the team consisted of three Labour peers it was irredeemably compromised as regards any claims to independence. Finally the terms of reference were flawed, narrow and did not clearly enunciate or oblige investigation into key issues to have emerged from the report, while leaving the three Labour peers to determine what should and should not be investigated. The inquiry, in short, will be a politicised one. It will likely exclude any consideration of the relationship between senior staff and others within the party such as MPs or members of the House of Lords. It will be very easy for an inquiry like this simply to slap wrists for loose talk in personal emails or for a fall guy to emerge, leaving any broader plot unexamined. As it stands, the inquiry is fatally flawed, Ellis read. Moreover other key questions are left unanswered such as the power to compel witnesses, the timescale, the secretariat, and whether or not the findings will be published in full. In short, Ellis concluded, this inquiry will be a whitewash. No surprise there. In Tesco social distancing seemed to have collapsed. An impatient woman with an empurpled face stepped over the line of yellow tape on the floor and pushed past the couple who were in the next marked-out area. At the check-out a fat man in shorts ignored the blue circles on the floor, which identified where shoppers should stand, and went and stood behind the woman in front of him in the queue. Later Ellis went to the bottle bank to dispose of many empty glass food jars and a handful of wine bottles. The child threw her sloth and chuckled.

She then threw her teddy bear. The joy of throwing! That evening Ellis watched episode six of the first series of *Better Call Saul*, the one in which the viewer learns there is a seeping bullet hole in Ehrmentraut's left shoulder and, in a flashback, how he came to acquire it. In bed he continued with the sequel. It lacked the concentrated intensity of the earlier book, Ellis felt. It was far less compelling, although the language still resonated in a style that would make any modern literary agent flinch. The source of the alarm never recognised and even the alarm itself unremembered, he read, as the actual stroke of the bell is no longer remembered by the vibration-fading air. He read on to the end of the first part.

Wednesday 13th May 2020

A cold morning, with a silvery-grey sky. The sun obscured by a sheet of cloud. The state radio reported that new research showed how valuable moths were in pollinating nocturnally a variety of plants shunned by bees and butterflies. Online Ellis read an article by Jonathan Cook: 'With Corbyn gone, the Israel lobby is targeting Palestinians directly'. Ellis discovered that the aggressive pro-Israel lobby outfit, the so-called Campaign Against Antisemitism, claimed to have protested to the General Medical Council and Exeter University, accusing the well-known Palestinian activist Ghada Karmi of making a series of anti-Semitic statements. 'It is hard not to conclude that the CAA wishes to make an example of Karmi, in the hope that she can be stripped of her medical licence and disowned by Exeter University, where she was previously an honorary research fellow.' On Ben White's Twitter page Ellis read: This morning, Israeli soldiers killed a 15-year-old Palestinian child - Zaid Qaysia - during a violent raid on his southern occupied West Bank community, Al-Fawar refugee camp. He was shot in the head with live fire. Four other residents were injured. On the 10pm Sky News the arrival in Israel of the war criminal, US Secretary of State Mike Pompeo, who wore a face mask decorated with the Stars and Stripes, was juxtaposed with brief meaningless clips of mourners at the funerals of Zaid Qaysia and an IDF stormtrooper. The usual fatuous equivalence of the supine corporate media, thought Ellis. The child victim of a murderous occupation, and the violent representative of an army soaked in blood represented as somehow equivalent. In bed that night Ellis read more of the classic sequel to the classic novel. She stares at him, smoking, deliberately now. Deliberately she removed the cigarette and, still watching him, reaches and snubs it out in the ashtray, he read. Snubs? A misprint for stubs? he wondered. Or is this simply the American way? He put out the light and slept.

Thursday 14th May 2020

Cold and cloudy. It began spitting with rain. Ellis filled the washing machine with clothes and switched it on. New UK cases of coronavirus infection: 3,242. UK deaths: 33,186. Data from Public Health England at 07:58 BST. A wren perched on the fence, then shot off. The child drank from her plastic mug, then raised it: Cheers! The rain stopped and the sun came out but it was chilly outside. The postman brought a bank statement. That evening Ellis watched episode eight of *Better Call Saul*, the one about the discovery of institutional fraud in a network of care homes. The one where Jimmy searches for the shredded documents. In bed he continued reading the novel. The woman at its centre seemed to be in possession of a secret which might, perhaps, spare the life of the woman at its margins. Not that the wilderness's dark denizens, already dispossessed at Doak's Stand, were less inveterate now, but because this canoe bore not the meek and bloody cross of Christ and Saint Louis, but the scales the blindfold and the sword, Ellis read.

Friday 15th May 2020

Nakba Day. A blue Mediterranean sky, sunlight pouring down upon the houses and the green hedges. The child looked at her book of baby faces, which seemed to hold a special fascination. She burbled, as if reading out aloud the captions in a distorted form. Online Ellis read that the RSPB has been deluged with reports of birds of prey being illegally killed since lockdown began. There are multiple cases of protected species being shot, trapped or poisoned on or near estates managed for game-bird shooting. Birds targeted in the last six weeks include hen harriers, peregrine falcons, red kites, goshawks, buzzards and a barn owl. Dr Ruth Tingay of Raptor Persecution UK said: When will this government acknowledge the scale and extent of the problem and hold these shooting estates to account? Never, thought Ellis. Had he been a character in a novel he might well have suffered that involuntary spasm imposed on their prisoners by novelists and shrugged. At the fish shack he bought smoked haddock and a piece of cod. £17.43. In the afternoon he spoke on the telephone to Jennifer, the mental health doctor. That evening he watched another episode of the prequel to *Breaking Bad*. The one in which the electric lights are switched off at the law offices and the employees form up in lines and applaud. That night he read more of the sequel to the classic. He reached p. 127 and still the secret which represented the narrative suspense remained untold, although it gave the appearance of being on the brink of exposure. Because he wanted me to be contented, you see; and not only contented, he didn't even mind if I was happy too, the woman was saying. But Ellis was tired. He put out the light.

Saturday 16th May 2020

A grey cool morning. A sheet of cloud covering the sky. Ellis glanced at *The Times*. He looked through the TV guide to see if there was anything worth watching in the coming week. There was not. He spent much of the day reading. The child scrambled up the stairs, going much faster now than just a few weeks ago. Then she bumped her way back down, step by step, laughing. The sun shone. A sparrow picked at the red fat stick on the bird table. After eating a plate of vegetable pasta bake and a bowl of strawberries and icecream, Ellis watched *Ad Astra*. It was a disappointment. As so often with science fiction movies the spectacular special effects were like a gorgeous coating over a cake that was severely under-baked. The plot was thin, the characterisation threadbare. There were so many moments Ellis had seen before: debris shooting from a damaged space station, the astronaut being shaken in his seat, the explosion that hurls the spacecraft forward in a blaze of light. The astronauts going off alone to explore the mysteriously silent craft, only to die alone when meeting an unexpected malevolent creature. He went to bed. Now tell him, Ellis read, as he reached the teasing end of the next part of the classic novel's supposedly classic sequel.

Sunday 17th May 2020

The blue sky was strewn with ragged clouds. The state radio gave prominence to a speech by Barack Obama, which criticised the Trump administration's handling of the pandemic. The state radio also promoted the determination of the privatised Academy state schools to force their teaching staff back to work. Ellis spent much of the day drinking coffee and reading. It turned into a hot sunny day. He received two telephone calls on the landline. The child waved a yellow spoon and grinned when Ellis waved one back. Ellis pressed the buttons of the children's book which played a variety of noises: a barking dog, a sequence of piping notes, the beat of a drum. His evening meal was roast chicken with rice and salad, followed by a small bowl of strawberries and ice-cream. In the evening Ellis went to the nearest ATM to get out some cash. The High Street was deserted. The £10 notes which came out of the machine were brand new and clung together so that he had difficulty separating them to count them. That strange creature Michael Gove appeared on television, babbling that children and teachers must get back to work. He always half-reminded Ellis of a fish staring out from an artifical world through the dense curving inspection wall of an aquarium. Was it only last year that Gove had insisted that the world did not need that species he derisively referred to as 'experts'? Ellis went to bed. Friday, he read. The black day. The day you never start on a journey.

Monday 18th May 2020

It looked as if it would be another warm day. At 6.20am sunlight was brightening the yellow wall of the house opposite Ellis's study window. At 8.50am Ellis made a phone call, and another one at 11.20, and another one at 1.55pm. Ellis read an online review on a website which purported to be edgy and cool. The reviewer actually used that tired phrase 'darkly comic'. The review consisted not of any analysis or citation of the text but rather a gushing flow of adjectives which read like an author's self-penned blurb rather than criticism. That was the problem with the internet: the digital underclass could be every bit as banal, self-satisfied and self-serving as the privately educated gatekeepers of the corporate media. Elsewhere Ellis clicked on the link and read the latest critique by Media Lens, entitled 'An Illusion Of Protection: The Pandemic, The "Criminal" Government And Public Distrust of The Media'. Later, in the afternoon, he wrote some emails. He continued reading a biography. He ate hot rice and cold chicken, with salad. The phone rang. Total C-19 deaths in the UK to date: 34,796. So that the first word he ever spoke to her, Ellis read, was a promise delivered through a stranger. It was a quarter to midnight but he was too tired to wait for the news. He put out the light and slept, alone.

Tuesday 19th May 2020

A grey, dull morning, but warm. Ellis made a mug of tea. He checked his emails. He spent much of the day reading a paperback political biography. In the morning he received two calls on the landline. The first was from a woman who said it was a courtesy call. In the afternoon Ellis washed the kitchen windows, which had become spotted with marks and covered in swathes of cobwebs which were prominent when the morning sun illuminated them. Afterwards he had a bath. A black car drew up ouside the house next door and two women got out. He did not watch the Sky News that night. To stand, in this hot strange little room furious with frying fat, among the roster and chronicle, Ellis read. He was almost at the end of the novel, now.

Wednesday 20th May 2020

It would be exceptionally hot today, the weather forecaster announced on state radio. That seemed likely, Ellis reflected. Outside the sun blazed across the buildings and the gardens, and in the house it felt as warm as Spain or Italy. The news on state radio headlined the threat that the Coronavirus posed to sufferers from diabetes, and the decision of some local councils to oppose a return to work by primary schools. One third of all state schools had been privatised and were now run by 'academies' (i.e. groups of reactionary businessmen) but two thirds remained under the control of elected councils. It was another reminder of the uselessness of the Labour Party, or rather its right-wing nature, Ellis thought, that Blair and his followers had themselves colluded with and promoted the most backward-looking and anti-democratic aspects of modern conservatism. The capitalist workers party had long since detached itself from the workers. He went out to collect his emptied wheelie bin and met two neighbours. He chatted to them. A third neighbour walked by and greetings were exchanged. Ellis put more rubbish in the bin. The sun moved across the sky. The child seemed a little subdued but laughed when Ellis pressed the buttons in the book that made sounds: a beating drum, a panting dog, a barking dog… Ellis made a couple of telephone calls. He replied to an email. He went out to talk to another neighbour. The postman had left a parcel for her daughter. For lunch Ellis ate chicken salad, for his evening meal: tuna with borlotti beans. In the evening he continued reading a political biography. He learned from the internet that Tony Blair had been given a platform on state television to attack teachers for not wanting to return to work on June 1st. He also learned that Yvette Cooper had announced she'd be voting in support of the new Conservative immigration bill. Ellis wondered yet again why anyone who considered themselves a socialist would bother involving themselves in any way with an organisation like the Labour Party. Towards the end of the 10pm Sky News was footage of flooding in Bangladesh. Abnormally high temperatures at sea had caused very high winds and torrential rain. Nameless people stood beside brown surging water. In bed Ellis came to the end of the novel. Anyone to save it, said the central female character. Anyone who wants it. If there is none, I'm sunk. We all are. Doomed. Damned.

Thursday 21st May 2020

Ellis woke at 5.15am in a room filled with grey light. He dozed until 6 when he heard the boiler begin working. He went to the kitchen and switched the kettle on. It became another very hot day. Ellis went out and bought eggs, a chicken, a pot of marmalade. The child seemed subdued. Her consciousness seemed to have enlarged. In the park she was disturbed and frightened by her own shadow. A spider on the stairs produced an adverse reaction. In the garden a wood pigeon troubled her. Her mother took her indoors. The child seemed a little subdued but brightened and smiled broadly when Ellis pressed the button in the *One Hundred and One Dalmatians* spin-off children's book which played the sound of a barking dog. It was reported that the so-called Independent Office for Police Conduct had concluded that no criminal inquiry was required after it had taken eight months to drag out its so-called investigation into the diversion of public money and freebies and foreign trips to Jennifer Arcuri. The so-called Independent Office for Police Conduct's so-called Director General, Michael

Lockwood, said: We found no evidence to indicate that Mr Johnson influenced the payment of any sponsorship monies to Ms Arcuri or that he influenced or played an active part in securing her participation in trade missions. Cripes, no! The very idea! Ellis looked up who ran the so-called Independent Office for Police Conduct and was unsurprised by what he saw. As a state-funded body it bore some resemblance to the so-called Equalities and Human Rights Commission. Elsewhere online he learned that the ABC circulation figures scheme was in its death throes. The *Daily Telegraph* had already dropped out, and now the Murdoch press had withdrawn its titles. The newspaper industry did not want to expose the collapse of its readership. The internet had massively damaged it. Ellis saw that daily sales of the *Guardian* were down from 130,000 to 106,000 since the lockdown. A risible figure. Ellis watered some pots. Supper that day was cheese soufflé with new potatoes and broccoli, followed by a small bowl of strawberries and ice-cream. In bed Ellis read a few of the opening pages of *The 7th Function of Language*, translated from the French by Sam Taylor. Superintendent Bayard encounters Simon Herzog and is less than impressed by his world. But Herzog, plainly, is Sherlock Holmes.

Friday 22nd May 2020

Ellis was woken in the dark early morning by the sound of torrential rain beating down. He falls asleep again. When he gets up at 6am the morning is cool and the pale sky overcast. He makes himself a mug of tea and goes to sit at the computer, where he writes this sentence. The day passes. He spends much of the day reading a political biography. That evening the breaking news is that the infamous government adviser Dominic Cummings flouted the lockdown restriction and drove 264 miles from London to Durham in March. The infamous BBC Tory toady Laura Kuenssberg instantly retorted to the journalist Pippa Crerar who broke the story: *Source says his trip was within guidelines as Cummings went to stay with his parents so they could help with childcare while he and his wife were ill - they insist no breach of lockdown*. Or as one person sarcastically tweeted: Laura to the rescue. Another: They were so ill but managed a five-hour car journey. Someone else retweeted Kuenssberg's response to the journalist tweeting the exclusive news that Professor Neil Ferguson was resigning from SAGE after his lover visited him during the lockdown: *That's a hell of a story...* Yes, Kuenssberg's hypocrisy and political bias was not only blatant, so, too, was the insolence of the BBC in its contempt both for public opinion and for widespread criticism of its enduring deference to power. That evening in bed Ellis continued reading *The 7th Function of Language*. A pomo detective story which wittily recycled the Holmes/Watson relationship, evidently.

Saturday 23rd May 2020

It was bright and sunny at 6am but later clouded over. It was a windy morning with a chilly edge to the gusts that tore through the trees of the neighbourhood. Later that morning it was reported that Michael Rosen was out of intensive care after 47 days. His wife Emma-Louise Williams tweeted: His recovery is continuing on the ward & will take time. Rosen, it was reported, had been receiving treatment at Whittington Hospital in north London. On 22 March Rosen had described his illness: 'Can't stop my thermostat from crashing: icy hands, hot head. Freezing cold sweats. Under the covers for bed-breaking shakes.' It remained windy all day. There were nine people standing at intervals outside the store. It was a lengthy wait to go inside. The child stood at the open back door but did not run out onto the lawn. She played with an empty biscuit tin. Ellis continued reading the lengthy political biography. At lunchtime he ate asparagus and poached egg. He glanced at *The Times* review section. In bed that night he read as far as the meeting with Giscard and the box on his desk.

Sunday 24th May 2020

Grey and cold. Ellis slept until 8am. He listened to the state radio headlines. Steve Baker MP called on Dominic Cummings to step aside to stop further damage to the government over its response to the pandemic. Ellis went to put the kettle on and draw back the curtains. Later, dressed, he went out to water some pots. Online he read a piece about the letters of Monica Jones. It remained a grey, cloudy day. The child seemed a little subdued, though she grinned when Ellis pressed the buttons on the book that made sounds. On television Boris Johnson stood by Dominic Cummings. He had done nothing wrong, he insisted. The Twitterati seethed. Ellis felt pleased he was under no obligation to express opinions for a body of followers. It was an addiction best avoided. The landline rang and Ellis held a short conversation. Later he pruned a buddleia. In the evening he watch *La La Land*, followed by Sky News. Reading *The 7th Function of Language*, in bed, Ellis gets as far as the funeral of Roland Barthes.

Monday 25th May 2020

A hot sunny day. Ellis pruned some plants. He extracted some nails from lengths of wood and put the wood in the new shed. He did some sweeping. Later in the day he tied up some stray loops of climbing rose and then watched the live statement by Dominic Cummings. It was followed by a sequence of softball questions from Laura Kuenssberg, Robert Peston, Beth Rigby and other corporate journalists. The most absurd of Cummings's threadbare excuses, Ellis felt, was the one about driving to Barnard Castle to test out his eyesight. Twitter was full of people pointing out that the date in question was his wife's birthday but not a single one of the overpaid corporate toadies asked Cummings about this amazing coincidence. That evening Ellis ate cold chicken, rice and salad. Afterwards he did some watering. In bed he read as far as the spasms which shook poor Hamed's body.

Tuesday 26th May 2020

Sunlight filled the kitchen at 6.20am but later the sky clouded over. Ellis made himself a mug of tea and sat in his favourite armchair, continuing to read the immense political biography. The landline rang and he held a short conversation, which included the topic of house prices and trains to London. On the fence opposite a large sparrow repeatedly attempted to mount a smaller sparrow. Congress was not achieved. From the internet Ellis learned that a government minister, someone he had never heard of, had resigned in protest at the continuing employment of Dominic Cummings as a top government adviser. He read the jokes on Twitter. BARNARD CASTLE - TWINNED WITH PIZZA EXPRESS WOKING. Very good… He watched the first episode of the final series of *The Affair*. In bed that night Ellis read: The opposition is non-existent. The system is locked in place.

Wednesday 27th May 2020

A grey cloudy hot day. Ellis wore a T-shirt. He discovered that the *Guardian* website was now blocking readership of its news, demanding reader-registration before allowing access. Mentally (but not physically) he shrugged. He could live without what the *Guardian* had to say on anything. Outside, workmen fitted a new window and a new glass door. He read more of the political biography, before turning to another large book on an issue of pressing concern. The child waved a cushion and hid behind it, then grinned as Ellis did the same. Ellis discovered that, underlining the Labour Party's abrupt lurch to the right, a Blairite reactionary, David Evans, had been appointed as the new general secretary of the Labour Party. The Zionist 'Jewish Labour Movement' was in ecstasies. That evening Ellis ate spaghetti with salad, and then watched the next episode of *The Affair*. Oddly, like the first series of *Better Call Saul*, it featured a talking toilet. In *The 7th Function of Language* Julia Kristeva and Philippe Sollers give a party. Althusser rocks up with Hélène.

Thursday 28th May 2020

Blue sky, sunshine, warm. Ellis tried to find Left commentary on the appointment of David Evans, without success. Labour Party member Richard

144

Seymour appeared mute. As did many others. Ellis did however discover a retweet by slippery Owen Jones of a statement by the majority of the executive of Wavertree CLP standing by MP Paula Barker "in her attempts to rebuild relations between our party and the Jewish community". It concerned an article which Paula Barker MP had written for the *Jewish Telegraph*, 15 May 2020. She had written: "It was the post war Labour government, following the destruction and brutality of the Second World War, that supported and advocated for the self-determination of the Jewish people on their ancestral lands". Presumably this buffoon had never heard of the racist Jews Theodor Herzl or Chaim Weizmann, or the invention of 'the Jewish people', or the preposterous historically-unsustainable superstition of 'ancestral lands'. Paula Barker MP had written: "This year marks 100 years since the affiliation of Poale Zion to the Labour Party". True enough - Zionist colonialism and British imperialism were at the heart of early Labour Party politics. Paula Barker MP had written: "Upon my election to Parliament, one of my first acts was to sign up to the International Holocaust Rememrbance Alliance definition of antisemitism in full as an individual MP". Paula Barker MP had written: "The scourge of antisemitism within our ranks must be routed out". Yet time and time again it had been pointed out that *genuine* anti-Semitism scarcely existed in the Labour Party. What pudgy right-wing Paula Barker MP really meant was grovelling to reactionary Jewish organisations and routing out anyone who dared criticise Israel. Paula Barker MP had chattered emptily about supporting "the establishment of a Palestinian nation" while adding: "I will always be steadfast in my support of Israel's right to exist, and the self-determination of her people". This cretinous woman plainly didn't understand the first thing about Zionism. Paula Barker MP had written, "It is important we educate the next generation of the scourge of racism and where it can lead if left unchallenged". The ironies of that remark reverberated across a century of Palestinian dispossession at the hands of violent racist Jews with the enthusiastic support of the Labour Party and its associated trade unionists. Ellis learned that Paula Barker MP was previously the regional convenor for UNISON and the full-time UNISON branch secretary for Halton Council. Why were so many trades union bureaucrats fat, thick women? wondered Ellis. He had a vague memory of the grotesque bloated female trade unionist who had helped to eject Tony Greenstein from the Labour Party. Paula Barker MP received support from Charlotte Nichols MP, Labour member for Warrington North, and Kim Johnson, Labour MP for Liverpool Riverside. On the Twitter page of Ben White Ellis read: *Despite the Covid19 outbreak - & in what human rights NGO @btselem concluded is "deliberate…sheer abuse" - Israeli soldiers have been shooting rooftop water tanks in Palestinian village Kafr Qadum. 24 tanks damaged since start of April, some repeatedly.* Not on BBC News, obviously. Not mentioned by Paula Barker MP, obviously. She wouldn't want to cause offence to Britain's

Zionist community. Ellis went shopping and bought almond croissants, milk, plain yogurt, white crispy rolls and a newly released DVD. The sun burned down. The child played under a sheet draped to create a shady play space on the lawn. She stirred pretend food in a plastic pot, and put the plastic spoon to her lips. That night Ellis watched the third episode of Series 5 of *The Affair*. On Sky News there was a shot of Minneapolis in flames, after the killing of George Floyd. Floyd, a 46-year-old black man, had been handcuffed and placed face down on the road surface, while a white cop kneeled on his neck for several minutes as Floyd pleaded that he could not breathe. Black men in the USA were like Palestinians in Israel. They were murdered quite casually, with no sanctions on the perpetrators. The circumstances of George Floyd's death had been filmed on a mobile phone. As a piece of technology the mobile phone was of inestimable value in exposing police behaviour. Ellis remembered how the standard fog of police lies had been dispersed by a single piece of footage showing the circumstances in which Ian Tomlinson had died in London. In bed Ellis read of Simon Herzog's haircut and his pursuit of the cop with the missing finger.

Friday 29th May 2020

Another hot bright day, blue sky, blazing sun. Ellis rose at 6.30am and drank a mug of tea. He went to his computer. He discovered that Irm Hermann had died, aged 77. It was a death which passed without notice in the British corporate media. The child played with her new crayons. She held up a red crayon and a yellow crayon and chuckled. In the street outside a woman with long black hair and wearing shorts walked by pushing a buggy in which sat a small child. A dog was tied to the buggy. An older child, a girl, perhaps three years old, stood on a small wheeled platform at the back of the buggy, causing the woman to bend over her in the stooped posture of a pensioner suffering from osteoporosis. *Waffle doggee*, sang the girl. Ellis recognised the words and the melody. In the High Street a man of around thirty parked in the disabled bay, sprang out, and brushed past Ellis, who was about to enter Tesco. The man hurried inside ahead of him. A Dominic Cummings type, Ellis thought. Ellis bought tomatoes, mushrooms, blueberries, salmon, a sliced brown loaf and a bottle of Tesco Finest Picpoul de Pinet, 2019 vintage. It was not as good as the 2018 vintage, Ellis thought, when he tasted it later. On the internet he read an article by Adam Raz entitled **When Israel Placed Arabs in Ghettos Fenced by Barbed Wire**. It revealed that in 1948, during the Nakba, Palestinians were ejected from their homes and placed behind barbed-wire fences in zones called 'ghettos' and 'concentration camps'. That night Ellis watched a film set in Newcastle. It was the second film he'd watched set in that city. The first was *Get Carter*. Afterwards he looked at the newspaper front pages, displayed on Sky TV a little after 10.30pm. Then he switched off the television. Ellis had no wish to listen to the two pundits discussing the stories in the corporate press, least of all the slippery Ash Sarkar, who belonged to the Owen Jones school of equivocal leftism. In bed that night, prior to sleep, Ellis read the chapter about the Logos Club, followed by the short one-paragraph chapter beginning: This story has a blind spot that is also its genesis: Barthes' lunch with Mitterrand.

Saturday 30th May 2020

Another hot bright day, blue sky, blazing sun. The state radio reported fresh disturbances in the USA over the killing of George Floyd. Ellis drank tea, then ate a bowl of cereal. He watered four indoor plants, then drank a cappuccino. He went online. The state broadcaster's website headline was CLASHES AS PROTESTERS ACROSS US DEMAND JUSTICE - a textbook example of the BBC's utter inconsistency as a transmitter of information. It would never transmit what happened in Gaza two years ago as ISRAELI TROOPS MASSACRE PALESTINIAN PROTESTERS DEMANDING JUSTICE. On the contrary, it infamously chose to represent a day-long massacre as a mere matter of 'clashes' between two forces, one signifying disorder and the other signifying security, order, legality. Another top story for the vacuous BBC was that Forbes had dropped Kylie Jenner from its billionaire list. But then the BBC had long used froth and celebrity gossip as a screen for blood, bombings and British state terror in all its incarnations. Ellis searched the state broadcaster's website for information about the latest number of UK deaths from Coronavirus but was unable to find any. Its *Coronavirus: Daily update* included more important matters such as *Remi Wolf on how she makes music videos in lockdown*. It only took a few minutes in the BBC's digital company to reinforce the acute loathing which Ellis felt for this smug, poisonous self-perpetuating institution. Ironically, Ellis then went on Ben White's twitter page at 10.13am and discovered that just two minutes earlier Ben White had posted, above photographs of two individuals: *Israeli occupation forces have gunned down and killed two unarmed Palestinians in the past 24 hours. Iyah Hallak (L) was on his way to the school he attended. Fadi Samara (R) was going to pick up his wife & children. Experience indicates that there will be no accountability*. Ellis went back to the BBC news website. Naturally this latest atrocity by the Jewish state went unreported. Instead, there was only: *'Cannabis' burned during worship by ancient Israelites - study*. It was the usual uncritical recycling of a press release, with no acknowledgement that Zionist archaelogy had a long history of erasing the true history of Palestine in a desperate attempt to establish a bogus connection between this land and its current sectarian Jewish occupiers. So uncritical was the fawning BBC News report that it failed to name the archaeologists who had produced this amazing discovery, nor even identify the journal in which it had been reported. The sun rose across the sky. The child ran around in her dress with a design of many lemons. Ellis went shopping. In Tesco he bought a *Times*, some hot cross buns, coffee and yogurt. The customers waited patiently in their individual zones marked out with yellow tape. Then a middle-aged middle-class man in shorts waddled into the store. He walked into the zone of the nearest customer, who shouted angrily at him 'Distance!' The man ignored the warning and walked through the zones of the other customers, reached for a bottle of wine, and went to join the checkout queue. A classic Dominic Cummings-type, Ellis reflected. This was not the first time he'd witnessed this behaviour in Tesco and he decided not to shop there again. It was unquestionably the most shambolic store in the High Street, as far as social distancing was concerned. That evening in bed he read a few more pages of *The 7th Function of Language*. He usually goes to the Drogheria Calzolari or the Osteria del Sole, the porter says, in perfect French.

Sunday 31st May 2020

Another hot bright day, blue sky, blazing sun. Ellis sawed two lengths of wood to make batons for some new curtains. The child hugged her doll. There was a commotion in the garden as a blackbird attacked a jackdaw. Protecting the contents of its nest, perhaps. Ants swarmed up two legs of the garden bench and ran along the crossbars. The television news was all about the Black Lives Matter protests in the USA. As always with corporate television 'news' it was all spectacle rather than context or analysis. Cordelia Lynch, Sky's reporter, did mention 'police violence' - a term no British television reporter would ever contemplate using about their own country. The cop digs the spoon into the eye socket, Ellis reads in Laurent Binet's novel.

Monday 1st June 2020

Another hot bright day, blue sky, blazing sun. Ellis drank a mug of cappuccino. He went on Ben White's Twitter page. *Last night, Iyad Hallak was laid to rest after being killed by Israeli forces on Saturday. Disturbing details have emerged: - fatal shots were two bullets to the chest - Israeli cops raided the family home & beat Iyad's sister.* 14 minutes ago (time 08.53) Ben White tweeted: *"a bitter blow for justice & demonstrates Israel's complete disregard for the importance to promote human rights" @Amnesty now expects courts to rubber stamp authorities' 'secret evidence'-based travel ban imposed on Palestinian staffer Laith Abu Zeyad.* Ellis followed the link to the Amnesty website, where he read about the case. Heba Morayef, MENA Regional Director at Amnesty International, said "Today's hearing demonstrates the Kafkaesque nature of Israeli justice for Palestinians, who are denied fundamental due process, such as the opportunity to effectively challenge the state's evidence… Palestinians living under occupation are already trapped in a system of control, that touches every aspect of their lives and severely limits their movement. This travel ban confines Laith to an even smaller area and puts him in the long list of Palestinian and Israeli human rights defenders who have become a target for the authorities. It is a fundamental part of the right to a fair trial that an accused should be able to view the evidence against them. But Palestinians living under Israeli military occupation are stripped of such basic civil and political rights and face systematic oppression on a daily basis…" And now it is 09.23 and 13 minutes ago Ben White tweeted a short piece of film, with a link to an online report on the *Haaretz* website: *Newly released videos show Israeli forces in Kafr Qaddum, occupied West Bank, slashing car tires & tossing tear gas canisters into a Palestinian family home. The village holds weekly anti-occupation protests that are typically met with violent repression.* Ellis belatedly discovered that the anti-Palestinian MP for Canterbury, Rosie Duffield, had been exposed for breaking the lockdown and had resigned her shadow cabinet position. In the town centre it was busy. Later, Ellis observed a pair of magpies sat companionably on the branch of a holly tree. The child grinned at the cartoon face Ellis had drawn in a notebook, and gurgled 'Baby!' Later, a neighbour burned rubbish, suffusing the gardens with an acrid stench. Ellis closed the windows. He watched another episode of *The Affair*. He learned that Cole had died in his seventies, in 2058. In bed the last sentence Ellis read before turning out the light was: The man in gloves ends up falling asleep in a row between seats.

Tuesday 2nd June 2020

Another hot bright day, blue sky, blazing sun. By June, said the President on 30 March, the US 'will be well on our way to recovery'. Confirmed US cases: 1,816,070. Current US death toll: 107,478. In the UK the death total passed 50,000, confirming Britain's status as one of the countries worst hit by the pandemic, and worse than Italy, France and Spain. In the USA protests continued about the killing of George Floyd. Ellis watched film of a man driving a tanker into a crowd of protesters on a closed-off freeway. The driver turned out to be a Trump supporter. Police rushing to the scene fired tear gas at protesters standing in small peaceful groups on the grass along the edge of the freeway. Another piece of film on Twitter showed a cop firing a tear-gas cannister at point blank range into the face of a protester. The American police seemed out of control, assaulting and arresting anyone on a whim. The sun continued to blaze down. The child chuckled when Ellis showed her the drawing he'd done of a smiley face. 'Baby!' she said. Ellis drew a tree. 'Tree!' Later Ellis put out the wheelie bin, for collection the next day. He watched another episode of *The Affair*. Sierra leaves her baby in the car while she attends an audition. She gets the part of Madame Bovary. She has sex with the director in a toilet cubicle. Later, high on coke, she crashes her car into a parked truck. The baby is uninjured. Noah asks Helen to return to him. She says she doesn't love him any more. A beautiful young woman turns up at Sasha's. He gives her $25,000. She is the daughter of his deceased fiancée. Ellis wondered if Sasha was being blackmailed. He suspected that the relationship with Helen would soon collapse. In bed he read as far Althusser's strangulation of his wife and his autobiography *The Future Lasts Forever*. In it Althusser wrote that the biggest mistake of his life was not turning up when granted an interview with Mao. The italics are mine, wrote Binet, of the words *the biggest of my life*. Ellis put out the light.

Wednesday 3rd June 2020

Cloud, grey, dull, cool. Ellis went to the bank and then to buy some groceries. The High Street was busy. On a small grassed area of public land beside a closed café a bearded man in his twenties sat on the ground, while half a dozen police officers stood beside him. Police cars were parked alongside. He looked to be a homeless man, whose sleeping roll lay beside him. Ellis wondered why the cops were harassing him, as he looked harmless enough and was not obviously commiting any kind of offence. In retrospect Ellis wished he'd taken a photograph, although he knew from bitter experience that cops did not like being photographed and usually became aggressive when any attempt was made. He had once been unlawfully detained by a moronic bully in uniform who claimed that his photography in a public place was an illegal act. Home again, Ellis drank coffee and surfed the net. He looked at footage of an Australian TV crew being hit by cops in Washington D.C. He watched another episode of *The Affair*, the one in which Joanie sees the police report on her mother's death and predicts the loss of Montauk to the sea and is ejected from her home by her angry husband. In *The 7th Function of Language* Slimane asks Foucault if he can come with him to Ithaca.

Thursday 4th June 2020

It had been raining in the night, Ellis realised when he glanced out of the window. It was a cool grey overcast day. He put laundry in the washing machine and set it to economy wash. He spent the morning indoors, reading and making notes. Sparrows skipped around the back garden. The child seemed a little subdued but brightened when Ellis showed her his drawing. 'Baby!' she chuckled. It began to rain. In the evening Ellis watched the next episode of *The Affair*. On the Sky TV press review the front pages of all the UK papers on display were blacked out in those sections which reproduced the face and name

150

of the new suspect in the Madeleine McCann case, one Christian Brückner. In *The 7th Function of Language* Derrida arrives at the cafeteria at Cornell, accompanied by Paul de Man.

Friday 5th June 2020

Ellis woke in the dark early hours, hearing what might have been the whisper of rain. But in the morning it was hard to tell if it had really rained in the night. It was a cold morning, overcast. A little after nine it began raining. It became a day of sunshine and showers. The state broadcaster reported that 40,261 people had now died in Britain from the coronavirus. Ellis watched a short clip of film of police in Buffalo pushing a solitary 75-year-old man to the ground. As he lay there blood poured from his ear. The man was removed in an ambulance and was later found to have suffered a severe head injury. An initial statement from Buffalo police department said the man had tripped and fallen during a skirmish involving protesters. Another short piece of film showed police in Indianapolis savagely beating a woman in a T-shirt. Ellis ate spaghetti bolognaise, re-heated in the microwave. Searle, Ellis read, is sitting in the exact centre of the tiered seating. The lone man in the middle of the crowd: it's like a scene from Hitchcock. Ellis listened to the midnight news, then put out the light and fell asleep.

Saturday 6th June 2020

A bright sunlit morning but cold, with a strong wind blowing. A pair of jackdaws pecked at the moss on the tiles of the house opposite. Ellis drank tea and scanned the internet. He read about the background of the newly appointed BBC Director General, Tony Davie. Privately educated, former Vice President, Marketing and Franchise for PepsiCo Europe, no journalistic experience whatever, a former Deputy Chairman of Hammersmith and Fulham Conservative Association, twice stood as a Conservative councillor, not elected. On the 'Ducksoap' website Ellis read that Davie's first role at the BBC was Director of Marketing, Communications and Audiences - appointed in 2005. He pushed the BBC toward business chasing-ratings and saw only audience numbers, not quality. Davie's market-oriented philosophy will erase innovation and lower the standard of information and education, Ellis read on Ducksoap. Reduction in quality will be most visible in news programming, the website asserted. Driven by the combination of ignorance and fear of Tory cuts, the BBC's interpretation of balance and impartiality in news broadcasting, concepts that were woefully misunderstood by Davie's predecessor Tony Hall, will become more warped. Investigative reporting and intelligent analysis will be further reduced in favour of news-as-entertainment, with ill-informed charlatans espousing offensive nonsense as guests on Newsnight or Politics Live. Ellis switched to the *Daily Mail* website, which reported that before Davie worked for the BBC he made his name in marketing by turning Pepsi blue. A day of sunshine and showers. The temperature dropped. Ellis began to feel cold and put on a thicker jumper. Sky News at 10 headlined global protests about the police killing of George Floyd. Crowds blockaded the White House. Demonstrators were kettled by helmeted cops in Whitehall. Ellis went to bed. At the far end of the empty room, a pianist plays Ravel half-heartedly, Ellis read. It should be pointed out that it is mid-afternoon in midwinter and, while there is no cholera outbreak, the weather is not particularly conducive for swimming.

Sunday 7th June 2020

It was unusually cold for June. Ellis put on his warmest winter shirt and the thick jumper. The state broadcaster reported that in London fourteen people were arrested and 10 officers injured after a small group of protesters became "angry and intent on violence". The BBC, as always, uncritically recycled a police handout, in much the same way that it always gave the Israeli version of events in occupied Palestine. I stand with you and I share your anger and pain, said the Mayor of London Sadiq Khan, who had in fact not attended the protest but stayed in, expressing his support in a tweet. Blood-spattered Metropolitan Police Commissioner Dame Cressida Dick, who herself was reponsible for the violent killing of an unarmed man, said that the London protests were "unlawful". On Twitter Ellis discovered the truth: protesters penned in by the cops as a punishment were shouting "Let us go! Let us go! Let us go". On Twitter Ellis read a tweet by Michael Abberton: *The use of horses against protestors has a long and bloody history in the U.K. It's deliberately inflammatory as a result. They are used to instil fear and it inevitably leads to unrest. It should be stopped.* Michael Abberton's tweet was accompanied by four illustrations. The first showed what Ellis believed was probably Peterloo. The second was a famous photograph from the great 1984-5 miners' strike, which showed a mounted officer leaning over to smash his truncheon against a woman with a camera (a photograph which no British newspaper at the time would publish, least of all the fawning spineless supposedly liberal *Guardian*), the poll tax protest in Trafalgar Square, and Whitehall on 6 June 2020. On Twitter Ellis discovered the truth: the police had attacked the demonstration by riding into peaceful protesters, sending them scattering. It was the old, old story. Those who defend themselves against unprovoked assault are demonised by the BBC News. It was Orgreave all over again, when BBC News had quite deliberately and cynically reversed the footage. "Zippy" tweeted: *BBC propaganda spin: "After one officer was injured Downing St said violence was unacceptable." The officer collided with a traffic light.* Later it rained, a soft light rain that went on for half an hour. The child looked at a picture book, tried on a hat, then cuddled her mother. In the afternoon Ellis drilled some holes for the curtain baton. He opened a window to speak to a friend who had brought him some Assam and Earl Grey tea. Later, on Twitter, Ellis learned about the toppling and disposal of the statue of Edward Colston in Bristol. He instantly thought of those statues in London which celebrated murderers, psychopaths and war criminals. There was Havelock's in Trafalgar Square and Orde Wingate's on the Embankment. As *The 7th Function of Language* approached its end the action moved to Venice. Simon and Bayard encounter Umberto Eco on the Piazza San Marco.

Monday 8th June 2020

Cold and grey but no rain. Ellis went into the bakery to buy four croissants. When he turned to leave he saw that the pavement outside was filled with cops. They were waiting for him to leave before entering. The nearest cop stood by the door, just inches away rather than two metres. Ellis hurried past. In the supermarket he bought bananas, apples, blueberries, yogurt, Lurpak, chocolate, milk and a tub of icecream. Later, Ellis went online. He had never been to Bristol and had never heard of Edward Colston. From Twitter he learned a great deal about the sanctification of a man responsible for the deaths of thousands of slaves. Ellis noted that those who were scandalised by the removal of this statue were invariably individuals who enthusiastically supported arms sales to Saudi Arabia, Egypt and Israel - three torture states which were no slouches when it came to the violent repression of human rights. Although overcast it did not rain. The child held a biscuit tin on top of her head and grinned. Then she hid it behind her back. In the afternoon Ellis did a little pruning and then sorted through some boxes of books. Then he had a bath. It is raining in Paris, he read that night in bed. The celebrations have begun at the Bastille. Not many pages to go, now.

Tuesday 9th June 2020

Cloudy bright, cool. Seven years since Iain died. Ellis went out and bought some celery, tomatoes, a cucumber, cheese and rice. Afterwards he went to the bottle bank, and then bought cod and Dover sole. Home again, he drank a capuccino and ate a plain croissant with some dollops of apricot jam. The child grinned at Ellis's drawing of a smiley face. Later, Ellis pan-fried Dover sole. In *The Affair*, Noah tracked Eden down and confronted her, gripping her by the arm. The TV news showed scenes from George Floyd's funeral. In bed Ellis came to the final pages of the *The 7th Function of Language*. It is never too late to try to change the course of the story, he read. And then that final twist, on the lip of the crater.

Wednesday 10th June 2020

A cold, grey day. Ellis stayed indoors, reading. He ate houmous on softbread
with salad for lunch, with a glass of water. Afterwards, sliced apple with plain
yogurt. In the afternoon he painted a section of ceiling white, where steam rising
from a shower had discoloured it. Supper was cheese soufflé with new potatoes,
cabbage and carrots, followed by sliced nectarine with yogurt. In *The Affair*
Noah's career began to implode with the publication in *Vanity Fair* of
allegations of sexual harassment. Smoke drifted across L.A. In bed Ellis read the
opening pages of a new novel. But I did not sleep, the chapter ended. For it was
that night, as the false dawn broke, that I saw the first signal from outer space.

Thursday 11th June 2020

A cold grey day, with light rain in the late afternoon. In the morning Ellis went
out for a 24-pack of toilet rolls. Much of his day was spent reading. The child
played with her soft toy dog. In the evening it rained continously. In *The Affair*,
Noah encouraged Helen to follow him across a wilderness to escape the
spreading fire. Things are truly progressing! (Ellis read in the novel he held in
bed). End of footnote.

Friday 12th June 2020

Another grey day. Ellis went shopping and bought potatoes, blueberries, apples,
a quiche, yogurt, rolls, a bar of chocolate, two packs of coffee, milk, kitchen roll.
In the bakery he bought four croissants. He talked to a neighbour, who was
sitting on a bench drinking coffee. Later, he wrote a letter to a friend. The child
spoke some words. Toes. Tree. Baby. Ellis lay on the sofa and napped. Later,
online, he read about a controversy involving J. K. Rowling and a tweet. Her
first husband admitted he had slapped her but denied abusing her. Ellis watched
the final episode of *The Affair*. I therefore never rested, never slept, in order to
continue my pursuit of the Communists, he read in his bedside novel. I plotted
against them, organized attacks on them, and gave witness against them.

Saturday 13th June 2020

It was a hot morning, getting hotter. Ellis went out for a *Times*. He read some of
the newspaper while drinking coffee. Later he began reading a new political
biography. After that he did a little painting - domestic rather than artistic - and
then did some sweeping. Outside he scattered a little ant powder by a pot which
had become home to some. He rescued a large black beetle which had become
entangled in a spider's web. On the internet he watched film of two police

officers who were demanding details from a middle-aged black couple who had just returned to their house in Ipswich in their BMW. The film had received two and a half million views. Ellis put weeds and other garden cuttings in a bag which had once held compost. Somewhere in the neighbourhood someone was employing an electric saw. The child pushed her toy buggy with Polly sitting in it. She had learned to walk backwards. On the internet there was footage of far-right protesters - all white and male - attempting to break through a line of police in central London. A link on Twitter led Ellis to the forensic archaelogy analysis of the killing of Mark Duggan in Tottenham. It was a location Ellis knew well. He had never believed the police version. It seemed obvious to Ellis that the gun had been planted at the location where it was ostensibly discovered. Once again the IPCC investigation had been exposed as the standard whitewash. On a mobile phone, on Duo, Ellis talked to three other screens. Later, he pan-fried some cod and ate it with mashed potato, fried tomatoes and peas. He went to bed at 9.45pm, feeling very tired. Outside there was still lots of daylight. Ellis reached the end of chapter twenty-two. "Can you explain that?" asked my outer-space friend. "I will indeed explain."

Sunday 14th June 2020

Cloudy and cool. More than 100 arrests after violent London protests involving the far right. MP Tobias Ellwood said the photograph of a man urinating beside the memorial to PC Keith Palmer was "abhorrent". Boris Johnson has commissioned a review into the two metre social distancing rule, to be completed by 4 July, when pubs and restaurants reopen. Atlanta's police chief has resigned after the shooting dead by police of a black man, Rayshard Brooks, 27, on Friday evening. On Twitter Ellis followed a link to Asa Winstanley's article on the *Electronic Intifada* website about the new Israeli ambassador to Britain, Tzipi Hotovely. A 41-year-old extremist, she is a pro-settler activist who has said that there are "no Palestinian people". She claims that the entire West Bank belongs to Jews alone. She has supported a Jewish extremist group that seeks to destroy Jerusalem's al-Aqsa Mosque compound - Islam's third holiest site. She has also supported the work of Lehava, a government-funded anti-miscegenation group which attacks relationships between Arabs and Jews. She has said it is important to "prevent mixed marriages". Speaking to a US pro-Israel lobby grouyp in 2017, she attacked American Jews for marrying non-Jews: "American Jews are losing it big time. I see the numbers, I'm in the foreign ministry: 80 percent of American Jews assimilate." Asa Winstanley finished: *As such an open advocate of Zionist settler-colonialism and racism, Tzipi Hotovely will be a true representative of the state of Israel in the UK*. Ellis read a retweet by Asa Winstanley of a comment by Joe Sucksmith: *Important to be able to cut through the bullshit at times like this. Starter for 10 is Nick Lowles, founder of*

Hope not Hate, which claims to be "anti-fascist" yet spent 4 years amplifying bogus charges of antisemitism against Jeremy Corbyn. Put simply: he's a fraud. On Twitter one thing leads to another and soon Ellis had stumbled upon a tweet by Dave Berkeley, who wrote: *Coincidentally, Hope not Hate was headed by ex MP, Ruth Smeeth, who previously worked as campaigns manager for BICOM, the pro Israel propaganda org funded by billionaire arms dealer Poju Zabludowicz.* 'Frank' tweeted: *I saw through them the moment they started the Corbyn smears. They are a front organisation for interests that have little to do with fight against hate. It's pure coincidence when they say something reasonable (they have to do that sometimes to stay credible with the gullible).* Next he read a long thread by Fuad Alakbarov on the crimes and racist views of Winston Churchill. The child pushed her buggy, then tottered into the garden. That evening Ellis watched *Four Weddings and a Funeral*. In bed he read the words: I wanted her to help me teach him to be very careful of what he said, to guard his tongue, and to speak of such things only in a whisper.

Monday 15th June 2020

A hot sunny morning. Ellis was up making tea at 6.10am. He read through some notes and then had a bowl of cereal. Later he went shopping and bought milk, yogurt and dishwasher cleaner. He unexpectedly met two friends and held a short, socially-distanced conversation. Much of the day he spent reading a political biography. The child seemed to be troubled by the heat and an emerging new tooth. She touched her ear and then cuddled her plastic dog on wheels. Later Ellis brought the washing in, did some watering, and then pan-fried some Norwegian salmon, whch he ate with boiled new potatoes and peas. Afterwards he washed-up. On the internet he read Matt Kennard's tweet posted some eight hours earlier: *Ruth Smeeth - former Labour MP exposed as a US embassy informant and ex-staffer for Israel lobby group BICOM - is new CEO of Index on Censorship. On top of this, Index received $430,187 from CIA cutout National Endowment for Democracy in last 4 years. Another one bites the dust.* By 20.22 the sun had vanished and a cold mist had started to creep across the neighbourhood. It was the first day of the big London stores reopening after the lockdown and the TV news showed crowds flooding in to make purchases. Social distancing had evidently collapsed, judging by the queues and the jostling shoppers. "That interpetation never so much as crossed my mind," the character said in the novel Ellis was reading in bed. "We don't punish you for what crosses your minds but for what crosses the big man's mind," was the reply.

Tuesday 16th June 2020

Another bright sunny morning. Blue sky with, in the east, just a faint, fast-ebbing screen of pale cloud. It is reported that there have now been more than 8 million confirmed cases of Covid-19 infection worldwide. Somali-born US congresswoman Ilhan Omar has announced the death of her father from the virus. 100 new cases of infection are reported from Beijing. A very hot day. Ellis remained indoors, reading and writing. In the evening he watered some plants. She was young and beautiful, he read in the novel he was reading in bed. And, even more important, she knew just how to converse with men.

Wednesday 17th June 2020

Cloudy, warm. Ellis made himself a mug of tea. Online he read a piece by Robert Mackey on *The Intercept* website, about the 75-year-old protester Martin Gugino, who was pushed over by two police officers outside City Hall, Buffalo, New York. His lawyer told CNN that his client is unable to walk and has a cracked skull. Robert Mackey's article was headlined **Trump's New Favorite Channel, OAN, Keeps Lying About Buffalo Protester Assaulted by Police**. It began: *ONE AMERICA NEWS, a far-right cable channel that rounds up internet conspiracy theories for its viewers, has spent the past week trying to smear Martin Gugino, the 75-year-old Catholic peace activist who was assaulted by Buffalo police officers at a protest against police brutality, and remains hospitalized with a brain injury. The channel's obsessive focus on Gugino is part of a wider effort to tarnish protests against racism and police violence that OAN has pursued for years.* Ellis read on. Echoing an OAN report that treated the musings of a conspiracy theorist in Florida as evidence, Trump told his millions of followers that Gugino might have been a professional ANTIFA provocateur who had thrown himself to the ground to make the police look bad, after trying to jam their radios. OAN tried to cast doubt on the severity of Gugino's injury, citing unidentified medical experts. But the blood pouring out of his ear after the fall was consistent with the fracturing of his skull. The film of the incident reveals a very audible thud when his head hits the pavement. In a third report OAN claimed, falsely, that it had evidence Gugino was an active member on anarchist messaging boards. Another bogus claim was that the mayor of Buffalo had described Gugino as having a reputation in the town as being someone who caused trouble, 'an agitator' and someone who encouraged looting. Ellis read that this utterly false claim had been repeated by Fox News and the UK *Independent* newspaper website. Ellis read this last revelation with interest, as it was the *Independent* which some three years ago had first run the utterly false story that Jeremy Corbyn supporters had assembled outside the home of the MP Stella Creasy to intimidate her. That wholly fraudulent story had been eagerly taken up by the rest of the corporate media, not least the Corbyn-hating *Guardian* and the Corbyn-hating BBC. Ellis read on. The piece by Robert Mackey included footage shot by Antonio Wells of a bellicose foul-mouthed man dressed as a protester who was probably an undercover cop. It raised yet more questions on top of the basic one that the Buffalo police had sent a large number of police in riot gear against a 75-year-old Catholic peace activist and two young protesters sitting on the steps of City Hall. Next, a post by Ben White on his Twitter page led Ellis to a new report by B'tselem about the al-'Ofoq Teachers Housing Association complex on land belonging to the villages of Zawata, Ijinsinya and a-Naqurah, north-west of Nablus. It includes 174 single-family two-storey residences designed for teachers at government schools. A teacher who purchases an apartment receives a foundation grant and must complete the construction independently. The complex consists of two compounds, each with its own gate. Four are currently occupied in each compound. The road from Route 60 to Zawata was damaged by tanks and military vehicles after the second intifada of 2000. The military began using the compound for training exercises, usually for a day or two every two or three months. About two years ago the military stepped up the frequency and exercises are held once a month for three or four days at a time. During the training the soldiers create a commotion, move around the homes, enter vacant ones, shoot stun grenades and flare bombs, and sleep in empty homes. When the training is over they leave behind a trail of ammunition, unexploded ordnances and filth. On Sunday 5 April 2020, some 150 soldiers raided the complex for three days. They used live fire, hurled stun grenades and flare bombs, and ran among the houses shouting and disrupting the residents' lives. On Thursday 16 April 2020, around 3:30am, soldiers raided four inhabited homes in the western compound for the first time. They broke down the front doors of two homes whose occupants were away. The soldiers forced the inhabitants who were present to wait out in the street as they ransacked their homes, using dogs. This occurred despite the pandemic. And so it went on, this terrorism. Just like Nazis, the Jews enjoyed humiliating the *untermenschen*. They broke down doors. They emptied wardrobes and drawers and tore away bedding. The Jews left their bootprints across the floor. They threw the children's toys around. *Everyone knows they're not really looking for anyone. Their goal is to scare us and make us leave.* Next Ellis followed another link on Ben White's Twitter page, to an article by Ofer Aderet on the *Haaretz* website. It reported on the suppressed history of the Haganah, which was formed 100 years ago. For example, in the summer of 1939 members of the Haganah murdered two men and a woman and injured a young girl and a toddler in the village of Lubya in the Lower Galilee. They were shot at home in the night. Among the murderers was Yogal Allon, later head of the Palmach, and IDF general, and Education and Foreign Minister. The man who planned the murders was Nahum Shadmi, a senior Haganah member, a future IDF Colonel, and later president of a military appeals tribunal and a Mapai Party activist (forerunner of the Labour Party). Shadmi's son Issachar was commander of the Border Force brigade whose members carried out the 1956 massacre in the Arab town of Kafr Qasem. *The full history of the Haganah will not feature in the centenary celebrations, and is not well known to the public or part of the high school curriculum. This aspect has been excluded from museums, parades, and the official and state-sanctioned history books.* On November 25 1940 the British ship *Patria* was blown up by the Haganah. It sank, killing some 250 Jewish passengers and several British servicemen. In February 1946 the Haganah targeted British police stations across the country. In one bombing three British women and a child were killed. There was the bombing in January 1948 of the Semiramis Hotel in Jerusalem's Katamon neighbourhood by the Haganah's Moriah battalion. The blast was meant to kill Abd al-Qadir al-Husayni, commander of the Arab militias in the Jerusalem area. The Haganah placed explosives in the hotel basement and detonated them. Husayni was not in the building but dozens of Arab civilians were. The exact number of dead and injured is unknown. One report said 26 dead, 60 injured. Most of the dead were from the Christian Abu Suawan family, including women and children, as well as the Spanish vice-consul, who lived at the hotel. The Jewish newspaper *Davar* reported the bombing but justified it as having dealt with a 'nest of killers'. A popular song among Palmach members in those days celebrated 'castrating Mohammed'. This alluded to an Arab from the town of Beisan (now Beit She'an) who was suspected of trying to rape a kibbutz member. Yogal Allon, later head of the Palmach, and IDF general, and education and foreign minister, was once again involved. He organised the abduction and castration of the nameless Arab. The crime was carried out by Yohai Ben-Nun (a future naval commander), Amos Horev (a future IDF general) and president of the Technion [Israel Institute of Technology] and Yaakov Cohen (later a member of all three intelligence agencies). The team was briefed by a Jewish doctor in Afula on how to castrate the Arab in a way that ensured he lived, in order to terrorise others. The three men dressed as Arabs, broke into the man's home, dragged him to an open area, and castrated him. This had the effect of "terrorizing the local Arabs" gloated Yaakov Cohen, in a book published by the Israeli Defence Ministry. The May 1948 massacre of Arabs in the village of Ein al-Zeitun, near Safed, by the Palmach's Third Battalion, has been erased from history. Dozens of Arabs were captured. Two days later, with their hands bound, they were executed. Afterwards Ellis watched a short piece of footage of 30 Israeli military jeeps pouring into the Palestinian town of Ramallah and firing stun grenades after midnight, to disturb and terrorise the population. The hearts of these Jews were consumed by hatred. It was a scene you would never see on the craven BBC News service, which since its inception had been keeping reality muffled, walled-up, or at best twisted into strands that served state power. Ellis drank a cappuccino and ate a slice of toast and honey. In the afternoon the temperature dropped. Ellis watered some pots, although he thought he could smell rain in the air. But no rain fell. In bed he read: He kept on digging and digging, so the story goes, to the east, to the north, to the south, and to the west, until finally he completely uprooted the tree. But still he found no treasure. Then six more sentences and the novel was over.

Thursday 18th June 2020

Ellis woke in the darkness, hearing rain hiss down outside. Eventually he fell asleep again. When he woke at 7.15am it was still raining. Later the rain stopped. On *The Modern Novel* website he read a review of the novel he'd just completed reading. The child was in a bubbly mood, lively and animated and beginning to articulate words with a new fluency. Young brown blackbirds skipped around the garden. The death of Vera Lynn was announced. Joshua arrived, later than anticipated. He stayed for a little over an hour, then left. The 10pm Sky News included footage of Vera Lynn singing before a large RAF audience. In bed Ellis began reading *Flaubert's Parrot*.

Friday 19th June 2020

A bright sunlit morning. The High Street was busy and lined with parked cars, every space taken. Ellis bought two almond croissants, a chocolate croissant, and a plain croissant. He went to the bank. He considered going into the bookshop but saw there were people inside and so walked on. On the internet he discovered that President Trump had retweeted a tweet by Max Blumenthal, who reproduced the retweet under the line: *Framing this one*. The tweet ran: Donald J. Trump Retweeted **Defund The Police**@MaxBlumenthal: *John Bolton, a notoriously mendacious enemy of all living beings on the planet, is discovering what every other great Republican hope of the Resistance has: liberals will eagerly lap up any piece of hysterical Cold War propaganda if they think it can be leveraged against Trump.* The next day Trump deleted his retweet, evidently having been informed that Max Blumenthal was not a supporter. Elsewhere on the net Ellis finally found a review of the new Dylan album *Rough and Rowdy Ways* that was less than 100 per cent reverential. He listened to Dylan singing 'I Contain Multitudes', which confirmed his sense that this was not an album he was in any hurry to purchase. He started listening to the JFK song but gave up after a couple of minutes. It clouded over and grew cooler. For lunch Ellis ate asparagus with a poached egg and a slice of bread, followed by a sliced apple with plain yogurt. The child was a little subdued and spent the day clinging to her mother. Perhaps it was the pain of a new tooth pushing through. Later Ellis had a bath. The death of Ian Holm was announced. On the internet Ellis read the latest post on Tony Greenstein's blog: Hundreds at Zoom Meeting Say - **Stand up to Starmer Help Build the Campaign for Free Speech on Palestine & Zionism in the Labour Party** Greenstein once again attacked the illusions of that vast swathe of the Left still besotted by Corbyn's ghost. *Corbyn was both cowardly and stupid. Despite 30+ years of work over Palestine Corbyn never got it. Never understood how malicious and vindictive the Zionist movement is. Never understood that Zionism isn't a nice friendly form of Jewish identity but it is the ideology that dictates the ethnic cleansing of Palestinians. Corbyn **voluntarily** adopted the IHRA definition after Theresa May because he thought he was being clever to wear the Crown of Thorns. He came to realise that the crown can be a heavy burden. Corbyn introduced the fast-track expulsion procedure and lied that it would only apply to the most 'egregious' cases whereas it applies now to every 'anti-Semitism' case. All of us have borne a heavy load but we are determined that the fake anti-Semitism narrative will not win out. Truth will prevail.* Ellis ate cold chicken with potato salad and a green salad, washed down with a glass of water. Afterwards he ate rhubarb crumble with ice-cream. He began watching *Alien.* In bed he read to the end of Chapter 3 of *Flaubert's Parrot.* The novel was dedicated 'To Pat', who was presumably Pat Kavanagh, a member of that literature-smothering species, literary agents. Her client list had been rich with profitable nonentities and sleek mediocrities. Ellis remembered wandering randomly in a roughly clockwise direction around Highgate Cemetery and coming across her rather large gravestone. He had been amused at the time by its size and also that it bore the words WIFE OF JULIAN BARNES, as if this added to her lustre.

Saturday 20th June 2020

Another bright sunny morning. Ellis had first woken in a grey light and seen that it was only 4.35am. Thereafter he'd drifted in and out of consciousness. The state radio was promoting the reduction of safe distancing from two metres to one. Later, after 7.30am, two history professors argued about a statue in Edinburgh, which commemorated a slave trader who had been influential in delaying abolition. The first history professor, a flabby liberal, blathered about the need to keep it, but with an instructive plaque. He had been involved with Edinburgh Council in producing such a plaque. This had been going on for three years and for some reason the plaque had not yet been attached to the base of the statue. The second history professor said the statue should be removed. It was a celebration of the slave trader and no plaque could alter its existence as a memorial set up to admire a man who had traded profitably in death, racism and human misery. The drippy liberal said that next stately homes would be torn down! It was a classic debating strategy - change the subject. Stately homes may well have been set up out of the profits of the slave trade - *Mansfield Park,* anyone? - but they were not commemorations of that activity, merely the luxury proceeds. As such they could be reclaimed for everyone. Ed Miliband's mansion tax (a modest proposal which had produced a tsunami of foam-flecked wrath from the billionaire class and any number of whining multi-mansion-owning celebrities, including Griff Rhys Jones) had been the tiniest step in the right direction. A land tax on the ruling class was many centuries overdue, but plainly would never happen under the corrupt and reactionary Labour Party. Ellis finally climbed out of bed at 8.10am. Outside a man in a puffa jacket wandered by, towing a small dog. Young blackbirds snatched the tiny, budding fruit of a pear tree. The day grew hotter. The child tottered around the garden. She played with her new watering can, tipping out water from the spout and chuckling. Ellis dead-headed two rose bushes. Later he replaced the defective lock on a bathroom door. He finished watching *Alien*. He learned from the internet that some scenes of the alien had involved a suit worn by a very tall, thin Nigerian. In the evening Ellis ate risotto, followed by apple crumble and ice-cream. He watched *Sliding Doors*. He had forgotten that in one of the parallel lives Helen dies. He missed the news headlines and was bemused to see live coverage of a major incident in a park in Reading. The Sky journalists blathered on, saying nothing at all about what had happened but merely describing over and over again how police had sealed-off the park, how the police helicopter was circling overhead, how there were reports of a stabbing. This was some three hours after the incident. Ellis went on Twitter and immediately learned that three people were dead. He watched a short, blurry piece of footage which showed emergency workers - police perhaps - gathered around three separate figures on the ground, while others ran forward to assist. He went to bed and finished Chapter 4, read all of Chapter 5, and the first four pages of Chapter 6.

Sunday 21st June 2020

A cool, grey overcast morning. Ellis woke to the memory of two strange dreams. In the first he'd been a member of the Rolling Stones and there had been problems with a truculent Keith Richard. Ellis had been called upon to assist with the vocals, which had left him aghast, since he could neither sing nor remember the words to a single Stones lyric. The second dream had involved a distorted version of the decapitated android scene in *Alien*. A man's face dripping with milk. But in this version the face was attached to a half-clothed body. The big floppy underpants were exposed and cradled a single glistening turd. A Freudist would have a field day with this dream, Ellis reflected. Light rain was a possibility later in the day, the state radio asserted. The news headline remained the killing of three people in Reading but it was now stated that it was not believed to be a terror attack. President Trump had spoken to a crowd of supporters in Tulsa, but numbers were reduced and there were many empty seats. Six members of his campaign team had become infected with Covid-19. Ellis listened to the BBC's Sunday newspaper round-up. It included a fawning account of how photographs of Prince William were in all the papers, pictured with his children. The announcer's voice was thick with the syrup of sycophancy. Ellis climbed out of bed and went downstairs. He boiled the kettle and made a cup of tea. Then he went to see what the *Mail* online website had to say about the killings in Reading. Ellis learned that the three victims were members of a group of a dozen middle-aged men who had been sitting on the grass, drinking and chatting. Their attacker was reported to be a 25-year-old 'Libyan'. The *Mail* put the man's nationality in apostrophes, which seemed to indicate uncertainty. There were the usual banal utterances by various politicians regarding their shock and concern and their praise for the emergency services. It was something of a genre, with stock conventions. These same politicians invariably supported arms sales to murderous tyrannies and torture states. Eating a bowl of cereal, Ellis read an article by Ajit Singh on the Grayzone website. It began: *A leading Hong Kong "pro-democracy" figure, Jimmy Lai, has denounced nationwide protests in the United States against police brutality and systemic racism, which were sparked by the police killing of an African-American man, George Floyd. Lai's views reflect a significant segment of the city's protest movement, who affirm the exceptionalist myth of the US as a beacon of "freedom and democracy".* Ellis read on. He learned that another leader, Joshua Wong, had carefully avoided making any specific criticism of Trump or the movement's Republican sponsors in Washington. He learned that Jimmy Lai is a billionaire media tycoon who is a major financial and media backer of Hong Kong's protest movement. He read that much of the protest movement in Hong Kong has lionized Washington, upholding the US government and Trump as their "liberators". *It is clear that Hong Kong's "pro-democracy" movement and Black Lives Matter are separate movements with radically different political ideologies and aims.* On Asa Winstanley's website Ellis read a retweet of a tweet by Jews Sans Frontieres responding to a tweet by Janet Daby, the Labour MP for Lewisham East, who wrote that she was "Really pleased" to be involved with the Zionist anti-Palestinian propaganda outfits the Jewish Labour Movement, the Board of Deputies, the Jewish Leadership Council, and the Community Service Trust. It remained overcast and cool. The child played with a tube of paint and a tube of toothpaste. The state radio news performed a somersault. It reported that the attack in Reading *was* a terror attack. Ellis went for a walk. It looked as if it might rain so he packed a light raincoat in his rucksack. Back home he began watching *Aliens*. On the TV news the killer was reported to be a 25-year-old asylum seeker. On the TV news a photo was shown of the killer holding a baby. In bed Ellis read Julian Barnes's blistering attack on Dame Enid Starkie, distinguished Reader in French Literature at the University of Oxford and Fellow of Somerville College. Starkie could not speak French fluently, was a bumbling incompetent where biography was concerned, and showed herself to be an utterly inept reader and interpreter of *Madame Bovary*. Ellis continued and read the first six and a half pages of Chapter 7 before he put out the light and fell into a deep and untroubled sleep.

Monday 22nd June 2020

Another bright and sunny morning, with a cloudless blue sky. It felt warm. The state radio solemnly announced that a minute's silence would be held at 10am for the victims of the Reading attack. The 'minute's silence' culture was getting out of hand, Ellis felt. It was a manipulative and sentimental attempt to impose Solemn Thoughts in a society which was structured on violence. Ellis went shopping. He bought bananas, blueberries, yogurt, white rolls, milk. A man stood blocking the supermarket aisle, yapping on a phone. Two staff members made no attempt to speak to the man. Ellis in the end walked past the idiot. He added a packet of sandwich bags and a large kitchen roll to his basket. When it was his turn to pay the machine repeatedly declined his card. The manager was called. Ellis was sent to another till to pay. The manager explained that the machines regularly malfunctioned since they had been reprogrammed to accept payments of up to £45 instead of £30. Ellis went to the bakery to buy four croissants. Later he went home. Meanwhile Avon and Somerset Police were vindictively pursuing the identities of 15 people who they wished to interview in connection with criminal damage to the Edward Colston statue in Bristol. Detective Superintendent Liz Hughes said that "in the eyes of the law" a crime had been committed and the force was "duty-bound to investigate without fear or favour". A risible statement, since pressure had been applied by the Home Secretary, Priti Patel. Tucked away at the end of the news was the revelation that three pedestrians had been run down and killed in Cumbria by the driver of a car. The massacre happened on Abbey Road, Dalton-in-Furness, at about 14.30 BST on Sunday. The driver of the Peugeot, a 47-year-old local man, was arrested on suspicion of drinking and driving and three counts of causing death by dangerous driving. And that was that. The massacre had gone unreported on the 10pm Sky TV News because the corporate media is indifferent to most forms of violent death. British policing has always been institutionally car-supremacist, with a very relaxed attitude to speeding. British policing has always been contemptuously indifferent to anti-social obstructive car parking. There would be no minute's silence for these dead walkers, whoever they were. The identity of the killer driver wasn't being mentioned. It would be interesting to know if the driver had previous convictions for motoring offences but of course the corporate media had no interest in such trifles. The Green Party, which of any party ought to have a policy on such matters, was characteristically mute. But then anyone who thought the Green Party was some sort of radical alternative to the Labour Party was as delusional as those people who thought the Labour Party was somehow socialist. Searching for information later in the day Ellis learned that the victims were a father and his two children who had been run down and killed while walking on a footpath at Ruskinville Bridge. The drunk speeding driver was at the controls of a silver Peugeot 206. The driver had driven east from Barrow to Dalton, a journey of some 39 miles. By mid-day the BBC had ceased all reference to the Cumbria massacre. The dead of Reading were all that the corporate media cared about. For sensible commentary you had to turn to Twitter. Nick Forster commented that drunk drivers kill and injure a lot more of us than terrorists. True, reflected Ellis. Yet police traffic patrols have been massively reduced this century. Rod Hewitt commented: *Sentencing in these 2 cases will be interesting: Reading stabbings: Three people dead after Forbury Gardens attack. Driver held after three pedestrians die in Cumbria crash.* True, Ellis reflected. The drunk killer would invariably be treated far more leniently than the knife killer. The drunk killer would almost certainly have his freedom to drive restored to him by Britain's car-centric judicial system. The odious Keir Starmer had oozed his sympathy for the families and loved ones killed in Reading. He had nothing to say about the Cumbria massacre. No votes there. Ditto slithery Lisa Nandy. It grew hotter. The child ate half a banana and then two strawberries. She responded to stimuli. *Nose.* She touches her nose. *Ears.* She touches an ear. *Head.* She touches the crown of her head. Ellis ate an almond croissant and read the *Times* obituary of Ian Holm. He discovered Holm had once been married to Penelope Wilton. Later, Ellis pan-fried some cod and tomatoes and ate it with boiled potatoes and peas, followed by a bowl of strawberries with vanilla icecream and yogurt. He watched more of *Aliens*. On the 10pm Sky News the grieving father of the American man killed in Reading was interviewed. In the half hour that followed there was no mention whatever of the violent killing of the father and his two children by the drunken motorist. They might almost have been Palestinians, so indifferent was the corporate media to their fate. Ellis went to bed. We look at the sun through smoked glass, he read. We must look at the past through coloured glass.

Tuesday 23rd June 2020

A bright warm sunny morning. Ellis woke at 5.45am. He went to the kitchen and made himself a mug of tea. Then he read for half an hour, before eating a bowl of cereal. He made a cappuccino and read until 7.30am. The news had coverage of the third victim of the Reading stabbings. The massacre of the father and his two children by a drunk driver was blanked out by the corporate media. It had already gone down the memory hole. A visitor called and stayed for some 25 minutes. Ellis drank more coffee. The child picked dandelions in an overgrown part of the park. Back home again the child played with half of a broken wooden peg. The temperature rose. The Prime Minister announced further relaxation of the lockdown. The owner of a pier was interviewed and was delighted. The owner of a pub was interviewed and deplored the fact that the reopening was scheduled for a Saturday. A Monday would have been better, he said. Ellis ate quiche with potato salad and green salad, followed by strawberries and ice-cream. In London he carried her round the Great Exibition, Ellis read. He put out the light and slept.

Wednesday 24th June 2020

Ellis woke at 5am and finally got out of bed at 5.45am. He made himself a mug of tea and continued reading a political biography. After breakfast he went for a walk. A bird - some sort of small finch - skipped along the road ahead of him. Finally it flew off. A woman ran past, dressed in black lycra. She wore a wristband with a device to record her exercise. She was sweating copiously. The sun rose in the sky and it became hotter. Monica and her husband were approaching from the opposite direction. A short conversation, then on. Back home Ellis read on Twitter: *@Reuters: Israeli troops kill Palestinian who attempted car-ramming in West Bank: police https://reuters.com/article/us-isr.* This was a classic corporate news fabrication. It was a lie. It was fake news. *Ben White @benabyad: Ahmed Erekat, 27, shot dead today by Israeli occupation forces at a checkpoint. He was going to pick up his mother & sisters from a salon, ready for his sister's wedding tonight. Israeli spox: he was driving "quickly towards the direction" of border cop* And: *Ben White @benabyad: "Israeli police spokesman Micky Rosenfeld said Erekat "got out of the car and approached officers who responded by shooting" him".* So, an execution. And *Ben White @benabyad: "The director of the Palestinian Red Crescent Society in Bethlehem confirmed that a soldier prevented Palestinian medical personnel from approaching the man and was left to bleed"* And: *Noura Erakat@4noura: Ahmed Erekat, 27, beautiful young man. A son. A brother. Fiancée. My baby cousin. Israeli cowards shot him multiple times, left him to bleed for 1.5 hours and blamed him for his death. Tonight was his sister's wedding, his was next month. We failed to protect him. I am so sorry.* The landline rang. Soon afterwards a vehicle parked outside and the driver emerged. Ellis made coffee. It grew hotter. Mid-day. One. Two. Ellis read some newly arrived emails. Later he talked to a neighbour in the street. Later he returned to Twitter. *Ben White@benabyad: "Hundreds of Palestinian citizens of Israel protested on Monday in the Negev region to denounce the Israeli government policy of house demolitions and evacuation orders in the village of Khirbet al-Watan."* Ellis read about the EU's equivocation regarding the Israeli plan to annex the West Bank. *The European Union is Israel's largest trading partner, with nearly a third of Israel's exports going to the bloc. Belgium is among the countries that feel the EU could use this leverage, and has asked the European Commission, the EU's executive, to draw up a list of possible punitive measures on Israel, including on trade, an EU diplomat said. Amongst possible countermeasures* *being discussed in private in Brussels are suspending Israel's privileged EU trade agreement, banning imports from settlements, and cutting Israel out of scientific research and student exchange programmes, EU diplomats say. EU foreign policy chief Josep Borrell said in February that annexation "if implemented, could not pass unchallenged". However, the lack of consensus means he has been unable to flesh out what any such challenge might contain. By contrast, the EU agreed swiftly in 2014 to impose hefty economic sanctions targeting Russia's financial, energy and defence sectors when Moscow seized the Black Sea peninsula of Crimea from Ukraine – land that Russia still holds. "Big countries never had a problem imposing counter measures against Russia over Crimea's annexation, so why can they not do it on Israel? We need coherence," Simon Moutquin, a Belgian Green lawmaker, told Reuters. EU diplomats, officials and experts point to a strong presence of pro-Israel advocates in Brussels, with at least 10 lobby groups opening offices in the city over the past 17 years as Israel looked to bolster its international image in the wake of the second Palestinian intifada and three wars in Gaza. Israel's ties have improved with the Visegrad Group, an alliance combining Hungary, the Czech Republic, Slovakia and Poland, which carries its own weight within the EU. In Viktor Orban, Netanyahu has found an ally prepared to block statements or actions critical of Israel, even in the face of heavy pressure from other European capitals, EU diplomats say. "Hungary ... will continue to oppose unilateral and unjust international political approaches against Israel," Hungarian Foreign Minister Peter Szijjarto wrote on Facebook on June 10.* On the *Independent* website, Ellis read: *Hemmed in by an Israeli military base & Wall, Aida refugee camp may be the most exposed community to tear gas in the world. Youth centre director & resident Anas Abu Srour writes on tear gas as a form of physical & psychological subjugation. I've been hit with tear gas almost every day of my adult life – this is what it feels like https://bit.ly/2BBU1Oc.* So, Ellis thought. Jews are gassing the Palestinians… On the news Bournemouth beach was shown to be packed with holidaymakers. Scientists warned of a second coronavirus wave. The Housing Secretary Robert Jenrick stoutly denied any wrongdoing in connection with his approval of a massive housing development on the site of the former Westferry Print Works in East London. In bed that night Ellis reached the end of Chapter 8. I climbed into my car and drove off, he read.

Thursday 25th June 2020

Ellis woke at 5am and got up 45 minutes later. He drank a mug of tea and continued reading the political biography. It was another hot sunny day without a cloud in the sky. On Twitter he read *Remi Kanazi@Remroun: A military checkpoint is itself violence. Controlling, harassing, strip searching, and*

167

abusing Palestinians at checkpoints is violence. There is no innocence in population control and land theft. Earlier Remi Kanazi had tweeted: *Israeli occupation soldiers aren't civilians or victims. They are violent, heavily-armed apartheid pushers whose main purpose is to subjugate Palestinians, colonize land, and transfer native resources to usurping Israeli settlers.* Two days earlier Remi Kanazi reproduced a communication he had received from Twitter: *Hello, We have received a complaint regarding your account, @Remroun, for the following content. Tweet ID:127339001 11040378880 Tweet text: In case anyone forgot: From the river to the sea, Palestine will be free. We have investigated the reported content and could not identify any violations of the Twitter rules (https://support.twitter.com/articles/18311) or German law. Accordingly, we have not taken any action at this time. Sincerely, Twitter.* Interesting, thought Ellis. The complaint had evidently emanated from Germany. It was a German Wikipedia editor who some years ago had deleted Wikipedia's 'Ellis Sharp' entry. Zionists shut down debate and criticism wherever and whenever they could. The sound of a workman's drill pierced the morning. The child was in an ebullient mood and roared with laughter when Ellis attempted to sing 'Twinkle Twinkle Little Star'. On the Sky News website there was a top story of the day: **New Lamborghini sports car crashes in West Yorkshire twenty minutes into first trip.** The story was based on a tweet by the West Yorkshire Police Roads Policing Unit, which reproduced two photographs of the aftermath of the crash. *M1 Ossett today - it's only a car! But on this occasion a 20 minute old brand new Lamborghini that stopped due to mechanical failure in lane 3 them [sic] hit from behind by an innocent motorist.* It was tweeted with the hashtag *#couldhavecried*. The story on Sky ended with the sentence: *Lamborghinis are typically worth between £125,00 and £211,000.* All in all this was a classic instance of the alliance between the car-supermacist corporate media and the car-supremacist police. That it was actually the Roads Policing Unit which talked of "an innocent motorist" exposed yet again what a malignant and dangerous force the police were. They promoted violence in all aspects legitimised by the state. What was the top speed of this obscene machine? In a world racing towards human extinction the very existence of vehicles like these on the public highway was the perfect symbol of astounding complacency. It grew hotter. Ellis drank a glass of water. Online he became aware of a new day's Twitter storm. Rebecca Long-Bailey@RLong_Bailey had tweeted *Maxine Peake is an absolute diamond* with a link to an interview on the website of the *Independent* between the actress Maxine Peake and Alexandra Pollard: https://www.independent.co.uk/arts-entertainment/films/features/maxine-peake-interview-labour-corbyn-keir-starmer-black-lives-matter-a9583206.html The interview inluded this: "Systemic racism is a global issue," she adds. "The tactics used by the police in America, kneeling on George Floyd's neck, that was learnt from seminars with Israeli secret services." This comment needless to say produced the usual froth of outrage from the usual band of apologists for Israel. *Oh my*, squealed John Rentoul. Slithery Stella Creasy emerged to identify *casual antisemitism*. Her Zionist partner Dan Fox added a sneer. Nick Timothy joined the chorus. Tracy-Ann Oberman fizzed. Dave Rich squeaked 'There is a deep well of antisemtic conspiracism that blames Jews for every calamity.' And on it went. Vile Oz Katerji. Repellent Ian Austin. Individuals who postured as Leftists joined in. Ally Fogg, for example: @AllyFogg *Going to get this off my chest all in one go: I love Maxine Peake but mentioning Israel as she did was painfully stupid & wrong. It will be welcomed only by those who want to see Jews at the centre of all evils & by those who want to see antisemitism at the heart of left politics 12:35 pm · 25 Jun 2020* Supporters of Maxine Peake supplied a link to Amnesty International: *Baltimore law enforcement officials, along with hundreds of others from Florida, New Jersey, Pennsylvania, California, Arizona, Connecticut, New York, Massachusetts, North Carolina, Georgia, Washington State as well as the DC Capitol police have all traveled to Israel for training. Thousands of others have received training from Israeli officials here in the U.S. Many of these trips are taxpayer-funded while others are privately funded. Since 2002, the Anti-Defamation League, the American Jewish Committee's Project Interchange and the Jewish Institute for National Security Affairs have paid for police chiefs, assistant chiefs and captains to train in Israel and the Occupied Palestinian Territories (OPT). These trainings put Baltimore police and other U.S. law enforcement employees in the hands of military, security and police systems that have racked up documented human rights violations for years. Amnesty International, other human rights organizations and even the U.S. Department of State have cited Israeli police for carrying out extrajudicial executions and other unlawful killings, using ill treatment and torture (even against children), suppression of freedom of expression/association including through government surveillance, and excessive use of force against peaceful protesters. Public or private funds spent to train our domestic police in Israel should concern all of us. Many of the abuses documented, parallel violations by Israeli military, security and police officials. The Department of Justice report cited Baltimore police for using aggressive tactics that "escalate encounters and stifle public cooperation." This leads, the report said, to use of unreasonable force during interactions for minor infractions, such as quality of life matters. Furthermore, the report details how an overall lack of training leads to excessive force being used against those with mental health issues, juveniles and people who present "little or no threat against others," such as those already restrained. For years, Amnesty International has found Israeli military, security and police forces responsible for the same behavior. In one case, a 28-year-old Palestinian man, not suspected of any crime except being present during a raid, was killed in what appears to have been an extrajudicial execution by Israeli forces, including an*

169

undercover police unit, during a raid on al-Ahli hospital in Hebron November 2015. Eyewitnesses report that when Israeli forces entered the hospital room where the suspect was recuperating, they immediately shot his cousin. There was no attempt to arrest him or to use non-lethal alternatives before shooting him dead. This is one example among many. https://www.amnestyusa.org/with-whom-are-many-u-s-police-departments-training-with-a-chronic-human-rights-violator-israel/. In response to this tsunami of froth two hours later Rebecca Long-Bailey@RLong_Bailey tweeted: *I retweeted Maxine Peake's article because of her significant achievements and because the thrust of her argument is to stay in the Labour Party. It wasn't intended to be an endorsement of all aspects of the article.* Frank@AhoFrank retorted: *Rebecca, not only did you not do yourself a favour, you helped smear Maxine Peak, by validating the notion that she said something wrong or unacceptable and that therefore there must be something dodgy about her. Another good person given to the smearers as target practice* And Silvi Vee@Allanastweets commented: *You did nothing wrong in the first place, Rebecca. But you've been here before and lost a lot of support in the process. It's time to decide what you feel about an article, a situation, a person. Allowing some to bully you into making apologetic statements is not a good look.* And Vanity Ⓥ@VanityXv commented: *And there I was thinking you'd grown a backbone.* Ellis moved on. He became aware of a new piece by Craig Murray: **Truly Shameful BBC Israeli Propaganda**: *In a genuinely outrageous piece of victim blaming, BBC News just blamed Palestinian intransigence in refusing to accept Israeli annexation of the West Bank for the deaths of Palestinian children caused by the Israeli blockade of medical supplies to Gaza. This is a precise quote from the BBC TV News presenter headline at 10.30am:* "The lives of hundreds of sick Palestinian children are being put at risk because of the latest downturn in relations between their leaders and Israel last month. The Palestinian President said his government was giving up on past peace agreements because of Israeli plans to annex parts of the West Bank. That decision stopped co-operation on many security and civil matters including medical and travel permits." *There followed a heart rending piece by BBC Middle East correspondent Yolande Knell featuring Palestinian children in Gaza dying of varous medical conditions and their distraught mothers. The entire piece very plainly blamed Palestinian officials for the situation. The BBC did not blame Israel for placing a blockade illegally preventing pharmaceuticals and medical supplies from entering Gaza – the basic reason the children cannot be treated at home. The BBC did not blame Israel for blockading in illegally the civilian population of Gaza, so that these children cannot freely leave for treatment in Europe without Israeli clearance. The BBC did not point out that the proposed annexation of the West Bank is illegal, has been condemned by the UN Secretary General and by 95% of the governments of the world, and will precipitate great violence. No, the BBC*

170

blamed the Palestinians. *"Accept the illegal annexation of still more of your land, or small children will die and it will be your fault".* That is a line the BBC are perfectly happy to push out on behalf of Israel. It is an astonishing moment for the UK state propagandist. It is important we do not ourselves become complacent at this absolutely unacceptable behaviour.
https://www.craigmurray.org.uk/archives/2020/06/truly-shameful-bbc-israeli-propaganda/. Ellis did not return to the internet until 16.57 when clicking on Twitter he encountered the headline: **Rebecca Long-Bailey sacked for sharing article that contained an antisemitic conspiracy theory**. A spokesman for Labour leader Keir Starmer said he had sacked her because "The article Rebecca shared earlier today contained an antisemitic conspiracy theory". Dame Margaret Hodge tweeted *This is what rebuilding trust with the Jewish community looks like.* Marie van der Zyl was ecstatic, as was Jonathan Goldstein, chair of the Jewish Leadership Council. Oliver Kamm was delighted. Fence-sitting, slithy Owen Jones gyred and gimbled in the wabe, remarking *Starmer's team should have settled for Long Bailey saying sorry, that sentence about the Israeli army is wrong.* Nick Cohen was delighted by the sacking. Bonnie Greer was scandalised by what Maxine Peake said. Slithy Miriam Mirwitch frothed how she was heartbroken by *a dangerous conspiracy theory.* And a wit using the pseudonym Han Matcock tweeted: *So stating a verifiable fact that some US police forces are trained by Israelis is now antisemitic. We are officially through the looking glass. The Labour party is finished.* Ellis came across a new piece by Basit Mahmood on the newsweek.com website. *A commissioner at the U.K. equalities watchdog failed to declare her donations and fundraising activities for the Conservative Party, Newsweek International can reveal. Pavita Cooper, who is a commissioner at the Equalities and Human Rights Commission (EHRC) made donations totalling £7,000 to a Conservative MP and to the Conservative Party itself.* Not really a surprise. The EHRC was a right-wing ruling class organisation, not some sort of impartial body. Meanwhile a further 149 coronavirus-related deaths were reported in the UK, bringing the death total to 43,230. Bournemouth Beach was crowded and featured as a top news story for raising the likelihood of a second wave of coronvirus infection. The second story on the 10pm Sky News was the firing of Rebecca Long-Bailey. The story was framed entirely according to Zionist ideology, and the Zionist Mike Katz was invited to comment. In bed Ellis read a few pages of the chapter on The Flaubert Apocrypha. The epigraph to this chapter made him think once again of Israel. It is not what they built. It is what they knocked down. It is not the houses. It is the spaces between the houses. It is not the streets that exist. It is the streets that no longer exist.

Ellis woke at 4.50am and got up at 6am. It was another bright sunny morning. He drank tea and read Daniel Finn's new article on the *Jacobin* website: **Jeremy Corbyn's Opponents Burned the House Down to Stop Him - Now Keir Starmer is King of the Ashes**. It included a critique of the Equalities and Human Rights Commission (EHRC), which in May 2019 announced a formal investigation of the Labour Party, in response to submissions from the tiny pro-Israel propaganda outfit, the Campaign Against Antisemitism, and the pro-Israel so-called Jewish Labour Movement. The EHRC's *criteria for launching investigations are strictly political, in the worst sense of the term*, wrote Finn. He observed the EHRC's reluctance to investigate the Conservative Party for racism. The Muslim Council of Britain (MCB) first asked the EHRC to investigate the Conservative Party in May 2019. The EHRC didn't even bother to reply. The MCB asked again in November 2019. Finn commented *The Conservative Party is racist in every conceivable way*. He cited a number of examples. *By dragging its heels, the EHRC ensured that the Tories would go into last year's election campaign without the stigma of being officially investigated for racism. The MCB submitted a new dossier in March 2020, with exhaustive documentation of Tory racism, but the EHRC could only say that it was "actively considering what, if any, action" it might take. Two months later, it ceased "actively considering" anything and authorized the Conservative Party to investigate itself. To describe this as a case of double standards would be the understatement of the decade. It is objectively impossible for anyone to believe that the Labour Party merits investigation for racism, yet the Tories do not. Instead of protecting the rights of ethnic minorities, the EHRC is functioning as a protective shield for racism in high places.* Later in the article Daniel Finn reminisced how *it's barely six months since a motley crew of celebrities signed an open letter urging people not to vote for Labour, supposedly because of concerns about antisemitism. They issued no such appeal against a vote for the Conservatives, implicitly granting their approval to the party of Windrush and the "hostile environment". Instead of being laughed out of town, these pompous hypocrites received front-page treatment from the liberal press.* Finn went on to observe that the consortium which took over the ailing *Jewish Chronicle*, keeping on its editor Stephen Pollard, was headed by the former director of communications for Theresa May, the ex-Labour MP John Woodcock, and none other than John Ware, responsible for the mendacious Panorama programme on the Labour Party and supposed anti-Semitism. Ellis finished reading the article. There was nothing he disagreed with. But what was lacking was any acknowledgement of Jeremy Corbyn's failures as a leader, any interpretation of the term 'the Jewish community' and any analysis of the corporate media, especially the BBC and the *Guardian*. Nor did Finn mention the fact that the EHRC's governance involved right-wing Jews. Corbyn's multiple failings as a leader included appeasing his critics, disloyally dumping old comrades and allies, a lack of pugnacity, and sheer strategic ineptitude. Above all, he revealed himself to be shallow and intellectually vapid. But the catastrophe of Corbyn's unsuitability for leadership was still nowhere admitted on the Left. At 7am Ellis listened to the 'Today' programme. Jon Lansman was on, supposedly to defend Rebecca Long-Bailey. He was hopeless. The interviewer, Justin Webb, framed the dialogue in classic Zionist terms. Why did people pick on Israel, say, and not Iran or Russia? Ellis could think of two replies to that. One was that neither Iran nor Russia was involved in training US cops in techniques of repression. The second was that Israel was above all the creation of the British state. The creators and implementers of the Balfour Declaration were cynical racist imperialists, who believed it would be good for the British Empire to have a European Jewish settler state take control of Palestine. It would protect the Suez Canal. The natives must not be permitted either democracy or a state, or for that matter weapons. It clouded over. Ellis went into the back garden and picked up the large open black plastic box which he used for storing used glass bottles. He brought it into the kitchen and set it down. To his alarm there was motion in the box, something alive. Another movement and Ellis saw that it was a frog. He quickly picked the box up, took it outside, and gently tipped it. The frog hopped out and fled back into its world. Ellis took the box back indoors. He went shopping and bought potatoes, tomatoes, avocadoes, bananas, yogurt, milk and a large kitchen roll. Next he visited the bottle bank and deposited a handful of glass jars and wine bottles. By nine it had started pelting with rain. Soon it was pouring down. Ellis went to one more shop, for a bag of apples. Back home again Ellis drifted on through the Twittersphere. Asa Winstanley tweeted: *More than anything, Rebecca Long-Bailey, Jon Lansman, John McDonnell and - yes - even Jeremy Corbyn himself all brought this disaster for the Labour left on themselves. The moment they bought into the "Labour antisemitism crisis" lies, it was all over.* Drifting on, Ellis came across a tweet by the author Philip Pullman, applauding Keir Starmer's decision to sack Rebecca Long-Bailey. Ellis was indifferent to Pullman's fiction and now his indifference was coloured by the knowledge that Pullman was just another wealthy reactionary. Next he read a thread by a Jew called Sara Gibbs, another slithery pseudo-liberal who was keen to connect Maxine Peake's remark to *a widespread far-right conspiracy theory that Jews are trying to start a race war & given that there have been multiple incidents of Jews as a collective being blamed for anti-Black racism.* What is this woman on about? Ellis wondered. There was the usual vacuum of reference when a Zionist apologist began heaping up excuses for a violent racist colonialist settler state. She wrote of *falsehoods about the state of Israel rooted in long-held antisemitic tropes* (eh?) and *an age-old blood libel where historically Jews have been accused of secretly orchestrating disasters.* The usual blustering Zionist apologetics completely disconnected from the facts of the case. No surprise to learn that this woman writes for *Have I Got News For You*, the programme which provided a platform for Boris Johnson to become a national figure, and which also allowed Jimmy Saville and Nigel Farage to project themselves as amiable and amusing clowns. Yousef Qandeel tweeted: *Just like on the ground, Israeli occupation of the Labour Party seems to have reached the point of annexation.* Linda Grant was with Starmer - no surprise that this *Guardian* resident Zio was part of the mob. Ditto the ubiquitous David Schneider, who linked to a piece he'd written on the *Independent* website on 9 May 2019, **Here's how to talk about Israel without sliding into antisemitism**. It begins with an anecdote about someone writing *Free Palestine* on an exhibition commemorating the Holocaust. Schneider was scandalised that someone thought "all Jews, even those who died in the Holocaust" were "somehow responsible for Palestinian suffering". But this was, as ever, reference-free. What exhibition, where, organised by whom? It evaded the reality that Holocaust memorial was, almost invariably, orchestrated by Zionists for the purpose of maintaining a sense of perpetual Jewish victimhood. Ironically, Schneider's article was illustrated with 14 photographs headlined **Protests against Labour antisemitism** (as if the phenomenon *actually existed*, rather than being a moral panic concocted by Jewish racists). The photographs included people who were prominent pro-Israel fanatics, as well as right-wing Blairites like Chukka Umunna and Stella Creasy. Schneider then proceeded to give his first tip: *(1) Be precise in your language. Avoid saying "Zionist" or "Zionism".* Oh really? That's a bit like saying *"when discussing the German state 1933-1945 do not use the term 'Nazi' or 'Nazism'.* Schneider claims that these phrases are *too often used by hardcore antisemites to mean simply Jew.* No evidence for this claim is supplied. Besides, apart from the fact that Zionism was a political movement with a history and an agenda - the seizure of Palestine - it is important to use the term precisely because it distinguishes between Jews who support Israel and define their identity by adherence to the sectarian Jewish supremacist colonial state and those Jews who do not. A Zionist who is *fighting to achieve justice for Palestinians* is a tautology, just as much as a *Jewish and democratic state* is. *(2)Do not assert that Israel is controlling everything or paying money to MPs, celebrities or the media to act as they do.* Eh? Ellis had never encountered any such claims on the Left, so Schneider was setting up a straw man. Schneider was however fudging the fact that Israeli did invest heavily in propaganda on a variety of levels. It lured unprincipled rock musicians like Radiohead and Nick Cave to come and perform on stolen land in venues to which Palestinians were denied access. MPs *did* receive money from supporters of Israel. Keir Starmer had received a substantial donation towards his leadership campaign and had refused to identify where that tainted campaign finance came from. *(3) Don't conflate Israel and Jews.* Hilarious. Zionists do this all the time. *If you see someone talking about Jews, antisemitism or the Holocaust and find yourself leaping straight to Israel-Palestine, think again.* And there we have it. Zionists can equate all Jews with the interests of Israel, racist Jews can squeal "anti-Semitism!" everytime anyone dares to criticise Israel, and the Holocaust has become part of the weaponry of Israel, but anyone who dares to join the dots is labelled as a racist. Holocaust memorial has, in reality, long been a tool for promoting Israel. That the 75th anniversary of the liberation of Auschwitz should be officially commemorated by world leaders at Vad Yashem in Israel was a sick joke. Israel originated in the same blood-and-soil ideology as Nazism. *(4) Avoid the terms "Israel lobby" and especially "Jewish lobby".* Another rhetorical trick by Herr Schneider. No one on the Left uses the latter term; no one on the Left should be denied the use of the first entirely accurate term. *(5) Don't accuse Jews of dual loyalty to Israel and the UK.* No, don't do that. Only accuse Zionists of this. *(5) Don't compare Israeli actions to the Nazis unless it's incredibly specific and historically justified.* And yet Zionism, like Nazism, has genocide in its DNA. From the very beginning the Zios dreamed of expelling *all* the Arabs from Palestine, in the same way that Hitler and the Nazis wished to expel all the Jews from Germany. Both ideologies believed in *Lebensraum*, achieved at the expense of an inferior people. Besides, the Nazi analogy is usually made in response to the atrocities which continue week after week. Palestinians gunned down like dogs. High-tech weaponry decapitating babies. That kind of thing. The kind of thing you never hear a squeak about on the part of David Schneider and all the others. *(7) Don't ask every Jew to condemn Israel in every tweet or comment they make.* Eh? Another preposterous straw man. In any case it's not possible to tell someone is Jewish on Twitter, unless they make a point of asserting their identity. *Jews need to be reassured at a time of rising antisemitism.* But even this last sentence is inflected with Zionism, since Britain is one of the safest places in the world to be a Jew, Zionism depends on generating the fraudulent idea that Jews are perpetually on the brink of a second mass extermination, and lastly, in those parts of the world where anti-Semitism really does exist the leaders of those states have no warmer friend than Israel. And what did David Schneider have to say about Starmer sacking Rebecca Long-Bailey? He supported it! Another example of anti-Semitism! Schneider, of course, belonged to a rabble of Jews who were always insisting it was perfectly OK to criticise Israel and yet whenever anyone did, suddenly, mysteriously, it was anti-Semitic. The same crew invariably remained silent about the latest Israeli atrocities. A passing remark by an actress evoked a tidal wave of indignation. The massacre of unarmed civilians or the latest house demolitions produced not a whisper of comment. Ellis went outside and did some weeding. The sun emerged. It was a hot afternoon. The child played with a wooden spoon. 'Bubbles,' she said, so

Ellis blew her some bubbles. Later Ellis made a cappuccino. Suddenly Rebecca Long-Bailey's demise was no longer news. **Man shot dead by police after several stabbed in Glasgow city centre.** Ellis went into the kitchen and scrubbed some Jersey Royal potatoes. Later he ate Dover sole with the potatoes, boiled, peas and tomatoes. Afterwards he ate half a nectarine, with sliced banana, blueberries, vanilla ice-cream and yogurt. **Coronavirus: UK reports 186 more COVID-19 deaths as daily count rises by more than a fifth.** The number of people who have tested positive for the virus in the UK now stands at 309,360, and the number who have died is 43,414. On the Sky News at 10pm it was stated that the events in Glasgow were not terror-related. A group of supposedly left-wing Labour MPs (Ellis laughed hollowly, or would have done had he been a character in a work of fiction) had been to see Keir Starmer regarding the firing of supposed left-winger Rebecca Long-Bailey. He had told them he wasn't changing his mind, and they had dutifully crept away. In bed Ellis finished Chapter 9 and began reading Chapter 10. Perhaps some final confirmation that mankind itself was ineradicably corrupt, he read. That life was indeed just a gaudy nightmare in the head of an imbecile?

Saturday 27th June 2020

Cool, grey, overcast. Ellis went out early shopping. He bought a *Times* and some groceries. He pushed a DVD through the letterbox of a friend who lived about a mile away. Home again, he ate a bowl of cereal with a sliced banana. Later in the day he read a critique by Daniel Finn on Twitter (26 June 2020 3:21pm) of the *New Statesman*'s Stephen Bush, who had written a defence of Keir Starmer's sacking of Rebecca Long-Bailey. Daniel Finn@DanFinn95 wrote: *Stephen Bush won a certain reputation among Labour supporters after 2015 for displaying basic professional competence in his reporting on Corbynism— something that eluded most reporters. But he always set that professionalism aside for the "Labour antisemitism" controversy. 1/ Bush apparently believes that racism in the Tory Party has not been "sufficiently acute" to warrant an EHRC investigation. Of course, he knows full well the EHRC's criteria for launching investigations have nothing to do with objective merit: it's about political expediency. 2/ Bush plays with words to insinuate that there was something sinister about Maxine Peake's comment, in which she drew a connection between two forms of state racism that have a well-documented ideological and material affinity, including the sharing of repressive techniques. 3/ The Israeli military is a brutal occupation force: fact. US police forces have received training from it: fact. The particular technique used by the officers who killed George Floyd is also routinely used by Israeli soldiers: fact. All glossed over blandly by Stephen Bush. 4/ Peake's suggestion that there was a direct causal link is a plausible inference, not an established fact (but certainly not a "conspiracy theory").* *What's beyond question is this: US police forces learn methods of racist repression from the IDF. It's all on the public record. 5/ "Why didn't she talk about Britain or France?" Bush demands to know. Those states have many crimes to answer for, but unlike Israel, they don't rule directly over an oppressed, stateless people, whose occupied land they claim as part of their own national territory. 6/ The IDF's main function, for many years now, has been to keep its boot on the necks of the Palestinians, both literally and metaphorically. The fact that US police forces are learning lessons from the South Africa of our time is extremely pertinent to the anti-racist cause. 7/ If US police forces had been receiving training from the apartheid regime in the 1980s, nobody would have dared accuse critics of "placing South Africa at the heart of a global nexus of various ills". Nor would they have split hairs over the precise content of that training. 8/ There's a palpable fear on the part of Peake's critics that anti-racist protests in the US will spill over into sympathy for the Palestinians as they face perhaps the bleakest moment in their history: isolated, downtrodden, facing a powerful state with a superpower behind it. 9/ Palestinians have seen the few politicians willing to champion their democratic rights—Jeremy Corbyn, Ilhan Omar—viciously slandered by charlatans. They need (and are entitled to) our support. Maxine Peake understands that, and she deserves nothing but praise. 10/ We've been told repeatedly that antisemitism can be inferred from a "pattern of behaviour": people don't have to say "I hate Jews". This inferential method can be—and has been—shamelessly misused, but there's nothing wrong with it in principle. Let's apply it here to Bush. 11/ From his "pattern of behaviour" (one that long precedes this article), from what he has said & neglected to say, it's reasonable to conclude that Bush thinks Palestinian lives have less value. His wilful blindness to anti-Palestinian racism is a form of that racism in itself. 12 /Bush's subjective feelings on the subject are of no real interest. Objectively, he is linking arms with anti-Palestinian racists as they try to snuff out any expression of solidarity with Palestinian democratic rights, giving their bogus talking-points a veneer of legitimacy. 13/ Pay no heed to the comfortable people who are anxious to erect firewalls between different struggles against oppression. Listen to the people with the boot on their neck instead: 14/ Listen to the people who know what a real anti-racist struggle looks like (and who know all too well how worthless the platitudes of establishment liberals are when it comes to the crunch).* Daniel Finn then linked to an article by Ronnie Kasrils, identified as 'a former South African government minister and a leading member of the African National Congress during the apartheid era': https://www.theguardian.com/commentisfree/2019/apr/03/israel-treatment-palestinians-apartheid-south-africa. In this article Ronnie Kasrils wrote: Israel's repression of Palestinian citizens, African refugees and Palestinians in the occupied West Bank and Gaza has become more brutal over time. Ethnic cleansing, land seizure, home demolition, military occupation,

bombing of Gaza and international law violations led Archbishop Tutu to declare that the treatment of Palestinians reminded him of apartheid, only worse. The parallels with South Africa are many. The Israeli prime minister, Benjamin Netanyahu, recently said: "Israel is not a state of all its citizens … Israel is the nation state of the Jewish people – and them alone." Similar racist utterances were common in apartheid South Africa. We argued that a just peace could be reached, and that white people would find security only in a unitary, non-racist, democratic society after ending the oppression of black South Africans and providing freedom and equality for all. The anti-apartheid movement grew over three decades, in concert with the liberation struggle of South Africa's people, to make a decisive difference in toppling the racist regime. Europeans refused to buy apartheid fruit; there were sports boycotts; dockworkers from Liverpool to Melbourne refused to handle South African cargo; an academic boycott turned universities into apartheid-free zones; and arms sanctions helped to shift the balance against South Africa's military. This is required huge organisational effort, grassroots mobilisation and education. Similar elements characterise today's BDS movement to isolate apartheid-like Israel. Ellis ate avocado salad. He began watching *Minority Report*. In bed that night he read to the end of Chapter 10. Do not forget that *brassière* is the French for life-jacket.

Sunday 28th June 2020

A bright sunny morning. Ellis went out at 7.10am. He bought a lettuce, strawberries, ice-cream, milk, and other items. By 8.26am clouds had appeared in the sky. When he went on Twitter he was greeted by the message: Happy Birthday, Elon Musk. Ellis read some posts by Louis Allday, Richard Seymour and Daniel Finn [@DanFinn95]. The child played with a push-along plastic butterfly on a stick that opened and closed its wings when in motion. Afterwards she pushed a supermarket trolley. Later Ellis drove the others to a beach. He helped build some sandcastles. The beach was busy but not crowded. Lunch was quiche with salad and slices of brown bloomer, followed by strawberries and ice-cream. In the afternoon it rained on and off. On Twitter he read a retweet by Richard Seymour of a retort by Alex Sobel, Labour & Co-operative MP for Leeds North West, who described himself on Twitter as 'Shadow Minister for Tourism & Heritage/Husband/Father/Jew', in which Sobel sneered at a tweet by #BlackLivesMatterUK: *As Israel moves forward with the annexation of the West Bank, and mainstream British politics is gagged of the right to critique Zionism, and Israel's settler colonial pursuits, we loudly and clearly stand beside our Palestinian comrades FREE PALESTINE.* Alex Sobel produced one of the standard Zionist defences for anyone who criticised Israel: *I'm looking forward to your support of the West Papuan people who's* [sic] *occupation started 5 years earlier.* Etc, etc. To which 'The Justin Horton Show'@ejhchess had replied: *Show me another people, other than the Palestinians, with whom solidarity is delegitimised unless you show a similar record of solidarity with some other people first. What Alex Sobel is doing here is racism.* In an accompanying tweet 'The Justin Horton Show' wrote: *This is the whole problem with the why-are-you-singling-out-Israel business (which has itself, become "omnipresent"). It singles out the Palestinians. It stigmatises them and their supporters, and them alone.* In an accompanying tweet 'The Justin Horton Show' commented: *You can say all you like that it's alright to criticise Israel but the necessary, inevitable consequence of demanding people's bona fides in this way is that criticism of Israel is not just muted but delegitimised.* In an accompanying tweet 'The Justin Horton Show' added: *If critics are placed under suspicion in this way as a matter of routine then the whole business of objecting to the subjugation and dispossession of the Palestinians is similarly placed under suspicion.* In an accompanying tweet 'The Justin Horton Show' commented: *So if you ask me who else have I objected to, before I object to what Israel does, the answer will be that it's none of your business. I won't make any performative declarations for you.* In an accompanying tweet 'The Justin Horton Show' commented: *We've been singling out the Palestinians for more than seventy years now. That's the reality, and it's a reality that may come horribly to a head next month. And all the hounding of their sympathisers has helped that happen.* Ellis had never heard of Alex Sobel before. He was struck by just how many Labour MPs were avid defenders of a violent, racist settler state saturated in the blood of the dispossessed, built on theft, and maintained by gerrymandering and extreme repression. The wind increased in speed, shaking the trees. It began raining again. Ellis watched a few minutes of the 10pm Sky News but quickly grew bored. A photograph of the Prime Minister doing a press-up was shown for so long that Ellis momentarily had the illusion that it was live footage and the pose was being held long enough to demonstrate just how fit and strong our great leader was. What a remarkable man blond-haired Big Brother was! Ellis switched off the television and went to bed. Such was the fierce gallantry of which Gustave was capable, he read. He would not, I am sure, have understood the significance of the convolvulus.

Monday 29th June 2020

A dull, cloudy day. Strong winds were forecast later in the day. The state radio sang the praises of the government's programme for schools. £1 billion would be spent on building projects! Another glorious statistic! Pay attention, Winston Smith! Later there was an interview with Michael Rosen, about surviving his Covid-19 infection. The physical impact was profound. He was still weak. He'd been in an induced coma for seven weeks. Later Ellis went out to buy tomatoes, quiche, a loaf of brown bread, four crispy white rolls. After that he went to the fishmonger and bought smoked haddock, cod and two salmon fillets. The child played with a spoon and then with a soft toy giraffe. Later in the day it was reported that Iran had issued an arrest warrant for U.S. President Donald Trump and 35 others over the killing of top general Qassem Soleimani and has asked Interpol for help, Tehran prosecutor Ali Alqasimehr said today, according to the Fars news agency. Alqasimehr said the warrant had been issued on charges of murder and terrorist action. This was not reported on the Sky 10pm news, or, as far as Ellis could tell, by BBC News. In bed he reached the end of Chapter 11. Slip your fingers down my wrist once more. There, I told you so.

Tuesday 30th June 2020

Cold and grey. On the 'Today' programme a woman described how her husband, Mal, had been in an induced coma for eleven weeks. Weeks ago she and her two teenage children had been invited to say their farewells. His chances of survival were negligible. But amazingly he had survived, although he had lost fingers and toes through amputation and he might well in the future require dialysis. There was an also an interview with Dame Cressida Dick, the blood-spattered Commissioner of the Metropolitan Police, whose responsibility for the execution of Jean-Charles de Menezes was tactfully never mentioned by the kind of fawning corporate news journalist employed by the BBC. Dick referred at one point to *so-called* Black and Minority Ethic people. The prefix was revealing, Ellis felt. At the end of the programme, the last item before the 9am news headlines, was an interview with Candice Carty-Williams and Bernardine Evaristo. The former had won the 'Book of the Year' prize for *Queenie* and the latter had won the Author of the Year prize. They were the first black authors to win these prizes. Ellis looked up *Queenie* and read that it was *The "painful and comic" story of a 25 year-old black woman living in London, straddling two cultures and slotting neatly into neither…its eponymous protagonist works at a national newspaper where she's constantly forced to compare herself to her white middle class peers. As the novel opens, we find her in the middle of a messy break up from her long-term white boyfriend, and seeking comfort in all the wrong places.* The book was marketed as *a black Bridget Jones.* Ellis looked up Candice Carty-Williams and discovered she was from the world of publishing, having served internships with Melville House, 4th Estate and William Collins, as a marketing executive at the HarperCollins imprint 4th Estate, and then at Vintage as a senior marketing executive. She was also a mentor on the Penguin Books 'Write Now' scheme. Candice Carty-Williams has also written for *Vogue*, the *Sunday Times*, *i-D*, *Refinery29*, *BEAT Magazine* and *Black Ballad*. In January 2020 she began writing a weekly books column for the *Guardian*. Ellis made himself a cappuccino and ate a toasted and buttered hot cross bun. That evening he watched the second episode of the second series of

The Split. Afterwards, in bed, he read Chapter 12 of *Flaubert's Parrot.*

Wednesday 1st July 2020

Cold, grey, overcast. On the state radio there was an interview with Husam Zomlot about the impending Israeli annexation of the occupied West Bank. Ellis had never heard of Zomlot. It transpired that he was head of the Palestine Mission in London. A Fatah hack. He was a poor speaker. He seemed still in thrall to the fantasy of 'the two state solution'. There was some blather about 'the peace process'. It was feeble, mushy stuff. Ellis made himself a cappuccino. The child seemed a little subdued. Her mother lay on the floor and she climbed on her back. She took hold of some of her mother's hair and began to pull on it. She chuckled. It was an amusing game. Outside it remained overcast and dull. Coronavirus cases worldwide: 10,599,525. Deaths: 514,298. In the UK: 312,654 known cases of infection; official death total 43,730. Ellis went out and bought some limescale cleaner, a loaf of bread, mushrooms, strawberries. Later that day it rained. For the main meal of the day: cheese soufflé, boiled potatoes, broccoli, cauliflower, mushrooms, followed by strawberries with ice-cream and yogurt. He watched two more episodes of *The Split.* The belligerent high-powered lawyer representing the devious controlling black TV celebrity - was that Duck Face from *Four Weddings and a Funeral*? Ellis did some research on the internet. Yes, it was! In bed Ellis read Chapter 13 and SECTION A of Chapter 14.

Thursday 2nd July 2020

The sun pushing through streaky layers of thinning cloud. Ellis did not wake until 6.50am, which was late for him. The state radio was describing the growth in Coronavirus death and infection in the United States. Lord Heseltine waffled about how to get the economy moving again. Something about Hong Kong. The corporate media loved Hong Kong. Brave fighters for democracy standing up against brutal China! The same media which was silent about British complicity in mass killings in the Yemen. The same media which sanitised the massacre of unarmed Palestinians by the Israeli army as 'clashes'. It never ended, the reproduction of one set of values - imperialist, reactionary, inhumane - at the expense of the opposite set of values. Climate catastrophe was the greatest issue of all, yet the corporate media mentioned it intermittently, and even then it was usually marginalised. A small item on page nine. A brief item towards the end of half an hour of visual infotainment. And later, on Twitter, he read on MSM_Critique@MSM_Critique: *Last night Saudi and UAE forces bombed Sana'a, they used UK and US war planes to do this. UK and US military personal assist with targeting, weapons procurement and mission briefings.*

Without UK and US assistance this bombing would stop within days. And elsewhere Ellis read that the High Court had ruled that the Venezuelan government was not entitled to the £820 million of gold reserves which the Bank of England held on behalf of Venezuela. The unelected Juan Guaidó, who declared himself acting President of Venezuela last year, asked the Bank of England not to hand the gold over to the Maduro government. A lawyer for Venezuela's Central Bank pointed to the fact that the UK has an ambassador in Caracas and that the Maduro-appointed Venezuelan ambassador to London remains in her post in London as proof of the UK's recognition of the Maduro government. Another lawyer for Venezuela's Central Bank commented that this judgement entirely ignored "the reality of the situation on the ground" saying that Mr Maduro's government was "in complete control of Venezuela and its administrative institutions". This episode showed yet again that the British judiciary was highly politicised under its spurious mask of objectivity and impartiality. Judges were predominantly white males from wealthy conservative backgrounds. They could be relied upon to serve capital, state power and imperialism in its many incarnations. It began to rain. The child wore a baseball hat, back-to-front. She nibbled a rice cracker. The rain gurgled down the waste pipes on the outside of the house. Ellis pan-fried salmon steak, with hand-cut chips, tomatoes and boiled peas. Afterwards: strawberries and blueberries with vanilla ice-cream. He watched the fifth episode of the second series of *The Split*. In bed he reached the final chapter of *Flaubert's Parrot*. We continued through the museum until we reached the room containing the parrot, Ellis read. Overcome by fatigue he put out the light and fell into a deep sleep.

Friday 3rd July 2020

A warm, cloudy, blustery day. Ellis did not wake until 7.10am. He spent much of the day in hard physical labour, excavating a trench. He talked briefly to a neighbour. For lunch he ate an egg salad with a slice of buttered stoneground bread, followed by a sliced Granny Smith's apple with yogurt. The child had fun emptying a cupboard in the kitchen. The state broadcaster reported the easing of British restrictions on international air travel. On Twitter Ellis learned that Stanley Johnson, the Prime Minister's father, had travelled to Greece, in defiance of lockdown restrictions. Ellis had a bath and changed. The wind seemed to be blowing more strongly. A little before 8pm it began raining. From the internet Ellis learned that Sir David Starkey had made a racist remark. Acording to BBC News: *Starkey told an online show hosted by conservative commentator Darren Grimes that slavery was not genocide, because of the survival of "so many damn blacks".* The *Independent* website was altogether more accurate: While speaking about the Black Lives Matter protests, the 75-year-old, who specialises in Tudor history, said: "Slavery was not genocide otherwise there wouldn't be so many damn blacks in Africa or Britain, would there? An awful lot of them survived." Helen the Zen@helenmallam tweeted: *David Starkey, Boris Johnson, Nigel Farage, Katie Hopkins - all notorious racists, all made household names by the BBC.* Lee@MXOFO tweeted: *Can we also remember that David Starkey, in addition to being a despicable racist, is also a sub-average historian. His books are distinctly pedestrian and unoriginal.* Craig Murray tweeted: *David Starkey has been known to the BBC as a racist for at least nine years. But you cannot be too right-wing for the BBC and it has never stopped them inviting him on to spread his poison.* In the kitchen Ellis listened to Van Morrison singing 'Almost Independence Day'. Later, Ellis watched the final episode of *The Split*, series 2. In bed he finished the novel. At the Museum of Natural History the narrator of *Flaubert's Parrot* gets to view the three last remaining Amazonian parrots in the collection and reflects that perhaps one of them is the one that belonged to Flaubert. Ellis read on the back cover that the novel had been shortlisted for the Booker Prize in 1984. It did not win.

Saturday 4th July 2020

Grey, warm, overcast, windy. Outside, Ellis felt a dusting of very light rain. Minutes later it had ceased. The state broadcaster spoke of the reopening in England today of pubs, restaurants, hairdressers and cinemas. A publican was interviewed. He hoped it would be a sunny day. Ellis looked up who had won the 1984 Booker Prize. It was Anita Brookner, for *Hotel du Lac.* Confirmed UK cases of Covid-19 infection: 284,276. New cases 544. UK deaths: 44,131. On Twitter, Ellis read zampa.info@info_zampa: *It is a bitter irony that the UK anti-semitism witch-hunt - ostensibly a campaign against discrimination and oppression - is in large part about protecting Israel's apartheid discrimination and oppression.* For his lunch he ate toasted cheese with salad, followed by a sliced apple with yogurt. Ellis continued with his digging, then had a bath. A neighbour called. The telephone rang. Happy Independence Day! The child sat in a foamy bath, playing with her three plastic boats. That evening Ellis watched the first two episodes of *The Salisbury Poisonings*. Nina from *The Split* was the cop's wife - not such a juicy role, although it grew in the second episode. And the greatest Shakespearean actor of the age - Jonathan Slinger - popped up as a top Porton Down scientist. It was slick entertainment, full of dramatic phone calls, people running, flashing blue lights, army vehicles. But many of the mysteries of this affair went unacknowledged. It was like BBC News. It invited no questions and did not even acknowledge that questions existed. Afterwards Ellis watched the 10pm Sky News. It was supposedly *Super Saturday*. A street in Soho was pictured, packed with people drinking, talking and flouting the social distancing rule. Ellis went to bed.

183

Sunday 5th July 2020

Ellis woke a little before 6am, then lay in a half-sleep until 7am. The state radio reported the concerns of a Police Federation spokesman that young people were indifferent to social distancing. The state broadcaster publicised a 5pm national street display of support for the National Health Service, involving the clapping of hands and (no doubt) the hitting of pans with spoons. Another fatuous display of orchestrated unity, straight out of *Nineteen Eighty-Four*. It was designed, of course, to deflect from the Tory government's catastrophic mishandling of the pandemic. Ellis would not be participating. Ellis wondered how many of those who involved themselves in this exercise knew of the history and origins of the NHS, and of the politicians and vested interests which had bitterly opposed and obstructed the establishment of this service. A blowy day, cloudy-bright. The child held a picked flower, a weed. Ellis chatted to a neighbour about plumbing and paint. Supper was roast chicken with microwaved rice, boiled sweetcorn, followed by strawberries, nectarine and ice-cream. He watched the third and final episode of *The Salisbury Poisonings*. It was oddly moving. Ellis wondered how much of it was true. The poignant human drama masked all kinds of questions. Why did the Skripals collapse simultaneously? Why was Detective Sergeant Bailey's family not affected by the contamination of their home? Was the sealed perfume bottle containing novichok a back-up supply? Why would you need such a supply if only a tiny amount of novichok was lethal? And there were other dimensions which the programme did not go near. It seemed very likely that Skripal had continued to be involved in intelligence work since being allowed to leave Russia. Perhaps in fifty years the full story would emerge. Ellis could not be bothered to watch the 10pm Sky News. He went to bed.

Monday 6th July 2020

A blue sky at 6.50am. But it was still windy. When Ellis left the bedroom the door slammed shut behind him. He made himself a mug of tea. Once dressed he went out to post an envelope containing a cutting from Saturday's *Times*. As he slipped the envelope into the pillar box mouth his hand brushed the edge. He realised he should have worn gloves. Someone infected with Coronavirus might have done the same just ten minutes earlier. Or perhaps (very much less likely, though) a dodgy Russian had sprayed novichok on the surface. It clouded over and looked as if it might rain. The child wore an apron and pushed a broom across the floor. Then she put on her red hat. In the afternoon it rained. The rain stopped and the sun came out. Ellis did some more digging. He felt tired and had a bath. That evening he ate microwaved rice with cold chicken and salad. He read some old newspapers. He watched Sky News at 10pm. It led with the story of how Bianca Williams, a black athlete, and her partner Ricardo dos Santos and their baby, had been in their car when it had been stopped by police in London. The police had no valid reason for stopping the car. They had stopped it on suspicion because it was an expensive vehicle being driven by a black man. The police were aggressive. One of the officers drew his truncheon. After a verbal confrontation, in which Bianca Williams had declined to step out of the car leaving her baby behind, the couple were dragged out and handcuffed. Some of it was filmed on a mobile phone. The episode followed a sequence of similar episodes in recent days and weeks. Later the Sky reporter Beth Rigby conducted a fawning interview with Andrea Leadsom. It was about the economy and business. Beth Rigby had all the edge of a cushion. No wonder politicians were always willing to be interviewed by her. Ellis went to bed.

Tuesday 7th July 2020

The sun shone through a scattering of light cloud. On the state broadcaster David Lammy MP was asked about the Bianca Williams incident. He was told that the Metropolitan Police's Professional Standards unit had investigated and decided that the officers had done nothing wrong. David Lammy asked them to look at it again. That was the sum of his response. What a feeble, useless individual Lammy was, Ellis thought. A typical Labour MP. Devoid of critical intelligence, devoid of even the faintest spark of radicalism. A purveyor of sludge and fudge. Dampening down dissent and anger - that was what the Labour Party existed for. The Parliamentary Labour Party was stuffed with careerists, mediocrities and reactionaries. Ellis went off and made himself a cappuccino. Later, on Twitter, he came across a link to the Metropolitan Police statement about the Bianca Williams incident. But the link did not work. The Met had evidently withdrawn their first attempt to justify the actions of their officers. Ellis remembered the case of Jean Charles de Menezes, 27, executed by the Metropolitan Police at Stockwell underground station on 22 July 2005. As soon as the Met knew they had shot dead a wholly innocent man the Met's PR team sprang into action. The corporate media was fed a number of lies, to cover-up the gross incompetence of the Met. It was reported that Menezes had been challenged outside the station and had ignored police and ran inside. Menezes had jumped over a turnstile. He ran down the escalator. He was wearing a large winter coat on a hot summer's day. His behaviour was highly suspicious. And so on. All these were outright fabrications but these lies, amplified by the corporate media, served to muffle what had occurred. In fact de Menezes was wearing jeans and a light denim jacket. He was very visibly not a suicide bomber. That the officer in charge of this state excution was Cressida Dick only served to underline how violent, corrupt and rotten was the British state. Instead of being sacked, she was promoted! (That was the Met, displaying its characteristic arrogance and contempt for the public.) She was then giving an honour! And now she was Commissioner! Naturally no fawning corporate journalist ever dared to remind viewers or listeners of what occurred fifteen years ago. The bloodstains which were splashed across Dick's uniform were never adverted to. The execution of Menezes had also been steeped in racism. The officers following him that day reported that he had 'Mongolian eyes'. The officers who shot him claimed they had first challenged him. The officers claimed they shouted 'Armed police!' *Alas* none of the passengers in the carriage supported these claims. Eleven bullets were fired into Jean Charles de Menezes, seven into his head. It was later revealed that hollow-point bullets had been used, which explode inside the victim. The corpse of Jean Charles de Menezes was unrecognisable. The post mortem report, written by Dr Kenneth Shorrock five days after the shooting, recorded Menezes as vaulting over the ticket barriers and running down the stairs. Dr Kenneth Shorrock told the inquest he had been told this by a police officer, but, *alas!* he could not remember which one. The movements of Menezes and the police officers following him should have been extensively captured on CCTV. But, *alas!* the footage on the bus was strangely incomplete. This was perhaps the result of vibration, which had prevented several cameras on the bus from working. Remarkably, *alas!* there were problems with the CCTV cameras on the train carriage and *alas!* also on the station platform. Any suggestion that that the Metropolitan Police was involved in a wide-ranging conspiracy to pervert the course of justice is naturally inconceivable, unspeakable, unwriteable. The following year Cressida Dick was promoted to Deputy Assistant Commissioner and in 2010 she was awarded the Queen's Police Medal. The Metropolitan Police tactic of shooting Jean Charles de Menezes was, it later transpired, based in part on advice from the murderous Israeli armed forces. It was odd, thought Ellis, how the toxic poison of Zionism leaked into so many aspects of British life. He made himself another cappuccino. A light rain fell all afternoon and in the evening. Ells finished reading Saturday's *Times* and read some more of the new issue of *Private Eye*. He watched the 10pm news headlines, then switched off. In bed he read for a while, then put out the light and fell into a deep sleep.

Wednesday 8th July 2020

A warm grey morning, the sky almost white, a soft continuing drizzle falling. This day is the 48th anniversary of the assassination of Ghassan Kanafani and his teenage niece Lamees Najim by Jewish barbarians. Child murder does not stir the conscience of this type of Jew, the Zionist. From its beginnings, political Zionism was always a sly, violent, racist ideology, which attached itself to imperialist power. The killing of Ghassan Kanafani was one of the great cultural crimes of the twentieth century, and it is virtually unknown in Europe, Britain, the USA and those other cultural zones where bad Germans and bad Russians are the enduring focus of selective and complacent state and intellectual remembrance. Ellis went online and read a piece by one Esther Walker published on the website of the *Times of Israel.* He read *Esther Walker is a final year History BA student at King's College London.She is part of the KCL Israel Society and is the CAMERA on Campus Fellow at King's.* The blog post turned out to be an attack on the King's College London Action Palestine (KCLAP) for publishing a piece on Ghassan Kanafani by Elias Khoury. By so doing KCLAP, wrote Esther Walker, "has once again proven to be a society vehemently bent on demonising Israel at all costs, even going as far as to actively promote and glorify antisemitic conspiracy theorists such as Khoury, and the intellectual mouthpieces of terrorism such as the late Kanafani." What was remarkable (and yet typical) about this rancid Zionist outpouring was Esther Walker's passing reference to Khassan's "death in 1972". No details, naturally. The accurate term would be assassination (along with the murder of Kanafani's teenage niece, Lamees Najim). But killing children has never stirred the conscience of Jews who are Zionists. The Zionists only want one child martyr - Anne Frank. They want Lamees Najim erased from history, along with Palestine. The Zionist Esther Walker wrote, "Despite not necessarily yielding *[sic]* a gun or a knife himself, Kanafani's literary works have undoubtedly justified and inspired brutality - the Lod Massacre being just one example." On this specious basis it is OK to murder intellectuals and writers. This kind of fanaticism and moral blankness is characteristic of the morals of the so-called "Jewish community", thought Ellis. The same gang who piously use Holocaust memorial as an intoxicant for their trembling sense of victimhood. Ghassan Kanafani's writing, wrote Esther Walker, "reveals the weakness of the Palestinians' fight - a prolonged conflict based on falsities and a warped history". And yet, of course, it was predominantly Jewish historians who had exposed the ugly, violent and racist origins of the Jewish state. On Twitter Ellis read a post by @ZaatarOuZeit: *Ghassan Kanafani was assassinated on this day, 48 years ago. His assassination marked the start of Israel's assassination campaigns against Prominent resistance figureheads, such as Kamal Udwan, Kamal Nasser, Wael Zueiter, Youssef Najjar, Ali Hassan Salameh, etc.* On Twitter, posted on the account of Alex Shams, Ellis came across an interview with Ghassan Kanafani, conducted in Beirut in 1970 by Richard Carleton, an Australian. *The history of the world is the history of weak people fighting strong people,* said Kanafani. He proceeded to shred the easygoing banalities of the interviewer, who was a characteristic corporate journalist. Why not end the violence? Why not talk to the Israeli leaders? *That kind of conversation between the sword and the neck, you mean? I have never seen any talk between a colonialist case and a national liberation movement.* On Louis Allday's Twitter account Ellis came across this tweet of 8 July 2019: *Kanafani's ability to express himself like this and present the Palestinian cause so adeptly to different audiences in both English and*

Arabic is exactly why the Israelis murdered him. Elsewhere on Twitter the day's big issue was 'A Letter on Justice and Open Debate' published by *Harper's Magazine*. It was an assemblage of pious platitudes deploring 'the restriction of debate' and complaining that 'it is now all too common to hear calls for swift and severe retribution in response to perceived transgressions of speech and thought'. Plaintively it cried out: 'We need to preserve the possibility of good-faith disagreement without dire professional consequences.' It was all very vague and none of the generalisations was connected to a single example of what was being meant. Alarm bells started to ring the moment Ellis looked at the list of signatories. A rabble of celebrities, reactionaries and belligerent Zionists, peppered with one or two liberals and, astonishingly, Noam Chomsky. Ellis was even more surprised to see that Media Lens had given this letter the thumbs up. The letter had wailed on behalf of 'journalists who fear for their livelihoods if they depart from the consensus' and yet surely the whole thrust of the Media Lens analysis was that corporate journalists only functioned at all by adhering to the medium's orthodoxy. Every prominent BBC news journalist came from a similar class background, was wealthy, and operated within the same framework of values. Ellis assumed that this ludicrous letter had been spawned by the fuss surrounding a recent controversial tweet by the cold, Corbyn-hating, multi-millionaire J. K. Rowling. (Rowling, le Carré, McEwan - how they all loathed the man who stood for a more humane foreign policy and an increase in income tax for people like themselves.) On Twitter there was no shortage of commentary observing the stark hypocrisy of certain signatories, who had themselves tried to hound, sometimes successfully, pro-Palestinian academics from their jobs. A tweeter, **thearetical@Thearetical** rather neatly summed it all up. *That #HarpersLetter is ridiculous, intentionally vague, and exceptionally inconsiderate. Disappointed to see names on there that I formerly respected. If nothing else, it highlights the paradox of liberal intellectuals— "hold power to account, certainly…as long as it's not mine".* Ellis ate a cheese roll. He returned toTwitter, where Ben Norton had tweeted: *My take on this stupid Harper's letter: Hell yeah, let's bring an actual open debate to the US media! Start with giving a platform to anti-imperialists… Oh wait, that's never gonna happen. Because they don't actually care about free speech. They just don't wanna be criticized.* Ben Norton had also tweeted: *This farce of a letter is signed by a bunch of warmongers and actual war criminals who control corporate media narratives and have never had their free speech stifled. Ever. Also a big chunk of these signatories support locking up journalist Julian Assange.* Norton also tweeted: *Key signatures on this extremely stupid Harper's letter (1/2):* **War criminal:** *-David Frum* **Imperial propagandist war hawks:** *- Anne Applebaum -Anne-Marie Slaughter -Bari Weiss -Shadi Hamid -Michael Walzer* **Actual CIA agent:** *-Gloria Steinem* **Jeffrey Epstein associate:** *-Steven Pinker.* And: *Key signatures on this extremely stupid Harper's letter (2/2):* **Total** *intellectual fraud / sophist snake oil salesman*: -Francis Fukuyama **Sweatshop defender**: -Matthew Yglesias **Awful musical influence**: -Wynton Marsalis **Lol**: - Yascha Mounk **Perpetually disappointing**: -Noam Chomsky Outside it had stopped raining. Later Ellis pan-fried Dover sole with tomatoes, mashed potatoes, boiled peas, followed by strawberries and ice-cream. He watched the first two episodes of *Line of Duty*, the first series. He went to bed. He read for a little while, then slept.

Thursday 9th July 2020

Another damp, grey, overcast morning. The state radio was extolling the marvels of the Chancellor's mini-budget. £10 off a meal in participating restaurants in August! The offer did not tempt Ellis. He had never particularly enjoyed eating out, except perhaps outside, in pub gardens, in warm sunshine, with good beer, fish and chips, and good company. Fine food had never really interested him. Mid-morning he went shopping. Bananas, blueberries, strawberries, yogurt, milk, ice-cream. Later he did some digging. It began to rain. He had a shower and changed. He watched the 5pm briefing, given on this day by the culture secretary, Oliver Dowding. Journalists asked questions and Dowding waffled and huffed and puffed. Later Ellis ate a chicken casserole. He watched episode 3 of *Line of Duty*. He went to bed and read a few pages of a book by an author he had grown to dislike intensely, then slept.

Friday 10th July 2020

Ellis lay in bed, a little drowsy. Outside he could hear two people laughing. A dog-walker holding a conversation with someone else on the far side of the street. Grey and dull but a pale watery sunlight was trying to leak through. On the state radio the proprietor of a chain of leisure centres was explaining how new safety procedures had been introduced. But the issue of changing rooms in swimming pools was not addressed and corporate journalist Martha Kearney never bothered to ask. You could always rely on a BBC journalist to avoid the difficult questions, no matter what the topic. Softball questioning, it was called. Pleasant and fuzzy and always falling back on a shared 'common sense'. Never being difficult to anyone except, perhaps, a trade union leader defending strike action, or someone outside the acceptable framework of the BBC News ideology. Later Ellis went to the bottle bank. No one anywhere seemed to be wearing facemasks. In the afternoon it began to rain. The child had a temperature and seemed subdued. A Covid-19 test was recommended, and was duly performed. Calpol brought the temperature down a little. Ellis pan-fried salmon, tomatoes, hand-cut chips. He watched the final two episodes of series one of *Line of Duty*. It was a very watchable drama, although the final episode ended with a flurry of over-simplistic closures. In bed he read a few more pages of a careless and annoying book. *It is relatively normal round here for people to fly their own tiny private aeroplanes*, smirked the smug author, who lived in Suffolk. The book had been loaned to him by a friend and Ellis was anxious to get it read so that he could return it.

Saturday 11th July 2020

Bright and sunny but with a slight coolness on the edge of the warmth. Ellis drank a cappuccino and read Jonathan Cook's article **Writers' open letter against 'cancel culture' is about stifling free speech, not protecting it**. Later it clouded over. The coronavirus test proved negative. But the child still had a temperature and continued to be subdued. She loaded her buggy with four soft toys. Ellis spent much of the day digging. In the evening he ate pasta with vegetables in a cheese sauce. He watched the first two episodes of *Mrs America*. It was okay, nothing special. Light entertainment. What had happened to Tracey Ullman, wondered Ellis. She looked as if she had been dipped in chocolate. On the 10pm TV news a reporter stood beside a derelict well which had been examined earlier that day by Portuguese police searching for the remains of Madeleine McCann. Ellis went to bed and read a few more pages of the irritating book.

Sunday 12th July 2020

Bright and sunny. Ellis listened to the state broadcaster's 7am news bulletin. President Trump had worn a facemask in public for the first time. The number of UK border staff was to be increased in preparation for Brexit. It had been suggested that the dead footballer Jack Charlton be given a posthumous knighthood. Ellis later went online to catch up with Ben White's tweets. On 9 July Ben White@benabyad tweeted: *Israeli occupation forces arrested 18 Palestinians in pre-dawn raids today, including yet another university student.* That same day he tweeted: *Birzeit University statement, 22 June: "More than 80 students are currently held in Israeli prisons...and thirteen students are still being held in Al-Moscobiyyeh interrogation centre. One staff member and assistant researcher is also under detention."* The next day he tweeted: *Last night, Israeli occupation forces shot & killed Ibrahim Mustafa Abu-Yaaqoub outside the village of Kifl Hares & injured one other.* The casual slaughter of Palestinians by the Jewish state's army continued, muffled by the silence of the BBC and the rest of the corporate media. Ellis went out to return some books to his local library, which had recently re-opened. He did some shopping. Raspberries, milk, yogurt, Rinse Aid… The child was still subdued. She lay in her mother's arms, her eyelids flickering. Soon she was asleep. Later Ellis read

Peter Beinart's essay, 'Yavne: A Jewish Case for Equality in Israel-Palestine'. That evening Ellis dined outdoors. Roast chicken, rice, salad. Later he watched the third episode of *Mrs America*. This was quite enough, he felt. Corporate television was never very good at dramatising politics. He would watch no more. *Line of Duty* was far more engaging. In bed he finished reading the annoying book. He began a new book, *From New York to California*. This was more like it! After only a couple of pages Ellis laughed out loud. *What are you laughing at?* Ellis read out the sentence.

Monday 13th July 2020

A bright sunny morning; cloudless blue sky. Very warm. The state radio talked of the changes which would come with Brexit. There would be new border controls. The state radio reported that the Trump administration had criticised Anthony Fauci, a member of the White House coronavirus task force, for his criticisms of the US handling of the pandemic. Dr Fauci had said the USA was not 'doing great' when compared to other countries. Brett Giroir rejected Dr Fauci's assessment, saying: 'He looks at it from a very narrow public health point of view.' The USA has a quarter of the almost 13 million coronavirus cases around the world, and is currently experiencing a surge of infections in many states. Globally, more than 230,000 news cases were reported yesterday, the World Health Authority says. Globally there have been 12.9 million confirmed cases since the outbreak began, with 568,000 deaths. The child seemed better today. She grinned and played with a toy shopping bag. Ellis went online. He came across Yair Wallach's interesting response to the Peter Beinart article. Ellis ate a plate of cheese on toast. As he did so, spilling crumbs, he read on the website of the *Observer* an interview with Nicola Barker **The offbeat novelist on the difficulty of writing novels about writing novels – and sitting on her roof to watch the sun rise.** Nicola Barker described her work in progress: *An epic Victorian novel which is now three different books that I'm writing at the same time.* **Who is the living author you most admire?** *I have to say Ali Smith, because I love her joyfulness, her energy, her integrity. It's just so easy to love everything about her. The whole package.* Ellis walked past a restaurant, which was crowded, every outdoor table taken. Some of the diners were only a metre away from the next table. It was a warm evening. People lingered in the High Street. Ellis returned home. He ate cold chicken with boiled potatoes and salad, followed by a bowl of raspberries, blueberries and sliced nectarine, with ice-cream spread on top. In bed he read more of *From New York to California*. He was enjoying it greatly. But then he came to these words: *I was reminded of a time when I'd been walking in Timna Park, in Israel's Negev desert, and in particular how I'd been fascinated there by…* A sentence like that immediately cast a shadow over the text. It raised questions. There was a tradition of people reporting what a marvellous/interesting/delightful/fascinating time they'd had on their holiday in Israel. These people were often apologists for Zionist terror. Ellis read a few more pages then put out his bedside light.

Tuesday 14th July 2020

The 7am news. The wearing of facemasks was to become compulsory in English shops as from a week on Friday. Non-compliance might be punished with a £100 fine. The state radio had an interview with the Mayor of London, Sadiq Khan. He boasted that on the London underground a similar measure had produced 90% compliance. That did not sound impressive. Scientists say the UK could see 120,000 new coronavirus deaths in a second wave of infections this winter. 'This is not a prediction - but it is a possibility,' said Professor Stephen Holgate, a respiratory specialist from University Hospital Southampton NHS Trust. Research suggests that the virus can survive longer in colder conditions and is more likely to spread among people indoors. Ellis drank tea and ate a bowl of cereal. He went online and looked up the author of *From New York to California* on the internet. *As well as writing novels, I have worked in the UK film and TV industry for nearly twenty years...* So perhaps it was for work purposes. Ellis looked up Timna Park on Wikipedia and read *The Jewish National Fund, a non-profit organization that aids in the development of Israel, funded the creation of many of the non-historic tourist and family attractions and activities in the park.* It was another reminder that Wikipedia was an utterly unreliable resource on anything at all to do with Israel, politics or anything that was debatable. The JNF was at the heart of the Zionist dispossession of Palestine and had been long before the ethnic cleansing of 1948. Its mission was to 'redeem' land for Jews, in perpetuity. It was the grateful recipient of the massive land thefts of 1948. *From New York to California* was plainly an imitation of *The Rings of Saturn*, but far more comic in tone. The comparison once again made Ellis wonder why the biography-in-progress of Sebald still hadn't been completed and published. In less than six months time it would be the nineteenth anniversary of Sebald's death. That was a long time to wait for a biography of a well-known writer widely regarded as being of classic status. Ellis this day revisited the site of Sebald's sudden death. A grey morning and a dull location, despite the rural setting. A place without echoes, drenched in particulates and fumes. The noise of passing vehicles moving at 50mph. In the afternoon, feeling exhausted, Ellis lay down on the sofa and fell asleep. When he woke it was ten to five. He made himself a cup of tea. The child was much better today. That evening he watched the first two episodes of the second series of *Line of Duty*. It was compelling viewing, although the body count was improbably high. It was a myth that being a police officer was a dangerous, high-risk occupation. More people died on building sites, much more regularly. The death by violence of a police officer on duty was relatively rare in Britain. But it was a clever idea to approach the tired genre of crime fiction through the lens of an anti-corruption police task force. In bed Ellis read the sentence: *They all came here, attracted to an empty sky and an empty land and no one to watch them thrive or fail.* It was strange how the pervasiveness of the mythology of violent colonising Jews contaminated even the most innocent of sentences, he thought. He put out the light and fell quickly into a long sleep.

Wednesday 15th July 2020

Bright and sunny. Ellis woke at 6.50am. He listened to the 7am news headlines. The spread of Coronavirus infection in Blackburn was the top story. Later it clouded over. The child held up a stone. 'Stone,' she said. She chuckled. She was better. Ellis walked a circular route, calling in to buy some shopping on the way. He wore a facemask in the store, the only person to do so. He bought new potatoes, tomatoes, a loaf of bread, yogurt. In the afternoon it began raining. He learned that Judy Dyble had died. He ate two sausages, boiled potato, cabbage. He watched two more episodes of *Line of Duty.* The plot was now preposterous but it was easy to suspend disbelief while watching the adrenalin-pumping sequence of events. Keeley Hawes, who had seemed guilty, now appeared innocent. But would there be a further twist? Ellis couldn't be bothered to watch Sky News. He went to bed and read as far as the chapter titled 'Scolt Head'.

Thursday 16th July 2020

Grey and cool. It looked as if it might rain later. Ellis went out at 8.15am to post a letter. Later he drank a cappuccino and surfed the internet. He learned that the *Guardian* was planning to sack yet more employees: *110 in departments such as advertising, Guardian Jobs, marketing roles, and the Guardian Live events business, with 70 coming from editorial. The editor-in-chief, Katharine Viner, and the Guardian Media Group chief executive, Annette Thomas, said in a joint statement to staff that the pandemic had created an "unsustainable financial outlook for the Guardian" with revenues expected to be down by more than £25m on the year's budget.* The reason for the *Guardian*'s massive drop in purchasers of hard copy was naturally not acknowledged, let alone analaysed. Ellis could only project from his own experience: a loyal, lifetime reader who stopped buying the newspaper when in August 2014, amid the latest Israeli high-tech massacre of Palestinian civilians, it chose to run a full-page vile, defamatory Zionist advertisement attacking Hamas for 'child sacrifice' and claiming it used children as human shields. Even *The Times* had declined to run the advert, on the grounds that the wording was 'too strong' and might 'cause concern' among its readers. Since that year the *Guardian* had lurched even further to the right. Its all-consuming hatred of Jeremy Corbyn in his role as new leader of the Labour Party was a matter of record. Together with BBC News, the *Guardian* had aggressively promoted the fabricated claim that Labour under Corbyn was seething with anti-Semitism. Sadly, Corbyn's weaknesses as a leader (timidity and a lazy disinclination to engage with detail) repeatedly allowed his enemies to destroy him. The *Guardian* was a rancid Blairite in-house journal which had evidently alienated a vast swathe of its readership. The last ABC circulation figures indicated daily sales were down again, bobbing around the 100,000 mark and exposing an immense decline from the 4 million plus circulation it had once enjoyed. Elsewhere, Ellis read about the latest desperate efforts of the Israeli state to defame Palestinian activism. *Online profiles describe him as a coffee-lover and politics junkie who was raised in a traditional Jewish home. His half-dozen freelance editorials and blog posts reveal an active interest in anti-Semitism and Jewish affairs, with bylines in the* Jerusalem Post *and the* Times of Israel. *The catch? Oliver Taylor seems to be an elaborate fiction.* Taylor claimed to be a student at the University of Birmingham, but the University had no record him. What's more, the fake 'Oliver Taylor' uses a synthetic image: *experts in deceptive imagery used state-of-the-art forensic analysis programs to determine that Taylor's profile photo is a hyper-realistic forgery - a "deepfake".* In an article in US Zionist propaganda outlet *The Algemeiner*, Taylor had accused London academic Mazen Masri and his wife, Palestinian rights campaigner Ryvka Barnard, of being 'known terrorist sympathizers'. It was Mazen Masri who drew international attention in 2018 when he helped launch an Israeli lawsuit against the surveillance company NSO on behalf of alleged victims of the company's phone hacking technology. *Six experts interviewed by Reuters say the image has the characteristics of a deepfake. 'The distortion and inconsistencies in the background are a tell-tale sign of a synthesized image, as are a few glitches around his neck and collar,' said digital image forensics pioneer Hany Farid, who teaches at the University of California, Berkeley. Artist Mario Klingemann, who regularly uses deepfakes in his work, said the photo 'has all the hallmarks. I'm 100 percent sure'.* On the Media Lens twitter page Ellis came across a recent tweet by **Andrew Neil**@afneil: *Devastating resignation letter from senior @nyt journalist Bari Weiss, who says, in effect, that the Twitter lynch mobs now edit the New York Times.* There was a link to the website of *Spectator USA*, which reproduced the letter, prefaced by the comment that *Weiss was much loathed by many of the paper's younger and more militantly 'progressive' staff. Today, Weiss announced that she is indeed leaving America's most famous publication. Her excoriating departure letter is worth quoting in full.* Ellis duly read the letter. What a crock, he thought. It boiled down to two things. One was unsubstantiated claims of bullying - claims which always needed to be taken with a very large pinch of salt when made by an apologist for Israel. Secondly, it was a long whine about being criticised on Twitter. And that was always the problem for corporate journalists. Their corporate platforms supplied them with a large audience but Twitter offered readers the chance to respond. Some responded by politely exposing the said corporate journalists for inaccuracy or hypocrisy or for political bias. Bullying was often the word used by those who had simply been criticised. Ellis laughed hollowly at Weiss's pious assertion of 'the necessity of resisting tribalism' - a bit rich for a someone who had dedicated her career to an aggressive defence of Israel. Like many privileged and reactionary individuals, Weiss wallowed in a sense of victimhood. Laughably, she cast herself as Winston Smith. 'My own forays into Wrongthink have made me the subject of constant bullying by colleagues who disagree with my views. They have called me a Nazi and a racist; I have learned to brush off comments about how I'm "writing about the Jews again".' The Jews? Or perhaps Israel? An analysis of the subject matter of Weiss's articles in the *New York Times* would be helpful. Bari Weiss wrote: '*New York Times* employees publicly smear me as a liar and a bigot on Twitter.' You'd think she might quote some examples, but none were supplied. Her Zionism leaked into her long whinge: 'We attached an editor's note on a travel story about Jaffa shortly after it was published because it "failed to touch on important aspects of Jaffa's makeup and its history". But there is still none appended to Cheryl Strayed's fawning interview with the writer Alice Walker.' Although there was no detail supplied, and Ellis had never read these pieces, he could guess what she objected to. And so it went on. Weiss never reflected on all the voices and opinions which the *New York Times* had been excluding for decades. She ended up quoting Adolph Ochs, but where the *New York Times* was concerned Ellis felt Phil Ochs was more pertinent. *Love me, I'm a liberal.* A song which never dated. Ellis read some of the responses to Andrew Neil's preposterous tweet. **Henry Tanguy**@HenryTanguy wrote: *She resigned -- she was not fired. She has tried to get colleagues fired for disagreeing with her views on Twitter. She (and apparently you) believe that free speech means that you get to pontificate from a prestige platform and not have to suffer any criticism. Ludicrous.* **spectacle, testicles, wallet and watch**@BilbarCooks wrote: *I'll be honest I don't reckon rich white people getting told off online is really comparable to lynching. It's actually quite a tasteless juxtaposition.* **Frank**@AhoFrank wrote: *I would say the kicking out of Chris Hedges was more devastating for the New York Times than the departure of that rather dim woman of whom nobody can explain what she has done to deserve all that attention.* **Mehdi Hasan**@mehdirhasan wrote: *The Bari Weiss resignation letter has so much wrong with it, but what stands out is the claim "centrists" are discriminated against. Centrists? They're the majority at @nytopinion! There are no pro-Bernie, pro-Palestinian or - dare I say it - pro-Trump columnists at the paper.* The sun tried to break through the clouds, without success. On the website of *The Grayzone* Ellis read a critique of Bari

Weiss by Max Blumenthal and Ben Norton (https://thegrayzone.com/2020/07/15/bari-weiss-cancel-culture-israel/), who wrote: *Before Bari Weiss branded herself as an avatar of free thought, she established herself as the queen of a particular kind of cancel culture. The 36-year-old pundit has dedicated a significant portion of her adult life to destroying the careers of critics of Israel, tarring them as anti-Semites, and carrying out the kind of defamation campaigns that would result in her targets losing their jobs.* They also wrote: *In her three-year career as an editor of the opinion section of the newspaper of record, Weiss devoted a significant chunk of her columns to attacking her left-wing critics, while complaining endlessly of the haters in her Twitter mentions (which is risible given her lamentation in her resignation letter that "Twitter has become [the Times'] ultimate editor").* Ellis went outside and did some digging. The child ate a low-sugar biscuit. 'Biscuit,' she said. She looked longingly at the tin where the adult biscuits were kept. They were sweeter. In the afternoon Ellis came across the Twitter debate about the sackings at the *Guardian*. There were those who thought the paper's financial crisis was a tragedy for the Left and those who regarded it as the deserved consequence of its contempt for its readership. **Louis**@Louis_Allday commented: *The function of the Guardian is to propagate imperialist propaganda with a leftist veneer on foreign policy & block even a minor shift to the left domestically, hence its campaign against Corbyn. It's pro-imperialist, pro-capitalist & is an enemy of anyone who wants real change.* Reading through more responses to the news about the *Guardian*'s financial difficulties Ellis was startled to come across a new tweet by **Laura Alvarez**@LauraAlvarezJC: *For our mental health and future it's important to stop buying the Guardian.* If Ellis was not mistaken this was Mrs Jeremy Corbyn. Tweet number 1283726451360047104. It's a shame Corbyn hadn't come out fighting against the *Guardian*'s regular sewage-flow of bogus Labour Party anti-Semitism stories when he was leader, Ellis thought. **Caitlin Johnstone**@caitoz wrote: *The Guardian is the single most destructive and despicable propaganda publication in the English-speaking world and the entire thing deserves to be completely obliterated.* **Matt Kennard**@DCKennard commented: *If the Guardian/Obs had engaged with and even faintly promoted the most exciting opening for the left in Britain in generations from 2015-19, I think its future could have been bright. Instead it dedicated itself to destroying Corbyn and smearing the movement. Suicidal decision. 11:32 am · 16 Jul 2020* **CEO of Antifa**@RebootedStef quoted from an infamous column by Nick Cohen which appealed to any person intending to vote for Jeremy Corbyn as leader to *stop being a fucking fool by changing your fucking mind.* This was the language of the Blairite neo-liberals who inhabited the *Guardian* and *Observer*. And as **CEO of Antifa** remarked: *What right-wing newspaper would print columns calling large sections of their readers 'fucking fools'? And the Guardian wonder why people on the left aren't* *rushing to defend them?* Later Ellis watched two wagtails at play. He ate baked vegetables scattered with cheese. He watched episodes five and six of *Line of Duty*. He found the last episode a little perplexing. He was still unsure who had ordered the hit on Tommy and his police guard. In bed he read the chapter about the night on Scolt Head, the chapter about Holkham beach, and the chapter about Wells-next-the-Sea. The author never mentioned where he left his bicycle at night, which seemed particularly odd where Scolt Head was concerned. Ellis fell into a deep sleep.

Friday 17th July 2020

Ellis woke at 6.10am. A bright sunlit day. The top stories on the state broadcaster's radio news were the rapidly increasing figures for Coronavirus infection and death in Brazil and alleged Russian cyberhacking. The last story was obviously a red herring (pun unintentional) designed to deflect attention from the forthcoming release of the long-delayed government report into supposed Russian interference in the last general election. The day became hotter. A tattooed Scotsman made a delivery. Ellis drank cappuccino. Someone wrote on Twitter that the *Guardian* was getting rid of its cartoonist, Steve Bell. If true, this made sense. Bell was probably the last socialist left on this Blairite rag. Later Ellis did more digging. To his surprise he found a spherical object about one inch in diameter. It felt heavy. It was plainly not a pebble. He had a strong suspicion that it was a musket ball. But from what period? Later, he searched the internet, without enlightenment. The child dragged her new blue chair along the ground. Then she tried pushing it, as if it had wheels. Next she went to a cupboard in the kitchen and took out a plastic box containing breakfast cereal in the form of tiny circles. She reached in and stuffed a handful of cereal into her mouth. That evening Ellis ate salad and pasta with a tuna sauce. He watched the first episode of series three of *Line of Duty*. It began with what appeared to be a loosely fictionalised version of the shooting dead of Mark Duggan in Tottenham in 2011. What was ludicrous about the drama was that it portrayed the police as rigorously investigating themselves. That made *Line of Duty* simultaneously both edgy - cops were shown as violent, unpleasant and corrupt - and tepidly reactionary (good cops weed out the bad cops). In bed Ellis read the short Walsingham chapter and the first page of the next one. But he was too tired to read any more. He put out the light and fell into a deep sleep.

Saturday 18th July 2020

Bright and sunny at 8am, cloudy and overcast by 9.50am. Ellis drank coffee and read the account on Wikipedia of the killing of Mark Duggan. Ellis did not believe that the police involved in that killing had set out to kill Duggan. But he did not believe that the circumstances narrated by the officers was remotely plausible. Ellis believed that Duggan had jumped out of the taxi holding his mobile phone, which the cops had mistaken for a gun. They had shot him. Since there seemed to be little dispute that Duggan had been transporting an illegal firearm which would have been used in the future for criminal purposes it seemed to Ellis unlikely that a jury would have convicted any of the cops involved. The gun was alleged to have been in Duggan's possession at the time of his killing. Mysteriously it had flown some 20 feet to a location behind a fence. The hasty removal of the taxi from the scene after the killing was quite extraordinary, yet no corporate journalist ever dared to ask why. The media were briefed that Duggan had shot at police from inside the taxi - a lie dutifully recycled by the BBC News, which could always be relied upon to pervert the truth, distort or lie when required to do so. The so-called 'Independent Police Complaints Commission' had naturally adopted a kneeling position throughout its risible 'investigation'. The Wikipedia article mentioned the Forensic Architecture analysis of the killing. Ellis found it online. It noted that *In the hours following Duggan's death, multiple news reports falsely described an incident in which an individual had opened fire, injuring an officer. The Daily Mail called Duggan a 'gangsta', while the Guardian reported an 'exchange of fire'.* What's more, *By 6 August, two days after his death, Duggan's family had still not been formally contacted by the Metropolitan Police.* In the aftermath a protest which began in Tottenham spread across the country, resulting in widespread damage to property, five deaths, 3,000 arrests and vindictive and punitive sentencing by the judiciary. Ellis watched the Forensic Architcture documentary. He was startled to discover that there was no evidence that Duggan had had his mobile phone in his hand when he was shot dead. From the documentary a reasonable suspicion might be that drawn that Duggan had been shot dead without in any way posing a threat. Perhaps the most astonishing revelation of all was that Forensic Architecture had discovered that the one piece of film of the aftermath of the killing had been tampered with, a section surreptitiously removed at the point where a particular officer might have entered the taxi and removed the gun. There seemed to be evidence of a conspiracy to pervert the course of justice. The documentary underlined just how feeble the supposedly 'independent' investigation had been, and how this investigation had reproduced false assumptions instead of analysing, challenging and exposing them. Almost nine years had passed. Ellis knew the spot where Mark Duggan had been gunned down. He had seen Tottenham burn. An unforgettable sight. He remembered the pair of police helicopters beaming their searchlights down. He remembered the long aftermath. The police vehicle parked there for hours, displaying enlarged images of the faces of suspects wanted for riot. Black faces, mostly. It was a hot day. The clouds rolled over, extinguishing the final glimmer of sunlight. Ellis went shopping. Milk, coffee, bananas, apples, plain yogurt. A pack of sausages. Breakfast cereal. To his fury an elderly man walked through the marked-out yellow zone that Ellis was standing in, jumping the queue while he was lifting a carton of milk off the shelf. Ellis had to suppress an urge to confront the man. A cretinous Conservative, most probably. Boris Johnson himself kept subverting the notion that in a pandemic social distancing should be maintained. Boris Johnson wanted business back on track, irrespective of the health risks to workers. Later, on the internet, Ellis read about the latest atrocity in the Yemen. A bombing raid involving the RAF had killed 24 civilians in al-Jawf province. But none of this was on BBC News, which continued to suppress the vicious, violent reality of British foreign policy. Ellis went out and watered some plants in pots. Afterwards he showered and changed. On the Twitter page of the novelist Benjamin Myers he read: *I don't know about other writers, but a review of ones* [sic] *book in The Guardian remains the pinnacle of achievement.* Wrapping up his sporadic and erratic readership of Twitter, Ellis came across Dr Louise Raw's sardonic comment on the *Guardian*'s financial crisis and the anguished appeals for donations and new subscriptions: *The Guardian is like an ex who drove you away with constant insults, laughed when you left, and is now drunk on your lawn screaming YOU RUINED MY LIFE SUSAN.* Very droll. The child played with four stones. 'Stone,' she said. She crawled on to her mother's back. 'Cuggle,' she said. That evening Ellis ate cheese soufflé with boiled potatoes, cabbage and broccoli, followed by strawberries, ice-cream and yogurt. As he ate he listened to Shawn Colvin's album *Uncovered*. Later, having loaded the dishwasher, he watched episodes two and three of the third series of *Line of Duty*. Having started with a fictionalised version of the killing of Mark Duggan, the series now incorporated the paedophile scandal involving the grotesquely obese Liberal MP Cyril Smith. The mixing of historical material with fiction reminded Ellis of a dreary play about the Labour Party by David Hare he had seen a few years ago. It featured a bit of fictionalised Kinnock, a bit of fictionalised Benn. Or so he remembered. What he chiefly remembered was how unsatisfactory Hare's representation of the Labour Party had been. But then Ellis had never had any regard for Hare. He was the dramatist of the liberal bourgeoisie. A critical analysis of his drama would surely reveal the same values as those propagated by the *Guardian*. And then of course there was that knighthood. Nothing was quite so revealing as the way in which so many of Britrain's supposed cultural elite fell to their knees to accept with gratitude an Honour bestowed by a blood-spattered government and a cretinous royalty. Ellis went to bed and read the chapter about Blakeney and the chapter about Cley-next-the-sea. The book was turning into an autobiography as much as a travel account. The influence of Sebald continued to be blatant. Ellis wanted to know much more about Sebald's private life and the foundations of his creativity, whereas he was essentially indifferent to what the author of *New York to*

California revealed about himself. This book increasingly resembled journalism - entertaining, slick, scattering nuggets of curious knowledge. But at heart strangely empty, devoid of profundity. It was like a ten-minute visit to a museum. You might marvel at the exhibits but you would depart having learned little or nothing. Ellis put out the light.

Sunday 19th July 2020

Warm but cloudy. Raindrops clung to the windscreens of parked cars, indicating a light brief shower in the night. Ellis walked the quiet streets. He returned home and wrote a letter. In the garden the child pulled off her mother's shoes. It was a dull day. Ellis continued reading an acclaimed history of Gaza by Jean-Pierre Filiu. He kept forgetting that Tzahal, sometimes Tsahal, which was not in the index of organisations or individuals, meant IDF. That evening he ate roast chicken with salad and basmati rice, followed by strawberries with ice-cream and yogurt. He watched two more episodes of *Line of Duty*. The body count became increasingly implausible, and the possibility of AC12 ever existing in the manner portrayed was surely tosh. But it was oddly compulsive viewing, by the tepid standards of BBC drama. In bed he read to the end of the second part of *New York to California*. At 11.35pm he put out the light.

Monday 20th July 2020

Bright and sunny. The alarm shrilled at 6.55am. Ellis lay in bed,listening to the headlines on the state radio. The government had signed deals for experimental virus vaccine doses. There were security concerns about the English Coronavirus track and trace system. There were rising tensions with China, with the imminent suspension of the extradition agreement with Hong Kong. Ellis went to the bank, which was empty. He went to a supermarket and bought milk, bread, Lurpak, salad dressing, rice, two types of cheese, a quiche, potatoes, two packs of salmon. He wore a facemask, as did two other shoppers. Most did not. He went to the bakery for croissants and later ate an oven-warmed almond croissant, while drinking cappuccino and reading more of the news section of Saturday's *Times*. He read about Johnny Depp's tumultuous relationship with Amber Heard. On the internet he read of Ahmed Masoud's photographs of the Demolition Order which he'd placed on the Orde Wingate memorial on the embankment in London. It read **DEMOLITION ORDER - THIS MONUMENT THREATENS THE PEACE, SECURITY, RIGHTS AND CULTURE OF THE PALESTINIAN PEOPLE. #PalestinianLivesMatter #StopAnnexation** Ellis had long thought that if any statue in London deserved to be torn down (or in this instance erased) it was this disgusting monument to a psychotic murderer and torturer. Ellis continued reading Jean-Pierre Filiu's history of Gaza. The child played with her stone. It looked like rain but no rain fell. Ellis watered some pots. He ate cold chicken with mashed potato and salad. He watched the final episode of the third series of *Line of Duty*. The body count continued to rise to an improbable degree. In bed he read as far as the pages devoted to the Holiday Inn on the outskirts of Norwich, across the road from the cattle market.

Tuesday 21st July 2020

Ellis woke a little after 5am and dozed in the light-filled bedroom. At 5.45am he went to put the kettle on and draw back the curtains. A bright, sunlit morning with a cloudless blue sky. He went online and looked up the Holiday Inn described in *New York to California*. Ellis discovered there were no less than four Holiday Inns in Norwich, three of which were on the outskirts. It took him some time to work out that the author was referring to the one in the south of the city, not far from the Ipswich Road. It was not a part of Norwich that Ellis knew, despite his long years of association with this city. Ellis went back to bed to listen to the 7am headlines. Then he drifted into semi-consciousness. A little after 8am he dressed and made a cappuccino. He drank it while reading material on the internet. From the Twitter account of Ahmed Masoud he learned that Carlos Ruiz Zafón had died last month. He was best known for his novel *The Shadow of the Wind* (*La sombra del viento*). The BBC described it as 'an international hit in 2001, published in 50 countries'. Ellis dimly remembered seeing it in bookshops at the time. He had scrutinised its prose, then put it down. Had his indifference been premature? Ellis went on Amazon. The gushing reviews put him off. The book sounded like populist Borges with a large helping of Umberto Eco, wrapped in a slick commercial narrative. Ellis had yet to find a Spanish writer he liked. He'd read Javier Marías's *A Heart So White* and not enjoyed it. The prose seemed tired ('my sense of impending doom'), the adjectives lazy. *Cadaverous*, for instance. Had the author ever seen a cadaver? Had his readers? There were moments that reminded Ellis of a Hollywood plot. *It was then that a memory returned to me.* Ah, yes. The conveniently remembered scene from many years earlier, recalled in lavish detail. There had been a time, directed by reviews in the *Guardian* and elsewhere, when Ellis read every acclaimed new novel. Not to have done so would have felt like missing out on the temper of the time. But now Ellis had grown indifferent to contemporary fiction. He was bored by it. The banal creative-writing-school prose, the plots which scattered little mysteries, sometimes a big mystery, which would be solved at the end. The twists. The sprawling sagas, where the chief character ended up in the USA. The social problem novels. The voices of the north. The novelists with a cute back story which could not but evoke a sigh from a bourgeoisie which always reminded Ellis of the Phil Ochs song about

201

liberals. Ellis felt as alienated as Malcolm Lowry had done in the 1950s. Why was this transient junk being published, reviewed, televised? Literary prizes were the final seal of approval, which proud beaming novelists wore like baubles. And in one rotting corner of this swamp, the Arts Council, rewarding the momentarily fashionable, the utterly mediocre. Ellis made a telephone call. The line was a blizzard of intereference and he had to ring again. The child held her dolly, Polly. Late afternoon Ellis drove to a street he knew well. He went for a walk with his companion. They held hands and talked of a day long ago. That evening Ellis ate lamb steak with boiled potatoes, broccoli and roasted beetroot, washed down with a glass of Freixenet cava. When the 10pm Sky News cut to President Trump's live press conference Ellis quickly grew bored. He switched off the television and went to bed. He finished the chapter on Norwich market and put out the light.

Wednesday 22nd July 2020

Ellis woke at 6.45am. He went to the kitchen and put the kettle on. Later he went on Twitter. The state broadcaster gloated that the Labour Party had agreed to pay 'substantial' damages to what it was pleased to describe as 'seven whistleblowers' who had featured in the state broadcaster's tendentious 'Panorama' hatchet-job on the supposed anti-Semitism infesting the Labour Party under Jeremy Corbyn. *The BBC's assistant political editor Norman Smith said the payout was an 'extraordinary moment' and underlined leader Sir Keir Starmer's determination to get to grips with the shadow of anti-Semitism hanging over the party.* Which was the kind of garbage you could expect from the state broadcaster, that regularly turned truth on its head. What the payout underlined was Sir Keir Starmer's determination to return the party to its historic support for the Jewish state, symptomatic of his wider support for nuclear weapons, Middle Eastern torture states and deference to whatever foreign policy goals Donald Trump might care to pursue. Sir Keir wanted Britain's shrill, bellicose Zionist community to know that it had no dearer friend in their determination to deny Palestinians equality. The BBC did not mention that the Labour Party's own lawyers had advised that this case could be won by the Party and there was absolutely no need to raise the white flag of surrender. **Chris Corbett**@ChrisCorbett3 commented *If Labour had won the case it would have knocked the antisemitism narrative for six. Five years of propaganda blown wide open. Starmer and his Blairite cronies couldn't have that..* Later, in bed, Ellis continued reading *New York to California*. He read the first two pages of the Thurne River chapter, then put out the light. It was gone midnight and he felt exhausted.

A cool, grey, overcast morning. A little after 9am there was a sudden short powerful downpour. Ellis read on Twitter that John Ware was planning to sue Jeremy Corbyn over the statement he had released on his Facebook page. Ellis tracked down the statement and read it. *Labour Party members have a right to accountability and transparency of decisions taken in their name, and an effective commitment from the party to combat antisemitism and racism in all their forms. The Party's decision to apologise today and make substantial payments to former staff who sued the party in relation to last year's Panorama programme is a political decision, not a legal one. Our legal advice was that the party had a strong defence, and the evidence in the leaked Labour report that is now the subject of an NEC inquiry led by Martin Forde QC strengthened concerns about the role played by some of those who took part in the programme. The decision to settle these claims in this way is disappointing, and risks giving credibility to misleading and inaccurate allegations about action taken to tackle antisemitism in the Labour Party in recent years. To give our members the answers and justice they deserve, the inquiry led by Martin Forde must now fully address the evidence the internal report uncovered of racism, sexism, factionalism and obstruction of Labour's 2017 General Election campaign.* Ellis followed the story on Twitter and came across Justin Schlosberg's online article *BBC Panorama Investigation Into Labour Antisemitism Omitted Key Evidence and Parts of Labour's Response*, which presented a critique of the programme and commented: *it was wrong to exclude the voices of others, including Jewish Labour members, who felt and thought differently. Worse still, the programme-makers chose to ignore abundant evidence that contradicted the accounts given by the "whistleblowers"* Ellis moved on to the Media Lens website, which retweeted **Yafa Jarrar**@YafaJarrar, who reported: *Israeli Occupation Forces invaded the home of and arrested Rania Elias, director of the Yabous Cultural Centre,one of the most important #Palestinian cultural centers in #Jerusalem and her husband Suheil Khoury the director of The Edward Said National Conservatory of Music.* And: *The #IOF raided their offices, including the music conservatory, and confiscated computers and documents. This attack on Palestinian Indigenous culture is part of the settler-colonial project as well as the process of protracted cultural genocide.* And: *This attack is an extension of Israel's erasure of Palestinian presence in Jerusalem for decades. This attack is an extension of Israel's attempts to erase Palestinians' lives, history and culture.* Ellis did not go out. He spent the rest of the day reading. In bed he read as far as the mooring of the canoe at Horsey Drainage Mill. Nearly at California, now.

Friday 24th July 2020

A bright sunny morning. Today was the day that the wearing of face masks became compulsory in shops in England. The BBC seemed to be doing its best to undermine the ban by advertising the fact that Sainsbury's and Asda would take no action against customers who flouted the ban. There were vox pop interviews with people who were contemptuous of the science. The BBC talked vaguely of people with breathing difficulties not having to wear a mask. Soon it clouded over. There were a few specks of rain but no more than that. At the place where Sebald died three cyclists waited to cross the A road. Ellis drank coffee in the garden. The child held up a small brown stone. Later she threw lightweight coloured plastic balls over the grass. Ellis picked them up and threw them into the air. The child grinned. Later Ellis went shopping. Everyone in the supermarket wore a mask. Ellis bought batteries, a bottle of red wine, milk, two boxes of tissues. By 6pm the clouds had ebbed and the sunshine was back. Ellis ate a cheese roll with three tomatoes and watched the first two episodes of the fourth series of *Line of Duty*. The 10pm Sky News had a live report from Portland, Oregon, where daily protests were growing against Federal agents who wore military-style uniforms and dragged Black Lives demonstrators away, forcing them into unmarked vehicles with blacked-out windows. In bed Ellis finished *New York to California*. He put out the light.

Saturday 25th July 2020

Ellis woke at 7.10am after a solid night's sleep. A grey, overcast day. Rain was forecast later. But the forecast was often wrong, so he put the washing-machine on. *The Times* ran a story headlined **Corbyn urged to snub cash from anti-Semitic donors**. It was a classic example of the corporate media's unceasing and fraudulent efforts to connect Jeremy Corbyn to anti-Semitism. The story began: *Jeremy Corbyn is facing calls to refuse donations from people who have expressed racist views on a crowdfunding page raising money for his legal costs.* The supposed 'racist views' amounted to a donor identified as 'Jack T' who donated £20 and wrote that Corbyn had been the target of 'people within the Labour Party working on behalf of the racist state of Israel'. And who was outraged by this statement? *Ian Austin, a former Labour MP, said that Mr Corbyn should refuse money from anyone who held such views.* Ian Austin! That slithery reactionary. An acolyte of the Zionist, Gordon Brown. Ian Austin, who in 2013 had wanted the government to subsidise parents who wanted to pay to send their children to private schools. Ian Austin, who demanded greater action to limit immigration, who wanted all immigrants to be fingerprinted, and who wanted a wide range of measures to be taken against immigrants. Ian Austin of the Labour Friends of Israel. Ian Austin, who in 2012 had been obliged to apologise after falsely claiming that a Palestinian human rights group, Friends of Al-Aqsa, were Holocaust deniers. Ian Austin who in the 2005-2006 financial year claimed £21,559 under the second home allowance, just £75 short of the maximum, and then went on to claim £22,076 in the next financial year, just £34 short of the maximum allowed. He also "flipped" his second-home designation just before buying a £270,000 London apartment. He claimed £467 for a stereo system for his constituency home. He spent £2,800 furnishing his new London apartment. In February 2019 Ian Austin resigned from the Labour Party and became an independent MP. Five months later the leader of the Conservative government, Theresa May, appointed Ian Austin as Prime Ministerial Trade Envoy to Israel. In November 2019 Ian Austin announced that he would not contest his seat at the forthcoming election. He urged his constituents to vote Conservative. In December 2019, shortly before the election, Labour supporters and members received a letter from Ian Austin, urging them to vote Conservative. This saga once again raised the question as to why the Parliamentary Labour Party contained so many right-wing mediocrities. In the afternoon E came round on her father's bicycle. Tomorrow she travelled to Edinburgh. In the evening it rained. Ellis ate a vegetarian risotto. He watched two more episodes of *Line of Duty*. In bed he began reading a trashy bestseller. The prose was excruciating. This exercise was not for pleasure.

Sunday 26th July 2020

Ellis woke at 6am. At 6.45am he made himself a cup of tea. It was a bright, sunlit morning. The news headline concerned the sudden government decision that anyone flying to England from Spain must quarantine themselves for a fortnight. The first half of the morning was spent reading and making notes. Afterwards Ellis went outside. It began to cloud over. Later he went in and drank a cappuccino. The child read her fingers and toes book. For lunch Ellis ate the remains of the risotto, warmed-up in the microwave. On Twitter there was discussion of the promise by certain individuals not to proceed with legal action against the Labour Party if, in return, Jeremy Corbyn was expelled. Elsewhere there was much tweeting about a black rapper for alleged anti-Semitic remarks. Ellis knew nothing of this person or his music or tweets. Rachel Riley had naturally joined in. But she had upset Jedward, who were indignant that she had mocked their music. Ellis had dimly heard of Jedward, although they had only registered on his consciousness at the height of their fame, some years ago. Elsewhere on Twitter, Richard Seymour was defending the SWP from the charge of anti-Semitism made by someone who claimed to be a former member. Ellis returned to the book he was reading. Later on he returned to Twitter and read Joe Sucksmith's criticism of Richard Seymour for his belated acknowledgement of the failure of what he called 'The wider "radical left" ' for evading the underlying politics of the 'anti-Semitism' campaign against Jeremy Corbyn. Seymour had said the wider radical left was 'either conspicuously silent or offering bromides. We didn't want to talk about it.' Alongside this sweeping generalisation was the claim that 'The people who wanted to really address the murky underlying political issues were often people who made a complete hash of it, like Livingstone, Williamson and the Skwawkbox left.' **Joe Sucksmith** commented: *I think we need to be clear that this is really quite dishonest. The "wider radical left" was simply silent on this. It *actively facilitated* the cancelling and reputational destruction of those who pushed back… And embedded within this disingenuous accounting is a really quite problematic elitism that pits the "radical left" against the "Skwawkbox left". The "non-crank left" against the "crank left", basically. So in this new, revisionist formulation, the "cranks" are accepted to have been substantively correct (de-crankification?), but nonetheless insufficiently skilled/educated to have not "made a hash" of addressing those "murky underlying political issues"…* **Wilf of the People** added: *We need to look at the LOTO staff & NEC. To throw out antiracists like Walker, Willsman, Chris W & Ken L was an act of almost deranged appeasement. I'd like to know the exact mechanics of how exactly this strategy came about, because it was a complete disaster.* Missing from all this, Ellis felt, was any acknowledgement of Corbyn's own character. Corbyn's timidity in the face of attack, and his increasingly absurd attempts to please his enemies - his grovelling before the Jewish Labour Movement was pitiful to behold - were central to the collapse of the Corbynite left. Probably his most corrosive legacy was his opposition to increased membership participation in the choice of parliamentary candidates. Corbyn was ultimately far more to blame for the catastrophe of his leadership. But it was true that at a time of crisis a section of the left was more intent on defending the expulsion of anti-Zionists than it was in criticising that assemblage of right-wing charlatans known as 'the Jewish community'. Richard Seymour, Ally Fogg, 'A Very Public Sociologist' (PhilBC), Ash Sarkar, and not least the slippery Owen Jones, were complicit in the expulsion of individuals like Marc Wadsworth and Tony Greenstein. Greenstein, in fact, was smarter than the lot of them. He saw from the very beginning where the strategy of appeasement would lead. He also saw that you cannot understand the fraudulent 'anti-Semitism' campaign without understanding the interference of the Israeli state in British domestic politics. Nor can you understand the politics of 'the Jewish community' without understanding Zionism. **Corbynism was a mirage** commented: *There's a hierarchy of awfulness in the faux-left. Bastani and Seymour are the least awful, Segalov the most awful. Sarkar is the most annoying. But they all joined the witchhunt or stayed quiet while it was underway. Never let them forget that. Not one is credible now.* Later Ellis stumbled upon PhilBC's enthusiasm for Tracy-Ann Oberman's promotion of #NoSafeSpaceForJewHate ("48 hours of race hate and not a swingle action ," wrote Tracy-Ann Oberman). A *swingle* action? Ellis, had he been a fictional character in a novel, would have laughed bitterly at PhilBC's pitiful politics. *You don't have to be an Oberman fan to support this. Great idea.* What a poltroon PhilBC was. To align himself with a rabble of howling Zionists. Ellis pan-fried cod and ate it with new potatoes and peas. In bed he continued reading the trashy bestseller.

Monday 27th July 2020

A dull wet morning, with intermittent flurries of light rain. Ellis went shopping. He bought strawberries, tomatoes, apples, cornflakes, a loaf of bread, two quiches, a six-pack of salt and vinegar crisps. Back home again he drank a cappuccino and ate a buttered croissant with a dollop of raspberry jam. A little after noon two old friends arrived. Coffee and conversation. Lunch, then a short drive and a walk. It was a blustery day. In the evening, after the friends had departed, he scrutinised the Twitter accounts of those people he read daily, or almost daily. Later Ellis went to bed, exhausted.

Tuesday 28th July 2020

Ellis spent the day reading non-fiction, skipping from one book to another. The child sang a lullaby to her doll. On the internet Ellis read Tony Greenstein's latest blog post, about Peter Beinart's abandonment of the Jewish state in favour of a single democratic binational state. In bed he continued reading the trashy novel.

Wednesday 29th July 2020

A bright hot sunny day. The child sang Happy Birthday and dry-washed her hands. She put a hat on her head, then placed another one on top of that. Ellis watered some wilting plants. He continued reading a book about twinned cities. On Twitter he came across **Coach Letterman**@3YearLetterman. Very droll. In the afternoon Ellis had a bath, then pan-fried two salmon steaks. Later he learned that coronavirus deaths in the United States today topped 150,000. In bed he read more of the bestseller.

Thursday 30th July 2020

Ellis got up at 6.30am. A bright hot day with a cloudless blue sky. He went shopping early. Red wine, white wine, lamb steaks, croissants. One individual defied the requirement to wear a facemask. He was bearded, fiftyish, with a substantial pot belly that curved down over his belt, surging forward like a frozen wave. The teenage girl at check-out said nothing as she took his payment. Later, on the internet, Ellis read a review of the new Taylor Swift album, *Folklore*. The reviews were enthusiastic. *Her voice is a translucent beam*, Ellis read. *Her syllables fall slowly, like ash.* On Twitter he read **Michael Crick@** MichaelLCrick: *Private Eye says Guardian editor @Kath Viner was paid £391,000 last year. That's more than twice as much as the Prime Minister. And Guardian CEO Annette Thomas gets £630,000 pa plus bonuses. Shome mistake surely? Or perhaps the Guardian's financial woes aren't as bad as I thought.* To which **James Morrow**@jamorro replied: *Appalling. I worked for Guardian for 22 yrs and was given choice of redundancy or being fired after a long period of RSI, signed off by company doctor. I was in my early 50s at the time and never got a long-term job. To see these people earning this amount makes me sick & angry.* Ellis hid his face behind a cushion and then peeped out. The child rocked with laughter. Ellis carried the child seat to the car. He watered some pots. He cooked a quiche. In bed he read a few pages of the bestseller.

Friday 31st July 2020

Ellis woke at 5.25am. He made a cup of tea. It was another warm bright sunny day. On the internet he looked to see what the biographical context of Joni Mitchell's song 'Conversation' was. One source claimed it was about Mark Volman of The Turtles, who at the time the song was written was in an unhappy marriage. At 7am Ellis went shopping. He'd hoped the shops would be quiet at this time but he was wrong. The supermarket was packed. He was unable to obtain soured cream so he went to another shop. He was told they no longer stocked it. Demand was insufficent. Later, on the internet, he read of the latest episode of Israeli repression of a Palestinian voice. *Occupied Ramallah, 30 July 2020 – At around 3:30 am, tens of Israeli occupation soldiers, accompanied by at least one dog, stormed the home of Mahmoud Nawajaa, the General Coordinator of the Palestinian BDS National Committee (BNC), near Ramallah, handcuffing, blindfolding and taking him away from his wife and three young children.* Mahmoud Nawajaa, 34 years old, was born in Yatta, south Hebron, and holds a master's degree in International Relations, Ellis read. The day grew hotter. The child threw a golf ball at Ellis and roared with laughter. Ellis flinched, then picked up the golf ball and rolled it back. The meal that evening was fish and chips, bought from a restaurant operating a takeaway service. That evening Ellis went to bed early.

Saturday 1st August 2020

Ellis woke at 5.30am. A little before 7am he went to the kitchen and switched the kettle on. It was cloudy but very warm. Later the sun came out. The child lay on Ellis's right leg and grinned as he raised it into the air. In the late afternoon Ellis read Tony Greenstein's latest blog post about Mark Elf and the Labour Party. It was a sign of the degenerate and reactionary state of the Labour Party that Mark Elf had been suspended by the Party. Some years earlier Ellis and Mark Elf had been in intermittent email contact on various anti-Zionist topics. In the early evening Ellis opened a recently purchased bottle of The Unexpected. The label on the wine was different. Comparing it to the label on a half-empty bottle of The Unexpected, 2018 vintage, Ellis saw that one of the four wines that made up the blend had been changed. Also, the new bottle lacked a year. Always a bad sign in a bottle of wine. Ellis sampled the new bottle. It was not as good as the 2018 bottle, he thought. He would not be buying this wine again. Ellis went to bed early and read a few pages of the bestseller.

Sunday 2nd August 2020

A hot bright sunlit day. Ellis went to W. H. Smith and bought a copy of the *Sunday Times*. **Emails reveal officers' fears of rogue SAS execution squad**. It was rare to read something like that in the corporate media. Ellis would read the story in a day or so. His first choice was the *Culture* supplement. He read Camilla Long's hatchet job on BBC TV's *A Suitable Boy*. He skipped the two pages dedicated to the Edinburgh Fringe, which he had never been to (along with Wimbledon, the Glastonbury festival, Glyndebourne, and numerous other core activities of the white middle and posh class). Ellis read with keen interest the approving review of the new Taylor Swift album. He read the review of the memoir by a woman whose husband had tried to murder her by tampering with her parachute. On the bestsellers list pages he read: *The Sunday Times Bestsellers list of July 12 included a title with sales that were subsequently found to be ineligible. The Hardback Fiction Chart should have shown John Grisham's* Camino Winds *in eighth position, Adele Parks's* Just My Luck *in ninth position and Stephen King's* If It Bleeds *in tenth position.* This alluded to the case of the author Mark Dawson, who had confessed to buying 400 copies of his own thriller *The Cleaner* in order to get it into the hardback fiction bestsellers list. It cost him £3,600. The internet was awash with indignation. Ellis found this hilarious. To these people it was as if the bestsellers list *really mattered*. It was as if somehow the publishing industry was democratic and fair and a fearless upholder of standards. Ellis moved on. His pulse quickened and the blood drained from his face, or would have done had he been a character in a thriller. He began reading Max Hastings's review of *Soft Power*. This was the opening paragraph of the review: *I once spent a grim morning in Gaza, hearing a procession of Palestinians denounce the iniquity of the United States for indulging Israel's occupation politics. Inside those hate-filled people's houses, however, I glimpsed their children sitting before televisions, gripped by*

Hollywood movies. What a dishonest and inhumane man Max Hastings is, thought Ellis. And what a coward. Hastings would never dare to write about hate-filled Jews, even though hate-filled Jews killed Palestinian civilians with remorseless, pitiless regularity. A journalist who wrote about hate-filled Jews would immediately face a storm of frothing outrage from the usual gang of British Zionists. Hastings, who liked to think of himself as a historian, was curiously indifferent to the history of European and American interference in Gaza. If anyone was entitled to hate it was the population of Gaza - two million people sealed up inside a vast prison camp, enduring the day-long whine of surveillance drones, the tyranny of unending repression which manifested itself as bouts of carnage and sadistic destruction, while throttling the population, denying it water, electricity, even sewage disposal. Hastings's point (and that of the book he was reviewing) was a trite one. Culture was a tool in influencing foreign populations. It had a propaganda utility. This point had long ago been made in *Who Paid the Piper?* by Frances Stonor Saunders. It clouded over. The child brought Ellis a toy ketchup bottle and a toy tin of tomatoes. Later he pushed her supermarket trolley around her as she whooped with laughter and ran up and down. In the evening there was a sudden unexpected downpour.

Monday 3rd August 2020

Grey and overcast, the atmosphere fresh, edged with a coolness. At 6.30am Ellis went downstairs. He made a mug of tea and a mug of coffee. The child handed him a plastic tree, a doll, a teddy and some toy tins of food. The sun came out. It became very hot. Ellis photographed a distant heron. Lunch today was quiche, salad, pitta bread, a houmous dip. In the evening Ellis caught up with some old copies of *The Times.* On the Sky News at 10pm the ubiquitous blood-spattered war criminal Tony Blair paid tribute to John Hume, newly deceased. But hundreds of thousands of Iraqis and others in the Middle East who had died as a direct result of Blair's politics and policies remained nameless and of no interest to the corporate media. Ellis went to bed at 10.15am, too tired to read. He fell asleep almost at once.

Tuesday 4th August 2020

A bright sunny day with a cloudless blue sky. Ellis made tea at 8am. On April 7th Ellis had written *On the Twitter page of Anthony Costello ('Ex-Director, WHO') Ellis read the prediction of the Institute for Health Metrics and Evaluation at the University of Washington, advisers to the World Health Organisation, which predicted 66,314 deaths in the UK by August 4th 2020.* That prediction had proved strangely accurate, if you added the surge in deaths above the statistical average to those credited to deaths from Covid-19. Credited deaths were 46,210, but 56,651 deaths had been registered in the UK where Covid-19 was mentioned on the death certificate, including suspected cases. Ellis learned that blood-spattered Blair was back again today, pontificating about the best way to combat a new surge in Coronavirus infection. The man just couldn't shut up. It became hotter. Ellis watered various plants. The child waved a wooden peg at Ellis and Ellis waved a green plastic peg back. In the evening it became windy and cooler, though the sun was still shining at 19.52. Ellis watched the first episode of series five of *Line of Duty*. He watched the 10pm Sky news. There had been a massive blast at the port in Beirut, with many dead and injured. The footage resembled a nuclear explosion. The Sky report suggested it was an accident, involving the storage of a dangerous substance. Ellis went to bed and read more of the bestseller.

Wednesday 5th August 2020

Ellis got up at 6am. A bright sunny morning. He went shopping. He bought the *Morning Star*. Social distancing had collapsed everywhere but the bank. Later that day he discovered that Louis Allday had closed his Twitter page to all but approved followers. As Ellis did not have a Twitter account it meant he could no longer read Allday's daily reflections. He moved on to Asa Winstanley's page. He learned that former deputy Knesset speaker Moshe Feiglin had expressed his satisfaction at the catastrophe in Beirut. He read Ali Abunimah's response to the news that a building in Tel Aviv would have the Lebanon flag colours projected on it in solidarity with blast victims: *You can't make it up. The murderous regime that has invaded Lebanon repeatedly, occupied Beirut and perpetrated massacres, murdered tens of thousands of Lebanese and Palestinians, and still cannot be cleared of suspicion in yesterday's disaster is feigning solidarity with Beirut.* The child played with a stone. The child stared at an apple and attempted to pronounce the noun. The child put on her red hat. Ellis listened to the Lana del Ray record *Honeymoon*. A syrupy, languorous summer album. In the *Morning Star* he read how Majed Abusalama and Ronnie Barkan were cleared of all charges following their punitive prosecution by the reactionary German state when they had protested against a visit to Humboldt University by Aliza Lavie, leader of the anti-BDS movement in the Knesset. Their colleague Stavit Sinai was found guilty of 'attempted assault' despite being punched in the face as she was dragged from the lecture hall. Last year the German parliament passed a resolution which branded the BDS campaign anti-Semitic, cutting off funding for organisations that actively support the boycott. That evening Ellis ate pan-fried cod with chips, peas and green beans, followed by strawberries and Cornish ice-cream. He watched episodes two and three of *Line of Duty*, series five. If Hastings was 'H' - there was the scene with him rushing to dispose of a laptop - why did he seem to be in debt and living in a tiny hotel room? In bed

211

Ellis read more of the bestseller.

Thursday 6th August 2020

Cloudy and overcast at 6.30am but by 07.51 the clouds had started to thin and the sun was shining. It felt very warm. Ellis read Asa Winstanley's new tweet: *What Israel has done to the @BDSmovement's Mahmoud Nawajaa is to intern him without charge or trial, or even access to a lawyer for the "crime" of standing up for his people's rights. This is not simply intimidation.* Needless to say this latest act of Zionist repression was ignored by the corporate media and craven BBC News, too busy amplifying new cold war propaganda against China and Russia. Sky TV had earlier in the year devoted night after night to protests in Hong Kong, where the police were actually quite soft with the demonstrators compared to the Israelis, who would have had no compunction about shooting Palestinians in the head, or in the leg. But violent Israeli repression was never shown on British TV. The broadcasters didn't want to upset the Board of Deputies of British Jews and the rest of the bellicose Zionist community. John McDonnell tweeted: *For constituents and others contacting me on the arrest of Mahmoud Nawajaa, let me say to them that I share their concerns at the intimidation of those who campaign for human rights wherever it is evidenced, be it in Saudi Arabia, Hong Kong or Israel.* Asa Winstanley commented: *Why is that the Palestinians are the only people in the world that even supportive politicians seem to feel obligated to bring other countries into the discussion when issuing even the mildest criticism of their oppressor, Israel?* It was a rhetorical question. John McDonnell was spineless. He had revealed his rubber spine when the posters stating ISRAEL IS A RACIST ENDEAVOUR had gone up at London bus stops, mocking the Labour Party's cowardly adoption of the Zionist IHRA's blatantly loaded 'new' definition of anti-Semitism, which was expressly designed to suppress pro-Palestinian activism. Cretinous John McDonnell MP had denounced the posters as 'anti-Semitic'. What's more there was that excruciating best-of-mates interview that Alastair 'dodgy dossier' Campbell had conducted with McDonnell. McDonnell and Corbyn were the Tweedledum and Tweedledee of a left radicalism that turned out to be composed of slush. It grew hotter. The child played with a serving spoon. Ellis went back to reading a lengthy political biography he'd temporarily abandoned some weeks earlier. In the evening he watched episode four of series five of *Line of Duty*. The insinuation that Hastings was 'H' grew ever stronger. Ellis watched President Macron on the 10pm news, surrounded by a crowd in Beirut. It struck Ellis how fluent the locals were in English. There was no shortage of commentary. There was also a mood of weary disgust. People wanted to leave Beirut. A woman said she wanted to go somewhere where there was no religion. Next was the face mask scandal, but this was fudged by concentration on the

212

inadequacy of the masks rather than the scandal of the procurement process. Ellis went to bed. He read three chapters of the bestseller, then put out the light.

Friday 7th August 2020

Ellis woke at 6.40am. He put the kettle on. It was going to be a very hot sunny day. The weather forecast suggested it would be hotter than the Caribbean. The tone of the corporate broadcasters was jovial. Hot weather was entertaining and amusing. No one mentioned climate catastrophe. But the looming climate disaster would make Covid-19 and the Beirut explosion seem trivial by comparison. Yet no one seemed to get it, apart from some scientists. The corporate media continued to warp social understanding of reality. But then so did 'literary fiction'. Jessica Elgot, Deputy Political editor at the *Guardian*, tweeted her latest story: *EXC - We have the leaked submission from the Labour staffers to the Forde Inquiry into that leaked Labour report on "hyper factionalism". In their legal submission, they are claiming the party 'misused private messages to portray party members as racist.'* She added: *It has also been confirmed that the Labour HQ officials, named in the report as insulting pro-Corbyn colleagues in WhatsApp groups are seeking damages against the party for misuse of data and libel, among other complaints.* Someone tweeted this salient sentence from Elgot's story: *They also say the inquiry should be abandoned given the damage already caused by the leaked report.* Peter Collins @pafcollins commented: *Very interesting that they want the inquiry stopped rather than defending their messages against the charge that they are racist and sexist and damaged Labour. Shame on the Guardian for cheerleading for these wreckers.* Michael BURN@MICHAEL 37656467 commented: *The Guardian trying to gaslight the Forde Inquiry on behalf of their Labour First/Progress wrecker mates?? Well I never - what a shock!! How are the actual words of abuse (recorded from the WhatsApp Gp) at Diane Abbot & Clive Lewis possibly open to 'wrong' interpretation??* Michael Burn added: *This is what the Guardian have been doing these last 5 yrs - spinning every Labour story on behalf of the right-wing faction that hates Corbyn & socialism. hence endless leaks/quotes from Coyle, Streeting, Phillips, Hodge et al to undermine Labour. Pathetic client journalism.* Ellis looked Jessica Elgot up on the internet. His search quickly brought him to Tony Greenstein's hatchet job: *Meet Jessica Elgot: the Guardian & former Jewish Chronicle 'Journalist' Whose Articles are Regurgitated Press Releases.* Greenstein remarked: *It's a sad commentary on the Guardian, which once boasted journalists like Michael Adams and David Hirst, that it employs a Zionist Presstitute.* FiveFilters.org commented that Jessica Elgot contributed at least sixteen articles to the *Guardian*'s anti-Semitism smear campaign against Jeremy Corbyn. Ellis remained indoors. He spent the day reading. On the TV news the Beirut explosion was the fifth item.

Soon it would disappear from news coverage and become as invisible as the war on the Yemen or the unending assault on the Palestinians. Ellis went to bed. Tonight he slept alone. There was so much that *Twenty-Twenty* left out. Including films watched, books read, pages written. The angle of a text was sometimes hard to establish. Ellis read more of the bestseller and then put out the light.

Saturday 8th August 2020

Hot but overcast. It was on this day that Ellis had the idea for a new novella. It would be called *Sudoxe*. It would be based around a 1960 movie, which adapted a 1958 novel. But it would also be in some aspect about the state of contemporary fiction, about the disenchantment he felt. The news topic of the day was the arrival of more migrants travelling across the Channel in inflatable boats. In the evening Ellis watched the penultimate episode of *Line of Duty*, fifth series. And then a few more pages of the trashy novel.

Sunday 9th August 2020

Very hot. Overcast. It looked like rain. But it had looked like rain yesterday and no rain had fallen. From the internet Ellis learned more about the killing of James Nash, described as a children's author, who had been shot dead in Hampshire by a man described as a paranoid neo-Nazi. The killer had escaped by motorbike and died in a crash. Meanwhile, not on the news, Mahmoud Nawajaa remained in detention. He was currently being held for another eleven days without charge and without access to a lawyer. He had been in detention since July 30th. Seized by military thugs, he was abducted from his home, blindfolded and handcuffed. The decision to extend his detention was made by an Israeli military court in Jenin on August 2nd, requested by the Shin Bet. No charges were laid against Mahmoud Nawajaa and no evidence was presented. Unnamed 'security reasons' were once again used to justify the arbitrary imprisonment of Palestinians. Naturally BBC News was silent about this repression. BBC News was only interested in repression by official enemies. China, say. Israeli military courts boast a 99.7 per cent conviction rate. An extraordinary statistic along with so much that the screeching Zionist lobby successfully muffled. The clouds melted away. Blue sky, bright sun, very hot. The child played with her ark, her plastic Noah and a lion. Simon Cowell was reported to have fallen from his electric bike. The black MP Dawn Butler tweeted that she had been stopped in a car being driven through Hackney by three white police officers. Ellis watched the footage. Nothing had changed where the Met was concerned. But there was silence from other Labour MPs. Ellis watched the final episode of *Line of Duty*. He had guessed that Gill

Biggeloe would turn out to be 'H', on the grounds that the plot would require a sudden twist and the only important character who had been with the series long enough was her. He was half-right. On the TV news that night a Sky reporter wandered around the waste land close to the epicentre of the Beirut explosion. The grieving family of a dead young woman paramedic was interviewed. A photograph was shown of her, young and beautiful with high cheek bones and smiling at the camera. When the item about the Coronavirus and the reopening of schools came on, showing Boris Johnson and a beaming teacher with children, Ellis switched off the television and went to bed. He read a few more pages of the bestseller.

Monday 10th August 2020

Blue sky, cloudless, a blazing morning sun. It was 08.01. And then, without noticing, it was 08.02. The temperature crept up into the thirties. Indoors, the child rummaged in her toy basket. She extracted baby doll. Ellis wrote a few paragraphs of *Sudoxe*. In the evening he watched the 'Babylon' episode of *Mad Men*. He'd seen the series twice and was surprised by how much he'd forgotten. In bed he read a few more pages of execrable prose used for information dumping.

Tuesday 11th August 2020

Hot but grey and overcast. The weather forecast predicted rain sweeping north from Kent. But at 13.15 it was hot and sunny. Ellis looked at a satellite photograph on the Twitter page of Ben White showing the Palestinian village of Bayt Sakarya, a community subjected to military rule and surrounded by illegal Jewish settlements. The adjacent illegal Jewish settlement of Alon Shvut is where Israel supreme court justice Noam Sohlberg lives. *A microcosm of apartheid*, remarked Ben White. Twenty-one hours earlier Ben White had tweeted some photographs, with the caption: *Israeli occupation forces demolished a Palestinian home in Khirbet Beit Zakariya village near Bethlehem earlier today. The house was destroyed on the grounds it lacked a permit that Israel systematically denies Palestinians.* The goal of the Israeli state, of course, was to make life unliveable for Palestinians. Ellis listened to *Ultraviolence*. In bed he read more of the bestseller.

Wednesday 12th August 2020

Another very hot day. Ellis spent the day sorting out CDs and building a CD tower. He caught up with an article in the *Times* headlined *'Blood batteries' fuel Musk fortune*. It was about the use of child labour and spectacular exploitation in

215

the mining of Cobalt, a key component in lithium-ion rechargeable batteries. Later, Ellis pan-fried some cod. He listened to a live Waterboys album. In bed that night he read a few more pages of the bestseller.

Thursday 13th August 2020

Another very hot day. Ellis went to the post office and sent a package first class to an address in Westminster. He bought a new toaster. Ellis read the instructions for his new toaster. The box showed a Union Jack and promised that this was a 'Great British' product. *Troubleshooting. Why is there a burning smell omitting from my toaster?* Omitting? Online Ellis read that Kamala Harris was an unprincipled and slippery careerist. Later, Ellis discovered that his toaster was wobbly. He realised that, of the four rubber supports, two were missing. Poor quality control. The child put on her red hat. Ellis put up a shelf. He listened to the first Roxy Music album. He ate sausages with mashed potato, boiled cauliflower and fried onion. He watched a few minutes of the 10pm Sky News programme, then went to bed. He could not be bothered to watch the latest servile reportage about a supposed 'peace deal' involving Israel and the United Arab Emirates. In bed Ellis read a few more pages of the trashy bestseller.

Friday 14th August 2020

In the night there was thunder and lightning and then a sudden short outburst of torrential rain. In the morning it felt fresher. But later it became hot and muggy. It felt as if it might rain but no rain fell. Ellis took the toaster back to the store. He visited a bottle bank and deposited a sack of wine bottles, cans and jars. Later he put up two more shelves, to hold his library of DVDs and CDs. From the internet he learned that Clive Ponting had died on 28 July. BBC News had evidently blanked out the fact of his death, which was what you'd expect from that decomposing organisation. The TV news was dominated by English holidaymakers rushing home from France to avoid the new 14-day quarantine restriction. In bed he read more of the bestseller, underlining many sentences.

Saturday 15th August 2020

Ellis slept badly. A car being parked nearby at ten to one wrenched him from his sleep. The slam of car doors, loud voices. He drifted through the night and woke at 7.50am. A cool grey morning with a light drizzle falling. Ellis read the day's *Times*. Tucked away on page forty he read near the foot of the page: ***US seizes oil from Iran bound for Venezuela:*** *The fuel on four tankers that Iran sent to aid Venezuela has been seized, the US Justice Department confirmed. "With the assistance of foreign partners, this seized property is now in US custody," the*

216

department said. It described the seizure as the largest yet of shipments from Iran. The department issued the warrant last month. *(AFP)* Ellis thought it was extraordinary how this act of war and of piracy has been marginalised by the corporate media and met with silence by the UK's corrupt governing class and its attendant media parasites. This year, of course, had started with the US terrorist assassination of Qassem Suleimani and nine others in his company. That afternoon Ellis watched *Blue Velvet*, which he hadn't viewed for many years. It had lost none of its edge. In the evening he watched *The Wife*. It was like a lot of modern movies - competently produced, well acted, slick, utterly lacking in substance, and leaning heavily on a plot twist. Ellis never wanted to see *The Wife* again. It was a movie he'd forget quite quickly. He went to bed and read more of the bestseller.

Sunday 16th August 2020

Hot and humid, grey and overcast. Ellis went to the library to take back two books and take four out. He talked to the librarian about *The Wife*. On the internet he became aware of dissatisfaction on Twitter at Sir Keir Starmer's inept performance as leader of the Labour Party. The Conservative Party was comfortably ahead in the polls. Donald Trump's younger brother had died. Of Covid-19? The cause of death was not reported. Ellis read that in 2007 the radical Green activist and writer Derek Wall had criticised Jonathan Porritt for taking 42 flights in a single year to attend meetings about the need for people to cut their emissions. Ellis read about what had happened to Sara Parkin, formerly of the Green Party. In 1996 she had joined with Paul Ekins and Jonathan Porritt to set up Forum for the Future, 'a registered charity and non-profit organisation that works in partnership with business, government and civil society to accelerate the shift towards a sustainable society. It has an annual turnover of around £5.2 million and employs 66 staff.' Paul Ekins now boasts an OBE, along with Sara Parkin OBE, while Jonathan Porritt has a CBE. Sara Parkin also served on the boards of the Environment Agency for England and Wales, the Natural Environment Research Council, the Leadership Foundation for Higher Education, the European Training Foundation, Friends of the Earth and the New Economics Foundation. She has aquired eleven honorary degrees. It was curious, thought Ellis, that despite all these careers in sustainability, carcentricity remained at the rotten heart of British urban transport planning, sales of 4X4s had increased spectacularly in recent years, cycling infrastructure was risible, and walking remained a marginalised and often dangerous activity across British cities, towns and villages. The child was oblivious to the world into which she had been born. She laughed and played with her soft toys. The owl, the giraffe, the penguin. At 6pm there was the distant roll of thunder. Soon afterwards it began to pelt with rain. The rain kept falling, hissing on the ground. Ellis finished watching *Blue Velvet: The Lost Footage*. Much of it was uninteresting but the final scene on the roof of Dorothy's apartment building was gripping, with a strange and haunting soundtrack. In the evening he watched *Exodus: Gods and Kings* as far as the plague of frogs. Tucked away at the end of the 10pm Sky News was the information that four young men had died in Wiltshire when a car being driven towards Calne crashed into a house at 3am in Derry Hill, near the Lysley Arms pub. The car then caught fire. A photograph of the crash site seemed to indicate that it was on a bend. The probability was that the car - the make and type was not identified by the incurious corporate media - was being driven at excessive speed by a foolishly reckless individual showing off to friends. The driver may or may not have been intoxicated as a consequence of drinking alcohol or taking drugs. But the truth would never emerge from the corporate media. One of the major forms of violence in British society was condoned by the governing elite, in Parliament, on the media and by the police. It was sanitised as accidental. Roads policing had collapsed, the ideology of British policing had always accommodated and condoned reckless and dangerous driving, and no one loved fast cars and bad driving more than the Conservative Party. Not that the Lib Dems or Labour were much better. In bed Ellis read more of the bestseller, furiously underlining the lies embedded in its information dumping.

Monday 17th August 2020

A bright sunlit morning with a blue sky at seven turned to a cool, grey, overcast day by 08.30. Ellis did a little writing, then devoted his time to the construction of a shelf unit to house CDs and books. At lunchtime he read Julia Lee's article **The US Brings State-Sponsored Piracy into the 21st Century**, on the Bloomberg website. Lee compared the unlawful US action to the state-sponsored piracy of Elizabethan England. The combined cargoes seized by the U.S. from the four ships are worth about $61 million, Lee wrote. Some of the money from the sale of the cargoes will in part be directed to the United States 'Victims of State Sponsored Terrorism Fund,' Lee wrote. Ellis had never heard of this fund - a grotesque concept, since the USA had long been the world's number one participant in state terrorism. Hot and close but no rain fell. The child played with her bowl of stones. In the evening Ellis finished watching *Exodus: Gods and Kings*. It was an oddly empty experience, filled with CGI spectacle that never seemed remotely realistic. There were too many characters whose appearance made them difficult to distinguish from others of their type and the characterisation was shallow. In bed Ellis read more of the bestseller.

Tuesday 18th August 2020

Cloudy, hot. Last night Israel bombed Gaza for the seventh day in a row -
something you would not know from BBC News. The corporate media was
massively interested in the protests in Belarus. This was the kind of protest it
adored. An official enemy! Commentators oozed outrage at police brutality. The
same kind of commentator who sanitised the massacre of unarmed Palestinians
as deaths resulting from 'clashes'. Ellis went shopping. He bought two packets
of nails, milk, three quiches. He deposited four glass items at the bottle bank. He
learned that the electricity supply had been shut down in Gaza. As usual, Twitter
was a much better source of information about the real world and for informed
opinion than most of the corporate media most of the time. Ellis fixed some
pictures to the wall of the child's room. The child rolled around on the sofa. In
the evening Ellis pan-fried two salmon steaks. The evening passed. He went to
bed.

Wednesday 19th August 2020

Cloudy, hot, sticky. Ellis went to the pharmacy to collect a prescription, then
went to buy fish, red wine, salt and vinegar crisps. He queued outside the bank.
He went to the library to collect a book. He bought six croissants from the
bakery in the High Street. The child played with her dolls, then decided her
collection of stones was more interesting. She took them out, counting them.
One. Two. Three. Ellis went online. Media Lens retweeted Lowkey
@LowkeyOnline's comment: *This is now the 8th night in a row Israel is
bombing Gaza. Still can't find one word of coverage by the BBC.* Media Lens
also retweeted Jonathan Cook@Jonathan_K_Cook who linked to a new item in
the Guardian and commented: *Michelle Obama strings together some platitudes
and thereby 'eviscerated' Trump, *reports* the* Guardian. *Obama, Biden, Blair -
these are the Guardian's heroes. Let's not pretend it aspires to anything more
than the neoliberal, planet-destroying status quo.* In the afternoon Ellis sawed
some wood to make more shelves. It began to rain. He drank a lager. The hours
passed. He went to bed and slept.

Thursday 20th August 2020

Cloudy-bright, warm. Ellis went to a supermarket. He did not enjoy the
experience. Later that morning he queued outside a shop. An old woman tried to
pass him. Ellis explained there was a limit to the number of shoppers allowed
inside and he was next. I only want to change a £20 note, the old woman said.
You'll have to wait, Ellis said. No one can go in until someone comes out. I
need a ten shilling note for the girl, the old woman said. Ellis realised she meant

a £10 note. Can you change a twenty for two tens, the old woman asked. Ellis examined his wallet. Yes, he said. He gave the old woman two £10 notes and she gave him a £20 note and walked happily away. And then an old man emerged from the shop and Ellis went in. He bought chicken breasts, cornflakes, Fruit & Fibre, and a tub of vanilla ice-cream. In the afternoon he put up shelves, which he later began to fill with books and CDs. It was hot. Wah-wah, the child said, meaning flower. Ellis changed from jeans into shorts. He ate cheese soufflé with cauliflower and mashed potato. The TV news wasn't worth watching. Ellis went to bed. He slept.

Friday 21st August 2020

Ellis went out to buy pitta bread, cheese, a pork pie. He deposited three bottles and a jam jar at the bottle bank. The wind grew in intensity. Two friends called by for coffee. They all sat at the back of the house and talked. Ellis helped the child try on her new red shoes. In the late afternoon Ellis went on the Twitter page of Ben White. He learned that the Israelis had murdered another Palestinian child: *Mohammed Matar, 16, died of his wounds Thursday after being shot by Israeli occupation forces late Wednesday in Deir Abu Mashaal village (northwest of Ramallah).* He learned that: *"Constant & alarming acceleration in home demolitions" over last couple months in occupied East Jerusalem. 89 homes demolished since Jan (+ 45 other structures); "demolitions in EJ have increased since 2016 and...2020 threatens to be a new record year".* He learned of a new report about the persecution of the Bedouin: *"Members of the Bedouin community in the Naqab are citizens...[but are treated] as enemies." "[Israeli] authorities are systematically working to demolish their homes & move them against their will from their ancestral land."* He learned of a new report into Israel's persecution of human rights organisations and activists: *An important report by @pchrgaza, an NGO that is itself one of the targets of such attacks on Palestinian activists and human rights defenders by the Israeli gov't and Israel advocacy organisations.* He read that: *Mothers of Palestinian youths from the same village, killed in 2017 & whose bodies remain held by Israel, came to express support for Mohammed's mother. Mohammed was shot by settler bypass road 465; Israel confiscated village land to construct the road.* Plus yesterday Israeli tanks shelled Gaza. And the Strip endured its tenth day of bombing. Or was it the eleventh? While BBC News remained silent, mute, despicably complicit in this repression. BBC News muffled truth and perverted understanding both of British and American foreign policy and the violent racist nature of the Jewish state. The wind roared in the trees. Ellis cut chicken into strips, with red onion. He fried them with mushrooms and soured cream. It was a Jamie Oliver recipe. As he cooked, Ellis drank a pint of Czech lager. As he ate, he drank a glass of Muscadet. By ten he was ready for bed.

At 7am the sky was overcast and a light rain had recently fallen. The cars outside were beaded with raindrops. But soon the clouds slid away to the east and the sun began shining from a clear blue sky. It was still windy but not nearly as fierce as yesterday. Ellis slipped on a paper facemask and went into W. H. Smith to buy *The Times*. It was 10am but the shop was deserted. Home again he scanned through the newspaper, drinking cappuccino and eating two home-baked cookies. On page 44 Ellis came across a classic of corporate media misrepresentation. *Israel returns fire on Gaza after rocket strike. Militants in Gaza fired rockets towards Israel, prompting retaliatory airstrikes, the Israeli military said. It is the biggest escalation of cross-border violence in months but no injuries were reported. Israel, which said it intercepted nine of twelve rockets, has closed its only commercial crossing with Gaza, banned sea access and halted fuel imports into the area.* (Reuters) Yet again the Jewish state was falsely cast as a victim, never as the aggressor. Nothing changed with the British corporate media. It pimped for power in all its manifestations. On twitter Ellis came across StanceGrounded@_SJPeace_ who tweeted: *10 consecutive nights of continuous bombings on a population of 2 million people HALF OF WHOM ARE CHILDREN and nobody is talking about this? Nobody cares?* A few people retweeted an article by Israeli journalist Gideon Levy, who wrote about how young Jewish soldiers gloated about maiming Palestinian protesters: *In the Gaza Strip there are 8,000 permanently disabled young men as a result of the snipers' actions. Some are leg amputees, and the shooters are very proud of that. None of the snipers interviewed for Hilo Glazer's frightening story in* Haaretz *(March 6) has any regrets. If they are feeling at all apologetic it's because they didn't spill more blood. One was mocked in his battalion with "here comes the killer". They all act like murderers. If their actions don't show it – more than 200 dead as a result of them – then their statements prove that these young men have lost their moral compass. They are lost. They will go on to study, to have careers and to raise families – and will never recover from their blindness. They disabled their victims physically, but their own disabilities are more severe. Their souls were completely twisted. They will never again be moral individuals. They are a danger to society. They lost their humanity, if they ever had it, on the shooting berms facing the Gaza Strip. They are the sons of our friends and the friends of our sons, the young people from the apartment across the hall. Look how they talk.* But this depravity surely had the support of most American and British Jews. The global silence of Jewish organisations and leaders on such matters was eloquent. *They recalled the number of knees they shot. "I brought in seven-eight knees in one day. Within a few hours, I almost broke his record." "He got around 28 knees." They shot at unarmed young men and women who were trying in vain to struggle for their freedom, an issue that couldn't be more just.* (https://www.haaretz.com/opinion/.premium-the-israeli-army-doesn-t-have-snipers-on-the-gaza-border-it-has-hunters-1.8637587) These Jewish psychopaths enjoyed the unstinting support of the leaders of the British Conservative, Labour and Liberal Democrat parties, as well as Donald Trump and Joe Biden. The wind speed lessened. The child had her afternoon nap. When she woke Ellis brought her the plastic teddy bear, the soft teddy bear, the seal and the cat. Miaow, he said. It remained a very hot day. Ellis ate fish pie for supper. He went to bed and read a few more pages of the bestseller.

Sunday 23rd August 2020

Overcast and cool. It looked like rain but according to the weather forecast there would be no rain today. Ellis smiled at someone's description on the internet of Jeremy Corbyn possessing 'the avuncular tone of a mild mannered vicar'. The child offered Ellis her plastic Homer Simpson figure. He took it, handing her a plastic dog. Then they handed back to each other Homer Simpson and the dog. In the evening it rained. Ellis watched 'Countryfile' for the first time. It featured Somerleyton Hall, where Sebald began his quasi-fictitious journey through Norfolk and Suffolk. Ellis read Jonathan Cook's article **How Israel wages its war on Palestinian history**. Israel's archives are being hurriedly sealed up precisely to prevent any danger that records might confirm long-sidelined and discounted Palestinian history, wrote Jonathan Cook. *Last month Israel's state comptroller, a watchdog body, revealed that more than one million archived documents were still inaccessible, even though they had passed their declassification date. Nonetheless, some have slipped through the net. The archives have, for example, confirmed some of the large-scale massacres of Palestinian civilians carried out in 1948 – the year Israel was established by dispossessing Palestinians of their homeland. In one such massacre at Dawaymeh, near where Palestinians are today fighting against their expulsion from the firing zone, hundreds were executed, even as they offered no resistance, to encourage the wider population to flee. Other files have corroborated Palestinian claims that Israel destroyed more than 500 Palestinian villages during a wave of mass expulsions that same year to dissuade the refugees from trying to return. Today's crimes of occupation – house demolitions, arrests of activists and children, violence from soldiers, and settlement expansion – are being documented by Israel, just as its earlier crimes were. Future historians may one day unearth those papers from the archives and learn the truth. That Israeli policies were not driven, as Israel claims now, by security concerns, but by a colonial desire to destroy Palestinian society and pressure Palestinians to leave their homeland, to be replaced by Jews.*(https://www.thenational.ae /opinion/comment/how-israel-wages-its-war-on-palestinian-history-1.1065932) Ellis went to bed and read a few more pages of the bestseller.

Cloudy bright, warm but with a slight chill in the air. Ellis wore his light summer jacket for the walk. He took photographs. Some were of the tall tree which had crashed to the ground, its roots ripped from the earth. Some were of the child, who ran along the path, grinning. Later, Ellis read Alan MacLeod's article **Media Show Little Interest in Israeli Bombing of Gaza** on the Fair.org website. *Israel is bombing Palestine again, although you likely wouldn't guess that from watching TV news. For the eleventh straight night, Israeli Defense Force warplanes have been bombing the densely populated Gaza Strip. Israel's bombs have caused considerable damage, forcing the shutdown of the area's only power plant.* The corporate media of the USA and Britain - AFP, CBS, ABC News, BBC News, the *Guardian*, etc etc - lazily recycled handouts from the Israelis. Nothing has changed, wrote Alan MacLeod, since Greg Philo and Mike Berry published their seminal books on media coverage of the conflict, *Bad News From Israel* and *More Bad News From Israel*. Sixteen years after their first study was published, corporate media appear to be following exactly the same playbook, wrote Alan MacLeod. The reporting on the latest round of attacks on Gaza follows the patterns we have often remarked on: downplaying Palestinian suffering and viewing the conflict from an Israeli state perspective. Ellis went to bed at 10.20pm. He read a few more pages of the bestseller, underlining with a ballpoint pen sentences which he would later comment on in *Sudoxe*.

Tuesday 25th August 2020

Ellis woke a little after 5am to the sound of torrential rain beating down. It continued to rain, on and off, for the rest of the morning. In the afternoon it brightened up and the sun came out. And then the wind started. On Twitter there was much sputtering about whether or not 'Rule Britannia' and 'Land of Hope and Glory' would be played at the audience-free Last Night of the Proms - another grisly cultural institution like Wimbledon, Royal Ascot and the Boat Race. The BBC, narcissistic as always, was bigging up the story, riding the wave of publicity. But the story was a fabricated one. No one from Black Lives Matter or any other group had demanded that these songs not be included. Meanwhile BBC News remained mute about 14 days of continuous Israeli bombing of Gaza, in the middle of a global pandemic. You could always count on the BBC to muffle and deflect reality with trivia. Meanwhile Owen Jones had denounced a tweet by Kerry-Anne Mendoza, which had apparently provoked a shrill outpouring of tweets reminiscent of the squawks from a rookery. *Lots of Jewish people got in touch with me about this tweet, expressed their distress, asked me to call it out as a left-wing commentator, which I gladly did. When minorities on the receiving end of bigotry ask for our support, we should listen to them.* A classically slithery Owen Jones tweet. He would surely end up as a Labour MP and, eventually, a member of the House of Lords. At a time when many people regarded Neil Kinnock as a man of the Left and an exciting radical Ellis had written a scorching satire, 'The Bloating of Nellcock', which had correctly forecast Kinnock's ultimate destination. Ellis gnawed on the remains of the half leg of roasted lamb. In the USA the shooting of unarmed black man Jacob Blake was condemned by presidential candidate Joe Biden, who called for 'an immediate, full and transparent investigation' and said that the officers 'must be held accountable'. The victim was filmed as he walked towards his car. As he opened the car door and prepared to enter one of two white cops from Kenosha Police Department, Wisconsin, shot him seven times in the back. The two officers involved in the shooting have not been arrested or suspended but placed on administrative leave, the Wisconsin Department of Justice said. On 25 May 2020 George Floyd died after a white police officer knelt on his neck for eight minutres and 46 seconds. In the evening the wind grew fiercer, shaking the neighbourhood trees, roaring between the houses. In bed Ellis read more of the bestseller. He was getting near the end now. That would be a relief. Outside the wind seemed to roar with greater intensity.

Wednesday 26th August 2020

Ellis woke at 6.25am and dozed, listening to the 'Today' programme. It supplied lengthy coverage of the Last Night of the Proms non-story. Climate catastrophe, the suffering of Gaza at the hands of the Israeli state, and the RAF's involvement in the bombing of Yemen were just three topics which the programme blanked out, as always. Reading a profile of Owen Smith, who was a central figure in the failed coup against Jeremy Corbyn's leadership in 2016, and who had just been appointed executive director of market access and external affairs for the drugs firm Bristol Myers Squibb, Ellis was interested to see that early on in his career Smith had worked for the 'Today' programme. Then again, this programme had once employed Rod Liddle. When Ellis pulled back the curtains he was surprised to see a trail of litter strewn along the road outside. Somebody's wheelie bin had blown over and the contents had been hurled by the wind some forty metres or so. When he was dressed Ellis went outside and cleared the litter up. He drank a cappuccino and went online. The Media Lens website drew attention to an article on the greenworld.org.uk website: **What can a swarm of locusts teach us about climate change reporting?** *Alan Story looks at how mainstream coverage of global environmental events continues to fall short of the standard required to accurately reflect the impact of the climate emergency.* The article deconstructed a recent Channel Four documentary, **Swarm Hunters**, about the arrival of billions of crop-eating locusts in East Africa. Alan Story pointed out that although the programme showed *what* was happening and *where* it was happening and *when* (this year, 2020) and who was involved in combating the locusts, it evaded the issue of *why* the locusts had arrived in such great numbers. Cyclones are the originators of locust swarms and climate change resulted in a 400 per cent increase in the frequency of cyclones in 2019 over the previous year. *This unusually poor Channel 4 Unreported World reportage is becoming ever more common these days. Open with some scene-setting drone photography, pack in lots of emotion-invoking sequences, but never present the real politics and real economics - let alone any science - that might offer or at least try to offer a serious and coherent explanation of what is happening on and to our planet. Keep it simple, stupid.* In the afternoon news broke that three protesters in Kenosha had been shot, two fatally, when a gunman opened fire. One person was shot in the head, another in the chest and a third man was seen on the ground, his arm almost severed by a gunshot wound. It appeared that the killer was a member of a group of white vigilantes who were heavily armed, some wearing body armour, who had arrived to counter-protest. On Twitter the shooter was identified as Kyle Rittenhouse. He was seen earlier being given water by riot police, who thanked him for being there. **Bishop Talbert Swan** tweeted: *A member of the white supremacist #BoogalooBoys shot multiple protesters in #Kenosha. Although he had an AR15 he was not confronted by police or SWAT but ignored & allowed to walk out of the area. @KenoshaPolice shoot unarmed Black men but see armed white men as allies.* To Ellis this was all strangely reminiscent of the occupied West Bank, where Palestinians were casually shot dead by armed Jews, and where the most fanatical kind of settler enjoyed the support and friendship of the depraved Israeli army and police. And just as the white supremacist militia believe that a new civil war is imminent, so the excuse for Zionist violence is that a new Nazi holocaust is just around the corner. Storm Francis was gone, now. The child wore her yellow boots. Later, as Ellis pan-fried cod and chipped potatoes he listened to the 6pm news on Radio 4. The account of the killings in Kenosha was fudged in classic BBC News fashion. And a BBC hack reminisced about how Jacob Blake was shot 'several times' by the cops. No, BBC hack. Be precise. Jacob Blake was shot SEVEN times in quick succession. Ellis switched off the radio and began listening to Roger Waters' *Flickering Flame* album. In bed he read more of the bestseller.

Thursday 27th August 2020

Grey, cloudy and cool at 7am, brighter later. By 9am the sun was pouring down. Ellis went to the store for yogurt, a loaf of bread, milk, red wine. He went to the bakery for almond croissants. He went to the bookshop. He had a sack of clothes,

CDs and books for the charity shop but a notice on the door said they were not accepting donations at present. He went to the liquor store and bought a bottle of champagne and some cans of lager. Later, at home, checking his receipts, he saw that the store had overcharged him. It was not the first time that this had happened but he couldn't be bothered to go back and demand a refund. From the internet he learned that Sir Ed Davey had been elected the new leader of the Liberal Democrats. On the Metropolitan Police website Ellis read: The following people all appeared at Highbury Corner Magistrates' Court on Tuesday, 25 August, charged with conspiracy to cause criminal damage: [A] Roger Hallam, 54 (14.05.66) of Putney Bridge Road, Wandsworth [B] Diana Warner, 61 (14.03.59) of Filton Avenue, Bristol [C] Ferhat Ulusu, 42 (15.04.78) of Mount Pleasant, Hackney [D] Holly Brentnall, 28 (06.09.91) of Clonmell Road, Haringey [E] Steven Nunn, 56 (22.07.64) of Longdon upon Tern, Telford. On the XR website Ellis read: On the 24th of August five members of the Burning Pink Party (BPP), formally known as the Beyond Politics Party, including Roger Hallam, Holly Brentnall, Diana Warner, Ferhat Ulusu and Anglican priest Steven Nunn, were arrested in their homes. They appeared in person at Highbury and Islington Magistrates court at 12 noon on Tuesday, charged with conspiracy to commit public nuisance and criminal damage, as well as breaking bail conditions. They are being held on remand until their plea hearing at the end of September. Four of the five arrested have also worked with Extinction Rebellion. Roger Hallam, co-founder of Extinction Rebellion who currently holds no formal role in the movement, along with Blythe Brentnall, a 28 year-old-journalist, Ferhat Ulusu, Steven Nunn and retired GP Diana Warner, have gone on indefinite hunger strike. The afternoon was cloudy and dull. It looked like rain. The child placed her doll in the toy pushchair. She took off her yellow boots. She took off her red hat, then replaced it, grinning, as Ellis put on his hat. It began raining, a few spots, then persistent rain. A sudden rise in UK Covid-19 infections was reported, with 1,048 new cases in the past 24 hours, bringing the total to 331,048, and the total of deaths to 41,493. The nights were suddenly drawing in. It was dark by 8pm. The 10pm Sky News lead story was Donald Trump's nomination as the Republican presidential candidate. Ellis couldn't be bothered to watch. He went to bed and read the trashy novel.

Friday 28th August 2020

Ellis lay in bed, listening to the 7pm headlines. The lead story was Trump again. His pitch was law and order. Joe Biden was presented as the man who would defund the police and open the way for the radical left. Ellis went to the kitchen and switched the kettle on. Later he went out for some vacuum cleaner bags, bananas and swing bin liners. The child stood in her toy tent and drank from her plastic bottle of milk. From Twitter Ellis learned that the Israelis were still bombing Gaza. Footage showed a pillar of smoke rising from an urban area. BBC and Sky News remained characteristically mute. Ellis ate sausage and bean casserole with boiled potatoes, followed by stewed apple and ice-cream. He read a few more pages of the bestseller.

Saturday 29th August 2020

Dull and overcast. It was spitting with rain at the place where Sebald died. The day dragged on. It was a bank holiday weekend and the roads were packed with cars. The gay neighbour came to his front door and Ellis was shocked by his appearance. He hadn't seen the man for quite a while. The neighbour had been in and out of hospital. Ellis had sent a card. The neighbour had lost a lot of weight. His face was skull-thin, his complexion pale. He looked like a man who was dying. Ellis watched *Laura*, which he'd not seen before. It wasn't really up there with the film noir classics, he felt. In bed he read more of the bestseller.

Sunday 30th August 2020

Ellis went for a short walk. It was warmer today. The child ran a comb through her hair. Ellis ran a comb through his hair. *Hair*, the child said, grinning. In the afternoon Ellis watched *The Night My Number Came Up* and in the evening *Leave Her to Heaven*. Then he read more of the bestseller.

Monday 30th August 2020

Ellis was woken in the night by the sound of someone repeatedly coughing. It was the sick neighbour. The cough was a strange raw animal-like cough, almost a roar, like something wounded and in pain. Ellis slept badly. He listened to the 7am news headlines on the 'Today' programme. It solemnly reported that an El Al jet bearing the word 'Peace' in Arabic, English and Hebrew had made an historic first flight to the UAE from Israel. Benjamin Netanyahu, reported the fawning BBC, had said that the Palestinians would no longer be allowed to have 'a veto on peace'. This Zionist claptrap was reported without comment or context. BBC News's latest little squirt of Zionist propaganda was in stark contrast to its absolute indifference to the daily bombing of Gaza. The new day was bright and sunny. The city centre was crowded. Ellis went into HMV and bought the new Taylor Swift album and *Joker*. He liked the song that was being played and he asked the assistant at the counter about it. The assistant went to look at the CD. He came back and said the band was Bear's Den and the album was *Red Earth & Pouring Rain*. Ellis went to look for it and discovered that the store was sold out. Later he watched *Hitchcock* and *Spellbound*. In bed he read a few more pages of the execrable bestseller. He just wanted to get it finished.

Tuesday 1st September 2020

A bright sunny day. Ellis sent a text and made a phone call. He listened to *Folkore* twice. The child said: 'Bubble.' Ellis went and got his yellow Double Bubble pot and blew some bubbles. The child grinned. 'Goodbye, bubbles,' Ellis said, putting the lid back on the pot. *Goodbye, bubbles* echoed the child. Ellis began watching *Joker*. He ate lasagna with salad, followed by raspberries and ice-cream. In bed he was too tired to read the bestseller. He fell asleep almost at once.

Wednesday 2nd September 2020

Ellis was woken at 6am by a yapping dog. The neighbour's, probably. He dozed awhile and then fell asleep. His alarm shrilled at 6.55am. He listened to the news headlines then went off to switch the kettle on. Eating a bowl of cereal Ellis watched *Joker* up to the point where the three bullies on the underground train are gunned down. It was a warm sunny day, a little windy. Ellis put out two loads of washing to dry. He spent the day writing. In the evening he pan-fried some cod and chips, eating them with peas. He finished watching *Joker*. The twist at the end seemed stale, he thought. It wasn't a movie he'd ever want to watch again. The headline news was the alleged attempted assassination of a Russian opposition leader by poison. Ellis reflected that the Israelis had been assassinating Palestinian political leaders for decades, to the absolute indifference of the corporate media. There was even a book about it by Ronen Bergman. Ellis went to bed. He underlined many more sentences in the bestseller.

Thursday 3rd September 2020

Ellis was woken by the sound of rain falling in the night. He drifted back to sleep. A little after 7am he went off to switch the kettle on and make tea. It was a grey, dull, overcast morning. The rain had stopped. Ellis went to the bakery for croissants and bought four. He went to another shop for Grape Nuts but they were sold out. An old aquaintance greeted him. Ellis did not at first recognise this friend, who, uncharacteristically, was wearing a baseball cap and a paper face mask. They talked about their families and about the virus. Afterwards Ellis went to the bottle bank and the library. Back home again he listened to *Folklore* while he attended to tasks in the kitchen. He did some writing. The postman delivered a package containing a book. In bed he read more of the bestseller, underlining many sentences. From Twitter Ellis learned that David Graeber had died suddenly in Venice, aged 59. Ellis ate Batchelors' chicken'n'mushroom pasta. It was glutinous but edible. Then raspberries, strawberries and ice-cream.

In bed he read more of the bestseller.

Friday 4th September 2020

Ellis woke at 6am. He went to the bathroom and emptied his bladder, then returned to bed and dozed until 6.45am. He put the radio on. A woman who opposed motor vehicle restriction measures to stop rat-running through residential areas was given a platform to publicise her ill-informed prejudice. Naturally the whole issue of car dependency went unmentioned and naturally there was no one on the programme to challenge this woman in an effective and well-informed fashion. The concept of 'traffic evaporation' also went undiscussed. There was almost no subject which this BBC News programme could not pervert in the interests of the status quo and corporate power. A grey dull day. The child played with a hair band. Ellis drew a face on a sheet of paper. *Cluck! Cluck!* the child cried. She began bouncing up and down on the sofa. She thought Ellis had drawn a chicken. Later Ellis began watching *Robin Hood*, the latest version, the one where Marian had a strong American accent. Nottingham, which appeared to be located in rolling French countryside, was as diverse as New York city. A tall black man could stroll around without attracting notice. The sheriff of Nottingham was dressed in 1930s fascist chic. The Irishman in the crowd, the one who'd engaged Marian's affections during Robin's absence, looked like Jamie Dornan. Ellis paused the film and looked at the cast list. It *was* Jamie Dornan! Ellis ate lamb steak with new potatoes and cabbage. In the evening he watched *Love Story*. The hero's father seemed familiar. It was only when the credits rolled that Ellis discovered it was Ray Milland. He'd seen him before in something. A Hitchcock movie, he thought. He'd have to look him up. In bed he read more of the abominable book.

Saturday 5th September 2020

Ellis woke at 6am and got up at 6.45am. It was a warm sunny day, the sky unbroken blue. Ellis finished watching *Robin Hood* while eating his breakfast cereal and drinking his first cappuccino of the day. The film was so bad it was entertaining. The credits rolled. Nottingham appeared to have been set in Croatia, or perhaps Hungary. When Ellis went to buy a *Times* he was told that the newspaper was unavailable because an Extinction Rebellion protest had prevented distribution. Ellis was delighted to learn this. There were plenty of *Guardian*s but Ellis preferred to do without a newspaper than buy that repellent Blair-worshipping rag. Lunch was eaten outside today - lasagne and salad, followed by Eton mess. The pleasures of eating outside in company were tempered by the repeated presence of wasps. It was a day when grey darkening clouds boiled up against a blue background. It looked like rain but no rain fell.

On Berners Street there were roadworks and tailbacks of cars held at the temporary traffic lights. By evening the clouds had gone and it was a warm mellow sunny end to the day. Ellis watched *All the President's Men*. It belonged to the days when the *Washington Post* would have appeared to be what it purported to be - feisty and independent and bravely facing up to power. That was before Noam Chomsky and *The Manufacture of Consent*. There were two moments in the movie that were revealing. One was the moment when the experienced journalist insisted there was no story in the Watergate burglary. The other was when Woodward announced he was a Republican. Nowadays, of course, it was impossible to see *The Washington Post* and *The New York Times* as anything other than corporate media, perverting the realities of US foreign policy, traducing the Palestinians, fawning over Joe Biden, blandly muffling the dread future of climate catastrophe. From the internet Ellis learned that Dawn Butler had tweeted her pleasure at the Climate Extinction action, a tweet she had then spinelessly withdrawn in the face of the frothing outrage of the usual opinionators. There was much blather about the freedom of the press. Ellis went to bed, exhausted. He was too tired to read. He put out the light and quickly fell into a deep sleep.

Sunday 6th September 2020

Cool and overcast. On the 7am news the BBC gave prominent coverage to the XR action against the Murdoch press and to the protests in Belarus. Ellis was interested to contrast the language of BBC news in covering Belarus with the completely different language the BBC had used in covering the March of Return protests in Gaza. The double-standards were blatant. BBC News was saturated in the ideology of its wealthy right-wing news presenters. For the first time since last winter Ellis wore a dressing gown when he went to make tea. Online Ellis watched the trailer of *I'm Thinking of Ending Things*. Later, he read some obituaries of David Graeber. It seemed Graeber died from internal bleeding. It was interesting to learn that he had once been hit by a plastic bullet fired by a cop during a protest in Quebec City. Graeber had been a professor at Yale University but his teaching contract was not renewed in 2005, for political reasons. According to the *Morning Star* website, Graeber tweeted in August that he had been 'sick for a month' with an illness that caused a 'weird soapy taste in my mouth, exhaustion, stomach [and] lung-ache'. Next Ellis turned to Stephen Mitchelmore's response to the thirteen novels on the 2020 Booker Prize longlist. 'I read descriptions of the contents of each and listened to the judges acclaim the list as "an excitingly diverse" selection full of "bold, fresh and accomplished" writing, without generating the slightest throb of interest,' wrote Stephen Mitchelmore.'I wondered if, after all these years, my appetite for novels had gone. Even if I had long lost faith in book prizes to bring to light novels that deserve more attention, this was a singularly dispiriting selection, as it appears to offer not the slightest challenge to the form, only indulgence in familiarity dressed up in colourful clothing.' Ellis read on to the end of the piece: https://this-space.blogspot.com/2020/08/the-end-of-literature-part-3.html Afterwards he re-read it, clicking on each of the links. A strange afternoon, weather-wise. One moment the sky was filled with louring black clouds evidently about to let loose cascades of pelting rain, and then the sun returned, pouring its light and warmth. Ellis put on a hat. *Hat*, the child said, grinning. The sun continued to shine. Soon the four pairs of jeans which Ellis had hung out to dry were ready to bring in. Ellis dipped into *The God Delusion*. Afterwards he finished reading the Leon Uris bestseller. What a vile book it was, and what made matters worse was that this poisonous racist fantasy had sold over a million copies, had inspired an influential movie, and was still getting 5 star reviews on Amazon. Ellis ate roast chicken with rice and salad, followed by stewed apples and yogurt. The top news story on Sky at 10pm was an apparently random attack by a knife-man in Birmingham. One person was dead and seven were injured. The police had not identified or caught the killer. The protests in Belarus were also given top billing. Ellis went to bed. He began reading *Selkie Summer*.

Monday 7th September 2020

Ellis woke at 6.20am. He dozed for a while then put the radio on. The BBC had sent a reporter to Yemen, but only to report on the Coronavirus infections there. As usual the role and long history of Britain and the RAF in breaking this state and its people went unmentioned. The weasel phrase 'Saudi-led coalition' was wheeled out, as it always was. Ellis went to make himself a mug of tea. It was a bright sunny morning. By 9am it had clouded over. Later there was a smir of rain. The High Street was crowded. The kangaroo court Julian Assange extradition hearing began today at the Old Bailey. It was another reminder that the British judicial system was the punitive arm of the ruling elite, committed to the maintenance of state terror and exploitation. Assange's crime was to expose the brutality of the US assault on Iraq. Wikileaks released a US army video showing how on 12 July 2007 AH-64 Apache helicopters fired 30-millimetre guns at a group of Iraqis in New Baghdad, killing Reuters photographer Namir Noor-Eldeen and his driver Saeed Chmagh. The video reveals the psychopathic delight of the American pilots in killing civilians. Among those hit were Saleh Mutashar, who was killed, and his two children, Sajad, 10, and Doaha, 5. The video showed how US military personnel actually behave, contrary to the fawning embedded coverage of corporate journalism. Fifteen civilians were murdered by the jeering American pilots, whose war crimes naturally went unpunished. Ellis read an online article on the *Press Gazette* website by Peter

Oborne. Oborne contrasted the UK media's indifference to Assange to how it would react if Assange had been a Chinese dissident facing extradition to Beijing. *There has been scarcely a word in the mainstream British media in his defence*, wrote Oborne. *The US is asserting the right to prosecute a non-US citizen, not living in the US, not publishing in the US, under US laws that deny the right to a public interest defence.* Ben Norton tweeted: *Should be a huge scandal: The husband of the judge overseeing Julian Assange's extradition case, a Conservative ex-defence minister, was involved with a lobby group attacking WikiLeaks and worked with a neocon think tank.. Major conflict of interest.* John Pilger tweeted a link to a speech he made today outside the Old Bailey in which he said: *He exposed the official-truth tellers in the media as collaborators: those I would call Vichy journalists.* A good phrase, that, Ellis thought. Pilger also attacked *the Judases on the Guardian*. Ellis reflected that no doubt Suzanne Moore would be along with a new column denigrating Assange from a crypto-feminist perspective. But since he avoided the *Guardian* website he would probably miss it, unless it attracted comment on Twitter from the accounts he visited. It grew greyer and colder. The child played with a pencil. Ellis ate cold chicken with boiled potatoes, grated carrot and some lettuce, followed by stewed apple and ice-cream. Sky News at 10pm didn't mention the Assange trial at all. Ellis went to bed and read more of *Selkie Summer*.

Tuesday 8th September 2020

Cloudy with a few glimmers of sunlight in the east. On the news it was reported that cases of Covid-19 infection were starting to rise among the 17-21 age group. There was concern about the spread of the virus in Leeds, where restrictions might be necessary. Ellis was at his desk by 7.20am, drinking a mug of tea. He read responses to *Tenet* on Twitter. Quite a few people didn't like it. Ellis didn't think he'd like it either, although doubtless he'd get round to watching it on a TV screen at some point. He hadn't liked *Inception* and he hadn't liked *Interstellar*. The trailer for *Tenet* reminded him of *Inception*. Big and glossy and full of wide-screen action, but hollow and impoverished at heart. By the sound of it *I'm Thinking of Ending Things* was a very much better and more interesting film. But he wouldn't be seeing that any time soon as he didn't subscribe to Netflix. Ellis looked at the Amazon website. He was startled to discover a contemporary novel which had over 52,000 customer reviews. *Perfect for fans of Barbara Kingsolver and Celeste Ng,* **Where the Crawdads Sing** *is at once an exquisite ode to the natural world, a heartbreaking coming-of-age story, and a surprising tale of possible murder.* Ellis went to the library to collect a book he'd ordered. Afterwards he walked to a house near his home to return a copy of *Good Housekeeping*. On the internet Ellis read that by the end of the century there would probably be a four-degree rise in the global temperature. He read about the latest events in the Julian Assange extradition hearing. He ate an apple. Later he drank another cappuccino and ate a slice of chocolate cake. The 10pm Sky news that night made no mention of the Assange extradition proceedings. The government had stated that as from Monday social gatherings of more than six people were banned. SAFE SIX punned the headline in tomorrow's *Metro*. In bed Ellis continued reading *Selkie Summer*.

Wednesday 9th September 2020

A dull grey morning. It was reported that Sir Ronald Harwood had died. The name stirred a dim memory. Ellis looked him up. Harwood was born Ronald Horwitz in 1934 in Cape Town. Sure enough it didn't take Ellis long to discover that Harwood was, as he told the *Jerusalem Post*, 'very pro-Israel'. Another morally blank Jewish intellectual happily enjoying the privileges afforded him by Israel and utterly indifferent to what violent racist Jews had done to Palestine and its population. In Harwood's case the irony of his ethical deficit was compounded by the fact that he'd left apartheid South Africa and had gone on to write drama about intellectuals and artists in Germany during the Nazi years. They dealt with, in his words, 'the conflict between art and politics and the agonizing personal and moral choices that had to be made by the protagonists'. Harwood had also collaborated with Roman Polanksi. 'He's a darling man,' gushed Haywood. Ellis learned that there had even been a biography written about Harwood, by W. Sydney Robinson. But it seemed Robinson had fallen out of love with his subject, referring to Harwood as a man characterised by 'that hard-earned smugness which is his own', who used theatre as 'a vehicle for self-aggrandisement' and who had an 'insatiable appetite for fame'. Ronald Harwood, it transpired, was another Jew who slandered and defamed those who spoke up for the Palestinians. 'I think there's a lot of antisemitism about at the moment, especially on the left. Corbyn is an anti-Semite, I think. There's a book out called *The Left's Jewish Problem* and it's mostly about Corbyn.' Ah yes, thought Ellis. That book. David Rich's whining assault on the ethical Left. Ellis read more. Harwood was also best mates with Harvey Weinstein. Another lovely man. 'When my wife was very ill on her death bed, Harvey said to me, "Ron, I've got a hospital in New York. We'll fly your wife over and give her the best treatment in the world. We'll move the Arabs out!" ' Ah, yes, *moving the Arabs out*. How light-heartedly these rich privileged Jews chuckle about such matters. No surprise to learn that Harwood was also chums with that reactionary crypto-liberal, John le Carré ("a lovely bloke"). In 2009 Harwood was one of 59 prominent British Jews who signed a letter protesting about Caryl Churchill's *Seven Jewish Children: A Play for Gaza*, first performed at the Royal Court Theatre in London. Other signatories included Maureen Lipman and Tracy-Ann Oberman. Ellis went for a walk in the park. He snapped off a seed-laden dandelion and blew on it. The child grinned. Then a young mother came along, pushing a pram. *Baby!* said the child. The baby and the child smiled at each other. Later, while the child had her afternoon nap, Ellis read Max Blumenthal's critique of those environmentalists who had sought to suppress the documentary *Planet of the Humans*. It exposed the links between a number of high profile Green campaigners - especially Bill McKibben - and 'climate-friendly capitalism'. It looked back to Al Gore, who, Max Blumenthal wrote, negotiated a notorious carbon offsets loophole at the 1997 Kyoto Climate Protocol that has been blamed for the release of 600 million tons of excess emissions. Naomi Klein declined to speak to Max Blumenthal. Ellis went to the supermarket. While he was there he received a message that an old friend had died. Cancer. Ellis finished making his purchases. People die and life goes on. There's a huge shock, and then a long forgetting. In the evening Ellis ate quiche and baked beans, with bread and butter. The corporate media continued to blank the Assange hearing. Towards the end of the news there was an item about melting glaciers in Iceland. Footage showed an ice cave in the dark interior of which a massive chunk of ice suddenly dropped, sending up a pillar of foam as it struck water. Ellis went to bed and continued reading *Selkie Summer*.

Thursday 10th September 2020

Ellis switched the radio on at 6.40am. The corporate news drifted past like dandelion seed, grey and insubstantial, afloat on hidden currents. There was an item about a citizen's assembly on climate change. The usual solutions were offered. Restricting car use in city centres. 'Discouraging' ownership of 4X4s. Increasing taxes on air travel. Conventional proposalswhich melted like Icelandic ice when they encountered corporate power in a corporate democracy. Ellis dressed. He read an online *Guardian* article **Biggest books of autumn 2020: what to read in a very busy year**. He skipped past non-fiction and read the fiction recommendations. The first was *a hard-hitting debut set amid London gang culture*. The next a novel in which *a mother and child escape a polluted metropolis for a dangerous experiment in living*. A slab of right-wing autofiction by Martin Amis. A poignant tale of interracial love. The heart-rending story of a family tragedy. *Bath to Borneo via Paris and Dublin*. DeLillo, Ferrante, O'Hagan, Kunzru, Coe, Boyd, Hornby. The exploration of a young Nigerian's gender identity. A feminist dystopia. A dissection of class and identity in Brexit London. A young woman comes of age in 1970s Uganda. A story of refugees arriving in Europe. The next Philip Pullman. A new Cormoran Strike book, as bloated and stiff as a week-old corpse rotting in a stagnant ditch. A crime novel by television celebrity Richard Osman. A family saga set in polyglot Toronto. The new novel by Susanna Clarke: *austere, otherwordly and profound*. A strangely revealing list, Ellis thought. An exquisite assemblage. He would read none of these titles. Not one. His interest was not remotely engaged by a single book in this list. Behind each author lurked a panting agent, eyes narrowed, desperately hoping for a best-seller. Ellis began watching *Planet of the Humans*. The thrust of its critique was that green renewable energy was fraudulent. Wind, solar panels and natural gas are not the solution. Renewable energy relies on fossil fuels for support, it's environmentally destructive, and above all it's about perpetuating the growing demand for energy. There was no technological fix for the crisis which faced humanity. Renewables are intermittent. They depend on nuclear power and coal. Renewable energy requires storage in batteries. But batteries degrade. Solar panels degrade. Solar and wind has limitations. Natural gas is required. Concrete and steel and glass are used in construction. An incredible amount of energy is required to manufacture green energy. Germany, touted for its high levels of green energy, is Europe's largest consumer of coal. Apple claims to be 100 per cent renewable. But nowhere runs on 100 per cent renewable energy. Green energy relies on toxic industrial processes. Cobalt mining in the Congo. Graphite production. Coal. Steel. Nickel. Sulphur hexafluroide. Copper. Concrete. Lithium. Tin. Cadmium. Lead. Petroleum. Environmentally benign? *No.* About the preservation of the fatal status quo. About maintaining unlimited economic growth. About the development of biomass plants - burning trees. But fossil fuel is required to fell the trees and make the wood chips. Biomass plants emit staggering amounts of pollution. Black soot, carbon dioxide. Rubber tyres are added to the wood. And creosote. Renewable energy grants are given to these toxic businesses. Biomass is not a renewable energy. But Bill McKibben of 350.org idolised wood chips. So did the Sierra Club. There was an explosion of biomass plants. But wood chips are a euphemism for trees. Biofuels are the latest fraud. The documentary exposed the equivocations of Green leaders on the subject of biomass. The documentary exposed how the Green movement in the USA had become co-opted by capitalism. Bill McKibben ('our nation's leading environmentalist') promoted a variety of major companies promoting the destruction of the planet. Al Gore was the pimp of corporate capitalism in Brazil. *The takeover of the environmental movement by capitalism is now complete.* That seemed to Ellis to be a reasonable conclusion. Bill McKibben was evasive and as forgetful as Richard Nixon when it came to the question of the funding of his 'Green' organisation. It was laughable that someone like Richard Branson postured as an environmentalist. The film showed the stupefying hypocrisy of an 'Earth Day' event, which was powered by a diesel generator and supported by corporate sponsors including Toyota and Caterpillar. So, what was the solution? Restricting consumption. But human beings retreat into cultural systems of denial. Belief systems eradicate anxiety. *The path to change comes from awareness. Infinite growth on a finite planet is suicide. Less must be the new more.* These points were all true. And the furious wailings from high-profile

Greens indicated that the film had touched a raw nerve. Bill McKibben surely had zero credibility after this hatchet job. Later, Ellis watched film of San Francisco swathed in a strange orange light, like a scene from Mars. It was the consequence of all the wildfires burning in the state. Oregon and Washington State were burning too. Smoke was drifting across the border, over Vancouver Island and the city of Vancouver. Ellis learned that his friend's funeral would be family-only, in view of the Coronavirus rules. In bed he read more of *Selkie Summer*.

Friday 11th September 2020

A warm sunny morning. Ellis drank cappuccino and ate toast and marmalade and surfed the net. He was disgusted but not surprised to discover that several of Keir Starmer's Labour front bench MPs had joined Labour Friends of Israel as newly appointed vice-chairs of the organisation that now includes a third of Shadow Cabinet members. LFI announced six new vice-chairs as follows: Rosie Cooper – MP for West Lancashire, elected in 2005. Chris Evans – MP for Islwyn, elected in 2010. Evans is parliamentary private secretary to Shadow Defence Secretary John Healey. Diana Johnson – MP for Kingston upon Hull North, elected in 2005. Peter Kyle – MP for Hove, elected in 2015. Conor McGinn – MP for St Helens North, elected in 2015. Catherine McKinnell – MP for Newcastle upon Tyne North, elected in 2010. McKinnell is co-chair of 'the all-party parliamentary group against antisemitism'. The new intake joins LFI's current parliamentary vice-chairs – Shadow Cabinet members Rachel Reeves and Jonathan Reynolds, front benchers Pat McFadden and Sharon Hodgson, plus back bencher John Spellar. Commenting on the new appointments, LFI chair Steve McCabe said: "I'm delighted to welcome my colleagues as new LFI vice-chairs. Together with our existing group of LFI officers, they demonstrate the widespread support for LFI that exists across the Labour party. The LFI officers group represents a wide range of parliamentarians, united by our support for Israel and a two-state solution. I look forward to working with our new vice-chairs – and all our supporters in Parliament – to continue to oppose antisemitism and stand up for Israel." As of July 2020, around a quarter of the Parliamentary Labour Party and a third of the Shadow Cabinet were members of the group, including Shadow Justice Secretary David Lammy and Shadow International Trade Secretary Emily Thornberry. Outside it grew hotter. Ellis went for a walk. The streets were busy. He went to the library but it was closed. The child was in an exuberant mood. A giddy kipper. In the evening Ellis read that Bahrain - another Arab dictatorship propped up by Britain and the USA - was to normalise relations with Israel. North-west America continued to burn. An 18-year-old youth was reported to have been arrested after spray-painting IS A RACIST on the base of the statue of racist Winston Churchill. It was a factual statement but Ellis felt strongly that the past tense would have been more appropriate. He ate Cumberland sausages with cabbage and boiled potatoes, followed by stewed apple, vanilla ice-cream and yogurt. The TV news headlines at 10pm were about new restrictions in Birmingham as a result of a surge in Coronavirus infections. Ellis went to bed and read more of *Selkie Summer*.

Saturday 12th September 2020

A cold, grey morning at 7am. An hour later the clouds had gone, the sky was blue, the sun was shining down. Ellis read a tweet by Nicholas Royle: *Tenet is Don't Look Now set in the future. With guns. Don't try to understand it. Feel it.* That made the movie sound more interesting than Ellis suspected it really was. He rather doubted that Christopher Nolan's lavish and glossy production could possibly match the atmosphere of Nicolas Roeg's seedy, desolate Venice. Or its piercing soundtrack. Or its strange supporting cast. The day grew hotter. In Oregon the fires were forcing mass evacuations. Ellis stared at a photograph of a burned-out trailer park. Parallel roads framed by ash rectangles in rows. Ellis sorted some books. He started writing a letter, then abandoned it. He read *The Times*, which had a one-page hatchet job on Extinction Rebellion. It reminded him of the stories they used to print about the Corbyn-led Labour Party. A piece stuffed full of anonymous sources and slander. The hours passed. The child dragged a comb through her hair. Ellis finished reading *Selkie Summer*. He ate vegetarian risotto. He watched *Judy*. In bed he read a few pages of a book about Van Morrison which he'd bought in a second hand bookshop in 2019.

Sunday 13th September 2020

A sunny morning, blue sky, a light scattering of cloud. A slight autumnal chill. BBC News blathered about the Last Night of the Proms. The news was not news at all. The real news was never on the news. The radio headline was all about Sir John Major and Tony Blair fretting about the Brexit bill and legality. To have blood-spattered Blair speaking out about legality, morality and the reputation of British governance was an irony so deep it was utterly beyond the mental horizon of those who managed and selected BBC News. Ellis ate a bowl of cereal and went online. He read the latest tweets by Steven Salaita. *What the West likes to conceptualize as "peace" is often just perpetuation of a barbarous world order.* That would make a fine epigraph to a book, Ellis thought. He read on, going backwards in time. *This "peace deal" between Bahrain and Israel is possible only because the Bahraini monarchy brutally suppressed a popular uprising with the aid of Saudi Arabia, the UK, and the USA.* The day grew hotter. The Angry Arab tweeted about protests in Bahrain against the agreement with Israel, and how this was being blanked by the corporate media. Ellis added

237

water to a cement mix and built some low steps. Later he took four books back to the local library and borrowed a new one. After that he sawed five lengths of wood into smaller lengths, three matching and two matching. The child played in the sun with her watering can. Ellis ate roast chicken with rice and salad, followed by stewed plums and vanilla ice-cream. He watched the first episode of *The Singapore Grip*. Afterwards, Sky News. Nothing about the protests in Bahrain but lots about the protests in Belarus. It was standard corporate news fare. The language of the report fizzed with indignation at this violent suppression of peaceful protest in Belarus. This kind of empathy was never available for the victims of official allies like Egypt, Israel, Saudi Arabia and the like. In bed Ellis began reading a new non-fiction book.

Monday 14th September 2020

Coronavirus infections continued to surge again in Britain, the USA, Brazil and India. On the radio BBC News was highlighting the latest Westminster bubble story, over unrest in some quarters of the Conservative Party about the Johnson government's Internal Market Bill, which broke international law. What signal does that send to Iran? fretted corporate pimp Martha Kearney, insinuating that Iran flouted international law. The programme had a particular obsession with Iran, which was regularly slandered. Israel, needless to say, was never mentioned as a serial flouter of international law. Israel could always rely on the BBC 'Today' programme to omit completely or, when required, sanitise its violence, racism and lawlessness. Ellis went out to post a letter. It was a bright warm sunny morning. He spent the morning writing. Later he mixed more cement and water. The child wrapped clothes around her head. Ellis read the latest tweet by John Pilger, about the Assange extradition proceedings. *Today in the Old Bailey I watched the grim farce of the US/UK attempt to extradite Julian #Assange. The bullying prosecutor is reduced to insulting the integrity of expert witnesses. Trapped behind glass, Julian is denied free access to his barrister. This is Britain's shame.* By 20.15 it was still surprisingly hot. On the news it was reported that the Internal Market Bill, which breached international law, had passed by 340 votes to 263. Despite corporate media talk of a rebellion only two Conservative MPs voted against the bill. Ellis went to bed at 10.30pm and read more of the non-fiction book.

Tuesday 15th September 2020

Another hot day. A cloudless blue sky. Ellis watched a chimney sweep's van pass by in the street. On a visit to California, President Trump dismissed climate change. It'll start getting cooler, you just watch, he said. I don't think science knows, actually. Ellis read that an Israeli occupation court has ordered that Al-

Qa'qa' Mosque in Jerusalem's Silwan neighbourhood be demolished because it was built without planning permission. In August 2020 Israel demolished 51 Palestinian properties in Jerusalem - something never reported on BBC News or the rest of the corporate media. Next Ellis read an article by Asa Winstantley on the Middle East Monitor website, titled: **Israel: A rogue state**. Winstanley began with the Trump administration's announcement that it was imposing economic sanctions on the chief prosecutor of the International Criminal Court (ICC), who had stated that the court was investigating possible US war crimes in Afghanistan, and Israeli war crimes in the West Bank and the Gaza Strip. In helping to sustain, fund, train, arm and encourage a racist, violent regime such as Israel, the US empire is also a world order of torture and injustice – much like the British empire was before it, wrote Winstanley. Every successive US President manages to be more pro-Israeli than the last. Barack Obama promised to give $38 billion in military aid to Israel over the course of the following decade. The threat of being made to face up to their crimes in a court of law is a very real one for Israeli officers, wrote Asa Winstanley. Until European countries began rewriting their universal jurisdiction laws in order to protect Israel, it was not an uncommon event for Israeli war criminals to have to avoid places like London. It was fifteen years ago that Doron Almog, a former major general in the Israeli army, had to return to Tel Aviv after landing in London. British police had been planning to arrest him for a war crimes case, but somehow, the Israeli embassy was tipped off and warned him not to vacate the plane. A judge had decided he had a case to answer. It was later revealed that British police had only made the decision not to board the plane because, allegedly, they were afraid they would be shot at by armed Israeli personnel protecting Almog. Next Ellis read a paper by Stef Lhermitte, Sainan Sun, Christopher Shuman, Bert Wouters, Frank Pattyn, Jan Wuite, Etienne Berthier, and Thomas Nagler published on the website of the National Academy of Sciences of the United States of America, entitled *Damage accelerates ice shelf instability and mass loss in Amundsen Sea Embayment*. The abstract began: Pine Island Glacier and Thwaites Glacier in the Amundsen Sea Embayment are among the fastest changing outlet glaciers in Antarctica. Yet, projecting the future of these glaciers remains a major uncertainty for sea level rise. The authors proceeded to explain the need for incorporating damage processes in models to improve sea level rise projections. The authors explained how they combined multisource satellite imagery with modelling to uncover the rapid development of damage areas in the shear zones of Pine Island and Thwaites ice shelves. The authors concluded that the results of their study suggested that damage feedback processes are key to future ice shelf stability, grounding line retreat, and sea level contributions from Antarctica. These feedback processes, currently not accounted for in most ice sheet models, can assist in improving sea level rise projections. Or, to put it another way, *things don't look good*. Next

Ellis read Craig Murray's account of yesterday in court at the Assange extradition hearing. *The mainstream media are turning a blind eye. Public access continues to be restricted and major NGOs, including Amnesty, PEN and Reporters Without Borders, continue to be excluded both physically and from watching online. It has taken me literally all night to write this up – it is now 8.54am – and I have to finish off and get back into court. The six of us allowed in the public gallery, incidentally, have to climb 132 steps to get there, several times a day. As you know, I have a very dodgy ticker; I am with Julian's dad John who is 78; and another of us has a pacemaker.* Craig Murray added: *I feel obliged to write this up, and in this detail, because otherwise the vital basic facts of the most important trial this century, and how it is being conducted, would pass almost completely unknown to the public. If it were a genuine process, they would want people to see it, not completely minimise attendance both physically and online.* The day grew hotter. The child once again put clothes on her head, to make a kind of covering. Ellis put the recyling bin out for collection tomorrow. In bed he read more of the non-fiction book.

Wednesday 16th September 2020

A cloudy morning. The Israelis had been bombing Gaza again. As usual BBC News reported this as 'retaliation'. BBC News said nothing about the continuing theft of Palestinian land. Ben White tweeted that the Brigadier General heading Israel's occupation authority in the West Bank had told the Knesset that the military has uprooted 43,000 trees planted by Palestinians in the past 20 years, including 7,500 in 2019. This was because they had been planted "illegally". That kind of reality was blanked by BBC News, which perpetuated a colonialist news agenda. The BBC was stuffed with mediocrities and reactionaries. It was top heavy with individuals on bloated salaries. Gary Lineker was paid an obscene £1,750,000 for his banal sports commentary. Zoe Ball was paid a stupefying £1,360,000 for blathering on a breakfast show. That grotesque lump known as Huw Edwards received £465,000. Fiona Bruce was on £450,000. The cretinous Vanessa Feltz was on £405,000. That smirking reactionary Emily Maitlis was on £370,000. The toady Andrew Marr was on £360,000. The shallow power-pimp Nick Robinson was rewarded with £299,999. For services to the Conservative Party, Laura Kuenssberg received £294,999. Empty-headed Jo Whiley received £280,000. Mishal Husain of the 'Today' sewer received £269,999. Martha Kearney was paid £255,999 for gently passing softball questions to politicians. Justin Webb likewise, minus 5K. For services to western imperialism Jon Sopel received £239,999 and Jeremy Bowen £244,999. James Naughtie was supposed to have retired but he had wormed his way back to collect £170,000. Add to that 106 senior BBC managers are paid more than the salary of the Prime Minister (£150,000). Later Ellis read some of Thomas

Paine's *The Age of Reason*. It was strange that this book was not a Penguin Classic. In fact there seemed to be no modern scholarly paperback editon at all. Ellis held the child's hand. He pointed to where a woman was blowing bubbles. Bubbles, the child said, entranced. But her toy cow she insisted on calling a sheep. Ellis ate pizza and salad, followed by stewed plums and yogurt. In the evening he watched part of *Cat People*, the remake, directed by Paul Schrader. Ellis did not bother watching Sky News at 10pm. He went to bed, too tired even to read.

Thursday 17th September 2020

Woken by the sound of something metallic, clattering. A cool and cloudy morning. Ellis dozed, listening to the 7am news headlines. Sleepy Joe had spoken of the need to protect the Good Friday agreement (or to put it another way: to ingratiate himself with the Irish American vote). Later, at ten to eight, after he'd shaved and dressed, Ellis heard an unctuous, earnest voice emanating from the radio. He recognised the tone at once. It combined treacle with smugness. It could only be Thought for the Day, in which a bland fence-sitter disgorged some conservative platitudes about a current news story. It invariably amounted to a propping-up of the status quo. Ellis would normally switch off but on this occasion the speaker was talking about Jews and the Nazi genocide. Apparently there had been a survey of young Americans which had exposed large areas of ignorance about it. Not a surprise, really. Most British adults were ignorant of huge swathes of history. But it could hardly be said that the Nazi death camps or the Second World War were marginalised subjects. Britain and the US were saturated in movies and books and television programmes about them. The Nazi Holocaust appeared on the curriculum. There were educational trips. The entire Zionist community was keen to promote the Nazi genocide as an alibi for the racist, sectarian, violent Jewish state. The purveyor of this treacle was revealed at the end to be one Dr Michael Banner. Ellis had never heard of Banner. He looked him up on the internet. Dr Michael Banner is Dean and Fellow of Trinity College, Cambridge. The Wikipedia entry (Ellis wondered if it was written by Banner himself) was reticent about his background and pre-university education. He began his glittering career at Balliol College. From then on it's The Establishment all the way. Stanley Hauerhas (Ellis had never heard of him) had once written that Banner was 'one of the brightest and most interesting young people doing ethics on the scene today'. So bright, in fact, that Banner had written a book on - Ellis laughed hollowly - the rationality of religious belief, as well as the revealingly-titled *The Practice of Abortion: A Critique*. The Trinity College website revealed that Banner 'also has an interest in matters to do with ethical investment and good business, and served for eight years on advisory boards for F&C Asset Management and Friend's Life, in the

City of London'. On Twitter Ellis saw that someone had criticised Banner for concentrating solely on Jews as victims and for not mentioning Romanies, gays or the disabled. Karen Pollock, Chief Executive of the Holocaust Educational Trust and relentless apologist for Israel, gushed that Banner's monologue was 'thought provoking and thoughtful'. But of course Banner's contribution to the 'Today' programme was utterly consistent with its political agenda. Yesterday Jews were bombing Gaza - a land which white racists had been bombing since 1915, making this the one-hundred-and-fifth year of violent colonial aggression against an almost entirely defenceless people. Not the kind of thing which is ever going to disturb the sleep of well-fed ethics-merchants like Dr Michael Banner. Travelling further into the internet Ellis discovered the story, in (where else) the Blairite *Guardian*. Almost half of those Americans aged 18-39 questioned in the study could not name a concentration camp. And so on. But go a little further and you discover that this is a survey commissioned by a Zionist organisation which claims to be seeking financial compensation 'to provide a measure of justice for Jewish Holocaust victims'. Or as Norman G. Finkelstein wrote a long time ago, 'the Holocaust industry has become an outright extortion racket'. At the very end of the *Guardian* Zionist propaganda item you discover that the survey is based on just 1,000 interviews across the entire USA, which has a population of 331 million. In other words, this survey lacks all credibility, even more so when its questions and answers have been set up and analysed by Zionists. Ellis moved on to the Twitter page of Asad Abukhalil, where he read: *What is the difference between an Arab leader and Arab dictator in Western media? Leaders are clients of US/Israel.* The sun came out. Ellis went for a walk. Taped to a lamp post was a poster advertising a six-week slimming course. If booked there was a bonus free week and a recipe book worth £4.95. Later Ellis watched *Cat People*, the remake with Nastassia Kinski. It was nowhere near as good as the original 1942 movie. That evening he sent emails to seven people and then went to bed.

Friday 18th September 2020

A bright sunny morning but with an autumnal chill. The news headlines were about the surge in coronavirus infections in England, the lack of testing equipment and the possibility of a new national lockdown. The day grew warmer. Ellis spent the morning writing. Mid-day he caught up with fresh information. Slippery Tom Watson, who devoted himself to undermining the Corbyn leadership, has become an adviser to corporate gambling business Paddy Power. Slippery Owen Jones has been given a platform in (where else?) the *Guardian* to plug his latest book, which purported to offer 'a nuanced understanding' of the Corbyn leadership. Ellis felt Jones had a point when he referred to *his pathological aversion to conflict, which initially defused Tory attack lines that he was a dangerous extremist, but led to a destabilising inability to take decisions.* But then Jones quickly reverted to being Jones the fence-sitting equivocator. *Those who insisted the antisemitism crisis was a smear campaign and nothing else – that Labour's opponents would always seize on it did not mean it was not a very real problem – not only caused pain to Jewish people but also helped strip away Corbynism's idealistic sheen.* Owen Jones propped up this nonsense with a link to supporting evidence in the form of… an opinion piece by Owen Jones. Such are the narcissistic circuits of Jones. Ellis clicked on the link, which was crammed with evidence-free assertions, and sobbed that *our failure to act leaves our Jewish sisters and brothers insecure, depressed and frightened.* Garbage, thought Ellis. The Jews who whined the most about Corbyn were the Zionists. Typically, Jones neither analysed the conservative tendencies of Britain's Jewish community, who, polls indicated, overwhelmingly voted Conservative, nor did he identify these trembling sisters and brothers. Probably he meant people like Michael Segalov and Rachel Shabi. Scanning Jones's Twitter feed Ellis was unsurprised to find this slippery crypto-Leftist announcing on 11 September *I'm on @BBCNewsnight tonight, BBC 2, 10.45pm, talking about my new book THIS LAND, and why Labour's terrible defeat means learning from mistakes, but not abandoning transformative policies that are more needed than ever.* And three days later *On @BBCRadio4 now: The Radical Agenda #Starttheweek with 'This Land: The Story of a Movement' author @OwenJones84.* Alongside Owen Jones was the rabid Zionist and *Times* hack 'Danny Finkelstein', otherwise known as Daniel William Finkelstein, Baron Finkelstein, OBE. The only fly in the ointment was that the person reviewing Jones's book for the *Observer* was the reactionary crypto-Left *Guardian* hack John Harris, who evidently didn't like his colleague. Harris wrote (13 September): *The other key story linked to the ugly underbelly of far-left politics was that of antisemitism: its presence among a nasty, credulous element of the party's new membership, the leadership's apparent tolerance of it, and past occasions when Corbyn had either shared the company of antisemites, or come dangerously close to apparently voicing age-old prejudices (witness the occasion when, in 2013, he took issue with unnamed "Zionists" who "having lived in this country for a very long time, probably all their lives, don't understand English irony" – on the face of it, a classic view of Jews as an eternally alien presence).* A grotesque but utterly characteristic distortion of the truth by that sewer-rag the *Observer* and its hack. Because, of course, Corbyn was replying to Zionists who had sought to disrupt a Palestinian solidarity meeting. One of those individuals was notorious. The idea that mocking Zionists was inherently anti-Semitic is the kind of trash that *Guardian* newspapers had been unloading ever since Corbyn had become leader. But then John Harris was yet another corporate pimp muffling the reality of Jewish violence in Palestine. He was scandalised by *Corbyn and Milne's refusal to entertain the idea of Labour officially embracing the entire text of the definition of antisemitism authored by the International Holocaust Remembrance Association* even though that supposed 'definition' was a cynical assemblage of rhetoric expressly designed to shield the crimes, sectarianism and inequalities of the violent racist Jewish state from criticism. As for the so-called 'International Holocaust Remembrance Association' - it supplied yet another example of the appropriation of the Nazi genocide for the vilest of political purposes. No one had degraded the memory of the Nazi genocide more than the kind of Jews behind this fraudulent 'Association'. Rancid, foul-mouthed Margaret Hodge is laughably described as 'an elderly Jewish MP'. It was, however, interesting to learn that John McDonnell had rushed to her defence. This reinforced Ellis's contempt for McDonnell and his equivocations. The only part of the Harris review that did ring true was the reference to Corbyn as *"endlessly indecisive": a man who, when faced with conflict, sometimes "didn't come into the office or answer his phone", "often did not seem fully present", and was "always difficult to prep for major interviews and debates".* It reinforced Ellis's view that Corbyn was shallow and lazy. At a time when strong, assertive leadership was needed, Corbyn revealed himself to be tepid and indecisive. And then we reach Harris's account of Jones's chapter on anti-Semitism. That old chestnut, the mural, is dutifully served up again - *a clearly anti-Jewish mural*, insists Harris, who blanks out those Jews who would disagree with him and who naturally omits to acknowledge the way in which the Israel lobby trawled huge quantities of ancient social media posts and then drip-fed them to the *Guardian* and BBC, guaranteeing that this would magically become national news. *Most remarkable of all is the absence of the BBC* Panorama *programme* Is Labour Anti-Semitic?*, aired the summer before the 2019 election, and full of complaints not only about the party's alleged indulgence of anti-Jewish prejudice, but the deep upset and hurt caused to Labour employees.* Most remarkable of all is the way in which this hatchet-job was contextualised by the leaked Labour report which exposed the politics of the Labour party bureaucracy, which actually wanted Labour to lose a general election. John Harris - a pseudo-Leftist even further to the right than Owen Jones. John Harris - a typical member of the *Guardian*'s resident rabble of reactionaries. Hadley Freeman. Jessica Elgot. Suzanne Moore. Jonathan Freedland. Ellis tied-up some roses. He felt tired and lay down for half an hour. Afterwards he read several pages of a psychological thriller. The child played with her plastic toys in the foamy bath. Numbers. A two. A nine. On the Sky 10pm News the top stories were all about the spreading virus and the latest restrictions. Later there was footage of the famine in Yemen. The British role in this atrocity was characteristically fudged. That the RAF was bringing daily misery to the Yemeni population was never mentioned. That the RAF was central to the Saudi bombing campaign was a fact too unspeakable for the craven corporate media. The Royal Air Force - one of the world's oldest terrorist organisations. Bombing civilians in the Middle East (and elsewhere) for over one-hundred years. A fact lost behind the blue and red smoke of the Red Arrows. Ellis had often wondered why, in a time of supposed austerity, the State could afford to finance the squirting of the most expensive coloured smoke in Britain. He went to bed.

Saturday 19th September 2020

Ellis woke at 6.30am and dozed until 7am, when he switched on the bedside radio. Dominic Raab's bodyguard had left his gun on a plane. US Supreme Court judge Ruth Bader Ginsburg had died. Tropical Storm Wilfred in the eastern Atlantic has used the last of the traditional names for tropical systems in a record-setting Atlantic hurricane season. Meteorologists will now have to use Alpha, Beta and other Greek letters for future storms. The only time this has been done before was in 2005, when Hurricane Katrina devastated New Orleans. Later, on the BBC News website, Ellis learned that the Labour Party had unveiled its new slogan: *A New Leadership*. A new leadership dedicated to capitalism, exploitation, imperialism and Zionism. *He won't be as much waving the Red Flag as the Union Jack*, tittered Iain Watson ('Political correspondent, BBC News'). Ah yes, the anonymous briefing: *As one Labour insider put it: "The brand has been trashed"*. Ah yes, *the brand*. Because, hey, politics is all about selling a commodity, innit. So - wait for it! - *there will be an emphasis on patriotism*. There will also be the usual reactionary banalities. Labour will stand for *Family, fairness, hard work*. Which translates, apparently, into *flag, forces, family*. In short, the Conservative Party! Yes, Labour will be saying goodbye to *old class labels*. Elsewhere on the internet Ellis read a statement from Mark Seddon about an open letter signed by various prominent British Palestinians which raised 'a significant number of hugely important issues, especially for the UK Labour Party'. It transpired that those bogus and reactionary 'Left' publications *New Statesman*, *LabourList* and *Tribune* had all refused to publish the letter. Mark Seddon wrote: *It would certainly appear that the bitter arguments around allegations of anti-Semitism in the Labour Party may be having the effect of shutting down advocates of the Palestinian cause, a cause with which the Labour Party has long identified. This, of course, may be one of the intended consequences desired by some of the protagonists. It should and must be resisted. I hope that publications such as these pick up these issues and give a platform to Palestinian voices calling for continued solidarity from Labour*. It was complete garbage that the Labour Party had 'long identified' with 'the Palestinian cause' except, at best, at the level of vacuous rhetoric. The letter stated, among other things: *We believe that an internationalist Labour Party has a special responsibility to redress the ongoing injustices against the Palestinian people, denied their right to self-determination during the British*

Mandate because of the role Britain played as a colonial power leading up to the 1948 Nakba, when Palestinians were forcibly displaced from their homes. Its authors wrote, *we remain deeply concerned about steps being taken which will only serve to shrink the space in the Labour party for British Palestinians and other members to assert their rights to campaign for an end to the oppression of the Palestinian people.* They added: *We note with concern statements made by the Labour leadership affirming support for the usage of the IHRA definition and examples, including within Labour Party disciplinary procedures, without reference to the concerns regarding the threat those examples pose to the rights of Palestinians and to party members advocating for justice for the Palestinian people. We are alarmed to note the stated intention of the Shadow Communities Secretary to urge all Labour-run councils who have not adopted the IHRA to do so, ignoring the evidence of how councils have previously used the IHRA to limit the rights of Palestinians, and of others advocating on their behalf.* But of course the Labour Party had a rotten record where imperialism, racism and the Palestinians were concerned. Corbyn's support for the Palestinians was an aberration, not the norm. Every Labour government there had ever been was keenly committed to torture, repression and Jewish supremacy in occupied Palestine. Ellis moved on and read a tweet by William Clare Roberts: *This looks bad: The faculty advisory board of the U of T's International Human Rights Program has resigned after an offer of the directorship was cancelled, apparently over the candidate's work on Israeli human rights violations.* Steven Salaita commented: *Yet another scholar has been screwed out of a job because of Zionist interference. As usual, the noisy paladins who bemoan the world-ending crisis of cancel culture are nowhere to be found when pro-Israel donors are the culprits.* The day wore on. The child made a blue banana out of Play-Doh. Ellis ate a vegetable pasta bake with garlic bread. He watched *Meet Me in St Louis.* It was difficult to understand why this saccharine tosh was regarded as a classic. It was basically a celebration of the homely values of the affluent white nuclear family and a reproduction of the marriage imperative for single young women. Released in 1944. A year of horrors. Ellis watched some of the 10pm Sky News, then went to bed.

Sunday 20th September 2020

Another bright hot sunny morning. Ellis woke at 6.30am, then dozed until 6.55am, when he turned the radio on, in time for the weather forecast, the news, and the review of the morning papers. He was intrigued that the review mentioned a piece in the *Sunday Times* attacking the BBC for paying James Naughtie a large sum of money for very little work. Plainly someone at Radio 4 didn't like Naughtie. Ellis had once been under the illusion that Naughtie had retired when he'd left the 'Today' programme. Not a bit of it. The overweight reactionary had bounced back from time to time with fawning interviews with selected writers, which amounted yet again to the BBC providing free national advertising to those writers favoured by the organisation's managerial elite. The kind of people who thought Hilary Mantel was Tolstoy. Later, while eating a bowl of cereal, Ellis put Naughtie's name into Google and clicked on the News option. **TAKING THE MIC *BBC slammed for paying Radio 4 host James Naughtie £175,000 for just 23 hours of air time*** This was on the *Sun* website. The BBC had released the salary figure but had evaded supplying any breakdown of what work Naughtie had done to be paid this sum. The *Sun* had done some research and discovered that Naughtie had done just 23 hours work, which worked out at a payment rate of £7,608 an hour. Ellis was with the *Sun* on this story. It provided another example of the BBC's lavish self-indulgence and its contempt for its critics and the general public. *Staff pay was up 3.5 per cent to £1.5 billion this year. Naughtie's huge pay dwarfs the Prime Minister's £150,402-a-year salary and up to £114,000 for a brain surgeon.* The sun rose in the sky. The child looked at her illustrated *Row, Row, Row the Boat* book. She chuckled when Ellis squeaked like a mouse, screamed at the crocodile and roared like a lion. Ellis went to the library, returning two books and borrowing two more. Later he read various online articles and reviews about Sasha Swire's forthcoming book *Diary of an MP's Wife*. Afterwards he went for a walk. It was a hot afternoon. Someone was burning cut vegetation. A cloud of blue smoke billowed across the road. There was a striking resemblance to Claude Monet's 'Path in the Fog'. Back home, Ellis ate re-heated pasta bake. He started watching *Gladiator*. He hadn't seen it for years. At 9pm he tuned into the second episode of *The Singapore Grip*. Afterwards he couldn't be bothered with Sky News. He went to bed and went on reading the non-fiction book.

Monday 21st September 2020

A mist lay across the neighbourhood at 7.30am but quickly burned away as the sun rose in the sky. It was going to be another hot day. Ellis read a feature by Gavin Lewis on the Monthly Review Press website https://mronline.org/2020 09/ 18/the-participation-of-uk-corporate-media-in-black-deaths/ Gavin Lewis criticised the BBC and the rest of the corporate media for its systematic bias in suppressing news of state violence against black people. In 2017, Paris was shaken by demonstrations protesting the alleged rape of a Muslim man by a policeman with a baton, wrote Gavin Lewis. It was ten days before BBC News 24 acknowledged the events and, even then, refused to report on the specifics of the allegation. Instead, only a single sentence was offered on the website: "Violence has broken out at a protest in Paris in support of a young black man who was allegedly assaulted by police." Gavin Lewis compared this with other forms of misrepresentation. He described how the BBC and mainstream UK media ran the story of a supposedly significant pro-Israel anti-Corbyn protest taking place outside the Labour Party headquarters on September 4, 2018. In reality, the action consisted of just ten all-white protesters—who were therefore easily identifiable as habitual pro-Israel activists. *The BBC and most of the corporate media used visual imagery composed in tight shots, falsely implying a much larger group of pro-Israel protesters, supposedly amassed outside the limits of the photographic frame. The hundreds attending a simultaneous actual multicultural demonstration in support of Corbyn and Labour were not given the same treatment or prominence in reports.* Gavin Lewis observed that *compared to instantly accepted claims of anti-Semitism, repeated instances of anti-Black racism—even fatal instances—are always downplayed and treated as dubious. To do otherwise would reveal the systemic nature of Western oppression. As a consequence, there is a constant absenting, paring, and rewording of such events by Western media elites.* It was a very good article, of the kind you would never expect to find in Blairite outlets like the *Guardian* or *Observer*. Ellis discovered that yesterday the *Observer* had a run a fawning interview with slithy Owen Jones. The Observer remarked: *The antisemitism crisis, which you recount in painful detail, amounts to a portrait of protracted political dysfunction.* Yet again, for the billionth time, the corporate media claimed that there was an 'anti-Semitism crisis' when there was no such thing. It was an evidence-free 'crisis'. It was confected. It was a hoax. It was created by Jewish racists and their reactionary allies. Owen Jones said none of this in response. Owen Jones said *Yes.* That was the first word of his response. How Ellis detested Jones, whose prominence in the *Guardian, Observer* and at the BBC rested entirely on his usefulness to the status quo and the ruling elites. If Owen Jones was genuinely a radical he would be marginalised by the corporate media. Jones once again indulged in windy generalisations: 'I think there was a lack of very basic emotional intelligence in some sections of the left in terms of engaging with the collective trauma of the Jewish people,' said Jones. 'And the same with Israel. There is an emotional connection that many Jewish people have with Israel and you just cannot ignore that.' No, I don't want to ignore that, Jones. I want to cause as much offence as possible to these people. Jews who have an emotional connection with Israel need to be told to stop wallowing in their sanctimonious enjoyment of victimhood. The Jewish state is, and always has been, a sectarian horror. The Jewish state has no right to exist. The Jewish state is not a democracy. It is a gerrymandered settler state. Owen Jones has nothing to say to the people of Gaza. He has nothing to say to those Palestinians who live inside the Zionist state. Owen Jones does not support the Boycott, Divestment and Sanctions Movement. Owen Jones is a careerist. Perhaps, thought Ellis, he will end up as a Labour MP. Quite possibly he will end up in the House of Lords. Clave Dements tweeted: *It's a real shame Mark Fisher namechecked him in Exiting the Vampire Castle. He turned out to be chief*

248

vampire. Exactly. Mark Fisher's essay, sadly evidence-free and without links to underscore his assertions, indicated the limitations of Fisher's politics. Plenty of people on social media had sniffed out the hypocrisies and careerism of Owen Jones. Fisher was in denial. Fisher ran to Jones's defence. The thrust of Fisher's essay seemed to be disdain for the rough and tumble of social media. Ellis went further down the rabbit hole. He came across an article by Micah Uetricht entitled 'The Beginning of the End of Capitalist Realism', on the *Jacobin* website, 30 January 2019. It was a tribute to Mark Fisher. 'I wish Mark could have held on because the nightmare of capitalist realism that he spent much of his life wrestling with is finally beginning to break,' wrote Micah Uetricht. 'We can see it wherever we look. Capitalist realism is beginning to break in the United Kingdom, where Jeremy Corbyn is on track to become the next Prime Minister. We can see capitalist realism beginning to break here in the United States, in the wild successes of Bernie Sanders. Perhaps we can see it nowhere better than in Rep. Alexandria Ocasio-Cortez's Twitter account.' Ellis clicked on a link in Micah Uetricht's piece, which connected him to various tributes to Mark Fisher by friends and associates published on 11th March 2017 on the *Los Angeles Review of Books* website. Ellis read the tribute to Mark Fisher by Roger Luckhurst. *I loved his haughty dismissal of the entire output of W. G. Sebald in two words: "Bourgeois kitsch!"* As for Ben Wheatley's *High-Rise.* He praised it in *forthright revolutionary language.* Ellis learned that Fisher used to hang out with Ellie Mae O'Hagan. Who in turn is a great pal of Owen Jones. Ellie Mae O'Hagan, who on 26 February 2017 on medium.com, published an article entitled *How do you solve a problem like Corbyn?* She revealed that when the Labour leadership race began in 2015 she planned to vote for Andy Burnham. Her article asserted that 'Corbyn is doing badly'. She attacked him for 'excessive hostility' to the media. She lambasted his personality, contrasting him with 'conscientious, brilliant people' like Matt Zarb-Cousin and James Schneider. She attacked Corbyn for seeming 'utterly disinterested in meeting the challenges that face him'. (The semi-literate Ms O'Hagan presumably meant 'uninterested'.) She cited a hack on the *Observer* who had attacked Corbyn for inheriting 'a brand...and he made it worse'. Ah yes, the Labour Party as *a brand.* Politics, for people like Ellie Mae O'Hagan, is all about selling a product. She goes on to cite - surprise, surprise! - Owen Jones. She insists she isn't a Blairite but confides that 'Blair was an impressive politician in many ways'. She wants Corbyn 'to chase the Remain vote'. She drivels that 'The Labour Party is in perhaps the worst mess it has ever been in', indicating how shallow her knowledge of Labour Party history is. Then again maybe she's never heard of Ramsay MacDonald. Then again it's no surprise that this peddler of soft-left rhetoric that ingratiates itself with the status quo finds herself in the happy position of having her blatherings published by the *Guardian*, the *New York Times*, the Murdoch press and the reactionary *New Statesman* or that she is paid to appear on BBC News, Newsnight, ITV News, Channel 4 News, Murdoch's Sky and elsewhere. The corporate media was awash with shallow mediocrities like Ellie Mae O'Hagan. They were commercially successful because they served power, not because they were talented, or clever, or thoughtful, or insightful, or interesting. Their supposed 'Left' identity functioned within accepted parameters. They never went outside the corporate frame. They never transgressed. The day grew hotter. It was reported that the Conservative MP for Devizes, Daniel Kruger, described as a close ally of Boris Johnson, had travelled from Hungerford to Paddington by train without wearing a mask, as required by law. A fellow passenger with a Twitter account had photographed him and posted the image on the social media site. The *Daily Mail* reported that on his own website Kruger had stated that he *detests the Rule of Six, the compulsory face mask, the Covid Marshalls and the snooping on your neighbours.* Confronted with the evidence of him flouting the facemask rule Kruger claimed to have 'forgotten'. Ellis made another mug of cappuccino. The child held up a bunch of keys. Keys, she said. It was a warm evening. Ellis watched the first episode of *Us*, the latest BBC drama for the white middle classes. It was about a white middle class couple going on a European trip as their marriage hangs in the balance. It had been filmed before the pandemic and the scenes all now seemed a little odd. A pandemic was like a revolution. Suddenly the old world was shaken up and re-arranged. Nothing was quite the same anymore. It was standard BBC fare. The production values were high. It was entertaining in an unchallenging, sofa-slump kind of way. Ellis went to bed and read the non-fiction book.

Tuesday 22nd September 2020

The last of the hot sunny days, according to the weather forecast. Ellis got up at 7.30am and went out early to post a card first class. He spent the morning drinking cappuccino and writing. The Labour Party was having an online annual conference, without the membership. The new leader made a speech. The *Guardian* gushed: *Significant sections of the speech sought to recast Starmer as a different leader to Corbyn, based not just on perceived competence but Starmer's repeated references to his patriotism, for example his family's pride when he was awarded a knighthood at Buckingham Palace for his previous work as Director of Public Prosecutions.* It was risible, Ellis thought. And futile. That kind of strategy had never worked in the past and would not do so in the future. As if to underline his credentials as a reactionary and a Zionist Starmer was introduced by Ruth Smeeth, the former Labour MP for Stoke-on-Trent North, who had lost her seat in December's election. Ruth Smeeth, who was about as nasty and right-wing as you could get in the Labour Party. Incredibly, Starmer was still going out of his way to perpetuate the great anti-Semitism fraud: *Starmer stressed his efforts over combating anti-Semitism in Labour, saying the party was becoming a competent, credible opposition. I ask you: take another look at Labour. We're under new leadership.* Who could doubt it? An ineffectual Leftist had been replaced by a wooden Establishment marionette. George Galloway tweeted: *He is a dalek, a desiccated calculating machine in which the batteries are slowly dying.* And Michael East@MichaelEast1983 tweeted a photograph of the two together, enjoying a meal: *Amazing how close Keir Starmer is to Ruth Smeeth, who has been funded by the Israeli lobby and identified in leaked cables by Wikileaks as a "strictly protect – US informant."* She's married to Michael Smeeth of the allegedly CIA-funded British-American Project. Ellis finished watching *Gladiator*. He ate a sausage casserole. He went to bed and finished the non-fiction book.

Wednesday 23rd September 2020

Pouring with rain. At the place where Sebald died a sign had gone up, advertising HALLOWEEN SPOOKTACULAR. Ellis drank coffee. He checked to see if he had any new emails. No. The child wore yellow boots and jumped delightedly in the puddle. She grew tired on the walk and Ellis carried her on the final stretch. Ellis came across the twitter account of David Glasgow @dvglasgow. David Glasgow wrote: *OK so this is a really great answer by Judith Butler on "cancel culture".* He reproduced part of a recent interview Judith Butler had given to the *New Statesman*. Butler had been asked about the notorious open letter on so-called "cancel culture" in *Harper's*. The one in which J. K. Rowling, Bari Weiss and others had whinged about being the victims of criticism and intolerance. Judith Butler commented: some of those signatories were taking aim at Black Lives Matter as if the loud and public opposition to racism were itself uncivilised behaviour. Some of them have opposed legal rights for Palestine. Others have [allegedly] committed sexual harassment. And yet others do not wish to be challenged on their racism. Democracy requires a good challenge, and it does not always arrive in soft tones. Judith Butler's comment, as reproduced by David Glasgow, ended: *When one has not been heard for decades, the cry for justice is bound to be loud.* It was a rather odd formulation of Butler's, Ellis felt. What was 'legal rights for Palestine' supposed to mean exactly? Weiss, like many prominent Jews, was a pathological apologist for Israel, keen to defend her privileges as a member of the supremacist religion in a sectarian state. There was no atrocity which people like her would not to seek to justify or muffle. The rain stopped, started again. It grew dark. There have been 6,178 new Coronavirus cases reported - the highest daily total in four months and the third-highest since the pandemic began. There would be no charges against the cops who repeatedly shot black woman Breonna Taylor in her own home in Kentucky. Ellis went to bed and read some pages of a book by Patricia Highsmith.

Thursday 24th September 2020

Raining. Ellis got up at 7.30am. It was much cooler. He put on a long-sleeved shirt. Online he read a tweet by Matt Kennard@kennardmatt: *Labour's Shadow Foreign Secretary @LisaNandy has never once tweeted about Yemen where 10 million children face starvation in the world's worst humanitarian disaster, a man-made crime in which the British government is majorly complicit.* Next Ellis read a report by Craig Murray about Day 16 of the Julian Assange extradition hearing: *It has been clear to me from Day 1 that I am watching a charade unfold. It is not in the least a shock to me that Baraitser does not think anything beyond the written opening arguments has any effect. I have again and again reported to you that, where rulings have to be made, she has brought them into court pre-written, before hearing the arguments before her. I strongly expect the final decision was made in this case even before opening arguments were received. The plan of the US Government throughout has been to limit the information available to the public and limit the effective access to a wider public of what information is available. Thus we have seen the extreme restrictions on both physical and video access. A complicit mainstream media has ensured those of us who know what is happening are very few in the wider population. Even my blog has never been so systematically subject to shadowbanning from Twitter and Facebook as now.* The rain stopped and the sun came out. The child played with a set of keys. That evening Ellis ate cheese soufflé with broccoli and boiled new potatoes, washed down with two glasses of red wine. He had a bad cold. His nose and eyes streamed and he had a sore throat. Afterwards he ate a bowl of raspberries with ice-cream and yogurt. He watched *Les Diaboliques*, guessing the twist. In bed he read more of the Patricia Highsmith book.

Friday 25th September 2020

Heavy rain, with strong winds forecast later in the day. On the 'Today' programme the presenters chuckled over the press story about how Benjamin Netanyahu and his wife took suitcases of dirty laundry with them when they visited the White House, in order to get them cleaned for free. Not on the 'Today' programme was the revelation that companies controlled by Chelsea football club owner Roman Abramovich had donated tens of millions of pounds to an Israeli settler group responsible for driving Palestinian families out of their homes in Jerusalem. The billionaire Russian oligarch was granted Israeli citizenship in 2018. Four companies he controls in the British Virgin Islands have contributed more than £74 million to Elad, a Jewish group trying to oust

Palestinians from the neighbourhood of occupied East Jerusalem called Silwan. The rain continued all day. A gale tore at the trees in the locality. A policeman was reported to have been shot dead in Croydon. Leaves showered everywhere. Ellis read an online article by Richard Sanders on the Middle East Eye website, entitled *'The wrong sort of Jew': How Labour pursued complaints against elderly Jewish opponents of Israel.* It began with the July 2019 BBC Panorama stitch-up, *Is Labour Anti-Semitic?* Panorama spoke to party member Ben Westerman, the only Jewish official on the complaints team, who it reported "was confronted with the very antisemitism he'd been sent to investigate". Westerman told Panorama that, after one interview had finished, he was asked by one of those present: "Where are you from... Are you from Israel?" The interviewee Westerman spoke to that day appears to have been a woman called Helen Marks. As part of Labour Party procedure, she was allowed a "silent witness" who could observe, but not participate in, the interview, for which she chose her friend Rica Bird. With Westerman's permission, they recorded the conversation. The programme omitted to mention that Marks and Bird, both 74, are Jewish. Neither, they said, knew that Westerman was Jewish. At the end there is an exchange that closely matches the one described in Panorama – except that there is no mention of Israel. Westerman was among the contributors to the Panorama programme who in July received an apology and financial compensation from the Labour Party which had initially described them as being "disaffected former employees" with "political axes to grind". The party says it now accepts this description was "defamatory and false". The incident involving Marks and Bird, wrote Richard Sanders, is an example of one little-reported aspect of the Labour antisemitism story – the frequency with which Jewish party members find themselves the centre of investigations, often on what they regard as the flimsiest and most tendentious of grounds. It is a trend that appears to have gathered pace since Keir Starmer took over as Labour Party leader in April 2020, continued Richard Sanders. The article described the case of Stephen Solley, a retired QC and former chair of the Bar Human Rights Committee. He is Jewish, a Labour Party member and a critic of Israel. On 28 January he received a campaign email from Miriam Mirwitch, chair of Young Labour, the party's youth section, and a candidate for the London Assembly. "I know what it's like to face antisemitism every day," Mirwitch wrote, identifying herself as a national committee member of the Jewish Labour Movement. "I've had to fight antisemitism both inside and outside the Labour Party," she said. Solley told Richard Sanders: "I got this just a week after Holocaust Remembrance Day. I thought this was the most offensive thing. She lives in modern north-west London. It's absurd. Of course she doesn't face antisemitism every day. It's just whipping up anxiety. I was really upset by it." He replied to Mirwitch with a short, simple email. "The Jewish Labour Movement is, in my opinion, a force for ill and something of a con in that it is destructive of socialism. It is a pro-

Israel, anti Palestine group. It becomes imperative to vote against you." Twenty-three minutes later, wrote Richard Sanders, Mirwitch wrote to Solley's former chambers, accusing him of anti-Semitism. She also wrote to the Bar Standards Board. Both rejected her accusations. But three days after sending the email, Solley received notification from the Labour Party that he was under investigation for anti-Semitism, an investigation that appears to be ongoing. Solley is aware that by speaking out he may have contravened the party's demand that he "keep all information and correspondence relating to this investigation private." But Solley said he didn't care. "If they really want to expel the Jewish former chair of the Bar Human Rights Committee so be it." The article went on to compare Jewish Voice for Labour, which claims over 1,000 Labour Party members, a third of them Jewish, with the aggressively pro-Israel Jewish Labour Movement, which claims 3,000 members, although how many are Jewish is unclear, as is the number of those who are not members of the Labour Party. The key line of division between the two organisations, wrote Richard Sanders, is the International Holocaust Remembrance Alliance definition of anti-Semitism adopted by the Labour Party in September 2018. The definition is opposed by JVL. "The IHRA definition is hopelessly vague, muddled and open-ended," Avi Shlaim told Richard Sanders. "It deliberately conflates anti-Zionism with antisemitism in order to deter legitimate criticisms of Israel. It has 11 'illustrative examples' of antisemitism. Seven of them relate to Israel. That's the giveaway. Antisemitism is hatred of Jews as Jews. That's all we need." Criticism of the IHRA definition focuses in particular on example number seven: "Denying the Jewish people their right to self-determination, e.g., by claiming that the existence of a State of Israel is a racist endeavour." Ellis remembered that on the day the Labour Party cravenly signed up to this Zionist fraud, a group in London put up posters in the panels at some London bus stops stating ISRAEL IS A RACIST ENDEAVOUR. Ellis also remembered that John McDonnell MP had stupidly denounced this as - wait for it - 'anti-Semitic'. With comrades like McDonnell and Corbyn it was hardly surprising that the Left in the Labour Party had been routed by the Right. But few on the Left seemed to acknowledge this. As he took in more of the Richard Sanders article Ellis was astonished to read Avi Shlaim's comment that "Zionism began as a national liberation struggle of the Jewish people - an anti-racist movement in fact". It was a bizarre assertion, since Zionism from its inception was a reactionary and virulently racist colonial ideology. Shlaim, it appeared, believed that Israel only became a "colonial enterprise" following the occupation of the West Bank and Gaza Strip in 1967. Ellis was disappointed in Avi Shlaim, for whom he had previously had a certain regard. The article continued, and highlighted another case involving an elderly Jew placed under a Notice of Investigation. "It's Kafkaesque," she says. "You are not told who is accusing you. And you are not allowed to discuss it with anyone. So you receive this devastating letter – and are immediately isolated." In short, the Labour Party was a thoroughly rotten institution, which Corbyn had made no attempt to reform during his short tenure as leader. The article revealed that 'a significant proportion of its committee' is now under investigation. Ellis had a streaming cold. He went to bed and dozed. At 4pm he had a bath and then dressed. He began watching *The Boston Strangler*, but grew bored by it and fast-forwarded it to the end. He ate spaghetti bolognaise with salad followed by apple crumble and ice-cream. By 7.15pm it was dark outside. Later there was a power cut. Ellis lit some candles and sat in a chair, waiting for the power to return. It came back on again in time for him to watch some of the 10pm Sky News. The blood-spattered Commissioner of the Metropolitan Police had the chutzpah to mourn the death of an innocent man by shooting. Ellis went to bed and began reading Derek Marlowe's *Echoes of Celandine*, which Nicholas Royle had recommended as *one of the best novels by England's best ever novelist*.

Saturday 26th September 2020

Grey, cold, raining. A day for staying in. Ellis could manage without his Saturday *Times* if he really had to. Besides, he only bought it for the TV guide. The child played with a carton of milk, trying to remove the screw-top lid. Having failed, she investigated the drawer of the desk. It contained a variety of pens and pencils. Ellis went online and read some reader-reviews of the September 2018 *Reece Witherspoon Hello Sunshine Book Club* choice. What makes this a fabulous read are the rich descriptions, the language and the languorous pace that, just like the waterways, move the story along at just the right tempo, wrote one anonymous admirer. The setting comes to life beautifully. The writing and storytelling has been compared to the work of Barbara Kingsolver and I can really see why! The title comes from common parlance in the area and means ...far in the bush where critters are wild, still behaving like critters... I was sad when this book came to an end and it is still vibrantly with me, a couple of weeks down the line. It indeed has all the hallmarks of a future classic! But, Ellis noted, there were dissenters. Absurd plot, dreadful dialogue, terrible sex scenes - absolutely nothing to recommend this over-acclaimed novel. I was expecting something exceptional but was completely underwhelmed. I felt the the characters were underdeveloped and the plot rushed and implausible. The dialogue is ridiculous, the love scenes are stitched together out of worn-out clichés, and the suspension of disbelief required of the reader is just asking way too much. It continued raining. On the Radio 4 news programme at 5pm Ellis listened as Andrew Neill was allowed to promote his forthcoming TV news channel, claiming that it would offer a much-needed alternative to the left-leaning mainstream news channels of the BBC, ITV, Sky and Channel 4. The interview was preceded by another Corbyn-bashing episode in which Neill challenged Corbyn on his support for the IRA. The question was lengthy and was more like a criminal indictment. Corbyn's reply was truncated by the BBC, which once again could barely conceal its hostility to him. Neill's absurd proposition that the corporate media was somehow the repository of progressive values - a media which was currently blanking all coverage of the Assange extradition proceedings, which was currently failing to report on the atrocious state of the people of Yemen (and on the rare occasions that it did, muffled the RAF's complicity in and responsibility for mass murder), which regularly adopted the missionary position in the face of Britain's dull, parasitical royal family, which comprehensively blanked coverage of British military repression and its activities on behalf of US imperialism, and which could always be relied upon to represent Palestinians as truculent, violent irrational Arabs, and their bigoted, murderous Jewish oppressors as incarnations of virtue and rationality - was not for a moment challenged by the BBC's softball interviewer. But then the interviewer shared the same values as Andrew Neill. What was not mentioned was that Neill's TV channel was obviously intended to be the British equivalent of Fox News, and would be publicising the views of far-right ideologues, Zionists and racists, with a view to normalising bigotry, hatred and illiberalism. It would be a TV channel pitched at UKIP members and *Daily Mail* readers. No doubt in due course Owen Jones would put in an appearance, giggling along with Alastair Campbell and Jacob Rees-Mogg. The rain stopped. Ellis went into the kitchen to peel some potatoes. That evening he watched *Hidden Figures*. In bed he read a few pages of *Echoes of Celandine*. Outside, the wind had picked up speed, making the TV aerial clank against the chimney which supported it.

Sunday 27th September 2020

Grey, cold, wet. Autumnal. Fallen leaves everywhere. Drizzle. The store was empty. People aren't coming out today, the proprietor said, gesturing at all the unsold newspapers. Ellis drank coffee and glanced at the *Sunday Times*. The child drew shapes on her new whiteboard, then wiped them off. Bye bye, she said, and then drew more shapes. These she also erased. Bye bye! Ellis drank a second cappuccino. He read that over 50 actors, writers, playwrights and journalists had signed a letter deploring the 'hate speech' directed against J. K. Rowling. 'J K Rowling has been subjected to an onslaught of abuse that highlights an insidious, authoritarian and misogynistic trend in social media.' Ellis glanced at the list of signatories. Where the famous ones were concerned, it was the usual crowd of faux liberal reactionaries, multi-millionaires, Zionists and right-wing hacks. There was the actor Griff Rhys Jones, who Ellis recalled had led the brave struggle of the super-rich when the Labour leader Ed Miliband had proposed a mansion tax. A mansion tax! It transpired that Rhys Jones owned three mansions. How he frothed at the prospect of contributing a fraction of his wealth to benefit those who did not enjoy his own agreeable housing arrangements. Ellis wondered how many of those signing this letter also owned two or more homes. Then there was Sir Tom Stoppard, who had long been a pitiless Tory and a dear friend of Rupert Murdoch. There was the grotesque bloated Zionist tweeter and third-rate actress, Frances Barber. For Frances Barber to deplore unkind words on Twitter was beyond satire. There was the genre novelist Ian McEwan, who had declined to oppose the invasion of Iraq and who had written a meretricious novel mocking those who had opposed it, while extolling the merits of apathy and consumerism. There were novelists Ellis was completely indifferent to - Lionel Shriver, Susan Hill, Philip Hensher. There was, perhaps a little surprisingly, Francis Wheen, yesterday's man, slithering into reaction in old age. There was the comedian Alexander Armstrong, who had all the substance of candy-floss. There were right-wing faux-left hacks like Nick Cohen and Joan Smith. It was Nick Cohen, Ellis recalled, who, in his *Observer* column, had addressed those planning to vote for Corbyn as Labour leader with the words *Just. Fucking. Don't.* (or something like that). For Cohen to deplore abusive language by others was kinda ironic. There were others who Ellis was vaguely aware of (Andrew Davies, Craig Brown, Sam Leith) and some he thought he'd probably heard of (but without being entirely sure): Amanda Smyth, Trezza Azzopardi, Jane Thynne, Maureen Chadwick, Amanda Craig, Jane Harris, Julie Bindel. There were others Ellis had never known existed: Graham Linehan (writer), Ben Miller (actor), Simon Fanshawe (writer), James Dreyfus (actor), Frances Welch (writer), Arthur Matthews (writer), Russel Celyn Jones (writer), Aminatta Fornia (writer), Kaths Goots (musician), Ann McManus (writer), Eileen Gallagher (writer), Jimmy Mulville (producer), Lizzie Roper (actress), Stella O'Malley (writer), Nina Paley (animator), Abigal Shrier (journalist), Rachel Rooney (writer), Tatsuya Ishida (cartoonist), Lisa Marchiano (writer), Zuby (musician and writer), Debbie Hayton (journalist), Gillian Philip (writer), Jonny Best (musician), Manick Govinda ('arts consultant'), Magi Gibson (writer), Victoria Whitworth (writer), Dr Mez Packer (writer), Grace Carley (producer), Malcolm Clark (television producer and director), Shirley Wishart (musician), Charlotte Delaney (writer), Nehanda Ferguson (musician), Justin Hill (writer), Birdy Rose (artist), Jess de Wahls ('textile artist'), Mo Lovatt (writer), Simon Edge (novelist). It was good to have a list like this. It meant Ellis could boycott their books, their TV shows, their art. Of course with public letters like this it was always as interesting to see who had not signed as who had. Tom Burke hadn't, for example. Holliday Grainger hadn't, for example. Of course they may not have been asked... Ellis ate lamb steak with new potatoes, cabbage, onion and pepper. He watched the third episode of *The Singapore Grip*. Afterwards he watched the Sky 10pm News. He was astonished to see that it began with a report of a probable war crime in Yemen. A Sky TV team consisting of Middle East Editor Zein Jafar, producer Ahmed Baider, and cameraman Kevin Sheppard, fronted by reporter Alex Crawford, travelled hundreds of kilometres along dry riverbeds and through rocky, inhospitable terrain and winding mountain paths to reach the remote village of Washah near the Yemeni-Saudi border. This is a poor community with no running water or electricity. They then walked up narrow hill trails to the site of an airstrike on a family home. *We were the first outsiders to reach the site,* explained Alex Crawford, *and the first independent journalists to examine the area and talk to multiple eyewitnesses as well as survivors of the massacre. The mud and stone home was now rubble. There was very little left of it. But it was still strewn with personal items from the Mujali family who once lived there.* The bomb killed nine people instantly - six of them children. Among the debris was a metal cooking dish, toys, a baby's bib, small trousers for a toddler. The crowd of neighbours who gathered round the Sky team were angry as well as shocked. They showed the Sky team photographs taken after the bombing. *Many of them were the blackened and grubby faces of the dead children, many without limbs, some barely recognisable as humans.* "Body parts landed on my roof," one older man said. "I live up the hill there,' he said, pointing. "I'd never seen anything like it." Others pointed down the valley: "A leg ended up there. And an arm there." *This was a massacre. Nine people died on that day. Six of them were children. There were no adult men amongst the dead or injured. There were only three survivors - a young mother who was breastfeeding her baby son and a teenage boy.* The Sky team tracked down the survivors, who were now living hundreds of kilometres from Washah. They learned that the family had been gathering in the house for their midday meal. It was around 1pm on Sunday 12 July when the attack happened. The young mother, Nora Ali Muse'ad Mujali, said she had been breastfeeding her baby son in the corner of the house when the bomb hit. Her young daughter was next to her. "I was in shock. The house was destroyed. I was searching for my daughter. But she was dead. Then I saw my sister-in-law and she was dead too. I just picked up my son and screamed for help." The bomb came from a jet circling the village. It was a targeted attack. No other house in the village was touched. After the massacre the jet continued to circle for another 15 minutes. The deliberate targeting of civilian and non-military sites is a war crime under international law. The bomb fragments at the scene appeared to be from a GBU-12 fin-guided 500lb bomb, manufactured in the USA. Human rights investigators have details of over 500 attacks on civilian targets by the US-UK-Saudi dictatorship alliance. The Royal Air Force is instrumental in the murder of children. It is complicit in attacks on hospitals, schools, health facilities and homes. Confronted by the Sky report the British government's response was bland and banal. It was in no danger of having its imperial deceits and atrocities challenged by the leader of the Labour Party. Ellis went to bed. He read a few

258

more pages of *Echoes of Celandine.*

Monday 28th September 2020

Grey, cold, dull. Ellis went out early to post a letter in time for the 9am
collection. Later he began assembling a bookcase from a kit. At lunchtime he
caught up with some of the commentary surrounding Congresswoman
Alexandria Ocasio-Cortez's acceptance of an invitation from a Zionist front
organisation calling itself Americans for Peace Now to a commemoration of the
former Israeli Prime Minister Yitzhak Rabin. Ellis came across a link to an old
online article about 'the true Yitzkak Rabin': https://www.alternet.org/amp/i-
would-see-gaza-drown-sea-remembering-true-yitzhak-rabin-20-years-after-his-
assassination-0-2647285146, published on 5 November 2015. It pointed out that
in 1988, Yitzkak Rabin had boasted of his achievements as the Defence Minister
who enacted the "broken bones" policy to suppress the first Palestinian
Intifada. "They also know: 260 Palestinians were killed in the last two months!"
he proclaimed to boisterous applause from his audience. "7,000 were wounded!"
Rabin bragged. "18,000 were arrested!" He continued boastfully, "5,600 are
currently in prison. Are these trivial numbers? Are these trivial numbers?" Rabin
was only ever interested in what he described as 'an entity which is less than a
state' for the Palestinians. He had no interest whatever in co-existence, only in
control. It was Rabin's idea to wall off the Gaza Strip. A few months later this
great humanitarian and liberal said: "I would like to see Gaza drown in the
sea." But then genocide has always been inherent in the Zionist project. Many of
Rabin's central strategic ambitions have been fulfilled, the article asserted.
Thanks to the siege of Gaza and the construction of a vast concrete wall severing
the occupied West Bank from Jerusalem, his vision of hard separation has
become a reality. The Palestinian Authority and Hamas are governing in the key
Palestinian population centres, embracing a form of limited autonomy beneath
Israeli occupation. And as the conditions of basic life in Gaza deteriorate to
catastrophic levels, some of the coastal enclave's most desperate residents are
literally drowning [https://euobserver.com/justice/125652] in the sea. Rabin's
involvement in Zionist violence dated back to 1948, when he had issued a
written order to the Yiftach Brigade, a Zionist militia: "The inhabitants of Lydda
must be expelled quickly, without regard to age." Some Palestinians took refuge
in Lydda's Dahmash mosque, where Rabin's men massacred around 120
civilians. In 2013, Yerachmiel Kahanovich, a fighter in the Palmach Zionist
militia, told an Israeli interviewer about what they had done. "Sometimes we
had to shoot one or two, and then the rest got the message and left on their
own," Kahanovich said. "You need to understand: if you didn't destroy the
Arab's home, he will always want to come back," he added. "When there is no
home, no village, there is nowhere to return." Kahanovich was present at a

massacre. The dead were "all scattered on the walls," he recalled. Asked how many, Kahanovich replied, "I don't know. Many. I didn't count. I opened the door, saw what I saw, and closed it." Audeh Rantisi was 11 years old when Israeli soldiers ordered his family out of their home in Lydda on 13 July 1948. He recalled how in the summer heat "Women in black *abbahs* and heavily embroidered Palestinian dresses hysterically clutched their infants as they stumbled forward to avoid the expected spray of machine gun fire." Over three days without food, water and in the heat, many would die, until finally trucks came to transport the survivors to Ramallah. "Our death march was over," Rantisi wrote. "Our life as refugees had begun." Two decades after the Lydda Death March, in June 1967, Israel occupied the West Bank and Gaza Strip, completing the Zionist takeover of Palestine. Twenty more years would pass until in December 1987 an unarmed popular uprising broke out in the West Bank and Gaza against Israel's brutal military occupation. As Defence Minister and effective military dictator over millions of Palestinians, Rabin embraced his task of crushing the intifada. He publicly ordered Israel's army to use "force, might and beatings" – as well as live ammunition that took the lives of young Palestinians almost daily for years. One piece of film, widely broadcast at the time, showed Israeli soldiers methodically beating two Palestinian youths using rocks, trying to break their bones. The two boys, both 17, were cousins, Wael and Osama Jawdeh. Israeli army Lieutenant Eldad Ben-Moshe testified that his commander Colonel Yehuda Meir told him to "break the arms and legs" of Palestinians "because the detention camps are full". Another officer, identified as Lieutenant Colonel Zvi, testified that Rabin himself "told me to lash into them forcefully and beat them" without restraint in 1988. Like an old Nazi, Yitzkak Rabin never once expressed regret for his crimes. Like innumerable Israeli war criminals and murderers, Yitzkak Rabin never had to face trial for his crimes. Alexandria Ocasio-Cortez's initial agreement to participate in an event honoring this vile individual is telling, even though she later retracted it. Next, Ellis read an online article by Amjad Iraqi, which criticised 'The Myth of Rabin the Peacemaker'. (https://www.972mag.com/yitzhak-rabin-oslo-accords-aoc/) His persona as a "warrior-turned-peacemaker" is almost exclusively centered on the final four years of his life, five decades of which were defined by hawkish and militaristic views, wrote Amjad Iraqi. This cult of personality, dotingly crafted by the Zionist left in Israel and liberal Zionists in the United States, has particularly relied on a counterfactual argument: that had he not been killed, Rabin might have helped to bring about a two-state solution. From 1993 to 1995 Israel initiated the construction of over 6,400 housing units in settlements. In that time Israel also demolished at least 328 Palestinian homes and structures — including in East Jerusalem. The result was that Israel's settler population rose by 20,000, and Palestinians were displaced in the thousands, while Rabin sat at the plastic negotiating table. Oslo simply restructured the occupation and minimized the cost to Israelis. The newly created Palestinian Authority suppressed opposition on Israel's behalf. The Paris Protocol allowed Israel to control the Palestinian economy and resources. As critics like Edward Said warned, the accords were always an illusion. The myths around Rabin, wrote Amjad Iraqi, have distracted from his most egregious fault: his belief in Jewish supremacy in Palestine, and his will to commit atrocities to pursue it. Next Ellis read two tweets by Asa Winstanley. 26 September: *It's been more than a week and @jeremycorbyn still hasn't said a word about this open letter by British Palestinians (including a former Labour councillor) objecting to their censorship by the Labour Party.* And: *He has, however, found time to post about getting a song about Dennis Skinner into the charts.* The child ran into the playground. She wore her yellow boots and yellow raincoat. She went to and fro on the swing, grinning with delight. That evening Ellis watched the second episode of *Us*, the latest BBC easy-viewing comedy for its ageing centrist white middle class audience. It had its moments. On Sky News Alex Crawford visited victims on the other side of the Yemen civil war. There was footage of hideously maimed children who had picked up landmines. Landmines! Sky did not consider the matter of who manufactured them, or who sold them, or the politicians who were complicit in this trade in barbarism. Politics was not permitted to intrude upon human interest. The horror lacked context. Historians were never interviewed for this kind of news. A writer like Mark Curtis, who could have offered enlightenment on the conflict, was shunned by the corporate media. Ellis went to bed and read a few more pages written by Derek Marlowe.

Tuesday 29th September 2020

Muggy, drizzling, a damp autumn day. Ellis got up when 'Thought For The Day' started. The thinkers were invariably Zionist fanatics, Anglican bores or banal smoothies from some other faith. You didn't even have to understand a word these thinkers uttered to know it was 'Thought For The Day'. It was the tone. Privately educated verbs. Syllables marinated in syrup. The thinkers invariably oozed their prejudices coated in sugary self-satisfaction and smugness. Paltry conservative platitudes paraded as if profound. Today it was Anne Atkins, described as a novelist and commentator. Ellis had never heard of her. 'In my gap year,' gushed Atkins, 'I was privileged to smuggle Bibles behind the iron curtain'. Ellis left the room. Drinking coffee and gazing at his computer Ellis realised it was six months to the day that he'd recorded in *Twenty-Twenty* what he'd learned from the corporate news: *The deputy chief medical officer, a rather lacklustre woman named Jenny Harries, says it could be six months before life in the UK returns to normal. The number of dead from the virus in Britain has reached 1,228. The numbers would get worse over the next week, possibly two, and then we are looking to see whether we have managed to push that curve down and we start to see a decline, said the deputy chief medical officer.* Had life in Britain returned to normal? No. How many have now died? 42,014. How many have been infected? 443,044. The drizzle faded. Ellis made a phone call. Later he looked up novelist Anne Atkins, never having heard of her before. A self-styled 'controversialist', her Wikipedia entry exposed what a prejudiced Christian dullard she was. On Amazon she was the author of *An Elegant Solution.* It had earned a five star review from Simon Ratsey: **A 21st century thriller, it deserves recognition as a masterpiece and portrait of our times.** *While the build-up of tension became almost unbearable at times, the denouement was exactly as it needed to be.* Simon Ratsey had reviewed three other titles on the Amazon site: Ruth Valerio's *Saying Yes to Life,* a theology book published by SPCK (five stars), Ruth Valerio's *Just Living: Faith and Community in an Age of Consumerism* (five stars), and Tom Wright's *Simply Good News: Why the Gospel is News and What Makes it Good* (five stars). But 'Cricket enthusiast' asserted that Anne Atkins's novel contained inaccuracies and poor proof reading. 'Amazon Customer' explained that the book had been purchased as a mother's early Christmas present. 'She has been glued to it and thoroughly swept along with the pace of the story.' Elsewhere on Twitter Ellis learned that it had been decided not to prosecute any of the paratroopers involved in the Bloody Sunday massacre, apart from one, known as Soldier F. The British state continued to look after its own. *In 10 mins on Bloody Sunday, 30 Jan 1972, 21 British paratroopers fired 108 times at unarmed protestors in Derry. 26 civilians were shot. 14 died, 12 injured & 2 more run down by army vehicles.* Elsewhere Ellis read that Mark Elf, AKA *Jews Sans Frontieres,* had responded to a tweet by the BBC's Daniel Sandford regarding criticism that the corporation was blanking out the Assange extradition hearing. Sandford wrote: *The case is being covered by our World Affairs unit. I have been in a few hearings, and it is slightly repetitive at the moment. It will return as a news story.* Mark Elf wrote: *Wow, a BBC journo is using "slightly repetitive" as an excuse for not publicising the Julian Assange affair. The constant repetition of lies about #LabourAntisemitism was no problem for the Beeb. @BBCNews and @guardiannews were the main offenders.* Ellis watched the first episode of the latest BBC drama, *Life.* He went to bed and read a few more pages of Derek Marlowe's novel.

Wednesday 30th September 2020

A bright sunny morning. Today's BBC 'Thought For The Day' provided a platform for yet another rabid Zionist, this one in the familiar shape of Giles Fraser. He was plugging a book called *Why We Drive* by Matthew Crawford. Later, the 'Today' programme plugged the forthcoming return of the Spitting Image puppet show. It was described as bravely satirical, which was itself satire.

The humour of Spitting Image would lie in its feeble mimicry of selected politicians and celebrities. It would have all the edge of a bald tyre. It would spinelessly avoid politicians and subjects which were taboo - Netanyahu, the Chief Rabbi, Israel, the RAF's terror campaign in Yemen. It would be softball satire. In later years the politicians would explain how they purchased their own puppet, out of affection. Spitting Image would be as cosy and bland as a speech by Sir Keir Starmer. Later, Ellis looked up *Why We Drive*. It appeared to be an apologia for carcentrism, with a chapter denouncing cycling campaigners. Ellis couldn't be bothered to buy the book to find out. Anything which Giles Fraser liked, and which had received a rave review on *Unherd*, was plainly right-wing trash. The weather forecast was for rain sweeping across England. Ellis went out and bought some fish. It did not rain, then or later. At lunchtime he watched Sky's edited version of the Trump-Biden debate. It was predictably unenlightening. Trump was his usual bullying self, voicing the fantastic lie that he had paid 'millions' in tax, rather than $750 for the year in question. Trump claimed, preposterously, to be the enemy of big pharma. Biden focused his gaze on the viewer, pitching himself as the father of a patriotic soldier who had done his duty in Eye-rack. The child played with a crayon. In the evening Ellis cooked smoked salmon and fried some handcut chips. He had a bath. He watched the 10pm Sky News. There was an interesting segment about the forgotten racist history of Bristol. Apparently in the 1960s a local bus company refused to employ black drivers, on the grounds that this might upset white passengers. Black activists organised a strike, which forced the company to change its policy. The Labour government under Harold Wilson later brought in legislation in 1965, making such discrimination unlawful. It was a good example of how change came not from the top but from below. Protest and dissent preceded action by Parliament. Ellis went to bed. He read a few more pages of *Echoes of Celandine*.

Thursday 1st October 2020

It was grey and cloudy and raining, but warm for October. Ellis went to the bank, the supermarket and the bottle bank. Later he read *Observer* reviewer Hannah Beckman's tweet about *Three Hours* by Rosamund Lupton: *I gasped my way through it in two breathless sittings.* Later, from an article on the *Electronic Intifada* website written by Omar Karmi, Ellis learned that the *Lancet*, under its spineless editor Richard Horton, had capitulated to pressure from a Zionist after publishing a letter, 'Structural violence in the era of a new pandemic: the case of the Gaza Strip' written by David Mills of Boston's Children's Hospital, Bram Wispelwey of Boston's Brigham and Women's Hospital, Rania Muhareb, formerly of the Palestinian human rights group Al-Haq, and Mads Gilbert of University Hospital of North Norway (Volume 396, Issue 10255, 26 September–

2 October 2020, p. 882). It ran: Hope for improving health and quality of life of Palestinians will exist only once people recognise that the structural and political conditions that they endure…are the key determinants of [Palestinian] population health. As the world is consumed by the spread of coronavirus disease 2019 (COVID-19), it should be of no surprise that epidemics (and indeed, pandemics) are disproportionately violent to populations burdened by poverty, military occupation, discrimination, and institutionalised oppression. Structural violence rooted in historical, political, and social injustices determines health patterns and creates vulnerabilities that hamper the effective prevention, detection, and response to communicable disease outbreaks. In the occupied Gaza Strip, the convergence of these forces in the era of a pandemic have the potential to devastate one of the world's most vulnerable populations. The colonial fragmentation of the Palestinian people and their health systems, combined with a neoliberal development framework implemented during the past decades, has created a profound dependency on aid, placing health care at the mercy of increasingly restrictive international donor politics. Since 2007, Israel has imposed a crippling land, air, and sea blockade over the Gaza Strip's 2 million Palestinians, 1.4 million of whom are refugees, subjecting them to extreme crowding in one of the world's most densely populated regions. As a result, the Gaza Strip faces high levels of poverty, unemployment, food insecurity, and lacks sufficient clean water while the blockade disrupts medical supply chains, curtails the movement of patients and health workers, and severely inhibits medical capacity-building and public health development. Preventive measures and containment of COVID-19 will be extremely difficult now that the pandemic has reached the Gaza Strip. While prisoners in Iran and elsewhere are temporarily being released to protect them from contained spread, for Palestinians, living in what is described as the largest open-air prison in the world, there is nowhere to go—unless, of course, they are granted their legal and moral right of return. Guided by our moral values and professional obligations, the international community must act now to end structural violence by confronting the historical and political forces entrenching a cyclical, violent, and mutable reality for Palestinians. A COVID-19 pandemic that further cripples the Gaza Strip's health-care system should not be viewed as an inevitable biomedical phenomenon experienced equally by the world's population, but as a preventable biosocial injustice rooted in decades of Israeli oppression and international complicity in the struggle for the health, fundamental rights, and self-determination of all Palestinians. We declare no competing interests. This letter produced a furious response from Daniel Drucker, a Canadian endocrinologist, who took to Twitter on 29 March to excoriate *The Lancet* and its editor, Richard Horton. The craven Horton then spinelessly deleted the letter, earning the praise of Daniel Drucker: *We must commend the Editor-in-Chief, Dr. Richard Horton, for his swift decision to pull the Mills et al letter about Gaza*

from the Lancet Website Monday March 30. In a blog post, Drucker wrote: *Anti-semitism, anti-zionism, and anti-Israel invective, are highly related strains, and have proven to be repeatedly lethal. While grateful for the actions of the EIC at* Lancet, *we must ask-what motivation prompted the* Lancet *to publish this Letter in the first place? At a time when all countries are united in the same goal to battle a deadly pathogen, how did the* Lancet *perceive it was advancing its Global Health goals by publishing a one sided trope excoriating Israel, while once again ignoring the complicity of the terror state that regularly diverts hundreds of millions of $ into tunnels, rockets, armies, and militias, and away from health care and hospitals for its civilian population.* A classically froth-filled piece of rhetoric from an apologist for the Jewish state. A state which repeatedly murdered Palestinian medical personnel and bombed hospitals. Bram Wispelwey said it was "astounding" that *The Lancet* decided to publish a letter in response to an article that had already been taken down. "It just makes the whole situation more bizarre," Wispelwey said. "Publishing a response to a now 'disappeared' piece and allowing him to comment on its removal?" Wispelwey added: "Censorship and surveillance are classic methods of settler-colonial control." Rather than aiming for a false "balance" of viewpoints that fails to account for power differentials, Wispelwey said, we must "start recognizing, naming and resisting these forces in academic medicine and beyond". *The Lancet*, reported *the Electronic Intifada*, did not wish to comment. That night Ellis read a few more pages of *Echoes of Celandine*. He was nearing the end.

Friday 2nd October 2020

At 6.20am, drinking tea, Ellis learned that President Trump and his wife had tested positive for Covid-19. It was a dull grey day, with brief patches of watery sunlight. The choice for 'Thought For The Day' on the BBC 'Today' programme was Zionist fanatic and Trump-worshipper, the Chief Rabbi, Ephraim Mirvis. Ellis went to the children's playground. He pushed the child on the swing, then went on the see-saw with her. He helped her to the top of the activity frame and held her until she could safely slither down the slide. Her yellow boots impeded her progress but she liked it. *Again!* Rain did not fall until the afternoon. While the child napped, Ellis finished reading *Echoes of Celandine*. That evening he ate quiche with baked beans. In bed he began reading *The Uncollected Stories of Patricia Highsmith*.

Saturday 3rd October 2020

President Trump has been admitted to hospital. This is purely precautionary. It is a warm morning, with light rain. There was a queue outside the store. Ellis glanced through the reviews in the *Times*. The child played with the potato-masher and a spoon. That evening Ellis ate a cheese soufflé and watched *Trumbo*. A film about writing in which we are never shown any writing. We see the typewriter, the cigarettes, the glasses of whisky, the meetings with Hollywood producers and directors. But no writing. Or, for that matter, reading. The index of success is an Oscar. Yet Hollywood movies seem vastly inferior to European ones. *Spartacus* is hollow. *Exodus* is plodding, one dimensional, meretricious and racist. It's Zionist propaganda straight out of Goebbels Studios. Aftewards Ellis watched the 10pm Sky news. There was confusion about when Donald Trump first displayed symptoms of Covid-19. Was it as early as last Wednesday? Footage was shown of the President on the campaign trail last week, throwing baseball caps into the adoring crowd. Had he been sick then? It was revealed that Trump had required oxygen at the White House, prior to his hospitalisation. The front page of the *Sunday Telegraph* asserted the possibility that Trump was seriously ill. Ellis went to bed and read a few more pages of the Highsmith book.

Sunday 4th October 2020

Grey, warm, overcast, raining. Ellis did not wake until 8.45am. It was reported that President Trump had released a video of himself saying he was feeling fine. There were suggestions that the footage had been edited to remove coughing. In South-West France there had been very bad flooding. Ellis listened to Bach's Violin Concerto in A minor played by Kati Debretzeni with the English Baroque Soloists. The child wanted to go outside but it was raining. She stood by the glass door with her boots on and her pink rucksack across her back, looking out longingly. The rain continued all day. Ellis ate soup with bread and cheese for lunch and roast chicken with rice and broccoli for supper. He watched *The Party's Over*, a 1965 black and white film about beatniks in London. It was exquisitely filmed, in London locations. But the script was weak and the censorship of the era rendered the content tepid. There was a scene in which an unconscious woman at a party was stripped of her clothing, but its dramatisation was coy. It was unclear in the next scene whether or not she was being raped. But even this nerveless representation did not satisfy John Trevelyan, Secretary of the British Board of Film Classification, who found the film *unpleasant, tasteless and rather offensive*. In order to satisfy this pompous philistine the film-makers were obliged to make a series of cuts and supply a happy ending. Ellis looked up John Trevelyan, the Chief Censor. He was the son of a parson. He was awarded the CBE. It was said of him that he *never shrank from using his scissors, especially when it came to protecting the young*. Castration sponsored by the state was his thing. Film director Roy Ward Baker called him *a sinister mean hypocrite*. Later Ellis watched the latest episode of *The Singapore Grip*, followed by the 10pm Sky news. The news from the hospital was upbeat about the President. During the course of the bulletin the President's motorcade appeared and there was a glimpse of a masked Trump waving from behind a window. Ellis went to bed. He switched to *Little Tales of Misogyny* as his bedtime reading. He read the first ten tales then put out the light.

Monday 5th October 2020

Grey, wet, raining. On 'Thought For The Day' another reactionary academic theologian was wheeled out. He said he was praying for Trump. On the news it was stated that the President may be returning to the White House today. The rain continued. Over on Twitter, a sardonic tweet by Media Lens three days ago had provoked a response from one of its targets. Media Lens commented: *During the #JulianAssange hearing from 7 Sep to 1 Oct: No. of articles by Owen Jones mentioning Assange: 0 No. of articles by George Monbiot mentioning Assange: 0 Twitter: No. of times Owen Jones mentioned Assange: 1 No. of times George Monbiot mentioned Assange: 0.* No surprise there. Jones and Monbiot were the resident faux-Left at that Blairite publication *The Guardian* and their hypocrisies had been exposed many times before on social media. Today, stung by criticism, Monbiot asserted: *We need to be vibrant, heterodox, welcoming, broad and challenging. We pull together by embracing our differences, not purging them.* Which was slightly ironic, coming from an individual who regularly blocked polite critical tweets. In response to the specific point that he'd ignored the Assange extradition hearings, Monbiot commented: *This illustrates my point. There are hundreds of crucial issues on my mind at the moment. Julian Assange's trial is one of them. But is it more important than phosphate depletion? The occupation of West Papua? The Indus conflict? Why is this the essential box to tick?* It was a remarkable position for Monbiot to take, Ellis thought. In the first place, the Assange case involved a flagrant attempt by the United States government to punish a journalist who had exposed war crimes, as well as a wide variety of information which was embarrassing but hugely illuminating. Not least that former Labour MP Ruth Smeeth was an 'asset' to be 'protected'. This was the woman who was at the heart of the campaign to denigrate Jeremy Corbyn as an anti-Semite and destroy his leadership. In the second place, the legal justifications for the proceedings were highly questionable, involving an Australian citizen being prosecuted in Britain for matters which were not in any convincing way criminal and which in any case did not involve anything done in Britain. Thirdly, the way in which the proceedings had been conducted raised all kinds of questions about the judge. Finally, the persecution of a campaigning journalist was a blatant attempt to crush dissent and frighten other journalists into steering clear of security matters. The silence of the corporate media about the Assange case exposed where that media's role really lay in protecting power in all its manifestations. There was also the issue of the *Guardian*'s own tawdry role in the fate of Julian Assange. For George Monbiot to pretend that the Assange case was of lesser significance than the three news stories he mentioned was to exclude from discussion the central role of the corporate media in filtering public understanding of the modern world. When Ellis thought of Owen Jones and George Monbiot he thought of a recent tweet by Steven Salaita, 29 September: *Note the indisputable correlation between catering to Zionism (or strategically disposing of Palestine) and upward mobility in corporate media. We need not indulge or excuse anyone who accepts this terrible bargain.* The rain continued. Ellis took in a parcel for a neighbour who was out. The child ran around with her trolley of wooden bricks. Night fell. Trump still seemed to be in hospital. Perhaps by 10pm he would be out. But he was not. He would emerge later. Ellis went to bed. He laid aside *Little Tales of Misogyny* and began reading (re-reading) *Despair*.

Tuesday 6th October 2020

Ellis lay in the darkness, listening to Radio 4. The 'Today' programme supplied an update on the progress of David Cameron's 2016 scheme for a Holocaust memorial in central London. The chosen site was Victoria Tower Gardens, beside the Palace of Westminster. Lord Carlile had now objected to this location, saying that it would become 'a trophy site' for terrorists and a 'self-evident terrorism risk'. The plan had been rejected by Westminster City Council but the final decision will be made by the government following the ongoing public inquiry. Like the verdict of the judge on whether or not Julian Assange should be deported to the USA, the Johnson government's decision was utterly predictable. No one dared to stand up to the small, loud, whining voices of the Zionist community. Last week, the BBC continued, the new Zionist leader of the Labour Party, Sir Keir Starmer, told the Zionist *Jewish Chronicle* that the proposed Memorial and Learning Centre was 'vital'. He planned to emphasize the national importance of the project in a meeting with the grotesquely fat right-wing buffoon Lord Eric Pickles and the reactionary Labour Party clown Ed Balls, who are co-chairs of the UK Holocaust Memorial Foundation. This unnecessary memorial will waste £100 million of public money. 'The fight against intolerance and prejudice in our society, and the stain of antisemitism, goes on,' the Zionist leader of the Labour Party said. The memorial also has the support of the Zionist Gordon Brown, the blood-spattered mass-murderer Tony Blair and the oily Blairite Mayor of London, Sadiq Khan. Needless to say BBC News was, as usual, muffling the truth, which is that this monumental folly has nothing at all to do with the Nazi holocaust and everything to do with the Zionist appropriation of historic Jewish suffering for the purpose of promoting Jewish racism, sectarianism and violent land-theft in Palestine. It was also about promoting an image of the Jew as perpetual victim at a time when, in Britain,

Jews suffered no discrimination whatever and when, in Israel, Jews were among the most prejudiced and violent people on the planet. This farcical memorial was designed to flatter the self-regard of an affluent and reactionary community wallowing in a spurious and sanctimonious sense of victimhood. It would be a perfect symbol of Zionism, stealing a small and precious slice of greenery in central London and taking it over on behalf of the Zionist community. That in the process it would displace a small and rare memorial to the slave-trade only compounded the irony of this offensive project. This spurious memorial will make an apt twin to the monument to the Zionist serial killer and psychopathic religious fundamentalist Orde Wingate a short distance away along the Embankment, Ellis reflected. It began raining. Ellis went out. He waved at a distant friend in the High Street. At the supermarket he bought bananas, apples, two quiches, two yogurts, two packs of Lurpak, a packet of microwavable rice, two cartons of milk, two bottles of red wine, a pack of kitchen roll and two double-packs of tissues (on special offer). At the bakery he bought two almond croissants and two plain croissants. At the greengrocers he bought cooking apples and a punnet of strawberries. After this he went to the library. After this he went home. In the late afternoon the rain fell very heavily. Ellis watched a documentary about Fassbinder's *Despair*. Tom Stoppard had lips which were strangely twisted in one corner, as if he had suffered a stroke or the damaging consequences of an operation. In the evening Ellis read Jonathan Cook's devastating demolition of George Monbiot's excuses for being silent about the Assange extradition hearing. Monbiot's credentials as a fearless radical were well and truly shattered. He had turned out to be almost as slippery as Owen Jones. Which was a shame. Ellis used to respect Monbiot. Once he had even met him. On that occasion he had been impressed that Monbiot was clutching a copy of *War and Peace*. Or was it *Anna Karenina*? One of those two. It was many years ago. But perhaps it had just been a prop. Monbiot's credentials had now been battered on several fronts. The vegan who killed and ate a deer. The passionate opponent of flying, who insisted on the individual's responsibility to abstain from climate-destroying activities, but who had then flown to an important meeting on the far side of the Atlantic. Surely he could have kept his principles and video-conferenced? Monbiot was opinionated about Syria, yet his knowledge of the Middle East was zero. He'd become another corporate *Guardian* hack. He had declined to address the contradicition between his passionate environmentalism and his newspaper's long history of accepting advertisements which promoted 4X4s, cheap flights and a lavish consumerist lifestyle. He had declined to address the criticisms levelled by a site like Media Lens, whose critics he had petulantly blocked from reading his Tweets. When Corbyn was down, Monbiot had joined the jeering, bullying *Guardian* gang to kick the one political leader who might have brought about some of the changes he, George Monbiot, claimed were urgent. In bed Ellis read a few more pages of

Despair.

Wednesday 7th October 2020

The alarm went at 6.55am. Ellis listened as the 'Today' programme reported that the Unite union was cutting its affiliation money to the Labour Party by 10 per cent. Len McCluskey, General Secretary, expressed dismay that Unite funds had been spent by Labour paying damages to whistle-blowers who contributed to a Panorama programme about Labour's handling of the anti-Semitism crisis, asserted the BBC. This was classic misrepresentation since the 'whistleblowers' were no such thing and there was no 'anti-Semitism crisis'. That supposed crisis was the biggest hoax in modern British political history and the BBC had been deeply complicit in promoting it. McCluskey was right to say 'we shouldn't have paid them anything'. But McCluskey was himself part of the problem, capitulating on the IHRA definition, failing to articulate a coherent analysis of the poisonous influence of Zionism over the Labour Party, and even now indulging in the delusion that withdrawing a small of amount of money from the party would somehow influence the rabidly Establishment reactionary Sir Keir Starmer. McCluskey wanted a socialist programme, which he saw as vital to a Labour victory in 2024. Well, thought Ellis, he sure as hell isn't going to get it. In recent days Labour MPs had voted to support a Bill designed to protect from prosecution British troops who tortured and murdered, and had also abstained on a Bill designed to legalise a range of activities by undercover police (and others) which were currently illegal. Rape, for example. The spurious justification for protecting abusive cops was, needless to say, 'security'. A warm sunny day, a brief interlude between wet grey ones. Ellis did some writing. He finished watching Fassbinder's adaptation of *Despair*. It was no masterpiece. It was sluggishly paced and over-stylized. The dramatic intensities seemed histrionic. The plot was paltry and simplistic. It was visually sumptious and it had an impressive cast but in the end this wasn't enough. In the evening it began to rain. Ellis read a few more pages of Nabokov's *Despair*.

Thursday 8th October 2020

Ellis woke at 6.59 am and turned on the radio. Two British alleged members of the ISIS execution quartet known as 'the Beatles' had been deported from the Middle East to the USA to stand trial. The Vice-Presidential debate had occurred. The BBC reminded listeners that the next US president, whoever that might be, would be the oldest in American history. It was reported that a fly had landed on the head of the current Vice-President. Prince William had uttered some platitudes about climate change. Tonight Scotland were playing Israel at Hampden Park in Glasgow in a European qualifiers match. Why, wondered Ellis, was this Middle Eastern settler state permitted to play in a European football match? Admittedly Israel was full of European racists who had emigrated there to enjoy their sectarian privileges as members of the master religion, but that still didn't justify this repugnant state's presence in a football tournament which was supposed to be European. Moreover, the Israeli army was infamous for deliberately shooting to maim peaceful protesters, including footballers. It was another example of how the odious, fanatical and repressive Jewish state had been permitted to embed itself in modern British and European life, without comment. This football match was no better than one played with a team from Nazi Germany. It sanitised atrocity and normalised a state which had absolutely no right to exist. In the days of apartheid South Africa, sporting matches had been regularly disrupted by protesters. That tradition needed to be revived for matches with Israel, Ellis thought. On the Twitter page of Ben Norton Ellis read that NATO-backed Azerbaijan is using Israeli cluster munitions to bomb Armenian civilians in Artsakh / Nagorono-Karabakh. Amnesty International had identified Israeli-made M095 DPICM cluster bombs - a weapon banned under international humanitarian law. Cluster bombs are inherently indiscriminate weapons, and their deployment in residential areas is absolutely appalling and unacceptable, said Amnesty's Denis Krivpshee. But Azerbaijan could rely on the BBC to block all reporting of this crime. Elsewhere on Twitter, Jeffrey Kaye stated that in 1952 the USA used anthrax spread by insects and feathers in NE China, utilizing methods pioneered by the Japanese bioweapons war criminals they had just amnestied. Sarah Cooper, an American comedian and writer whom Ellis had never heard of, but who had 2.3 million followers, tweeted BIDEN 2020: HE WON'T TRY TO KILL YOU. Ben Norton replied: *(Asterisk): Unless you live in: Venezuela, Nicaragua, Cuba, Syria, Yemen, Palestine, Iran, Iraq, Afghanistan, Russia, China.* The day grew cooler. Twilight. The child put on her mother's boots. Ellis pan-fried some cod. He watched *The Hole*, a rather under-valued thriller, he felt. (Admittedly, on the negative side, one of the cast was that dreary right-wing contrarian, Laurence Fox.) At the end of the 6pm Radio 4 news it was revealed that Louise Gluck had been awarded the Nobel Prize for Literature for her poetry. Gluck was a professor at Yale, apparently. Ellis had no memory of ever having read any of her work. On the 10pm Sky TV news there was a long feature about a Zimbabwean student who described how he had been seized and beaten by men he believed were working for the government. It supplied yet another example of how the corporate media was always willing to focus on human rights abuses by states which were outside the British and American zone of influence, and almost never on those states which were allies. Israel knew full well that its regular repression of Palestinian civilians would never be reported by Sky TV or BBC news. In bed Ellis read a few more pages of *Despair*.

Friday 9th October 2020

A bright sunny morning, but chilly. There was frost on the grass. The flood plain was coated by a layer of mist a couples of metres deep. It was an exquisite scene which cried out to be photographed. Ellis went on, without using the camera which he had with him. Ditchingham churchyard was the final destination on my walk through the county of Suffolk, W. G. Sebald revealed in his most-imitated book. Later, while I was waiting for Clara in the Mermaid, it occurred to me that Ditchingham Park must have been laid out around the time when Chateaubriand was in Suffolk, Sebald wrote. But today it would not be possible to pursue Sebald's ghost to the bar of the Mermaid, where he waited for his wife to arrive by car. The pub closed some years ago and became a Balti takeaway. But on this bright October morning it looked as if the Balti House was itself defunct, despite the sign on the wall. The building was boarded-up and in a state of decay. The wooden window frames were rotting. The paint was peeling away. It seemed strangely apt that the last building Sebald visited on the itinerary set out in *The Rings of Saturn* should now be a very visible symbol of the transience of things. At lunchtime the child ate microwaved slices of pizza. Afterwards she ate a banana. In the afternoon she slept for two hours, from 1pm to 3pm. About 4.20pm it began to rain heavily. On Twitter, *literaturersupporter* wrote: *when I met W G Sebald and Susan Sontag, I was awestruck. They seemed like marble gods come to live.* (sic) Ellis discovered the Twitter account of Adam Scavell. Later he read about an Israeli historian, Adam Raz, who had written a book about the massive theft of Palestinian property by Jews in 1948. Ellis read that Adam Raz was the author of three books, including one on Herzl, and one about the 1956 Kafr Qassim massacre. But perhaps these titles were all in Hebrew and had never been translated. Ellis could find no trace of them on the Amazon website. Today would have been John Lennon's 80th birthday, had he not been murdered. In the evening Ellis watched the end of *A Hard Day's Night* on BBC 4, while waiting for the repeat of an old 'Top of the Pops' tribute to Lennon's greatest songs, curated by Yoko Ono. It did not come at the advertised time, 9pm, but thirty minutes later. When the programme was introduced there was a brusque acknowledgement of this by the introducer but naturally no apology. The BBC's arrogance even extended to an institutional indifference to its own advertised broadcasting schedule. It was followed by the repeat of a documentary about John Lennon and Yoko Ono in New York. Ellis watched part of the programme, then grew bored and went to bed, where he read more Nabokov.

Saturday 10th October 2020

A bright crisp sunny morning. The Radio 4 news reported that the rabid Zionist actress Maureen Lipman had been made a Dame. This was the perfect reward for a woman whose regular frothings about anti-Semitism belonged to pantomime. Ellis went for a flu jab, afterwards buying a *Times*, a loaf of bread, a chicken, a packet of sausages, six eggs, a box of Fruit & Fibre breakfast cereal and two packets of frozen peas. Later the sky clouded over and it began to rain. The child played with a twelve-inch ruler. On the fourth page of the news section of the *Times* Ellis read the headline **Universities may lose funding over antisemitism**. Naturally the story was not about anti-Semitism at all but about reactionary Jews seeking to suppress any criticism of racist Israel by defining any criticism of Israel as racist as anti-Semitic. The usual dreary loop, which the corporate media and the nastiest and most right-wing elements in establishment British politics had been encouraging for years. That repulsive, whining body known as the Union of Jewish Students had discovered that only 29 British universities had adopted the spurious and muddled 'new' definition of anti-Semitism promulgated by that right-wing entity calling itself the International Holocaust Remembrance Alliance (leading figure: that bloated right-wing buffoon Eric Pickles). *80 said that they would not adopt it. Some said it was not necessary and others considered it an infringement of free speech.* Outrage on the part of the Zionist community! Naturally these Jewish bullies go right to the top to seek support for their bullying on behalf of the racist Jewish state. Enter that cretinous Tory, the infamous Gavin Williamson, who currently holds the post of education secretary. *Williams has threatened to cut universities' funds if they refuse to adopt an internationally agreed definition of antisemitism. The education secretary wrote to vice-chancellors to say he was shocked and disappointed that so few universities had recognised the International Holocaust Remembrance Alliance (IHRA) description of antisemitism.* Ha! An interesting slip, thought Ellis. Because the ludicrously verbose and incoherent 'definition' is indeed a description, not a definition. *He said there were too many antisemitic incidents on campuses and that it was seen in some student communities as less offensive than other forms of racism.* Complete garbage, of course. The usual Zionist hysteria, devoid of any reference or factual basis. Gavin Williamson has directed the Office for Students *to consider imposing a regulatory condition of registration or suspend funding from universities which have not signed up to the definition.* That evening Ellis watched *The Disappearance*, an adaptation of Derek Marlowe's *Echoes of Celandine*. The geography of the novel was changed, shifting the action to Montreal and Suffolk, England. The plot was also radically transformed at the end. The movie was oddly slow and brooding, with a single haunting extract from Ravel's Piano Concerto in G Major played throughout. It was easy to understand why upon its release in 1977 it was a flop. It was too slow, too undramatic, the characters were not engaging. It was hard to care that the protagonist's promiscuous wife had gone from his life. The contract-killer plot lacked plausibility. But despite its manifold failings the film lingered in the mind. Its silences and absurdities lent it a certain charm. The movie locations were haunting. The film had a dream-like quality. Afterwards, in bed, Ellis read more Nabokov.

Sunday 11th October 2020

Bright, sunny and warm. On the internet Ellis came across a new tweet by *The Jerusalem Post*: *You may not like #Trump, but you can't deny that this presidency has been a success, good for #Israel, and good for the Middle East.* On the *Skwawkbox* website Ellis came across the news that for the second time this year, the *Jewish Chronicle*, its editor and one of its writers had apologised and paid 'substantial' damages for publishing histrionic fake news in a series of articles about a left Labour activist, Nada al-Sajani. The *Chronicle*, which also paid Ms Al-Sanjari's legal costs, accepted that all its accusations were 'completely unfounded'. The paper and its hacks are repeat offenders, said the article on *Skawkbox*. Earlier this year, the *Jewish Chronicle* apologised and paid damages to Liverpool pensioner and Labour activist Audrey White for a 'litany of lies' and was hammered by its own regulator IPSO for its failure to check the accuracy of its claims, to withdraw its lies even when challenged, or even to cooperate with IPSO's investigation. As in the Al-Sanjari case, the *Chronicle* didn't even try to defend its claims or conduct in court. Last year, the paper also paid damages plus legal costs to the British-based Palestinian charity *Interpal*, after the *Chronicle* falsely claimed it was associated with terrorism. The *Jewish Chronicle* was bailed out of its financial woes earlier this year, the *Skwawkbox* reminded its readers, by a consortium including John Ware, who made last year's *Panorama* programme alleging antisemitism in the Labour Party, former Labour MP John Woodcock, who now works for the Johnson government, former BBC executive and Tory spin doctor Robbie Gibb, and others. Ellis tapped the name Nada al-Sajani into Twitter search and was intrigued to get the message: *No results for "Nada al-Sajani" The term you entered did not bring up any results. You may have mistyped your term or your Search Settings could be protecting you from some potentially sensitive content.* The child held a green pen. She went into the kitchen, where she ran in circles, laughing. That evening Ellis watched episode five of *The Singapore Grip*. It was annoying watching a drama on ITV. There were the interminable commercials at the beginning and every seven minutes or so. This week ITV had decided to insert a small message in the top left hand corner of the screen. It was something to do with *Talk Britain*. Irritatingly, the message remained there during the opening minutes of each section, until it evaporated. The drama itself was chopped up into brief moments, for viewers with very short attention spans. The same sets were used interminably. The lavish timbered house with an immense lush garden. The street corner in Singapore, which was obviously a studio set. Ellis had grown bored by this adaptation. He was glad it would end next week and be over with. The only moment of interest was when Vera produced a book of translations by Arthur Waley and began reciting from it. At the next commercial break Ellis ran to fetch his own edition. It was one of the first books he'd ever bought. He had made a note inside the cover many years ago indicating the personal importance to him of 'Summer Song' by Wu Ti and 'The Waters of Lung-T'Ou' by Hsü Ling. Glancing again at this ancient paperback Ellis saw that the publishers had a Singapore office, at 36c Princep Street, Singapore 7. On the Sky News there was more about new Coronavirus restrictions, which would be announced tomorrow. There was nothing about the immense fraud involving over £10 billion of government C-19 related contracts awarded without tendering to a variety of tiny dodgy companies, which had been set up with £100 capital and immediately awarded £110 million contracts. The scandal was all over social media but was being shunned by the corporate media. As someone tweeted, it was as if the Mafia had been elected. Ellis went to bed. He read more Nabokov.

Monday 12th October 2020

Grey, bright, cool. Rain forecast for the afternoon. Ellis went to the bank to pay in a cheque and obtain some cash. Afterwards he walked to the Post Office. Upon entering he heard a man shouting at the female counter clerk. 'You can't ask me that!' The man resembled one of the characters in *EastEnders*. He had florid cheeks and a square head, with very little hair. It seemed that the woman had asked what was in the package he wished to post. It was a question which Post Office clerks had been asking for years. If you didn't wish to tell them what was in your parcel you could always lie. The man plainly was not someone used to visiting Post Offices with a parcel. The man was in a rage. He was adamant that he was not obliged to say what was in his package. The woman behind the counter quietly explained that he needed to, if he wished to post it. Ellis noticed that the man was not wearing a face mask, as required by law. The man gave up. He stormed out of the Post Office. As he left he screamed at the woman that she would regret it. He shouted that he would make this Post Office famous. 'Hundreds of thousands of people will know!' he shrieked. Ellis wondered what medium the man would use. He did not look like a news journalist. Probably he meant social media. Did he have a Twitter account and a million followers? Was he on Facebook, with hundreds of thousands of friends and admirers? Or did his threat have a sinister connotation? Would he back with a double-barrelled shotgun? Very unlikely, but you never knew. Ellis joined the queue. He had three items to post this day. Afterwards he went shopping, purchasing Grape Nuts, cheese, yogurt, cooking apples and bin liners. He bought the child a toy goat, to join her collection of native animals. In the evening he watched the final episode of *Us* and then some of the 10pm Sky News. And then to bed, to read more Nabokov.

Tuesday 13th October 2020

A louring morning, but without rain. Ellis went for a walk. Later he was
telephoned by a librarian. Online he discovered that on Saturday there had been
a protest outside the London office of an Israeli arms manufacturer. The report
in the *Morning Star* stated: *Five activists were arrested after spattering red
paint over the front of an Israeli arms firm's London office in a surprise attack
during a protest on Saturday. The group of women activists from the Palestine
Action network burst out of a car with fire extinguishers filled with paint,
spraying the facade of 77 Kingsway, Holborn, bright red. The multi-office
building is where Elbit Systems – Israel's largest arms company – has its
London headquarters. Paint also showered onto police officers and a group of
pro-Israel protesters defending the arms firm, who were standing in front of the
building at the time. Five people were arrested, including the driver of the car,
on suspicion of criminal damage and police assault, the Metropolitan Police
confirmed in a statement. Elbit supplies the Israeli military with more than 80
per cent of its drone fleet, including the Hermes 450 and 900, which have been
used to bomb civilians in Gaza.* Excellent news! Later Ellis read Tony
Greenstein's blistering attack on Professor Catherine Hezser of SOAS's Jewish
Studies Centre. The latest Zionist propaganda angle was to deny that Zionism
was a colonial enterprise. The hours passed. Ellis sorted some old files. The
child stood in her dungarees and watched an episode of the CBeebies
programme *Molly and Mack*. Periodically she jumped into the air, laughing with
delight. Ellis pan-fried some cod and chips, eaten with peas, fried tomatoes and
two glasses of white wine. Later he watched another episode of *Life*, in which
the dead wife was revealed to have been involved in a lesbian affair. Ellis
couldn't be bothered to watch Sky News. He went to bed.

Wednesday 14th October 2020

A bright morning of silvery cloud cover. Neither warm nor chilly. The child
wore her new coat from Tesco. Ellis read Ed McNally's review of Owen Jones's
new book *This Land*, on the *Jacobin* website. McNally exposed the poverty of
Jones's brand of socialism. Later, Ellis sorted some files and boxes of books. In
the evening he watched a documentary on Channel 5 about the murder of Jill
Dando. It was feeble stuff, recycling the story in a lazy, unquestioning way.
There was nothing about police incompetence or about Dando's private life.
There was a long interview with Michael Mansfield, which asked no pointed
questions. The only thing that was new and of interest was a long interview with
the woman who had first come across Dando's slumped body. This woman

was… strange. Was she really a friend, as she claimed? She said that she had been unable to go to the funeral. Ellis suspected that was because she hadn't been invited. Aftewards he went to bed.

Thursday 15th October 2020

Grey, cloudy, dry. Ellis went out to buy some rolls, red wine, milk, yogurt and croissants. He also took some books back to the library and borrowed a book. Home again, he drank cappuccino. Surfing the net Ellis came across Daniel Finn's hatchet job on Owen Jones, published on the *Jacobin* website on 3 July 2017. Finn had also exposed the sheer feebleness of Jones's politics, writing of the great anti-Semitism hoax: 'Owen Jones himself seemed to have little understanding of what was at stake. His only notable contribution to the debate was a fairly anodyne article in March 2016, which said that antisemitism was a bad thing and that the Left should oppose it, but raised no questions about why, exactly, the issue was gaining so much traction at this particular moment.' The sun came out, thin and watery. Ellis learned from social media that Keir Starmer had appointed a virulent apologist for Israel, Nita Clarke, to an advisory position. Universal Basic Cyber Unit tweeted: *Nita Clarke is a Blairite dinosaur and if she's in charge of looking at "the culture of the party" and building "an election winning organisation", you know what's coming. Anti democratic, top down, donor dictated, tabloid agenda following, PR, marketing and retail anti politics.* Frank Owen's Legendary Paintbrush tweeted: *Judging by her tweeting history, Nita Clarke's role in Keir Starmer's Labour Party is to facilitate a culture of transphobia, Islamophobia, anti-unionism, anti-socialism and warmongery. Yet another sign that Starmer blatantly lied when he claimed to be the "unity" candidate.* Ellis watched *To The Devil A Daughter* and *The 7.39*. In bed he read some Dennis Wheatley.

Friday 16th October 2020

A grey day. The park was full of dog-walkers. The child went on the swings, the seesaw and one of the slides. For lunch she ate fish fingers, tomatoes and a fruit yogurt. On the news it was reported that daily coronavirus cases had risen to 27,900. On the *Very Public Sociologist* blog Ellis read the latest post about the Covert Human Intelligence Sources (Criminal Conduct) Bill, which had passed with 313 voting for it, 98 against. 200 MPs abstained, including most of the Labour Party under orders from Keir Starmer himself, while 34 opposed - several resigning their front bench positions in the process. *Why then? Who is Keir trying to appease or, at the very least, impress with his reasonable, responsible government-ready opposition? The only ones left are the Tory papers. Carrying on his charm-the-press round, offering measured, process*

criticisms of the bill...telling them his criticisms come from a place of
fundamental loyalty to the system, not outright opposition à la Corbyn and
Corbynism. In return, the hope is they'll continue going easy on him, ensuring
the next election is a more benign environment for Labour than the last four
contests. If this is the game, the leader, his office, and all the people he listens to
are more naive about the character of British politics than I feared. David
Lindsay commented: *When, exactly, was Keir Starmer a "human rights lawyer"?*
That one goes unquestioned, but it is drivel. He had much the same line of work
as Kamala Harris, who withheld exonerating evidence on death row prisoners
until after they had been executed. She would have been proud of him tonight. If
she had ever heard of him. Everyone on the Left, or even just in the unions,
knows that we are under surveillance, and the rest, all the time. But most
Labour MPs have no left-wing, or even just trade union, background. And
Starmer is even worse. He comes from the other side. Where he remains.
Elsewhere, Ellis read about The Overseas Operations Bill, which is intended to
protect British armed forces from prosecution for torture and other human rights
abuses committed more than five years earlier. Peter Oborne wrote: *Labour*
under Starmer has abstained from voting on this disreputable legislation. Indeed,
Starmer sacked Nadia Whittome from her role as a Parliamentary Private
Secretary for voting against the bill. Again and again, Starmer takes the line of
least resistance - the expedient position. He's not defining himself against
Johnson. He's defining himself against Corbyn. Elsewhere, Ellis read the cri de
coeur of Joëlle Gergis. She described the third mass bleaching event recorded on
the Great Barrier Reef since 2016. *This time, the southern reef – spared during*
the 2016 and 2017 events – finally succumbed to extreme heat. The largest
living organism on the planet is dying. As one of the dozen or so Australian lead
authors involved in consolidating the physical science basis for the United
Nations' Intergovernmental Panel on Climate Change (IPCC) Sixth Assessment
report, I've gained terrifying insight into the true state of the climate crisis and
what lies ahead. There is so much heat already baked into the climate system
that a certain level of destruction is now inevitable. What concerns me is that we
may have already pushed the planetary system past the point of no return. That
we've unleashed a cascade of irreversible changes that have built such
momentum that we can only watch as it unfolds. Joëlle Gergis wrote: *what really*
worries me is what our Black Summer signals about the conditions that are yet
to come. The revised warming projections for Australia will render large parts
of our country uninhabitable and the Australian way of life unliveable, as
extreme heat and increasingly erratic rainfall establishes itself as the new
normal. Later, Ellis learned that Tom Maschler had died. He read the obituary in
the *Guardian*. Somewhere, Ellis had a letter from Maschler, rejecting a non-
fiction book proposal. That was in the days when publishers read letters and
submissions, rather than letting agents do the screening. Ellis ate pizza and

coleslaw. He went to bed early and fell into a deep sleep.

Saturday 17th October 2020

A warm bright morning. Radio 4 news made the beheading of a French history teacher its top story. The emphasis was on *Islamist terror*. Yet again it showed how the representation of violence was mediated by the BBC and other organisations which packaged that product known as *news*. Some victims were privileged; most were marginalised or completely ignored. Some perpetrators of violence were identified, others were permitted to commit their crimes in the knowledge that BBC news would not mention them (or would even seek to sanitise or justify them). State violence could usually rely on the co-operation of the BBC, unless, of course, the state was an identified enemy. Ellis got up. He did some writing, while defrosting two freezers. The landline rang and he talked for fifteen minutes. He continued writing. The sun came out, then it rained, then the sun came out again. He ate soup, bread and cheese for his lunch. Afterwards, he did more writing. He went to bed late and quickly fell asleep.

Sunday 18th October 2020

A day of cloud, bursts of sunshine, intermittent light drizzle. Ellis spent the morning writing. For lunch he had soup with bread and cheese, followed by sliced apple and yogurt. The corporate media was giving enormous prominence to demonstrations in France in the aftermath of the beheading of a history teacher. People were out there supposedly defending freedom of speech. But France was a state where 12 pro-Palestinian protesters received criminal convictions for wearing 'Boycott Israel' T-shirts and for handing out fliers that read *Buying Israeli products means legitimising crimes in Gaza*. This was regarded by the authoritarian and reactionary French judiciary as inciting 'discrimination, hatred or violence towards a person or group of people' - the usual spurious 'anti-Semitism' loop, whereby anti-racists who criticised the racist Jewish state were the criminals. The protesters were targeting Israel not Jews but the ruling was another reminder that judges are poisonously reactionary. French Zionists gloated that France had 'the most effective legislation on BDS today'. That evening Ellis watched the final episode of *The Singapore Grip*. It was in the end a lacklustre adaptation and it was a relief to be done with it. Ellis went to bed and read some Dennis Wheatley.

Monday 19th October 2020

Cloudy-bright (as the old camera aperture setting used to say). Ellis spent the morning writing. Later, at one o'clock, the sun came out. On the 972 website he read an article by Natasha Roth-Rowland, 'Why the "Pallywood" myth endures' (https://www.972mag.com/pallywood-trope-second-intifada/). It was subtitled: A lasting legacy of the Second Intifada is the pernicious idea that Palestinians cannot be trusted to narrate their experience of Israeli oppression. The article began with the Israeli murder of 12-year-old Muhammad al-Durrah and his father, Jamal, at Netzarim Junction in Gaza, on September 30, 2000. It supplied graphic evidence of the murderous and psychopathic mentality of racist Jews with powerful modern weapons. In response a Zionist industry sprang up seeking to denigrate this footage and other film evidence of this sort, suggesting that it was staged. The *hasbara* term "Pallywood" was coined by Richard Landes, an American medievalist scholar. The "Pallywood" charge has been liberally applied to incidents from Israeli airstrikes in Gaza to the fatal shooting of two Palestinian teenagers during Nakba Day protests in 2014, wrote Natasha Roth-Rowland. *It has become a trope whose intention is to* a priori *cast doubt on any accusations of cruelty or use of excessive force by Israeli security forces, above all when they are caught on film. Indeed, according to the logic of the "Pallywood" slur, the very fact that violence has been documented on video is more reason to doubt its existence, not less.* In short, thought Ellis, many Jews subscribe to Holocaust denial, but of their own colonial variety. Later Ellis read a piece by Ben White (14 October) on the *Middle East Eye* website, which asserted that the racism of Israeli settlers was not an aberration but simply a manifestation of an apartheid state. *The racism of Yitzhar settlers can only be understood as part of, rather than extraneous to or exceptional from, historic and contemporary policies implemented and supported by Israel's political and military leadership, judiciary, and a majority of its Jewish public. The exclusion and removal of Palestinians from land and communities by violence, legislation and de facto practice, is an integral part of Israel's history, beginning with the displacement caused by pre-state Zionist settlers and the ethnic cleansing of the Nakba.* The hours passed. The child used a potty for the first time. She seemed to like the idea. The first effort was a great success. The second one less so. This time the urine went on the floor. 'Baby,' said the child. She meant her soft toy baby was responsible for the mishap. Ellis ate chicken and mushrooms with basmati rice. He drank two and a half glasses of red wine. That evening he watched the first episode of *Roadkill*, the latest BBC drama. It was slick and watchable, although Ellis felt that it was derivative and, since it was written by David Hare, would probably fizzle out and become a disappointment. In bed he read a few more pages of *The Haunting of Toby Jugg*.

Tuesday 20th October 2020

Ellis did not wake until 8.20am. He switched on the radio and lay in the gloom listening as the sports section of the BBC 'Today' programme came on. Within seconds Ellis found himself listening to yet another propaganda effort by the BBC to sanitise the vile and barbaric Jewish state. The BBC sports journalist Rob Bonnet was interviewing the cyclist Chris Froome. Bonnet kept repeating the phrase 'Israel Start-Up Nation'. Froome, it seemed, was now cycling on behalf of Israel. Ellis waited to hear Bonnet challenge Froome on the morality of becoming the propaganda asset of a violent apartheid state whose troops deliberately maimed young Palestinians by shooting them through the legs with high-powered rifles. So depraved were some of these Jews that they even boasted of the numbers they had shot in a single day's duty. Needless to say Bonnet never challenged Froome. Had he been around when the England football team attended the Nazi Olympics and infamously gave the Hitler salute, Rob Bonnet would have talked about nothing but football. But Israel Start-Up Nation was not even a conventional cycling organisation. It had specifically been set up for propaganda purposes, to normalise violent ethnic cleansing. Ellis knew that because he looked it up. Billionaire owner Sylvan Adams makes no secret of his desire to use his cycling team *to project a positive image of Israel to the world.* 'Yes, the team does act in an ambassadorial role. The team is there to project tiny Israel on to the world stage.' His team are 'riding in our blue and white colours, we have the name Israel emblazoned on the front of the jersey and the riders know that'. *This, then, is Chris Froome's new role: part cyclist, part ambassador for Israel.* Ellis hoped that if this outfit ever cycled in Britain it would be regularly disrupted by protesters waving Palestinian flags. He would gladly do it himself if Froome ever came anywhere near his home. This episode indicated that the average sports professional was a narcissist, greedy for fame and material advancement, and utterly devoid of ethics. It was the same for rugby and cricket in the era of apartheid South Africa. Reading on, Ellis learned that Froome's ethics-free deal would make him cycling's top earner, with sponsorship deals adding to annual sum of around 5 million euros. Ellis learned that Sylvan Adams was born in Canada in 1958. In 2015 he emigrated to Israel, enjoying his privileges as a member of the master religion in a Jewish state which denies citizenship to its Arab population. That this Canadian Jew should be promoting Israel as a 'start-up' nation was chutzpah indeed. Israel is a nation built on violent theft and its prosperity has depended on theft, violence and the cynical exploitation of its captive Palestinian population. It has been subsidised throughout its tawdry existence by British imperialism and then American and European imperialism. Israel Start-Up Nation is the perfect symbol of the moral corruption and rot at the heart of corporate sport, the corporate media, and the degenerate democracies of the USA, UK and Europe, as well as the ethical void at the heart of modern Judaism. Ellis turned to Asa Winstanley's twitter page. Commenting on the victory of the Left in the Bolvian election, Asa Winstanley remarked: *I still can't get over "non-elected conservative government" as @AP's scummy euphemism for Bolivia's fascist coup regime.* Ellis went shopping. He bought cheese, yogurt, rice, rolls, dessicated coconut, ground almond, milk and wine. At the bakery he bought an almond croissant, a chocolate croissant and two plain croissants. Later Ellis did some writing. For lunch: soup, bread and cheese, followed by yogurt and an apple. In the afternoon he emptied a box of books. For supper: cheese soufflé, cabbage, mashed potato, with a glass of water. That evening he watched episode four of *Life*. Ellis had started to find it oddly compelling. He went to bed and finished reading the Wheatley book.

Wednesday 21st October 2020

The alarm went at 6.55am. Ellis listened to the weather forecast and the news headlines, then got up. He drank tea and ate his breakfast. Later, dressing, he listened to 'Thought For The Day'. Today's speaker was Rabbi Jonathan Wittenberg. Ellis had never heard of him. The Rabbi began by praising Gordon Brown for a recent speech about helping young people financially during the pandemic. There followed some banal pieties about how important young people were. At 8.30am Ellis went out. It was raining and the roads and pavements were dotted with pools of water. At the bakery he bought three plain and two almond croissants. Fresh bakery supplies were being brought in by a man who was not wearing a face mask. Soon afterwards, on the other side of the road, Ellis spotted a librarian he knew. But she did not recognise him as she was staring ahead and besides he had his hood down against the rain. Ellis went into another store and bought packets of Corn Flakes and Fruit & Fibre, a jar of Colman's Mustard and a tub of cornflour. He went home, where he drank a cappuccino, ate a plain croissant with butter and blackcurrant jam, and went online. He learned that Rabbi Jonathan Wittenberg had been born in Glasgow in 1957, had read English at King's College, Cambridge, and had thereafter spent two years in Israel. He had gained a rabbinic qualification there from his teacher Dr Aryeh Strikovskyl. On June 28th 2013 Rabbi Jonathan Wittenberg had written about 'Four days in Israel, where it's wonderful to be'. Rabbi Jonathan Wittenberg purported to be a liberal and expressed concern about 'the deeply troubling bill about the Negev Bedouin. Let ancestral lands be kept, villages be recognised. Painful, worrying.' The stuttering grammar was revealing, Ellis thought. What could not be articulated - what could not even be *thought* by Rabbi Wittenberg - was that the entire Jewish state was built on the ancestral land of the Palestinians. Historically, European Jews had *no connection whatever* with Palestine and Zionism was a racist colonial ideology constructed out of Biblical fiction. The treatment of the Bedouin was not an aberration. It was entirely consistent with every aspect of the Jewish state - a state which the majority of the world's Jews evidently supported. Every time Wittenberg visited Israel he was exercising his privileges as a Jew in a sectarian Jewish terror state.

The Rabbi was basically just another mealy-mouthed liberal, whose pious concerns concealed a pitiless refusal to accept that the Jewish state had no right to exist. Israel was a grotesque anomaly in the modern world. No wonder he was an admirer of the arch Zionist, blood-spattered Gordon Brown, who had been brought up by a religious fundamentalist fanatic. Next Ellis caught up with the news about Dominic West. The gloating, lip-smacking tabloid media had published photographs of West enjoying a convivial touchy-feely kissy-kissy weekend in Rome with Lily James. West's wife Catherine Fitzgerald was reported to have left the marital home and gone to stay with her parents in Ireland. Lily James was reported to have pulled out of an appearance on the Graham Norton Show. The media scented scandal. The *Daily Mirror* referred to the couple's *intimate getaway*. What a delightful distraction from the pandemic, the collapse of the world's climate, and starvation and child-deaths in Yemen! *Dominic was spotted smooching Lily during a three-day sun-soaked trip in the romantic city earlier this month.* The child was in a voluble mood, babbling away. Ellis read through some old copies of the *Times*. In bed he began reading Malcolm Gaskill's *Witchfinders*.

Thursday 22nd October 2020

BBC Radio news informed listeners that US intelligence believed that Iran and Russia were interfering in the US presidential election. Needless to say the BBC did not express the slightest scepticism about this slab of propaganda from an intelligence source infamous for its long history of lies and fabricated stories. That BBC News was the echo chamber of power in all its manifestations was evident from every bulletin, every day of the year. What possible difference could it make to Iran whether Trump or Biden won? Biden was every bit as much of an imperialist as Trump. It had recently emerged that one of the reporters on the 'Today' programme was the Honourable Sarah Smith, daughter of the deceased reactionary Labour leader John Smith (an oily creep who had been no friend of the workers, and who had energetically prosecuted them in his role as a lawyer). Ellis had once written a short satire about John Smith, in which the Labour leader had defended the slave trade on the grounds that it was good for Britain; he'd received a rapturous response from the party's annual conference attendees. Soon after the story was written, Smith had prematurely died, and so the story had been published posthumously, in the magazine *Casablanca*. The morning sun cast long shadows and the sun seemed to exaggerate the colour of the natural landscape, as if it had been tweaked and tinted on a computer screen. In the park Ellis pushed the child on the swing and then carried her to the red roundabout and the yellow see-saw. Going online he discovered that Len McCluskey had provoked the usual tsunami of froth from the Zionist rabble who specialised in sniffing out anti-Semitism. McCluskey had told Peter Mandelson to go away and 'count his gold'. This was an obvious reference to the Mandelson's accumulation of wealth by exploiting his networking connections with the super-wealthy. Peter Mandelson had never been identified as a Jew. Indeed, his father was an atheist. But his paternal grandfather was the founder of the Harrow United Synagogue. On these tenuous grounds, and even though McCluskey was plainly talking about Mandelson's dodgy financial history, the usual suspects fizzed with hyper-indignation. Needless to say the rather dim McCluskey had then proceeded to grovel and apologise for any hurt caused to a mob of Zionists. It was McCluskey, of course, who had capitulated on the IHRA definition of anti-Semitism, once again demonstrating the rubber spines of those supposedly on the Left when faced by shrill Jewish racists. Reading further on the internet Ellis came across the curious case of Eluned Anderson. This young woman had been standing to be chair of Young Labour, backed by the Zionist 'Jewish Labour Movement'. She boasted that she was 'a North West regional ambassador for the Holocaust Education Trust and involved with the TUC Young Workers Forum'. Someone had discovered that this woman, who had accused Corbyn of anti-Semitism, had in January 2019 tweeted: *Look I know they were evil bastards, but Eichmann and a young Ribbentrop were incredibly good looking.* Needless to say the Zionist rabble who were daily outraged by imaginary anti-Semitism rushed to defend Eluned Anderson. Needless to say she was in no danger of being expelled from the Labour Party. Ellis ate a cheese roll with two tomatoes and a packet of salt and vinegar crisps, followed by an apple. That evening he watched the news, which was largely about the Covid-19 second wave. From Dingle in Ireland came a report that the harbour's dolphin, which had been entertaining tourists for years, had vanished. In bed Ellis read more of the book on witch-hunting.

Friday 23rd October 2020

A bright, sunny morning. Ellis lay in bed until 8.30am. Later, as he ate his breakfast cereal, he read an article by Cameron Laux, 'The challenging books we need right now,' on the BBC Culture website. There are many skeletons in our literary closets, wrote Cameron Laux, expressing the standard BBC belief that what applies to the individual afforded a platform by the BBC applies to everyone. *War and Peace* and *Moby-Dick* 'often put people off because of their length'. Oh really? Length didn't seem to matter where the plodding historical melodramas of Hilary Mantel were concerned, or for that matter J. K. Rowling's latest Cormoran Strike crime novel. Then there are those other unread long books like *In Search of Lost Time* or *Ulysses*, wrote Cameron Laux. They 'have become a byword for daunting, modernist, experimental writing that is unintelligble without resorting to scholarly notes'. Oh really? Lazy Laux had plainly made not the slightest effort to read Joyce, let alone easy-peasy Proust. Laux's idea of a great long book is Don DeLillo's *Underworld*. 'Instead of trying to swallow the whole thing, like a snake eating a buffalo, it is possible to sample the book instead.' A lot of literary writing nowadays used the language of consumption and eating, Ellis reflected. Laux recommends *The Prologue*, about baseball, 'one of the great bravura performances of modern prose'. Ellis did not ever wish to read any fiction about baseball. Another part of *Underworld*, 'Part One, Long Tall Sally' is 'more accessible, and more likely to pull you in'. This book attracted praise from no less a person than David Foster Wallace (chummily referred to as 'DFW'). Wallace wrote that DeLillo had 'taken some truly ballsy personal risks'. As an admirer of 'risk-taking' Cameron Laux recommends Zadie Smith's *NW*, 'one of the defining novels of its time'. Smith has, we are told, 'a marvellous ear for dialogue'. *NW* is *devastating*, a *challenging* read, *a subtle and beautiful book*, it is worth picking up *even if it demands your full attention*. Cameron Laux has useful tips for readers faced by a long novel. *It is a good idea not to bite off more than you can chew. One reader got through Roberto Bolaño's hefty masterpiece 2666 by reading a few pages a day over the course of months.* It is worth the effort, for you, the reader, will receive *a glimpse of some kind of sublime*. Eh? Cameron Laux finishes by chatting to Zadie Smith, who helpfully supplies a list of 'very interestingly shaped' books. It includes *99 Glimpses of Princess Margaret* by Craig Brown. Later Ellis read Tony Greenstein's assault on Richard Seymour's article on fascism. Greenstein contended that Seymour had a poor grasp of German social history during the Nazi era. Pursuing the subject on Twitter Ellis stumbled upon a tweeter named Sabrina Miller, a Jew, who was a student at the University of Bristol. This repulsive woman was plainly seeking the dismissal of sociology Professor David Miller by orchestrating a campaign against him for his criticisms of Israel. She was Bari Weiss reincarnated. "Some Jewish students have been feeling intimidated by what he's been teaching for months," she wrote. As evidence she produced "A Jewish student in his class, who spoke on the condition of anonymity." And what did this anonymous individual have to say? "I was scared because I am one voice and felt I couldn't stand up to him or tell him what he was saying was wrong." Pathetic. Apparently Miller dares to assert that the Community Security Trust is part of the Zionist movement. Well, *it absolutely is*. Dave Rich and his organisation are whining apologists for Israel. The existence of the CST is predicated on the notion that Britain seethes with anti-Semitism and physical danger for Jews. The Union of Jewish Students is also part of the British Zionist establishment - a whiney assemblage of reactionary comfortable middle-class young Zionist Jews wallowing in fake victimhood. What was disturbing, however, was to learn that in December 2019 the University of Bristol had signed up to the spurious IHRA definition of anti-Semitism. That certainly made Miller vulnerable, as the IHRA definition and its examples were expressly designed by Zionists to degrade and abuse the Nazi holocaust by using it to shut down criticism of Israel. How loathsome and disgusting the bullying and fanatical so-called "Jewish community" had become, Ellis thought. How intellectually corrupt and vapid the University of Bristol had been in signing up to a Zionist diktat. Ironically it was reminiscent of nothing so much as the abject capitulation of the German academy to Nazism in the 1930s. Continuing to surf the net Ellis came across a reference to a new publication by Steve Cushion and Merilyn Moos, *Anti-Nazi Germans*. On a blog called A Trumpet of Sedition (which stirred a dim memory of something Coleridge had said as he slithered rightward, disavowing his younger radicalism) Ellis read an interview with the authors. Merilyn Moos said that the book in part stemmed from her family history. My father was an active and socialist German anti-Nazi who fled and lived, said Merilyn Moos. But many of his comrades did not, and I wanted to draw attention to the reality of grass-roots German resistance to Nazism. Moreover, added Moos, the historiography of the Nazi period has shifted many times since 1945. But the Eichmann trial and the increasing domination by Israel over the Middle East legitimated a new take on Nazism: that it was the Jews who were the Nazis' main target and moreover, that most Germans, if not perpetrators, were "bystanders". But even superficial research into the early years of the Nazi Party reveals that from the very beginning their main target was the organised working class. Moreover, continued Moos, there has been a further shift towards seeing Jews as "victims" which justified any crimes that Israel committed. In fact, with minute exceptions, the many "historical Jews" who were involved in the struggle against Nazism did so as part of, generally, a Communist movement, and sometimes as anarchists etc., not primarily as Jews. The old adage that Jews went like sheep to the slaughter is as false as that most Germans were bystanders, Merilyn concluded. She went on to describe how in 2018 she had been invited to speak at a commemoration at Brandenburg for the victims of euthanasia who were gassed there in 1940. One of those victims was her aunt. It was held on a patch of ground next to where the gassing had taken place, before an invited and very respectable gathering. But two of those invited individuals were local councillors who represented the far-right Alternative für Deutschland (AfD). The organisers were upset that three protesters had turned up who stood at the edge of the gathering with a banner protesting about AfD. The organisers called the police to get them removed. Merilyn Moos said: So the two people I was staying with and I walked up to the demonstrators. I had been the main speaker, so carried some "weight" and the police, observing me walking up and standing right next to them, swerved away. I then confronted the organiser as to why the AfD had been invited. The organiser shrugged and said something like: "All councillors were invited. What was I supposed to do?" I tell this story because of what it reveals. The organisers saw the AfD representatives as legitimate, unlike the antifascists. Now what

286

period of twentieth-century German history does that remind me of? Ellis came offline. The child scribbled with a crayon. In the kitchen Ellis pan-fried two salmon steaks. The news that night had vox pop interviews with people in Nashville. A bearded man with circular spectacles, described as guitar-maker to the stars, said he thought Biden had the edge in the debate. Two women in a bar said Trump had done best. They were Trump supporters. In Lagos unrest seemed to be spreading but there were complaints that the protests had been hijacked by hoodlums who were using roadblocks to extort cash from drivers. It was hard to get a sense of the reality when the coverage was so impressionistic and patchy. Surely there were academics who specalised in modern Nigerian society and politics whose views could have been sought? In bed Ellis read more of the book on witch-hunting.

Saturday 24th October 2020

Lying in bed listening to Radio 4 some time after 7am Ellis was astonished that there was a report on the harvesting of olives in the occupied West Bank. But it turned out to be the usual BBC fudge, which actively muffled and misrepresented reality. The harvest had been poor this year, as a result of excessive temperatures. There was mention of 'clashes' with Jewish settlers. A Jewish settler was allowed to speak about permits and the law. There was no mention of the institutional sectarianism of Israeli land law. BBC News never supplied the historical context. It distorted and misrepresented truth and reality via a screen of impressionism, omission, inequality of point of view and, from time to time, outright fabrication. Attacks on Palestinian land by settlers were mentioned, without detail. Then the show moved on. The word 'Zionism' was never used. Ellis realised that this item was really there to allow the BBC to defend itself against the charge that it never mentioned the Palestinians. But of course it had done so in a largely meaningless way and the item had been slotted in before 7.30am on a Saturday morning, when the radio audience was only a fraction of what it would be on a weekday. Later, a bland Anglican bishop made fun of a working class man's accent. Ellis dressed. He wrote: *Lying in bed listening to Radio 4 some time after 7am Ellis was astonished that there was a report on the harvesting of olives in the occupied West Bank.* He read the reviews section of the *Times*. Reviewing *Roadkill* the Murdoch pimp Hugo Rifkind (privately educated, son of plummy Tory Sir Malcolm Rifkind) managed to drag in a sneering attack on yesterday's man, Jeremy Corbyn. He mentioned 'that very racist mural that Jeremy Corbyn liked so much…The one with all those, er, ethnically distinctive plutocrats sitting at a table that rested on the backs of the world's exploited poor'. But of course this sarcasm was a standard piece of corporate media fabrication. Far from *really liking* the mural, Corbyn had barely been aware of its existence. As a regular supporter of grassroots protest he had naturally agreed to add his name to protests against the erasure of a striking piece of street art. This was an obscure act of solidarity, apparently done on a Facebook page.the art work in question showed kneeling figures - plainly the oppressed masses - supporting a platform, on which sat a group of prominent twentieth century bankers (identifiable if you knew your bankers). The bankers were not all Jews and the artist denied any anti-Semitic intent. The noses were potato-knobbly, not hooked. As satire or politics it was dubious only in so far as it leaned towards generalised conspiracy theory - the majority manipulated by a powerful elite - rather than class war. But all this was basically irrelevant. The key issue in this supposed controversy was why this miniscule years-old episode in Corbyn's political history had been located, saved and then released to media acclaim at the precise moment that it was. The answer, of course, was that it was produced and orchestrated by the Zionist lobby for the express purpose of supplying ammunition to the corporate media in its daily efforts to defame and destroy Corbyn. That evening Ellis watched the first episode of the adaptation of *Emma* starring Romola Gairy. Afterwards he watched a BBC documentary about Maggi Hambling. Outside, the wind howled. In bed he read more of the witchcraft book.

Sunday 25th October 2020

A bright sunny morning. Ellis woke, remembering a strange dream in which Maggi Hambling had hidden behind his sofa. Ellis went out to deliver a birthday present and card, and then went for a walk. The child played in her tent. Later Ellis lunched on soup, bread and cheese. He finished emptying a box of old files. From the internet he discovered that Labour MP Stephen Kinnock had been reprimanded for speaking out in the House of Commons debate about the illegal settlements in the West Bank, arguing that importing goods from these settlements allowed Israel to profit 'from the proceeds of crime'. Lisa Nandy, the Party's Shadow Foreign Secretary, confirmed at a meeting with the usual rancid right-wing Jewish communal organisations last week that Kinnock had been given a 'dressing down' over this speech made on September 24. Sources say Sir Keir Starmer was 'infuriated' with the tone of the MP's speech. Kinnock, it was reported, had been reprimanded for his speech. "Lisa made no secret of the fact that she and the leader were angry with Kinnock - especially after all the work that has been done to try to restore Labour's relationship with the Jewish community. Mr Kinnock has a long record of singling out Israel with over-the-top criticism." On YouTube Ellis listened to various versions of 'Darkness, Darkness'. The best of the lot, he thought, remained that old one by Iain Matthews. After that he watched 'Pinky in the Daylight'. That evening he watched the second episode of *Roadkill*, then went to bed.

Monday 26th October 2020

A bright sunny morning. Ellis went shopping. He bought croissants from the bakery; stewing steak and a pork pie from the butchers; milk, vegetables and ground almond from the supermarket. The child played with her toy bottle of milk, pretending to drink it. Online, Ellis read about the latest Israeli atrocities. A Palestinian teenager had died of his injuries after being savagely beaten by Israeli forces near the town of Turmus-Ayya northeast of Ramallah. The Palestinian health ministry said that Amer Abedalrahim Snobar arrived at the hospital after being "severely beaten on the neck". The medical centre reported that the injuries to Snobar's neck were consistent with being beaten with the butts of Israeli soldiers' rifles. In a statement, the Palestine Liberation Organization (PLO) accused Israeli troops of "a monstrous act of brutality against a defenceless young man whose only crime was being Palestinian". Senior PLO official Hanan Ashrawi said in the statement that Sanouber had been "bludgeoned" by Israeli troops. Snobar hailed from the village of Yatma, south of the occupied West Bank city of Nablus. This Jewish barbarism naturally attracted no attention in the British or American media, and Jewish organisations were silent. Elsewhere, on the *Middle East Eye* website, Ellis read that Abdullah Maarouf typically tends to his olive grove at this time of year, the start of the olive harvest season in Palestine. But this year, however, 55-year-old Maarouf is forced to sit at home. Maarouf lives in the village of Deir Ballut, in the northern governorate of Salfit, in the occupied West Bank. He says his land was once "a paradise". Today, it has become a wastewater swamp, due to the sewage that runs from the illegal settlement of Leshem nearby. Maarouf and his family of 50 members own 20 dunams (two hectares), home to about 400 olive trees, some of which date back to the Roman period. Their trees produce two tonnes of olive oil each year. "We can no longer reach our land, nor can we harvest the olives. The settlement sewage water has drowned the land completely," Maarouf said. *Illegal Israeli settlements discharge millions of cubic metres of wastewater into the West Bank every year. A large amount of the wastewater is untreated sewage that flows into Palestinian valleys and onto agricultural land. About 10 dunams of the land's original size were confiscated for the settlement area, which they are now forbidden from accessing. Settlers also previously attacked the land and cut down 200 olive trees that were about 25 years old. Deir Ballut is surrounded by the illegal settlements of Leshem, Peduel and Beit Aryeh-Ofarim, all of which release sewage that ends up on the village's agricultural land.* But of course this kind of barbarism, Ellis reflected, enjoys the unequivocal support of the British government and the official opposition. The day passed. Ellis went to bed, where he read a few more pages of the witchfinders book.

At the very end of the news BBC Radio 4 revealed that Sir Keir Starmer had knocked a cyclist off his bike in London on Sunday. Ellis went out shopping. He did not enjoy the experience. More and more people were indifferent to social distancing. Home again Ellis went online. As the Starmer story unfolded on social media more information came to light. Starmer had been driving a 4X4 - a grotesque vehicle for personal mobility in central London. Starmer had left the scene before police arrived. The cyclist had been taken to hospital. The police had phoned Starmer's home but had been unable to speak to him. A message was left that he needed to report to as police station about the collision. This he duly did. The criticism was made on social media that he had left the scene before the police had had any chance to breathalise him. It began to rain. The child was reluctant to eat the stew placed before her. She asked for a banana but then declined to eat it. She ate some orange instead, and then some cake and yogurt. Ellis read several pages of the latest issue of *Private Eye*, then went to bed, where he read several pages of *Witchfinders*.

Wednesday 28th October 2020

A bright sunny morning. The child played with sand, picking it up and running it through her fingers. In the afternoon it clouded over and rained. Online Ellis learned more about the killing of 16 year old Amer Abdel-Rahim Snobar on the evening of Saturday 24 October. He was helping a 17-year-old friend move his broken-down car near the village of Turmus'ayya, located northeast of Ramallah, when Israeli forces arrived at the scene. The friend fled on foot and hid in trees, where he witnessed the Jewish soldiers surround Amer. Amer was placed in a chokehold, beaten and killed. An autopsy found that the cause of death was probably asphyxiation resulting from strangulation. There was also substantial bruising and wounds on the child's chest and abdominal area. The killing of George Floyd on 25 May had resonated around the world. The killing of Amer Abdel-Rahim Snobar went unreported by the Western media. Amer's killers enjoyed the protection of governments, media and all the main Jewish organisations in the US, UK and EU. The Holocaust-memorial-mongers had nothing to say because official Holocaust memorial was instituted precisely to protect and promote Jewish racist violence in Israel. That was its major function. 'Israeli forces routinely use excessive and lethal force against Palestinian children,' said Ayed Abu Eqtaish of the Defense for Children International - Palestine. 'As long as systemic impunity is the norm and the international community remains complicit, Israeli forces will continue to torture and carry out extrajudicial and unlawful killings against Palestinian children.' The brutal murder of Amer Abdel-Rahim Snobar was carried out by six Israeli soldiers.

One placed a baton against his throat to choke him. Then the other Jews began cursing and beating Snobar with their fists and weapons. The child screamed and cried in pain. After about four minutes the screams stopped. He was dead - murdered by psychopathic racist Jews no different to Nazis who enjoyed the immunity supplied by the institutionally violent sectarian Jewish state and its supporters - the USA, Britain, the EU, and Jewish organisations around the world. The last child the Jews killed was on August 19, when Mohmmad Damer Hamdan Matar, aged 16, was shot dead by soldiers. On Ben White's Twitter page Ellis learned that in just two weeks during October, Israeli settlers burnt or damaged over 1,000 olive trees in the occupied West Bank. Meanwhile the shallow, self-promoting mediocrity Ed Balls had attacked Corbyn over supposed anti-Semitism. Ellis ate lasagna and salad, followed by apple crumble and ice-cream. In bed he read a few more pages of *Witchfinders*.

Thursday 29th October 2020

A wet, grey morning. The *Guardian* and the BBC headlined with excited anticipation the imminent report of the Equalities and Human Rights Commission's investigation of supposed anti-Semitism in the the Labour Party. Ellis watched Chris Williamson's video about the history of the EHRC. This right-wing quango was created by Tony Blair with Trevor Phillips as its leader. Today, leading figures in the Commission were right-wing Jews David Isaacs and Rebecca Hilsenrath. Williamson summarised the EHRC as a 'right-wing attack dog'. A light rain continued to fall. The child gleefully jumped up and down in the puddles in the car park. She was wearing her yellow boots and a new pink coat from Tesco, with a mock-fur-lined hood. Later in the day Ellis read the first responses to the EHRC report. Later still he learned that Jeremy Corbyn had been suspended from the Labour Party for stating that the issue of anti-Semitism had been greatly exaggerated for factional purposes. Louis Allday tweeted: *Lenin had it right about the Labour Party 100 years ago – "a thoroughly bourgeois party, because, although made up of workers, it is led by reactionaries, and the worst kind of reactionaries at that, who act quite in the spirit of the bourgeoisie".* Joe Sucksmith tweeted: *To be honest, I didn't think Starmer had it in him to suspend Corbyn. He's gambling the Labour Left will throw a tantrum, but ultimately come to terms with it. It's a fair bet, sadly.* Ellis downloaded the EHRC report and began reading it. *Investigation into antisemitism in the Labour Party.* The title itself was loaded. It treated the prejudice as a matter of fact, not as an allegation (an allegation, moreover, stemming from two aggressively Zionist organisations). It also used the Zionist spelling of anti-Semitism. It talked of but failed to define 'the Jewish community'. It spoke of 'growing public concern about antisemitism in the Labour Party' but supplied no evidence to substantiate that claim. It acknowledged the leaked internal Labour Party report but then, incredibly, said: 'It was not proportionate for us to require the Labour Party to provide the evidence underlying the report'. It assumes that 'Jewish Labour Party members' are Jewish and members of the Labour Party but in fact neither necessarily holds true, therefore the assertion that such individuals may have suffered 'indirect discrimination' is absurd. The report never defines what anti-Semitism is. It alludes to 'Jewish community stakeholders' - almost certainly rancid reactionary groups like the Board of Deputies of British Jews. Having failed to define the prejudice it purports to be investigating, it also fails to establish any hierarchy for the seriousness or otherwise of the expression of prejudice (physical violence, threats of physical violence, job discrimination, or verbal or written expressions). It says 'Social media was the source of most complaints of antisemitic behaviour: of the 70 complaints that we investigated, 59 concerned social media. This shows how vital it is that this form of antisemitic behaviour is tackled.' Ellis waited to see what examples would be supplied. The Party was ordered by the Jewish-run EHRC to 'Engage with Jewish stakeholders'. The usual rabble of screeching Zionists, in other words. That the EHRC was part of the problem was revealed by its admission that 'This investigation was prompted by complaints made to us by Campaign Against Antisemitism (CAA) and the Jewish Labour Movement (JLM) in the summer and autumn of 2018'. That the EHRC report is a Zionist stitch-up is shown by the ludicrous and irrelevant statement that in April 2018 'over 20 elected representatives (including MPs, peers and councillors) resigned from the Party in 2018 and 2019, citing a failure to tackle antisemitism in their reasons'. That these unidentified indivduals were a motley crew of Zionists and right-wingers united by their adoration of Israel is not mentioned by the EHRC. By the usual circular logic of Zionism evidence of 'anti-Semitic incidents' supplied by Zionist organisations (which characteristically exaggerated such incidents, and devalued their measuring by defining criticism of Israel as anti-Semitic) is treated as bona fide evidence. And what evidence did the EHRC manage to come up with? 'We found that the Labour Party, through its agents, committed harassment against its members in relation to Jewish ethnicity in the case of two individuals, Ken Livingstone and Pam Bromley.' The report cited: 'Local Rossendale Borough councillor, Pam Bromley, posted on Facebook: "Had Jeremy Corbyn and the Labour Party pulled up the drawbridge and nipped the bogus AS [antisemitism] accusations in the bud in the first place we would not be where we are now and the fifth column in the LP [Labour Party] would not have managed to get such a foothold ... the Lobby has miscalculated ... The witch hunt has created brand new fightback networks ... The Lobby will then melt back into its own cesspit." Nothing wrong with those remarks, you might think. But the EHRC decided that the reference to 'the fifth column in ther LP' meant Jews. It plainly didn't. It meant the right-wing malcontents, most of whom weren't Jewish. In short, by p.28 the EHRC report had established itself as garbage. Next evidence: 'Suggesting that complaints of antisemitism are fake or smears. Labour Party agents denied antisemitism in the Party and made comments dismissing complaints as 'smears' and 'fake'. This conduct may target Jewish members as deliberately making up antisemitism complaints to undermine the Labour Party, and ignores legitimate and genuine complaints of antisemitism in the Party.' No, it doesn't. Those who whined the loudest about anti-Semitism were the Zionists. Next, the EHRC distributed some stale crumbs from the Zionist table: 'In media interviews in April 2016, Ken Livingstone, a Labour Party National Executive Committee (NEC) member, made reference to social media posts made by Naz Shah MP. Naz Shah's posts included a graphic suggesting that Israel should be relocated to the United States, with the comment 'problem solved', and a post in which she appeared to liken Israeli policies to those of Hitler'. Nothing wrong with that. Shah had taken the graphic from a Zionist site (which was trying to make the point that Israel was so small, so weak). It was a joke. 'Naz Shah apologised for her comments in Parliament and conceded that they caused "upset and hurt to the Jewish Community".' Yes, she did, demonstrating a lack of spine that would later be reciprocated by Corbyn and McDonnell. Yet again, the 'Jewish Community' meant the usual rabble of Zionists. 'Ken Livingstone repeatedly denied that these posts were antisemitic and sought to minimise their offensive nature. In his denial, Ken Livingstone alleged that scrutiny of Naz Shah's conduct was part of a smear campaign by "the Israel lobby" to stigmatise critics of Israel as antisemitic, and was intended to undermine and disrupt the leadership of Jeremy Corbyn MP.' Livingstone was, of course, one-hundred-per-cent correct. The EHRC report simply echoes Zionist propaganda. The EHRC report takes very seriously the feelings of unidentified snowflakes: 'Labour Party members told us that the comments by Ken Livingstone in relation to Naz Shah (referred to above) caused shock and anger among Jewish Labour Party members. They felt his comments were appalling, highly offensive and very distressing'. Well, the JLP was rabidly anti-Corbyn and rabidly pro-Israel, so it's hardly surprising its right-wing membership didn't like the sound of a few home truths. The EHRC report continued, page after page, to accumulate fresh garbage. By p.79 Ellis came to a reference to 'antisemitic posts on social media', including 'How can we not have empathy with the Palestinians when they are up against these murdering, Zionest [sic] bastards. Their NAZI masters taught them well'. That's a criticism of Zionist murderers, not a criticism of Jews. What was missing from the report, Ellis suddenly realised, was any reference to all those Jews who had been expelled from the Labour Party on spurious grounds of anti-Semitism or, when that charge was difficult to uphold, for 'bringing the party into disrepute'. And on it went, a report devoid of evidence. Then it became sinister as it emerged that this tinpot quango had legal power which it intended to use: 'Following that investigation the EHRC is satisfied that the Labour Party has committed the following unlawful acts (Unlawful Acts): 1. The Labour Party committed unlawful harassment of its members, contrary to section 101(4)(a) of the Equality Act 2010, related to race (Jewish ethnicity), through the acts of its agents Ken Livingstone and Pam Bromley (as further set out in Chapter 3 of, and Annex 2 to, the EHRC's report of the investigation titled: 'Investigation into antisemitism in the Labour Party' (Report)).'. At times the report became literally laughable. How Ellis chuckled when he read another example of Pam Bromley's supposed anti-Semitism: 'A huge sigh of relief echoes around Facebook' (comment accompanying a shared BBC News story with the headline 'Israeli spacecraft crashes on Moon', 12 April 2019). In short, the EHRC used the Zionist device of conflating criticism of Israel with criticism of Jews. The report was a Zionist document - hardly surprising when it emerged from a Commission dominated by right-wing Jews. The hours passed. Ellis waited with interest to see what slippery Owen Jones would have to say. Finally it came, as slithery and vacuous as you might expect from this faux leftist: *This has to be pulled back from the brink. The EHRC report's solid recommendations need urgent implementation. The whole left needs to accept antisemitism in Labour caused genuine distress and hurt to Jews. Corbyn's suspension just means Labour's forever war will go on and on.* Not that Len McCluskey was much better. More grovelling to the Zios, with empty platitudes about defeating the evil of anti-Semitism, more grovelling to Keir Starmer urging him to 'unite the party behind the implementation of the EHRC's important recommendations', and a desperate plea to members not to leave the Labour Party. On social media there was a cascade of tweeters stating they were resigning from the party and cancelling their direct debits. This was countered by the usual loyalists urging people to stay and fight and asserting that mass resignations of the Left were what Starmer wanted. But the Labour Party was the party of Margaret Hodge, Rosie Duffield, Stella Creasy, Wes Streeting and the pro-war, pro-Israel, pro-austerity right. A PLP of Blairite mediocrities and reactionaries. That evening Ellis watched Sky news at 10pm. The Coronavirus pandemic was now spreading across Europe again, evidently as a result of the relaxation of the earlier restrictions. Three people had been murdered in a Catholic church in Nice by a lone wolf jihadi fanatic, a young Tunisian, who had been shot but not killed by the police. Jeremy Corbyn had been suspended from the Labour Party. Ellis learned from social media that on the BBC radio programme 'The World at One' Angela Rayner had put the boot in, asserting that Corbyn had 'a blind spot' regarding anti-Semitism. Rayner was another shallow mediocrity, all personality and no intellect. Aaron Bastani tweeted that he would be doing the Sky press review, so Ellis stayed up to watch him. He'd never watched Bastani peform live before. And how amazingly useless he turned out to be! He blathered. He praised the EHRC's 'brilliant' report. He said not a word about Chris Williamson's strange absence from the report (but then

Bastani and his slithery Novara Media outlet had joined the witch-hunt against Williamson, for reasons of expediency). He said nothing about the report's conflation of criticism of Israel with anti-Semitism or the fact that it only named two names. Ellis switched off the TV and went to bed.

Friday 30th October 2020

Ellis woke soon after 7am. On the radio Corbyn ally James Schneider was attempting to defend the former leader of the opposition. He was hopeless. Yet again a supposed leftist began from the assumption that the crisis was about anti-Semitism when it wasn't. It was about Zionism. Schneider blabbered on. An hour later Sir Keir Starmer popped up. It would be wrong for the Leader to get involved in disciplinary matters, he said, as if somehow the decision to suspend Corbyn had been taken without his involvement. Naturally the right-wing softball interviewer allowed him an easy ride. Later, on social media, Ellis came across a tweet by Richard Burgon MP, a supposed socialist. *Labour members from across the country have contacted me deeply upset at the decision to suspend Jeremy. I agree and I'll be working for his reinstatement. Let's move foward together to fight antisemitism, all forms of racism and Tory attacks on all our communities.* Pathetic, thought Ellis. The Labour left was going to capitulate, that was obvious. Elsewhere on Twitter Ellis came across more responses. Michael Gove - yes! Michael Gove! - tweeted *All of us should be concerned about what has happened in the Labour Party in recent years. And today's EHRC report underlines that. There are still important questions for Keir Starmer and so I have written to him seeking answers.* The so-called left Zionist Rachel Shabi tweeted *The EHRC produced a strong, solid document. It shows that the issues Jewish people and others were highlighting as problems within the Labour party were, in fact, problems. Please read it.* Well, Ellis had done. And it showed no such thing. Shabi added: *Antisemitism is often pernicious and many still struggle to understand what it is. The EHRC report helps to clarify in several areas, especially on denialism. Please read it.* By this Kafkaesque logic, if you deny that the problem identified by racist Jews is a problem then you are the problem. This circular logic existed from the very start of the anti-Semitism hoax. Slithy Owen Jones, replying to incoherent Shabi, tweeted *Brilliant analysis.* Ellis went shopping. The first store he entered stated : *Only one family member to enter.* He was unsurprised to enter and find three family members shopping in a group, while the store staff said nothing. The next store said : *Maximum of 30.* Home again Ellis went online and was delighted to see that Tony Greenstein had tweeted about the latest events in the right's takeover of the Labour Party. *Starmer Declares War on the Left – It's About Time to Declare War on Him - We Demand the Reinstatement of Jeremy Corbyn* was the title of Greenstein's article (https://azvsas.blogspot.com/2020/10/

starmer-declares-war-on-left-its-about.html). The EHRC is **not** an anti-racist body, wrote Greenstein. *Its Commissioners are taken from the corporate and banking world with the odd lawyer thrown in. It is an organisation of the liberal Establishment that has been mobilised to drive a wedge into the Labour Party using identity politics to disguise its purpose. It is a body that has said next to nothing about the Windrush scandal, done nothing about the 'hostile environment' policy of the Tories, it has said nothing about stop and search, refugees or institutional racism. Why? Because it is itself an institutionally racist body. As Simon Woolley, a former Commissioner wrote, the EHRC doesn't have one single Black or Muslim Commissioner. It is stuffed with liberal and corporate do-gooders. Woolley wrote 'I've been particularly stuck by the huge gulf between the EHRC and the new generation of young Black Lives Matter activists'. The EHRC is utterly irrelevant to the victims of racism in Britain today. It is a body whose sole purpose is in incorporating and blunting the anti-racist message. It is as much our enemy as Boris Johnson.* Greenstein added: *When the EHRC first proposed its investigation it should have been vigorously opposed as an intrusion by a State body into a democratic political party. What has happened is the kind of tactic used in police states. The State has effectively sought to neutralise a radical political party.* Greenstein contrasted the EHRC's investigation into the Labour Party with its reluctance to address racism in the Conservative Party. The EHRC, wrote Greenstein, has fought shy of doing anything about an openly racist party led by someone who believes that Black people are *'picanninies'* with *'water melon smiles'. Unlike 'anti-Semitism' in the Labour Party Islamaphobia in the Tory Party is part of its DNA. Yet this useless body has kept its mouth shut for fear of losing what's left of its grant.* Greenstein's critique got better and better. *Sure there is some antisemitic prejudice if you look hard enough but as the EHRC Report concedes most of it is in social media. No one has ever died from a tweet but plenty of Black youth have died in Police custody yet Starmer has nothing but praise for the Police.* As for the former Labour Leader: *Corbyn himself laid the basis for what has happened. His opposition to Open Selection at the 2018 Labour Party Conference and then his decision at the 2019 Party Conference to support 'fast track' expulsions which we were assured were only for 'egregious' cases but which have since been used in EVERY 'anti-Semitism' case laid the basis for his own suspension.* Greenstein linked to the *LabourList* website, which reported that: Constituency Labour Parties have been warned by Labour's general secretary David Evans not to "question the competence" of the Equality and Human Rights Commission or reject its report, *LabourList* can reveal. *He has also told CLPs that their social media accounts must not be used to comment on the investigation or the report, and accounts where comments or discussion is usually allowed they should be "closely moderated" or access "temporarily suspended". The general secretary has warned that motions seeking to* *"question the competence of the EHRC to conduct the investigation"* or to *"repudiate or reject the report or any of its recommendations"* are *"not competent business"...* Evans told local parties over the summer that they should not allow motions relating to the Panorama settlement or the EHRC report, nor should they *"repudiate"* the International Holocaust Remembrance Alliance definition of antisemitism. Greenstein commented: It is crucial that local parties defy Evans and go ahead and condemn the report and Sturmer with it. That is what Momentum should be calling for, not unity with the devil. Greenstein then went on to address the EHRC report, calling it 'an insubstantial tract'. *At 130 pages is remarkable for the fact that it is shallow and superficial, lacking in substance. Its main focus is the alleged failure of Labour's disciplinary and complaints processes. Whereas it took me 3 days to read Labour's leaked report on Anti-Semitism the EHRC Report was a breeze. There is nothing in it apart from procedure. The EHRC has produced a mouse and yet Starmer willed it on as a means of attacking the Left. Its failures are manifest to anyone who isn't cerebrally challenged.* Greenstein had noticed what Ellis had noticed: the report never defines what anti-Semitism is. Instead of adhering to the classic definition - hostility to or prejudice or discrimination against Jews - the Commission concentrated on what might be 'offensive' to unidentified Jews, *regardless of whether or not it was true.* The Commission never addressed who exactly the Jewish Labour Movement or the so-called Campaign Against Antisemitism are or what they represent. Not once did the EHRC consider the traditional application by Zionists of the term 'anti-Semitism' to those campaigning for Palestinian rights. Disgracefully, the EHRC report singles out Ken Livingstone, who pioneered anti-racism in local government. The report once singled out Chris Williamson but then retracted its criticisms after the threat of legal action. Greenstein added: The Report completely decontextualises the allegations whilst insinuating that anyone denying that there was an anti-Semitism problem was themselves anti-Semitic! This is called 'denialism' which is the logic of the Salem Witchhunt, when women and men were hanged for witchcraft in Massachusetts. As Elizabeth Purdy wrote: 'Those who publicly questioned the guilt of a defendant were likely to be accused of witchcraft themselves'. Greenstein added: *There is repeated talk of 'Jewish community stakeholders'. It never once explains who these might be but we can assume it means the Trump-Tory-supporting Board of Deputies. A body which cheered on the Israeli army as they mowed down unarmed Palestinian protesters in Gaza. They blamed the death of medics and children on the victims and they then profess to be concerned about anti-Semitism.* Greenstein noted that *Nearly all their examples of 'anti-Semitism' consist of social media posts. This simply trivializes anti-Semitism. Racism is about what people do not what they post on Twitter. No one has ever died from a tweet but plenty have died from Israeli bullets.* Moreover: *Despite saying that they took evidence from Jewish Voices*

for Labour there is no evidence of this. The EHRC comprehensively disregarded the voice of anti-Zionist and non-Zionist Jews. Tony Greenstein knew this from first-hand experience: *I wrote to the EHRC's Investigation repeatedly offering to give evidence. They were not interested. I told them that as the first Jewish person to be expelled I might have a different perspective on the fake anti-Semitism affair. They made it clear that they weren't interested.* Greenstein noted how politicized this spurious 'investigation' had been from the start: *The EHRC said they launched their 'investigation' because of 'serious public concern about allegations of anti-Semitism'. It is strange that serious public concern about Police stop and search, the Windrush deportations and other acts of state racism merited no such concern. In fact there was no public concern about Labour anti-Semitism. It was a narrative of the Tory press and the Labour right-wing.* Greenstein noted the dubious legal basis for the investigation: *The legal basis of its inquiry, that the Labour Party was an association under the Equality Act 2010 omits the fact that it is a political party and allegations of 'anti-Semitism' were weaponised, e.g. the allegations at Oxford University which had been made by Alex Chalmers, a former intern of the Israel Lobby organisation BICOM.* He added: *By definition a political party is not a sports club or other voluntary association. The EHRC is an organ of the state. It had no right to interfere and in essence take sides in a political dispute inside the Labour Party. It was Corbyn and Formby's stupidity which prevented them telling the EHRC to mind their own business.* Greenstein was well placed to critique the report, since he is mentioned indirectly in it: *The Report also mentions that I was suspended yet given no details of the allegations against me, despite requesting information on several occasions. It reports that I successfully obtained an injunction. However what the report does not do is mention that I am Jewish (it didn't mention me by name).* This dishonesty is characteristic of this shoddy report. And so it went on. Greenstein's was by far the most comprehensive and incisive analysis of this bogus report, but it would undoubtedly be doomed to the margins by the rabble of faux Leftists like Owen Jones, Rachel Shabi, Aaron Bastani et al. Ellis put 'tony greenstein' into twitter search and at the top of the page was a tweet from someone posted 23 minutes ago linking to Greenstein's blog post and praising it. Ellis scrolled down, then returned to the top of the page - only to find that the tweet praising Greenstein and linking to his blog post had been erased. How very, very curious. It was almost as if Twitter was aggressively censoring links to Greenstein's blog posts. Next Ellis discovered that on the *Middle East Eye* website there was a critique of the EHRC report by Richard Sanders and Peter Oborne, pointing out that for two-thirds of the period under investigation, Labour HQ and the complaints procedure were under the control of individuals hostile to Corbyn and seeking to undermine him. *In large measure Corbyn is being held responsible for the failures of party officials who were not just his political opponents, but also among his principal accusers when it came to allegations of antisemitism ... The EHRC's failure even to reference the significance of the transfer of power at party HQ between February and April 2018 has facilitated obfuscation and lazy reporting.* Sanders and Oborne were apparently present at the press conference called by the EHRC on Thursday morning, when the report was published. They report that *Not one journalist probed the inconsistencies, contradictions or omissions of the report.* Later, Ellis came across more froth from that ubiquitous mediocrity, Ellie Mae O'Hagan. She twittered *please please news producers please stop inviting Ken Livingstone and Chris Williamson on broadcast media. It is grossly irresponsible.* Ah, yes. Shutting down dissent. What you'd expect from someone who describes herself as *'Strategic comms consultant, commentator, author-to-be. Regular contributor @guardianopinion.* The corporate media was infested with snivelling crypto-radicals like O'Hagan. Her frothings were matched by the vacuous rhetoric of dim-witted Michael Segalov, who wanted *a sombre day of reflection on the experiences of Jewish people in the UK and the prejudice, abuse, discrimination and hurt we face.* Oh please. No one wallowed in spurious victimhood more than Jews like Segalov. Murray Jay Siskind retorted: *It's the most blatant of witch hunts. Yet you still don't have the guts to call it, because you're a weak careerist.* Quite. It looked increasingly like rain but no rain fell. The child played with her Play-Doh. Her mother fashioned her a cat. Later, online, Ellis read a tweet by Owen Hatherley praising an article on the *Tribune* website. Hatherley wrote: *this is as always properly clear about what has happened and what the stakes are.* Ellis clicked on the link. The article was by Ronan Burtenshaw. It began by saluting the EHRC report as 'a sober and earnest document which focused on procedural issues'. Burtenshaw wrote: 'The most damning finding – of harassment – related to two cases where representatives of the party, former mayor Ken Livingstone and a Lancashire councillor, had made antisemitic comments'. No, they hadn't. Once again a supposed Left journalist was swallowing whole the garbage around this manufactured 'crisis'. It was a pitifully inadequate response to the Zionist-inflected report, the rancid complainants behind the report, and that slippery, reactionary entity known as 'the Jewish community'. Burtenshaw stated: *Labour is, indeed, in a civil war. But only one side is fighting. The Left has thus far remained largely disorganised and timid. This must change.* Pathetic. The Left inside and on the fringes of the Labour Party was intellectually impoverished and contemptibly opportunist. A little after 5pm one of the Jews who'd set out to destroy Corbyn, Jonathan Freedland, used his platform in the *Guardian* for a fresh assault: *Labour and anti-Semitism: once again it's all about Jeremy Corbyn.* Freedland, as usual, wrote as the self-appointed representative of 'British Jews'. He hailed the reactionary EHRC as 'a neutral legal arbiter'. He cited 'one community figure' - unidentified, naturally - who confided that a Corbyn-led Labour Party in power would surely 'discriminate against Jews once in government, when they would have the full power of the state at their disposal'. Amazing. At best a Corbyn government might have restricted arms sales to Israel, although even that would have no doubt upset the delicate sensitivities of the British Jewish establishment, for whom no racist atrocity by the Jewish state was not to be excused, defended or justified. Freedland went on to say he'd had a chat with 'EHRC executive director Alastair Pringle'. Pringle had told him of 'hundreds of [files]...they were absolutely atrocious. The language, the behaviour - it was shocking'. It was rather extraordinary, Ellis thought, that a top man at the EHRC should be feeding the Zionist Freedland with titbits that formed no part of the Report. The Report contained nothing to substantiate Pringle's anecdotes. Besides, how could anyone be sure that this alleged material had anything at all to do with Labour Party members? How could we be sure that the content was as shocking as Pringle claimed? It was a generalised anecdote with not a single example supplied. And as was obvious from the EHRC report, any criticisms or jokes about Israel were deemed to be an attack on Jews. There followed the usual misrepresentations by Freedland, warming up the old, putrefying sediment of the Zionist smear campaign (the most bizarre of which involved Corbyn's Introduction to the economist J. A. Hobson's book on imperialism). Ellis baked two smoked-salmon steaks. He watched episode two of the adaptation of *Emma* starring Romola Gairy. He watched the 10pm Sky news. There was footage of a building collapsing during an earthquake in Turkey. There was an impressionistic account of the campaign against Trump in Florida, centred on 'suburban women'. There was film of florid, wooden Keir Starmer justifying the suspension of Corbyn. The footballer Nobby Stiles had died at the age of 78. He was famous for his footballing achievements for Manchester United and for his lack of teeth. He was shown holding his false teeth in his hand at the end of a triumphant match. Nobby was an abbreviation of his first name, Norbert. It transpired that Nobby had suffered from dementia since the age of 61 and that there was a high incidence of this disease among retired professional footballers. Damage to the brain from repeatedly heading the ball was a likely cause. It also transpired that Nobby had been impoverished in later life and felt abandoned by his old and now fabulously wealthy football club. Ellis switched off the television and went to bed. He read a few more pages of *Witchfinders*.

Saturday 31st October 2020

Ellis woke at around 6.45am and lay in the gloom listening to 'Farming Today'. A pumpkin farmer said his trade this year was down eighty-per-cent. A representative of the National Farmers Union spoke of worries about the year ahead in relation to finding workers for seasonal picking. The end of free movement on 31st December meant that East Europeans would no longer be able to come here to work in the fields. Later, Ellis went online. Owen Jones wanted 'the whole left accepting the hurt and distress caused to Jewish people by antisemitism' and cretinous Jennie Formby spoke about the need to 'rebuild relations with the Jewish community and mend the hurt and pain that has been caused'. This futile grovelling to the bellicose Zionist lobby never ended. The sun came out. The sky was blue. The child emptied out a cupboard of empty tupperware boxes. She wore her new size 5 red shoes. That evening Ellis watched the remaining two episodes of *Emma*. Romola Garai was the best Emma he'd seen, Ellis thought, and the adaptation was also superior to others he'd viewed.

Sunday 1st November - Tuesday 3rd November

Malware gobbled three and a half days of writing which Ellis had foolishly failed to back up. So it goes. As he looked back he tried to remember what he'd written. On Sunday morning, lying in bed, he'd caught the opening of 'Sunday Worship'. The programme was supposed to be devoted to religion but it started with the rabid Trump-supporting Zionist Marie van der Zyl attacking Jeremy Corbyn and what she claimed was the surge in anti-Semitism which had occurred in the Labour Party under his leadership. This gargantuan fabrication naturally went unchallenged by the fawning BBC hack. When Ellis looked at the Wikipedia entry on van der Zyl he was not surprised to read that it was 'last edited by Philip Cross'. The notorious Philip Cross, Wikipedia's licensed right-wing vigilante, who devoted every day of the year to doctoring entries for prominent campaigners on the Left, while massaging entries for those on the Right. Later, on the internet, Ellis discovered that today's *Observer* newspaper carried no less than three vicious assaults on Jeremy Corbyn. There was a sputtering editorial, a foam-flecked piece by the odious Ruth Smeeth, and a lengthy diatribe by the Blairite war-lover, Andrew Rawnsley. Ellis was amused to see that Smeeth couldn't even be honest about her CV. Her narcissistic column ended with the claim that she 'left Parliament in November 2019'. It didn't say she was booted out by her constituents the following month. It was extraordinary that a shallow right-wing mediocrity like Smeeth had been appointed chief executive of Index on Censorship. Or perhaps not, when you saw who was involved. Ellis looked up this organisation and discovered that its chair was Trevor Philips, its company directors included David Aaronovitch, and its patrons included conscience-free Margaret Atwood, long-term Tory Sir Tom Stoppard and, disappointingly, Michael Palin CBE. The organisation was funded by, among others, the Arts Council, the *Daily Mail*, the anti-Palestinian EU, the rabidly reactionary *Evening Standard*, Facebook, Google and others. *From the beginning, Index declares its mission to stand up for free expression as a fundamental human right for people everywhere.* Except Palestinians, natch.

Ellis wondered what Index had had to say about the murder of Ghassan Kanafani on 8 July 1972. He strongly suspected nothing at all. The murder of a Palestinian novelist hadn't troubled the conscience of western liberals then, nor had it since. The next day, Monday, was dominated by corporate media coverage of the US Presidential election. It poured with rain. Ellis went out to a bookshop, a greengrocers, a supermarket and a bakery. That evening it was reported that a major terrorist attack was happening in central Vienna, with six locations under simultaneous attack. By the end of Tuesday 3rd November it became clear that in fact it was a lone wolf attacker, who had shot dead four people before being killed by the police. On this day the *Guardian* ran yet another assault on Corbyn and the supposed crisis of antisemitism. On this occasion it was a joint production by David Feldman, professor of history and director of the Pears Institute for the Study of Antisemitism, Birkbeck, University of London; Ben Gidley, a senior lecturer in the department of psychosocial studies, Birkbeck (who had been outed some years ago by Mark Elf as the individual behind the Zionist blog 'Bob from Brockley'); and Brendan McGeever, a lecturer in the department of psychosocial studies, Birkbeck. It was an intellectually shoddy piece. It began with the ludicrous assertion that *The report was a vindication for those who struggled to combat antisemitism in Labour*. No, it wasn't. What was striking was just how thin the 'evidence' amounted to. The EHRC took it upon itself to assert that 'legitimate' criticism of Israel was acceptable but that it was unlawful to engage in 'criticism of Israel that was antisemitic'. But the EHRC failed to define what it meant by this. Is the factual assertion 'Israel is a racist endeavour' anti-Semitic by the EHRC's standards? The EHRC doesn't say. What it does say is that Councillor Pam Bromley's reference to 'the fifth column in the LP' [Labour Party] is anti-Semitic because it refers to Jews. This is a bizarre and ludicrous reading of what Pam Bromley wrote. It's perfectly obvious that the term 'fifth column' as used by Pam Bromley is not about Jews. The second example the EHRC supplies is that it is anti-Semitic to suggest 'that complaints of anti-Semitism are fake or smears'. And yet many of them *were*. The EHRC analysis of anti-Semitism is Zionist to its rotten core. *Naz Shah's posts included a graphic suggesting that Israel should be relocated to the United States, with the comment 'problem solved', and a post in which she appeared to liken Israeli policies to those of Hitler. The comments made by Naz Shah went beyond legitimate criticism of the Israeli government, as she acknowledged, and are not protected by Article 10. Neither is Ken Livingstone's support for those comments.* This is exceptionally sinister. A state body where right-wing Jews occupy senior positions is now determining that criticism of this sort is illegal and not protected by Articles 10 and 11 of the European Convention of Human Rights (ECHR), which ostensibly protect freedom of expression and freedom of association. (The Human Rights Act 1998 brought the ECHR directly into UK law.) *Articles 10 and 11 are* particularly relevant when considering whether conduct should be regarded as harassment, as conduct which has the effect of violating a person's dignity or creating an intimidating, hostile, degrading, humiliating or offensive environment for them. What this boils down to is that whiney middle-class British Zionists who don't like the violent and sectarian Jewish state to be criticised can claim that they feel offended and hurt by such criticisms and can shriek illegal prejudice. Or as the EHRC report puts it: Labour Party members told us that the comments by Ken Livingstone in relation to Naz Shah (referred to above) caused shock and anger among Jewish Labour Party members. They felt his comments were appalling, highly offensive and very distressing. They said the effect of these comments was humiliating, denied the victims' experience, diminished the issue, and had the effect of stirring up and fuelling hatred for Jews. Labour Party members also told us that Pam Bromley's conduct, including the Facebook posts above, contributed to a hostile environment in the Labour Party for Jewish and non-Jewish members. In short, you mustn't upset a Jewish anti-Palestinian racist. That this circular logic was hailed as 'damning' by the corporate media tells you everything you need to know about the hollowing out of liberalism by the poison of Zionism. Intelligent analysis was nowhere to be found on the soft Left, which simply rolled over and accepted it. The finding that the Labour party has breached equality law is historic gloated David Feldman, Ben Gidley and Brendan McGeever. Yes, it certainly was. Zionists were edging closer and closer to shutting down all pro-Palestinian political activity, with the ultimate goal of locking up anyone who dared to criticise Israel. Later, Ellis watched the final episode of Life, which, he felt, fizzled out, and became implausibly upbeat and feel-goody. The 10pm Sky News was dominated by the US election, and consisted of nothing more than the usual stenographers engaging in impressionistic chatter. Ellis went to bed.

Wednesday 4th November

A bright sunny morning. The US election results were so far indecisive and indicated a narrower lead for Biden than the polls had suggested. Ellis went for a walk. Later he learned that Twitter had permanently suspended the account of David Icke, described by the *Guardian* as 'the conspiracy theorist'. *A spokesman for the social media platform said Icke had violated its rules regarding coronavirus misinformation. The move follows the decision by YouTube and Facebook to terminate Icke's accounts in early May for the same reason. Famous medics including Dr Christian Jessen and former junior doctor Adam Kay have called on social networks to remove Icke from their platforms. They are backed by the Centre for Countering Digital Hate (CCDH), which claims his conspiracies over Covid-19 have been viewed more than 30m times. The Countdown presenter Rachel Riley celebrated Icke's departure from the the popular website, tweeting: "The UK's foremost hate peddler/conspiracy grifter has finally been chucked off Twitter."* Ellis looked up the so-called Centre for Countering Digital Hate. It was based in East Finchley and appeared to have a strong Zionist aspect. Its patron was... the shrill Zionist harpy Rachel Riley. Ellis felt it unlikely that Index on Censorship would be rushing to protect Icke's freedom of speech. Shutting down people like Icke delighted the liberal centre, of course, which plainly failed to appreciate that such actions merely confirmed the views of those who felt that sinister, powerful, secret forces were being utilised against them. Ellis browsed Twitter to read commentary on the US elections. He learned that there were two other candidates apart from Biden and Trump. Jo Jorgensen, libertarian, had pushed the Green into fourth place. She'd got more than one per cent of the vote, it seemed. On the face of it her policies looked attractive. Anti-imperialist, against the 'war on drugs'. Truly libertarian. Twitter was filled with furious Democrats shrieking abuse at anyone who had voted for her instead of Sleepy Joe. Danny DeAndre tweeted: *Love when people try to tear me down for voting for Jo Jorgensen. Love her policies and issues. Fuck off if you say a waste of a vote, just because I'm voting for someone I believe in. i don't play the lesser of two evils games.* The day grew older. The child sang the duck song and went Quack! Quack! Then she ate a peanut butter sandwich. Ellis tucked into a lamb steak with mash and cauliflower. Later he learned that 492 new coronavirus deaths had been reported in the UK today, the highest daily total for 5 months. By 10pm Sky News was forecasting a Biden victory. Trump looked downcast and unusually orange. A woman who had attempted to remove her 97 year old mother from a care home had been arrested by police. Mobile phone footage of her was shown, handcuffed in the back of a police car. Ellis went to bed and read more of *Witchfinders*.

Thursday 5th November

Ellis woke at 7.30am. Counting was continuing in the key American states. He went out to the bakery and bought some croissants. After that he went for a walk, during which he encountered the electrician who had wired up his room of books. Later, he went online. He read tweets by Branko Marcetic, forecasting that Biden would be a very weak president, under a cluster of epochal crises. *Biden, who is mentally well past his prime, has neither the kind of loyal base and grass roots fervor, nor the reserves of charisma and inspiration that, say Obama did, to try overcome divided government. Not sure what follows a failed or conservative Biden administration.* Marcetic tweeted: *The election is over and people can stop pretending. Faced with a 1932-style scenario, the party this time, succeeded in stopping FDR and picked Al Smith instead.* Ali Abunimah tweeted footage of Trump supporters screaming *Stop the count!* in Detroit, Michigan, commenting: *If these right wing fanatics trying to stop vote counting* in Michigan were in Venezuela or Bolivia they'd have the full support of Joe Biden and Nancy Pelosi as "pro-democracy activists." Ellis learned that Facebook had suspended the account of The Freud Museum in London, for breaching its community standards. The Museum had advertised a discussion of psychoanalysis and conspiracy theory. Josep Borrel Fontelles, High Representative of the EU for Foreign Affairs and Security Policy/Vice-President of the EU Commission wrote *We need to fight Islamist terrorism together*, to which Ali Abunimah retorted: *You would never catch the EU using a term like "Judaist terror" to describe the crimes of Israel and its fanatical Jewish settlers. But stigmatizing Muslims is totally normal for EU leaders like Josep Borrel Fontelles.* The hours passed. Ellis finished watching *The Ninth Gate.* A neighbour let off fireworks for his children. By 20.53 the total of electoral college votes won by the two main presidential candidates was: 253 for Biden, 214 for Trump. By 10.40pm there was still no decisive result. Ellis went to bed and read a few more pages of the witchfinders book.

Friday 6th November

Bright and sunny. Ellis woke to a 6.50am alarm. Incredibly, there had been no new results in the US presidential election. It was a hot day for November (another unspoken sign of climate catastrophe). Donald Trump alleged that fraud was occurring, to deprive him of victory. Samantha Power, former American ambassador to the UN, with a pleasant job at Harvard, tweeted: *He's going full Robert Mugabe.* Heba Hersi retorted: *Reminded of the time Samantha's motorcade killed a 6-year-old Cameroonian child (Toussaint Birwe). She didn't bother to stop or care and kept it moving.* Steven Salaita tweeted: *As of now, Biden leads Trump by approximately 3.8 million votes, more than the population of 22 states (and DC). Yet we still await a winner, either of whom will continue plundering the world's poor and vulnerable on behalf of a predatory ruling class. Hell of a "democracy."* Owen Jones tweeted: *The corporate media has failed us. Help me build something new.* Ellis clicked on the link. It turned out to be an invitation to watch Owen Jones pontificate on video. It had three levels of charge: *Grassroots* (£3 a month plus VAT), *Comrade* (£5 a month plus VAT), *Solidarity* (£10 a month plus VAT). A cruel smile crossed Ellis's face. He chuckled, reading Ben Norton's retort: *Liberal opportunist and The Guardian of Blairism columnist Owen Jones—who worked behind the scenes to undermine Corbyn from day 1 and supported the fake "anti-Semitism" witch hunt—wants you to give him money. Hint: Don't do it.* But dim-witted John McDonnell MP tweeted in response to Owen Jones's begging bowl: *Great initiative. We need a pluralist media and this is another terrific step in achieving it. I urge people to back this next step in securing the democratic media we need to combat the corporate establishment control of so much of our* print and broadcast media. **jackie seaton** wrote: *but he is part of the corporate media....* **macheather** replied to McDonnell: *Week by week you really are slipping down in my estimation. I'm starting to understand why you were not named on a certain list.* (This was presumably a reference to the list of MPs denounced for alleged anti-Semitism following the suspension of Corbyn.) **Jam Tart** commented: *Owen Jones spends a lot of time getting paid by the mainstream media and I can't recall him complaining much.* **John Ellison, Socialist, Blues guitarist** wrote: *Pointless sharing a media site that has restricted reading.* **Rob Macfarlane** wrote: *Shameless grift. Monetising an echo chamber to keep pushing the same narrative, to the same people, to keep them clapping like seals after a fish, getting their worldview reinforced by an intellectual lightweight. No better than the right wing chumps doing the same thing.* **AJ 'Ace' Rimmer, Space Adventurer, BSC** wrote: *Yeah cause no-one's thought of starting a private patreon before. I'm sure this one belonging to a shameless gatekeeper always willing to subordinate his principles for the sake of his career will be a real game changer.* He added, directing his comment at John McDonnell MP: *Mind you you'd know a a bit about subordinating your principles.* **Alan** @wakeyrule wrote: *No chance, Jones has more faces than the town hall clock.* **3.5%** wrote: *Rumour has it, his contract* [at the *Guardian*] *isn't being renewed. Hence this publicity.* **F Eckersall** wrote: *Pluralist media? The Owen Jones Channel?* **Catherine**@catherhutch wrote: *Hmm, Owen Jones has spent the last few years blocking everyone who disagrees with him, including on Corbyn. It's going to be 'pluralist media' for those who agree with Owen.* **Pike Slay** wrote: *Anything touched by Owen has the stench of duplicity. Stay well clear.* And while Twitter was suspending some popular accounts for breaching its rules, Max Blumenthal sarcastically pointed out that one US senator for Florida did not have a problem. *Reminder that the account of @marcorubio, who called for the murder of Venezuelan President Nicolas Maduro on Twitter, is still active.* The sun crossed the sky. The rooms filled with warmth. The child climbed on to the shelving unit, wearing her yellow boots. Then she came down and climbed on to her mother's back. Ellis watched an old documentary on the actor Oliver Reed. By 10pm there was still no decisive result in the Presidential election but it seemed that victory for Joe Biden was a certainty. Donald Trump looked downcast and deflated. His air-punching ebullience was gone. Ellis went to bed and continued reading the witchfinders book.

Saturday 7th November

A bright sunny morning. Still no decisive result in the presidential election, although it seemed plain that Biden had won. Asad Abukhalil sarcastically tweeted: *It deeply saddens me that Husni Mubarak, the late Egyptian tyrant, is not alive to see the victory of Joe Biden. After all, Biden once called him "family"*. Ellis read a few more of Abukhalil's tweets. They included: *one of the drawbacks of a Biden victory is that the establishment will be back, in full force. And with a Democratic administration, the bombs will fall over the heads of Arabs and Muslims peppered with repulsive sanctimonious, self-righteous, and moralistic rhetoric.* And: *For the liberals and Arabs who are celebrating Biden's victory, remember me the next time the "liberal" administration launches a war in the Middle East. It won't be long.* And: *Trump administration has revived Balfour's colonialist attitude,' says PLO's Dr Hanan Ashrawi*, with Abukhalil's retort: *Revived? You mean that colonialist attitude (it is a doctrine and not a mere attitude) did not exist and shape the thinking of US administrations before Trump? I can't believe how the current PLO leadership views US policies.* Next Ellis read Ali Abunimah's retweet of a tweet by Dan Cohen @dancohen3000, who linked to a *Haaretz* article headed *Biden victory will free Israel from Trump's sinister soul* and commented: *Israel killed more Palestinians under Obama/Biden during the 51-day assault on Gaza than it did throughout the entire Trump era. Trump's sinister soul isn't the fundamental problem. Zionism is.* **Media Lens** tweeted sarcastically about today's *Guardian* editorial: *Everything you need to know about the Guardian: 'Joe Biden looks to have done enough to win the White House... He will have to reassert America's role as the global problem-solver.'* At 4.30pm, as twilight spread, the news came that Biden had won Pennsylvania, supplying him with enough electoral college votes to become President. On the tiny screen of a mobile phone Ellis saw the child playing in her bath, grinning and babbling. She took hold of her mother's hair. Throughout 2020 Ellis had seen more of the child on a phone screen than in person. Later he pan-fried cod and tomatoes and boiled some potatoes and frozen peas. Dessert was raspberries, ice-cream and yogurt. Ellis watched the biopic, *The Invisible Woman*. He realised he'd seen it before. The 10pm Sky News showed scenes of ecstatic Americans demonstrating their delight that Trump had been defeated. The vox pop interviews included disgruntled Trump supporters, who held protests beside highways. One woman screeched that Biden represented socialism, would put up taxes, and would allow immigrants to pour into the country. Ellis smiled sardonically as reporters kept referring to 'unsubstantiated' claims of voter fraud by Trump's team. These same reporters had never once used that word in connection with the tsunami of slanders against Jeremy Corbyn when he was Labour leader. Nothing was more unsubstantiated than the anti-Semitism slur yet not a single reporter had ever subjected it to scrutiny. Even now, incredibly, it was treated as a matter of sober historical truth rather than the concoction of fraudsters and liars working on behalf of their beloved Zionist state. Ellis went to bed and read more of the witchfinders book.

Sunday 8th November

A bright sunny morning. Ellis listened to the 8am news. The far-right Jewish extremist Lord Sacks had died. Sacks, former chief rabbi of the United synagogue, the largest movement of orthodox Jewry in Britain, was the perfect symbol of the hypocrisy and ethical blankness of mainstream British Jewry. The solemn tributes recited on BBC News failed to mention his active high-profile participation in the 'March of the Flags' march, when thuggish bullying Jews marched through Palestinian neighbourhoods in Jerusalem screaming 'Death to Arabs'. The solemn tributes did not mention Sacks's trip to Hebron to dance with the local representatives of the murderous IDF in a city which was the perfect symbol of the violent Jewish colonial jackboot against the Palestinian throat. The solemn tributes did not mention how Sacks was an ethically blank and immoral intellectual, for whom no atrocity carried out by Israeli Jews could not be excused and sanitised. In short, Jonathan Sacks was no better than a Nazi intellectual and the world was well rid of this oily, velvet-tongued fraud. Ellis went online to see what the twitterati had to say about Biden. Benjamin Netanyahu tweeted: *Congratulations @JoeBiden and @KamalaHarris. Joe, we've had a long & warm personal relationship for nearly 40 years, and I know you as a great friend of Israel. I look forward to working with both of you to further strengthen the special alliance between the U.S. and Israel.* Via the Media Lens twitter page Ellis came across Glenn Greenwald's article on the new president and his liberal fan base who had worked for *a goal as banal and uninspiring as empowering a septuagenarian career-politician — the centrist-authoritarian author of the 1994 Crime Bill, the credit card industry's most loyal servant, and key Iraq War advocate — along with his tough-on-crime prosecutor-running-mate* whose governance would enshrine the policies of *the painfully ordinary and mediocre corporatist and imperialist Democratic Party.* Or to put it another way: *none of Trump's actions and policies are in some new universe of savagery, lawlessness, or radicalism when compared to those who preceded him in power.* Glenn Greenwald added: *And even if Trump has lied more frequently and more blatantly than prior presidents — a conclusion I would probably accept — how do those lies compare to the one sustained over many years, from liberals' most currently beloved neocon pundits and journalists, that convinced Americans that Saddam Hussein was pursuing nuclear and biological weapons and was in an alliance with Al Qaeda and thus likely responsible for the 9/11 attack, leading to the invasion and destruction of a country of 26 million people and, ultimately, the rise of ISIS?* He went on: *the grotesque historical revisionism that seeks to erase and whitewash the far worse moral evils, acts of violence and assertions of lawlessness that preceded him, all in order to propagate myths of American Exceptionalism and, worse, to rehabilitate the reputations and careers of the political and media cretins who perpetrated them.* He added: *which acts of Trump's compete with the destruction of Iraq, or the implementation of a global regime of torture, or the "rendition" kidnappings and CIA black sites and illegal domestic eavesdropping under Bush and Obama, or imprisoning people for decades with no due process, and on and on and on.* Greenwald's searing critique was in stark contrast to Naomi Klein's pitiful tweet that *The fall of tyrants must be celebrated, it's a human right! Profound thanks to all the grassroots groups who did deep organizing to make this happen and who will be pushing hard every day for the new admin to do whatever it takes to get us all to safety.* This combined stupid exaggeration - Trump was not a tyrant but democratically elected - with obtuse naivety regarding the future course of a Biden administration and the likelihood of 'grassroots groups' having the slightest impact upon it. Far sharper was **Anna** @bademjanbitch, who remarked that *the liberal establishment and their media pundits lampooning trump for contesting the election result are the same people who launched an equally delusional conspiracy theory in 2016 the second the outcome didn't go in their favour.* **Mark Curtis** tweeted: *What a relief for centrists - now the US can continue ruling the world by force using pleasing language.* **Joe Sucksmith** commented: *How long before the Biden administration drone strikes a wedding?* The day grew sunnier and hotter. From the site **Tweets MPs delete** Ellis belatedly discovered that dim-witted Jeremy Corbyn had at 2.46pm on 7th November retweeted Owen Jones's tweet celebrating what he intimated was a massive response to his digital begging bowl: *Absolutely overwhelmed by the response to this. It allows me to hire media workers on union wages during a massive recess...* Few noticed this latest evidence of Corbyn's folly. But **Populist Clave** noticed, and commented: *I reckon it was Laura. She's nobody's fool.* Meanwhile the child played with her plastic dinosaur and sang a song about dinosaurs. Ellis had celery soup for lunch. Later he read **Jeremy Carbon** @MarkJDoran's tweet: *Folks, Jonathan Sacks -- 'Rabbi Lord Jonathan Sacks', to use his whole phoney title -- was an oily little bastard who defended a whole range of totally fucking horrible things, racist apartheid Israel included. We shall not see his like again -- unless we're *very unlucky*...* **Stephen Latham** agreed: *What amazes me is that he organised those racist Flag marches used to intimidate Palestinians, yet he was awarded a tenure as Professor of Law and Ethics, and invited on the Moral Maze on Radio 4. Our society and institutions must be deeply corrupt.* David Rosenberg's old hatchet job on Sacks was cited. As chief rabbi, wrote Rosenberg, he talked a lot about "unity" in the Jewish community but sowed the opposite. One of his first initiatives as chief rabbi was a Jewish unity walkabout in Hyde Park, only he got into hot water for his decision to exclude the Jewish Lesbian and Gay Helpline, which supported marginalised and discriminated-against Jews, from participating in it. Nothing, if not consistent, he spoke out later against the right of gay men and lesbians to marry. Sacks's extremist politics were signalled by the assistance he gave to Donald Trump's right hand man, Mike Pence, to write a speech delivered in the Knesset coinciding with Trump's provocative decision to move the US embassy to Jerusalem. Sacks worked tirelessly on behalf of evil. At the height of Operation Pillar of Defence in Gaza in November 2012, in which 174 Gazans were killed by Israeli bombing and many hundreds more wounded, Sacks completed another "Thought for the Day," on the BBC's right-wing 'Today' programme. BBC presenter Evan Davis, addressing him familiarly as Jonathan, asked: 'Any thoughts on what's going on over in Israel and Gaza at the moment?' Sacks sighed and said: 'I think it's got to do with Iran actually.' At this point, co-presenter Sarah Montague quickly whispered: 'We're live.' Sacks's stupidity and bigotry was exposed for all to hear. But perhaps the most disgusting aspect of Sacks's undistinguished life was his involvement in the "March of the Flags" (Israeli flags). Haaretz's correspondent Bradley Burston once described it as "an annual, gender-segregated, extreme-right, pro-occupation religious carnival of hatred, marking the anniversary of Israel's capture of Jerusalem by humiliating the city's Palestinian Muslims," in which marchers have "vandalized shops in Jerusalem's Muslim Quarter, chanted: 'Death to Arabs' and 'The (Jewish) temple will be built, the (Al Aqsa) Mosque will be burned down,' shattered windows and door locks and poured glue into the locks of shops forced to close for fear of further damage." Rabbi Sacks extended a "personal invitation" to diaspora Jews to join him on a trip to Israel which includes "leading" the March of the Flags on Jerusalem Day and "dancing with our brave [Israeli Defence Force] soldiers" in the settler enclave inside Hebron. *Haaretz pleaded with Rabbi Sacks not to attend, saying: "One of the world's most respected rabbis sends a message of normalisation and acceptance of the occupation by the mainstream Jewish community. He ignored them and did help to lead the March of the Flags, together with the new Chief Rabbi Ephraim Mirvis, who also enjoys putting the boot into Corbyn regularly, and whose dinner guests on the night before Theresa May became leader of the Conservative Party were indeed Ms May and her delightful husband.* [https://morningstaronline.co.uk/article/you-were-never-my-chief-rabbi-bruv] The reactions to the death of this deeply unpleasant Jewish fanatic exposed the sanctimonious hypocrisies of the atrocity-supporting mainstream Jewish and religious communities. The Zionist temple to remembrance of the Nazi holocaust, Yad Vashem @yadvashem, tweeted: *Yad Vashem mourns the loss of Rabbi Lord Jonathan Sacks. @rabbisacks worked tirelessly for the betterment of the Jewish nation worldwide. Rabbi Sacks was a true friend of Yad Vashem, working together to raise awareness about the Holocaust and to fight antisemitism worldwide.* Proving yet again that the Zionist establishment has no sense of irony and is utterly unfit to memorialise the sufferings of Jews at the hands of a blood and soil ideology with many parallels to Zionism. Ellis was fascinated to discover that this moral blankness extended well beyond Judaism.

Thus Remembering Srebrenica@SrebrenicaUK tweeted: *We are deeply saddened to hear the news of Rabbi Lord Sacks. Rabbi Sacks showcased his support for Remembering Srebrenica and spoke about the importance of educating on the genocide in Bosnia. Our heartfelt condolences go out to his loved ones and the Jewish community.* But the erasure of Palestine and its people - hey, that was fine. The Hampstead Synagogue @HampsteadShul tweeted: *We are deeply saddened at the news tonight of the passing of Emeritus Chief Rabbi Lord Sacks z'l. His towering intellect and eloquence earned him admiration worldwide as an outstanding teacher of Torah and a wonderful ambassador for the Jewish people.* Another example of the ethical deficit inherent in mainstream modern Judaism. Ellis was interested to see **The Methodist Church** @MethodistGB blubbering *We are very sad to hear of the death of Rabbi Lord Jonathan Sacks and send sympathy to the Jewish community, his family & friends. He was a highly respected theologian and philosopher, committed to developing understanding between different faiths. May his memory be a blessing.* Ellis had briefly been raised as a Methodist - a dull, austere religion - but his coins for the collection plate, alas, had been diverted by Satan, who had placed a chewing-gum machine near the place of worship. Ellis remembered that his friend Keith had told him how the Norwich branch of the Palestine Solidarity Campaign had been prevented from meeting in a Methodist church hall when the usual gang of lying, bullying Jews had shrieked that the group was anti-Semitic. The Methodist Church had promptly capitulated to Zionism. And how very, very apt that the tsunami of tributes to Sacks should come from perhaps the most blood-spattered criminal admirer of all: **Tony Blair Institute** @InstituteGC: *"Jonathan was a wonderful friend, a beloved mentor, a philosopher of extraordinary insight & of course a religious leader respected well beyond the Jewish community & well beyond the shores of Britain." Read Tony Blair's tribute to Rabbi Lord Sacks.* Ellis went for a walk. The sun began to sink. A vast flock of geese went honking past overhead. There were lots of people around. It wasn't like the last lockdown at all. Ellis guessed that this new lockdown would fail dismally. Returning home, returning to twitter, Ellis read Paul O'Connell's tweet: *A minor thing, but the majority of pundits on mainstream news channels usually have bookshelves full of biographies, which speaks to an understanding of politics and historical change being the work of "great men", and explains why most of their analysis is court gossip.* A very good point, Ellis thought. That evening he dined on roast chicken with microwaved white rice, gravy and broccoli, followd by stewed apple, ice-cream and yogurt. At 9pm he watched the final episode of *Roadkill*. He felt the best ending would be if the truth-tellers were crushed and the lying, devious careerist Peter Lawrence ended up as prime minister, and sure enough that was what happened. Realism. The character was plainly loosely based on Boris Johnson, just as the prime minister he ousted was a hybrid of Theresa May and Margaret

Thatcher. It was the first drama by David Hare that Ellis had seen which he'd felt was remotely plausible and which he had thoroughly enjoyed. The news supplied sycophantic commentary on the murderous imperialist hawk Joe Biden as the blood-spattered old hypocrite went to church surrounded by a gang of armed bodyguards. Donald Trump was filmed playing golf and waving at a handful of forlorn supporters standing at the junction of the road leading to the golf course. TRUMP THE GRUMP was the headline in tomorrow's *Metro*. Ellis went to bed. He was now on the penultimate chapter of the witchfinders book. The catalogue of false confessions brought about as a result of torture, bullying and broken people was beginning to become a little tedious. Perhaps the only interest lay in the unusual names which the supposed witches gave to their satanic imps. Ellis put out the light and went to sleep.

Monnday 9th November

Ellis lay in the gloom listening to the 'Today' programme. Justin Webb and Martha Kearney. Corporate journalism at its smoothest. Disinformation at its most charming. Lies coated in velvet. Ellis didn't start paying attention until the review of the corporate papers. Today's focus of these corporate pimps was, perhaps predictably, on tributes to Lord Sacks. A gush of oil which coated the Palestinian blood upon which this Jewish fanatic's career had floated. Worse still, these tributes were followed as 'Thought for the Day' by a personal tribute from Sacks's successor, Chief Rabbi Ephraim Mirvis. Ellis reflected how extraordinary it was that a fundamentally decent and humane man like Jeremy Corbyn had been repeatedly defamed as a racist monster, while a vile racist sectarian Trump-worshipping extremist like Jonathan Sacks was represented by the BBC and corporate presstitutes as a lovely man. Ellis went out. A light mist hung over the neighbourhood. It looked as if it had rained in the night. Ellis spotted a friend and stood in the street having a brief conversation. The bakery was sold out of plain croissants. The high street seemed busy. The supermarket was crowded and few were taking any notice of social distancing. Ellis felt unsafe at the check-out. As often happened, the person behind ignored the marked-out zones for waiting and came and stood right behind him. The man then leaned forwards to take an energy drink from a shelf. Ellis was glad to be out of the store. He felt sure this half-assed lockdown would fail to work. It might reduce the level of infection a little but it would do nothing to make the country a safe place in which to live and work. Back home again Ellis went on the *Electronic Intifada* website to read about Joe Biden's support for Israel. Ali Abunimah described how back in 1986, Biden said that Israel is "the best $3 billion investment we make…Were there not an Israel, the United States of America would have to invent an Israel to protect our interests in the region," Biden asserted. In 2007 Biden said: "Israel is the single greatest strength

America has in the Middle East. When I was a young senator, I'd say, 'If I were a Jew I'd be a Zionist,'" Biden added. "I am a Zionist, you don't have to be a Jew to be a Zionist." When Israel killed an average of 11 children per day during its summer 2014 assault on Gaza the Obama-Biden administration resupplied Israel with weapons. During its 51-day assault, Israel killed more than 2,200 Palestinians. The Obama-Biden administration sprung into action to thwart Palestinians from seeking justice for Israeli war crimes at the International Criminal Court. Biden has pledged *not* to move the US embassy from Jerusalem back to Tel Aviv. *One of the Obama-Biden administration's final acts was to reward Israel's settlement spree and massacres with the biggest military aid package in history – a minimum of $38 billion over 10 years.* On the twitter account of Paul O'Connell, Ellis read: *In 2017 French socialists and trade unionists developed the slogan: "Vote Macron now, get Le Pen in 2021" - that's pretty much how I feel about the election of Biden, a feeble restoration candidate who will pave the way for far worse than Trump in the years to come.* At 5pm the Prime Minister made a statement. Ellis did not bother to watch it. It was reported that a successful new vaccine had been announced. It was 90 per cent effective. On the face of it, that sounded like a large margin of failure. Ellis sat in an armchair, reading. The child put a coat on her soft toy baby, then put on her own coat, with help from her mother. Ellis ate cold chicken with mashed potato, cauliflower and carrot, followed by cold stewed apple with yogurt. He finished Malcolm Gaskill's book *Witchfinders*. He began watching the film *Clouded Yellow*. In bed that night he began reading *An Expensive Place to Die*.

Tuesday 10th November

A dull, grey misty morning. The two big stories of the morning were the Covid-19 vaccine and the Martin Bashir scandal. It was alleged that the BBC reporter had used faked bank statements to ingratiate himself with Diana Princess of Wales and her brother, in order to get an exclusive interview. The graphic designer at the BBC said he thought he'd been asked to produce this material as a studio prop, not to mislead the Princess. He had reported his concerns to his line management. Bashir had been interviewed by the head of news, Tony Hall, and after a cosy chat it had been determined by Hall that no wrongdoing had occurred. Instead, the BBC decided to freeze out the whistleblower, whose contract was not renewed and who never again was used by the BBC for graphic design. Hall had later become a member of the House of Lords and the BBC Director General. It was further evidence that the BBC was rotten from top to bottom. Ellis was pleased to see that *Defund the BBC* had started to appear on Twitter. Meanwhile Keir Starmer's crackdown on the Left in the Labour Party received no coverage on the BBC or in the *Guardian*. Tom Mills tweeted: *Let's just imagine for a second the media response if Corbyn had not only suspended*

Tony Blair, but decreed that no constitutency party could even discuss his suspension. The British corporate media was equally uninterested in events in Bolivia. The imperialist American media was. Aaron Maté retweeted the *New York Times* tweet *Bolivia's former president, Evo Morales, returned to the country on Monday, a year after his failed attempt to keep power tore the nation apart and sent him into exile*, commenting: *The creativity that goes into writing propaganda like this is truly impressive. If we were challenged to formulate a way to avoid saying "coup in response to a democratic election that led to a far-right junta & state terror", few of us could come up with something so dishonest.* Ellis went out. He bought some kitchen roll and borrowed a book from the library, which had re-opened, with a window service. Back home again he read about the unveiling on Newington Green in London of a statue sculpted by Maggi Hambling to commemorate Mary Wollstonecraft. It was condemned by a variety of prominent women for featuring the figure of a nude woman. Caitlin Moran (or Caitlin Moron as Ellis preferred to think of her) was against the statue. No surprise there. You would expect no less from a Rupert Murdoch puppet. Ellis pan fried two Norwegian salmon steaks. Later he watched part two of the ITV documentary *Diana: Revenge of a Princess*. The revelations of the graphic designer were left to the end. Most of the programme consisted of extracts from the Diana interview framed by commentary from those uninvolved in filming it, or elderly royal corespondents, who blathered about how historic this interview had been. They made it sound like the greatest event in twentieth-century world history. The 10pm Sky News had three stories. One was about the new vaccine, one was about the resignation of a leading official from the world of corporate football after he had used inappropriate language in public ('coloured' footballers) and the third was about Trump's refusal to concede he'd lost, and the reluctance of senior Republicans to say anything about the impasse. In bed Ellis read a few more pages of *An Expensive Place to Die*.

Wednesday 11th November

A bright dry day. Ellis went for a walk. From the internet he learned that 532 people died yesterday of the virus. This has not been mentioned on the 10pm Sky News. Ellis read that the Labour Party had started a campaign *for airlines to give Speedy Boarding to Armed Forces heroes*. On Twitter **It's real** @StefGotBooted commented: *Do they honestly think people can't see through this? This is just going to alienate two sets of voters, those on the right who don't like being treated like fools and those on the left who hate this sort of flagshagging.* **Deleverage4ever** @deleverage4ever wrote: *Squaddies are all scum and beyond salvage, on top of that they are demographically insignificant and will never be a wedge issue. These moronic statements are neither ideological or pragmatic, just pure stupidity with zero payoff* **Gift** @Jgiftmacher commented: *Coming from a forces family, there's nothing less convincing than this performative bullshit. You're just insulting everyone's intelligence now. It's pretty obvious this is another "values" fish for votes that'd rather fucking shoot you.* Ellis learned of Louis Allday's article on Joe Biden and proceeded to click on the link and read it: https://www.ebb-magazine.com/essays/the-false-hope-of-a-biden-presidency.

Allday wrote: *It should be plainly stated that by any meaningful and honest measure, Biden is a monster who has caused an incalculable amount of suffering over his many decades as a senior official of the US empire.* He continued, noting that *Biden is a racist authoritarian at home and an enthusiastic and unapologetic imperialist abroad. On environmental issues, in spite of the hopes that liberals are already investing in him, Biden is little better. During the campaign he repeatedly announced that he will not ban fracking and his adviser on energy issues, who served as Energy Secretary under Obama, is a notorious lobbyist for the fossil fuel industry.* Allday concluded: Such is the incredible power of the media to continually re-invent and sanitise public reputations, that virtually all of this lamentable record is simply cast aside and intentionally obscured. Later Ellis learned that a report by parliament's Joint Committee on Human Rights had concluded: *We find that the Equality and Human Rights Commission (EHRC) has been unable to adequately provide leadership and gain trust in tackling racial inequality in the protection and promotion of human rights.* The day wore on. Ellis ate soup with a chicken sandwich for his lunch, followed by sliced apple and yogurt. In the afternoon he continued reading his library book and sorted out some old photographs, throwing most of them away, along with their negatives. The child was starting to learn the names of colours. Red. Blue. Green. Supper was two baked potatoes with baked beans. Returning to the internet Ellis caught up with an editorial in the online *Morning Star*. It concerned the latest tactical use of the charge of anti-Semitism against the Left. *Labour movement activists may have thought they had entered the Twilight Zone on Friday evening on hearing that Roger McKenzie, one of British trade unionism's leading figures, is being accused of anti-semitism. McKenzie is running for the leadership of Unison — one of the two biggest unions in the country — and the existence of a "lengthy dossier" that has been submitted to the Labour Party about him has conveniently been leaked just as ballots are landing on doormats. It might seem rather brazen to level accusations of racism against one of the trade union movement's best known black leaders in the year that Black Lives Matter swept the world. Especially given McKenzie's long history of anti-racist campaigning and the passion with which he has always challenged racism — a passion informed by personal experience of racist abuse directed at him and his family from childhood onwards. McKenzie was the first black person in TUC history and in Unison to hold a regional secretary post, became Unison's first black assistant general secretary and, if elected, would be the union's first black general secretary.* On the Twitter page of Ali Abunimah Ellis read: *Oh look! Biden's "Muslim outreach" adviser @FarooqMithha, from pro-Israel Muslim group @EmgageAction, is on the Pentagon transition team. Pretty soon Farooq will be "reaching out" to Muslims with cruise missiles and drones.* On the website of the *Huffington Post* Ellis learned more about the latest Zionist assault on socialists. *Labour Against Antisemitism has urged the party to suspend Unison assistant general secretary Roger McKenzie for sharing social media posts that compared Israel's treatment of the Palestinians to the Holocaust and that suggested anti-Jewish hatred was being exaggerated to undermine Jeremy Corbyn's leadership. The union official stands accused by the group Labour Against Anti-Semitism (LAAS) of breaching party rules on conduct that conflicts with the International Holocaust Remembrance Alliance (IHRA) definition of anti-Semitism. A lengthy dossier of allegations submitted to the party includes Facebook and Twitter posts shared by McKenzie that compared Israel's "apartheid" and "Zionist colonisation" to the Sobibor concentration camp. He is also accused of sharing articles that included claims that Gaza is "an Israeli-administered ghetto", that talked of "Corbyn's enemies [and] the anti-Semitism row they manufactured" and that referred to "the inherent racism of Israel (and its founding ideology of Zionism)". Other posts featured cartoons depicting Gaza as a prison camp, a comparison that Jewish groups find offensive as it suggests a reference to the Holocaust.* Ellis felt that as much offence as possible should be caused to that rabble of anti-Palestinian bigots, racists and fanatics which went under the rubric of 'Jewish groups'. The great anti-Semitism hoax - a hoax as spectacular and effective as the Zinoviev letter - once again involved not actual physical assaults on Jews but *hurt feelings* on the part of Jewish racists. Tough. Ellis watched the 10pm news headlines, then had a bath. In the bath he listened to the BBC radio 10pm programme. It was every bit as poisonously misleading as any other BBC news programme. A softball interviewer allowed a former American government hack to blather about the US mission to support democracy around the world - a direct inversion of the truth. In bed Ellis read several chapters of *An Expensive Place to Die*. The chapters were very short.

Thursday 12th November

Ellis woke at 5.50am. He listened to a farming programme which described efforts to save sugar beet from aphids. The 6am news headline, typical for the BBC, concerned the resignation of an adviser to Boris Johnson. Ellis had never heard of this individual. It was court politics - bickering among the inner circle. The BBC was as little interested in the latest spectacularly bad coronavirus figures for deaths and infections as it was in climate breakdown or the Jewish state's pitiless and ceaseless savagery against the Palestinians. Ellis switched off and drifted back to sleep. When he woke again it was quarter past eight. A man named Eddie Jaku was being interviewed about his concentration camp memoir. He was 100-years-old and had survived Auschwitz. Later, once he was dressed, Ellis looked up Eddie Jaku. After the war he had emigrated to Australia. Last September he had been approached by Pan Macmillan, who wanted to commission him to write a memoir. He had declined. 'I didn't want to write a book because there are so many books [by survivors]' Baku had explained. But Pan Macmillan persisted. *They saw the potential for a powerful and candid memoir, in which glimmers of hope shine even in the darkest of hours.* What's more Auschwitz is a hot, profitable topic. There have this year been a string of fiction and non-fiction titles in the top ten with the word Auschwitz in the title or as the central subject. The profits from Eddie Jaku's book were being donated to the Sydney Jewish Museum. Ellis looked at the museum's twitter account. On 2nd June the museum had tweeted: *The rights of others are everyone's concern. In the light of the death of #George Floyd and similar injustices in our own country, Australia, we are reminded not to stay neutral, to keep questioning and working for equality and humanity, and to stand up for the oppressed.* Admirable sentiments. But of course there was one repressive and discriminatory state where Jews were usually either silent about its crimes or fiercely supportive of them. Indeed, on 27 January the Museum retweeted a tweet by **Auschwitz Memorial** which stated: *Auschwitz Survivors walk through the 'Arbeit macht frei' gate on the day of the 75th anniversary of the liberation of the camp.* Among the first of the figures to walk past was a man wearing an Israeli flag. Auschwitz has become a place where Israeli teenagers go to be psyched up before compulsory military service, to make them feel OK about shooting Palestinians. When the Israeli army raided the Talkarm refugee camp no soldier objected when told to inscribe identification numbers on the forearms and foreheads of blindedfolded Palestinian prisoners. When soldiers at a checkpoint outside Nablus ordered a local Palestinian man to take up his violin and 'play a sad song' not one of the Jews intervened to stop him being humiliated. Instead they gathered round him and mocked him. The incident was captured on film by Machson Watch, an organisation of Jewish-Israeli women who monitor some of the checkpoints. But these kinds of event never find their way on to the websites of all those sanctimonious Zio-controlled organisations dedicated to Holocaust memorial. Next Ellis read three tweets by Paul O'Connell: (1) *Important to understand that Starmer's restoration regime was never about winning the next election (that was never a possibility) - it's all about "course correction" and restoring Labour as the dependable junior partner for managing the affairs of British capital.* (2) *Winning the next election was never a possibility because it would require Labour to win an additional 123 seats, an electoral swing of 10.3 percentage points - those around Starmer,* and on the right of the party more generally, are smart enough to know this is not happening. (3) *In contrast the campaign of restoration is proceeding apace, facilitated by the failures during the Corbyn era to make meaningful changes to internal party democracy, & by the ongoing delusions of Labourist "unity" - in short order it will be as if the Corbyn moment never happened.* Publishing news: Ellis learned that the Zionist and warmonger Gordon Brown had signed a deal with Simon & Schuster to produce a book on Seven Major Challenges Facing The World. That was one ineluctably destined for the remainders bin. Other book deals of the day were for works described as empowering, touching, powerful and deeply moving, intoxicating and magical. Next Ellis read Sarah Lazare's tweet: *I analyzed Biden's Pentagon transition team and found that one third of its members work for think tanks, organizations, or companies that either directly receive money from the weapons industry—or are part of the arms industry themselves.* Ellis learned that two days ago *The European Union and the State of Israel held their 13th High Level Seminar on combating racism, xenophobia and antisemitism online, via videoconference. The EU-Israel seminar, which took place today (Tuesday) is a unique annual forum that brings together European and Israeli civil servants, policymakers, experts, international organisations and non-governmental organisations to discuss best practices and measures to combat racism, xenophobia and antisemitism. The discussion of today focused on hate speech in the digital sphere and its impact to the real world, as well as possible measures to address the challenges of online hatred.* How utterly grotesque that the EU was colluding with the fanatical Jewish state to suppress Palestinian advocacy online (for that was what this hypocritical charade was all about), Ellis thought. He read on. *The Political Director of the Israeli Ministry of Foreign Affairs, Alon Bar, indicated in his introductory remarks: "The digital sphere opens the unlimited opportunity to proliferate hate ideology of all kinds. Research shows that the internet has become the main outlet for circulation all types of Antisemitism. The sad reality has proven that a straight line connects the virtual and the physical world. Governments have the responsibility and the means to face this challenge, using the IHRA definition as a tool to identify and mark the problem. Coalition building between governments, civil society and the technology companies is an important tool."* Once again the Nazi genocide was being debased and degraded by Jews who sought to use it to suppress criticism of Israel. *Paul Nemitz, Principle Advisor Justice and Consumers (EU Commission) stated: "To ensure safety of its users, the digital highway needs rules. The spike of antisemitic and racist hate speech in the course of the COVID pandemic has increased the urgency. With its upcoming proposal for a Digital Services Act, the European Commission aims for a harmonised, clear set of due-diligence obligations for online platforms, redress mechanisms, accountability measures, and cooperation obligations with public authorities. The Act will also ensure greater*

318

transparency on how platforms moderate content, on advertising and on algorithmic processes." Yes, the EU would be at the forefront of censoring the internet on behalf of Zionism and the priorities of the high-consumption planet-destroying European bourgeoisie. *Katharina von Schnurbein, European Commission Coordinator on Combatting antisemitism and fostering Jewish life said: "We need to encourage states, organizations and the technology companies to adopt the IHRA definition. Israel and the European Commission will continue to work closely in the dialogue with the Tech companies in order for them to implement the much needed tools to handle the massive amount of data in this context."* No surprise to learn that it was a German who was at the forefront of promoting Zionism. Ellis read an illustrated tweet by **Sk Boz** @skkboz: *Japanese protesting expansion of American military bases on Okinawa get dragged off by the police today. The protest that will never be the headline feature on BBC.* **The New York Times** tweeted: *By refusing to concede defeat and hurling unfounded accusations of electoral fraud, Mr. Trump has adopted some of the anti-democratic tactics commonly employed by leaders like Robert Mugabe of Zimbabwe and Nicolas Maduro of Venezuela. https://nyti.ms/2Iwh9RH* **Max Blumenthal** retorted: *This piece of State Department propaganda contains zero evidence that Nicolas Maduro has lost or stolen an election, because none exists. And it legitimizes Juan Guaido, the author of two failed military coups. The NYT loves anti-democratic coups against Official Enemies.* **Max Blumenthal** tweeted: *The US condemned Venezuela's 2018 election before it even happened and threatened candidates with sanctions for daring to participate. It knew Maduro would win, so it worked to delegitimize the democratic process itself. Then it launched a coup. The New York Times supports this.* **Max Blumenthal** criticised Yanis Varoufakis for writing for the *Guardian*. He tweeted: *Building and supporting independent, editorially uncompromised media institutions would be a better use of energy than left-washing those like The Guardian that are institutionally aligned against us.* Ellis caught up with the latest depravity committed by Jews in occupied Palestine. Amira Hass in *Haaretz* wrote: *The Civil Administration gave the families living in the Palestinian hamlet of Khirbet Humsa in the northern Jordan Valley just 10 minutes to remove their possessions from the tents last Tuesday.* The Jews arrived in force to destroy the settlement, leaving 11 families – 74 people, including 41 children – homeless. This kind of brutality had the total support of Joe Biden, Keir Starmer, and the European Union. *In terms of the number of people made homeless, this is the largest demolition operation carried out by the Civil Administration since 2010. In terms of the number of structures that were torn down, it is the most extensive demolition operation since 2016, knocking down 11 tents and huts used as living quarters, 29 tents and shelters for sheep (about 1,000 animals), plus 10 sheep pens, three sheds, nine tents used as kitchens, 10 portable toilets, two solar panels, 23 water* tanks, plus stalls and feeding troughs for the sheep. Sacks of animal feed were ruined. Two tractors and Awawda's Subaru were confiscated. The Abu al-Kabash and Awawda families lease land owned by people from Tamun and Tubas. On this land they erected their simple dwellings, and there they also grow wheat and barley for their own needs. But Israel declared the area a "firing zone" and that is COGAT's explanation for the massive demolition, as it has been for many of the recent demolitions and restrictions imposed by Israel on Palestinian construction and movement in the West Bank. Firing Zone 903 alone, where Humsa is, took 80,000 dunams (about 20,000 acres) of land from Palestinians in the northern West Bank. Since 2018, the residents of Humsa have had to evacuate at least 20 times due to military exercises in the area. "Israel didn't leave us any land to plant. Without our sheep, we'll become beggars," says Yusef Abu Awad. "Israel does not want us to have our own source of income. It wants us to work for the Israelis." Photographers were stopped by soldiers, so there is no footage of the demolition itself. The demolition was in violation of international law but Israel has known from the moment of its bloody birth that it can flout international law, supported by the USA, the UK, the EU, and Jewish organisations around the world. The Holocaust memorial mongers will also have nothing to say about this fresh barbarism. Holocaust memorial has a purpose, and it is not about learning from the past. Homeless, dispossessed Yusef Abu Awad said: "What's new here? They don't know what Israel is? They don't know that Israel wants to get rid of us and bring more settlers here instead?" But of course they do. They do, they do, they do. Ellis went out. He went to a supermarket for wine and then for a walk. The sun, very low in the sky, cast elongated shadows. The child held up her muddy yellow boots. Boots, she said. She held up two pieces of coloured paper. Blue, she said. Green. Ellis ate a cheese soufflé with broccoli and mashed potato. He watched the trailer for *In Harm's Way*, with Otto Preminger standing in the studio set of a burning ship. He seemed to be imitating Alfred Hitchcock. On the television England played Ireland in a friendly. Three nil. Ellis walked across the room. He had no interest in football. He sorted old photographs in the next room instead, destroying most of them. The 10pm Sky News featured an interview with the head of the company which had produced the new coronavirus vaccine. It was reported as a marvel that this man, a Turkish German, lacked a television set and cycled to work. The daily infection rate for the virus had reached a new record, with 33,470 cases reported today in Britain. There was anxiety that Brexit might impede the swift transport of the vaccine. In bed Ellis read more Len Deighton.

Friday 13th November

A dull wet morning. Ellis woke just before 6am and listened to the headlines.

They were all about Dominic Cummings leaving Number 10 at the end of the year. He switched off the radio and drifted back to sleep, finally getting out of bed at 8.10am. As he drank his morning tea he heard the voices of children as they went by on their way to school. Ellis cruised the net. On the website of Rampant Magazine he read a list identifying Kamala Harris's past reactionary activities: https://rampantmag.com/2020/08/31/kamala-harriss-history-a-list/ *2016: At an AIPAC speech in 2017, Harris cited her biracial background as a reason for supporting sending tens of billions in military aid to Israel. But interracial marriages between Palestinians of the West Bank and Gaza with Israeli citizens are illegal in Israel. 2017: Harris cosponsored Senate Resolution 6, which objected to a UN Security Council resolution adopted in 2016 that declared Israeli settlements a violation of international law. She has proudly pointed out that this was the first resolution she cosponsored as a senator. 2018: At the 2018 AIPAC Policy Conference Harris boasted: "As I child, I never sold Girl Scout Cookies, I went around with a Jewish National Fund box collecting funds to plant trees in Israel."* But the Jewish National Fund is a quintessential Zionist organisation, which has always sought to obtain Palestinian land, 'redeem' it for Jews, and henceforth ban Arabs from farming or living on it. It is an absolute symbol of Jewish supremacism, racism and sectarianism. And those trees which are planted are there to cover up the ruins of the villages which were emptied and destroyed by violent Jews in 1948. Elsewhere on the net Ellis learned that the Highgate branch of Sir Keir Starmer's own local party had passed a motion on the suspension of the former Labour leader, by 33 votes to 29. It reads: "This branch/CLP expresses its solidarity with Jeremy Corbyn. Jeremy is a lifelong campaigner against racism and antisemitism. We believe that unity, not division, is important for the party to make progress and effectively challenge racism, fascism, antisemitism and harassment in what ever form this may take." It was revealing, thought Ellis, that almost half of these Labour members wouldn't support Corbyn. Later that day it was reported that the Yorkshire Ripper had died. Later still Dominic Cummings abruptly left Downing Street, contradicting his earlier statement that he would remain until the end of the year. Ellis went out. He posted a card and went to a supermarket. After that he called in at a bookshop to pick up a book he'd ordered. After that he went for a walk. The sun had slipped below the horizon and lights were on in many of the houses. That evening he ate spaghetti bolognaise with sliced carrot and apple. He read a library book. From the internet he learned that one of the vilest people in the Labour Party, Luke Akehurst, had topped the poll in the list of successful candidates for the National Executive Committee. Turnout was 27.4 per cent and 135,000 people voted, down from 293,000 in 2018. In bed Ellis read more Len Deighton.

A wet gloomy morning. Ellis got up at 7.45am. As he drank his mug of tea he read Ed McNally's tweet about Luke Akehurst: *I wonder if people will stop pretending *any* reference to the pro-Israel lobby is suspect now the director of an organisation called 'We Believe in Israel' sits on Labour's NEC. probably not!* Ammar Kazmi tweeted: *Luke Akehurst is the director of We Believe In Israel (part of the BICOM pro-Israel lobby group). He supports the Iraq war and the actions of the US in Vietnam, said he could 'justify arms sales' to Saudi, and defended the Freikorps who killed Rosa Luxemburg. 'Moderate'.* And: *In other words, if you believe in oppressing Palestinians, killing millions of brown people, supporting brutal dictatorships, and murdering Jewish socialists, that makes you a 'moderate' in today's Labour Party.* And: *We've been calling out Luke Akehurst's racism and vile comments for years, but no action has ever been taken.* Joe Sucksmith tweeted: *Leftists calmly analysing the NEC results as if a rabid anti-Palestinian racist hasn't just topped the poll. Hello?* Joe Sucksmith tweeted: *Johanna Baxter, witch finder general, back on the NEC. But sure, this is a great result for the left.* Joe Sucksmith tweeted: *Laura Pidock will make some great points on the NEC. Then the right will win the vote. That's the beauty of having a majority - you don't need to win the argument.* Joe Sucksmith tweeted: *The left was always going to win most seats on the NEC. Point was that, under STV, the right would also win seats. And, as anticipated, they've won enough for a majority. That's the only thing that matters. Time for the left to ditch this unreformable, reactionary beast.* **Mark W. Clark, Esq** tweeted: *So if the Labour NEC elections were undertaken under a single transferable vote system why hasn't the Labour Party signed up to that for as a policy goal for other elections such as the General and locals?* **Aaron Bastani** tweeted that 6,000 votes had been removed from the count. He tweeted a letter from Siobhain McDonagh MP urging her local members to vote for Luke Akehurst. She described him as follows: 'A former Hackney councillor, a cancer survivor and a dad, he has never been anything but a devoted Labour Party member.' Elsewhere on the internet Ellis caught up with an old *Electronic Intifada* interview with Max Blumenthal. *The negation of Palestinian lives has been German policy since the days of Konrad Adenauer [chancellor of West Germany from 1949 to 1963]. In those days Israel had no problem to negotiate on Holocaust reparations with the head of the chancellery, Hans Globke, who was a known Nazi in the Third Reich. This cash flow from Germany went directly to the Israeli occupation machine that has made the Palestinians indirect victims of the Holocaust.* The day grew gloomier. Ellis ate warmed-up spaghetti bolgnaise with a slice of buttered brown bread. Afterwards he ate a sliced apple with yogurt. He drank a cappuccino and read the reviews section of the *Times*. The child played with her potty. She asked for water to be put in it.

Then she placed her toy horse and toy cow in the potty. Afterwards she took a wet wipe and gave them a clean. Then she scrambled upstairs. She asked her mother to bring her blue plastic chair. Then she used the chair to try and climb over the bars of her cot. She could not manage it. Her mother lifted her into the cot. She put a blanket over her head. Pee-boh! Ellis sorted more years-old photographs, destroying most of them. His intention was to thin out his possessions. There was too much clutter from the past. Later his mobile phone rang and he talked for almost an hour to the person who'd phoned him. On the 10pm Sky News the big stories were the continuing spread of the coronavirus, President Trump's motorcade passing through Washington past a big crowd of his supporters chanting *Four more years!* and the fallout from the abrupt departure of Dominic Cummings. Apparently Cummings regularly referred to the Prime Minister's fiancée Carrie Symonds as 'Princess nut nuts'. Ellis went to bed and read more Len Deighton.

Sunday 15th November

The wind howled, making a strange scratching sound in the chimney that ran through the bedroom. When Ellis got out of bed at 8.10am he saw that outside torrential rain was falling. Rust-coloured autumn leaves lay everywhere. Ellis played one of his Glenn Gould CDs. Gould's rendition of Bach's Fugue in B minor on a theme by Tomaso Albinoni was perfect for a moment like this. Ellis spent the morning reading a library book. For lunch he had leek soup, with bread and cheese, followed by a sliced apple with yogurt. In the afternoon he caught up with the latest repression carried out by the Jewish state, courtesy of Ben White's twitter page. *Israeli forces, guards, & settlers launched avg. of 10 attacks per month on West Bank kindergarten & school students, staff & facilities Jan 2018-June 2020. "Israel's policies and practices toward Palestinian schools have created an environment of constant fear that traumatises children, while abandoning its obligation under international law to not commit attacks on education". "These included soldiers' raids on schools, harassment, arrest and assault of children in schools & at checkpoints, firing towards children and blocking teachers & students from reaching schools...[as well as the] demolition of schools and confiscation of equipment". Report: Israeli occupation forces arrested 446 Palestinians in the month of October, 2020, including 63 children. 68 'administrative detention' orders (no charge or trial) were issued in October by Israeli military authorities.* The rain stopped and the clouds melted away. The sun shone from a blue sky. The child went up and down on the swing. The play area was deserted, apart from one other parent and child. That evening Ellis ate sausage casserole, washed down with two glasses of red wine. He watched *Small Axe*, a drama about the Metropolitan Police's harassment of the black-run Mangrove Café in Notting Hill, which

climaxed with an Old Bailey trial. In bed he read more Len Deighton. Ellis
turned off his bedsight light. After listening to the midnight news headlines - the
Prime Minister, Boris Johnson, was self-isolating after coming into contact with
an infected person - he fell asleep.

Monday 16th November

Bright and sunny. Ellis got up at 8.10am. A bright sunny morning. Ellis went
online. Joe Sucksmith sarcastically tweeted *Novara's "finest"...* retweeting
Aaron Bastani's sycophantic tweet: *Starmer came across really well on Desert
Island Discs on a personal level (Three Lions choice aside). How he spoke
about his wife in particular was really moving. Why are his handlers keeping
this side of him out of the public eye?* That Bastani tried to promote himself and
his media outlet as an alternative to the corporate media was laughable. The
Bastani-Owen Jones-Ash Sarkar spectrum was entirely devoid of the critical
socialist rigour that was to be found on the social media accounts of Ed McNally,
Paul O'Connell, Daniel Finn, Louis Allday, Asa Winstanley, Tony Greenstein
and numerous others. Including Steven Salaita. From Salaita's twitter page Ellis
learned that Pharrell Williams ('launching a new MasterClass on racism') was
the pimp of violent racist repression. Or as SLANK @DabSquad_Slank put it
(retweeted by Steven Salaita) *Pharrell is a Zionist who helps raise tens of
millions for the IDF, if he actually gave a fuck abt racism & social justice he'd
stop fund raising for apartheid.* There was a link to an article by Randi Nord (13
November 2018) on the Mint Press News website. **BEVERLY HILLS,
CALIFORNIA** — *Just two weeks before Israel pounded Gaza with bombs last
night, over 1,200 celebrities came together to raise a record-breaking $60
million to support the Israeli Defense Forces and Israel's occupation of
Palestine at a gala called Friends of Israeli Defense Forces (FIDF).* Some of
these celebrities Ellis had never heard of. Some he had. They included Ashton
Kutcher, Andy Garcia, Ziggy Marley (son of Bob), Arnold Schwarzenegger and
Seal. The bright morning began to cloud over. The child wanted help to put on
her pink shoes. Shoes, she said. Then she began to look at her *Spot* books. After
that she climbed the stairs. Ellis received a text. He went out. He bought milk,
brown sugar, lemon bleach. Then to the bakery to buy almond and plain
croissants. Afterwards he went for a walk. He observed a figure of indeterminate
gender lying on a bench, staring at a mobile phone. Lunch was once again soup
with bread and cheese, followed by a sliced apple with yogurt. Ellis had a bath.
When he returned to social media he learned that a black student at the
University of Manchester had been seized by aggressive security guards who
had pushed him up against a wall. The incident had been filmed. It was alleged
that they had said he did not look like a student and had spoken of drug-dealing.
From social media Ellis learned that one of the successful left candidates for the

NEC, Gemma Bolton, had now, with the usual calculated timing, been accused of anti-Semitism. In 2018 she had tweeted that Israel was an apartheid state. Naturally the rancid and reactionary *Jewish Chronicle* had inflated this non-story into news. That night the 10pm Sky News top story was about an American vaccine which boasted a 95 per cent success rate in providing protection against Covid-19. Meanwhile questions were raised about the flouting of social distance advice by Boris Johnson and his associates. Ellis went to bed and read a few more chapters of *An Expensive Place to Die.*

Tuesday 17th November

It had rained in the night. A dull cloudy morning. BBC News regarded the biggest news of the day to be Boris Johnson's remark that Scottish devolution was Tony Blair's biggest mistake as Labour leader. Sir Malcolm Rifkind was invited to comment at length. A cosy chat with Nick Robinson. Naturally Blair's greatest crime, the invasion of Iraq, was not mentioned. As he ate his breakfast cereal Ellis went online. **Sharon** tweeted about the *Jewish Chronicle* non-story concerning Gemma Bolton: *I think they know it will go nowhere but it's specifically designed to belittle and embarrass her.* Next Ellis read an article by Rus Azhdar on the *Jacobin* website. It was about the background to the suspension of Labour Party activists in Bristol West, for speaking out in support of Jeremy Corbyn following his suspension from the party. The new Starmer-appointed general secretary, David Evans, suspended Corbyn, wrote Rus Azhdar. *Evans relied on rules established by the previous general secretary and Corbyn ally, Jennie Formby. They stated that branches "should not engage in debate about disciplinary matters in a way that might jeopardise confidentiality or due processes." In a fit of the scope-creep typical of the Labour bureaucracy, Evans extended this into a blanket gagging order on any discussions of disciplinary procedures. This did not, however, stop Starmer and co from publicly defending the decision; in truth, the demand for silence applied only to us ordinary members.* At the end of his article Azhdar wrote: *Rumour has it that the Right is likely to de-escalate tensions and readmit Corbyn in a few weeks' time — hoping the experience will leave him and his supporters chastened and cowed.* But the most revealing part of the article, Ellis felt, was this indictment of Corbyn's utter uselessness as a Left leader: *It's important to note how vital it is for the apparatus to suppress criticism of unelected regional officials who rule the party. Despite five years under Corbyn's leadership, the Left achieved next to nothing in terms of transforming the party's internal structures — and still less in rooting out the right-wing from positions of power.* Ellis went out. He bought lemon juice, pine nuts, cod and salmon. Later he went to the pharmacy. Back home again he drank a cappuccino, ate an almond croissant and read the *Morning Star*. Its front page story was about the black Manchester university student. Later Ellis went online. He discovered that Suzanne Moore had left the *Guardian*. The reactionary liberal chatterati blubbered in sympathy. Reading about all this on Twitter, Ellis discovered that, referring to the extremist Jonathan Sacks, Moore had written 'We are depleted by such a loss'. No we're emphatically not, thought Ellis. The world was well rid of that smug and smarmy bigot. As Ellis read more he learned that the *Guardian* had come in for criticism for publishing an obituary of Peter Sutcliffe. Julie Sheppard tweeted: *As someone living in West Yorkshire at the time, I would have preferred to read the obituaries of the women Sutcliffe murdered. He terrorised my life and the lives of other women for years.* On the twitter page of Louis Allday, Ellis read Allday's comment on the Gemma Bolton story: *It's clear that it's not just Corbyn that is under attack, but the entire future of the Palestine solidarity movement in the UK is at stake. Concession after concession will soon reach a point where any condemnation or criticism of Israel & Zionism will be called anti-Semitism.* As the sun set that day the sky was astonishingly beautiful - the clouds like ribs, flooded with a strange pink-purple colour that reminded Ellis of a painting he'd once seen by Edward Lear. The child ate a bowl of *Cheerios*. Online Ellis learned about the latest blunder by the thoroughly useless Jeremy Corbyn. He had made a statement on Facebook which amounted to yet another abject surrender to the Zionist lobby. 'I regret the pain this issue has caused the Jewish community and would wish to do nothing that would exacerbate or prolong it.' (Then just *shut the fuck up*, thought Ellis.) 'To be clear, concerns about antisemitism [spelt the preferred Zionist way, Ellis noted] are neither "exaggerated" nor overstated". The point I wished to make was that the vast majority of Labour Party members were and remain committed anti-racists deeply opposed to anti-Semitism. I fully support Keir Starmer's decision to accept all the EHRC recommendations in full and, in accordance with my own lifelong convictions, will do what I can to help the party move on, united against anti-Semitism which has been responsible for so many of history's greatest crimes against humanity.' Ellis thought: dim-witted Corbyn *still doesn't get it*. This shallow social reformist has been a catastrophe both for the Left and for those seeking justice for the Palestinians. Needless to say the Trump-worshipping Zionist hoodlums of the Board of Deputies of British Jews were not placated. That screeching Zionist harpy Marie van der Zyl called it a 'pathetic non-apology'. On twitter Justin Schlosberg attempted to defend Corbyn's abject surrender asserting that 'concerns are not exaggerated and overstated' IS NOT the same thing as saying 'the problem has not been overstated by political opponents'. To which the somewhat smarter Joe Sucksmith commented: 'This totally misses the point. His original statement was fine. Issuing anything further was superfluous and could only convey a rowing back. Plus this "concerns vs levels" distinction" is somewhat contrived. Were the BoD's "concerns" not overstated. Of course they were'. At 6.25pm, as Ellis was baking smoked salmon, frying chips and boiling peas, the radio reported that Corbyn's suspension from the Labour Party had been lifted. Back online Ellis read more social media. The author of an admiring book on Corbyn, **Alex Nunns** tweeted: 'Jeremy Corbyn's readmission is a huge climbdown from the leadership and a victory for the left. His statement released today didn't alter his original words— no grovelling. He clarified that he didn't mean concern about antisemitism was overstated, as opposed to the scale of it'. **Freecitizen864** replied: 'Huge victory for the left? What planet are you on. We are getting beaten from all sides and all the left can do is cry "unity". #DumpLabour #DefundLabour #CrushStarmer' **Fencelt** tweeted: 'Christ , a victory for the left?! Brilliant language betraying an attitude which has learnt nothing from the disaster of Corbyn's leadership. Enjoy your (pyrrhic) victory'. The usual rabble were furious that Corbyn had been readmitted. Karen Pollock, Chief Executive of the risible Holocaust Educational Trust, tweeted: 'This sends an appalling message. "Zero tolerance" either means zero tolerance or it's meaningless. The scathing report from the EHRC less than three weeks ago outlined a stream of racism and discrimination by the Labour Party on Jeremy Corbyn's watch. Yet here we are. 2/ Once again Corbyn has failed to take responsibility and the Labour Party have let him off the hook. Ends'. Demonstrating yet again that holocaust memorial was not in fact about learning from the Nazi genocide and that the last person to learn anything from that atrocitywas sanctimonious Israel-worshipping Karen Pollock. The headline in the online *Daily Express* was: **Owen Jones turns on Corbyn as he slams ex-Labour chief's 'lack of emotional intelligence'** *Guardian columnist Owen Jones has criticised the "lack of emotional intelligence" shown towards Labour's anti-Semitism scandal by people like Jeremy Corbyn.* It reported that Jones had appeared on BBC Politics Live to say "He expressed his regret, and I think that's an important clarification. What's so tragic about this whole saga is the focus should have been on the Labour Party and the Left uniting around the implementation of the EHRC recommendations". Well, thought Ellis. You could always rely on oleaginous Owen to cloud the waters on behalf of Zionism. What was *actually* tragic was that a lifelong anti-racist like Corbyn had cravenly capitulated to a howling gang of Trump-worshipping Jewish liars, racists and apologists for Israel, who had successfully defamed him because of his timidity and unwillingness to confront Jewish extremism head-on. How revealing it was that instead of challenging the Zionist witchfinders, Owen Jones aligned himself with them. Jones sobbed about "the hurt and distress that's been caused to Jewish people, not just in the party but across the country, by the existence of anti-Semitism…All the way through this there's been this problem of a lack of emotional intelligence". On and on he drivelled. "If it ends up that people on the Left become the guys getting defensive over anti-Semitism on TV, there's no future for the Left in this country." A sentence triply devoid of truth. In the first place no one on the Left was *defending* anti-Semitism. In the second place Left defenders of Corbyn were almost *never* on TV (unless you counted fellow fair-weather Jonesean slitherers like the *Novara Media* crowd). And finally the Left had no future in the Labour Party because it had dismally failed to confront the aggressive campaigns of the Zionists. The Labourist Left was intellectually impoverished, organisationally inept, devoid of strategy and, crucially, not prepared to confront Jewish racism and reactionary Jewish organisations, who played the Jewish-victim card and time and time again used Nazi genocide as an alibi for atrocities carried out by Israeli Jews. Zionism remained a taboo subject. *Zionism is the ideology of one of the most violent, brutal, shameless and mass-murderous projects of military colonialism in modern history. The *real* meaning and definition of Zionism is that which most closely corresponds to the realities on the ground at present, historically and as these trends continue into the future.* Ellis came upon this in the comments appended to Nimer Sultany's article *Against Appeasement: What's wrong with Zionism?* a link to which had been provided, with a recommendation, on the Twitter page of Louis Allday. Needless to say Corbyn's readmission to the party was a big story on the Sky News 10pm bulletin. For comment Sky turned to the rabid right-winger Ian Austin, member of the House of Lords, laughably identified by a caption as an 'Anti-Extremism Campaigner'. The Corbyn story was the first item on the review of the papers which followed. The commentators were a strangely inarticulate and predictably reactionary young woman who wrote editorials for (where else?) the *Observer*, and a loon from *Spiked*. Once again coverage was 100 per cent against Corbyn with no voices to articulate a genuine analysis of the situation. The Zionist poison had spread everywhere in the corporate media and among its favoured chatterati. Ellis went to bed and read more Len Deighton. The novel was nearing its end, with crisp Chandleresque repartee and a desolating description of a journey across some of the old Great War battlefields along the Western front. Ellis put out the light and went to sleep.

Wednesday 18th November

Elis woke at 7.20am and lay in the gloom of the curtained bedroom. Predictably, at 7.30am, the BBC 'Today' programme led with the Corbyn story. The chosen person to comment on it was the Zionist harpy Marie van der Zyl of the Board of Deputies. She sputtered and frothed and was given the usual easy ride by her supine softball questioner. Listeners to the 'Today' programme would never know that van der Zyl admired Donald Trump or that the Board of Deputies was a right-wing Tory body or that the anti-Semitism story was a gigantic hoax. For 'balance' there was the less than adequate James Scheider (although in fairness to Scheider it had to be said he was much better than an equivocator like Owen Jones). Ellis went out and bought a *Morning Star*, a loaf of bread, some rolls, a pack of mixed salad and a pack of tomatoes. At 11.25am Ellis learned that Sir

Keir Starmer had decided not to restore the whip to Jeremy Corbyn. Ellis went for a walk. The sun shone. He walked along the route of the old railway line, now used by cyclists and pedestrians. Home again he went online. Ali Abunimah tweeted: *We can't fight the Israel lobby's smears and lies against @jeremycorbyn more than he wants to fight them himself, which is not at all apparently.* Abi Abunimah added: *I'm not saying this to be harsh. It's just a practical reality. Instead of rallying his many supporters and fighting back, @jeremycorbyn just keeps capitulating and appeasing, thereby undermining those exposing the facts about the lies and smears against him.* Abi Abunimah added: *Imagine if @jeremycorbyn joined up with @DerbyChrisW and others to rally people on left to fight back against smears and lies of Labour right and its embedded Israel lobby. They'd create a real force. But Corbyn just wants to sit on back bench for Sir Keir Starmer KCB QC MP MI5.* John McDonnell MP tweeted about Starmer's decision to deny Corbyn the whip: *This is just plain wrong & will cause more division & disunity in party. Jeremy's gone through the formal procedures & decision has been made properly. I appeal to everyone that surely it's time to move on & start working together to implement the EHRC.* Abi Abunimah retorted: *The fault also lies with you @johnmcdonnellMP, you thought you could appease away the lies and smears and throw a few people under the bus and it would all be fine. You'd better go along with this or you'll be next.* Slippery, pop-eyed Rachel Shabi, in fine fence-sitting style, tweeted: *Removing Corbyn's whip is nonsensical and wrong. Also: Corbyn should never have made his statement about the EHRC report, leading to this sorry mess. It could all have been avoided, if both current and ex leader had been wiser. But, well, here we are.* Richard Seymour replied: *In all seriousness, at what point do you think it *would* be permissible to state the patently obvious? When, if not at precisely the point when people are talking about it?* Mark Steel, indicating that he'd finally parted company with the socialist sensibility he'd once possessed, retorted: *If Corbyn was stating the patently obvious, why does he have such little support on this issue? It appears most people can't be persuaded to agree with something patently obvious.* Tony Fletcher replied to Mark Steel: *You should perhaps get out more! It is true he has very little support among BBC journalists, and some noisy types on Twitter, but most people seem to me to support him.* Mark Steel replied: *Sadly, at the last election it appears most of the population was made up of BBC journalists and noisy types on Twitter, whereas you and your mates couldn't quite swing things the other way.* How low Steel had sunk, Ellis thought. Ellis had once queued for a talk by Paul Foot on Byron's *Don Juan*. In those pre-internet days it was not always easy to obtain books and Ellis had gone all over London before he'd found a bookshop with a copy of the plump Penguin edition. He had taken his copy with him to the talk. As he stood there a voice behind him cried 'Blimey! Here's a man has found a copy!' Ellis turned and saw that the speaker was Mark Steel. He had basked in the warm

329

glow of the attention of someone who in those days was a star of the hard and virile left. What a delightful and amusing comrade Steel was! But then Mark had suddenly and unexpectedly walked out of the Socialist Workers Party, broken up with his SWP partner, and written a memoir about his life in politics. The book had been roundly denounced in SWP publications. Ellis had bought a copy. It was very funny, occasionally careless with the facts (Steel cited a Libertines song but, scandalously, got the title wrong) and quite incisive about a malaise inside the Party. The SWP, Ellis learned, was dishonestly inflating its membership figures. That kind of thing was a minor sin - all political parties did that - but a revolutionary party ought to be transparent about itself and not lie to the membership. Steel described a collapse in the revolutionary fervour and organisation of the old days, and at the time it seemed all too true. Once upon a time you saw SWP posters everywhere in British cities, and *Socialist Worker* sellers were ubiquitous in towns and cities on a Saturday. Incredibly, Ellis had once even encountered a *Socialist Worker* seller in Hunstanton. In retrospect Steel's book had anticipated all too accurately the eventual implosion of a party which had died at the hands of an ageing, ossified, self-perpetuating clique who were as resistant to party democracy as any Labour Party right-winger. The rape scandal had exposed all too vividly the rot inside the party and its cult-like aspect. In spite of that, Ellis still missed the SWP for its efforts to create a radical left culture and for its unrelenting and all too accurate critique of the dead-end of Labour Party reformism and the illusion of radical social transformation via parliamentarianism. But it was one thing to leave the party on ethical and political grounds. It was quite another to compromise your principles in the service of self-advancement and the quest for celebrity. Shame on you, Mark! Ellis opened a bottle of wine. It was 5pm. The child played with her wooden tortoise. That evening Ellis watched *Breakfast at Tiffany's*. The 10pm news featured the latest twist in the Corbyn saga. True to form, for comment Sky turned to Gideon Falter of the so-called Campaign Against Anti-Semitism. It was another reminder that the campaign against Corbyn had nothing whatever to do with anti-Semitism. In bed Ellis finished *An Expensive Place to Die*.

Thursday 19th November

Ellis woke at 6.10am. At 6.40am he turned on the radio. At 7.30am the 'Today' programme continued its tradition of vilifying Jeremy Corbyn and giving a platform to Zionists, while denying any opposing point of view. Today the person chosen to comment on the refusal to readmit Corbyn to the Parliamentary Labour Party was foul-mouthed reactionary Margaret Hodge. She wallowed in her fake Jewish victimhood. Later, Ellis went online. He learned that the right-wing Jew Philippe Sands had appeared on the poisonously reactionary BBC Newsnight show to put the boot into Corbyn. No surprise there. Sands, laughably described as a 'Human rights lawyer', was always willing to promote the cause of Zionism. He had supplied fulsome praise for the cover of Zionist Julia Neuberg's vicious little book *Antisemitism* ('Passionate, principled and necessary'). *Antisemitism* was devoted to slandering Palestinian activism. As he was online Ellis learned of another development in the assault on Corbyn. The rabid Zionist Gordon Brown had been granted a platform by ITV to demand that Corbyn 'make a full apology. No ifs, no buts, no caveats, no qualifying sentences. He has got to admit he got it wrong.' **The Flying Rodent** sarcastically tweeted: *Moving into full Confess And The Beatings Will Stop mode now, and I'm sure we can all recall how often giving critics what they want has cheered them up and calmed them down.* Elsewhere on the internet Ellis came across Glenn Greenwald's tweet: *I've never seen a more flagrant, repellent and cynical exploitation of anti-Semitism in my life than its disgusting use to smear Corbyn because of a lack of alternatives for how to defeat him. Nothing has trivialized this cause more than what British Blairites have done.* Next Ellis came across the latest example of the lamentable inadequacy of the so-called 'left' in the Labour Party. It transpired that Rebecca Long-Bailey, interviewed on ITV by the Zionist Robert Peston, had said *that Jeremy Corbyn may need to apologise to have the @UKLabour whip restored.* Joe Sucksmith commented: *Christ this is bad. With friends like these, Corbyn really doesn't need enemies does he?* **Petr G. Tarasov** @tarasoviets added: *That was hard to watch. Everybody indulging the delusion. When will the penny drop that no amount of appeasement will ever be enough?* **Ian Westell** wrote: *It's amazing anyone put any faith in any of them. What a wasted five years!* Joe Sucksmith also put the boot into Mark Steel: *"Corbyn doesn't have much support within the corporate media, therefore I conclude he doesn't have much support more generally". That's "leftist" Mark Steel's take. Mark Steel who writes for and makes a living from... the corporate media.* The author **Tom Mills** @ta_mills wrote: *I like Mark, but the only way this could seem like a sensible reading is if you've remained more or less aloof from left politics for last five years.* **John Wight** @JohnWight1 wrote: *The Labour Party is far too broad a church to be sustainable any longer. Pro-Palestinian activists in the same party with apologists for apartheid. Antiwar voices alongside pro war. Neoliberals alongside socialists. The party's over. #Corbyn* **Matt Kennard** @kennardmatt wrote: *Have you noticed that every progressive voice given access to the broadcast tv news shows melted on Labour's "antisemitism crisis" and Julian Assange? That's not a coincidence. It's a club. And the club has rules.* **Matt Kennard** wrote: *Labour's new "independent complaints process" is the pièce de résistance of the witch-hunt against the left and pro-Palestinian activists. Just watch.* Ellis moved away from political commentary. Book news. Michael O'Mara books is to publish a *captivating* new biography of Queen Elizabeth II and her sister Margaret. And the Booker Prize ceremony this year is to feature *star speakers* Barack Obama, the Duchess of Cornwall and Kazuo Ishiguro. A blood-spattered war criminal, a royal parasite and a writer indifferent to the company he keeps. Then Ellis learned that the Zionist Jewish Labour Movement had advertised star speakers for its One Day Conference on 29 November: Lisa Nandy, Andy Burnham, Angela Rayner, David Miliband, Ruth Smeeth, Margaret Hodge, Louise (drop that 'i'!) Ellman, Keir Starmer. Ellis went for a walk. When he returned home he went online. Louis Allday wrote: *Labour & the Conservatives are completely united on the issue of imperialism. The only criticism Labour has of this obscene new military build up is that its plans for Britain to "be a force for good in the world" aren't detailed enough.* He retweeted a tweet by Lisa Nandy: *Keir_Starmer is right. Britain must once again show global leadership and be a force for good in the world. But this is a spending announcement without a strategy. Global Britain must be more than a slogan.* Louis Allday added: *Perpetuating the ridiculous idea that Britain ever has been a force for good or ever could be by spending billions of pounds on the military is offensive and ahistorical.* Louis Allday continued: *The UK care sector is collapsing, child hunger/poverty rampant and worsening, an ongoing pandemic and mass job cuts and Starmer's only response to the govt dedicating 16.5 billion pounds to the military (ie war) is to endorse it and demand more details. There is no opposition.* Louis Allday concluded: *Even by Labour's own myopic electoral ambitions, this is an enormous missed opportunity but it seems pretty clear that gaining popularity/votes is not actually Starmer's primary objective given how keen he is to support virtually whatever the govt announces.* Louis Allday commented: *At what point are people going to accept that the idea or hope they have of what the Labour Party is/could be bears no relation whatsoever to its historical role, contemporary position or its future. It's an irredeemably pro-imperialist party, it always has been & will remain so.* Observing today's revelation that *The United States will label the Boycott, Divestment and Sanctions campaign, which seeks to isolate Israel over its treatment of the Palestinians, as antisemitic* Louis Allday noted that *Mike Pompeo and Owen Jones are now on the same page re- BDS then.* He retweeted his tweet from 29 Mar 2018: *Owen Jones' justification for his opposition to the @BDSmovement is that it could "end up indiscriminately targeting Jewish people". This is a fundamentally disingenuous & illogical argument that conflates a boycott of Israeli companies & organisations with "Jewish people".* Allday wrote: *Jones constantly talks about passionately supporting "Palestinian justice" which is an odd and deliberately vague phrase that doesn't really mean anything and crucially, commits to nothing.* Allday wrote: *Jones won't even offer his support to the peaceful, Palestinian-led BDS movement, condemns Hamas' resistance, writes awful articles and yet he has the gall to say "history will damn those who stood in the way".* The child munched her way through a large apple. On the TV news that night Ellis learned that today's total for

Coronavirus infections was 22,915 with 501 deaths. There was a story about Priti Patel and bullying. The report into complaints of her behaviour to her civil servants had been leaked. It sounded like the standard Whitehall whitewash. The evidence was plainly overwhelming since the substance of the complaints was grudgingly acknowledged. But whoever had compiled the report had conveniently concluded that any bullying on her part had been 'unintentional'. Ellis switched off the TV. Back online he caught up with a tweet by Margaret Hodge. *I hope she dies soon. Dumb bitch. Member of a rich & powerful Jewish dynasty. Mossad agent. Liar. Rat. Old cunt. Snake. Nazi. Traitor. Zionist stooge. Evil personified. Cancer. Zionist hag. Pig. Infiltrator. Racist witch. Controlled & funded by Israel. Palestinian child murderer.* Hodge alleged that she was the victim of these remarks but supplied no evidence that her claim was genuine. She supplied no evidence of where these remarks might be found. If on Twitter, why not display them? Ellis regarded Margaret Hodge as a thoroughly untrustworthy and deeply unpleasant individual with an execrable political history. Hodge added: *This abuse is not normal. This is why zero tolerance matters. This is why people have to take responsibility for their actions.* Which was a bit rich coming from someone who had been widely reported as screaming 'You fucking racist and anti-Semite!' at Jeremy Corbyn. Yet no one seemed to be identifying her as the sanctimonious hypocrite that she indubitably was. On the contrary, her tweet was amplified into a throbbing fable of victimhood by the corporate media, including Sophia Sleigh in *The Evening Standard* and Aidan Radnedge in *Metro*. The rhetorical technique used by Hodge - collage - was a meretricious one in the hands of Zionists. It was noticeable that Hodge made it all about Israel. Which was what the anti-Semitism fraud had been about all along. Ellis received an email. It was about this year's Booker Prize winner, Douglas Stuart. Ellis hadn't watched the ceremony and had been indifferent to the shortlist. *Christ, how can anyone win a Booker writing shitty prose like this*, the email began. There followed a quotation from the novel *Shuggie Bain*. 'Thatcher didn't want honest workers any more; her future was technology and nuclear power and private health. Industrial days were over, and the bones of the Clyde Shipworks and the Springburn Railworks lay about the city like rotted dinosaurs.' The quotation continued. Ellis saw what the Glaswegian sender of the email meant. *Shite, as we say in Glasgow: pure shite.* Ellis went to bed and began reading *Breakfast at Tiffany's*.

Friday 20th November

Ellis did not get out of bed until 8.15am. Later he went out. He bought some bananas, tomatoes and two kitchen rolls. He went for a walk. The sun shone. Everywhere was busy. The Coronavirus lockdown rules were being flouted on a large scale. You would barely notice that there was a lockdown on at all, were it not for the closed clothes shops, the closed hairdressers and the closed charity shops. For lunch Ellis ate a roll, cheese and soup. The child pulled her mother's hair, then tried to climb on the sofa. Help, she said. Glenn Gould played the Goldberg Variations. Paul O'Connell@pmpoc tweeted: *Britain's political and media class are a genuinely odious collection of sociopaths, careerists, sycophants and craven lickspittles.* **Media Lens** retweeted a tweet from two years ago: *Corbyn was first elected as an MP in 1983. The first story ever to be published in a UK national newspaper with the words 'Corbyn' and 'antisemitism' appeared in the Guardian on August 13, 2015.* Ali Abunimah noted that *The EU-Israel Association Agreement is conditioned on Israel respecting human rights, so Israel and EU violate it every minute.* He added: *Israel's criminal occupation regime violates Article 2 of EU-Israel Association Agreement every minute. You are depraved to celebrate enriching war criminals to commit more crimes against Palestinians. EU is a full participant in Israeli land theft, torture & murder. #EUtoICCC.* The 10pm Sky News began with stories about preparations for innoculating Britons with the Coronavirus vaccine. Next was the Priti Patel bullying story. For an independent assessment of her bullying Sky turned to… her special adviser. He said what a lovely person she was. Ellis went to bed and read a few more pages of *Breakfast at Tiffany's*.

Saturday 21st November

The alarm went at 6.50am. Ellis heard the end of a farming programme. It reported on protests at Ramsgate about the cruel and degrading conditions of the live animal exports which went through the port. One protester said she had been a sheep farmer and that farmers would be horrified to see how the animals were treated after they'd been sold. Another woman spoke of huge quantities of evidence of maltreatment which was regularly submitted to the relevant authorities, MPs and the government. It was a dull grey morning. When he went online Ellis discovered that 11 hours ago Angela Rayner had tweeted: *Happy Birthday @JoeBiden I hope you are having a lovely day.* Ed McNally commented: *Given Rayner has derided Corbyn for having "a more international view of things" than her, the pathetic Biden birthday tweet is interesting. Begging for recognition from a senile warmonger is well and good, but standing with freedom struggles around the world is dodgy.* Paul McConnell tweeted a link to Michael Doyle new article 'The Labour left's deference strategy has failed' (https://www.conter.co.uk/blog/2020/11/20/the-labour-lefts-deference-strategy-has-failed). Contemplating Labour Party history, Michael Doyle looked back at how *Routinely, the media would report allegations that mostly referred to offensive social media posts from a minuscule number of party members and supporters, followed by the assertions that 'Jeremy Corbyn has a blind spot',* *'the Labour leadership is not dealing with the problem' and 'Labour under Corbyn has created a haven for antisemites'... This campaign was replete with the bizarre spectacles of life-long racists being brought into TV studios to be the moral arbiters on Labour's antisemitism problem, with the media framing the issue as a problem unique to Labour... Despite the protestations of his accusers, that their charge of antisemitism against Corbyn was not related to the defence of the Palestinian cause, the accusations against him mostly revolved around this issue.* Michael Doyle scrutinised the feebleness of the Corbyn project's media outriders. On the BBC This Week programme, the host, Andrew Neil asked Aaron Bastani "why is antisemitism endemic in the Labour Party?" *Rather than say it was not, and then refer to the YouGov poll commissioned by the Campaign against Antisemitism group, one of the most hostile critics of Corbyn on this issue, that showed that antisemitism in the Labour Party had* slightly fallen *under Corbyn, Bastani conceded the point, and then proceeded to give a convoluted and unconvincing explanation related to a "digital culture bleeding into a mass membership party".* Michael Doyle added: *as documented in Owen Jones' new book, his close allies John McDonnell and Andrew Fisher implored Corbyn to adopt the IHRA in full. Fisher is quoted in Jones' book saying "it is f**king ridiculous to not adopt the IHRA when your party is accused of having an 'antisemitism problem".* That, in a nutshell, was the pitiful stance many senior leftists around the Corbyn project took on an issue that was being used to delegitimise pro-Palestinian activism and to destroy the Corbyn leadership.* The sheer ineptitude and flabbiness of the Labour left was exposed yet again by its feeble response when Corbyn was suspended from the party by Starmer. *It consisted mainly in online petitions and pitiful calls by leading figures like John McDonnell and Momentum founder Jon Lansman for diplomacy and calm.* The hours passed. Ellis could hear in the street or a nearby garden a barking dog. Ellis read an essay about a shipwreck off the Isle of Wight in 1876. Next he read Gerard Manley Hopkins's poem 'The Wreck of the Deutschland' and then the chapter about this poem in the Hopkins biography by Robert Bernard Martin. Next he glanced at a novella published in 1898 about a massive ocean liner colliding with ice in the Atlantic. For lunch Ellis ate soup, a roll and cheese. For his evening meal: pan-fried cod, fried mashed potato, and salad. He watched two documentaries in the American 'Unsolved History' series. The first debunked conspiracy theories about the death of Princess Diana. The second debunked conspiracy theories about the death of Marilyn Monroe. On the Sky News that night the newscaster asserted that Joe Biden had 'ambitious plans' to combat climate change. That seemed to Ellis to be a perfect example of how corporate news consisted of propaganda, not accurate, objective or questioning reportage. Joe Biden was appointing a host of advisers and future government staff from the fossil fuel world. This was not the action of a President who would reverse or slow down the planet's accelerating and

catastrophic over-heating. After the news Ellis read Tony Greenstein's latest blog post. It was entitled: 'You Can't Unite with a Rattlesnake: the Left Will Never Defeat Starmer as long as it accepts his "Anti-Semitism" narrative'. *For the past 5 years, Momentum and Corbyn have repeatedly tried appeasing the Labour Right and the Zionist Jewish Labour Movement. The more they gave them the more they demanded. The more they apologised, the more ground they conceded,* wrote Greenstein. *Starmer, unlike Corbyn and the Campaign Group/ Momentum,* Greenstein continued, *is not stupid. Cunning, deceitful, dishonest but not stupid. From the beginning of his leadership he has repeated his promise to 'tear the poison of anti-Semitism out of Labour by the roots'. That was what justified the sacking of Rebecca Long-Bailey and Lloyd Russell-Moyle and the dressing down of Stephen Kinnock. Not once has any member of the stupid left challenged his narrative.* Greenstein contined: *Starmer wanted the EHRC Report to be as bad as possible in order that he could wield it as a weapon. As it turned out the EHRC Report was insubstantial and evasive. Despite ignoring the evidence of Jewish Voices for Labour and my own offer, as the first Jewish person to be expelled, to give testimony its Report was a botched political stitch up. The suggestion that Ken Livingstone and Pam Bromley had been guilty of harassment is not worth the paper it is written on. Political speech and denying that there is an anti-Semitism problem is not harassment. It would be laughed out of court. That is why Starmer and his glove puppet, David Evans, have been so concerned to prevent local Labour parties discussing the Report.* Greenstein asked: *What was the response of Momentum to the suspension of Corbyn? Was it to call for Starmer to go? Was there a call for defiance of David Evans declaration that discussion of the suspension was not 'competent business' for Labour parties? Andrew Scattergood, Momentum's Co-Chair issued a statement that 'This suspension risks politicising Labour's response to antisemitism.' Where have they been? The 'anti-Semitism' campaign has been political from the start. It has been the means by which the Right has progressively undermined Corbyn.* Greenstein continued: *It is the inability of the Labour Left to come to grips with the Zionists' anti-semitism hoax which sealed Corbyn's fate and is now consigning the Labour Left to oblivion. It is a consequence of their acceptance of pro-imperialist politics in combination with identity politics.* Greenstein added: *On a personal level I have no sympathy for Corbyn. I consider him a disloyal, treacherous fool who had it within his power to become Prime Minister and he threw it all away by throwing his own supporters to the wolves. Corbyn knew, more than most, that the ritual accusation of 'anti-Semitism' is levelled at all Palestine solidarity supporters.* Ellis was in complete agreement with Greenstein. Corbyn had been a catastrophe for both the Left and for the cause of the Palestinians. Greenstein went on: *On any objective analysis the campaign against 'anti-Semitism' was always about Israel and Zionism. In December of 2016 Corbyn voluntarily proposed the adoption of the IHRA's 38 word definition of anti-Semitism? The idiocy of Corbyn beggars belief.* Greenstein added: *To compound his idiocy and cowardice Corbyn opposed Open Selection at the 2018 Labour Conference. Once again he appeased his enemies.* Greenstein concluded: *Victory can still be salvaged from defeat but unfortunately the Campaign Group and Corbyn himself is so lacking in any Marxist or class politics that they are blown hither and thither in the gusts of capitalist reaction. Of one thing we should be clear. The Labour Party has been captured by Zionist and imperialist supporters who are as dedicated supporters of neo-liberal capitalism as Boris Johnson.* Greenstein was so much smarter and more lucid than posturing careerists like Owen Jones, Aaron Bastani and Ash Sarkar, Ellis felt. He went to bed and read more Truman Capote.

Sunday 22nd November

A bright sunny morning. Ellis woke at 8.15am. On BBC Radio 4 someone was solemnly explaining how the internet had resulted in the loss of elite narrative. The old *objectivity* (yes, the BBC person actually used that word!) had (whimper) gone. It was classic BBC smuggery. The notion that the corporate media and corporate publishing was the repository of impartiality, high values and truth-telling, the objectivity of which was now seriously put at risk by subjective, unreliable social media, was laughable. Every tweet by Media Lens challenged the poverty of that banal construction, demonstrating how these media were saturated in unacknowledged systems of value and belief and that their core function was to protect power and commerce. But the man on the radio was not only complacent, he also - interestingly - symbolised *anxiety*. Social media was a democratic space. Its content was often far more informative, truthful, newsworthy and solidly analytic than the infotainment of the BBC, Sky and all the other hegemonic institutions. This was why Google, Facebook and Twitter were beginning to introduce creeping censorship. They were shutting down the voices of dissent. The Silicon Valley billionaires were deeply embedded in the ruling class and its rapacious capitalism and imperialism. Ellis drank a cappuccino and went online. Richard Seymour, supplying more evidence of his slow slither to the right, retweeted a *New York Times* article. *The revolution eats its children. They Championed Venezuela's Revolution. They Are Now Its Latest Victims.* Yes, once again that voice of imperialism, the *New York Times*, carried an article attacking Venezuela's leader Nicolás Maduro. Ellis next read Ben Norton's tweet on this topic: *Neoliberal imperial mouthpiece the NY Times, which regurgitates CIA lies and has opposed every socialist movement everywhere, is amplifying Venezuela's so-called "left opposition" to attack the elected socialist govt from the "left" and right at the same time. Information warfare.* Ben Norton added: *US "leftists" (usually Trotskyites and socdems)*

often insist on constantly criticizing actually existing socialist govts in the
Global South that are under siege by imperialism. Well, CIA stenographer the
NY Times is now weaponizing these same "left" criticisms against Venezuela.
Cruising on across the choppy waters of Twitter, Ellis came upon Aaron Maté's
tweet of 19 November 2020: *Did intellectual coward @GeorgeMonbiot respond*
to me on promoting a Bellingcat hoax; dismissing ex-OPCW chief José Bustani;
attacking @TheGrayzoneNews & denigrating OPCW whistleblowers? The
answer is no, because @GeorgeMonbiot is an intellectual coward. Ellis cruised
on. Max Blumenthal tweeted: *Genocide advocate and notorious bone-breaker*
Effie Eitam - who said Palestinians "are creatures who came out of the depths
of darkness... We will have to kill them all" - has been nominated to lead
Israel's Yad Vashem Holocaust memorial museum. Ellis cruised on. Joe
Sucksmith retweeted the tweet of the ubiquitous-on-corporate-media 'liberal'
Zionist Rachel Shabi: *I spoke with Radio Scotland this morning: how has*
Labour's latest row over antisemitism been handled? Badly, by everyone. In full
here from 8.15am https://bbc.co.uk/programmes/m00. Joe Sucksmith
commented: *A more pertinent question: how has the phoney antisemitism crisis*
been handled by the liberal, optics-obsessed left? Answer: fucking horrendously,
by all of them. And, sadly, it continues, as neatly demonstrated here by Shabi.
Ellis read more tweets by Joe Sucksmith. *Novara folk still use "Labour*
antisemitism crisis" as though it was an organic crisis, cynically used by the
right to discredit the left, ie a chronology of crisis followed by weaponisation.
This analysis is demonstrably wrong, but it's the price of admission to the
Sunday papers. He added: *I shouldn't need to explain why it's wrong, but for the*
avoidance of doubt... Yes, some genuine cases of AS were "weaponised", but the
important point is that the narrative of "crisis" was itself a *construction*... He
continued: *... A fraud created and propagated by a network of individuals and*
groups united by their opposition to Corbyn and the emergence of a left,
Palestine-supporting Labour Party. Zionist groups undeniably played a pre-
eminent role - the BoD, JLC, JLM etc., but this is the "unsayable". He continued:
As in, "unsayable" if you want the Sunday paper invites to keep flowing. Next
Ellis came upon a tweet by Laura Parker @ParkerCiccone. It was about the
Hong Kong activist Joshua Wong, who was on trial there. *Incredible courage.*
The whole Labour movement should stand with @joshuawongcf & send
messages of solidarity. @Keir_Starmer @OpenLabour
@PeoplesMomentum@socialistcam @Younglabourint. Ed McNally
@edmcnally96 retorted: *The whole Labour movement should probably not stand*
with a guy who calls covid the "Wuhan Virus". Julian PD @JuJo_PD wrote:
Joshua wong is hong kongs farage... Julian Cole @Julianpcole wrote: *I haven't*
heard you speaking out against the ongoing inhuman detention of Julian
Assange. @joshuawongcf is funded by evangelical homophobes. He would have
been locked up long ago if he'd been here funding and organising violent

overthrow of UK govt. Hypocritical double standards. J @d1fferentangle wrote: *I rather not show any solidarity with an anti-mainland chinese racist thank you very much.* Josh Jackson @JoshuaYJackson wrote: *Joshua Wong is a dangerous separatist who is allies with ultra right US politicians & spreads racist hatred against mainland Chinese. His supporters also shut down BLM rallies & attacked trade union offices. He has nothing to do with the labour movement.* In just a few minutes on the internet Ellis learned far more than he ever did listening to BBC News or watching Sky. What was never shown on the British corporate media was non-violent Palestinian resistance to the Israeli terror state or the violence of Jews in uniforms and the settlers. Ellis had dimly heard of Laura Parker. He looked her up on Google. Predictably, perhaps, there was a gushing *Guardian* profile of her. The paper talked of 'the hard left', a faction to which Parker ostensibly belonged. But - wait for it - the *Guardian* hack found her 'calm, accomplished, amiable. Everybody likes her. The Blairites in her constituency Labour party (Vauxhall) like her'. Hardly surprising, Ellis thought, since this woman appears to be shallow as a puddle by a lamp post. Ellis came to the end of the *Guardian*'s sycophantic profile and laughed hollowly as he came up against the newspaper's newly angled begging bowl. ***Joe Biden has won****, renewing hope for the US and the world. The result of this historic presidential election offers fresh promise for democracy and progress. Now is the time to support a free press, and the Guardian's independent, truthful journalism.* Really, Ellis thought, the *Guardian* sounds just like the BBC: staring into the mirror, constantly congratulating itself for its beauty and brilliance. *If you can, support the Guardian today, from as little as £1.* Jeepers-creepers! They really are desperate, Ellis thought. Out of the blue he remembered the time a one-legged man with a wooden crutch had lurched towards him on a street in Southsea. 'Help me, help me!' the man had cried, reaching out. 'I don't want money'. The man had collapsed against him and Ellis had felt obliged to support the poor wretch, who claimed he just needed assistance to get a little further along the street. The man's grip upon him tightened, rather like those of the tentacles of the giant squid in *Voyage to the Bottom of the Sea*. Once he was firmly locked in the man's embrace Ellis became aware that people in the street were laughing. Perhaps they knew the beggar and his ways. Because, of course, the man was not remotely in need of assistance in his locomotion. On the contrary, he was an accomplished hopper on his crutch. What he wanted was money. He pressed his whiskery repellent face close to Ellis and demanded a quid. Ellis was happy to give this abominable individual a one pound coin simply to be liberated from his noxious clutch. Returning to Google, Ellis discovered that 'Laura Parker is a Labour activist. She was Momentum's national co-ordinator until 2019, and previously worked as private secretary to Jeremy Corbyn'. She left to become a leading participant in a group seeking to reverse the Brexit referendum result. There she had evidently cosied-up to Keir

Starmer. On 19 February 2020 she had posted an article on the Labour List website, 'Laura Parker: Why I'm backing Keir Starmer for Labour leader'. How Ellis laughed reading her opening words! 'I am backing Sir Keir Starmer because he has placed unifying the party at the heart of his mission'. And so it went on. No wonder the Left was in the doldrums when people like Laura Parker occupied leading positions in the Labourist movement. Ellis went on to read a plug for a book on Cuba by Helen Yaffe. Louis Allday wrote: 'I wanted to write a proper review of this book, but this mess of a year means I might not get round to it. In short, I can't recommend it highly enough! A brilliant, thoughtful and deeply informative look at Cuba (with a focus on the post-Soviet period).' Allday added: 'It's the perfect, informed antidote to the crude anti-Cuba slander of people like Richard Seymour and Owen Jones'. Meanwhile the child played with a sheet of *Frozen* stickers, peeling them off one by one. Ellis connected to YouTube on his phone and played 'Let It Go'. The child adored this song. Ellis baked a quiche and ate it with Heinz baked beans. Later, he read the tweet from BBC Politics @BBCPolitics: *Shadow Chancellor Anneliese Dodds tells #Marr that dealing with anti-Semitism in the Labour party "is more important than any other consideration".* An incredible statement, Ellis thought. It showed how far the Zionist poison had contaminated every aspect of the Labour Party and its leadership of reactionary dullards. Under Sir Keir Starmer the party would not rest until it had expelled or crushed into mute submission every member who dared to criticise apartheid Israel. Elsewhere Sana Saeed tweeted: *Reminder that Gaza is the size of Detroit and Israel does target civilian infrastructure and defines Hamas targets rather broadly.* Finally, Ellis read a tweet from UN Special Procedures @UN_SPExperts: *UN experts condemn #Israel's demolition of the homes and property belonging to a #Palestinian Bedouin community in the northern Jordan Valley of the West Bank, amid a significant rise in property demolitions across the occupied territory. Learn more: http://ow.ly/SjXE50Cpgma*
The tweet was accompanied by a poignant image of a small Palestinian child holding her soft toys amid the rubble of her home. It was the kind of scene which the corporate media of Britain, Europe and the USA would never permit their viewers or readers to see. The daily barbarism of the Jewish state was a taboo topic. Ellis went to bed. He read a few more pages of Truman Capote, then put out the light.

Monday 23rd November

A bright cold sunlit morning. Ellis went for a walk. When he came back he discovered that a friend had pushed a DVD through the letterbox. The sun was very low in the sky. The child was out of sorts. She pointed at something she wanted which was out of reach on the sideboard but every object which was offered to her she rejected. Ellis read through some old copies of the *Times*. When he reached page 86 of the news section (14 November) he came to a fawning platitudinous tribute by Ephraim Mirvis, Chief Rabbi of the United Hebrew Congregations of the Commonwealth, to the recently deceased Zionist fanatic, Rabbi Lord Sacks. According to Mirvis, Sacks was 'a truly great person, someone who has unquestionably changed the world for the better'. An utterly grotesque assertion. Sacks (metaphorically) waded in blood. His silence about the suffering inflicted upon Palestinians said everything about that smug, velvet-tongued hypocrite. Sacks was certainly a man who could have reduced the amount of human suffering in the world. Instead he chose to expand it. He was a man devoid of any moral sense. Ellis moved on to the glossy magazine. There was a fawning and superficial profile of Kamala Harris - classic corporate media sycophancy. Ellis glanced at it and moved on. There was almost nothing in this gleaming trash he wanted to read. It included an ingratiating interview with an actress Ellis had never heard of - Erin Doherty. She had played Princess Anne in the TV series *The Crown*. There was nothing quite like getting a part in *The Crown* to expose an actor or actress as an obsequious toady. Ellis remembered reading a profile of Olivia Colman, in which the actress had spoken with reverence of her deep admiration for the Queen. Erin Doherty belonged to the same mould. PRINCESS ANNE IS MAGNIFICENT. I'M KIND OF IN LOVE WITH HER. That was the headline to Andrew Billen's interview. A puff piece. It transpired that Doherty had acted in the Young Vic's 2019 revival of *My Name is Rachel Corrie*. According to Andrew Billen, Rachel Corrie was 'the 23-year-old American activist killed by an Israeli soldier on the Gaza Strip'. Crushed to death by a Russian immigrant wielding an armoured bulldozer. The brutal murder of Corrie had produced the usual excuses for Zionist atrocity by the Israeli state, reactionary journalists and that entity known as 'the Jewish community'. The Alaskan composer Philip Munger wrote a cantata in Corrie's honour titled *The Skies are Weeping* but in their usual bullying fashion Israel-worshipping Jews put a halt to its premiere on 27 April 2004 at the University of Alaska Anchorage. A local rabbi screeched that the cantata 'romanticised terrorism'. The Israeli state later murdered the film-maker James Miller, the student Thomas Hurndall and the aid worker Iain Hook. Fact: the Jewish state murders with absolute impunity, protected by the US government, the British government, the Conservative Party, the Labour Party, the Liberal Party, and the European Union. Ellis caught up with the *Sunday Times*, October 18 2020. Its lead story was about Caitlin McNama, 32, who said that while working for the Hay literary festival in Abu Dhabi she had been sexually assaulted by Sheik Nahyan bin Mubarak Al Nahyan, the Minister of Tolerance (sic) in the United Arab Emirates cabinet, and a member of Abu Dhabi's ruling family. What interested Ellis about this ugly episode was the light it shed on the degenerate state of British intellectual life. No writer of conscience would consider attending an arts event put on by a seedy dictatorship in the Middle East. But the darlings of corporate culture seemed to possess the ethics of a lamp post. Writers were as narcissistic as actors. Those who had scuttled off to the festival included Bernardine Evaristo, Wole Soyikna, and Jung Chan. No solidarity from these self-promoting writers with Ahmed Mansoor, poet, sentenced to ten years in prison for social media posts 'insulting the status and prestige of the UAE'. No surprise to learn that on the board of the Hay festival is Philippe Sands, laughably described as 'the renowned writer and human rights barrister' (oh, and Zionist). Via the *Media Lens* Twitter page Ellis learned about a new publication, 'Seeing Through The Rubble: The Civilian Impact of the Use of Explosive Weapons in the Fight Against Isis'. It was the latest report, 46 pages in length, from Airwars (https://airwars.org/). Ellis looked up the organisation and learned that it was 'a not-for-profit transparency organisation which monitors military actions and related civilian harm claims in conflict zones, and Dutch peace organisation PAX'. Ellis downloaded the report (https://airwars.org/wp-content/uploads/2020/10/PAXAirwars-Through-the-Rubble.pdf). He would immerse himself in it at a later date. In the meantime he read the summary. The report examined the consequences of the US-led air campaign against Isis since 2014, focusing on Raqqa in Syria and Mosul and Hawijah in Iraq. Ellis learned that the primary effects of explosive weapons are caused by the blast wave and fragmentation of the warhead after detonation. These cause injuries such as the bursting of hollow organs (ears, lungs and the gastro-intestinal tract), brain damage when the brain crushes into the side of the skull, and burns and projectile wounds from weapon fragments. Airwars and PAX estimate that between 9,000 and 12,000 civilians died in the fighting — "with most killed by explosive weapons with wide area effects." The report notes "despite declaring that it had struck more than 900 targets in Mosul during the battle for the city, the official UK position remains that no civilians were harmed in its own urban strikes". The report considered the Syrian city of Raqqa. Airwars and Amnesty International conservatively estimated that at least 1,600 civilians died as a result of coalition strikes on the city. The local monitoring network *Raqqa is Being Slaughtered Silently* reported that 90 per cent of the city had been levelled in the fighting, with eight hospitals, 29 mosques, five universities, more than 40 schools, and the city's water irrigation system all destroyed. The report concluded that "The great majority of both the urban destruction and civilian harm in Raqqa resulted largely from the actions of just one party to the fighting: the United States". Far from not being newsworthy, or of no interest to the British public, the report included very important information about the huge loss of civilian life caused by US and British military intervention in Iraq and Syria. But, typically, this report was shunned by the corporate media of Britain and the USA. It was as if it never existed. Elsewhere on the internet Ellis came across a revealing exchange between Dave Robinson and the reactionary editor of right-wing faux-Left rag the *New Statesman*. Dave Robinson @davidrobbo66 tweeted. *The argument that the BoD takes an equally tough line on antisemitism within the Tory party as it does within Labour is nonsensical. Ditto the Jewish Chronicle. Ditto the EHRC. Antisemitism on the left is shameful but let's not pretend that the discourse on the matter is balanced.* Stephen Bush @stephenkb retorted: *Has the EHRC received a submission from the Campaign Against Antisemitism, the Jewish Labour Movement and Labour Against Antisemitism? The answer is no, so the "ditto the EHRC" argument is nonsensical.* What was revealing about this exchange was that Bush actually took seriously the so-called Campaign Against Antisemitism, the so-called Jewish Labour Movement and so-called Labour Against Antisemitism. Of course these outfits haven't complained about anti-Semitism in the Conservative Party. That's not their purpose. Elsewhere Ellis came across a tweet by Jess Barnard, the newly-elected chair of Young Labour. On it she published a statement about the control-freakery of the party bureaucracy under Keir Starmer. *On Saturday, following a vote of the Young Labour National Committee, a decision was reached to publish a statement in opposition to the removal of the whip from Jeremy Corbyn MP. Earlier today, I received an e-mail from Labour's head office ordering me to remove this statement "immediately" and alleging that Young Labour had "missused" Labour "branding" to provide "commentary on factional disputes".* There was much more. Elsewhere Ellis learned that Starmer intended to block left-leaning Ian Murray of the Fire Brigades Union from becoming Chair of the NEC, according to the convention that when the Chair stood down the Vice-Chair was the replacement, and instead appoint elderly reactionary Margaret Beckett to the position. Elsewhere, Ellis learned that Labour's chief whip had asked Jeremy Corbyn to "unequivocally, unambiguously and without reservation" apologise for claiming that the scale of anti-Semitism in the party was "dramatically overstated for political reasons". In a letter obtained by the PA news agency, Nick Brown said the former Labour leader's response to a damning Equality and Human Rights Commission (EHRC) report caused "distress and pain" to the Jewish community. Mr Brown, writing to Mr Corbyn on Monday, said that to inform an investigation into whether the Islington North MP broke the party's code of conduct he had asked him to "unequivocally, unambiguously and without reservation apologise for your comments made on the morning of 29 October 2020, in particular for saying 'One anti-Semite is one too many, but the scale of the problem was also dramatically overstated for political reasons by our opponents inside and outside the party, as well as by much of the media', which caused such distress and pain to Jewish members of the Labour Party and the wider Jewish community?" Brown also asked Mr Corbyn to confirm that he would remove or edit his response – which he posted on Facebook, and asked for an assurance that he would co-operate fully with the party as it seeks to implement the EHRC's recommendations. And so this preposterous Zionist witch-hunt continued. The poison that had started with the Balfour Declaration was still eating like a foul acid through British politics one-hundred-and-three years later. Ellis watched the news headlines on Sky, then went to bed. He drew close to the end of *Breakfast at Tiffany's* but decided to leave the final pages for tomorrow.

Tuesday 24th November

A dull damp morning. A woman called Lucy Yardley was being interviewed on the radio. Ellis was struck by her persistent use of high raised terminals. Later he looked her up on Google. Lucy Yardley OBE CPsychol FBPsS is a Professor of Health Psychology. Also on the 'Today' programme was one of the BBC's cadre of imperialist pimps, who was enthusing about Joe Biden's foreign policy appointments, including Antony Blinken. Ellis went out at 7.28am with a bag of clothes for a charity and positioned it at the front of his property. Some eighty minutes later a small white van stopped there but Ellis did not see who got out of it. The van drove off and the bag had gone. Ellis ate his breakfast cereal at the computer. He read some tweets by Daniel Finn, who commented on yesterday's news of the letter from the chief whip to Corbyn. *Deranged, Kafkaesque nonsense worthy of a Stalinist show trial: "You must apologize for saying something that is incontestably true and erase the evidence of you saying it." Corbyn should chuck this rancid communication in the bin and get his lawyers on the case.* Daniel Finn added: *The only proper response to this from left-wing Labour MPs would be to repeat the substance of Corbyn's statement—not simply defend his right to say it—and challenge their incompetent, feather-brained leader to suspend them, too. Escalate the crisis for Starmer, don't back down.* Fat chance, thought Ellis. The spines of the parliamentary Left were every bit as rubbery as Corbyn's. Ellis chuckled. He was chuckly as the child. He'd just discovered the twitter account of Moby Duck [https://twitter.com/amphitryoniades] The posts of someone with a sense of humour. Next he read a tweet by Paul O'Connell. *Labourism encourages such wilful blindness, and even now the left of the Labour Party are calling for "common sense and compromise" to prevail - the hangman does not compromise with the condemned - labourism is a perilous dead end.* Someone else tweeted that the so-called Socialist group in the Labour Party hadn't tweeted for five days. Their cowardly silence said everything. Ellis went for a walk. The bookshop window displayed copies of the new book by the blood-drenched war criminal, Barack Obama. Later, home again, Ellis followed a link to a digest of an article by one Francesco Belcastro, with the enticing title 'Sport, politics and the struggle over 'normalization' in post-Oslo Israel and Palestine. *This article uses sport as a theoretical tool to analyse Palestinian–Israeli relations in the post-Oslo era. It does so by looking at two major sport events,* the start of the Giro d'Italia cycling race and the Israel–Argentina football match. These two events were scheduled to take place in Israel and the Occupied Territories within a month of each other, in May and June of 2018, respectively. Despite frequent claims of its 'neutral' and 'apolitical' nature, sport is closely intertwined with issues of identity, representation, community and nation. Next Ellis turned to Max Blumenthal's twitter account. He mentioned a tweet by Matthew Duss praising Joe Biden's foreign affairs appointees. *I knew Matt would eventually grovel for a job in some Democratic admin when he wrote this review of my book yrs ago in a centrist journal, positioning himself as a sensible moderate taking on an anti-Zionist & a Likudnik - painting both as equally extreme.* Ellis followed the link to Duss's 2015 review article on the *Democracy* website, which was entitled 'American Progressives and Israel'. Duss considered Joshua Muravchik's *Making David into Goliath: How the World Turned Against Israel* and Max Blumenthal's *Goliath: Life and Loathing in Greater Israel.* Astonishingly, this centrist chump was, it turned out, foreign policy advisor for Sen. Bernie Sanders. No wonder Sanders' position on Israel was so flabby. Next Ellis discovered that another pro-Palestinian tweeter had been closed down by Twitter at the behest of the Zionist lobby. *After being falsely smeared by @StopAntisemites as a Jew hater for her BDS activism & also made the target of trolls from 4chan, Twitter suspends @oliviakatbi. Just like in the US where we supposedly have a 1st amendment, speech rules are bent to silence BDS supporters on Twitter* wrote Alex Rubinstein, who Blumenthal retweeted. Blumenthal added: *Stop Antisemites is run by Liora Rez, a stooge of Canary Mission blacklist backer @AdamMilstein.* Meanwhile Kevin Gosztola @kgosztola commented that *On April 21, 2017, days after WikiLeaks founder Julian Assange was expelled from Ecuador embassy and arrested, Blinken said he would have loved to have seen Obama admin find a way to charge Assange.* Jake Sullivan @jakejsullivan tweeted: *President-elect Biden taught me what it takes to safeguard our national security at the highest levels of our government. Now, he has asked me to serve as his National Security Advisor. In service, I will do everything in my power to keep our country safe.* But Ellis learned from twitter: Jake Sullivan in 2012: "Al Qaeda is on our side in Syria". Max Blumenthal commented: *After Jake Sullivan chirped to his boss about Al Qaeda being "on our side in Syria," he advocated for more covert arms shipments to the Syrian insurgency the jihadist group was leading. Expect more wise moves like this in the months and years to come.* Ben Norton tweeted*: the reality is 90% of the policies of these Biden administration cabinet officials are going to be the same. They're all neoliberal warmongers. The bipartisan consensus will continue.* Aaron Maté tweeted: The Washington Post *just published an article called: "Washington's aristocracy hopes a Biden presidency will make schmoozing great again." They quickly changed it to "Washington's establishment." Someone must've worried how the plebs might* *react.* The *World Index* published a list of *The most dangerous places to travel in 2020.* 1. Libya 2. Syria 3. Iraq 4. Yemen 5. Somalia. Someone tweeted: *Another thing the top 5 have in common is that they have all been bombed by the U.S.* Ben Norton tweeted: *There were two more massacres of human rights activists in just 12 hours in Colombia. 303 social movement activists have been killed in *76 massacres* so far in 2020. But they happened in US client state Colombia, not Venezuela, so don't expect outrage.* Aaron Maté tweeted: *Really looking forward to celebrating a special holiday this Friday: honoring the two-year anniversary of @lukeharding1968's blockbuster report for the @guardian, under editor @KathViner on Paul Manafort's multiple secret meetings with Julian Assange in the Ecuadorian embassy.* This was sarcasm. Luke Harding's exclusive was a notorious fraud. It was classic fake news. Harding had allowed himself to be the sewage pipe for the discharge of a fabricated story from the murky world of 'intelligence'. But Kath Viner had stubbornly refused to acknowledge the newspaper's grievous error. Viner had the classic arrogance of the corporate journalist. The financial rewards for pimping for the status quo were substantial. Kath Viner was rewarded with £391,000 a year. Ellis took a break from the internet to continue reading a book he was reviewing. When he returned he learned that the so-called 'Left' had stormed out of today's meeting of the National Executive Committee of the Labour Party, because of the stitch-up over the position of chair. 'New Labour' Iraq-war-supporting Margaret Beckett had been elected. No surprise to learn that slithery 'unaligned' local party representative Ann Black, Scottish Labour leader Richard Leonard, and GMB reps Tom Warnett and Kathy Abu-Bakir all voted in favour of Beckett for chair. You could almost always rely on a Labour Party trade's unionist to be a reactionary. The blood-spattered reactionary Margaret Beckett had fully supported the last murderous Israeli invasion of Lebanon. Moreover her snout was well and truly deep in the trough. She had claimed £72,537 expenses for her THIRD home. She was at the same time a property owning landlord. She'd claimed £600 for hanging baskets and pot plants. She had in December 2015 urged the bombing of Syria, supporting Cameron against Corbyn. And once the news was out the fat property developer Jon Lansman tweeted *Get over it!* (how on earth had this grotesque, obese and politically-slippery slob ended up as one of Corbyn's best mates? It supplied yet more evidence of Corbyn's poor judgement.) Ellis turned to the Twitter account of Louis Allday, who'd written: *A lot of time-wasting debates wouldn't be needed if much of the UK/US Left had ever fully come to terms with the scale & depravity of the war crimes those two countries have committed against Iraq & what the implications of that should be for everyone who was involved in them.* Louis Allday added: *During Israel's war on Lebanon in 2006, Margaret Beckett - then Blair's Foreign Sec. & new chair of the NEC - blamed Hezbollah, fully backed Israel & like the US, refused to call for a ceasefire, allowing the war to go on, as Israel massacred Lebanese* *civilians on a daily basis.* Louis Allday added: *She also voted consistently for the war on Iraq. The salient point here being, it's virtually impossible to find a senior member of the Labour Party without blood on their hands because it is an imperialist party, it's not just Iraq - it always has been and it always will be.* Ellis continued reading a book. Later, he baked cod and tomatoes, which he ate with fried chips and peas. He watched *Lunch Hour.* Later, in bed, Ellis finished *Breakfast at Tiffany's* and began *Answered Prayers.*

Wednesday 25th November

A bright dry morning. Ellis went online. His first Twitter account of the day for perusal was Ed McNally's. But today he read: *These Tweets are protected Only approved followers can see @edmcnally96's Tweets. To request access, click Follow.* Next Ellis turned to Louis Allday, who retweeted a story from NBC News: *8 million Americans slipped into poverty amid Coronavirus pandemic.* Allday wrote: *They didn't 'slip' into anything, they were pushed.* Louis Allday retweeted a story from ABC News: President-elect Joe Biden: *"In calls from world leaders...I've been struck by how much they're looking forward to the United States reasserting its historic role as a global leader."* Louis Allday translated: *Under Trump's leadership...the superficial mask of American liberalism dropped entirely... Biden's win is...the start of a concerted effort to lift that mask back up, restore America's image and get back to the business of imperialism disguised as 'global problem-solving'.* Louis Allday cited Carnegie Europe (evidently a crypto-left think tank) which offered up a paper entitled 'A Feminist Foreign Policy to Deal with Iran? Assessing the EU's Options'. It was, as Allday observed, quite literally feminist imperialism in its demand that 'a regime built on discrimination against women' needed to be dealt with by the benign EU, whiuch should put 'human security and human rights at the center of the discussion'. Except, of course, when the discriminator was the Jewish state. That pampered torture regime would go on getting trade deals, weapons and subsidies. Louis Allday cited Deepa Kumar: *"As several Third World Feminists have argued, a historical weakness of liberal feminism in the West has been its racist, patronizing attitude towards women of color who have been seen less as allies/agents and more as victims in need of rescue."* Deepa Kumar went to the heart of the matter: *"It is liberalism's understanding of the state as a neutral body, rather than as a coercive apparatus used to advance capitalism and empire, which is at the root of such perspectives."* Ellis moved on. Jonathon Shafi tweeted: *As we stand on the brink of Starmer voting through a Brexit deal, it should be clear that the "People's Vote" was primarily designed to undermine the left. Starmer opposed a Corbyn-led Brexit only to end up supporting a Tory Brexit led by Johnson.* Paul O'Connell retweeted an old tweet of his own: *Periodic reminder that the "People's Vote"/Stop Brexit "movement" was, in* large part, an anti-Corbyn/anti-socialist initiative led by the reactionary middle and upper classes - here's Gina Miller in early 2019 making that quite clear. He cited an interview in which Gina Miller had remarked: 'I was more worried about Corbyn than I was about Brexit.' Meanwhile Suzanne Moore was everywhere. **'Client Journalism' Expert** @ClientJournoExp tweeted: *"I'm being silenced!" cries Suzanne Moore from a national newspaper.* Ellis followed a link to an article by Ellen Scott on the *Metro* website https://metro.co.uk/ Author/ellen-scott/13th June 2020, titled 'A guide to DARVO, the gaslighting response people give when they're called out for bad behaviour'. *DARVO is an acronym that describes the typical response of a guilty person when they've been accused of bad behaviour. It's traditionally referred to in discussions of a perpetrator of sexual crimes, such as rape or physical abuse, but is a pattern that pops up in many other situations in which people are called out for something negative. It stands for Deny, Attack, and Reverse Victim and Offender.* Ellen Scott described the various stages, which concluded with the 'Reverse Victim and Offender' stage. It was prophetically relevant to a narcissistic whinger like Suzanne Moore. *The accused person will turn things around and say that actually, they're not guilty of doing something terrible. In fact,* they *are the ones being treated poorly… they might focus their statement on how they feel 'bullied' by the accusations, so those reading feel that the person who has been called out is actually the victim, facing online abuse rather than being challenged on their actions.* The *Daily Telegraph* tweeted: *Having left* **The Guardian** *after months of feeling hounded, columnist @suzanne_moore explains how women are the main victims of the Left's cancel culture.* **jonathan nunn** @demarionunn sarcastically tweeted: *the suzanne moore "my cancellation hell" tour of 2020/2021 dates have been announced 25/11 - Daily Mail 26/11 - Unherd 1/12 - Daily Telegraph 4/12 - New Statesman 12/12 - The Spectator 17/12 - Quilette 30/12 - Question Time 3/1 - Joe Rogan Experience 9/1 - The Guardian (again).* **Duncan Hothersall** tweeted: *It seems to me that Suzanne Moore's problem was that she *wasn't* cancelled, she was just disagreed with. She ended up having to cancel herself in order to be able to emerge triumphant and get the adulation she is now receiving from those determined to ignore that stubborn fact.* **Bryn** @brynismyname tweeted: *Suzanne Moore has been silenced! And in being silenced she has been interviewed by… three major publications? The arrogance and lack of insight dripping from the articles is palpable.* Reading the *Media Lens* twitter page, Ellis came across a link to the latest article by Jonathan Cook, on the *Middle East Eye* website. *Trenchant criticism of Israel - of the kind so urgently necessary – is now increasingly off-limits. Instead western states are actually defaming and outlawing even the most limited forms of grassroots, non-violent action against Israel, like the BDS movement.* Jonathan Cook added: *In the 1970s Israel made efforts to obscure its ideological character, it has long since abandoned such pretence. In 2018 Israel* passed the Nation-State Law, https://www.middleeasteye.net/news/israel-passes-nation-state-law-enshrining-jewish-supremacy, *making its apartheid explicit. The law affirmed superior legal rights for Jewish citizens over a large minority of Palestinian citizens.* Jonathan Cook went on: *We have now reached the point where, as Pompeo's statement underscores, it is criticism of Israel and Zionism that is viewed as racism. In this topsy-turvy worldview, nuclear-armed Israel is the victim, not the Palestinians who have been dispossessed and ethnically cleansed by Israel for decades. This derangement is so entrenched that last year the House of Representatives passed a near-unanimous resolution – pushed by the Israel lobby group AIPAC – denouncing any boycott of Israel as antisemitic. Some 32 US states have passed legislation uniquely denying First Amendment rights to those who support a boycott of Israel in solidarity with oppressed Palestinians. Other states have similar legislation in the pipeline. The German parliament passed a resolution last year that declared boycotting Israel – a state occupying Palestinians for more than five decades – comparable to the Nazi slogan "Don't buy from Jews". Bonn has the power to deny public funds to any group that supports, however tangentially, such a boycott.* Jonathan Cook added: *The IHRA definition is now widely accepted in the West, making it all but impossible to mount a defence against the malicious characterisation of support for Palestinian rights as equivalent to hatred of Jews. Antisemitism is the insidious charge that sticks to anything it touches. The stain is all but impossible to remove. Which is why those standing up for human rights – and against racism and oppression – are going to find themselves ever more aggressively condemned as antisemitic.* Elsewhere on the internet Ellis learned that Chuka Umunna and Luciana Berger had both been recently employed by PR firm Edelman, an outfit used by the Saudi dictatorship to sanitise the destruction of the Huwaitat tribal community. The rubble of their homes will be the site of a new megacity. It grew dark. The child played with a jewellery dish. Ellis came across an article by Paul Waugh on the Huffington Post website. It was headlined **McDonnell Urges Corbyn To 'Calculate The Pain' Caused To Jews In Anti-Semitism Row.** The thoroughly useless and deeply damaging MP John McDonnell had *urged Jeremy Corbyn and Labour to "keep on apologising" to Jewish people for the pain caused by anti-Semitism in the Pa*rty. In a new podcast McDonnell made clear that *the case numbers were not relevant and the key was to acknowledge the impact of abuse on the UK's Jewish community.* "Numerically, the number of cases of anti-Semitism within the Labour party might be small, but that's not the issue. It's the pain," he said. What utter garbage, thought Ellis. The existence of *any* anti-Semitism in the party had *never* been the issue. The issue had always been Palestine and the cynical use of the charge of racism by the so-called 'Jewish community'. The cretinous McDonnell went on digging the hole deeper. "The anti-Semitism issue has been a nightmare, we've got to come out of this nightmare. It's been a really dark night," he said. *McDonnell's remarks echo those of Momentum founder Jon Lansman, who told the LabourList website this month the personal pain he felt at Corbyn's remarks and their timing.* These two individuals had the intellectual awareness of a carrot. A thought which Ellis accepted was deeply offensive to carrots, a tasty and useful vegetable, which could not in any way be held responsible for a certain similarity in skin tone to the complexion of the 45th President of the United States of America. *McDonnell said that he worried that many younger Labour members who flocked to the party under Corbyn were now leaving it over the anti-Semitism row and its consequences.* No, they were leaving because the Party was back in the hands of the pro-war, pro-austerity, gerrymandering right wing. "I'm saying that you've got to stay in, and take us to the next level of these struggles. Accept that our generation, my generation made mistakes around this. And we need to move on." Struggles? What struggles? The PLP was stuffed with corrupt reactionary careerists, and the self-styled Socialist Group had the firmness of blancmange and the fighting spirit of a slug. **JamieSW** @jsternweiner tweeted: *McDonnell says: facts don't matter, all that matters is that people feel "pain". This as the JLM is characterising branch motions that criticise the Party's response to the EHRC as "harassment and intimidation" that impacts "mental and physical wellbeing".* Dim-witted Aaron Bastani replied: *McDonnell is a politician. That's not meant as a criticism but it's why he's different to Corbyn, who really isn't. Once you get that you understand a lot.* The fatuity of Bastani was remarkable. (Thinking about it, 'The Fatuity of Bastani' would be a good title for a satirical short story, Ellis felt. But his days of writing satirical short stories were probably over.) JamieSW retorted: *His advice on this issue has been consistently awful, even by those opportunistic standards.* Matt Kennard @kennardmatt joined in, tweeting: *The establishment had two main methods of destroying Corbynism: Brexit and the "antisemitism crisis". McDonnell called both of them catastrophically wrong, strategically and morally. Corbyn needs to stop listening to him asap.* Sienna Rodgers tweeted her knowledge of an email from the so-called Jewish Labour Movement. *The email offers practical guidance in light of a "growing level of harassment and intimidation taking place" including motions condemning the party's actions in responding to the EHRC and subsequent events. Advises members to put their mental and physical wellbeing first.* So now the Zionists equated motions passed at CLP meetings with 'harassment and intimidation'. The impudence of the JLM was boundless and the feebleness of the Labour so-called 'Left' in responding to it was no less remarkable. Ellis glanced at the 10pm Sky headlines and decided not to watch the programme. He went to bed and read a few pages of *Answered Prayers*.

Dull and grey. Ellis discovered that Ed McNally @edmcnally96 was back. McNally had been listening to the BBC 'Today' programme. He tweeted: *Ideology doesn't get more naked than Nick Robinson asking Sunak on #R4today if he's "tough enough" to bring back austerity.* On a similar theme, Paul O'Connell tweeted: *The richest MP that has ever sat in parliament, in a government that has squandered billions in handouts to their mates, is telling us that we all have to tighten our belts and lower our expectations to pay for the crisis of capitalism, while the rich go on getting richer.* Adverting to the Suzanne Moore saga, Solomon Hughes tweeted: *All Labour Branches have been banned from even discussing Jeremy Corbyn's suspension, after many branches voted to say he should be re-admitted. That's the big headline about 'free speech crisis,' not some newspaper columnist resigning of their own free will.* Ellis learned that the *Guardian* yesterday refused to publish Steve Bell's comic strip mocking Keir Starmer in the role of a dominatrix, pictured with a whip alongside Jeremy Corbyn. Sycophantic Ash Sarkar tweeted: *I feel very, very lucky to work alongside @piercepenniless. I don't think there's a better, more mellifluous or precise writer on the British left.* Roger Errington @rjerrington retorted: *'Optics Left' stick together + crawling to the Boss. This is an Establishment-friendly anti-Corbyn pro-McDonnell's triangulation piece which praises Owen Jones, barely mentions the rancid neoliberal MSM - or Starmer - and is the worst form of early revisionism. I'd shun Novara...* Whereas Andrew Fisher @FisherAndrew79 wrote: *As you'd expect from @piercepenniless, this is astute, thoughtful and beautifully written on the Corbyn project and the recent books about it.* To which Roger Errington replied: *God not you too, Andrew. It's an 'Optics Left' Establishment-friendly piece which favours the 'antisemitism' smear, slags off your old Boss & praises McDonnell's treacherous disastrous triangulation with the Blairites. You've finally shown which side you're on - it's not the Left.* Andrew Fisher retorted: *What rubbish. Antisemitism was and remains a problem on bits of the left. It doesn't slag off Jeremy, it's balanced about his period as leader. Jeremy and John remain friends, and I remain friends with both of them. Being a divisive twerp does nothing for the left.* It was a cold day. Ellis did some gardening. Later he began reading a hardback. He watched *Rebel Without a Cause*. He watched the 10pm Sky News and the first sixty seconds of the papers review. The big story was angry reaction to the tier system of restrictions before Christmas. Business owners in the hospitality trade spoke of their sense of injustice. **ALL WIGHT FOR SOME**, quipped the *Sun*, alluding to the Isle of Wight and Cornwall, where the lowest national level of restrictions were to be applied. **THE NORTH SEES RED** punned the huge headline in *Metro*. Ellis went to bed and read a few more pages of *Answered Prayers*.

Friday 27th November

Ellis did not get out of bed until 8.30am. It was a bright crisp sunny morning, with frost on the roof tiles, car windows iced-up, and a mist hanging over the streets. Ellis ate his breakfast cereal sitting at his computer. Ed McNally's Twitter page alerted him to the latest example of Keir Starmer's war on the Left and internal Labour Party democracy, such as it was. Evidently it was now forbidden to discuss matters of urgent political concern at Labour Party meetings. David Evans, General Secretary, had instructed that 'motions which seek to repudiate the findings of the EHRC or question its competency to conduct the investigation remain not competent business for branches or CLPs'. Moreover 'other motions (including expressions of solidarity, and matters relating to the internal processes of the CLP) are providing a flashpoint for the expression of views that undermine the Labour Party's ability to provide a safe and welcoming space for all members, including our Jewish members'. The poison of Zionism just went on spreading, wider and deeper. Ed McNally commented: *Labour banning members from discussing the EHRC's 'competency' sends a pretty clear and grim signal given the recent appointment of a hard-right Islamophobe as a commissioner, and the findings about its total failure to do anything about anti-Black racism.* McNally also reproduced part of the LRB review article by James Butler, which Ellis had been unable to read since it was hidden behind a paywall. Novara's finest had written: 'the leader's office would prefer to avoid factional conflict'. Yes, thought Ellis. With Novara supplying the analysis no wonder the Left in Britain was in such a stunted and horizontal state. Ellis's sense of alienation from the prevailing literary and political culture of his society was acute. He went outside and did some weeding. Later he watched the child on a mobile phone screen as she played with her nativity set. She began drawing on the face of baby Jesus. Ellis baked salmon and boiled some potatoes. He listened to the 6pm Radio 4 news. He learned that the Jewish state had carried out another act of terrorism, murdering Iranian scientist Mohesen Fakrizadeh on Iranian soil. BBC News did its best to justify the assassination, referring to a 'covert nuclear weapons programme'. A claim devoid of any evidence. For comment the BBC selected, unbelievably, Benjamin Netanyahu. The calculated insolence of the BBC news propaganda machine was of astounding proportions. Naturally this act of state terrorism was greeted with silence by hypocritical western states and the US government. Ellis remembered that this year had begun with an act of state terrorism against Iran by the US, which had murdered Qassem Suleimani. The United States of America - the world's number one rogue terror state, closely followed by its belligerent ally, Israel. Both receiving every encouragement from the UK and the EU. Meanwhile it was revealed that a bunch of Labour MPs had set up an organisation called 'Love Socialism'. On Twitter Ed McNally scrutinised its membership and their past history, and sarcastically summarised it as: *Love Socialism, Love Brussels, Love NATO. Much grassroots, very radical!* He added: *It's funny, given Love Socialism's attack on 'top-down, bureaucratic, authoritarian tendencies', that: a) its leading members happily abstained on Spycops and Overseas Ops bills. b) among the supporters are a group of MPs whose seats were stitched up by Unite-Momentum fixers.* He added: *For people wondering what coheres Love Socialism: none of the SCG MPs listed as supporters on its website signed the SCG statement opposing Corbyn's initial suspension.* Elsewhere, Ellis read more about Jewish barbarism: *87 Palestinians will be evicted from their homes in East Jerusalem after a court ruled in favor of right-wing Israeli settler groups. They have lived in the Silwan neighborhood for decades. Nearly 11,000 Palestinians in the occupied West Bank have been displaced since 2009.* Ellis began watching *Song of Summer.* In bed he read the sentence: Walleyed, pipe-sucking, pasty-hued Sartre and his spinsterish moll, De Beauvoir, were usually propped in a corner like an abandoned pair of ventriloquist's dolls.

Saturday 28th November

A piano piece by Chopin tinkled downstairs. The sun shone from a sky that was mostly cloudy. Ellis made himself a cappuccino and took it through to the living room. Later he looked to see if Ed McNally had had anything to say today on Twitter. Ellis learned that Nadia Whittome MP (a member of that assembly of shallow parliamentary hucksters who liked to identify themselves, laughably, as the Socialist Campaign Group) had roundly denounced her own constituency party for passing a motion (presumably in support of Corbyn) which she asserted was 'clearly out of order'. Her objection was overruled by the chair of the meeting. 'The atmosphere and tone of the meeting that proceeded was wholly unacceptable,' she complained, 'leading to a Jewish member of the Labour Party feeling they had no choice but to leave the meeting'. Doing a Ruth Smeeth, Ellis suspected, although as usual where this kind of thing was juicily said no detail was supplied. By 10.23pm last night Lee Harpin of the *Jewish Chronicle* was gloating: 'Breaking: I understand that the Chair of Nottingham East CLP has been suspended tonight. This is prompt and effective action by the @UKLabour leadership'. Ellis read Michael Walker, @michaeljswalker, who had tweeted: *Of the @novaramediaa gang I was always the most keen to give @Keir_Starmer a chance. It's now clear: He's shifty as f*%k.* Who was Michael Walker? wondered Ellis. He clicked on the photograph and realised Walker was the bald-headed one who'd appeared in a fatuous video about anti-Semitism, which Corbyn had stupidly endorsed. Ellis only knew about Michael Walker's tweet because the infinitely smarter Asa Winstanley had replied: *It was always clear that Starmer was a right-winger, you were just refusing to* acknowledge that obvious fact. *Anyone taking £50,000 from the Israel lobby and declaring themselves a supporter of "Zionism without qualification" was never going to be a genuine socialist.* On Sky News a typical corporate news journalist spoke about 'the Iranian regime'. The word 'government' was not permitted for official enemies, no matter how democratic they might be. This presstitute - Ellis had switched off before the name came up - would never refer to 'the Israeli regime', still less 'the Israeli apartheid regime'. And the marvel was that it was all internalised. No one told these hacks what to say. They did it quite voluntarily. They knew the conventions and strictly adhered to them. As he consumed a bowl of lunchtime soup Ellis read Tony Greenstein's latest post: 'Obituary - the Death of an Establishment Bigot - Rabbi Dr Jonathan Sacks (8 March 1948 - 7 November 2020)'. As always, the prodigiously well-informed Greenstein did not disappoint. *He was a pretentious windbag who wrote over 20 books without saying anything worthwhile. Sacks flattered to deceive and created an aura of profundity..* And: *Sacks was a vehement Zionist and opposed to anything remotely approaching a universalist outlook. He used his academic background in philosophy in order to legitimise Jewish chauvinism and particularism. His academic learning was employed to defend Jewish exceptionalism, muddying it with a commitment to interfaith 'dialogue'.* And: *It says a lot about the intellectual poverty of the organised, synagogue-going British Jewish community around the United Synagogue, that someone like Sacks was treated with veneration. Sacks was an intellectual fraud posing as someone with deep insight into the human condition.* And: *Sacks was a bigot who dressed up his prejudices in flowery language, sophistry and semantics.For all his fine, measured words, he lent his weight to the sanitizing of bigotry and racism.* And: *Jonathan Sacks, with his affected profundity and learning, was an Establishment courier, flattering those with privilege and power but with nothing to say to the dispossessed. He was a man with little in the way of original thought. He simply repackaged the mundane.* This was, thought Ellis, undoubtedly the only accurate obituary to appear. Afterwards, on the twitter account of Daniel Finn, Ellis came across a link to an old article which noted that at the Jewish Labour Movement Labour leadership contest hustings Peston asked if all the candidates would regard the statement "Israel, its policies, and the circumstances surrounding its creation are racist" as anti-Semitic. All answered yes. It demonstrated just how reactionary and intellectually impoverished the so-called Left candidates like Rebecca Long-Bailey actually were. It clouded over and the sun vanished. The night drew in. The child looked at the Christmas tree. Ball, she said. Ellis clicked on Craig Murray's blog and read his today's post: 'The State You May Not Criticise'. It concerned yet another outfit, 'The All-Party Parliamentary Group Against Antisemitism'. Andrew Percy MP, Co-Chair, Catherine McKinnell MP, Co-Chair, and Dr Lisa Cameron MP, Vice-Chair, had jointly written to Amazon to complain that

'Alexa' was emitting anti-Semitic answers to questions. Examples were listed, including one citing material on Craig Murray's blog. The complainants pompously informed Amazon that they had contacted the Home Secretary, Priti Patel, and the police, inviting them to see if there had been criminal 'breaches of communications or racial incitement legislation'. Craig Murray wrote: It is worth looking at precisely what the MPs are complaining of in my case. Let's look at the exact passage: "Question: Is Israel guilty of war crimes? Answer: Here's something I found on the web: according to www.craigmurray.org.uk, ethnic cleansing on a massive scale and serial human rights abuse, including war crimes, yes, Israel is guilty of these atrocities." Murray commented: I maintain that the answer given from my website is self-evidently true and highly capable of proof. It states fact which a large majority of the public would recognise as true. Yet I am told by a journalist from the *Times* who contacted me, that on the basis of this incoherent letter from self-selecting MP's, Amazon have blocked Alexa from quoting my website. This is only a tiny example of the removal of access to dissenting opinions – dissenting as in not conforming to the wishes of the political Establishment, although not diverging from objective truth. The trend towards this censorship on the internet is massive. Murray noted that Lisa Cameron is an SNP MP, adding that the SNP's large cohort of MPs at Westminster had become very comfortable there with their life of privilege and large income, and had lurched further to the right. The SNP had now dumped its commitment to unilateral nuclear disarmament. Land Reform has been reduced to the foundation of a Scottish Land Commission which can put public money towards other funds raised by community groups to buy out great landlords in specific tracts at an assessed "market price". *The great success of the much touted land reform is that it has put £5 million of public money straight into the pocket of the Duke of Buccleuch, for some tiny and insignificant portions of his vast estates, marginal and despoiled moorland he was probably glad to be shot of. The Chair of Buccleuch Estates, Benny Higgins, is also economic adviser to Nicola Sturgeon.* From the *Media Lens* website Ellis learned that slithy Owen Jones had written a new article on the Labour Party for today's *Guardian*. Referring to the aftermath of the publication of the risible EHRC report, Jones sobbed: 'This protracted dispute is causing genuine hurt and distress to Jewish people across the political spectrum'. Ah, more hurt feelings - but no names. Evidence-free, as always. But to be fair to Slithy, it was useful to be reminded that Starmer's political operation – charged with running relations between the leadership and 'stakeholders' - vampire hunters! - including the Parliamentary party, unions and NEC – is run by Jenny Chapman and Matt Pound. Pound is the deeply repellent individual pictured on social media alongside vile Luke Akehurst and one Marlon Solomon, wearing ZIONIST SHITLORD T-shirts. As for Jenny Chapman. *A supporter of war and the military. Generally voted against higher taxes on plane tickets. Generally voted against a statutory* register of lobbyists. *Almost always voted against limits on success fees paid to lawyers in no-win, no-fee cases.* Yes, we get the picture. A classic Labour Party MP - no friend of the poor, the organised working-class, the environment, or those unfortunate enough to live in countries which the US chooses to bomb or to invade. Ellis read to the end of Slithy's column. It was as shallow and vacuous as you might expect. Absurdly, Jones claimed that 'The left is far more powerful than it was before 2015: in the parliamentary party, in the unions, in the membership, in civil society through institutions such as Momentum…' Garbage. It ended with an instruction to this mythical 'left', which, according to Slithy, needed to 'untangle discussions of its progressive vision to end inequality from the evils of antisemitism'. Jones was pure poison, Ellis felt. A slippery fence-sitting, fair-weather careerist. Another crypto leftist who diluted and deflected. Ellis ate a cheese soufflé with mashed-potato and cauliflower. He watched *Yesterday*. He went to bed. It makes one *wonder* about Beckett, thought Truman Capote's avatar, and his pretentious aloofness, austerity. I guess I would have been pretty interested in her swag, he offered, by way of analysis.

Sunday 29th November

A dull damp morning. Ellis drank a mug of tea in bed while listening to the 8am headlines. Later he came across a tweeter named Ollie Daly, who sarcastically retweeted Owen Jones: *Here's my new interview with @piersmorgan: on the Tories' disastrous handling of the pandemic, on trans rights, "cancel culture" and egg emojis.* To which Daly responded: *Ah don't you love creating independent left media to give a platform to voices generally ignored by the media such as *checks notes* Piers Morgan…* The corporate media had been utterly silent about Starmer's efforts to suppress support for Corbyn from constituency Labour Party branches but now that a bogus anti-Semitism spin could be placed on the matter reactionary BBC News naturally sprang into action. **Nottingham East Labour CLP chair suspended after Corbyn motion row. The chair of a Labour group has been suspended after a motion at an online meeting described as "clearly out of order" by the area's MP was passed.** *The Nottingham East CLP broke party rules with a motion calling for the restoration of the whip to Jeremy Corbyn, the BBC understands. One Jewish party member said he felt the atmosphere was so "hostile" he had to leave. Steve Lapsley, 50, a local Jewish constituent, said he tried to raise concerns about the discussion going ahead but the chairperson did not stop it. He said six months ago he had been told by another Labour member "we do not want Jews in the party". He said at Friday's meeting a member who witnessed that denied there was any anti-Semitism in Labour. Mr Lapsley added: "It was very triggering. The suspension of Jeremy Corbyn has really upped the anger." Local MP Nadia Whittome said: "I am disappointed that a motion that was clearly out of order* *made its way on to the agenda. I take the EHRC report into Labour anti-Semitism very seriously, as should all our members, given the pain caused to Jewish communities and that the report found the Labour Party to have broken the law."* **Catherine clarke #RestoreTheWhip** @Catheri22274003 tweeted: *Another false outrage of AS from a witch-hunter general, Steve Lapsley, and encouraged by a supposedly left-wing MP, Nadia Whittome, If someone says they have never seen AS within the party, maybe, just maybe, they have never seen AS within the party!* There was a link to a Labour election pitch by Steve Lapsley, who had claimed that 'My politics are unashamedly left…I ask for your vote as a left, independent-minded candidate'. But Lapsley was a Zionist and a member of the right-wing Jewish Labour Movement. His election leaflet indicated he had once tweeted using the twitter address @enrages. Three years ago, it transpired, he had tweeted on 27 July 2017 at 6:29pm about another Labour Party member: 'She's as Jewish as a lobster hanging on to a foreskin'. Who 'she' was was unclear but Ellis suspected it might well be Jackie Walker. More recently, now tweeting as Steve Lapsley @stevelapsl he had on 17 November 2020 tweeted of Jewish Voice for Labour, 'this organisation are [sic] a disgrace and should be nowhere near any structures of the Labour Party. They have done more damage than anyone. Proscription is a blunt tool, but necessary here'. Ellis went for a walk. When he returned he drank a cappuccino and ate a slice of toast and honey. He read David Rosenberg's tweet from yesterday: 'Tomorrow is the UN International Day of solidarity with the Palestinian People (instituted 1977). The daily oppression of Palestinians in the Occupied Territories has multiplied since then. How will labour's leaders @Keir_Starmer @AngelaRayner be marking this anniversary in 2020? They will be speaking at an event jointly organised by Labour Friends of Israel + the Jewish Labour Movement'. Ellis discovered that addressing this reactionary rabble Angela Rayner said: 'If I have to suspend thousands and thousands of members, we will do that. Because we cannot and we will not accept an injury to one, because an injury to one is an injury to all.' Ed McNally tweeted: 'Angela Rayner is so serious about anti-racism that she's speaking at an event co-hosted by a group that denies the Nakba and blames Palestinians shot in the back by Israeli snipers for their own deaths.' **Rob** @carregydefaid tweeted: 'It's nice of Angela Rayner to mark Palestine Solidarity Day by telling a JLM crowd that she'll gladly halve the Labour Party for the crime of showing solidarity with one of the only real politicians in the party to show meaningful solidarity with the embattled Palestinians.' **Shabbir Lakha** @ShabbirLakha tweeted: 'I'm never going to stop reminding Momentum that they backed Angela Rayner over Richard Burgon for deputy leader, because it's the kind of shitty politics that got us to this position.' **Kerry-Anne Mendoza** tweeted: 'Imagine if during a day of international solidarity with the oppressed of Apartheid South Africa, the Labour leadership opted instead to spend the day with white supremacists.

That's what Keir Starmer and Angela Rayner are doing today. #FreePalestine #PalestineDay'. **Ammar Kazmi** @AmmarKazmi tweeted: 'A disgraceful way of approaching political debate here from Angela Rayner. She is talking about conducting a purge, let's be clear about that: there is no other way to describe this'. Ellis read more about this squalid episode: *Labour deputy leader Angela Rayner has called on members to "get real" about antisemitism within the party and warned that "thousands and thousands" could be suspended if they fail to do so. Addressing the Jewish Labour Movement one-day conference this morning, Rayner talked about a local Nottingham East Labour meeting on Friday that led to a Jewish member saying he felt forced to leave. The local party considered and passed a motion calling for the Labour whip to be restored to Jeremy Corbyn – after general secretary David Evans had said such motions would be ruled out of order. Local Labour MP Nadia Whittome issued a statement to "put on record my stated objection to the motion this evening". Commenting on the events, Rayner said: "We're on it, by the way. I want people to know that there as been suspensions and we're on it and we are supporting Nadia, the MP there who spoke out and I completely commend her for doing that. Our members need to get real about this, our Labour members. If they don't think antisemitism is within the Labour Party and that there's problems now, then there's really no place for them in the Labour Party. If they think making people feel unsafe or unwelcome in our meetings is a response to the EHRC report, then they need to be out of our party immediately. People need to understand what our Jewish community have been through." The deputy leader added: "We should have a bit of humility... We should be listening and aware of how hurt and upset people are. I feel really, really angry actually that there's been scenes like that in our CLP meetings. If I have to suspend thousands and thousands of members, we will do that. Because we cannot and we will not accept an injury to one, because an injury to one is an injury to all. That's what we say in our movement. It's about education as well. It's about having this approach where we don't accept that people – you know, we have debates but there's no debating what the EHRC said."* David Rosenberg commented: '"An injury to one is an injury to all" said @AngelaRayner at a conference co-run by Labour Friends of Israel, who blamed the massacre of 100s of Palestinians and wounding of 1,000s at Gaza border protests on Palestinians themselves. **Mrs Gee Ex Labour #WeAreCorbyn** @earthygirl011 tweeted: 'Angela Rayner has basically weighed up her career prospects & decided the well-documented Israel lobby is more powerful & useful than socialism'. **The Party's Over** @dascott66 tweeted: 'Long passed the point of reasonable debate or arguments about party procedures/rule book technicalities. All out war was declared five years ago. A failure to understand that was, and remains, "the left's" greatest weakness...' **Chris Clee** @CcleePolitical tweeted: 'Angela Rayner is just Tom Watson with better hair'. **The Cat In The Hat #We Are Corbyn**

@frankevans074 tweeted: 'Angela Rayner is the Labour Partys answer to Jo Swinson'. **Socialist** @Mark_Profound tweeted: 'Starmer goes further down the rabbit hole with each passing day. And now he's taken Angela Rayner with him ...' **Liam Shrivastava** @LiamShrivastava tweeted: 'I wonder if Angela Rayner thinks there's also no point in debating the EHRC's recent report on the hostile environment which failed to serve a compliance notice on the government, despite having found they broke the law...' **The Lefty Crank (Ex-Labour)** @theleftycrank tweeted: 'So @AngelaRayner has declared war on freedom of speech and defending your reputation against liars and racists if you are a @UKLabour member. This is utterly disgusting and proves that Labour is no longer a safe place for Socialists and anti-racists'. Someone tweeted a link to an old article by Nicky Hutchinson on the *New Socialist* website, May 13th 2020. 'Angela Rayner, whose working-class background, accent and career as a union official will be held up as indicators of socialism by those who (deliberately or otherwise) understand none of those things...Illusions of Rayner's radicalism are a precise echo of how 90s journalists mistook connections with trade union leaderships for a commitment to radical socialism'. In the afternoon Owen Jones acknowledged that it was a day of solidarity and tweeted: 'Remember the suffering of the Palestinian people. Support their right to national self-determination and an end to all annexations. Demand sanctions on Israel until the occupation ends'. It was classic Jones, devoid of substance. The 'suffering' went unidentified, as did those responsible for it. And what was meant by 'their right to national self-determination'? A Palestinian state alongside Israel? If so, that was the classic delaying tactic of so-called left Zionism. And those hypothetical sanctions were aimed at 'the occupation' not at the existence of Israel as an apartheid state dedicated to the expulsion of every last Palestinian. Besides, what did Owen mean by 'the occupation'? The West Bank, probably. But what of Gaza? And those Palestinians who lived as second-class citizens within Israel? Slithy Jones did not support BDS. Nor, evidently, did he support a single state based on equal rights for all citizens. Jones's greasy solidarity ignored the spurious and sectarian 'right of return' for Jews, just as it failed to mention the right of return for the Palestinian refugees, and compensation for what had been stolen from them. To remind us all that the Blairites were always unprincipled reactionaries, Andy Burnham was another anti-Palestinian careerist who popped up at this meeting to express his support for Zionism and his solidarity with the hard Right: "There has been a cultural problem in the Labour Party going back a long time". He concluded: "I trust Keir and Angela to sort it out". Returning to the Middle East, Ellis read Mark Curtis @markcurtis30, who tweeted: 'If Iran were suspected of being behind the terrorist assassination of the head of Israeli nuclear weapons in Jerusalem, we'd be on the verge of war amid 24/7 coverage of righteous indignation in every TV studio in country. The media follows the state'. Ellis learned that the great journalist Robert Fisk had died.

Guardian presstitute Jessica Elgot @jessicaelgot was quick to urinate on the memory of a courageous journalist who'd travelled to war zones and who'd exposed Israeli crimes and hypocrisies. She tweeted: 'Great piece by @OzKaterji, hard to read even having heard all similar stories about Fisk. Like so many, he was inspiring to me as student & so depressing the evidence that he fabricated so much and how he was so badly on wrong side of history on Syria'. Aaron Maté @aaronjmate replied: '*Guardian* deputy editor promotes a hit piece by a deranged Syria regime change troll on the late, great Robert Fisk. Always instructive to see the best journalists of our time attacked by colleagues. Fisk had accomplishments & integrity, so is naturally reviled by those who don't.' The child chuckled as Ellis put a puppet on his hand and waggled the head and hands. Bear, she said. Ellis ate stew with mashed potatoes and sprouts. At 9pm he watched the latest Steve McQueen drama in the 'Small Axe' series. It dramatised the early life of Leroy Logan, a black man who'd joined the Metropolitan Police in the 1980s and repeatedly encountered racism and hostility. But the ending was open-ended and unsatisfactory. Ellis had assumed that Logan had been driven out of the force. But later online he discovered that Logan had risen to the rank of Superintendent and been given an MBE. That didn't sound remotely radical. This was the celebration of identity politics over class. Logan had joined the police to change attitudes but what had he changed? Nothing at all. The Met was still racist. One in four of all young black people in London had been stopped and searched by the Met during the first national lockdown. Racial stereotyping remained pervasive throughout British policing. The police force was largely made up of poorly-educated white, working-class males, who colluded with the system against the wider interests of their class. Steve McQueen seemed devoid of a radical political sensibility. A successful black man, he was celebrating individual success which shone a light on racism but did nothing whatever to challenge it effectively. Ellis went to bed. Aces thumbnailed another kitchen match, and blew it out, he read.

Monday 30th November 2020

It had been raining in the night. Ellis drank tea and went online. He discovered that the dullard Labourist Andrew Fisher had written a piece for the *Guardian*, attacking the Tories. 'Now they are coming for Britain's liberal institutions: the BBC, the Electoral Commission, the EHRC, the FoI Act and those pesky "activist lawyers".' Leaving aside the morality of writing for this particular newspaper, it showed how enfeebled Fisher's politics were. The notion that the BBC was somehow on the left was a classic liberal delusion. Fisher obviously didn't bother reading *Media Lens*, for had he done so he could not write such drivel. And the notion that the right-wing Zionist-inflected EHRC was a liberal institution displayed a crass ignorance of the history of this Blairite quango, the sinister powers of which were being used exclusively against pro-Palestinian activism. But then Fisher was the fool who'd urged Corbyn to quench Zionist bellicosity by signing up to the cynical and coldly-calculated redefinition of anti-Semitism. How dim Corbyn had been to regard someone like Fisher as a useful advisor on strategy. Ellis turned to the Twitter page of Louis Allday. He learned that on February 14th 2020 slithery Aaron Bastani had tweeted that *after 1945, and given what was happening before, Israel was inevitable and entirely justified (my view).* Yet another reminder that the Novara crowd were lickspittle careerists. They were so unprincipled that they ought to be Labour MPs. Quite possibly this was the direction that some of them were heading in. Or columns in a Rupert Murdoch publication. It began raining. The child looked out of her bedroom window. Black car, she said. Ellis went out shopping. It was still raining. He bought bananas, cheese, yogurt, tinned tomatoes, milk and kitchen roll. He stood by a farmer's stall, which had apples for sale. A woman mistook him for the farmer and enquired about the apples. Ellis explained that he was a fellow customer, not the vendor. Ellis bought some apples. Afterwards he went to the newsagents and bought the latest issue of the *London Review of Books*, £4.75. It came wrapped in sealed transparent bag, with a free copy of a paperback collection of essays, *The Meaninglessness of Meaning.* A trite, clickbait title. Back home Ellis glanced at the paperback. Several of the contributors were dead. He'd known one of them. He turned to the LRB. First he read the review of *Shuggie Bain*. The reviewer saluted the writing as being 'often exquisite; its mode realism with gothic touches'. Ellis scrutinised the first sample of Douglas Stuart's prose which was offered up. It described the lighting of a cigarette: 'Agnes reached across the mattress for her cigarettes, she lit one and sucking loudly, she coaxed the end into a blazing copper tip'. Ellis felt that there should have been a full stop after 'cigarettes'. Did anyone drawing on a cigarette really make a noise or was 'sucking loudly' simply there because behavioural spasms (of which the most unrealistic and commonest of all was the shrug) were required as narrative punctuation for the actions of literary puppets such as this woman, Agnes? As for 'a blazing copper tip,' that seemed both in thrall to the showy prose required of the genre of Literary Fiction and also unrealistic. The end of a cigarette glows red, not copper. Besides, it was all surplus to requirements. Why not just write: 'Agnes reached for her cigarettes. She lit one.'? Ellis went back to the start of the magazine, which displayed the lengthy review by Novara's James Butler of the two books about the Corbyn years, by *Times* hacks Pogrund & Maguire and *Guardian* hack Owen Jones. The weakness of Butler's politics and analysis were made glaringly obvious by his treatment of the anti-Semitism saga. Butler solemnly regarded 'the anti-Semitism crisis' as *real* rather than confected by the aggressive Zionist lobby and their natural allies in the reactionary Parliamentary Labour Party. 'The anti-Semitism crisis cannot be explained away,' asserted James Butler. Oh yes it can, and it has been. Butler simply obfuscates, having nothing to say about the Israel lobby and the history of its propaganda techniques, or the reactionary condition of modern British Jewry, or the cynical and degrading use of the Nazi genocide to provide an alibi for Jewish colonial racism and violence. Ellis had been contemplating taking out a subscription to the *London Review of Books*, as an alternative to buying the *Times* on Saturday for its review section, but having discovered that its fiction reviewing was of poor quality and that it employed people like James Butler to offer up political analysis, he decided against. He might as well stick with the *Times*. Later, Ellis came across Daniel Finn's response to Owen Jones's *Guardian* piece about the Labour Party. Finn remarked: 'Unfortunately, this article evades the main issues at stake. It tacitly urges the left to revert to a failed strategy of unwarranted concessions and apologies that just added fuel to the fire, instead of challenging the false narrative around "Labour antisemitism" directly…in practice it amounts to a call to dodge around this controversy in the name of pragmatism, allowing falsehoods to go unchallenged instead of taking them on directly. It's the approach that has largely prevailed since 2015, and it's been ruinous'. Outside, the wind increased in strength and rain fell. Ellis spent much of the rest of the day reading. He ate a mix of vegetables and melted cheese for his evening meal, washed down with a glass of water. He watched the 10pm Sky News. He went to bed and read as far as the words: Ann Hopkins was definitely racing her motor in the Grand Prix manner.

Tuesday 1st December 2020

Ellis woke to the sound of rain. Later he went shopping, purchasing some live yogurt, a bloomer, a pot of strawberry jam, two cartons of milk and three rolls of Christmas wrapping paper. After that he went for a walk, calling in at the library on his way home to collect a book he'd ordered. The sun shone. Ellis drank a cappuccino and went online. He came across a website called *Spotlight*, which had an illuminating update on events in Nottingham East. According to some of those present at this meeting: 'There was only one interruption during the meeting. This arose when one member stated that in his personal experience he had never witnessed any anti-Semitism in any of our meetings. As he continued with his personal view, another member shouted out – in a manner that some found to be aggressive – that he himself had suffered personal, anti-Semitic abuse from the person speaking, who was taken aback and stated that this wasn't true; the Chair intervened and tried to calm things down. At this point the member who had interrupted declared that he no longer felt safe at the meeting and left.' Ellis had been under the impression that this was an assembly of people in a room. Thinking about it, it couldn't have been, of course, because of the lockdown restrictions. So, this had been a zoom meeting! This threw into perspective the claims of Steve Lapsley that he felt intimidated. In fact, according to this account, Lapsley was the one who was shouty. The account went on: 'The atmosphere of the meeting immediately became tense and uncomfortable and many were very upset by it. It should be noted that there had been no anti-Semitic behaviour or language at the meeting. Several members then spoke of their concern for the member who had left and the Chair stated that she had reached out to him to check that he was ok'. Amazingly: 'Additional concerns have arisen by the discovery that someone present was sending out live information – including members' names – to a journalist known to be hostile to Jeremy Corbyn and his supporters, who was live-tweeting this information.' The journalist was Lee Harpin of the *Jewish Chronicle*. A Zionist hack with very considerable form. What's more, where Steve Lapsley was concerned, 'It has also been noted that the member who left has changed his narrative on social media to stating that the member he accused had "witnessed an anti-Semitic attack" on him rather than had attacked him personally.' Ellis discovered that Nottingham East was the constituency previously represented by Chris Leslie, who walked out of the Labour Party in February 2019 to set up a new party, with fellow reactionaries Chuka Umunna, Lucretia Borgia, Mike Gapes etc. Fifteen minutes after the end of the meeting its chair, Louise Regan, discovered from journalists that she had been suspended. The rotten Right was back in control of the party, and intended to hunt down and expel anyone who dared to show the slightest sign of sympathy for Palestinians or hostility to Israel. Ellis came across a tweet by Chris Hazzard @ChrisHazzardSF who tweeted, in relation to Pat Finucane 'As a QC who specialised in human rights issues, it's very odd that the leader of the Opposition at Westminster, Keir Starmer, hasn't said a word about the Govt's failure to announce a public inquiry into the state's illegal killing of a fellow human rights lawyer. Remarkable even'. Not really. Starmer was the living incarnation of the capitalist-imperialist State. Ellis saw that Richard Seymour had retweeted a begging letter from *Novara Media*: 'Here at Novara Media, we've got big, big plans for 2021. But to make them happen, we need to increase donations by £5,000 a month by Christmas.' Ellis laughed coldly, mirthlessly, a cruel smile spreading across his face. He turned again to James Butler's long article in the *London Review of Books*. Butler had written that 'the statement by Momentum's founder, Jon Lansman, that he felt ' "used as a Jew" to defend the party, but was left without support afterwards, should be a source of shame'. Oh really? In an essay Lansman had demanded that the Left stop using the word 'Zionism'. To justify this preposterous demand Lansman cited an obscure law professor at the University of Kent, Didi Herman, who claimed to have once been an anti-Zionist (but who supplied not a scrap of evidence of any pro-Palestinian activism). She had complained 'The identification of a generic Zionism with *nothing but* racist practice in Israel entrenches an understanding of zionism not just as a dirty word, but as a pariah form of thinking unrelated to any other'. Eh? Zionism had always been a racist and sectarian ideology which sought a 'homeland' *exclusively* for Jews. When Ellis looked up Didi Herman he discovered that her philosophising about Zionism had been demolished some time ago by energetic, brilliant Tony Greenstein. Greenstein had written: 'Yes, Jews in Europe had a legitimate desire for a homeland. When fleeing the Czarist pogroms they found one - in Britain and the United States. That's why Palestine was a racial dream that has turned sour'. That pudgy wealthy property-developer Lansman should be playing the Jewish victim card was laughable. Jon Lansman was an overweight intellectual mediocrity and yet another of Corbyn's ill-chosen allies who had helped annihilate 'the project'. James Butler likewise seemed to have all the intellectual depth of a tadpole. He wrote: 'The EHRC's statutory inquiry into Labour is a sober, conservative and often lawyerly examination of the problem'. No it isn't. Butler simply ignores the history and structure of the EHRC as a compromised and partisan State body. Its report is striking for its *failure* to discover evidence of anti-Semitism and deeply sinister in its conclusion that to say that claims of anti-Semitism have been exaggerated constitutes unlawful harassment of Jews. This is Matthew Hopkins territory, not analytical rigour. James Butler puts the boot into Ken Livingstone, as one might expect of a careerist lickspittle. Livingstone, like Corbyn, has a record of anti-racist activism which puts a keyboard warrior like Butler to shame. How hilarious that in a publication dated December 3rd 2020, Butler should assert that 'even now, the leader's office would prefer to avoid factional conflict'. James Butler was a moron. Starmer had been attacking the Left, even in its flabbiest incarnations, from the moment he became Leader. Butler's banal and stunted politics shine through yet again when he writes that the oleaginous John McDonnell 'emerges in both books as the most serious and determined politician in the Corbyn circle…He was willing to make the necessary compromises…it is hard not to wonder, along with [Owen] Jones, whether he isn't the Labour left's "lost leader".' Dismal. Pathetic. Pitiful. Ellis remembered all too well McDonnell's hopeless response to the BBC's bullying Nick Robinson's demand that he deplore the shocking intimidation of saintly Stella Creasy by thuggish Corbynistsas. The story was completely fraudulent but the useless McDonnell duly deplored it. Even after it was exposed as fake news, McDonnell never once brought it up in subsequent media interviews. He had all the fighting instincts and dexterity of a slug. And when some Palestinian activists mocked Labour's craven capitulation to the fraudulent redefinition of anti-Semitism by the Zionist IHRA, sticking up posters at London bus stops reading ISRAEL IS A RACIST ENDEAVOUR, McDonnell cravenly condemned them as 'anti-Semitic'. McDonnell had all the principles and socialist consciousness of a stick of candy floss. And there was, of course, the little matter of McDonnell's cosy smiley-smiley interviewwith blood-drenched, unrepentant Blairite warmonger Alastair Campbell. But none of this mattered to the careerists, opportunists and narcissists of *Novara Media*. Ellis drank a glass of red wine, and then a second one. That evening, in bed, he finished reading *Answered Prayers*. The final word on p. 164 began a sentence which made no sense: 'As burglar, but now even Nini admits that Ann must have done it.' Eh? Ellis re-read the sentence. He realised that the final line on p. 164 - 'burglar, but now even Nini admits that Ann must have done it. As' - had been repeated, making it the top line on page 165. The top line on this next page should actually have read: 'you may recall, if you followed the case, the Hopkinses went to a'. Slovenly Penguin had first published *Answered Prayers* as a Penguin Books paperback in 1993, repackaging it as a Penguin Classic in 2001. They had gone on printing the book, with this glaring error, ever since. Penguin Classics didn't give a toss about textual accuracy. But it had always been like this with slovenly Penguin. For forty years they had published *Nineteen Eighty-Four* with a glaringly inaccurate last chapter, in which instead of writing "2+2=5" Winston Smith had written "2+2= ". For many years Penguin had published editions of *Heart of Darkness* which, on the very first page, referred bafflingly to 'varnished spirits' (Conrad had written 'sprits'). Penguin had first published *Under the Volcano* as a Penguin paperback in 1962. The text contained a number of errors which had never been corrected. The defective text was still being published by Penguin some 58 years later. It was a reminder that corporate publishing was as indifferent to the writing of its authors as it was to literary quality. Ellis read the first couple of pages of *Humboldt's Gift*, then turned out the light.

Wednesday 2nd December 2020

A bright crisp morning. Ellis woke shortly before 7am. He listened to the weather forecast and then the headlines. The Pfizer vaccine had been declared safe by the UK regulatory authority. Later, Ellis ate his bowl of breakfast cereal - he would soon need to buy another packet of Shredded Wheat - and went online. He learned that Maggie O'Farrell's *Hamnet* had been named Waterstones' Book of the Year 2020. Next he went on Ed McNally's twitter page only to encounter once again the message *These tweets are protected Only approved followers can see @edmcnally96's Tweets*. He went for a walk. It was cold outside. He met two people he knew and chatted briefly about the pandemic and its effect on families and Christmas. Later, Ellis read on the website of *The Bookseller* that Michal Shavit, Jonathan Cape's publishing director, had acquired UK and Commonwealth rights to Claire-Louise Bennett's novel *Checkout 19* from Peter Straus at Rogers, Coleridge and White. The novel will be published in autumn 2021. Described as a "deeply felt, original and devastatingly moving" novel, it *follows a young woman who finds herself in love, in conflict with life and death, and in a life made of books, where the act of turning the page is a way of carrying on living. "Fearlessly inventive in its form, merging linguistic ingenuity and a searing emotional depth, the book explores class, the notion of freedom, adolescence, transcendence, sexual politics and artistic synthesis."* Michal Shavit said: "I have long been in awe of Claire-Louise Bennett's writing and I couldn't be more excited to be publishing her at Cape and Vintage. She is without a doubt one of the most exciting writers of her generation and this novel is one of the most beautiful and moving books I have ever read. It's ultimately a novel about girlhood and womanhood and what it means to be a whole when there are so many individual pieces that make up each of our cosmoses. It's about freedom and passion, about longing and desire, about men and women, creativity and belonging, all the things that make us human and that pull us between the opposite poles of life and death." Claire-Louise Bennett said: "Writing it turned out to be incredibly exhilarating and freeing. Michal Shavit's response to it was astute and impassioned—I was bowled over." Battered by adjectives, Ellis wasn't at all sure what this novel was *about*. He also wondered how *fearlessly inventive* its *form* would turn out to be. He went into the kitchen and baked some salmon, which he ate with mashed potato and peas. He watched the second episode of Dan Snow's Dam Busters documentary on Channel 5. There was footage of Guy Gibson's beloved dog. Ellis noticed that a corporate hack like Snow carefully avoided mentioning the name of the dog. Gibson was a hero, after all. Best not to be reminded of other aspects. In a similar fashion the corporate media liked populist wartime subjects, where the emphasis was on courage, ingenuity, British pluck. Other aspects of the RAF's history were never to be discussed. From the perspective of British foreign policy - or from that of the many Arab civilians it had spied-on, machine-gunned, bombed and massacred- the RAF was one of the world's most enduring and successful terrorist organisations. It had been instrumental in suppressing democracy in the Middle East for almost a century of its violent existence. Ellis went to bed and read several more pages of *Humboldt's Gift*.

Thursday 3rd December 2020

Grey and damp. Ellis did not wake until 8.15am. On the 'Today' programme there was some woman - she sounded like a garrulous teenager - talking about herself. She had a strange accent, soft, on the verge of a lisp, but it seemed unattractive, or the voice did, in its relentless self-obsession. As he dozed Ellis gathered that this woman was an artist. He was startled but somehow not at all surprised when the narcissist was revealed to be Tracey Emin. An artist startling devoid of any talent or significance whatever, Ellis felt. He had seen her silly and characteristically self-regarding tent at the Sensation exhibition, an occasion when the Royal Academy allowed itself to be used as a warehouse for the remarkably bad taste and poor judgement of the deeply unpleasant Charles

Saatchi. Ellis had seen the dead shark, too - another piece of trash. Later he read Gareth Porter's article on the *Grayzone* website, 'How Israel deployed an intelligence deception to justify killing Mohsen Fakhrizadeh.' Referring to the assassination of Darioush Rezaeinejad, Gareth Porter wrote: 'The deployment of absurd assertions backed by paper-thin evidence to justify the cold-blooded murder of a young electrical engineer with no record of nuclear weapons involvement illuminated a Mossad modus operandi that has reappeared in the case of Fakhrizadeh: Israeli intelligence simply gins up a narrative centered around fictional ties to a nonexistent nuclear weapons program. It then watches as the Western press uncritically disseminates the propaganda to the public, establishing the political space for cold-blooded assassinations in broad daylight'. Yesterday's *Financial Times* reported that Mossad and associated agencies were estimated to have assassinated some 2,700 individuals. A dark, wet day. Ellis went to the bank, the bottle bank, the library, the supermarket. He returned home. The child held up a book. Ellis held up a red book. What colour is your book? he asked the child. Blue book, she said. The correct answer. Ellis drank a mug of tea and read a book. Later he ate bangers, mash and purple cabbage stir fried with apple. He watched the third and final episode of the Dam Busters documentary on Channel 5. On the 10pm Sky News Dr Anthony Fauci was interviewed. He intimated that the British regulatory approval of the Pfizer Coronavirus vaccine had been too hasty. He explained that the United States took longer to approve drugs because they wanted the public to have complete confidence in any new vaccine. Ellis went to bed. He opened *Humboldt's Gift*. The buster muffler was so loud that though the car filled the lane there was no need to honk. You could hear us coming. That second sentence was redundant, Ellis felt. He read on. For a while it was a double concerto, but presently I was fiddled and trumpeted off the stage. Ellis struggled to keep his eyes open. He put the book away and turned off the light.

Friday 4th December 2020

A wet dark morning. Ellis woke at 6.35am. On the radio a woman from the Herefordshire Wildlife Trust was talking about the unlawful destruction of a mile-long stretch of the River Lugg. She said that all bankside and riverside habitats had been completely obliterated after the river and its banks had been bulldozed, straightened and reprofiled into a sterile canal. Wildlife affected by the damage included otters, salmon, crayfish and lampreys. The woman on the radio was circumspect about who had vandalised this protected site but appeared to have a culprit in mind. Later, Ellis went online to find out more. The Trust appealed for action, saying that a 16-tonne bulldozer had been used by individuals who knew very well that the river had been designated a Site of Special Scientific Interest. 'The bankside trees are all grubbed out and burnt, the river gravels have been scraped away, and the beautiful meanders of the river have been straightened and reprofiled.' The Trust said that repairing the damage and restoring natural process and wildlife to this landscape would take decades. Ellis spent the morning reading. In the afternoon he went out to buy eggs, apples and a *Morning Star*. Later, he read more about the vandalism of the protected site. It turned out that the Environment Agency had been first alerted to what was occurring at this site on 26 November, when it started, but the supine and toothless Agency had done nothing. It was only when massive destruction had been accomplished that this thoroughly useless Agency moved in. This struck Ellis as a major scandal, which ought to result in the sacking of top officials at the Agency. But since the Johnson government was rotten to the core with corruption this seemed unlikely. TV gardener Monty Don, who lives nearby, said: 'It breaks my heart but is all too typical of the ignorance, arrogance and sheer wanton destruction of those privileged to care for our countryside'. The clear implication was that this destruction had been carried out by whoever owned the land beside the river. But then all the main four parties - Tories, Labour, Lib Dems and SNP - had always represented the landowning class over the people. Meanwhile that sewer of Zionism known as the *Jewish Chronicle* was today obliged to publish its seventh apology in three years: Following an article published in print on March 13, 2020 headlined "Hampstead chair thanked 'Jewish Question' activist", and online on 10 March 2020, headlined "Hampstead and Kilburn Labour chair thanks ex-member who was expelled for 'sickening' comments about Jews", Gerald Downing complained to the Independent Press Standards Organisation that the newspaper had breached Clause 1 (Accuracy) of the Editors' Code of Practice. IPSO upheld this complaint and has required the *Jewish Chronicle* to publish this decision as a remedy to the breach. The article reported that Mr Downing had been expelled from the Labour Party after making "sickening' comments about Jews" and that these comments had been discussed in Parliament. The complainant said that the article was inaccurate; he had been expelled from the Labour Party for publicly supporting another political party, not for making comments about Jews, sickening or otherwise. The complainant provided official Labour Party letters to IPSO which supported this position. He also said that no comments he had made about Jewish people had been discussed in the House of Commons. IPSO found that it was significantly inaccurate to report that the complainant had been expelled from the Labour Party for making "sickening" comments about Jews which were raised in Parliament, and particularly where this featured in the headline of the online article, it had failed to take care not to publish inaccurate information in breach of Clause 1. By accessing this rag online Ellis learned that Prince Charles, Tony Blair and Gordon Brown and the Archbishop of Canterbury Justin Welby would be participating in a digital tribute to Rabbi Lord Sacks to be aired on Sunday evening. A royal clown, a blood-drenched war

criminal and his Zionist associate, and an old Etonian Anglican would solemnly honour the memory of a racist mediocrity. The programme would also feature contributions from the oily Zionist Chief Rabbi Ephraim Mirvis, the Israeli President Reuven Rivlin and Lady Sacks. It would mark the end of the 30-day period of forgetting since the departure of Emeritus Chief Rabbi, who to the betterment of this world departed it on November 7, aged 72. The programme would be hosted by that weird cyclophobe, Lord Winston. Leading Orthodox American Jewish organisations, morally blank and fully signed-up to Jewish exceptionalism and the immiseration and dispossession of the Palestinians, have also produced a video in his memory. At 20.28pm Ellis went on the Twitter page of Ben White and read: Israeli occupation forces have killed 15-year-old Palestinian child Ali Ayman Saleh Nasr, while suppressing a protest against settlement expansion in Al-Mughayyer near Ramallah. He was shot "in the stomach with live ammunition". Next Ellis caught up with a new report from *Defense for Children International - Palestine*. The 73-page report was titled "Isolated and Alone: Palestinian children held in solitary confinement by Israeli authorities for interrogation".
(https://d3n8a8pro7vhmx.cloudfront.net/dcipalestine/
pages/5323/attachments/original/1606920678/Solitary_Report_2020_FINAL_02
1220.pdf) The report analysed patterns of arrest, detention conditions, and interrogation practices by Israeli authorities. Over a four-year period, between January 1, 2016 and December 31, 2019, DCIP documented 108 cases where Palestinian children detained by the Israeli military were held in isolation for two or more days during the interrogation period. Evidence and documentation collected by DCIP overwhelmingly indicate that the isolation of Palestinian children within the Israeli military detention system is practised solely to obtain a confession for a specific offence or to gather intelligence under interrogation. Solitary confinement has been used, almost exclusively, during pre-charge and pretrial detention. The practice is not generally employed after children have been convicted and are serving their sentences. Isolation of Palestinian child detainees typically follows a military arrest and transfer period, during which many children are subjected to physical violence and other forms of ill-treatment. While in isolation, child detainees are without meaningful human contact, as interactions with others are often solely with their interrogator. The conditions in isolation cells are commonly characterized by inadequate ventilation, 24-hour lighting, no windows, unsanitary bedding and toilet facilities, and hostile architectural features such as wall protrusions. During interrogation, Israeli military law does not afford Palestinian minors the right to have a parent or lawyer present. The interrogation techniques are often mentally and physically coercive, frequently incorporating a combination of intimidation, threats, verbal abuse, and physical violence with a clear purpose of obtaining a confession. In all 108 cases documented by DCIP, Israeli authorities interrogated Palestinian

369

child detainees without the presence of a lawyer or family member, and children were overwhelmingly denied a consultation with a lawyer prior to interrogation. Israel has the dubious distinction of being the only country in the world that systematically prosecutes between 500 and 700 children in military courts each year. DCIP estimates that since the year 2000, Israeli military authorities have detained, interrogated, prosecuted, and imprisoned approximately 13,000 Palestinian children. Of the 108 cases documented by DCIP between January 1, 2016 and December 31, 2019: • The average duration of isolation was 14.3 days. • Nearly 40 percent (43 children), endured a prolonged period of isolation of 16 or more days. • All cases were Palestinian boys aged between 14 and 17 years old. • In the majority of cases, Palestinian child detainees were unlawfully transferred to detention and interrogation facilities located inside Israel operated or controlled by the Israel Prison Service (IPS) and Israel Security Agency in violation of the Fourth Geneva Convention. At least 52 children were held at Al-Jalame (also known as Kishon) interrogation and detention center; at least 29 children were held at Petah Tikva interrogation and detention center; at least 32 were held at Megiddo prison; and at least 14 were held at Al-Mascobiyya interrogation and detention center. In 86 cases (80 percent), children held in isolation reported being subject to stress positions during interrogation, most commonly having their limbs tied to a low metal chair for prolonged periods, a position they described as acutely painful.• DCIP finds that the physical and social isolation of Palestinian children for interrogation purposes by Israeli authorities is a practice that constitutes solitary confinement, which amounts to torture or cruel, inhuman, or degrading treatment or punishment under international law norms. On the *Haaretz* website Ellis read a story about how the barbaric Jewish state hangs on to the corpses of dead Palestinians. Since April 2016, Israel had added 68 more bodies of Palestinians to those it refuses to return for burial to their families, which it is holding for purposes of bargaining or deterrence. Among the bodies are those of seven men who died of illness during incarceration over the past four years, including one detainee who had not even been tried. The total number of bodies held by Israel is unknown but estimates are as high as a few hundred. Since January 2020, Israeli authorities have added 17 more Palestinian bodies to the total already being held. These are the crimes which Rabbi Lord Sacks spent his self-satisfied and privileged life defending. Ellis went to bed. The suspense claws at my heart, he read. Actually, standing on my head did relieve me.

Saturday 5th December 2020

The alarm woke Ellis at 6.50am. He dozed in the dark, half-listening to the weather forecast and the news headlines. Brexit negotiations had stalled. There would be a meeting between Boris Johnson and Michel Barnier. Later that day hailstones pelted down. For a minute or so it looked as if snow had fallen. Ellis read about a controversy involving the Booksellers Association and the new website Bookshop.org. It was claimed that there was discontent among booksellers and publishers regarding the role played by the Booksellers Association in promoting the new website, along with the requirement that participating bookshops must be BA members. James Daunt, who runs the independent book chain Daunt Books, said he had declined to sign up to this new organisation. He was concerned about its accumulation of customer data and what he claimed was a lack of transparency. Kieron Smith of Blackwell's said he did not think Bookshop.org was good for customers or the industry. It rained, then the sun came out. Ellis spent much of the day reading. Returning to the internet, he read Tony Greenstein's latest blog post, about Alasdair Henderson, who led the EHRC investigation into supposed anti-Semitism in the Labour Party. Henderson's tweets revealed that he liked a variety of hard Right individuals and hard Right views. His politics were exposed as someone on the far Right. That he should have led an investigation into racism was a scandal but as usual the corporate media, not least the BBC, muffled this extraordinary revelation. The two latest appointments as EHRC commissioners - David Goodhart and Jessica Butcher - exposed the rotten and reactionary politics of this establishment organisation. Later, Ellis drank a lager and ate a curry. He looked again at the end of a novel which had lingered on the edge of his mind. It was done; it was finished. Yes, she thought, laying down her brush in extreme fatigue, I have had my vision. Ellis switched on the TV. The ubiquitous 'liberal' Zionist Rachel Shabi was on Sky's review of tomorrow's papers, along with a *Telegraph* hack. Ellis had no interest in listening to what either of them had to say. He went to bed. He sat up late reading *Humboldt's Gift*. He read the final sentence of the third paragraph of the unnumbered chapter and then put out the light. The death question itself, which Walt Whitman saw as the question of questions.

Sunday 6th December 2020

Ellis woke in gloom at 7.45am and turned on the radio. Patchy showers were forecast. There was a trailer for the news programme at 9am. Among those reviewing the papers would be the noxious reactionary Trevor Phillips. The corporate media gave saturation coverage to right-wingers like Phillips. Only recently he'd had two full pages in the *Times* to attack the Left. BBC News reported that Millwall supporters had booed when players had taken the knee ahead of the Championship match with Derby. Much outrage. But no comment at all that the Premier League had just signed up to the anti-Palestinian racist redefinition of anti-Semitism set up by the Israel lobby with the express purpose of defaming individuals and organisations seeking equal rights for Palestinians in apartheid Israel. There was also an anti-Semitism story in the bulletin. Roald Dahl's family had apologised for the author's anti-Semitic remarks. It was also reported that the singer Rita Ora should have been in quarantine when she broke lockdown rules, having flown to Egypt on 21 November in a private jet to perform at a five-star hotel. She should have self-isolated for 14 days but instead threw a 30th birthday party at a London restaurant on 28 November. From Twitter Ellis learned that the poisonously reactionary Union of Jewish Students was delighted that the University of Birmingham had signed up to anti-Palestinian racism by adopting the Zionist redefinition of anti-Semitism. Ellis was reminded of how swiftly and how easily after 1933 German academia had capitulated to the Nazis. Ellis also learned that the European Commission against Racism and Intolerance, an outfit of the Council of Europe, also took this risible, cynically calculated and incoherent redefinition seriously. It was a cold morning. The sun began shining. Word count told Ellis he'd so far written184,280 words. But the mere fact of recording this changed the figure. And each time he added the new figure, the figure changed. A Shandean predicament. Ellis warmed an almond croissant in the oven and then went off to do some off-line reading. The sun crawled along the skyline, casting long shadows. The child put a red sticker on her jumper. Ellis formed his fingers into the outline of a duck. His thumb and forefinger formed the beak. The beak opened and closed. The child sang the song about what the little duck said. The hours passed. The UK recorded another 231 Covid-19 deaths and 17,272 more cases. Ben Jolly's twitter account was suspended by Twitter, along with two other Left tweeters. Silicon Valley's slow censorship of the Left was proceeding apace at every level - YouTube, Google, Twitter, Facebook - while celebrities (J. K. Rowling and other wealthy reactionaries) responded to criticism on the internet by screeching about 'cancel culture'. The corporate media was happy to provide a platform for, and to amplify, the whining of the rich and powerful, for whom even the mildest and most rational of criticism was denounced as 'bullying'. Ellis watched the last in the Small Axe series, about a writer named Alex Wheatle. The drama was scrappy and incoherent, Ellis felt. More black identity politics, which was no politics at all. He watched the news - the vaccine, Brexit negotiations, the Millwall booing, Roald Dahl's anti-Semitism - and went to bed. The fact that the Premier League had signed up to a definition of anti-Semitism engineered on behalf of Jewish state racism was not mentioned. Ellis read a few more pages of the Bellow novel. To his surprise, he was enjoying it.

Monday 7th December 2020

Ellis woke at 6.25am and dozed, half listening to the radio, until 'Thought for the Day', which forced him out of bed. It was a frosty, misty morning. The house felt cold. Ellis ate a bowl of cereal and went online. The child balanced a coaster on the head of soft toy baby. Ellis balanced a coaster on his head, with a small plastic horse standing on the coaster. The child grinned. Ellis went for a walk. A bright sunny morning, but cold. The last-ditch Brexit negotiations dragged on. There was talk of level playing fields, safety nets, balls in courts, glide paths. Glide paths? Ellis searched for the artificial Chrismas tree and the box of Christmas decorations. He located them. Plus some old unused rolls of Christmas wrapping paper. He ate a soufflé with mashed potato and swede, with diced purple cabbage, washed down with a glass of water, followed by stewed apple and ice-cream. In the evening Ellis attended to some Christmas cards, which needed to be posted abroad. On Sky News this night there was fawning coverage of the royal progress through the land made by the publicity-addicted gormless Duke and simpering Duchess of Cambridge. Ellis went to bed. We were speeding eastward on Division Street, Ellis read. He felt tired and put out the light.

Tuesday 8th December 2020

Ellis woke a little before 7am and turned on the radio. He dozed. He learned that the Millwall team would not 'take the knee' at their next match on Tuesday but would instead link arms with the opposing team, Queens Park Rangers. This sop to the yobs among the Millwall fans was dressed up as a magnificent gesture of solidarity rather than an abject capitulation to racists. An outfit called Kick It Out (AKA Kick Racism Out of Football) was thrilled by this surrender. This stirred a memory. Later Ellis went online and his suspicions were confirmed. When the Premier League had signed up to anti-Palestinian racism in the form of the absurd, loaded and muddled Zionist redefinition of anti-Semitism, Sanjay Bhandari, chair of Kick It Out, said that the League was setting an example as 'a massive global brand' and called on the whole of football to sign up to it. Ellis distrusted anyone who spoke of branding, apart from the little matter of Bhandari's ignorance of Zionism. Jonathan Goldstein of the so-called Jewish Leadership Council - one of a network of Zionist outfits - welcomed the Premier League's capitulation to Zionist propaganda. Goldstein, revealingly, said that the definition did not prevent criticism of Israel that was 'valid and proportionate'. Ah, yes. Harmless chatter about the chimera of a Palestinian state was acceptable. But doubtless talk of the Nazi-style excesses of the IDF would not be. Ellis discovered that Ed McNally's tweets were protected again. Presumably he'd been getting abuse from the usual suspects. Meanwhile Yair Wallach had tweeted: *Universities who adopted the IHRA have typically done so as a decision of the very top echelon of the university (senior management team, board of trustees), often without consultation with the academic community.* An interesting revelation. It was a bright sunny morning. The child waved a set of keys, then picked up a notebook. Ellis picked up his notebook and drew a face.

The child grinned. She went to her toy pushchair, in which was sat a soft toy Waffle dog. She pushed it into the kitchen. Miss Polly went with her. Ellis returned online. He read Daniel Finn's latest tweets. *The Guardian's Jessica Elgot has strong views about journalists who (allegedly) "fabricated so much". But she includes a crude fabrication of her own about Corbyn's response to the EHRC, in a fawning puff piece about Margaret Hodge and her call for censorship of social media.* Elgot's fondness for fiction had perhaps been marinated during her years of service for *The Jewish Chronicle*. Elgot had reported of Jeremy Corbyn: *he said the EHRC report into antisemitism in the party had overstated the problem.* Well, actually, he hadn't. Elgot was fibbing. Finn added: *The "Labour antisemitism" media narrative relies upon countless fabrications like this one—some minor, some major—all pointing in the same direction, piled up on top of each other over the course of several years. And liberal media outlets are among the worst offenders.* Finn added of Elgot's fabrication: *And now they've corrected it (while still quoting selectively from his statement). Funny that these errors just happen in one direction, isn't it? And no explanation of how this "mistake" over something so basic could happen in the first place.* Ellis went on to Paul O'Connell's twitter page, where he read: *The main union representing academic staff in universities opposes the adoption of the IHRA definition of anti-Semitism because it would undermine free speech and support for Palestinian rights - so of course, Labour support it.* O'Connell quoted from an article by Kate Green MP, Shadow Secretary of State for Education. Ellis had never heard of Kate Green. It transpired she was another member of that assemblage of unprincipled careerists and reactionaries known as the Parliamentary Labour Party. Ellis read her article. 'Universities gave several reasons for not adopting the definition, the most frequently discussed being protection of academic free speech. I understand the importance of freedom of speech and thought in our universities. However, freedom of expression does not mean freedom to abuse.' Trite, false and impudent, Ellis thought. This Green woman was a bully, too. Her article contained a clear threat. Sign up to Jewish racism or you will suffer financially. 'I am pleased to say that this is a cross-party issue. The Office for Students – the regulatory body for UK universities – has announced that it will explore what practical steps can be taken to ensure wider adoption of the IHRA definition across universities. This includes the possibility of placing further conditions on funding. I sincerely hope such unwelcome action is not needed, and that universities recognise that failing to adopt the definition is letting down their students, staff and the wider communities that they serve'. Zionism continued to seep across British society, fouling everything it touched. And the Labour Party was now as repellent as it had ever been. Ellis went on to read Asa Winstanley's latest article, about the economic costs of the Israeli siege of Gaza. 'A new report on the Gaza Strip by a United Nations (UN) agency makes for sobering reading. The UN Conference

374

on Trade and Development (UNCTAD) reports that the economic cost to Gaza of the Israeli siege since 2007, along with a series of major military assaults, amounts to no less than $16.7 billion,' Winstanley wrote. Naturally BBC News would not be mentioning this report. Winstanley reminded readers of the overall context to the siege - the unexpected victory of Hamas in the 2006 elections, followed by the Dahlan coup attempt. 'In addition to putting Palestinians "on a diet", Israeli planners have another deadly euphemism they like to use – "mowing the lawn". This is a rather disgusting, dehumanising way to describe their periodic wars against the population of the Gaza Strip.' Next Elllis read the latest *Electronic Intifada* article, about the murder of 15-year-old Ali Ayman Saleh Nasser by the infamously brutal Israeli army. Ayman Saleh Nasser was fatally shot in the stomach in the central West Bank village of al-Mughayyir on Friday during a protest against Israeli land theft in the area. The child was observing the protest. Ellis baked salmon and fried some chips, which he ate with coleslaw. Later, he watched part one of the Channel 5 documentary about Lindy Chamberlain, the woman whose baby was snatched from a tent by a dingo at a campsite beside Uluru (then known as Ayers Rock). It was a compelling saga about prejudice, mob hysteria, an incompetent police force, and a reactionary Northern Territory administration which sought to repair supposed damage to tourism by orchestrating a case against an innocent woman. In bed that night Ellis read more Bellow. He reached the line: "Take the order, Giulio," he said.

Wednesday 9th December 2020

A dull morning. Ellis went out to buy fish, bananas, potatoes, yogurt, milk and a bar of white chocolate. Back home he went online and read a new tweet by Daniel Finn, referring to a piece on LabourList by Paul Thompson and Frederick Harry Putts: 'Love to be lectured about hard-headed thinking from people whose view of geopolitics has all the flinty realism of a letter to Santa Claus. One of the authors helped workshop the "talking about capitalism is antisemitic" into British media discourse, so no surprise there.' Ellis belatedly learned that David Lammy MP had tweeted: 'Winston Churchill was a pioneer of human rights.' An utterly absurd and quite false statement. Chris Hazzard @ChrisHazzardSF tweeted: 'Winston Churchill's brutal imperialism was fuelled in part by a disgusting white supremacism that ran through his every fibre - he was no pioneer of human rights - he was a serial abuser of human rights across the globe!!' Someone retweeted an old 23 Jul 2019 tweet by David Schneider @davidschneider about Boris Johnson: 'I for one welcome our new lying, racist dog-whistling, incompetent, principle-free, bullshitting, back-stabbing, British-citizen-in-Iran-incarcerating, white-supremacist-befriending, business-fucking, reality-fucking, countrycidal maniac overlord' and the retort by top British barrister and Jew, Jeff Samuels @JeffSamuels16: 'And yet despite all that he's still better than that cunt Corbyn'. Ellis went offline then later returned. Brad Parker @baparkr tweeted: 'I began working at @DCIPalestine in January 2013. In that time we've documented 155 Palestinian children killed by Israeli forces with live ammo or crowd-control weapons. Israeli investigations are a PR move. Systemic impunity is the norm.' Ellis read the latest tweets and retweets by Louis Allday. He learned that Egypt's military dictator Sisi had been awarded France's highest honour, the legion d'honneur, in Paris in the presence of Macron, who also threw Sisi a gala dinner. The depravity of the French government shone through at moments like this, along with the EU's fundamental and enduring contempt for democracy and human rights. At 9pm Ellis turned on Channel 5 and watched the second half of the Lindy Chamberlain documentary. It was a remarkable programme about a massive miscarriage of justice. But the miscarriage had not been accidental but rather a calculated one, involving the Northern Territory administration, the police and 'experts' whose expertise was highly questionable. Afterwards Ellis watched the news headlines. The top story was Boris Johnson's mission to Brussells. The latest deadline was Sunday. The Sky commentator said a deal seemed unlikely. Ellis went to bed. Later, as tiredness dragged at his eyelids, he read: A space was cleared. Twice the slender Kennedy, carelessly elegant, tossed the ball.

Thursday 10th December 2020

Ellis woke a little before 8am and switched on the radio. The news was all about Brexit. Ellis dressed and went out to post some Christmas cards. Later he went online and read Sai Englert's new article on the *Middle East Eye* website criticising the British government's attempt to impose the Zionist definition of anti-Semitism on British universities. This is an extraordinary definition of anti-Semitism, attempting to impose specific limits on the discussion of Zionism and Israel's crimes in Palestine, wrote Sai Englert. *For the millions of Palestinians expelled during the creation of Israel in 1948, besieged in Gaza or under military occupation in the West Bank, or for those who live within Israel's borders and are targeted by more than 65 discriminatory laws, the idea that Israel is a democratic nation is, at best, laughable. In an academic context, the imposition of a definition that describes these facts about the history of Zionism in Palestine as antisemitic is a direct assault on the academic freedom of those working on these issues, as well as on the civil rights of all those campaigning for solidarity with the Palestinian people. While Israel is further institutionalising its structural racism and the second-class status of its Palestinian citizens through measures such as the 2018 nation-state law, the IHRA's working definition is attempting to silence international criticism.* Ellis went out and bought a *Morning Star*, two oranges, a pack of pancakes, a loaf of bread, a pack of white flour and a tub of vanilla ice-cream. He bought eight apples from the man at his stall in the market place. He went into the bookshop to collect a book he'd ordered. Ellis returned home. A dull grey day. Ellis went online and read the latest tweets and retweets on Asa Winstanley's Twitter account. He learned that on 27 February 2020, referring to the Labour Party, Aaron Bastani had tweeted that 'hearing & reading the things I have in recent days I wouldn't feel welcome in the party as a Jewish person'. Bastani had gone on to tweet: 'calling a Jewish MP a "disruptive Zionist" is clearly unacceptable. If I was called a "disruptive Iranian stooge" I'd feel that was unacceptable. That has happened, of course, and its [sic] not the end of the world, but this isn't the rhetoric of a healthy, diverse party'. Bastani's enfeebled politics stood exposed yet again, since 'disruptive Zionist' was a term which was either accurate or inaccurate. It was not a slur but a description. As someone responded: why is it outrageous to call an MP a Zionist if they self-identify as a Zionist? It was telling that Bastani confused a political ideology with a state. Next Ellis read Timothy Garton Ash's article on 'The Future of Liberalism' on the website of *Prospect Magazine*. Once again a cruel smile appeared on Ellis's face and he laughed mirthlessly as he read: 'The victory of Joe Biden in the US presidential election gives a fragile opening for liberal renewal... In Britain, a populist Conservative government faces a Labour Party with a new, left-liberal leader, Keir Starmer. In France, Marine Le Pen remains a serious threat to Europe's leading liberal renewer, Emmanuel Macron'. Oh *please*... Blather, blather, blather blathered Timothy. (You would expect a British liberal to be called Timothy, somehow.) Ellis's smile deepened. How he laughed, coldly - so coldly that his laughter might have been used to store the new Pfizer vaccine - as he read Timothy's grumble that 'liberalism itself has come to be viewed as the ideology of the rich, the established and powerful'. Well, yes. And also the ideology of the imperialists, the invaders of foreign countries, the enablers of torture. And lurking within Timothy's liberalism, what do we find? Another version of the STRONG ON IMMIGRATION red mug that Ed Milliband flourished, along with Yvette Cooper. Timothy says 'we need to slow down the rate of change to *one that most human natures can bear*, while preserving the overall liberal direction of travel... This means, for example, limiting immigration, securing frontiers, and strengthening a sense of community, trust and reciprocity inside them'. In other words, pandering to racism and reaction. Blather, blather, blather. Timothy cries out in a squeaky voice, like a mouse in a cartoon, for *liberal patriotism*. More storage space for the vaccine! Timothy described 'the west's liberal wars, such as those in Afghanistan, Libya and Iraq', adding 'in each case military interventions were partially justified by reference to liberal ends'. Alas, things hadn't quite turned out to be entirely perfect but - liberals take heart! - 'To learn from these grim experiences does not require us to abandon the universalist aspiration to secure for other people the freedoms we enjoy ourselves'. Ash had never grasped that liberal rhetoric was the oily salad-dressing scattered across imperialist savagery. The motives for invading other countries were material. Even Eric Blair understood that, almost a century ago. But Ash's liberal baltherings - a slip but a marvellous coinage! - said not a word about US imperialism or the bloody record of the US in overthrowing democracies and promoting coups. Instead - it's official enemies time! - Timothy darkly informs us that 'Chinese influence now reaches deep inside liberal democracies, distorting our democratic processes and trying to use financial clout and outright bullying to impose self-censorship on journalists and academics, a process seen most dramatically in Australia. This calls on us to defend, in the heart of our own societies, such primary liberal values as freedom of speech and academic independence'. The vacuity of this kind of argument was exposed by a remarkable absence, namely any mention of the Palestinians and the blood-spattered bellicosity of Israel and the Zionist lobby. Nor did Timothy have a word to say about Jeremy Corbyn or the annihilation of a progressive and indeed *liberal* mild social-reformist manifesto at the hands of the Israeli embassy, the Zionist lobby, and the corporate media (not least the *Guardian* which regularly supplied voluble Timothy with yet another platform for his windy baltherings). Ash's politics were every bit as bland and balthery and fragrantly greasy as you might expect from a man who was Isaiah Berlin Professorial Fellow at St Antony's College, Oxford, and a Senior Fellow at the Hoover Institution, Stanford University. Isaiah Berlin was a Zionist and an ardent admirer of that sly, lying, devious Jew and enabler of Palestinian misery Chaim Weizmann. Isaiah Berlin was no friend of human rights or equality. He asserted that Jerusalem was the capital of Israel. He scampered off to collect the Jerusalem Prize, invented for PR purposes by the atrocity-saturated Jewish state. Isaiah Berlin voiced support for the two-state solution - that tactical fraud beloved of devious Zionists who effectively supported the status quo. In a humane liberal world there would be no chairs named after that old sectarian fraud. As for the Hoover Institution. Judging by Ash's politics perhaps the benefactor was J. Edgar... Ellis put Ash's full name into Google and added the word 'Israel' It supplied a feature in - where else? - the *Guardian*. Wednesday 26th July 2006. An opinion piece about the Middle East. Ellis began reading. Almost at once he discovered what a shoddy and ill-informed historian Timothy Garton Ash was. According to Ash a French mob had chanted 'à bas les juifs' as Dreyfus was stripped of his epaulettes. Except that they hadn't. That was an invention of the lying Jew Theodor Herzl. The mob hadn't howled 'death to the Jews' but 'death to traitors!' Herzl doctored the facts for propaganda purposes. You'd think an academic historian would know that. But it got much worse than Ash's slovenly incompetence as a historian. Ash went on to claim that Israel was the consequence of the Holocaust. No it wasn't. Political Zionism existed long before the Nazi Party. Zionism, a blood and soil ideology, grew out of exactly the same soil as Nazism. Ellis read on. Ah, so this is where this balthery wisdom is leading. Ash peddles the liberal Zionist propaganda line of 'a viable Palestinian state' alongside Israel. Which is like a liberal saying the solution to apartheid South Africa was a black state alongside a white supremacist state. Apart from its inherent reluctance to acknowledge the principle of equality, the 'two-states' fraud overlooked the essential fact that Israel had absolutely no interest in allowing a free and independent Palestinian statelet. It also rather overlooked what would happen to those Palestinians inside Israel. But that wouldn't bother balthery Timothy Garton Ash as he sipped a rather splendid sherry in the Senior Common Room before jetting off across the pond in Business Class. Palestine was always the acid test of a person's politics and Timothy Garton Ash revealed himself all too clearly for what he was - an insufferably smug, well-fed flabby liberal with a giant carbon footprint, whose life had been one of agreeable chit-chat in tranquil leafy institutions, and for whom Brexit was at most a disagreeable expression of democracy and a deeply felt matter which might well lead to one having to wait considerably longer in queues at passport control. It was time to listen once more to Phil Och's classic song 'Love Me, I'm a Liberal' which was timelessly relevant as a commentary on people like Timothy Garton Ash. It grew dark outside. The child held up a potato. Then she ate a banana. Ellis ate a pasta and vegetable mix, followed by apple crumble with ice-cream and yogurt. He sent some emails. Back on the internet he learned that the International Criminal Court had found that 'there is a reasonable basis to believe that from April 2003 through September 2003 members of UK armed forces in Iraq committed the war crime of wilful killing/murder pursuant to article 8(2)(a)(i) or article 8(2)(c)(i)), at a minimum, against seven persons in their custody. The information available provides a reasonable basis to believe that from 20 March 2003 through 28 July 2009 members of UK armed forces committed the war crime of torture and inhuman/cruel treatment (article 8(2)(a)(ii) or article 8(2)(c)(i)); and the war crime of outrages upon personal dignity (article 8(2)(b)(xxi) or article 8(2)(c)(ii)) against at least 54 persons in their custody. The information available further provides a reasonable basis to believe that members of UK armed forces committed the war crime of rape and/or other forms of sexual violence article 8(2)(b)(xxii) or article 8(2)(e)(vi), at a minimum, against the seven victims, while they were detained at Camp Breadbasket in May 2003. These crimes, while not exhaustive, were sufficiently well supported to enable a subject-matter determination on crimes within the jurisdiction of the Court. In this respect, the Office recalls the wider body of findings by other public authorities and institutions in the UK that hundreds of Iraqi detainees were subjected to conditions of detention and practices which amounted to inhuman or degrading treatment. Although the Office's findings may not be fully representative of the overall scale of the victimisation, they appear to correspond to the most serious allegations of violence against persons in UK custody. The Office has not identified evidence of an affirmative plan or policy on the part of the Ministry of Defence (MoD) or UK Government to subject detainees to the forms of conduct set out in this report. Nonetheless, the Office has found that several levels of institutional civilian supervisory, and military command, failures contributed to the commission of crimes against detainees by UK soldiers in Iraq. As set out in this report, despite the existence of standards of procedure in the MoD requiring detainees to be treated humanely, a number of techniques found unlawful in UK domestic law in 1972 and banned from use – especially in interrogations – re-entered practice through gradual attrition of institutional memory and lack of clear guidance. As the Baha Mousa Inquiry found, by the time of the Iraq war the MoD had no generally available written doctrine on the interrogation of prisoners of war, other than at a high level of generality. Instead, doctrine had largely become restricted to what was taught during interrogation courses, with varying degrees of understanding of what was permissible, as well as variations in emphasis and interpretation between different instructors. This spilled over into the early rotations of Operation Telic ("Op TELIC"), with UK service members holding differing views on what was permissible'. But, marvellously, the ICC decided there would be no prosecution - demonstrating once again that the ICC was a timid, cowardly organisation that declined to act against the superpowers, while continuing to drag its heels regarding the overwhelming evidence of serial Israeli war crimes. Jonathan Beale, BBC Defence correspondent, wrote: There is a palpable sense of relief inside the Ministry of Defence that the International Criminal Court will not be pursuing a case against the UK government over allegations that British forces in Iraq committed serious war crimes against Iraqi detainees. Elsewhere, Ellis learned that Palestinian writer, journalist and political activist Majd Kayyal was arrested by Israeli police at his home in Haifa on Tuesday morning. At 6am, police raided the home he shares with his mother, seizing Kayyal and his brother Ward, a student. After ransacking the home, the police confiscated the Kayyal brothers' computers and phones, and departed with Majd and Ward. They were then released following several hours of detention. Kayyal, 30, is a prominent voice in the Palestinian citizens of Israel community and has written for *Middle East Eye*. Upon their release on Tuesday evening, Kayyal wrote a Facebook post thanking people for their support, adding that the arrest was "complete nonsense and nothing but intimidation and repression, as usual, and just like it has happened with many young men and women in the recent period." Kayyal was born in northern Israel's Haifa, but his family were originally displaced from al-Birwa, a village in the Galilee known as the birthplace of Palestinian poet Mahmoud Darwish. They were expelled from it by Jews. The violence and sectarianism of Jews in Palestine continued in 2021. The Palestinians had endured over a century of dispossession and harassment. The police action was standard low-grade Israeli terrorism against peaceful activism. Ellis went offline and signed some Christmas cards. He watched the 10pm Sky News. Brexit. The pandemic. A brusque acknowledgement that Beth Rigby would be away for three months having breached the Coronavirus restrictions. Ellis went to bed. Humboldt waved his hands at me, he read.

Friday 11th December 2020

Ellis woke at 5am. At 5.30am he heard a man and a woman walk past in the street, talking loudly. He dozed. Later he switched on the bedside radio. Barbara Windsor had died. The BBC treated this news as if she had been a giant of the world of cinema and drama. Ellis dressed and ate his morning bowl of cereal. He went online. The *Bookseller* website reported the latest exciting news from the world of publishing. **O'Farrell is the critics' pick of 2020 as Hamnet, Mantel and Ferrante top the pile,** the headline said. A collation of the newspapers' books of the year round-ups show Maggie O'Farrell's acclaimed *Hamnet* out in front, Ellis read. He learned that Richard Osman's crime fiction debut *The Thursday Murder Club* was already the bestselling novel of the year after just three months on sale. In other news from the world of corporate publishing Jonathan Cape had won a 10-publisher auction for *Fire Rush*, the "phenomenal" debut novel by Jacqueline Crooks. Truly the world of commercial fiction was full of phenomena. A dull, wet day. Ellis went out and returned with a pack of birdseed. He spent much of the day reading. The child played with her new pink doll's bath. She poured in a bottle of imaginary water, then placed the plastic dog in the bath. Ellis ate warmed-up vegetable and pasta mix. He read three sections of the latest edition of the *Sunday Times*. Later, in bed, Ellis read: This was when Ricketts told him that Princeton would not renege. Money would be found. But this put Ricketts in the morally superior position. Was it the case, Ellis wondered, that sentences in fiction had grown shorter as the twentieth century had progressed? He put out the light and was soon asleep.

Saturday 12th December 2020

Ellis went out at 9am to post more Christmas cards. He encountered a couple. The woman had been pushing a pram containing a baby. She was followed by a man who was plainly her partner. He had a small black dog, a puppy, on a lead. The puppy had stopped, planted its four legs firmly in a truculent manner, and was refusing to walk any further. The man scooped up the dog. He said: I'll take it back. The woman continued while the man returned up the road. Ellis went on and posted his cards. When he came back he could see the woman in the distance. She had paused and was looking back. From the other direction came her now dog-less partner. Ellis turned off and lost sight of them. Today it seemed a lot less cold than previous mornings. He went indoors and ate his breakfast while reading Ammar Kazmi's lengthy online essay 'Lawfare, McCarthyism, and the EHRC'. The child played with her Play-Doh. A blue duck. Next Ellis watched the new Taylor Swift song 'No Body, No Crime' on YouTube. Later, Ellis read Paul McConnell's old article in the *Morning Star*, which argued that 'the decisive reason Labour lost the election is that over the last three years it shifted from being a party committed to respecting the result of the Brexit referendum, to being a party of Remain in all but name.' Paul McConnell added: 'There were, of course, a number of other important reasons, ranging from the undisguised bias of the mainstream media, the pessimism ingrained by more than 30 years of neoliberalism, and a concerted campaign of character assassination against Corbyn, carried out over the last four years, often with the support of many Labour MPs and disgruntled Blairites in the media. But Labour's changed stance on Brexit proved decisive as this was the key issue for many voters in the election, formed the core of the Tory election message (dutifully parroted by the media) and is reflected in the Leave-voting constituencies which Labour lost to the Tories.' Paul McConnell continued: 'Once Labour was successfully manoeuvred into backing a second referendum, the electoral logic of this position was to try to capture the disgruntled middle classes, who form the social base of the second vote/Remain bloc…The election, then, was lost because Labour chose to privilege the politics of the middle class, over that of large sections of the working class on the defining issue of Brexit.' Paul McConnell added: 'While the Brexit vote is complex, the majority of working-class people that voted for it (which was a majority of the working class that voted) are from areas that have witnessed industrial decline, poverty and marginalisation for decades…when they voted for Brexit, the establishment reacted immediately with efforts to de-legitimate and overturn the result'. In the 2019 general election, wrote Paul McConnell, 'having capitulated to the demands of reactionary liberalism and committed itself to a second referendum, Labour could not consistently present itself as a party of insurgent change and transformation, while playing the part of restoring the status quo ante on the Brexit issue'. Paul McConnell concluded: 'it is no mere coincidence that those most fervently opposed to Brexit are also those most hostile to Corbyn and the Corbyn project in Labour'. He wrote: 'celebrity commentators imparting bland slogans are no substitute for organised, educated cadres of committed socialists in our communities and workplaces. In doing this, we will need to develop media platforms that break with the individualism and narcissism of the current sea of podcasts, Patreons and niche publications'. Time passed. At 17.50 on this dark December day BBC Radio 4 was spewing yet more lies and venom about Jeremy Corbyn and anti-Semitism via the medium of an interview with Labour MP Kate Green. 'He needs to apologise,' said Green. Ellis looked her up. She represented Stretford and Urmston in Greater Manchester. Kate Green OBE was another colourless right-wing mediocrity of the type which infested the Parliamentary Labour Party. In 2016 she led Owen Smith's unsuccessful challenge for the leadership of the Labour Party. Before that she had worked for Barclays Bank (1982-1997) and for two years after that as 'a Whitehall and Industry Group secondee to the Home Office'. She then became a charity hopper, working as Director of the National Council for One Parent Families (2000-2004), before hopping off to become Chief Executive of the Child Poverty Action Group (2005-2009). She served as a magistrate in the City of London (1993-2009). In 2009 she was selected as the candidate for Stretford and Urmston and elected to Parliament the following year. She played the feminist card, claiming that Corbyn's attitude to sexism reinforced rather than addressed the root causes of gender inequality. Kate Green is a member of Labour Friends of Israel. Next Ellis read a review by John Booth on the *Lobster* magazine website of the books *Left Out* by Gabriel Pogrund and Patrick Maguire and *This Land* by Owen Jones. Booth exposed the shoddiness and dishonesty of all these authors in their account of the bogus anti-Semitism crisis. None mentioned the Israel-lobbying background of the Zionists at the forefront of the slander campaign. None of these authors mentioned the fact that the 'Enough is Enough' demonstration organised in Parliament Square by the Jewish Leadership Council was at the behest of an organisation whose chairman, Sir Michael Davis, just happened to be Chief Executive Officer and Treasurer of the Conservative Party. How typical that a sleek narcissist like Owen Jones should be silent about that rather substantial fact. Jones had nothing at all to say about the well-documented links between the Israeli embassy and those seeking to destroy Corbyn with spurious allegations of anti-Semitism. The name Shai Masot does not appear in Jones's account of the Corbyn years. John Booth pointed out that between 15 June 2015 and 31 March 2019, in the eight main newspapers in Britain, no less than 5,497 stories appeared about Jeremy Corbyn, the Labour Party and anti-Semitism. Owen Jones likewise had nothing at all to say about the BBC's vendetta against Corbyn. But then Owen Jones is part of the corporate media, just as the other two authors are. Ellis ate shepherd's pie and cabbage, then watched *A Night to Remember*. He was surprised to discover just how much James Cameron had ripped-off from this movie when making his *Titanic* extravaganza. In bed Ellis read as far as: He had lots of lawyers - he collected lawyers and psychoanalysts. Treatment was not the object of his visits with the analysts. He wanted to talk, to express himself. And then darkness, night, sleep's sweet oblivion.

Sunday 13th December 2020

Ellis woke at 5.20am. His mind was a cage of chattering monkeys. In time he drifted off again and woke just before 8am. The news. A hard Brexit loomed.

Ellis put on his military-style green shirt and then pulled over it a blue cardigan.
Blue and green
should not be seen
without a colour
in between
said an off-page voice, with an off-page smile. Later Ellis went out to deliver
some local Christmas cards. A dull grey morning. On the walk light rain began,
then fizzled out. Ellis discovered that a neighbour had died. Someone who lived
alone. Someone who had seemed quite well the last time he had spoken to her.
Death hits you like a fist to the chest. Sometimes just a light thud, sometimes
very much harder. And then the shock in time wears off and the days are filled
with distraction. And death becomes forgotten. And the gaudy carnival
continues. The walk round the neighbourhood had taken a couple of hours. Back
home again Ellis wrote an email and sent it. The child wore her cycle helmet.
Ellis read Tony Greenstein's latest blog post. For Palestinians the Star of David
is what the Swastika is to Jews, Tony Greenstein wrote. Ellis baked cod with
tomatoes. He watched the last programme in the 'Small Axe' series. It was far
superior to the two which preceded it in the series. The girl who made animal
noises and had big staring eyes was a wonderful actress. Ellis recognised the
booklet by Bernard Coard. He had a copy of it somewhere. It wasn't really his.
It had belonged to a progressive London teacher, who long ago he'd married.
Afterwards Ellis watched the news. The Brexit talks were to continue until the
end of the month. The final deadline. Except that every final deadline dissolved.
The yellow strip at the foot of the screen reported the death of John le Carré.
What a falling off was there, thought Ellis. A man who had once marched
against Bush and Blair on a dull London Thursday in a crowd which contained
Peter Capaldi and Ellis Sharp. Ellis had spotted Capaldi at the time, having only
recently seen him on television in *The Crow Road*. Back then Ellis had no idea
what the spy thriller writer looked like. Ellis remembered that day well. The
march had been diverted across Waterloo Bridge and then back across
Westminster Bridge, and then been obliged to stand and wait. A diversion to
give Ian McEwan and other reactionary sycophants from the world of culture
time to scuttle out of Number 10, where they had been taking tea with the First
Lady, Laura Bush, who had once killed someone and escaped all punishment by
virtue of her wealth and social position. But since that time le Carré had exposed
himself as being on the side of reaction, signing the toxic celebrities and minor
mediocrities letter denouncing Corbyn and Labour for anti-Semitism just before
the December 2019 General Election. Ellis could never forgive David Cornwell
for that calculated act against a possible social democratic government. At the
end of his life Cornwell had shown himself to be on the side of spivs, racists,
liars and the tax-dodging multi-millionaire class, and against humanity, equality
and justice. By 10.30pm Sky had found someone to speak about Cornwell. It

was the multi-millionaire reactionary Robert Harris, author of very successful potboilers. Harris had loathed Corbyn from the moment the possibility of his leadership of the Labour Party had arrived. Ellis remembered Harris writing in the *Sunday Times* urging everyone to sign up to the £3 scheme to vote against Corbyn. No surprise that a rich smoothie like Harris had formerly been a corporate television news reporter and later best mates with Cornwell. After Harris came the Sky papers review. This night it featured Mr Slithy himself! More pangs of nausea rocked Ellis's belly, like acid indigestion. Or might have done, had he been a 'character'. Ellis switched off the TV and went to bed. Jones nauseated him but there were no physical symptoms. A strange demonism revealed itself to her, Ellis read. But she was not intimidated.

Monday 14th December 2020

The headlines at 5am on the BBC World News were the extension of the Brexit talks and the death of John le Carré. 'He was an undisputed giant of world literature,' the newscaster said. Ellis disputed that. Cornwell was no more than a commercially successful writer of competent spy thrillers. He was the Eric Ambler of his generation. His books had grown longer and stodgier. It was a case of J.K. Rowling Syndrome. John le Carré's publishers were plainly terrified of suggesting edits. If you told a profitable writer he was verbose he'd go to another publisher. And corporate publishing was all about commercial success and dividends. It was not about writing or literature. Ellis switched off the radio and drifted in and out of consciousness. He switched on again at 7.45am. At some point Robert Harris came on air, ladling out adjectives. Later, Ellis dressed and ate his breakfast. Later, he talked to a neighbour. Next, Ellis went shopping, buying bananas, cheese, yogurt, a loaf of brown bread, a bottle of red wine and two cartons of milk. Later, he went for a walk. Back home again he had his lunch - soup, bread and cheese, followed by an apple, sliced, with yogurt. Ellis composed two email letters. The child played with her Play-Doh. Cup! she said, wanting her mother to make a Play-Doh cup. The result was more like a goblet without a stem. Ellis heard a knocking sound. It was the boiler, which seemed to be in the throes of some kind of metallic distress. He lowered the temperature control and the knocking ceased. Stew for supper, with mashed potato and cauliflower, washed down with a glass of water. On the Sky News at 10pm the latest Coronavirus restrictions were the top story. London to enter Tier Three at midnight tomorrow. Bad news for the hospitality sector. An unhappy pub owner was interviewed. It was reported that there was to be a Christmas lockdown in Germany, the Netherlands and the Czech republic. Meanwhile the Brexit talks continued. Ellis went to bed. Maybe he thought he was Rameau's nephew or even Jean Genet, Bellow had written.

Tuesday 15th December 2020

Ellis woke at 5.50am. He listened to the radio for 40 minutes, then switched off and drifted back to sleep. When he woke again it was approaching 8am. A man whose wife had dementia was being interviewed about his distress at being unable to visit her at Christmas in the care home where she lived. Later a government minister was interviewed, insisting that there would be no Christmas lockdown. Ellis ate his breakfast. Paul O'Connell tweeted: Liberals - the handmaidens of fascism. Louis @Louis_Allday tweeted: Just noting that during the First Intifada Jeffrey Goldberg served as an IDF prison guard and personally assaulted Palestinian detainees. Ellis went out. He bought a *Morning Star* - the last one in the rack! - a packet of Shredded Wheat, two bottles of red wine and two packets of dishwasher tablets. Then he went for a walk. The sun was low in the sky. His shadow elongated itself before him as he walked northward. A good twenty feet or more in length. Back home again he went on the internet. Somebody called Luke de Pulford tweeted: This is huge. Thank you so much @chiefrabbi for your willingness to invoke the excruciating memory of the Shoah to defend the #Uyghur people. NOW will the @GOVUK listen? This was a reference to an article on the *Guardian* website by the Zionist Ephraim Mirvis - *As Chief Rabbi I can no longer remain silent about the plight of the Uighurs*. Ellis laughed coldly at the notion that a man with Mirvis's foul record cared about human rights. He also noted de Pulford's use of the term 'Shoah' - the preferred Zionist word for the Nazi genocide. Steve W StevenW69808657 replying to @chiefrabbi tweeted: On issues where he has real influence: Apartheid Israel, its occupation of Palestinian land & intermittent mass slaughters of Palestinians, the Chief Rabbi doesn't just shirk "responsibility", he indulges in apologetics, solicits for weapons & meets & grins with the perpetrators. Simon Cohen @Desuetudine replying to @chiefrabbi tweeted: Says a Chief Rabbi who publicly backed one of the most Right Wing Governments in modern British history, supported the hideous defamation of Corbyn that was even condemned by the most orthodox Jews as a political misuse of antisemitism and disinformation. Ellis strongly agreed with those sentiments. He watched the news headlines. The five days of Christmas get togethers would not be changed by the government, despite majority public support for a lockdown and the fearful predictions of scientists that it would result in a new surge of infections in January. It was hinted that a Brexit trade deal might yet be arranged. Ellis went to bed. At the age of ten I had dismantled the machine and put it together again, he read. And then the darkness.

A grey, overcast morning. Ellis watched a new Ryan Adams video, featuring aerial shots of Birmingham, Alabama. He recognised the Sloss site. He had once explored its rotting innards. A marvellous place, full of rust. Entropy incarnate. How Tarkovsky would have liked it! Ellis went on the Amazon site and read: Ryan Adams' first album in three years, *Wednesdays*, is purely raw, vulnerable, and honest. The music takes you on a deep dive exploring the complex heart of Ryan Adams, through a journey of love, pain, and heartbreak. The album so effortlessly creates an immediate connection with anyone who has ever experienced love lost - the type of love that haunts you in quiet places of your mind. While the lyrics walk you through the vast emotional layers of grief, they also remind you of the rich memories of a love that will forever remain a part of you. *Wednesdays* will be available on CD and LP March 19th. The LP will include an exclusive two extra tracks. 1. I'm Sorry And I Love You 2. Who Is Going To Love Me Now, If Not You 3. When You Cross Over 4. Walk In The Dark 5. Poison & Pain 6. Wednesdays 7. Birmingham 8. So, Anyways 9. Mamma 10. Lost In Time 11. Dreaming You Backwards. Later, Ellis went shopping. In the supermarket he bought milk, chocolate, Lurpak, loose tea, coffee and other items. He noticed a male customer without a mask, and three staff without masks. In another shop he bought a Christmas pudding. Home again Ellis read John Pilger's latest article, about a visit to the Armed Services Memorial in Staffordshire. The names of more than 16,000 British servicemen and women are listed. The literature says they *died in operational theatre or were targeted by terrorists*. On the day I was there, wrote John Pilger, a stonemason was adding new names to those who have died in some 50 operations across the world during what is known as *peacetime*. Malaya, Ireland, Kenya, Hong Kong, Libya, Iraq, Palestine and many more, including secret operations, such as Indochina. John Pilger added: 'Not a year has passed since peace was declared in 1945 that Britain has not sent military forces to fight the wars of empire. The investigative journalist Phil Miller recently revealed in *Declassified* that Boris Johnson's Britain maintained 145 military sites – call them bases — in 42 countries. Johnson has boasted that Britain is to be "the foremost naval power in Europe". In the midst of the greatest health emergency in modern times, with more than 4 million surgical procedures delayed by the National Health Service, Johnson has announced a record increase of £16.5 billion in so-called defence spending – a figure that would restore the under-resourced NHS many times over. Exploring the serenity of the National War Memorial, I soon realised there was not a single monument, or plinth, or plaque, or rosebush honouring the memory of Britain's victims — the civilians in the "peacetime" operations commemorated here. There is no monument to the Palestinian children murdered with the British elite's enduring connivance. Two weeks ago, Israel's military chief of staff and Britain's Chief of the Defence Staff signed an agreement to "formalise and enhance" military co-operation. This was not news. More British arms and logistical support will now flow to the lawless regime in Tel Aviv, whose snipers target children and psychopaths interrogate children in extreme isolation. Perhaps the most striking omission at the Staffordshire war memorial is an acknowledgement of the million Iraqis whose lives and country were destroyed by the illegal invasion of Blair and Bush in 2003. ORB, a member of the British Polling Council, put the figure at 1.2 million. In 2013, the ComRes organisation asked a cross-section of the British public how many Iraqis had died in the invasion. A majority said fewer than 10,000.' Next Ellis read Jonathan Cook's latest article on his website about the growing suppression of criticism of Israel across Europe. In Germany, for instance, 'Cultural associations, festivals, universities, Jewish research centres, political think-tanks, museums and libraries are being forced to scrutinise the past of those they wish to invite in case some minor transgression against Israel can be exploited by local Jewish organisations. That has created a toxic, politically paranoid atmosphere that inevitably kills trust and creativity. But the psychosis runs deeper still. Israel, and anything related to it, has become such a combustible subject – one that can ruin careers in an instant – that most political, academic and cultural figures in Germany now choose to avoid it entirely. Israel, as its supporters intended, is rapidly becoming untouchable'. The underlying aim, it seemed to Ellis, was to criminalise all pro-Palestinian activism. Darkness fell. The child ate a bowl of grapes and then a packet of carrot puffs. She said she wanted to watch an episode of Waffle the Wonder Dog. Ellis ate quiche with baked beans and mashed potato and swede, with a glass of water. At 9pm he began watching a Channel 5 documentary about the disappearance of Suzy Lamplugh. As I ran into the Chicago crowd, Ellis read in bed some two hours later, I felt my pegs slipping, the strings slacker, my tone going lower.

Thursday 17th December 2020

Ellis woke at 6.55am. A bright dry morning. BBC radio news dutifully recycled the latest US propaganda. A major computer hack believed to have originated in Russia. A Libyan wanted for the Lockerbie bombing. Lockerbie, Lockerbie, Lockerbie. Never *Vincennes*, *Vincennes*, *Vincennes*. Ellis went for a walk. Another bright sunlit morning. Later he went online again. In literary bauble news, David Constantin is to receive the Queen's Gold Medal for Poetry. In book profits news Richard Osman's *The Thursday Murder Club* (Penguin), *Pinch of Nom Quick & Easy* (Bluebird) and Barack Obama's *A Promised Land* (Viking) are all in the running for number one Christmas bestseller. In risible mediocrity news Hodder & Stoughton has commissioned a new book from reactionary *Guardian* 'political journalist' Matthew d'Ancona: *Identity,*

Ignorance, Innovation. In the complete-collapse-of-literary-standards news, in her first fiction acquisition as publishing director at Bloomsbury, Emma Herdman has bought *Metronome*, Tom Watson's debut novel. Further evidence of the irrelevance of the Booker Prize to good writing is revealed by the judging panel for next year, which will include former Archbishop of Canterbury Rowan Williams, 'writer and editor' Horatia Harrod and 'actor' Natascha McElhone. In Zionist propaganda news, TLS Books, the publishing imprint of the *Times Literary Supplement,* is to publish *Jews Don't Count* in February - a supposedly 'urgent' polemic on 'the realities of anti-Semitism' by David Baddiel. In the afternoon Ellis talked to two old friends. Later he baked some salmon and boiled potatoes and frozen peas. He ate stewed apple and ice-cream. He did some reading. He watched the 10pm Sky News. The virus. Brexit. Ellis went to bed. They disliked my style intensely, he read. They hated it.

Friday 18th December 2020

Ellis woke in the dark. 7.25am. He turned the 'Today' programme on. Propaganda for GCHQ. The Christmas puzzle. How solving the Christmas puzzle could get you employment at GCHQ. The sentimentalisation of state surveillance. That overworked adjective 'Orwellian' seemed apt. Then the sports news. Russia! The athletics doping scandal! The ban on Russian participation reduced from four years to two. Outrage. And then the news headlines. Brexit talks on a knife-edge again. Then Russia again. Hacking! An American imperialist given a softball interview by one of the 'Today' power pimps. Justin, was it? And then - Russia again! It was like a return to the bad old days of the Cold War. One day the BBC was propagandising against China. The next Russia. Sometimes Venezuala or Iran. This morning a BBC hack named Steve described his questions to Vladimir Putin at a press conference. He asked questions of the sort people like Steve would never dare to ask a Western politician. President Putin had replied that the West had lied about NATO's expansion plans. His point was ignored by the BBC. The intepretation placed upon Steve's interview was that 'Putin' (as the BBC called him) was a cold-hearted cynical monster. Well, maybe. But Steve would never dare to ask an American President those kinds of questions. BBC news reporters could always be relied upon to approach leaders of western imperialism, colonialism and militarism from a kneeling position. It was already plain that Joe Biden would receive nothing but deference from BBC news. He would always be 'Joe Biden'. The BBC angle was plain. Joe had difficult tasks ahead of him. He would do his best for freedom and democracy. Not on the 'Today' programme: Half of Yemen's population will suffer from hunger next year due to lack of international support, the United Nations warned on Wednesday. The spokesperson for the UN Secretary-General, Stephane Dujarric, told reporters: 'We're now helping only about 9 million people every month, down from a peak of 13 million earlier this year. More than 80 percent of Yemenis need humanitarian assistance and protection. Next year, more than half of all Yemenis will go hungry, and we expect 5 million people to be living just one step away from famine and about 50,000 people to be living in famine-like conditions.' The conflict has left 233,000 people dead and 80 per cent of the population – about 30 million people – dependent on aid, according to the UN. UNICEF Executive Director Henrietta Fore has described Yemen as the most dangerous place on earth for children: 'Yemen is teetering on the edge of complete collapse. Over 80 per cent of people require urgent humanitarian assistance and protection. Including 12 million children, whose lives are a waking nightmare. One child dies every ten minutes from a preventable disease. Two million are out of school. And thousands have been killed, maimed, or recruited since 2015. Just last week, 11 were reportedly killed, including a one-month-old baby'. And now for something completely different: the latest book prize news from the world of corporate publishing and its corporate allies. Professor Suzannah Lipscomb will chair the judging panel for the 2020 Costa Book of the Year prize, where she will be joined by vlogger Simon Savidge, actor Stephen Mangan and TV presenter Angellica Bell. The final nine-member panel that selects the overall Costa Book of the Year is made up of a chair of judges, a judge from each category panel and three other well-known people in the public eye who love reading. Book news for liberals who don't mind the odd splash of blood or the screams of torture victims in the night: Barack Obama has released a 17-strong list of his favourite books of the year, spanning memoir, fiction and non-fiction, including *Homeland Elegies* by Ayad Akhtar (Tinder Press), *How Much of These Hills is Gold* by C Pam Zhang (Virago) and Isabel Wilkerson's *Caste* (Allen Lane). Ellis went out. A grey, blustery day. He bought a swede, some onions, a head of broccoli, two parsnips and three large mushrooms. In the park the child went down a slide. Later, indoors, she ate some sliced pear. More snack, she said. Ellis went online. He read an article by the former Labour MP Chris Mullin, on the *Middle East Eye* website. Although it purported to be a defence of Corbyn, it demonstrated the lamentable poverty of the Labourist intellect. 'The rise of Corbyn also attracted a small number of far-leftists whose views were not in tune with Labour values,' wrote Mullin, adding 'and a relative handful of antisemites attracted by his record of support for the Palestinians. It is the latter who are the source of Labour's recent woes'. What bilge, what tosh, what utter garbage, thought Ellis. The source of Labour's recent woes were the rancid and aggressive Zionist lobby - the so-called 'Jewish community' - in alliance with the poisonous Labour right (a spectrum encompassing the Blairites and beyond). Mullin went on to confess, 'As it happens, I am not a Corbyn supporter. I did not vote for him in either of the Labour leadership elections'. Gosh. What a surprise. 'One of Corbyn's most attractive features is that, although he has been on the receiving end of a great deal of abuse, he never responds in kind,' wrote Mullin. Yes, thought Ellis, but the problem was Corbyn never responded at all. He was a disaster by virtue of his aversion to conflict. Such was his stupidity he even grovelled to the Jewish Labour Movement, begging them not to leave the party. And then we come to Mullin's classically Labourist fence-sitting: 'One difficulty for outsiders is that there are few heroes on either side'. Ah yes, the equivalence between the occupied and the occupiers. In Mullin's twisted perceptions, resistance by Hamas is the problem, because it wilfully invites 'inevitably disproportionate retaliation'. The victims are at fault. The violent provocations of the belligerent Jewish state are erased from consideration. The victims are at fault, at fault, at fault. Mullin displays a classic colonial mindset. It gets worse. 'One doesn't envy Starmer in having to deal with all of this. None of it is of his making.' Oh *please*. It gets worse. 'One can't blame Starmer for wanting to draw a line under it,' sobs Mullin, who shows himself to lack any kind of critical understanding of the remorseless Zionist lobby. His feeble conclusion is to hold out his hands in a gesture of helplessness - the classic fence-sitting liberal exhibiting the posture of the one who *understands* it all but cannot *do* anything in the face of all this unreasonableness. Muller whimpers: 'but has he?' Well, Starmer is planning to set up a body to deal with supposed anti-Semitism among Labour Party members which will be staffed by rabid Zionists and reactionaries, so plainly there will be a conclusion of sorts. Expulsions, expulsions, expulsions. It grew dark. The child bounced up and down on the sofa. She'll need a trampoline when she's older, Ellis thought. He ate chicken casserole with rice. Later he went back online. Joe Sucksmith's Twitter page led him to the latest verbiage by the ubiquitous Rachel Shabi. It was on *The Nation* website, headlined 'The British Labour Party's Anti-Semitism Problem'. 'Under Corbyn, Labour was seen as dismissive or slow to investigate complaints,' was an absolutely characteristic sentence by Shabi. *Seen by whom?* was the obvious question. A question which Shabi-journalism never asked. The words 'Zionism' and 'Israel lobby' appear nowhere in Shabi's shabby witterings. She speaks of 'the anti-Semitism crisis' as if it was real rather than fabricated. She solemnly asserts that 'October's EHRC report was a sobering verdict for a party that not only established the commission but also introduced the very law it was now deemed to have broken'. The EHRC's disinclination to investigate the Conservative Party said everything about that organisation. 'To read the report's full 130 pages is to comprehend both the scale of the problem and Labour's culpability.' Garbage. On and on it went, the usual stale material, stuffed with bland generalisations. Rachel Shabi, spokeswoman for 'Jewish people'. And at the end the real testament to Shabi's role as an acceptable pseudo-leftist, whose platitudes and pieties would never disturb the stupor of the liberal bourgeoisie: 'Rachel Shabi is a UK-based journalist, author, and broadcaster who has been covering the Labour Party for various publications including *The Guardian*, *The Independent*, and *The New York Times*'. Ellis watched the 10pm Sky News. The virus, a possible new lockdown, Brexit talks. He went to bed. As he followed me there I entered one of the stalls and was free at last to read Kathleen's letter, Ellis read.

Saturday 19th December 2020

The alarm went at 6.50am, dragging Ellis from his dream. It was raining. A miserable morning. He contemplated going out for a *Times* but decided against it. The headline news was about the new mutant strain of the virus which was more easily transmitted than the original Coronavirus and was believed to lie behind the recent surge in infections. On balance Ellis did not wish to risk death for the sake of learning what would be on TV over Christmas. He only bought the *Times* to read the Arts section and the TV schedule. He could manage without. Ellis was not short of reading material. He filled the washing machine with two pairs of trousers and a pair of jeans. He filled the blue plastic bulb with washing liquid and balanced it on top of the clothing. Then he switched the machine on and returned to his computer. The hours passed. The rain stopped and the sun came out. Ellis read Tariq Ali's article 'Starmer's War' on the *New Left Review* website. How much sharper Tariq Ali was as a political analyst than flabby columnists like Owen Jones, Rachel Shabi and the *Novara Media* gang. 'The weakest link turned out to be Corbyn's supposedly loyal ally and Shadow Chancellor,' Ali wrote. 'But John McDonnell – hailed by the soft left as 'the most radical politician of his generation' (see Jeremy Gilbert in OpenDemocracy, Owen Jones in the *Guardian*, James Butler in the *LRB*) – had already shown his colours at the time of the Manchester bombing in the run-up to the 2017 election.' Corbyn had connected the atrocity to British foreign policy, whereas McDonnell was terrified that the media would savage Labour over this. Polls indicated that the public agreed with Corbyn. 'The same knee-jerk conformism saw McDonnell and Diane Abbott, Corbyn's Shadow Home Secretary, join with the Labour right in dragging out the Brexit process,' wrote Ali. 'Disastrously, Corbyn's closest colleagues began playing around with notions of an unelected national-government coalition to stop Brexit. This was coupled with a *Guardian*–BBC barrage against Corbyn, insinuating he was an anti-Semite; what they really meant was that he supported Palestinian aspirations to statehood and opposed the US–UK neo-imperial wars in the Middle East.' Once Corbyn had gone he was replaced by establishment man Keir Starmer. Starmer had been rewarded with a knighthood for his work as the Director of Public Prosecutions, when he had ruled not to prosecute the police killers of Jean Charles de Menezes and Ian Tomlinson, or the MI5 and MI6 officers accused of torture in Bagram and elsewhere. 'Meanwhile he showed up during the all-night trials of those arrested in the 2011 London riots to praise the judges for their harsh sentencing. His office notoriously fast-tracked the extradition of Julian Assange,' Tariq Ali wrote. Meanwhile corporate stenographers had endlessly reiterated the same soundbites: 'under new management', 'serious', 'professional', 'capable', 'competent', 'responsible', 'sober'. (Ali missed out 'forensic'.) As for Starmer's purge on the Left: 'Starmer will soon have evicted more Jews from the Labour Party than any predecessor'. Ali looked forward wistfully to a new political grouping: 'An Independent Labour Party with even half a dozen MPs and a membership base of perhaps 50,000 – that number have left already since Starmer took over – could mark a real advance'. This seemed to Ellis unlikely. No Labour MP appeared keen to risk their neck - least of all J. Corbyn. A new party would need something other than 'Labour Party' in its title. Reading the piece Ellis remembered the time he had gone on a march through London in the rain. The protest, poorly attended, had ended up in Trafalgar Square. As he stood listening to the speeches Ellis suddenly saw that the figure standing right in front of him was Tariq Ali. A close encounter with a legend! From the 5pm radio news Ellis learned that Boris Johnson had cancelled Christmas. Richard Seymour angrily tweeted: *Last minute, after they surely *knew* what was coming. I've wasted hundreds on tests and tickets etc, and it's all down the toilet now.* Ellis ate chicken casserole and watched *The Astonished Heart*. It was, transparently, an attempt to repeat the *Brief Encounter* formula. But the film had been a flop. Ellis could see why. Noel Coward was miscast. It was hard to care about his love affair. The seductive other woman was too smooth, too self-assured. She lacked the guilt-ridden intensity of the wife in *Brief Encounter*. Noel Coward did not seem like the kind of man who would end it all in the way he ended it. Ellis watched the 10pm news. Afterwards he went to bed. And people's parlors, he read, are papered with these projections.

Sunday 20th December 2020

A sound like a shot woke Ellis around 3 am. It had been a strange, loud, cracking noise. He lay there in the darkness, waiting to see if further sounds would follow. When none came he eventually got out of bed and went to look out. The neighbourhood was silent and empty. Ellis returned to bed and drifted off again. At 8.15am he woke and turned on the radio. A sky pilot was imparting syrup wisdom and Ellis suddenly remembered it was Sunday. He made a cup of tea. A clear blue sky, the sun shining. Crisp. At 9am the news reported that Scottish police had announced they would not be enforcing the ban on people leaving or entering Scotland. A blatant invitation to subvert the new restrictions, Ellis thought. Later Ellis went online. The European Commission tweeted: We have agency and we have hope. We bought enough doses for everyone in Europe and soon the first vaccines will be authorised and vaccinations can begin. Ali Abunimah @AliAbunimah retorted: These @EuinIsrael racists also bought doses for every Israeli settler but not for the Palestinians they occupy and murder and whose land they steal and squat on. European Values = apartheid and racial eugenics. Earlier, Ali Abunimah tweeted: It appears that @EuinIsrael has hired @RaphaelAhren, the diplomatic correspondent of @TimesofIsrael, as its new hasbara officer. A good example of the cozy relationship between governments and the media that allegedly hold them accountable. Ali Abunimah added: This hire can't be worse than when @EuinIsrael hired a genocide advocate to promote EU-Israel relations, an egregious act they have never explained or apologized for despite all their regular, pious lectures about #NeverAgain. Later, Ellis came across some tweets by Daniel Finn. They demolished Rachel Shabis's piece in the *Guardian* which Ellis had read, scornfully, two days earlier. Shabi takes the EHRC and its report entirely at face value: a "sobering verdict," no less, wrote Daniel Finn. 'This is not the first time she's done this: she also uncritically endorsed the claims made in the BBC's Panorama documentary in July 2019. She then scolded the Labour leadership for stating that the central claims made in that documentary were demonstrably untrue and indeed the opposite of the truth, something that has become even more obvious since. As Richard Sanders & Peter Oborne pointed out, the findings of the EHRC report itself on Labour's disciplinary process tacitly contradict the Panorama documentary. It's logically impossible to endorse both. Instead of pointing out this discrepancy, Shabi simply moves on, seemingly with no reflection, to uncritically endorse the EHRC, ignoring the evidence of its crude partiality.' On and on Finn went, ripping apart Shabi's flimsy logic. 'Many of the EHRC's conclusions are eminently disputable: its claim to have identified "unlawful harassment", for example, is based on a tortuous chain of logic that would be very unlikely to hold up in court. The EHRC report clearly doesn't come anywhere close to substantiating the dominant media narrative about "Labour antisemitism", which is what Corbyn was really challenging with his statement. Shabi reproaches him for doing so.' Finn exposed the phoniness of Shabi's argument. 'She falls back on a now-familiar evasive formula, railing against "those leftists who dismissed the entire problem as a smear campaign", as if there are many people who believe there wasn't a single case of antisemitism in the Labour Party. It was the media narrative around "Labour antisemitism" that was a smear, or rather a compendium of smears, major and minor, empirical and conceptual. The Panorama programme that Shabi uncritically endorsed was the flagship of this effort, but there were countless others.' And then a tweet which Ellis felt should be retweeted across the internet a billion times. *There was no dramatic upsurge in antisemitism under Corbyn's leadership; antisemitism was not endemic in Labour; Corbyn did not encourage it or protect the guilty parties; Labour was not a "cold house for Jews" (still less an "existential threat to Jewish life in Britain").* Finn continued: 'Shabi archly dismisses "the numbers game", as if it makes no difference whether there were 50 or 50,000 virulent antisemites in the Labour Party. In effect, this means dismissing the idea of any empirical controls for the media narrative. It's a surrender to irrationality'. Shabi had also piously cited the example of Ilhan Omar. The main difference between the US and British cases, Finn remarked, is that Ilhan Omar stopped apologizing for things that didn't merit an apology (or never happened in the first place), and for the most part the US left rallied combatively behind her. He finished his twenty tweets with two searing observations which put Shabi back in her pitiful little box. *Corbyn's statement was right in every respect, and frankly it ill behoves people who thought that Iain McNicol & Sam Matthews were trustworthy sources to wag their finger at him while triangulating between truth and fiction. The idea that the EHRC report & the processes surrounding it can be a "positive step" for anti-racism in Britain is for the birds. The "Labour antisemitism" media narrative has functioned to protect & strengthen racism in British politics, as was always likely to be the case.* A car drew up outside. Later Ellis discovered that Leo Panitch had died of Covid-19, aged 75. He had vaguely heard of Panitch but never read any of his books. His impression was that Panitch was an academic radical who excited and interested a spectrum of opinion on the academic left. The sun shone. The child placed three straws into a plastic container, then took them out again. She put on her Waffle rucksack and pushed soft toy baby in her pushchair. Five o'clock. Radio 4 news reports that Coronavirus infections in the UK have risen to 35,928 recorded cases today. The total number of C-19 deaths currently stands at 67,401. The total number of cases for the UK this year is 2,040,147. Scottish police have performed a U-turn and will now have an 'operational presence' in the border areas of Scotland. As the evening wore on more and more European countries banned flights from Britain. Even the Bulgarians didn't want the Brits. And then Macron put a halt to freight entering from Dover on lorries. A devastating development. The TV news showed lorries backed-up and stationary on the motorway leading into the port. Towards the end of the 10pm Sky News there was footage of Sir Keir Starmer. He was standing at a podium across the top of which ran the message UNDER NEW MANAGEMENT. Behind the florid knight, on a wall, were the words Under New Management. The message was clear. I am not Jeremy Corbyn. I am the new manager. I believe in the capitalist state, a belligerent foreign policy, nuclear weapons and Zionism. On the papers review was Stephen Bush, yet another reactionary masquerading as a man of the Left. Ellis switched off and went to bed. Ronald, go away, he read. Let me alone. He read: the works which most of us are appointed to do are trivial - da-da-*da*, da-da-*da*, da-da-*da*. He read: objects would still be faintly visible in the winter dusk, etcetera. He read: some faces gain by misrepresentation. He put out the light.

Ellis woke at 6am. He dozed in the dark. At 6.59am he turned the radio on. The headline news was the disruption at Dover. Ellis lay listening. At some point a Lockerbie story came on. Today was the 32nd anniversary. Nick Robinson interviewed the Reverend John Mosey, father of 19-year-old Helga Mosey, who had been on the airliner when the bomb exploded as it flew over the small Scottish town. Trump's Attorney General, William Barr, had gleefully announced a decision to prosecute another obscure Libyan. The Reverend Mosey denounced the timing as disrespectful and insensitive. He questioned why the Attorney General had decided to bring charges at the very moment he left office. But what about the evidence? asked Nick Robinson, referring to a bomb timer fragment discovered at the scene. The Reverend Mosey explained that he had aquired a great deal of knowledge about the destruction of Pan Am flight 103. He had no faith in this supposed evidence. He regarded it fake. Nick Robinson brought the interview to a close. Outside it was dark and wet. It was still raining when Ellis dressed and ate his breakfast. On Twitter Ellis read Alex Macheras @AlexInAir Breaking: Morocco, El Salvador, Romania, join France, Germany, Italy & a long list of countries banning all travel to/from the UK. The BBC's Emily Maitlis @maitlis retweeted this with the comment "Banned from El Salvador .." Ed McNally @edmcnally96 commented: this is the kind of sneering racism you can expect from a state broadcaster who writes for *The Spectator* and is a regular at its parties. It rained much of the day. The child played with a plastic kitchen spoon. In the afternoon Ellis went out to return a magazine. Later, on the internet, he read: Union of Jewish Students @UJS_UK 'We are delighted that the University of Oxford has joined the growing list of UK universities adopting the IHRA definition of antisemitism. We want to thank Jewish students for their hard work, determination and for pressuring the university on this matter. Both the University of Oxford and University of Cambridge have taken this step to support their Jewish students. This should be an example to all other higher education institutes of the importance of adopting this definition. We will continue our work in ensuring all universities and Student Unions in the UK adopt this vital and comprehensive definition.' Well, Oxford and Cambridge had always incarnated the British ruling class, so perhaps no surprise there. Next Ellis read the University of Oxford's statement that the IHRA definition was useful 'as a guide to interpeting and understanding antisemitism'. On the contrary, it was a verbose and incoherent definition promoted by reactionary Jews for the purpose of suppressing criticism of Israel. It said a great deal about the intellectual poverty and moral vacuity of the University of Oxford that it had capitulated to pressure. Ellis watched the 10pm news. A Polish lorry driver screamed abuse at two men in yellow jackets who stood in front of plastic cones blocking the entrance to the ferry route at the port of Dover. The driver aggressively drove forwards and it looked for a moment as if he would run the port workers down. The driver was incoherent with rage and frustration. There were shots of lorries parked on the motorway and at the roadside below a junction. Ellis went to bed. His twenty years of sleep, let me tell you, Ellis read, went straight to my heart.

Tuesday 22nd December 2020

A bright sunny morning, blue sky, warm. Ellis went to the library to return a book and collect one he'd reserved. After that he went for a walk. Next he went to the pharmacy. Home again he learned that female unemployment had hit 44 percent in Gaza. The child wrapped herself in a jumper and played pee-boh. Next she tried to climb into an empty cardboard box which was too small for that ambition. The day wore on. Ellis spent much of it reading a book. In the early evening he caught up with Daniel Finn's *Jacobin* article 'Jeremy Corbyn's Movement Was a Signpost for the Future, Not a Relic of the Past'. Daniel Finn analysed the result of the 2019 general election. For a start, 1983 was much worse in many ways than 2019, Finn argued. Back then, the Conservatives won a majority of 144, compared with 80. In 1983 Labour got 27.6% of the vote — its worst share for 65 years. In 2019 it got 32.2% — mediocre, but more than at the 2010 general election, when Alan Johnson was home secretary, or in 2015 under Ed Miliband. Corbyn, Finn asserted, won slightly fewer Westminster seats than Michael Foot managed in 1983, even though Labour's vote share was considerably higher, because the British electoral system tended to magnify small, geographically-concentrated shifts. The first of those shifts, in Scotland, preceded Corbyn's leadership. In 2010, Gordon Brown took forty-one seats for Labour in Scotland, despite winning just 29 percent of the vote across the UK. Five years later, under Ed Miliband, Labour was left with one Scottish MP. Although Corbyn led the party to a modest Scottish recovery in 2017, he could still only convert 40 percent of the UK vote into seven Scottish seats, with the SNP now well-established in former Labour strongholds. The year 2019 wiped out that halting progress. Scotland and the 'red wall' explain why Corbyn came home with fewer seats than Foot, Brown, or Miliband, despite outpolling them all, wrote Daniel Finn. Moreover in 2019 the party's change of policy over Brexit since 2017 was crucial. Labour had become associated with attempts to block or reverse leaving the EU. Labour's vote share in the 'red wall' seats was no lower than it had been in 2010. The real shift was the massive post-Brexit increase in support for the Tories, rising from 32 percent in 2010 and 2015 to 42 percent in 2017 and 47 percent in 2019. Labour, wrote Daniel Finn, managed to keep its head above water in 2017 by lifting its vote share dramatically across those constituencies, from 42 percent in 2015 to 50 percent two years later. But when the party reverted to its 2010 level of support (39 percent), it left the way clear for the Tories to capture Labour seats. An election polarized between pro- and anti-Brexit camps was always likely to be a disaster for Labour, and so it proved to be. Many voters, it seems, felt that Corbyn didn't seem to have any position at all on Brexit. He appeared to be not in control of his Party and he failed to spell out a clear position on Brexit. But in fairness, Finn argued, it was difficult to imagine that *any* policy could have delivered 40 percent of the vote for Labour in an election where Brexit was the primary issue. Add to that the reality that there was a concerted effort to depress the Labour vote, not merely from the partisan right-wing press, but also from broadcasters with a statutory obligation to remain impartial. A glaring example: the two most eminent figures in British current affairs broadcasting circulated a fake story to an audience of millions about a Labour member assaulting a Tory politician's adviser. Neither the BBC's Laura Kuenssberg nor Robert Peston of ITV faced any consequences for their grossly unprofessional conduct, nor did they seek to explain themselves. They relied on a tacit understanding among their colleagues that all bets were off until Corbynism had been vanquished, wrote Finn. Ellis ate baked cod with mashed potatoes and peas. He watched the 10pm Sky News. Dover, accumulations of parked lorries, bored lorry drivers, an agreement to reopen the port to drivers who'd been tested and were negative. Robotic Joe Biden saying he'd be tough with Russia over a recent cyber attack. But there was no evidence that the Russian state had been behind the attack. Needless to say Sky News did not remind its viewers that the US was a rogue state which had only recently approved the Israeli assassination of an Iranian scientist on Iranian soil. Sky News referred to 'the Putin regime'. But Putin was elected. Sky would never, ever, speak of the Netanyahu regime, even though Israel was not a democracy, and the Palestinians now formed a majority in the land from which so many of their families had been expelled. Ellis went to bed. The temptation to lie down is very great, he read, and then put out the light.

Wednesday 23rd December 2020

Ellis woke in the dark and switched on the radio. The blood-spattered international criminal Tony Blair was being 'interviewed' by Tory sycophant Nick Robinson. Robinson's tone was friendly, genial, deferential. Blair was speaking about the pandemic. He said everyone should receive just one dose of the Pfizer vaccine instead of two. That would spread the numbers of those protected from the virus. But Blair was not a scientist and knew nothing about licensing procedures. Blair's solution was not permitted under the licence terms. If Nick Robinson had bothered to be properly briefed about the virus he would have challenged Blair on this, but of course a slovenly and grotesquely overpaid hack like Robinson did not know this. It was a dark wet morning. The child could now answer the question: How old are you? The child put on a woolly hat.

Ellis spent much of the day reading. At Dover, Sky News reported, there was continuing chaos and gridlock. In the afternoon it continued raining and it was announced that more parts of England would be put into Tier 4 as from Boxing Day. Ellis went on Twitter and read the latest tweets by Ben White. 155 Palestinian children killed by Israeli forces "using live ammunition or crowd-control weapons since 2013". These have led to just 3 indictments. In one case, charges were later dropped. In second case, sentence was nine months. In the third - one month in military prison. UN rights experts condemned Israeli forces' killing of 15-year-old Ali Ayman Abu Aliya; he was "hit in the abdomen with a bullet from a 0.22 Ruger Precision Rifle, fired by an Israeli soldier from an estimated 100-150 metres". Ali was the sixth Palestinian child in the occupied West Bank killed in 2020 by Israeli forces using live ammunition. The statement adds that 1,048 Palestinian children have been injured by Israeli occupation forces between 1 November 2019 and 31 October 2020. Ellis followed the link to the UN statement. GENEVA (17 December 2020) – UN human rights experts today called for an impartial and independent investigation into the killing of a 15-year-old boy by Israeli security forces at a West Bank protest this month, saying they were deeply troubled by the overall lack of accountability for the killings of Palestinian children in recent years. "The killing of Ali Ayman Abu Aliya by the Israeli Defense Forces – in circumstances where there was no threat of death or serious injury to the Israeli Security Forces – is a grave violation of international law," said the experts. "Intentional lethal force is justified only when the security personnel are facing an immediate threat of deadly force or serious harm." On 4 December, Palestinian youths in Al-Mughayyir protested against the construction of a nearby illegal Israeli settlement outpost. Information gathered by civil society organisations and the UN Human Rights Office indicated that they had thrown stones at Israeli Security Forces, who responded with rubber-coated metal bullets, tear gas and, eventually, live ammunition. Abu Aliya was hit in the abdomen with a bullet from a 0.22 Ruger Precision Rifle, fired by an Israeli soldier from an estimated 100-150 metres. He died later that day in hospital. The human rights experts are unaware of any claims that the Israeli security forces were in danger at any point of death or serious injury. The experts said Abu Aliya was the sixth Palestinian child living in the West Bank to be killed in 2020 by Israeli security forces using live ammunition. According to information received, it is understood that 1,048 Palestinian children have been injured by Israeli security forces across the Occupied Palestinian Territory between 1 November 2019 and 31 October 2020. "Children enjoy special protected rights under international law," the experts said. "Each of these killings raises deep concerns about Israel's adherence to its solemn human rights and humanitarian law obligations as the occupying power." The Israeli Security Forces announced that they would conduct an investigation into Abu Aliya's killing. The human rights experts noted, however, that investigations by the Israeli Defense Forces of fatal shootings of Palestinians by its soldiers rarely result in appropriate accountability. Civil society organisations have documented the deaths of 155 Palestinian children by Israeli Security Forces using live ammunition or crowd-control weapons since 2013. Only three indictments on criminal charges have been issued for offences directly tied to those killings. In one case, the charges were subsequently dropped. In the second case, the responsible soldier reached a plea deal and was sentenced to nine months jail for death by negligence. In the third case, a soldier was convicted of not obeying orders and sentenced to one month in military prison. "This low level of legal accountability for the killings of so many children by Israeli security forces is unworthy of a country which proclaims that it lives by the rule of law," the experts said. "We call upon the Government of Israel to either conduct an independent, impartial, prompt and transparent civilian investigation according to international standards into this deeply troubling human rights record, or to allow an international, impartial and independent human rights review to be conducted," they said. "Such an investigation – domestic or international – must be directed towards ensuring that children living under occupation no longer face death or injury when exercising their legitimate right to protest, and that the culture of impunity for military misconduct is ended." Fat chance, thought Ellis. Israeli Jews have a long record of killing children. The American journalist Chris Hedges famously wrote that he had seen children murdered in conflict zones around the world but Israel was the only country where soldiers killed children for sport. The depravity of the Jewish state was boundless. Next, Ellis read Ben White's critique of the motives of those who orchestrated the so-called working definition of antisemitism (WDA) adopted by the so-called International Holocaust Remembrance Alliance (IHRA). The "architect" of the WDA was Mark Weitzman, director of government affairs for the Simon Wiesenthal Centre. It was in his capacity as the then-chair of IHRA's Committee on Antisemitism and Holocaust Denial, that Weitzman introduced and steered the definition to adoption. In stark contrast to those who claim the definition is not intended to censor Palestinians and their allies, wrote Ben White, Weitzman has openly welcomed its use in efforts to sabotage Israeli Apartheid Week events on university campuses. In a 2018 interview, Weitzman specifically cited the cancellation of one such event the previous year as an example of the "practical applications of the IHRA definition". At an event this past February, Weitzman declared that the Palestinian-led, civil society Boycott, Divestment, Sanctions (BDS) Movement "directly clashes with the IHRA definition". In a document on the WDA published this year, Weitzman wrote – approvingly – that "European countries who've adopted the definition have used it as the basis of legislation condemning anti-Zionism and BDS". But it's not just Weitzman, wrote Ben White. The text of the IHRA's WDA almost exactly reproduces a document with an older history – what was once known as the European Monitoring Centre on Racism and Xenophobia (EUMC) working definition of antisemitism. Andrew Baker, the American Jewish Committee's Director of International Jewish Affairs, was part of the group that drafted that original EUMC text. While some have tried to argue that the IHRA's reference to a "racist endeavour" is about the mere principle of Jewish self-determination, Baker has been clear that the reference is not at all theoretical. "When you suggest…that it's [the State of Israel] a racist endeavour, we're very clear, this is not criticism, this is a form…of antisemitism", Baker told a November online event. Another co-drafter of the original EUMC document was Dina Porat, head of the Tel Aviv University-based Kantor Centre. Under Porat's leadership, the Kantor Centre's annual report for 2019 cited the German and Austrian parliaments' description of the BDS Movement as antisemitic as constituting one of the year's "significant achievements". Lastly, Ben White drew attention to that grotesque individual, Eric Pickles. This obscenely overweight reactionary buffoon has been appointed as the UK government's 'Special Envoy for post-Holocaust issues'. Fatty also heads the UK delegation to the IHRA. According to the government, the Pickles-led delegation "played an active role in supporting IHRA's adoption in May 2016 of a working definition of anti-Semitism". The loathsome Pickles told an online event in September that "those who object to it [the definition] want to…be able to suggest that Israel is an apartheid state". In 2019, Pickles told a conference in Jerusalem: "BDS is anti-Semitic and should be treated as such". Ben White concluded: Those promoting the WDA stress that the definition allows for "legitimate" criticism of Israel. Yet the above evidence demonstrates that what constitutes 'legitimate' and 'illegitimate' is determined by individuals who believe the BDS Movement and discussion of Israeli apartheid to be beyond the pale. Ben White added: By now, there are numerous examples of censorship, attempted censorship, and various efforts to toxify and delegitimise efforts by Palestinians and their allies to discuss, and oppose, Israeli human rights violations. Ellis read more. British universities were capitulating to Zionism. In 2017, officials at the University of Central Lancashire banned an event scheduled to take place as part of Israeli Apartheid Week, citing the WDA. Mark Weitzman hailed the decision as "firm evidence" of the WDA's "vital role in the fight against antisemitism". According to Michael McCann of the Israel-Britain Alliance, an initiative launched by the Zionist Federation, "the words 'Israel Apartheid Week' are manifestly anti-Semitic and violate the IHRA". One Tory MP has suggested legislation to ban Israeli Apartheid Week. This goes wider than annual events, wrote Ben White. Law lecturer Lesley Klaff, Editor-in-Chief of the *Journal of Contemporary Antisemitism*, claimed in *The Jewish Chronicle* in October that to simply talk of Israel as a "settler-colonial society" – analysis based on a decades-old, wide-ranging, scholarly body of work – is the kind of claim "that the IHRA definition…stigmatises as antisemitic". Meanwhile, "right-wing activists" in the US "are attempting to spread new laws" that would "suppress criticism on public university campuses of Israel and its occupation of Palestinian territory", using a definition of antisemitism almost identical to the IHRA's WDA. Nor is it just on university campuses where the WDA is being used to shield Israel from criticism, observed Ben White. In 2018, for example, the European Jewish Congress and AJC urged EU officials to ban Palestinian human rights defender and BDS co-founder Omar Barghouti from addressing a meeting in the European Parliament, accusing him of "antisemitic hate speech" based on the WDA. Moreover only last year the Simon Wiesenthal Centre "condemned" a Somerset House exhibition featuring photos from Palestinian protests in Gaza, claiming that the "series description" was "one-sided" – and thus "violates" the WDA. Also in 2019, Tower Hamlets Council "refused to host a charity event in aid of Palestinian children…based on fears their criticism of Israel could breach antisemitism guidelines". The same year Gilad Erdan, the then-Minister for Strategic Affairs, praised the role of the WDA in combating BDS, and hailed "the ground-breaking resolution of the Bundestag recognising the anti-Semitic nature of BDS" as "the most important step yet," again based on the WDA. Meanwhile the chaos at Dover continued. The new Coronavirus figures were released: 744 deaths in the UK, the highest daily figure since April, and a record breaking 39,237 infections - the highest since the start of the pandemic. Ellis learned from the corporate media that Donald Trump had granted pardons to some American war criminals and that supermodel Stella Tennant had died unexpectedly at the age of 50. Ellis had never heard of her. He momentarily wondered what the cause of death was. There was, perhaps, a suggestion that the circumstances of this death were not for public scrutiny. Next Ellis half-listened to a radio discussion of the recently discovered mysterious radio signal apparently emanating from Proxima Centauri. As he listened Ellis read some tweets and a blog post by Steve Mitchelmore. These led him to look up reviews of the novel *Threshold* by a writer he had never heard of. It sounded interesting. Ellis learned from *National Geographic* magazine that Proxima Centauri was a small red star roughly 4.2 light-years away from planet earth. It was the star closest to the sun. Ellis learned from *Scientific American* that there was the very faint prospect that it is a transmission from some form of advanced extraterrestrial intelligence (ETI)—a so-called "technosignature". But perhaps not. Perhaps it would be like the movie *On the Beach*. The signal's cause would be a disappointment. On Amazon a five star review of *Threshold* read: *This author has totally contaged me with his puzzlement! This is a work that matters.* Ellis had occasionally contemplated writing a prose piece constructed entirely from Amazon reviews. But the unwritten always amounted to more than the written. And the unwritten was more truthful. Spaghetti bolognese he ate, with grated carrot and celery. Eaten with a glass of water and a vitamin D tablet.

199,907 words so far, Ellis noted. On Sky News that night at 10pm the corporate stories were an imminent Brexit deal, continuing chaos at Dover, and the new mutant strain of the virus in South Africa. In bed Ellis read as far as: Renata was greatly annoyed when I said that she must come to Coney Island with me.

Thursday 24th December 2020

Ellis woke at 6.45am. He could hear the low distant roar of the boiler. The 7pm news headlines were about the Brexit deal. Everything had been resolved apart from arguments over quotas for individual species of fish. The deal was bad news for British seed potato exporters. Exports of seed potatoes would be banned to the EU and to Northern Ireland. Laura Kuenssberg chattered emptily. The two 's's in her surname seemed apt. The twisted hiss of a Tory snake. BBC news asserted that drivers at the airport in Kent had been tested and were now heading for Dover. But that had been the news ten hours earlier on Sky TV. Had a single lorry been driven on to a ferry for France? No reporter, whether on Sky or the BBC, asked this simple question. It appeared that paralysis continued, but this was fudged by the corporate media. The programme grew worse. How absolutely characteristic of 'Today' to give publicity to shrill, smirking Rachel Riley. After 7.30am Riley was given a slot to call for censorship of internet trolls. Needless to say the BBC did not feature anyone to challenge Riley's agenda or to cite what Riley had written in her own tweets. But then Rachel Riley's hatred of Jeremy Corbyn had been matched by that of the 'Today' programme and its staff over the past five years. Nor, of course, was the underlying agenda even mentioned. This topic was partly about shutting down criticism of celebrities - the saintly J. K. Rowling came to mind - and very much more about closing down Palestinian advocacy. But BBC news never acknowledged that, just as it never acknowledged US or British imperialism, and just as it had for years suppressed or marginalised the reality of climate catastrophe. BBC News would lie to the bitter end, as the oceans spilled over the land and the forests burned to the ground. Ellis went on Twitter to see if there had been responses. There had. Bren @brenpage72 tweeted: *Seriously #R4Today! Tuned in to get an idea about #BrexitShambles to find you giving social media troll Rachel Riley unfettered airtime to play the victim after her vile trolling of Corbyn. Switched off.* Ellis came off Twitter. He learned that something called The Reading Agency had been given £3.5m 'as part of a government £7.5m funding package to tackle loneliness over the winter period. Funds will be used by the charity for its Reading Well project—a selection of books curated by health professionals—and its Reading Friends programme.' Books curated by health professionals? WTF? 200,452 words. Getting near the end of the month, getting near the end of the book. It would be a relief to stop. The obligation to record every day had become a burden and a diversion. The need to write. The need to put some kind of shape on shapelessness. Last night, looking for *A History of the World in 100 Objects* - he had eventually located it wedged between *Wolf Hall* and *The Curious Incident of the Dog in the Night-Time* - he had given up on the Mantel after forty pages but had enjoyed the other one - he had glimpsed, on the bookshelf behind his favourite armchair, wedged between *Book of Longing* and *Difficult Men*, Gabriel Josipovici's *What Ever Happened to Modernism?* It was time to re-read that book. The short answer to Gabriel Josipovici's question, perhaps, was corporate publishing. A writer who wanted to attract approval, favourable reviews, sales and their agreeable consequences - the large house and garden, the fast and spacious vehicles, the infinity pool - was a writer who knew the importance of a pacy plot with an unexpected twist, exquisitely drawn characters from a social spectrum agreeable to editorial directors and a style polished by a creative writing school, tweaked by a hotshot agent. Processed narrative with a cute conclusion. Reading group fiction. Bestselling litfic. A genre, competing with crime fiction. Ideally straddling both genres. A page-turner but pleasingly middlebrow. Paperbacks with covers bearing praise from the giants of our time. Barack Obama and other highly regarded intellectuals. It was a cold morning of sunshine and showers. The child ate a biscuit. Her nose was red from a trip to the park. Ellis went out to reposition a plant in a pot which had blown over in the night. Next he read an article on the *Financial Times* website. He learned that there were more than 77m cases of Coronavirus confirmed globally, with more than 1.69m people known to have died. Coronavirus had spread to all 50 states in the US. More than 18m cases and 309,441 deaths have been confirmed in the country. There are concerns, however, that reported Covid-19 deaths are not capturing the true impact of Coronavirus on mortality around the world, Ellis read. The FT has gathered and analysed data on excess mortality across the globe, and has found that numbers of deaths in some countries are more than 50 per cent higher than usual. In many countries, these excess deaths exceed reported numbers of Covid-19 deaths by large margins. In the afternoon it grew darker and began to rain. Ellis learned that a Brexit deal had been agreed with the EU. Later in the day it was reported that a further 39,036 confirmed Coronavirus cases had been recorded in the UK, with 574 deaths. Meanwhile Labour leader Sir Keir Starmer has announced that Labour will back the government's Brexit deal. EU Commission President Ursula von der Leyen said it had been a long and winding road and parting is such sweet sorrow but what we call the beginning is often the end and to make an end is to make a beginning. How very true, thought Ellis. The end is where we start from. And every phrase and every sentence is an end and a beginning. We die with the dying. 201,007 words. Getting closer all the time. Ellis ate a mushroom omelette, with broccoli. He watched *Blow-Up*. Interrupted by a loud unexpected heart-stopping crashing noise by the window. Ellis ran to switch on the outside lights. He saw at once the source of the disturbance. The rain-sodden string supporting the hag stones had snapped. The stones lay in a heap on a flagstone. Ellis went back to the movie. Then the news headlines. The Brexit deal. At 10.14pm Ellis switched to BBC2 to watch the M.R. James ghost story starring Peter Capaldi. 'Martin's Close' was okay but it was too postmodern, too jokey. The ghost was artfully constructed but the drama wasn't remotely scary. Ellis went to bed. I have never suffered from a knowledge handicap, he read. And then: The original is apparently true. Ten to midnight. Ellis switched off the light.

Friday 25th December 2020

Ellis surfaced in the dark, without mechanical assistance, at 7.15am. He switched on the bedside radio. A woman chattered away. He could tell it wasn't the news. You didn't get news on Christmas Day. She was replaced by a male voice. Ellis realised he was listening to the cast of 'The Archers' talking about themselves. It meant nothing to Ellis as he never listened to that long-running radio drama. The actor who played Ben talked about playing Ben. He chose a piece of music. 'Holding Hands' by the Magic Lantern. Ellis had never heard of the song or the group. The actor who played Ben was replaced by the actress who voiced the part of... It meant nothing to Ellis. The actress chose a song by the Tory-supporter Kate Bush. A song about December. Ellis rolled out of bed and went to make a cup of tea. As he drank it he watched the Magic Lantern song video on his phone. Yeah, 'Holding Hands' was not bad at all. The kind of song that could grow on you. Next Ellis listened to Ryan Adams on YouTube: 'Birmingham', 'I'm Sorry and I Love You', 'So, Anyways', 'Poison & Pain', 'Walk In The Dark', 'When You Cross Over', 'Who Is Going to Love Me Now, If Not You', 'Lost in Time', 'Mamma', 'Wednesdays'. Ellis was surprised to see only 11K views in the past two weeks for 'Mamma'. But then even a fine song like 'Birmingham' had received only 23K views. As for 'Lost in Time': only 847 views. As he listened to Ryan Adams Ellis looked at recent tweets by Louis Allday. I'd humbly suggest ignoring whatever vague statements politicians make on Twitter or Instagram (even if they're cooking in order to appear relatable) and look at their actual voting records & stances on key issues beyond the heavily managed 'progressive' image that they project, wrote Louis Allday. It's transparent AOC & 'the squad' are the means by which they want to keep people invested in the current system. She's not a socialist - she's a capitalist imperialist with some social democratic tendencies (which she'll likely drop) & it's dishonest to portray her otherwise, wrote Louis Allday. Just as Sanders' role was, the Squad's function is to perpetuate the fallacy that there's hope within the Democratic Party, offer the illusion of change/progress, constrain people's political imaginations/demands & forestall the growth of a genuinely socialist movement in the US, wrote Louis Allday. Ellis saw that two days ago, adverting to the criminal's vaccine solution, Paul O'Connell had tweeted: *Tony Blair is never trending for the reason you'd hope ...* Smiley face! Adverting to the Brexit news Paul O'Connell had retweeted Sky TV's tweet: *Labour leader Sir Keir Starmer says when the post-Brexit trade deal is brought before parliament "Labour will accept it and vote for it", adding that no-deal "is not an option".* Paul O'Connell tweeted in response: *It's absolutely right to laugh at the "Stop Brexit"/FBPE reactionaries who were taken in by this opportunist - but in truth, his side won the decisive battle they were fighting.* The child played with her new Christmas Day pink toothbrush. Then she played with some toy kitchen utensils. Then she opened another present. A basket of plastic fruit. Then she opened another present. She recoiled in terror and burst into tears. It was a soft toy dinosaur. Hurriedly another present was placed before her. It was quickly unwrapped. A large Mr Potato Head! The child recoiled in terror and burst into tears again. Her mother quickly put Mr Potato Head away. The soft toy dinosaur she cuddled. She persuaded her daughter to feed the dinosaur a plastic orange. At lunchtime Ellis ate roast chicken with sprouts, roast potatoes, sausages, chestnuts, sage and onion stuffing, roast parsnips, carrots and gravy. *Nashville Tears* played in the background. This was followed by Christmas pudding with brandy butter. The Israelis flew low over Lebanon, for the fun of terrorising people. Next the Israelis bombed a town in Syria. They knew the BBC would choose not to notice. At 3.25pm Ellis watched the Channel 4 alternative Queen's message. It was supposed to be a satire. And it was - but of a tepid, timid kind. Corporate television was toothless and deferential to power. It dared not address truth. It fed off parasites. It was itself a parasite. A vehicle exploded in Nashville. On Twitter there was much frothing about Brexit. The Israel-worshipper , Simon Schama emitted balthery huff-puffery about restrictions on freedom of movement. It was another reminder that Zionists didn't do irony or self-awareness. They were too busy glowing with a privileged righteousness and wallowing in a spurious victimhood as they defended their material privileges. Squealer Eddie Marsan joined in - a strange, tiny little man who resembled a venomous dwarf in a Grimm fable. 'Hate this jingoistic, racist, xenophobic, small minded, cowardly bullshit,' he'd screeched on Christmas Eve. Which was rich coming from someone for whom Israel could do no wrong. Meanwhile in occupied Palestine a Palestinian had been seized, suspected of the recent killing of a Jewish settler, Esther Horgen, in the West Bank. Samaria Regional Council Chairman Yossi Dagan said that in revenge the government should 'strengthen the settlement of Samaria'. Earlier Jews stormed through the Palestinian village of Huwara, waving the Israeli flag and hurling stones at local people. The dead woman's husband, Jewish settler Benjamin Horgen, said that 'we' should 'focus on what we do - bring more light'. These people were Jewish settlers. The Jews' army of occupation said it would 'reinforce troops in Judea and Samaria to enhance the defence of communities and roads in the region'. Zionist geography and violence imposed on what had once been a tranquil rural community. The Palestinian suspect's home was prepared for demolition. The *Times of Israel* wrote: 'Israeli authorities often take punitive action such as home demolitions even before a conviction in cases of terrorist attacks'. Ah, *terrorist attacks*. The rhetoric of the violent, terrorist occupier. All resistance is criminal. The occupier must be free to steal, to kill, to humiliate, without reprisal. The dead woman's husband, Benjamin Horgen, said 'we trust the security forces and the courts, and of course expect justice to be served to the fullest with the despicable murderer.' But there is no justice for the occupied. A Jew can murder with little fear of punishment. And who were the Horgens? Esther Horgen 'made Aliyah' from France some years ago. She was French. She evidently had no connection whatever with Palestine, outside a twisted colonialist theology. She was a white European colonial settler imposing herself on the land of a violently dispossessed people. She had chosen to join her fellow fanatics in the occupied West Bank. Her sectarian privileges as a Jew were based on state violence and religious fanaticism. It grew darker. Ellis ate some cold chicken with cranberry sauce and cold chestnuts. He watched *A Cry in the Dark*. A well-made film about an orchestrated miscarriage of justice, slovenly 'experts' and popular prejudice. Meryl Streep's performance was a tour de force, Ellis felt. And afterwards: the Sky 10pm news. The Queen's banal and platitudinous Christmas speech. Flooding in Bedford. The explosion in Nashville. Ellis went to bed. Gone! he read. She had taken it.

Saturday 26th December 2020

Ellis woke some time after 8am. He turned on the radio. Brexit. The fine print of the agreement. Future disagreements over trade would be resolved by tribunals. Human remains had been found in the wreckage in Nashville. A suicide? Ellis went for a walk. The road was flooded. Later he encountered a couple with two dogs. The animals had scarlet Christmas hats attached to their heads. Twitter had dried up as a source of information and instruction. The child clutched her dinosaur, which she had now befriended. She called it Roar. She put the handle of a wooden spoon in her mouth and waggled the spoon. Ellis put the handle of another wooden spoon in his mouth and waggled it. The child grinned. She took the spoon out of her mouth. Later Ellis read Joshua Leifer's article 'The Tragedy of Jeremy Corbyn' on the *Jewish Currents* website. It was a feeble piece. It spoke of 'the antisemitism' scandal ('anti-Semitism' spelt the preferred Zionist way) *as if there really had been one*. The article contained no statistics. It was the standard impressionistic tosh you could expect from someone on the flabby Left. The term 'vulgar anti-imperialism' was tossed into the mix, without any definition or examples. It cravenly - deferentially - unsceptically - spoke of 'the fears of Jewish leaders'. Tony Greenstein had offered *Jewish Currents* a reply to

Joshua Leifer's wafflings but they had declined to use it. Ellis read Greenstein's piece on his blog. Greenstein shredded Leifer in his characteristically pugnacious, well-informed way. Ellis ate ham, cold chicken, salad and mashed potato while listening to Asleep at the Wheel's *New Routes*. Afterwards: Christmas pudding with brandy butter and ice-cream. As he cleared the kitchen Ellis began listening to *An Evening of New York Songs and Stories*. Then back to the computer. 202,641 words. Getting there. That evening Ellis watched *The Heart of Me*. Paul Bettany was miscast, he felt. On Sky News this night at 10pm the show obsequiously featured staged photographs of Boris Johnson clinching the great Brexit deal at Number 10. The reporter in Downing Street held up a print-out of the document. More than 1400 pages. The reporter had not read it and so the contents remained vague. Then flooding and Nashville. The ubiquitous Rachel Shabi with her trademark smirk was doing the Sky papers review, with a brat from the far-right Spiked website. Ellis went to bed. I walked through the TWA tunnel, like an endless arched gullet or a corridor in an expressionistic film, Ellis read, and then I was searched for weapons and got on a plane to Houston. All the way to Texas I read occult books. There were many stirring passages in them, to which I shall come back in a while.

Sunday 27th December 2020

A noisy night of roaring wind and the repeated splatter of rain beating down in waves. Ellis did not sleep well. He dozed, woke, drifted. Just before 7am he turned on the radio. Beavers, a voice said, eat their own faeces for extra nutrition. Ellis hadn't known that. But did he want to know that before breakfast? Ellis learned that beavers were large animals, slow and cumbersome on land. Their ample supply of sharp teeth was enough to see off predators. A fox would retreat when up against a beaver. Beavers were now returning to rivers from which they had been absent for hundreds of years. And then the weather. Storm Bella was still passing over England but would be gone by nine or ten this morning. Ellis got up and looked out. No trees were down. Nothing had blown over in the night. He ate his bowl of cereal, trying hard not to think about the habits of beavers. The wind died down and the clouds rolled away. The sun began to glimmer in the dissolving clouds. The child put her wooden egg in the plastic pan and placed it on a ring on her toy stove. The dinosaur sat on the other ring. Next she found her toy fish. Moments later the fish had gone. Where is the fish? The fish is hiding in the kitchen! The child waggled a wooden spoon in her mouth again. Ellis did the same. The child removed the spoon and giggled. Ellis went for a walk. The sun glittered in numerous puddles. The shadows of trees stretched out four or five times their height. Middle-aged men in lycra peddled past. Two women accompanied a pram north. A woman with long hair walked a tiny dog. A yellow digger stood inert, switched off. Ellis thought of *The Terminator* and of Palestine. He returned home. He glanced at an article on the *Guardian* website by the banal narcissist Ellie Mae O'Hagan. 'To understand how 2020 changed me, we first need to turn the clock back to June 2019,' O'Hagan wrote. 'I had flown to Australia to take part in a fellowship programme. My friend (and *Guardian* columnist) Owen Jones was there for a conference that was happening at the same time.' Not concerned about their carbon footprints, then, Ellis thought. Climate catastrophe was of inferior signifance to the need for O'Hagan and Jones to bring their relentless baltherings to a wader audience. No typos there, gentle reader. The sun sank, as the sun does. Twilight became night. Ellis pulled the curtains together. He read Jonathan Cook's latest article on the *Mondoweiss* website, about Netanyahu's choice of Effi Eitam as the new director of Yad Vashem. 'Eitam, aged 68, lives in an illegal settlement in the Golan and has long advocated the ethnic cleansing of Palestinians from the occupied territories, as well as the crushing of basic civil rights for non-Jews inside Israel,' Cook wrote. An apt choice for a propaganda outfit like Yad Vashem, built on stolen land, Ellis thought. It also occurred to him later this day that *Twenty-Twenty* had come to resemble the writing careers of John le Carré and J. K. Rowling. Their early works were short but later their books had grown longer and longer. Looking back over his text, Ellis realised the earliest entries were quite short. But as the year had gone on the daily entries had expanded, fuelled by the emptiness of his days and the time devoted to Twitter and other internet sources. Ellis would be glad when 2020 and *Twenty-Twenty* were over. The impulse to record words each day had become a burden, a tiresome aesthetic obligation. An attempt to enlarge a paltry canon. An idea that there might be some kind of significance in this record. The sense of significance being eroded by a sense of futility. The pointlessness of the contemporary text. Ellis felt tired, barren. Enough posturing. He needed a drink. But before that he could not resist clicking on the Word Count option. 203,562. A good solid quantity. Tolstoyan in length, though not in substance. A work, at least, to equal in weight *The Thorn Birds*. That evening Ellis watched *The Year of Living Dangerously*. A rare film about Indonesia in the 1960s. The Jakarta method. An atrocity erased from history. The TV guide had eight pages of listings for every day of the week and serious literature and politics were nowhere to be found. Just trash, light entertainment and a handful of corporate pseudo-documentaries in all their glistening forms. Elis had watched an old DVD of the film. When he looked the movie up on Amazon he discovered that it was no longer available. The Sky News washed over him as he glanced at his mobile phone. He watched some of the flooding footage then went to bed. But now the whole Atlantic must have surged between us; or perhaps the communications satellite was peppered with glittering particles in the upper air, Ellis read. Anyway, the conversation crumpled and ended. Lights out.

A strange dream in the night. Ellis was on an empty bus. Then a woman boarded and came and sat next to him. Irritated by her perverse decision to sit next to him during a pandemic Ellis climbed over the back of the seat in front of him and moved up the bus. But more people flooded on to it. They sat down. No one was wearing a mask. Ellis remembered no more than that. A Coronavirus anxiety dream. Ellis woke at 8.10am. He heard the giggling, ingratiating voice of Nick Robinson as he chatted amiably to Michael Gove. Two Tories having an agreeable chinwag about Brexit. Ellis got up and went to make himself a mug of tea. He ate his breakfast cereal. Later that morning he went for a walk. There were puddles everywhere. Many were filled with dazzling sunlight. A lot of people out walking. Ellis saw a couple of friends approaching. He waited for them to draw level on the far side of the road. They held a short conversation. Later, as Ellis ate his lunch, he read an old interview with Arundhati Roy on the website of the *Boston Review*, 3 January 2019. It is interesting that countries that call themselves democracies— India, Israel, and the United States—are busy running military occupations, said Arundhati Roy. Kashmir is one of the deadliest and densest military occupations in the world. India transformed from colony to imperial power virtually overnight. There has not been a day since the British left India in August 1947 that the Indian army and paramilitary have not been deployed within the country's borders against its "own people": Mizoram, Manipur, Nagaland, Assam, Kashmir, Jammu, Hyderabad, Goa, Punjab, Bengal, and now Chhattisgarh, Orissa, Jharkhand. The dead number in the tens or perhaps hundreds of thousands. Who are these dangerous citizens who need to be held down with military might? They are indigenous people, Christians, Muslims, Sikhs, communists. The pattern that emerges is telling. What it shows quite clearly is an "upper"-caste Hindu state that views everyone else as an enemy. The interviewer asked Arundhati Roy: What do you make of the injunction against the use of violence in resistance from below? Arundhati Roy replied: I am against unctuous injunctions and prescriptions from above to resistance from below. That's ridiculous, isn't it? Oppressors telling the oppressed how they would *like* to be resisted? Fighting people will choose their own weapons. For me, the question of armed struggle versus passive resistance is a tactical one, not an ideological one. She remarked: In certain situations, preaching nonviolence can be a kind of violence. Also, it is the kind of terminology that dovetails beautifully with the "human rights" discourse in which, from an exalted position of faux neutrality, politics, morality, and justice can be airbrushed out of the picture, all parties can be declared human rights offenders, and the status quo can be maintained. The hours passed. The child hid in a corner. She put a towel over herself. Pee-boh! She held her toy phone, her dinosaur, her soft toy cat. Night arrived. Ellis ate baked salmon, rice, peas,

Christmas pudding with brandy butter. He drank red wine. 204,278 words so far. Soon be done. That evening he watched *The Favourite*. A second viewing. And then the 10pm Sky News. The first story was about the spreading Coronavirus. Over 40,000 new infections recorded today. But the government was still insistent that schools should reopen next week. Other news. Snow. The transfer of power in the US. Ellis went to bed. A major plot twist in Madrid. I was suffering over Renata, Ellis read. She marched off in boots and plumes, as it were, and left me figuring, in pain, what was what, and how, and what to do. And trying to guess what Z was.

Tuesday 29th December 2020

Ellis woke at 7.25am. He switched on the radio. Saintly Margaret Atwood was guest-editing the 'Today' programme, in the guise of an environmentalist. Atwood, who jetted around the world promoting her novels. Atwood, who'd jetted off to Israel to pick up a Zionist bribe, defying the appeals of Palestinians not to go. Greta Thunberg chatted to Atwood. There was discussion of the new US President. Atwood called him 'Joe'. Another of Atwood's guests was Prince Charles. I mean, *Jesus*. Was anyone from Climate Extinction on the show? Probably not, Ellis suspected. He couldn't be bothered to listen to find out. But 'bird girl' was. A rich kid who'd jetted around the world to spot rare birds. Book deal, corporate promotion. The contradictions between all this and a purported concern for the environment were never explored. Cognitive dissonance rules. Ellis paused. He was suffering a migraine attack. His vision shimmered. The proposed third runway at Heathrow would expose all this chatter for what it truly was. His vision restored Ellis ate a croissant with strawberry jam, washed down with a cappuccino. He went on Ed McNally's twitter page. McNally had tweeted a letter from the latest issue of the *London Review of Books*. It was a response to James Butler's fatuous review of the two Corbyn books. Colin Leys and Leo Panitch put the boot into the EHRC, describing it as 'a politically appointed body of amateurs which lacks political balance and is known for the publicly stated prejudices of several of its commissioners'. These two had written a book, *Searching for Socialism*, about the Corbyn years and its Bennite origins. According to the Verso blurb: 'They argue that while this defeat marked the farthest point to which the generation formed in the 1970s was able to carry the Labour new left project, it seems unlikely that the new generation of activists will quickly see any other way forward than continuing the struggle inside the Labour Party, so as to fundamentally change it'. Well good luck with that, Ellis thought. The Labour Party was beyond transformation and anyone who didn't learn that lesson was destined to waste and divert their energy and their time. The child did some drawing. Ellis went for a walk. It was very cold. Later he learned that a further 53,135 cases of Covid-19 had been reported in the UK in

411

the past 24 hours, along wth 414 deaths. He read an online article by Richard Seymour about the future of the Left in Britain. He seemed to mean the Left within the Labour Party. 'The moral high ground is a powerful currency on social media, but it proved completely useless when the Left was subjected to a campaign of vilification, claiming it was pervasively antisemitic and had turned Labour pervasively antisemitic. This demanded a rigorous response.' This was a bit rich coming from Seymour, who Ellis did not remember standing up for Chris Williamson MP, or for Ken Livingstone, or for Jackie Walker, or for Tony Greenstein, who had stood up to the howling Zionist mobs. Seymour himself had colluded and was still colluding with what was known as 'the Optics Left'. Seymour wrote, for example, that 'there is a fringe on the Left that is plainly drawn to conspiracist and sometimes antisemitic thinking'. As usual, there were no examples given. To be persuaded Ellis required links and citations. Seymour supplied none. 'It was necessary for the Left to engage with the realities of both antisemitism and the state of Israel and its violent ethno-nationalist politics,' wrote Seymour, as if there was some kind of balance between a virtually non-existent anti-Semitism (which in any case manifested on social media) and a bellicose 'Jewish community' which was ubiquitous in both the corporate and social media. Seymour lashed 'The "articulate" Left' - Ellis was baffled by this category - who on earth did Seymour mean? - which promised to 'defend Palestinian rights while opposing antisemitism – without concretely explaining how. This persuaded no one. It looked evasive because it was'. Ellis had no idea who or what Seymour meant. Then, tacked on at the end, was the apparent solution: environmentalism. 'Yet to make the most of this, the Left must also understand environmentalism as a democratic issue.' A platitude. And a final wagging of the retired SWP finger: 'no serious climate project, which must protect the survival of the whole species by changing how we work, travel, consume and recreate – our whole way of life – can work without mass public involvement'. How true! Smiley face. 205,187 words. Tomorrow and the day after. Then free of all this. Was Seymour still a member of the Labour Party? This question had been put to him on Twitter and he had not replied. Ellis spent the evening reading a book. At 10pm the Sky News. Reach for the Sky… Hospitals overwhelmed by Coronavirus infections. New government announcements tomorrow. An earthquake in Croatia, with a handful of deaths, including a twelve year old girl. Harry and Meghan make another desperate pitch for publicity, promoting their infant's words. But anyone can see that their Californian sojourn is bad for business. They are fading from view. The other brother and his wife are getting the coverage. Harry has lost the PR war. Ellis went to bed. The chapter ended with the words: "I'll pack a bag."

Ellis woke and it was dark, it was morning. He switched on the bedside radio. He dozed. He learned through drifts of half-sleep that the Oxford vaccine had been approved by UK regulators. It would be rolled out in the New Year. He learned that the British state had once sought to prevent the publication of Kim Philby's memoirs in *Paris Match* and divert justified criticism of the British intelligence service, by planting a fake story in the *Sunday Times* suggesting that France had been penetrated at the highest level by a Soviet mole. Harold Evans, the paper's editor, had happily agreed to serve the secret state by printing an entirely bogus story. The revelation was contained in a memo dated 3 January 1968 from Sir Denis Greenhill, a senior official at the Foreign Office. Greenhill had spoken to Evans, who 'seemed quite taken with the idea'. Sir Denis Greenhill also suggested that the *Sunday Times* examine a spy novel by Leon Uris called *Topaz*, about Russian intelligence operations in France, which Greenhill claimed was 'founded on fact'. Oh really? Leon Uris, the mendacious author of *Exodus*... The servile and unprincipled Harold Evans duly submitted his fictitious material and Sir Denis Greenhill was able to tell him that it was the view that the *Times* story was 'a pretty good effort'. The story was picked up by *Life* magazine as well and in April both publications carried the fabricated and false 'news' that a Soviet spy was working on President de Gaulle's staff. A fascinating saga. At 8.30am Ellis climbed out of bed and went to make tea. A bright sunlit morning, with a clear blue sky. Paul McConnell tweeted: On the day Starmer's Labour waves through the abysmal Tory Brexit deal, with a handful of Labour MPs likely to performatively vote against it, it's worth recalling that this was always going to be the endpoint of Labour capitulating on a "People's Vote". McConnell linked to an undated article he'd published in the *Morning Star* last year. In this article McConnell cited E. P. Thompson's hostility to the EU. Labour's position on Brexit has shifted from working for the best form of Brexit, in line with the result of the 2016 referendum, to now effectively being a party of Remain, McConnell wrote. A party that will campaign for a second referendum, in which it will argue the virtues of remaining in and reforming the EU, to pursue radical, transformative and internationalist politics. But the EU's treaties, and the myriad directives and regulations made under them, are virtually impossible to reform, McConnell argued. 'The problem is that policies made within the EU are constrained both by the constitutional framework which has been put in place and the class character and perspective of the main political actors (European Commission, Central Bank and Council). These insure that the policies adopted are in line with the interests embedded in the treaties, with the European Court of Justice there to police any deviation.' Paul McConnell concluded, prophetically: 'That the Labour Party could spearhead reform of the EU, already constitutionally nigh impossible before 2008, forging alliances with high-profile but irrelevant and inept figures such as Yanis Varoufakis, beggars belief. Far more likely, capitulation by Labour will signal the end of Corbynism as any form of transformative politics, the British right will be strengthened, the EU will become increasingly neoliberal and authoritarian, and the left here will have squandered a golden opportunity'. From Twitter Ellis learned that Michael Walker of *Novara Media* had two days ago tweeted: 'What are the arguments against completely closing schools for whole of January and shortening summer holidays from 6 to 2 weeks? It seems like a no-brainer to me.' Yet more evidence that the true destination of the gang at *Novara* was the corporate media in all its lucrative forms. Junwinator responded: 'If "no brainer" refers to an idea where no brain has been used, then yeah'. Nicola Guy tweeted: 'I cannot understand how a left wing pundit continually disregards the teaching unions in their opinion, very puzzling'. Craig The Cub tweeted: 'Maybe it's best to leave it to those who work in education/teaching who know what they are talking about'. Ellis went out shopping. It was a cold day. Back home he drank coffee. The sun shone down from a blue sky. The child played with her play-doh, cutting out shapes. A Christmas tree. A triangle. A circle. Her painting of baby dried in the kitchen. The hours passed. Taj tweeted: 'Extraordinary to see Labour MPs who pushed for a people's vote and continuously undermined Corbyn's leadership under the guise that he was not remain enough now voting for Boris Johnson's Brexit deal'. Elsewhere on the internet Ellis learned that SOAS (University of London) had refunded a Jewish student £15,000 in fees after he said he was forced to abandon his studies because of an alleged "toxic antisemitic environment". Noah Lewis, a Canadian, was enrolled as a student in the academic year 2018/19. He claimed that during his time at SOAS, Jews and people who were pro-Israel were labelled as "Zionists". Well why not? Ellis thought. Israel was a Zionist state. It was the incarnation of Zionism. It was the creation of people who called themselves Zionists. Noah Lewis alleged that anti-Semitic graffiti and symbols were found on lockers, desks and toilet walls. (Photographs, please, thought Ellis.) And many people publicly stated their support for the BDS movement, which promotes boycotts, divestments and sanctions against Israel, whined Noah Lewis. Well, yes, of course they would, thought Ellis. Students on the whole are prone to idealism. If you aren't going to be on the Left when you're a student, you probably never will be. Noah Lewis complained that when he stated his intention to write a dissertation on the "systemic biases that exist in the United Nations and target the state of Israel", he said fellow students had accused him of being complicit in covering up Israeli war crimes and had said that he was a "white supremacist Nazi". These anecdotes were self-explanatory, Ellis felt. He moved on. Daniel Fooks tweeted: 'Assange is going to lose his case on Monday. And yet most of the Left remain silent'. Later it was reported that the UK had recorded 981 coronavirus deaths in

414

the past 24 hours, with another 50,023 infections. The corporate media muffled the horror. The corporate media always did - except when suffering and victimhood was of political service to power. 206,244 words. Not long, now. Soon be all over, thankfully. The release from narrative. A liberation. To drift off into silence. To enter the void of absence. The words like worms' castoffs. Squiggles in rippled sand. Language disintegrates in time. Chaucer now largely unread, largely unreadable. Shakespeare's texts rusting away like the *Titanic*. Jokes and allusions which now nobody in the audience except a professor of literature understands. How lyrical. How melancholy. Ellis's keyboard offered itself as a commentary on evolving language. No less than ten of the letters had worn away - Ellis thumped the keyboard hard - and six other keys were barely visible. Words kept coming out wrong, mispelt, garbled. He had to keep the three QWERTY rows in upper case printed out on a sheet of paper and bobbing just below the surface of every fresh entry, to help him back to the surface of accepted language. Time, time. Ellis this evening watched *Frozen*. Let it go... The 10pm Sky News was about the Coronavirus crisis. It was not until 10.22pm that the passing of the Brexit bill in the Commons was briskly mentioned. A once all-consuming topic was now pushed to the margins by disease and death. This is how climate catastrophe would be later in the century. The big becomes the microscopic and the marginal blows in to the centre. Ellis went to bed. He reached the end of *Humbolt's Gift*. They must be crocuses. One of those artful low key endings. Ellis put out the light.

Thursday 31st December 2020

Ellis woke at 6am and then again at 7am. When the dullard Gavin Williamson came on the radio Ellis left the bed and went to make tea. A bitterly cold morning, blue sky, sun, everywhere outside white with frost. The last day of 2020! The final pages. For this relief... What a year. One of the sleaziest governments in recent British history had managed to kill over 70,000 Britons by mishandling the Coronavirus pandemic from the start. But its corruption, lethal carelessness, incompetence and cynicism had been muffled throughout by the billionaire press and the BBC. The process had been greatly assisted by a Labour Party whose membership had chosen a wooden Establishment knight of the realm as its new leader. Once elected, Sir Keir Starmer ('the unity candidate') had launched an aggressive war on the Left in the party, with a special animus against activists who dared to criticise Israel. Meanwhile on the coming Monday, beyond the terminus point of this text, the deportation of Julian Assange would surely be announced, to the whoops and chuckles of Marina Hyde and her associates at the *Guardian*. The circulation of that newspaper had sunk to around 110,000 copies a day. If it ceased print publication Ellis would celebrate. What a year. The activities of the British armed forces in places like Oman had passed utterly without scrutiny by the corporate media. A place like Bahrain was mentioned only in connection with motor racing. The barbarism of the Egyptian dictatorship went unmentioned. Likewise the innumerable crimes of the Jewish state. Likewise the role of the Royal Air Force in bringing misery, violent death and injustice to the people of Yemen. The biggest story of all - climate breakdown, the daily movement towards planetary apocalypse - was pushed to the margins and trivialised. In fiction, what novels and which writers from this year would be remembered in fifty years time, while the planet boiled and bubbled? Ellis had no idea. He'd be long gone. On this cold morning he felt nostalgic. He looked up Frank Key's Wikipedia entry and discovered it had been greatly expanded. Poor Paul. 29 January 1959 - 13 September 2019. Next he looked at Max's. After that he read Danny Birchall's tweets. The surname was familiar. Was he the son of Ian Birchall? In some way connected, Ellis felt. A link led him to a comment by J. F., who Ellis remembered well. And next - one by Sherri Yanowitz. A discussion of the STUFF THE JUBILEE badge of 1977. 'When I ordered 4000 badges from the Universal button company in Bethnal Green, they sort of laugh at me.' (sic) The Universal Button Company! Ellis remembered it well. He used to see it from the train, the overground, when going to Liverpool Street. The name had haunted him like a passion. It cast a giant shadow over *The Aleppo Button*. But there came a time when Ellis no longer remembered seeing the name. Had the business folded or had the sign merely vanished, painted over perhaps, or lost behind a new building? Or was it still there and it was merely Ellis's attentiveness to the sights of East London which had shrivelled? No quick way to check. It would be a long time before Ellis ever rode that line again. Perhaps never. And now it was no longer buttons which occupied his mind. It was parks. Itchycoo Park. MacArthur Park. Maryon Park. Rosa Parks. On and on Ellis roamed. Over the bridge of sighs and down into the dark alleyways and ditches of the internet. He came across Ian Birchall's poignant personal obituary of his lover, Bel. Ellis read it. He smiled at 'Nellie the Elephant'. Yes, what a catastrophe A.C. had turned out to be. To protect the Party he'd destroyed it. In his own way A.C. had been as much of a disaster for a fraction of the Left as J.C. And reading it, Ellis came across another name - Merilyn Moos. That rang a bell. Of course! S. C. And then on, to a reference to the North Middlesex Hospital. Ellis had once been operated on there. He still remembered the crust of blood on the wall by his bed, the man whose leg had been amputated who smoked in the ward, the Irish nurse who told the man that God had been displeased with him. A hellish place. He remembered the tall black chimney, the mortuary building. The odd, comical name of the surgeon who'd cut him open. There had been the brief dark incomprehensible vista of terminal disease, of death, or - they thrust a paper at him to sign before the operation - an unfortunate side-effect. Then the needle had gone in and he'd plunged into unconsciousness. It ended much later in

416

wakefulness, pain, blood. Ellis learned he had been spared. He was more or less okay, apart from the scar. In due course he left the hospital. Death had been postponed for later on in the narrative of his life. Ellis finished Birchall's piece, which was dated 1 September 2015. Ellis recorded this fact for *Twenty-Twenty*. Before he added a word here, a phrase there, he'd reached 207,019 words. A goodly assemblage of text, forsooth. He hardly ever went back to it. But when he did he was pleased to see that he had kept to the vow he had made on 30 May. Outside, the sun was still shining on the nothing new. The frost was not yet thawed on the stiff grass. In the afternoon Ellis went for a walk. The frost still hadn't thawed. It didn't look as if it would. He returned home. The child made shapes out of Play-Doh. For her it was a busy life, all go. Days of play, oblivious to the pandemic, to absences, to the planet's side without light. Ellis hadn't seen the child or her parents since October. He wondered when he would be able to see them again. Not for a while, it seemed. The hours passed. It grew dark. The latest statistics broke. 964 deaths in the past 24 hours and a record-breaking 55,892 infections - the highest figure since the start of the pandemic. A symbolic end to the year. Ellis read responses to the news that Sir Simon Stevens, Chief Executive of NHS England, had decided that those who had received the Prifzer jab would now be expected to wait 11-12 weeks instead of 3 for their second vaccination. This was allowed by the Medicines and Healthcare products Regulatory Authority changing its guidance. Dr Katrina Farrell tweeted: 'Just received an email cancelling my 2nd dose of the Pfizer vaccine. On the basis of UK government guidance. This means that the vaccine is not being delivered as licensed. I DID NOT consent to receive an off-label drug with NO evidence of benefit with a single dose'. Pfizer and BioNTech warned that two doses of the vaccine were required for maximum protection against Covid and that they did not have evidence that the first dose alone offered protection after three weeks. Azeem Majid, a professor of primary care and public health at Imperial College London and a practising GP, said he was shocked by the change of plan. The chair of the BMA's GP committee, Dr Richard Vautrey, called on the government to publish a scientifically-validated justification for the new approach. Some GPs questioned whether it was ethical to delay a second dose when patients had given consent for the first dose on the premise that they would receive the second three weeks later. The Doctors' Association UK said: 'A patient can't consent for a treatment then have the treatment changed without their permission, especially when the evidence is lacking'. Dr Vinesh Patel, spokesman for DAUK's GP committee, said using the trialled vaccination regime was a huge gamble. Ellis came off the internet. It was New Year's Eve. He ate quiche, with baked beans and purple cabbage, washed down with a tumbler of water. He did not plan to stay up to midnight. As he tidied up in the kitchen Ellis listened to Roy Orbison - a name that reminded him of something Max had once written. In the latest photographs on the internet Max was still slim and tall, with dark hair, and a faint resemblance to Nick Cave. But the face had aged. Ellis had a photograph somewhere of the three of them - Frank, Max, Ellis. They were standing by a trestle table in a park trying to sell postmodern texts to an indifferent gathering of people. Birds chattered in the nearby aviary. All over. Ellis shrugged, for the sake of a narrative spasm. It also kept a body fit, flexing shoulders like that. Roy Orbison mentioned rainbows, a sunset, a definitive ending. The song plucked at Ellis's weathered organ of circulation. Thank you for the days did too. And many more. This evening Ellis watched *Mansfield Park*, the version with Harold Pinter playing Sir Thomas Bertram. A fine adaptation. It made Ellis think that in 2021 perhaps he should reread some Austen. After the film: the Sky News at 10pm. The virus, the vaccine, the fireworks in Australia. Ellis barely watched. He checked for emails, then went to bed. Time for some new bedside reading. There were various choices. In the end he selected a novel which the *Literary Review* had described - it was cited on the book cover - as 'An elegy for a vanishing style of mind ... evoked with a masterly vividness'. Ellis wondered what the ellipses concealed. Another review asserted that 'choice bits of prose appear on every page, glittering like diamonds'. A reviewer who had died quite suddenly not long after his enthusiastic review believed the novel to be 'Vivid, very funny, very chattery...' The *Washington Post* said that 'The book rings with laughter and joy'. *Vanity Fair* saluted the author for having retaken 'the king-of-the-mountain position'. A curious encomium, Ellis thought. It mingled warfare with folklore. But perhaps that was what literary reviewing amounted to in the corporate media. Control of the mountain could not help but remind Ellis of *Frozen* and Princess Elsa's impressive mountain residence. Let it go... He began reading the novel. I have always had a weakness for footnotes, he read on the second page. Ellis read on. He attracted gifted students, he read. The book so far seemed a little slack, Ellis thought. His reading was then disturbed by the sound of fireworks. He looked at the clock: it was only 11.20pm. The explosions continued. Ellis left the bed and went to look out of the bedroom window. The fireworks were away to the south-west, perhaps half a mile away. A private party, surely. Someone had evidently spent serious money. These were not cheap rockets. They soared into the sky and then exploded, sending out spreading streamers of silvery and golden light. Sometimes the streamers crackled with emerald explosions. The racket pierced the tranquil night. Oddly, none of the neighbourhood dogs were barking. The streets were deserted, the roof tiles pale with frost. Bored by the display, Ellis went back to bed and continued reading. He felt mildly tired. A little while later, a good half hour before midnight, he put out the light. Most nights he fell asleep very quickly. This night was no exception.